W9-ADV-888

Rick Steves®

SCANDINAVIA

CONTENTS

Post-Pandemic Travels: Expect a Warm Welcome...and a Few Changes
Research for this guidebook was limited by the COVID-19 outbreak, and the long-term impact of the crisis on our recommended destinations is unclear. Some details in this book will change for post-pandemic travelers. Now more than ever, it's smart to reconfirm specifics as you plan and travel. As always, you can find major updates at RickSteves.com/update.

Welcome to Rick Steves' Europe

Travel is intensified living—maximum thrills per minute and one of the last great sources of legal adventure. Travel is freedom. It's recess, and we need it.

I discovered a passion for European travel as a teen and have been sharing it ever since—through my bus

tours, public television and radio shows, and travel guidebooks. Over the years, I've taught millions of travelers how to best enjoy Europe's blockbuster sights—and experience "Back Door" discoveries that most tourists miss.

This book offers you a balanced mix of Scandinavia's dynamic capital cities and cozy small towns. Along with enjoying open-air folk museums, a fjord cruise, and a *smörgåsbord*, you can bike across a sleepy Danish isle, walk on a glacier, steam in a Finnish sauna, and wander among Sweden's eerie, prehistoric monoliths. And for an exciting Baltic side trip, I've included Tallinn, Estonia's charming capital.

I advocate traveling simply and smartly. Take advantage of my money- and time-saving tips on sightseeing, transportation, and more. Try local, characteristic alternatives to expensive hotels and restaurants. In many ways, spending more money only builds a thicker wall between you and what you traveled so far to see.

We visit Scandinavia to experience it—to become temporary locals. Thoughtful travel engages us with the world, as we learn to appreciate other cultures and new ways to measure quality of life.

Judging by the positive feedback I receive from readers, this book will help you enjoy a fun, affordable, and rewarding vacation—whether it's your first trip or your tenth.

Happy travels! *Rick Steves*

SCANDINAVIA

Scandinavia—known for its stunning natural beauty, fun-loving cities, trendsetting design, and progressive politics—is one of Europe's most enjoyable corners. A visit here connects you with Viking lore, immigrant roots, modern European values, and the great outdoors like nowhere else. You'll gasp at breathtaking fjords, glide on a ferry boat among picturesque islands, and marvel at the livability of bustling capitals.

What exactly is Scandinavia? It's Denmark, Norway, and Sweden. Finland is a Nordic country (like its Scandinavian neighbors), while Estonia is a Baltic state. Together yet distinct, these five countries offer a fascinating look at northern Europe. Here's a snapshot per country:

Denmark, a flat peninsula with small islands and long bridges, is the smallest and most densely populated. Simply put, Denmark is cute. It feels like a mini-golf course inhabited by happy blond gods. Sights include lively Copenhagen, a passel of castles, Viking ships, Legoland, inviting towns, and adorable islands. Danes embrace the concept of *hygge*, which means enjoying the cozy simplicity of everyday life, like walking along the beach, or sharing a picnic of *smørrebrød* (open-faced sandwiches) with a friend.

Norway is a land of intense beauty, with steep mountains and deep fjords carved out and shaped by an ancient ice age. This sparsely populated country is long: Oslo, the capital, is as far from the northern tip of Norway as it is from Rome. Along with its personable capital, the country's highlights include the

The village of Balestrand on Norway's unforgettable Sognefjord; craft demonstration at Stockholm's Skansen folk museum

salty port of Bergen, colorful villages, and wildly scenic routes over the mountains and through the fjords. Norway's icons are all things Viking, wooden stave churches, knitted sweaters, and *lutefisk* (imagine fish Jell-O).

Sweden, a forested land of clear lakes and island chains, is the largest Scandinavian country and has the grandest capital. Stockholm is a public-service announcement for good living, and its Skansen open-air folk museum is Europe's oldest and best. Sweden's attractions are an archipelago cruise, historic castles, glassworks tours, pleasant cities, and exceptional museums. Though industrious, Swedes always make time for *fika*— a coffee break with pastry—a habit you'll quickly adopt.

Finland is flat, friendly, and underrated. Its capital city, Helsinki, holds its own among the Nordic capitals for its renewed waterfront, modernist architecture, steamy saunas... and ubiquitous slot machines. Finns love gambling. Helsinki is a popular port, with overnight cruises to and from Stockholm, and quick ferries connecting Tallinn, Estonia.

Estonia, a small Baltic country, has islands, marshlands, and patriotic singers. Estonians achieved independence from Russia in 1991 through their peaceful Singing Revolution. They specialize in global technology, while folk music remains dear to their hearts. The photogenic Old World capital of

How to Enjoy a Smörgåsbord

The Swedish *smörgåsbord* (known in Denmark and Norway as the *koldt bord*) is a Scandinavian culinary tradition. While the word *smörgåsbord* originally meant a "bread-and-butter table" and *koldt bord* means "cold table," today's smorgasbords are an abundant feast of appealing appetizers, hot and cold dishes, and desserts.

Seek out a smorgasbord at least once during your trip, just for the experience of seeing so much wholesome and tasty Nordic food spread out before you.

Locals indulge in a smorgasbord mainly at festive times such as the Christmas season, but anyone can dig into this all-you-can-eat buffet any time of the year at bigger hotels and on overnight ferries. It's always smart to reserve a smorgasbord in advance. You'll generally pay one set price for the meal, though fancier drinks may cost extra (confirm before imbibing).

Follow the simple steps below to make the most of your smorgasbord experience.

Skål! Smaklig måltid! Cheers! Enjoy your meal!

1. **Arrive hungry and take time to browse through the buffet** before you begin, so you can budget your stomach space. Think of the smorgasbord as a five- or six-course meal.

2. **Don't overload your plate.** Instead make a number of trips, taking a fresh plate and cutlery each time. Dish up small servings and pace yourself.

3. To signal to the waiter that you're finished with each round, **lay your fork and knife side by side** on the plate. If you're getting up but are not finished with your plate, cross your fork and knife in an X shape on the plate. ▶▶▶

A smorgasbord is all-you-can-eat, so survey your options before taking your portions, then return for more of your favorites; cross your fork and knife to signal that you're not yet done.

4. **Begin with the herring dishes** (pickled, smoked, and in white cream sauce, to name several), along with small boiled potatoes and crispbreads.

5. Next, **sample the other fish dishes and more potatoes.** Warm dishes include baked trout and salmon, poached fish, and shellfish. You'll likely see *gravlax*—salt-cured salmon served on crisp rye crackers with sweet mustard sauce.

6. **Move on to salads** (greens, coleslaw, potato salad, beets, and marinated or pickled veggies), egg dishes (omelets and deviled, topped with caviar or shrimp), and various cold cuts.

7. **Now for the hearty main dishes**— it's meatball time! Reindeer, other roasted meats, sausages, casseroles, stews, and pâtés vie for your attention. Add mashed potatoes, dumplings, pasta, or rice, and ladle on gravy. Condiments include jams (such as lingonberry and gooseberry), mustard, and horseradish.

8. **Sample Nordic cheeses:** semisoft Danish Havarti, creamy-yet-tangy Castello (a blue cheese), mild Jarlsberg (with holes), and Norwegian *geitost* (sweet, brown goat cheese that looks like earwax).

A typical smorgasbord includes a tempting herring sampler, Swedish meatballs with lingonberries, and cheeses.

9. **Room for dessert?** Enjoy seasonal fruits and peruse racks of traditional pastries, cakes, and custards.

10. **Cap your meal with coffee or tea,** or go with beer, wine, or spirits such as vodka or akvavit. ∎

Tallinn makes for an engaging visit—by ferry from Helsinki or overnight cruise from Stockholm.

Politically, Denmark, Norway, and Sweden are constitutional monarchies, each with a figurehead monarch who cuts ribbons, works with a democratically elected parliament and a prime minister, and tries to stay out of the tabloids. As for royalty, talk about keeping it all in the family: Each of Scandinavia's current monarchs is descended from Oscar I, king of Sweden and Norway (ruled 1844-1859). In contrast, Finland and Estonia have democratically elected presidents.

Of the five countries, all but Norway are in the European Union, though only Finland and Estonia use the euro. Norway, with the world's second-longest coastline (after Canada), resists EU membership, unwilling to share its offshore oil and fishing rights (and give up its stubborn appetite for whaling).

Scandinavia is rich, with a high standard of living, as American tourists learn the hard way. Residents pay hefty taxes but receive cradle-to-grave security in return. Generally speaking, citizens willingly share the burden for the common good. Studies consistently show that Scandinavians lead longer, healthier, and happier lives than the rest of the world. They're well educated, well traveled, and generally content. Talk with the people you meet; their second language is often English. They tend to speak their minds frankly and have a good sense of humor.

Danes win the happiness race; colorful buildings in Stortorget, Stockholm's oldest square

Everything about Scandinavia feels well designed, from its governments and transportation systems down to everyday objects. Furniture and appliances are both functional and beautiful: sleek, appealing, and efficient.

Summertime is Scandinavia's time to shine, when this "land of the midnight sun" enjoys 18 hours of daylight. Everyone finds a reason to be outside. Scandinavians love nature and outdoor activities: cycling, hiking, boating, and fishing. Given their pristine natural surroundings, they're environmentalists—valuing hydroelectric and wind power—and are committed to preserving resources for future generations.

Despite their ultramodern, progressive outlook, Scandinavians still honor their traditions. Parents tell their kids old folktales about grumpy, clever trolls, and gardeners dot their yards with ornamental gnomes. At midsummer, locals in traditional clothing dance around maypoles to the tunes of folk bands. At winter solstice and Christmas, they enjoy Yule cakes and winter beer. Scandinavia is sailing confidently into the high-tech future on the hardy ship of its Viking past.

Scandinavia's Top Destinations

This overview breaks Scandinavia's top destinations into must-see sights (to help first-time travelers plan their trip) and worth-it sights (for those with additional time or special interests). I've also suggested a minimum number of days to allow per destination.

Arctic Ocean

200 Kilometers

200 Miles

Arctic Circle

Norwegian Sea

PLACES COVERED IN THIS BOOK
▲▲▲ Must See
▲▲ Try Hard to See
▲ Worthwhile

RUSSIA

SWEDEN

FINLAND

NORWAY

Gulf of Bothnia

MORE ON THE SOGNEFJORD

GUDBRANDSDAL & JOTUNHEIMEN

NORWAY IN A NUTSHELL

BERGEN

OSLO

SOUTH NORWAY

HELSINKI

STOCKHOLM

TALLINN

ESTONIA

STOCKHOLM'S ARCHIPELAGO

North Sea

LATVIA

JUTLAND

SOUTHEAST SWEDEN

DENMARK

COPENHAGEN

Baltic Sea

LITHUANIA

CENTRAL DENMARK

RUSSIA

GERMANY

POLAND

DENMARK

▲▲▲Copenhagen (allow 2 days)

This vibrant capital hosts the *Little Mermaid* sculpture, the old-time Tivoli Gardens amusement park, and Renaissance King Christian IV's Rosenborg Castle. Wander from the irresistible, shop-lined pedestrian street called Strøget to the colorful little harbor of Nyhavn. Gawk at the eye-opening hippie enclave at Christiania and get an earful of the city's thriving jazz scene.

▲Near Copenhagen (1-2 days)

You have four good options: Roskilde, west of Copenhagen, has the excellent Viking Ship Museum and Denmark's royal cathedral. To the north of Copenhagen, opulent Frederiksborg Castle is the "Danish Versailles"; plainer Kronborg Castle has a dramatic waterfront setting; and the Louisiana Art Museum features lush sculpture gardens and modern art galleries.

▲▲Central Denmark (2 days)

The peaceful isle of Ærø harbors Denmark's best-preserved 18th-century village, Ærøskøbing. This small island is perfect to explore on a loop tour by bike or car. Between Ærø and Copenhagen is the busy town of Odense, with author Hans Christian Andersen's childhood home.

▲Jutland (1-2 days)

Denmark's second-largest city, Aarhus, has an appealing-to-stroll center, the impressive ARoS art museum, a prehistory museum (with a well-preserved Iron Age "bog man"), and an open-air museum of bygone Danish life. This family-friendly region also hosts the Legoland amusement park and the village of Jelling with its historic rune stones.

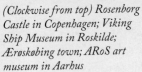

(Clockwise from top) Rosenborg Castle in Copenhagen; Viking Ship Museum in Roskilde; Ærøskøbing town; ARoS art museum in Aarhus

NORWAY

▲▲▲Oslo (2 days)

The compact core of Norway's capital holds an inspiring City Hall, harborfront promenade, striking Opera House, stirring WWII Resistance Museum, and outstanding National Museum (with Munch's *The Scream).* A quick ferry takes you to the Bygdøy district and museums dedicated to famous ships—Viking, *Fram,* and *Kon-Tiki*—plus the Norwegian Folk Museum. Just beyond the center, hundreds of bronze and granite statues adorn majestic Vigeland Sculpture Park.

▲▲▲Norway in a Nutshell (1-2 days)

This popular route connects Oslo and Bergen via train, bus, and ferry in a wonderfully scenic day brimming with pristine waterfalls, verdant forests, and steep mountains. To break the journey, you can overnight in a fjord town.

▲More on the Sognefjord (1-2 days)

The hamlet of Balestrand makes a cozy home base for fjord fun, with a stave church nearby. East of Balestrand, the serene Lustrafjord features another stave church and a glacier (the Nigard) you can walk on. This region, particularly Lustrafjord, is easier for drivers, but doable by public transit.

▲Gudbrandsdal Valley and Jotunheimen Mountains (2 days, best for drivers)

This lush valley northwest of Oslo has touristy Lillehammer and the excellent Maihaugen open-air folk museum. The rugged Jotunheimen Mountains offer the Lom stave church, lodge accommodations, fine hikes, and sweeping vistas. Drivers can follow a scenic valley-and-mountain route westward to reach Lustrafjord and Sognefjord.

▲▲Bergen (1 day)

The historic port town has a lively fish market, harborfront Bryggen quarter (with colorful buildings), interesting museums, and a funicular up a little mountain for sea-and-city views. Activities from Bergen include fjord cruises (plus an express boat to Balestrand) and bus tours to composer Edvard Grieg's home at Troldhaugen.

(Clockwise from top) Oslo's Opera House; kayaking on the Sognefjord; Bergen fish market; stave church in Lillehammer's Maihaugen open-air folk museum

(Clockwise from top) Royal pomp and circumstance in Stockholm; ancient burial mounds near Uppsala; Stockholm's tranquil archipelago; glassblowing in southeast Sweden

▲South Norway (1 day)

This region features the North Sea town of Stavanger, with a good petroleum museum and nearby Pulpit Rock, a dramatic promontory that attracts hikers and view seekers. Farther inland, the time-passed Setesdal Valley—lined with remote villages and humble sights—brings drivers to the port town of Kristiansand and the ferry to Denmark.

SWEDEN

▲▲▲Stockholm (2 days)

This splendid capital has charming Gamla Stan (historic Old Town island), a fun changing of the guard, and a stately City Hall with tower views. Sights include the superb Skansen open-air folk museum, astonishing Vasa Museum (17th-century warship), and fan-pleasing ABBA museum. The sleek port offers an archipelago cruise and overnight boats to Helsinki and to Tallinn.

▲Near Stockholm (1 day)

Choose among three good day trips: the lavish, royal Drottningholm Palace with its Baroque-era theater; the cute town of Sigtuna with rune stones and 18th-century buildings; and the university town of Uppsala, with its vast cathedral, Linnaeus Garden and Museum, and ancient burial mounds.

▲Stockholm's Archipelago (1 day)

Sweden's rocky garden of more than 30,000 islands is best seen by boat. You'll catch a glimpse from the overnight boat to Helsinki or Tallinn, but it's better if you get up close via the ferries that connect Stockholm's islands. You can visit several islands in one day and even stay overnight.

▲Southeast Sweden (2 days)

This sleepy region features two top towns. Pleasant Växjö has fine museums on Swedish emigration and glass making. Livelier Kalmar boasts a massive 12th-century castle and the nearby island of Öland, with sandy beaches and Iron Age monoliths. Sweden's Glass Country, between the two towns, is dotted with glassblowing hotshops and a historic paper workshop (easiest with a car).

FINLAND

▲▲Helsinki (1-2 days)

Finland's attractive capital is fun to reach on a scenic overnight cruise from Stockholm. Helsinki is a delight for its striking architecture, particularly its unusual churches and rival cathedrals. Other top sights are the bustling waterfront market, grand pedestrian boulevard, and museums ranging from art and design to history and folk culture. The fortress island guarding the harbor is a huge park—a joy on a sunny day.

ESTONIA

▲▲Tallinn (1 day)

This lively Baltic capital adds spice to a Nordic itinerary. Its quaint, fun-to-explore Old Town core is corralled by intact medieval walls. Sights include the Museum of Estonian History, the Russian Orthodox Cathedral, an open-air folk museum, and Kadriog Park, with a contemporary art collection. Tallinn is connected by boat to Helsinki (two-hour ferry) and Stockholm (overnight cruise).

Helsinki's Sibelius Monument—a forest of organ pipes in a forest of trees; Tallinn's Russian Orthodox Cathedral

Planning Your Trip

To plan your trip, you'll need to design your itinerary—choosing where and when to go, how you'll travel, and how many days to spend at each destination. For my best general advice on sightseeing, accommodations, restaurants, and more, see the Practicalities chapter.

DESIGNING AN ITINERARY

As you read this book and learn about your options...

Choose your top destinations.

My recommended itineraries (see the sidebars) give you an idea of how much you can reasonably see in 21 days, but you can adapt them to fit your own interests and time frame.

If you like to keep busy day and night, spend more time in the capitals, which offer plenty of sights, activities, and evening excitement. If you'd rather focus on smaller cities, the best ones—with enough sights to keep you entertained for a longer stay—are Aarhus (Denmark), Kalmar (Sweden), and Bergen (Norway). For tranquil villages, relax in Denmark's Ærøskøbing or Norway's Balestrand.

Nature lovers linger in Norway, basing in a mountain lodge or fjordside town to enjoy hikes, cruises, and dramatic scenery. If regal palaces and medieval castles thrill you, Denmark and Sweden deliver royally. And throughout this seafaring region, the maritime museums are excellent (and Oslo has the most).

For a stroll through traditional Old World culture, seek out an open-air folk museum. Every country has at least one;

these are even more meaningful if you have ancestral ties to the region.

Cruisers enjoy scenic fjord excursions and overnight boats (which connect Stockholm with Helsinki and Tallinn; and Oslo with Copenhagen). If cruising doesn't appeal, consider taking budget flights to Helsinki and Tallinn.

Connoisseurs of relaxation will find the most saunas per capita in Sweden and Finland. For family fun, Denmark's Legoland and Tivoli Gardens are tops.

In this land of attractive cities, colorful towns, and eye-popping natural beauty, photographers want to go everywhere.

Decide when to go.

Summer is a great time to visit. Scandinavia bustles and glistens under the July and August sun; all the major sights are open and in full swing. At these northern latitudes, the days are long—in Oslo, on June 21 the sun comes up around 4:00 and sets around 23:00. In many places, things don't kick into gear until about June 20, when Scandinavian schools let out. You'll notice crowds in July and August, but up here "crowds" mean fun and action rather than congestion. It quiets down when the local kids go back to school, around August 20.

Travel in May, early June, and September lacks the vitality of summer but offers occasional good weather and minimal crowds. Norway in particular can be pleasant from late May to mid-June, when the days are long but the tourist lines are short.

Unless winter sports are high on your agenda, winter is a bad time to explore Scandinavia. The region's metabolism slows down like a hibernating bear's, and many sights and accommodations close or keep a limited schedule, especially in remote fjord towns. The weather can be cold and dreary, and the days are short. Christmastime activities, such as colorful markets and Copenhagen's festively decorated Tivoli Gardens, offer some warmth during this chilly season.

For weather specifics, see the climate chart in the appendix.

Connect the dots.

Link your destinations into a logical route. Determine which cities you'll fly into and out of. Begin your search for transatlantic flights at Kayak.com.

Decide if you'll travel by car, public transportation, or a combination. The public transit system is sleek and reliable; in general, trains are faster and pricier than buses.

A car is fun for exploring the countryside, but is useless in big cities. Scandinavian regions best suited for a car are Norway's scenic fjord-and-mountain country, central Denmark (particularly the isle of Ærø, though it's also bikeable), and southeast Sweden (to visit glassworks and a papermaking atelier).

Overnight cruises can be a fun and efficient way to link Scandinavian cities. A cruise sounds pricey, but keep in mind you're paying for accommodations and transportation, combined with a memorable experience.

Gamla Stan, Stockholm's old town; wildflowers in the Danish countryside near Roskilde

Scandinavia's Best Three-Week Trip by Car, Train, Boat, and Plane

Day	Plan	Sleep
1	Arrive in Copenhagen	Copenhagen
2	Copenhagen	Copenhagen
3	Copenhagen	Copenhagen
4	Pick up car, visit Roskilde and Odense	Aarhus
5	Aarhus	Aarhus
6	Choose more time in Aarhus, a stop in Legoland, or earlier arrival in Ærø	Ærøskøbing
7	Ærø loop tour	Ærøskøbing
8	To Copenhagen, drop car, take direct train to Kalmar	Kalmar
9	Kalmar	Kalmar
10	Train to Stockholm (optional stop in Växjö)	Stockholm
11	Stockholm	Stockholm
12	Stockholm, night boat to Helsinki	Boat
13	Helsinki	Helsinki
14	Day trip to Tallinn by ferry	Helsinki
15	Morning flight to Oslo	Oslo
16	Oslo	Oslo
17	Pick up car, visit Lillehammer and Gudbrandsdal Valley	Jotunheimen Mountains area
18	Jotunheimen Mountains	Lustrafjord area or Aurland
19	Fjord cruise, drive to Bergen, drop car	Bergen
20	Bergen	Bergen
21	Fly home	

Notes: Flying into Copenhagen and out of Bergen (with a likely transfer in Copenhagen) can be wonderfully efficient. If you'd rather end your trip in Oslo, fly from Helsinki to Bergen, and explore Norway by car east to Oslo.

To see more of southeast Sweden, rent a car in Kalmar on Day 10 and tour the Glass Country and Växjö, where you can catch the train for Stockholm. Or stop in Växjö en route when you train from Kalmar to Stockholm.

With less time, instead of renting a car to link Oslo and Bergen, take the one-day Norway in a Nutshell train/fjord cruise/train trip between the two cities, trimming two overnights.

Flights are relatively inexpensive, given the time you'll save. For example, a two-hour flight connects Helsinki and Oslo, but it's approximately 22 hours by overnight boat (Helsinki to Stockholm) and bullet train (Stockholm to Oslo). Instead of taking a round-trip cruise, consider taking a leisurely boat one-way, then a quick flight back (or to your next destination).

To determine approximate travel times between destinations, study the driving map (in the Practicalities chapter or check Google Maps); visit Bahn.com for train schedules. Compare the cost of any long train or boat ride with a budget flight; check Skyscanner.com for intra-European flights.

Write out a day-by-day itinerary.

Figure out how many destinations you can comfortably fit in your time frame. Don't overdo it—few travelers wish they'd hurried more. Allow enough days per stop (see estimates in "Scandinavia's Top Destinations," earlier). Minimize one-night stands. It can be worth taking a late afternoon drive or train ride to settle into a town for two consecutive nights—and gain a full, uninterrupted day for sightseeing. Include sufficient time for transportation; whether you travel by car or train, it'll take you a half-day to get between most destinations.

Staying in a home base (like Copenhagen) and making day trips can be more time-efficient than changing locations and hotels.

Take sight closures into account. Avoid visiting a town on the one day a week its must-see sights are closed. Check if any holidays or festivals fall during your trip—these attract crowds and can close sights (for the latest, visit that country's national tourist website).

Give yourself some slack. Every trip, and every traveler, needs downtime for doing laundry, picnic shopping, people-watching, and so on. Pace yourself. Assume you will return.

Scandinavia's Best Three-Week Trip by Train, Boat, and Plane

Day	Plan	Sleep
1	Arrive in Copenhagen	Copenhagen
2	Copenhagen	Copenhagen
3	Copenhagen	Copenhagen
4	Train to Aarhus with stops in Roskilde and Odense	Aarhus
5	Aarhus	Aarhus
6	Train to Svendborg (via Odense), then ferry to Ærø	Ærøskøbing
7	Ærø	Ærøskøbing
8	Train to Kalmar	Kalmar
9	Kalmar	Kalmar
10	Morning train to Stockholm	Stockholm
11	Stockholm	Stockholm
12	Stockholm, night boat to Helsinki	Boat
13	Helsinki	Helsinki
14	Helsinki, afternoon ferry to Tallinn	Tallinn
15	Tallinn	Tallinn
16	Morning flight to Oslo	Oslo
17	Oslo	Oslo
18	Train and boat to Aurland	Aurland
19	Aurland to Bergen via fjord cruise	Bergen
20	Bergen	Bergen
21	Fly home	

Notes: To add Legoland, visit it between Ærø and Aarhus (and overnight in Billund).

If tight on time, you can link Oslo to Bergen without an overnight on the Norway in a Nutshell trip.

(Clockwise from top) Drinks and a view above Bergen; driving in Norway; floating wooden sauna in Sweden; ferries to Stockholm's archipelago

Trip Costs Per Person

Run a reality check on your dream trip. You'll have major transportation costs in addition to daily expenses.

Flight: A round-trip flight from the US to Copenhagen costs about $900-1,500, depending on where you fly from and when.

Public Transportation: For a three-week trip by public transportation, allow $650 per person. This covers a second-class Eurail Scandinavia pass (4-country, 6 days in 1 month), plus the cost of boat rides that aren't covered or discounted by the pass (such as Norway's Flåm-Aurland-Bergen route). The pass includes a discount on boat fares in the Stockholm-Helsinki-Tallinn triangle (without using a counted travel day). Consider the value of your time: Taking a short flight can beat taking a day-long train ride.

Car Rental: Allow roughly $300 per week (daily rates vary), not including tolls, gas, parking, and insurance.

Ferries: For the overnight cruises between Stockholm and Helsinki or Tallinn, allow about $100-125 per person for a one-way fare. The short Helsinki-Tallinn ferry costs $30-40 one-way. Look for discounts for rail-pass holders, students, families, seniors, and round-trip fares. ▶▶▶

AVERAGE DAILY EXPENSES PER PERSON

$215
Applies to cities, figure on less for towns

Lodging
Based on two people splitting the cost of a $180 double room (with breakfast)
$90

Meals
$20 for lunch, $40 for dinner, and $5 for coffee or ice cream
$65

City Transit
Buses, trams, subways, or taxis/Uber
$15

Sights and Entertainment
This daily average works for most people.
$45

Budget Tips

To cut your daily expenses, take advantage of the deals you'll find throughout Scandinavia and mentioned in this book.

A Eurail Scandinavia rail pass will save you money on train travel. City transit passes (for multiple rides or all-day usage) decrease your cost per ride.

Avid sightseers buy combo-tickets or passes that cover multiple museums. At sights, ask about discounted admissions, as many aren't posted. (Legoland offers discounted tickets online.) If a town doesn't offer deals, visit only the sights you most want to see, and seek out free sights and experiences (people-watching counts).

Some businesses—especially hotels and walking-tour companies—offer discounts to my readers (look for the RS% symbol in the listings in this book).

Reserve your rooms directly with the hotel. Some hotels offer discounts if you pay in cash and/or stay three or more nights (it pays to check online or ask).

Midsummer hotel discounts are possible but are generally offered only by the more expensive hotels. To save money, do as the Scandinavians do and stay in hostels (most have private rooms and great breakfasts). Or check Airbnb-type sites for deals.

It's no hardship to eat inexpensively in Scandinavia. The breakfasts offered at your lodgings are all-you-can-eat and so hearty that you'll need only a sandwich for lunch. Many restaurants offer reasonably priced lunch specials. Convenience and grocery stores sell a broad array of affordable to-go dishes, rescuing travelers shell-shocked by sit-down restaurant prices. Cultivate the art of picnicking in atmospheric settings.

When you splurge, choose an experience you'll always remember, such as a glacier walk or a smorgasbord. Minimize souvenir shopping; focus instead on collecting wonderful memories. ◼

Hiking the Nigard Glacier in Norway's Lustrafjord; foodie paradise in Oslo's Mathallen food hall

BEFORE YOU GO

You'll have a smoother trip if you tackle a few things ahead of time. For more info on these topics, see the Practicalities chapter and RickSteves.com, which has helpful travel tips and talks.

Make sure your travel documents are valid. If your passport is due to expire within six months of your ticketed date of return, you need to renew it. Allow up to six weeks to renew or get a passport (www.travel.state.gov). Check for current Covid entry requirements at your destination(s). You may also need to register with the European Travel Information and Authorization System (ETIAS).

Arrange your transportation. Book your international flights. Overall, Kayak.com is the best place to start searching for flights.

Figure out your transportation options: It's worth thinking about getting a rail pass (or buying essential train tickets online), renting a car, or booking cheap European flights. (You can wing it once you're there, but it may cost more.) If you plan to take an overnight boat between major cities in summer or on weekends, book it in advance (see "Connections" sections in destination chapters for details).

Reserve long-distance rail travel in advance. If you're doing the Norway in a Nutshell route in July or August, make reservations for the Oslo-Myrdal train, and consider reservations for the Myrdal-Flåm train (see the Norway in a Nutshell chapter). If you want to take your car on Denmark's Svendborg-Ærø ferry, reserve at least a week in advance.

Book rooms well in advance, especially if your trip falls during peak season or any major holidays or festivals.

Consider travel insurance. Compare the cost of insurance to the cost of your potential loss. Check whether your existing insurance (health, homeowners, or renters) covers you and your possessions overseas.

Call your bank. Alert your bank that you'll be using your debit and credit cards in Europe. Ask about transaction fees, and get the PIN number for your credit card. You don't need to bring the local currency for your trip; you can withdraw cash from ATMs in Europe.

Use your smartphone smartly. Sign up for an international service plan to reduce your costs, or rely on Wi-Fi in Europe instead. Download any apps you'll want on the road, such as maps, translators, transit schedules, and Rick Steves Audio Europe (see sidebar).

Pack light. You'll walk with your luggage more than you think. I travel for weeks with a single carry-on bag and a day-pack. Use the packing checklist in the appendix as a guide.

Rick's Free Video Clips and Audio Tours

Travel smarter with these free, fun resources:

Rick Steves Classroom Europe, a powerful tool for teachers, is also useful for travelers. This video library contains over 400 short clips excerpted from my public television series. Enjoy these videos as you sort through options for your trip and to better understand what you'll see in Europe. Check it out at Classroom.Rick-Steves.com (just enter a topic to find everything I've filmed on a subject).

The **Rick Steves Audio Europe app** makes it easy to download audio content to enhance your trip. Use the app to listen to audio tours of Europe's top sights, plus interviews from my public radio show with experts from Europe and around the globe. Find it in your app store or at RickSteves.com/AudioEurope.

Travel Smart

If you have a positive attitude, equip yourself with good information (this book), and expect to travel smart, you will.

Read—and reread—this book. To have an "A" trip, be an "A" student. As you study up on sights, note opening hours, closed days, crowd-beating tips, and whether reservations are required or advisable. Check the latest at RickSteves.com/update.

Be your own tour guide. As you travel, get up-to-date info on sights, reserve tickets and tours, reconfirm hotels and travel arrangements, and check transit connections. Visit local tourist information offices. Upon arrival in a new town, lay the groundwork for a smooth departure; confirm the train, bus, boat, or road you'll take when you leave.

Outsmart thieves. Pickpockets abound in crowded places where tourists congregate. Treat commotions as smokescreens for theft. Keep your cash, credit cards, and passport secure in a money belt tucked under your clothes; carry only a day's spending money in your front pocket or wallet. Don't set valuable items down on counters or café tabletops, where they can be quickly stolen or easily forgotten.

Minimize potential loss. Keep expensive gear to a minimum. Bring photocopies or take photos of important documents (passport and cards) to aid in replacement if they're lost or stolen. Back up photos and files frequently.

Guard your time and energy. Taking a taxi can be a good value if it saves you a long wait for a cheap bus or an exhausting walk across town. To avoid long lines, follow my crowd-beating tips, such as sightseeing early or late.

Prepare for border crossings. Border security between Norway, Sweden, Denmark, Finland, and Estonia may be a wave-through, but be prepared to show your passport. When you change countries, you change languages and currency (except between Finland and Estonia, which both use the euro).

Be flexible. Even if you have a well-planned itinerary, expect changes, strikes, closures, sore feet, bad weather, and so on. Your Plan B could turn out to be even better.

Attempt the language. Most Scandinavians—especially in the tourist trade and in cities—speak English, but if you learn some of the local language, even just a few pleasantries, you'll get more smiles and make more friends. Practice the survival phrases in this book, and even better, bring a phrase book.

Connect with the culture. Interacting with locals carbonates your experience. Enjoy the friendliness of the Scandinavian people. Ask questions; most locals are happy to point you in their idea of the right direction. Set up your own quest to discover the perfect fjord view, the tastiest pastry, and the coziest *hyggelig* experience. When an opportunity pops up, make it a habit to say "yes."

Scandinavia...here you come!

DENMARK

DENMARK

Danmark

Denmark is by far the smallest of the Scandinavian countries, but in the 16th century, it was the largest: At one time, Denmark ruled all of Norway and the three southern provinces of Sweden. Danes are proud of their mighty history and are the first to remind you that they were a lot bigger and a lot stronger in the good old days. And yet, they're a remarkably mellow, well-adjusted lot—organized without being uptight, and easygoing with a delightfully wry sense of humor.

In the 10th century, before its heyday as a Scan-superpower, Denmark was, like Norway and Sweden, home to the Vikings. More than anything else, these fierce warriors were known for their great shipbuilding, which enabled them to travel far. Denmark's Vikings journeyed west to Great Britain and Ireland (where they founded Dublin) and brought back various influences, including Christianity.

Denmark is composed of many islands, a peninsula (Jutland) that juts up from northern Germany, Greenland, and the Faroe Islands. The two main islands are Zealand (Sjælland in Danish), where Copenhagen is located, and Funen (Fyn in Danish), where Hans Christian Andersen (or, as Danes call him, simply "H. C.") was born. Out of the hundreds of smaller islands, ship-in-bottle-cute Ærø is my favorite. The Danish landscape

is gentle compared with the dramatic fjords, mountains, and vast lakes of other Scandinavian nations. Danes (not to mention Swedes and Norwegians) like to joke about the flat Danish landscape, saying that you can stand on a case of beer and see from one end of the country to the other. Denmark's highest point in Jutland is only 560 feet above sea level, and no part of the country is more than 30 miles from the sea.

In contrast to the rest of Scandinavia, much of Denmark is

arable. The landscape consists of rolling hills, small thatched-roof farmhouses, beech forests, and whitewashed churches with characteristic stairstep gables. Red brick, which was a favorite material of the nation-building King Christian IV, is everywhere—especially in major civic buildings such as city halls and train stations.

Danes are mainly of Scandinavian descent, with immigrants—mostly Turkish, Polish, Syrian, German, and Iraqi—making up 13 percent of the population. Greenland is home to the indigenous Inuit, and the Faroe Islands to people of Nordic heritage. Most Danes speak both Danish and English, with a small minority speaking German, Inuit, or Faroese.

The population is 75 percent Protestant (mostly Evangelical Lutheran), but only a small minority attend church regularly. The majority are ethnic Danes, and many (but certainly not all) of them have the stereotypical blond hair and blue eyes. Two out of three Danes have last names ending in "-sen." The assimilation of ethnic

Denmark Almanac

Official Name: Kongeriget Danmark—the Kingdom of Denmark—or simply Denmark.

Size: At 16,600 square miles, Denmark is roughly twice the size of Massachusetts). Its population is 5.8 million.

Geography: Denmark includes the Jutland peninsula in northern Europe. Situated between the North Sea and the Baltic Sea, it shares a 42-mile border with Germany. In addition to Greenland and the Faroe Islands, Denmark also encompasses over 400 islands (78 of which are inhabited). Altogether Denmark has 4,544 miles of coastline. The mainland is mostly flat, and nearly two-thirds of the land is cultivated.

Latitude and Longitude: 56°N and 10°E, similar latitude to northern Alberta, Canada.

Biggest Cities: Denmark's capital city, Copenhagen (pop. 1.3 million), is located on the island of Zealand (Sjælland). Aarhus (on the mainland) has 277,000, and Odense (on Funen/Fyn) has 179,000.

Economy: Denmark's modern economy is holding its own, with a gross domestic product of just over $355 billion. Denmark's top exports include pharmaceuticals, machinery, and food products. It is also one of the world's leaders in exports of wind turbine technology. The GDP per capita is about $59,000.

Currency: 6 Danish kroner (DKK) = about $1.

Government: Denmark is a parliamentary constitutional monarchy. Queen Margrethe II is the head of state, but the head of government is the prime minister, a post elected every four years. The 179-member parliament (Folketinget) is elected every four years.

Flag: Red with a white cross.

The Average Dane is 42 years old, has 1.8 children, and will live to be 81. Danes get five weeks of paid vacation per year, and their most popular vacation destination is Spain. The country routinely ranks in the top five in studies of the happiest nations.

groups into this homogeneous society, which began in earnest in the 1980s, is a source of some controversy. But in general, most Danes have a live-and-let-live attitude and enjoy one of the highest standards of living in the world. Taxes are high in this welfare state, but education is free and medical care highly subsidized. Generous parental leave extends to both men and women.

DENMARK

Denmark, one of the most environmentally conscious European countries, is a front-runner in renewable energy, recycling, and organic farming. You'll see lots of modern windmills dotting the countryside. Wind power accounts for 47 percent of Denmark's energy today. By 2030, the country hopes to free itself completely from its dependence on fossil fuels. About 60 percent of waste is recycled. In grocery stores, organic products are shelved right alongside nonorganic ones—for the same price.

Denmark's Queen Margrethe II is a very popular and talented woman who, along with her royal duties, has designed coins, stamps, and book illustrations. Danes gather around the TV on New Year's Eve to hear her annual speech to the nation and flock to the Royal Palace in Copenhagen on April 16 to sing her "Happy Birthday." Her son, Crown Prince Frederik, married Australian Mary Donaldson in 2004. Their son Christian's birth in 2005 was cause for a national celebration (the couple now have four children).

The Danes are proud of their royal family and of the flag, a white cross on a red background. Legend says it fell from the sky during a 13th-century battle in Estonia, making it Europe's oldest continuously used flag. You'll see it everywhere—decorating cakes, on clothing, or fluttering in the breeze atop government buildings. It's as much a decorative symbol as a patriotic one.

You'll also notice that the Danes have an odd fixation on two animals: elephants and polar bears, both of which are symbols of national (especially royal) pride. The Order of the Elephant is the highest honor that the Danish monarch can bestow on someone; if you see an emblematic elephant, you know somebody very important is involved. And the polar bear represents the Danish protectorate of Greenland—a welcome reminder to Danes that their nation is more than just Jutland and a bunch of flat little islands.

From an early age, Danes develop a passion for soccer. You may see red-and-white-clad fans singing on their way to a match. Despite the country's small size, the Danish national team does

DENMARK

well in international competition. Other popular sports include sailing, cycling, badminton, and team handball.

The Danish language, with its three extra vowels (Æ, Ø, and Å), is notoriously difficult for foreigners to pronounce. Even seemingly predictable consonants can be tricky. For example, the letter "d" is often dropped, so the word *gade* (street)—which you'll see, hear, and say constantly—is pronounced "gah-eh." Luckily for us, most Danes also speak English and are patient with thick-tongued foreigners. Danes have playful fun teasing tourists who make the brave attempt to say Danish words. The hardest phrase, *rød grød med fløde* (a delightful red fruit porridge topped with cream), is nearly impossible for a non-Dane to pronounce. Ask a local to help you.

Sample Denmark's sweet treats at one of the many bakeries you'll see. The pastries that we call "Danish" in the US are called *wienerbrød* in Denmark. Bakeries line their display cases with several varieties of *wienerbrød* and other delectable sweets. Try *kringle, snegle,* or *Napoleonshatte,* or find your own favorite. (Chances are it will be easier to enjoy than to pronounce.) To learn about two of Denmark's great cheap eats, the open-faced sandwich *(smørrebrød)* and the hot dog *(pølse),* see page 111.

For a selection of useful Danish survival phrases, see the next page. Two important words to know are *skål* ("cheers," a ritual always done with serious eye contact) and *hyggelig* (pronounced HEW-geh-lee), meaning warm and cozy. Danes treat their home like a sanctuary and spend a great deal of time improving their gardens and houses—inside and out. Cozying up one's personal space (a national obsession) is something the Danes do best. If you have the opportunity, have some Danes adopt you during your visit so you can enjoy their warm hospitality.

Heaven to a Dane is returning home after a walk in a beloved beech forest to enjoy open-faced sandwiches washed down with beer among good friends. Around the *hyggelig* candlelit table, there will be a spirited discussion of the issues of the day, plenty of laughter, and probably a few good-natured jokes about the Swedes or Norwegians. *Skål!*

Danish Survival Phrases

The Danes tend to say words quickly and clipped. In fact, many short vowels end in a "glottal stop"—a very brief vocal break immediately following the vowel. While I haven't tried to indicate these in the phonetics, you can listen for them in Denmark...and (try to) imitate. Three unique Danish vowels are æ (sounds like the e in "egg"), ø (sounds like the German ö—purse your lips and say "oh"), and å (sounds like the o in "bowl"). The letter r is not rolled—it's pronounced farther back in the throat, almost like a w. The d at the end of a word sounds almost like our th; for example, *mad* (food) sounds like "math." In the phonetics, ī sounds like the long i sound in "light," and bolded syllables are stressed.

Hello. (formal)	Goddag.	goh-**day**
Hi. / Bye. (informal)	Hej. / Hej-hej.	hī / hī-hī
Do you speak English?	Taler du engelsk?	**tay**-lehr doo **eng**-esk
Yes. / No.	Ja. / Nej.	yah / nī
Please. (May I?)*	Kan jeg?	kahn yī
Please. (Can you?)*	Kan du?	kahn doo
Please. (Would you?)*	Vil du?	veel doo
Thank you (very much).	(Tusind) tak.	(**too**-sin) tack
You're welcome.	Selv tak.	sehl tack
Can I help (you)?	Kan jeg hjælpe (dig)?	kahn yī **yehl**-peh (dī)
Excuse me. (to pass)	Undskyld mig.	**oon**-skewl mī
Excuse me. (Can you help me?)	Kan du hjælpe mig?	kahn doo **yehl**-peh mī
(Very) good.	(Meget) godt.	(**mī**-ehl) goht
Goodbye.	Farvel.	fah-**vehl**
zero / one / two	nul / en / to	nool / een / toh
three / four	tre / fire	tray / feer
five / six	fem / seks	fehm / sehks
seven / eight	syv / otte	syew / **oh**-deh
nine / ten	ni / ti	nee / tee
hundred	hundrede	**hoo**-nuh
thousand	tusind	**too**-sin
How much?	Hvor meget?	vor **mī**-ehl
local currency (Danish) crown	(Danske) kroner	(**dahn**-skeh) **kroh**-neh
Where is...?	Hvor er...?	vor ehr
...the toilet	...toilettet	toy-**leh**-teht
men / women	herrer / damer	**hehr**-ah / **day**-mah
water / coffee	vand / kaffe	van / **kah**-feh
beer / wine	øl / vin	uhl / veen
Cheers!	Skål!	skohl
Can I have the bill?	Kan jeg få regningen?	kahn yī foh **rī**-ning-ehn

*Because Danish has no single word for "please," they approximate that sentiment by asking "May I?," "Can you?," or "Would you?," depending on the context.

COPENHAGEN

København

Copenhagen, Denmark's capital, is the gateway to Scandinavia. It's an improbable combination of corny Danish clichés, well-dressed executives having a business lunch amid cutting-edge contemporary architecture, and some of the funkiest counterculture in Europe. And yet, it all just works so tidily together. With the Øresund Bridge connecting Sweden and Denmark (creating the region's largest metropolitan area), Copenhagen is energized and ready to dethrone Stockholm as Scandinavia's powerhouse city.

A busy day cruising the canals, wandering through the palace, and taking an old-town walk will give you your historical bearings. Then, after another day strolling the Strøget (STROY-et, Europe's first and greatest pedestrian shopping mall), biking the canals, and sampling the Danish good life (including a gooey "Danish" pastry), you'll feel right at home. Live it up in Scandinavia's cheapest and most fun-loving capital.

PLANNING YOUR TIME

A first visit deserves a minimum of two days. Note that many sights are closed on Monday.

Budget Itinerary Tip: Kamikaze sightseers on tight budgets see Copenhagen as a useful Scandinavian bottleneck. They sleep heading into town by train, tour the city during the day, and sleep on a boat or train as they travel north to their next destination. At the end of their Scandinavian travels, they do the same thing in reverse. The result is two days and no nights in Copenhagen (you can check your bag and take a shower at the train station). Considering the joy of Oslo and Stockholm, this isn't all that crazy if you have limited time (and can sleep on a moving train or boat). Consider taking a night train to Sweden with connections to Stockholm, or cruise up to Oslo on a night boat (see "Copenhagen Connections" at the end of this chapter).

Day 1
Catch a 9:30 city walking tour with Richard Karpen (Mon-Sat mid-May–mid-Sept). After lunch, catch the relaxing canal-boat tour out to *The Little Mermaid* and back. Enjoy the rest of the afternoon tracing Denmark's cultural roots in the National Museum and visiting the Ny Carlsberg Glyptotek art gallery (Impressionists and Danish artists). Spend the evening strolling with Copenhageners as you follow my Copenhagen City Walk.

Day 2
At 10:00, go Neoclassical at Thorvaldsen's Museum, and tour the royal reception rooms at the adjacent Christiansborg Palace. After a *smørrebrød* lunch, spend the afternoon seeing Rosenborg Castle, with Denmark's crown jewels. Spend the evening at Tivoli Gardens.

Christiania—the hippie squatters' community—is not for everyone. But it's worth considering if you're intrigued by alternative lifestyles, or simply want a break from museums. During a busy trip, Christiania fits best in the evening.

Orientation to Copenhagen

Copenhagen is huge (with 1.3 million people), but for most visitors, the walkable core is the diagonal axis formed by the train station, Tivoli Gardens, Rådhuspladsen (City Hall Square), and the Strøget pedestrian street, ending at the colorful old Nyhavn sailors' harbor. Bubbling with street life, colorful pedestrian zones, and most of the city's sightseeing, the Strøget is fun. But also be sure to get off the main drag and explore. Doing things by bike or on foot, you'll stumble upon some charming bits of Copenhagen that many travelers miss.

Outside of the old city center are three areas of interest to tourists:

To the north are Rosenborg Castle and Amalienborg Palace, with *The Little Mermaid* nearby.

To the east, across the harbor, are Christianshavn (Copenha-

The Story of Copenhagen

If you study your map carefully, you can read the history of Copenhagen in today's street plan. København ("Merchants' Harbor") was born on the little island of Slotsholmen—today home to Christiansborg Palace—in 1167. What was Copenhagen's medieval moat is now a string of pleasant lakes and parks, including Tivoli Gardens. You can still make out some of the zigzag pattern of the moats and ramparts in the city's greenbelt.

Many of these fortifications, and several other landmarks, were built by Denmark's most memorable king. You need to remember only one character in Copenhagen's history: Christian IV. Ruling from 1588 to 1648, he was Denmark's Renaissance king and a royal party animal (see the "King Christian IV" sidebar, later). The personal energy of this "Builder King" sparked a Golden Age when Copenhagen prospered and many of the city's grandest buildings were erected. In the 17th century, Christian IV extended the city fortifications to the north, doubling the size of the city, while adding a grid plan of streets and his Rosenborg Castle. This "new town" was the district around the Amalienborg Palace.

In 1850, Copenhagen's 140,000 residents all lived within this defensive system. Building in the no-man's-land outside the walls was only allowed with the understanding that in the event of an attack, you'd burn your dwellings to clear the way for a good defense.

Most of the city's historic buildings still in existence were built within the medieval walls, but conditions became too crowded, and outbreaks of disease forced Copenhagen to spread outside the walls. Ultimately those walls were torn down and replaced with "rampart streets" that define today's city center: Vestervoldgade (literally, "West Rampart Street"), Nørrevoldgade ("North"), and Østervoldgade ("East"). The fourth side is the harbor and the island of Slotsholmen, where København was born.

gen's "Little Amsterdam" district) and the alternative enclave of Christiania.

To the west (behind the train station) is Vesterbro, a young and trendy part of town with lots of cafés, bars, and boutiques; the hip Meatpacking District (Kødbyen); and the Carlsberg Brewery (plus the picnic-friendly Frederiksberg Park).

Most of these sights are walkable from the Strøget, but taking a bike, Metro, bus, or taxi is more efficient. I rent a bike for my entire visit (for about the cost of a single cab ride per day) and park it safely in my hotel courtyard. I get anywhere in the town center faster than by taxi (nearly anything is within a 10-minute pedal). In good weather, the city is an absolute delight by bike (for more on biking in Copenhagen, see "Getting Around Copenhagen: By Bike," later).

TOURIST INFORMATION

Copenhagen's TI, which bills itself as "Wonderful Copenhagen," is a blatantly for-profit company providing information only about businesses that pay hefty fees. While they can answer basic questions, their two most convenient offices—at the train station (daily 9:00-17:00) and on Vesterbrogade—are worthwhile mostly for their big racks of brochures and the free *Bus, Train & Metro Guide* map. You can pick up a free city map just as easily at many hotels and other places in town (main TI: May-June and Sept generally Mon-Sat 9:00-18:00, Sun until 16:00; shorter hours off-season, Vesterbrogade 4A, just up the street from the main exit of train station—across from the towering Radisson Blu Royal Hotel, good Lagkagehuset bakery in building; +45 70 22 24 42, www. visitcopenhagen.com).

Copenhagen Card: This card includes entry to many of the city's sights (including expensive ones, like Tivoli and Rosenborg Castle) and all local transportation in all zones of the greater Copenhagen area. It can save busy sightseers some money and the hassle of choosing the right transportation pass. If you're planning on visiting a lot of attractions (especially ones with steep entry prices) and are going to travel to outlying sights such as Kronborg Castle and Roskilde Cathedral, do the math to see if buying this pass adds up (419 DKK/24 hours, 619 DKK/48 hours, 759 DKK/72 hours, 889 DKK/96 hours, 999 DKK/120 hours; sold at the TI, online, and some hotels; www.copenhagencard.com).

Copenhagen Newspaper: The weekly English-language newspaper, *The Copenhagen Post,* has good articles about what's going on in town. Read it online at www.cphpost.dk (also available in print, sometimes free at TI or some hotels, or buy it at a 7-Eleven or newsstand).

ARRIVAL IN COPENHAGEN
By Train

The main train station is called Hovedbanegården (HOETH-bahn-gorn; look for *København H* on signs and schedules). It's a temple of travel and a hive of travel-related activity (and 24-hour thievery). Kiosks and fast-food eateries cluster in the middle of the main arrivals hall. From the main entrance, the **ticket office** is at

COPENHAGEN

Copenhagen

1. Pharmacy (2)
2. Launderette (2)
3. Bike Rental (2)
4. Bike Copenhagen with Mike

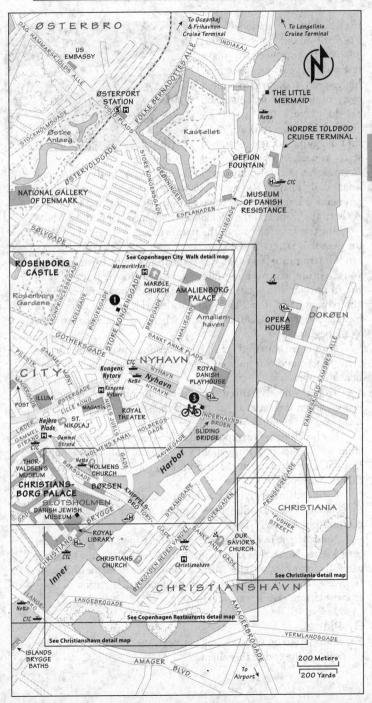

ØSTERBRO

DAG HAMMARSKJÖLDS ALLE

US EMBASSY

To Oceankaj & Frihavnen Cruise Terminal

To Langelinie Cruise Terminal

INDIAKAJ

ØSTERPORT STATION S M

OSLO PLADS

FOLKE BERNADOTTES ALLE

THE LITTLE MERMAID

Netto

STOCKHOLMSGADE

Østre Anlæg

ØSTERVOLDGADE

STORE KONGENSGADE

GRØNNINGEN

Kastellet

NORDRE TOLDBOD CRUISE TERMINAL

GEFION FOUNTAIN

H CTC

NATIONAL GALLERY OF DENMARK

ESPLANADEN

AMALIEGADE

MUSEUM OF DANISH RESISTANCE

SØLVGADE

See Copenhagen City Walk detail map

ROSENBORG CASTLE

Marmorkirken

MARBLE CHURCH

AMALIENBORG PALACE

Rosenborg Gardens

KONPRINCESSEGADE

ABELGADE

BORGERGADE

STORE KONGENSGADE

BREDGADE

1

AMALIEGADE

Amalien-haven

OPERA HOUSE

DOKØEN

GOTHERSGADE

SANKT ANNÆ PLADS

CITY

PILESTR.

GAMMEL MØNT

MAGEGADE

ØSTERGADE

NIELS JUELS GADE

CTC

NYHAVN

Kongens Nytorv

Netto

Nyhavn

NYHAVN

ROYAL DANISH PLAYHOUSE

KANNERKJOLD-SAMSØES ALLE

POST

ILLUM

Kongens Nytorv M

LILLE KONG.

MAGASIN

ROYAL THEATER

3

H

INDERHAVNS-BROEN

LÆDER.

GAMMEL STRAND

Højbro Plads

ST. NIKOLAJ

Gammel Strand M

HOLBERGS GADE

HAVNEGADE

SLIDING BRIDGE

THOR-VALDSEN'S MUSEUM

CTC

HOLMENS KANAL

Netto

HOLMENS CHURCH

BØRSGADE

Harbor

CHRISTIANS-BORG PALACE

BØRSEN

SLOTSHOLMEN

Danish Jewish Museum

KNIPPELS-BRO TORV.

GADE

STRANDGADE

OVERGADEN

PRINSESSEGADE

CHRISTIANIA

PUSHER STREET

GADE

ROYAL LIBRARY

CHRISTIANS CHURCH

H

CTC

OVERGADEN NEDEN VANDET

SANKT ANNÆ GADE

CTC

M

Christianshavn

OUR SAVIOR'S CHURCH

See Christiania detail map

Inner

CHRISTIANS

GADE

CHRISTIANSHAVN

LANGE-BRO

Netto

CTC

LANGEBROGADE

See Copenhagen Restaurants detail map

AMAGERBROGADE

VERMLANDSGADE

See Christianshavn detail map

ISLANDS BRYGGE BATHS

AMAGER BLVD.

To Airport

200 Meters

200 Yards

the back of the station (Mon-Fri 7:00-20:00; Sat-Sun 8:00-18:00). If you need to make reservations for an upcoming high-speed train trip (required even of rail-pass holders), you can do it here.

Within the station, you'll find **baggage storage** (go down stairs at back of station marked *Bagagebokse;* lockers and checkroom/*garderobe* both open long hours daily); pay **WCs** (right side of station); a branch of the recommended **Lagkagehuset** bakery (front of station); and lots more. At both the front and the back of the station, you'll find **ATMs.**

The tracks at the back of the station (tracks 9-10 and 11-12) are for the suburban train (S-tog).

Getting into Town: If you want to get right to sightseeing, you're within easy walking distance of downtown. Just walk out the front door and you'll run into one of the entrances for Tivoli amusement park; if you go around its left side and up a couple of blocks, you'll be at Rådhuspladsen, where my Copenhagen City Walk begins.

Hotels are scattered far and wide around town. It's best to get arrival instructions from your hotelier, but if you're on your own, here are some tips:

To reach hotels **behind the station,** slip out the back door—just go down the stairs at the back of the station marked *Reventlowsgade.*

For hotels **near Nørreport**, ride the S-tog from the station two stops to Nørreport, within about a 10-minute walk of the hotels. Bus #5C, which starts at the airport, also runs from the train station to Nørreport.

For hotels **near Nyhavn**, you can take the Metro three stops to Kongens Nytorv, within a few minutes' walk of Nyhavn. Or you can take bus #26 to Nyhavn.

Note: If you're staying near Nørreport (or near Nyhavn, an easy Metro connection from Nørreport), check the train schedule carefully; many local trains (such as some from Roskilde and those from the airport) continue through the main train station to Nørreport Station, saving you an extra step.

By Plane

For information on Copenhagen's airport, see "Copenhagen Connections" at the end of this chapter.

COPENHAGEN

By Boat or Cruise Ship

For information on Copenhagen's cruise terminals, see "Copenhagen Connections" at the end of this chapter.

HELPFUL HINTS

Blue Monday: As you plan, remember that most sights close on Monday, but these attractions remain open: Christiansborg Palace (closed Mon Oct-April), City Hall, Rosenborg Castle (closed Mon off-season), Round Tower, Royal Library, Our Savior's Church, Tivoli Gardens (generally closed late Sept-late March), both Harbor Baths (closed Oct-May), and various tours (canal, bus, walking, and bike). You can explore Christiania, but Monday is its rest day so it's unusually quiet and some restaurants are closed.

Jazz Festival: The Copenhagen Jazz Festival—10 days in early July—puts the town in a rollicking slide-trombone mood. The Danes are Europe's jazz enthusiasts, and this music festival fills the town with happiness. The TI prints up an extensive listing of each year's festival events, or get the latest at Jazz.dk. There's also a winter jazz festival in February.

Pharmacy: Steno Apotek is across from the train station (open 24 hours, Vesterbrogade 6C, +45 33 14 82 66). **Kongelig Hof Apotek** is at the other end of town, between Nyhavn and Amalienborg Palace (Mon-Fri 9:00-18:00, Sat 10:00-14:00, closed Sun, Store Kongensgade 45, +45 33 14 11 68). For locations, see the "Copenhagen" map, earlier.

Laundry: Møntvask is a good coin-op laundry with a location near Nørreport (50 yards from Ibsens Hotel at Nansensgade 84) and another several blocks west of my train-station-area hotel listings at Flensborggade 20 (both daily 7:00-21:00, see the "Copenhagen" map, earlier, for locations). *Vaskel* is wash, *tørring* is dry, and *sæbe* is soap.

Ferries: While in Copenhagen, book any ferries that you plan to take in Scandinavia. Visit a travel agent or book directly with the ferry company. For the Copenhagen-Oslo overnight ferry, contact **DFDS** or visit the **DSB Rejsebureau** at the main train station (see page 124 for details). For boats between Stockholm and Helsinki, see page 500. For the boat from Helsinki to St. Petersburg, see page 634.

GETTING AROUND COPENHAGEN
By Public Transit

It's easy to navigate Copenhagen, with its fine buses, Metro, and S-tog (a suburban train system with stops in the city). Be sure to pick up the *Bus, Train & Metro Guide* map at the TI for an overview of all your public transit options. Info: DinOffentligeTransport.dk.

For a helpful website that covers public transport (nationwide) in English, consult Rejseplanen.dk.

Tickets and Passes: The same tickets are used throughout the system. A 24-DKK, **two-zone ticket** gets you an hour's travel within the center—pay as you board buses, or buy from station ticket offices, convenience stores, or vending machines for the Metro. (Ticket machines accept most American credit cards with a chip, and most machines also take Danish cash; if the machine won't take your credit card, find a cashier.) You can also download the free Copenhagen DOT app to your smartphone. Assume you'll be within the middle two zones unless traveling to or from the airport, which requires a **three-zone ticket** (36 DKK).

If you plan to ride transit exclusively in central Copenhagen, the **City Pass Small** is a good value—and it covers the trip from the airport (80 DKK/24 hours, 150 DKK/48 hours, 200 DKK/72 hours, covers zones 1-4). If you'll be traveling to outlying sights too, including Roskilde, Frederiksborg Castle, Louisiana Art Museum, or Kronborg Castle, consider a **City Pass Large** (160 DKK/24 hours, 300 DKK/48 hours, 400 DKK/72 hours, covers all travel zones). You can buy a pass at some train and Metro stations or at CityPass.dk; it will be sent as a text message to your mobile phone.

For some visitors, the **Copenhagen Card** will be the best choice for its sheer convenience. It covers all public transportation in the greater Copenhagen area (including to Roskilde, Frederiksborg Castle, Louisiana Art Museum, etc.), canal boat tours, and admission to nearly all the major sights (see "Tourist Information," earlier).

Buses: While the train system is slick (Metro and S-tog, described later), buses serve many of the major sights in town every five to eight minutes during daytime hours. If you're not riding a bike everywhere, get comfortable with the buses. Bus drivers are patient, have change, and speak English. City maps list bus routes. Locals are usually friendly and helpful. There's also a floating Harbor Bus (described on page 49).

Bus lines that end with "A" (such as #2A) use quiet, eco-friendly, electric buses that are smaller than normal buses, allowing access into the narrower streets of the Old Town. Among these, **#2A** is particularly useful, going from Christianshavn to the main train station and Rådhuspladsen in the city center, then onward to points west.

Other, non-"A" buses, which are bigger and tend to be more direct, can be faster for some trips:

Bus **#5C** connects the airport more or less directly to the main train station, Rådhuspladsen, and Nørreport.

Bus **#23** runs a handy route right through the main tourist zone, from the main train station/Tivoli to the Østerport station with stops at Rådhuspladsen, Stormbroen (National Museum), Gammelstrand, and Kongens Nytorv (near Nyhavn).

Bus **#26** runs from the main train station/Tivoli to Nyhavn-broen (near Nyhavn).

Bus **#27** runs from the cruise ports of Oceankaj and Langelinie to the Østerport station, with a stop on Indiakaj, near *The Little Mermaid.*

Buses **#31** and **#37** run from the main train station to Christianshavn.

Metro: Copenhagen's Metro is simple, futuristic, and growing—the city is nearing completion of a multiyear Metro expan-

sion project; the new M3 City Circle line (Cityringen) has added 17 stations in the center. The Metro connects the airport and several stops within the city center: Nørreport (near Rosenborg Castle), Østerport, Marmorkirken (near Amalienborg Palace), Kongens Nytorv (near Nyhavn and the Strøget's north end), Gammel Strand (near Slotsholmen Island), Rådhuspladsen, the main train station, and Christianshavn. Nearly all recommended hotels are within walking distance of the main train station or one of these stops. For details on the Metro, including route maps, see http://intl.m.dk.

S-tog Train: The S-tog is basically a commuter line that links stations on the main train line through Copenhagen; for those visiting the city, the most important stops are the main train station and Nørreport (where it ties into the Metro system). Note that while rail passes are valid on the S-tog, it's probably not worth using a travel day. The S-tog is very handy for reaching many of the outlying sights described in the Near Copenhagen chapter.

By Boat

The hop-on, hop-off Harbor Bus (Havnebus) boat stops at the Black Diamond library, Christianshavn (near Knippels Bridge), Nyhavn, the Opera House, and the Nordre Toldbod cruise-ship pier, which is a short walk from *The Little Mermaid* site. The boat is part of the city bus system (lines #991 and #992) and covered by the tickets described earlier. Taking a long ride on this boat, from the library to the end of the line, is the "poor man's cruise"—without commentary, of course (runs 6:00-19:00). Or, for a true sightseeing trip, consider a guided harbor cruise (described later, under "Tours in Copenhagen").

By Taxi

Taxis are plentiful, easy to call or flag down, and pricey (39 DKK pickup charge and then about 8.50 DKK/kilometer—higher in evenings and on weekends). For a short ride, four people spend about the same by taxi as by bus. Calling +45 35 35 35 35 will get you a taxi within minutes...with the meter already well on its way. Uber does not operate in Copenhagen.

By Bike

Cyclists see more, save time and money, and really feel like locals. With a bike, you have Copenhagen at your command. I'd rather have a bike than a car and driver at my disposal. Virtually every street has a dedicated bike lane (complete with bike signal lights). Warning: Police routinely issue hefty tickets to anyone riding on sidewalks or through pedestrian zones. Note also that bikes can't be parked just anywhere. Observe others and park your bike among other bikes. The simple built-in lock that binds the back tire is adequate.

Renting a Bike: Your best bet for renting a bike is often your hotelier: Many rent (or loan) decent bikes at fair rates to guests.

For an (often) better-quality bike and advice from someone with cycle expertise, consider one of these rental outfits in or near the city center (see the "Copenhagen" map, earlier, for locations).

Københavns Cyklebørs, near Nørreport Station, has a good selection of three-gear bikes (90 DKK/1 day, 170 DKK/2 days, 240 DKK/3 days, 450 DKK/week; Mon-Fri 10:00-17:30, Sat-Sun until 14:00, closed Sun in off-season; Gothersgade 157, +45 33 14 07 17, www.cykelborsen.dk).

Copenhagen Bicycles, at the entrance to Nyhavn by the Inderhavnsbroen pedestrian/bicycle bridge, rents basic three-gear bikes (90 DKK/3 hours, 110 DKK/6 hours, 120 DKK/24 hours, includes lock, helmet-40 DKK, Mon-Fri 7:30-17:30, Sat-Sun 9:30-16:00, Nyhavn 44, +45 35 43 01 22, www.copenhagenbicycles.dk).

They also offer guided tours in English and Danish (120 DKK, not including bicycle, April-Sept daily at 11:00, 2.5 hours).

Using City Bikes: The city's public bike-rental program **Bycyklen** lets you ride white, three-gear "smart bikes" (with GPS and an electric motor) for 60 DKK/hour. You'll find them parked in racks near the train station, on either side of City Hall, and at many locations around town. Use the touchscreen on the handlebars to create an account. At their website (http://bycyklen.dk), you can locate docking stations, reserve a bike at a specific station, and create an account in advance. I'd use these bikes for a short hop here or there, but for more than a couple of hours, it's more cost-efficient to rent a regular bicycle.

Tours in Copenhagen

ON FOOT

Copenhagen is an ideal city to get to know by foot. You have several good tour options.

▲▲Hans Christian Andersen Tours by Richard Karpen

Once upon a time, American Richard Karpen visited Copenhagen and fell in love with the city. Now, dressed as writer Hans Christian Andersen in a 19th-century top hat and long coat, he leads 1.5-hour tours that wander in and out of buildings, courtyards, back streets, and unusual parts of the old town. Along the one-mile route, he gives insightful and humorous background on the history, culture, and contemporary life of Denmark, starting with the colorful Viking period and the royal family, up to current topics like Denmark's commitment to renewable energy and the core values that make Danes particularly "Danish" (150 DKK, kids under 12 free; departs from outside the TI, up the street from the main train station at Vesterbrogade 4A; mid-May-mid-Sept Mon-Sat at 9:30, none on Sun; no reservations needed for scheduled tours—just show up. Richard departs promptly—if you miss him try to catch up with the tour at the next stop at Rådhuspladsen).

You can also hire Richard for 1.5-hour private city tours, or of Rosenborg Castle or the National History Museum (price depends on number of participants, May-Sept, mobile +45 91 61 95 02, www.copenhagenwalks.com, copenhagenwalks@yahoo.com).

Hans Christian Andersen (1805-1875)

The author of such classic fairy tales as *The Ugly Duckling* was an ugly duckling himself—a misfit who blossomed. Hans Christian Andersen (called H. C., pronounced "hoe see" by the Danes) was born to a poor shoemaker in Odense. As a child he was gangly and high-strung, and he avoided school because the kids laughed at him. Instead, he spent his time in a fantasy world of books and plays. He loved playing with a marionette theater made by his father, sparking a lifelong love affair with the theater. In 1819, at the age of 14, he moved to Copenhagen to pursue an acting career and worked as a boy soprano for the Royal Theater. When his voice changed, the director encouraged him to return to school. He dutifully attended—a teenager among boys—and eventually went on to the university. As rejections piled up for his acting aspirations, Andersen began to shift his theatrical ambitions to playwriting.

After graduation, Andersen won a two-year scholarship to travel around Europe, the first of many trips he'd make and write about. His experiences abroad were highly formative, providing inspiration for many of his tales. Still in his 20s, he published an obviously autobiographical novel, *The Improvisatore,* about a poor young man who comes into his own while traveling in Italy. The novel launched his writing career, and soon he was hobnobbing with the international crowd—Charles Dickens, Victor Hugo,

▲Daily City Walks by Red Badge Guides

Five local female guides work together, giving two-hour English-language city tours. Their walks mix the city's highlights, back lanes, history, art, and contemporary social issues, and finish at Amalienborg Palace around noon for the changing of the guard (150 DKK, daily May-Sept at 10:00, departs from TI at Vesterbrogade 4A, just show up, pay direct, small groups, +45 20 92 23 87, www.redbadgeguides.dk, redbadgeguides@gmail.com). They also offer private guided tours year-round upon request.

▲▲Copenhagen History Tours

Christian Donatzky, a charming Dane with a master's degree in history, runs a walking tour on Saturday mornings. In April and May, the theme is "Old Copenhagen" (covering the period from 1100-1600); in June and July, "King's Copenhagen" (1600-1800); and in August and September, "Hans Christian Andersen's Co-

Franz Liszt, Richard Wagner, Henrik Ibsen, and Edvard Grieg.

Though he wrote novels, plays, and travel literature, it was his fairy tales, including *The Ugly Duckling, The Emperor's New Clothes, The Princess and the Pea, The Little Mermaid, The Snow Queen,* and *The Red Shoes,* that made him famous in Denmark and abroad as the "Danish Charles Dickens." Some stories are based on earlier folk tales, and others came straight from his inventive mind, all written in an informal, conversational style that was considered unusual and even surprising at the time.

Andersen's compelling tales appeal to children and adults alike. They're full of magic and touch on strong, universal emotions—the pain of being different, the joy of self-discovery, and the struggle to fit in. The ugly duckling, for example, is teased by his fellow ducks before he finally discovers his true identity as a beautiful swan. In *The Emperor's New Clothes,* a boy is derided by everyone for speaking the simple, self-evident truth that the emperor is fooling himself. (For commentary on Andersen's famous story *The Little Mermaid*—and what it might tell us about his life—see page 71.)

Despite his many famous friends, Andersen remained a lonely soul who never married. He journaled about unrequited love affairs with several women, including the famous opera star of the day, Jenny Lind, the "Swedish Nightingale." Without a family of his own, he became very close with the children of his friends—and, through his fairy tales, with a vast extended family of kids around the world. By the time of his death, the poor shoemaker's son was wealthy, cultured, and had been knighted. His rise through traditional class barriers mirrors the social progress of the 19th century.

penhagen" (1800-present). Those with a serious interest in Danish history will find these tours time well spent (100 DKK, Sat at 10:00, approximately 1.5 hours, small groups of 5-15 people, tours depart from statue of Bishop Absalon on Højbro Plads between the Strøget and Christiansborg Palace, English only, no reservations necessary—just show up, +45 28 49 44 35, www.historytours.dk, info@historytours.dk).

BY BOAT

For many, the best way to experience the city's canals and harbor is by canal boat. Two companies offer essentially the same live, three-language, one-hour cruises. Both boats leave at

Copenhagen at a Glance

▲▲▲**Tivoli Gardens** Copenhagen's classic amusement park, with rides, music, food, and other fun. **Hours:** Late March-mid-Sept daily 11:00-23:00, Fri-Sat until 24:00, also open daily 11:00-22:00 for a week in mid-Oct and mid-Nov-New Year's Day. See page 71.

▲▲▲**National Museum** History of Danish civilization with tourable 19th-century Victorian Apartment. **Hours:** Museum—Tue-Sun 10:00-17:00, Thu until 20:00, closed Mon; Victorian Apartment— English tours June-Aug Sat-Sun at 12:00, Danish tours Sat-Sun at 11:00, 12:00, and 13:00 year-round. See page 76

▲▲▲**Rosenborg Castle and Treasury** Renaissance castle of larger-than-life "warrior king" Christian IV. **Hours:** Mid-June-mid-Sept daily 9:00-17:00; mid-April-mid-June and mid-Sept-Oct daily 10:00-16:00, except closed Mon in April; shorter hours and generally closed Mon rest of year. See page 86.

▲▲▲**Christiania** Colorful counterculture squatters' colony. **Hours:** Guided tours at 15:00 (daily July-Aug, only Sat-Sun rest of year). See page 95.

▲▲**Christiansborg Palace** Royal reception rooms with dazzling tapestries. **Hours:** Daily 10:00-17:00, Oct-April closed Mon (and may close for royal events); stables and carriage museum open 13:30-16:00—longer hours possible in July; palace chapel open Sun 10:00-17:00, except daily in July. See page 79.

▲▲**Thorvaldsen's Museum** Works of the Danish Neoclassical sculptor. **Hours:** Tue-Sun 10:00-17:00, Thu until 21:00, closed Mon. See page 80.

▲▲**Museum of Danish Resistance** Chronicle of Denmark's strug-

least twice an hour from Nyhavn and Christiansborg Palace, cruise around the palace and Christianshavn area, and then proceed into the wide-open harbor. Best on a sunny day, it's a relaxing way to see *The Little Mermaid* and munch on a lazy picnic during the slow-moving narration.

▲Netto-Bådene Cruises

These inexpensive cruises cost about half the price of their rival, Canal Tours Copenhagen. Go with Netto; there's no reason to pay nearly double (50 DKK, mid-March-mid-Oct daily 10:00-17:00, runs later in summer, shorter hours in winter, sign at dock shows next departure, generally every 30 minutes, dress warmly—boats gle against the Nazis. **Hours**: Daily 10:00-16:00, Oct-April closed Mon. See page 85.

▲**City Hall** Copenhagen's landmark, packed with Danish history and symbolism and topped with a tower. **Hours:** Mon-Fri 9:00-16:00, some Sat 9:30-13:00, closed Sun. See page 73.

▲**Ny Carlsberg Glyptotek** Scandinavia's top art gallery, featuring Egyptians, Greeks, Etruscans, French, and Danes. **Hours:** Tue-Sun 10:00-17:00, Thu until 21:00, closed Mon. See page 74.

▲**Danish Jewish Museum** Exhibit tracing the 400-year history of Danish Jews, in a unique building by American architect Daniel Libeskind. **Hours:** Tue-Sun 10:00-17:00; Sept-May Tue-Fri 13:00-16:00, Sat-Sun 12:00-17:00; closed Mon year-round. See page 83.

▲**Amalienborg Museum** Quick and intimate look at Denmark's royal family. **Hours:** Early-July-early-Aug Tue-Sun 10:00-16:00; rest of year Tue-Sun from 11:00; closed Mon year-round except Oct. See page 84.

▲**Rosenborg Gardens** Park surrounding Rosenborg Castle, filled with statues and statuesque Danes. See page 92.

▲**National Gallery of Denmark** Good Danish and Modernist collections. **Hours:** Tue-Sun 10:00-18:00, Wed until 20:00, closed Mon. See page 92.

▲**Our Savior's Church** Spiral-spired church with bright Baroque interior. **Hours:** Church—daily 11:00-15:30 but may close for special services; tower—May-Sept Mon-Sat 9:30-19:00, Sun from 10:30; shorter hours off-season, closed mid-Dec-Feb and in bad weather. See page 94.

are open-top until Sept, +45 32 54 41 02, www.havnerundfart. dk). Netto boats often make two stops where passengers can get off, then hop back on a later boat—at the bridge near *The Little Mermaid*, and at the Langebro bridge near Danhostel. Not every boat makes these stops; check the clock on the bridges for the next departure time.

Don't confuse the cheaper Netto and pricier Canal Tours Copenhagen boats: At Nyhavn, the Netto dock is midway down the canal (on the city side), while the Canal Tours Copenhagen dock is at the head of the canal. Near Christiansborg Palace, the Netto boats leave from Holmen's Bridge in front of the palace, while

Canal Tours Copenhagen boats depart from Gammel Strand, 200 yards away. Boats leaving from Christiansborg are generally less crowded than those leaving from Nyhavn.

Canal Tours Copenhagen

This more expensive option does the same cruise as Netto for 99 DKK (daily March-late Oct 10:00-17:00, runs later in summer, shorter hours in winter, no tours Jan-Feb, boats are sometimes covered if it's raining, +45 32 96 30 00, www.stromma.dk).

Canal Tours Copenhagen also runs audioguided hop-on, hop-off boat tours (109 DKK/48 hours, daily late May-mid-Sept 9:30-19:00, shorter hours off-season), 1-hour evening **jazz cruises** (see "Nightlife in Copenhagen," page 104), and other theme cruises.

BY BUS
Hop-On, Hop-Off Bus Tours

Several buses with recorded narration circle the city for a basic 1.5-hour orientation, allowing you to get on and off as you like at the following stops: Tivoli Gardens, Gammel Strand near Christiansborg Palace, *The Little Mermaid,* Rosenborg Castle, Nyhavn sailors' quarter, and more. Cruise passengers arriving at the Langelinie Pier can catch a hop-on, hop-off bus there; those arriving at the Oceankaj Pier can take a free shuttle provided by the hop-on, hop-off tour companies (or their own cruise shuttle) to *The Little Mermaid*, where they can pick up a hop-on, hop-off bus.

The same company runs **City Sightseeing**'s red buses and Strömma's green **Hop-On, Hop-Off** buses. Both offer a Mermaid route: City Sightseeing tickets, 240 DKK, are valid 72 hours, and Hop-On, Hop-Off tickets, 250 DKK, are good for 48 hours; other routes include the Carlsberg Brewery and Christiania area (pay driver, 2/hour, May-mid-Sept daily 9:30-18:00, shorter hours off-season, buses depart near the TI in front of the Radisson Blu Royal Hotel and at many other stops throughout city, www.citysightseeing.dk or www.stromma.dk). Strömma's Hop-On, Hop-Off also offers a 250-DKK ticket that includes some bus stops and a cruise on their hop-on, hop-off canal boat.

Another operation—called **Red Buses**—does a similar Mermaid route (every 30-40 minutes, shorter hours off-season; 225 DKK/24 hours, www.redbuses.com).

BY BIKE
▲Bike Copenhagen with Mike

Mike Sommerville offers three-hour guided bike tours of the city. A Copenhagen native, Mike enjoys showing off his city to visitors, offering both historic background and contemporary cultural insights along the way (April-Sept daily at 10:00, second departure

Fri-Sat at 14:30 in summer, must book all tours in advance; 300 DKK includes bike rental, price same with or without a bike, 50-DKK discount with this book—maximum 2 discounts per book and must have book with you, cash only; participants must have good urban biking skills). All tours are in English and depart from his bike shop at Sankt Peders Straede 47, in the Latin Quarter (see the "Copenhagen" map, earlier, for location). Mike also offers private tours; details at www.bikecopenhagenwithmike.dk.

Copenhagen City Walk

This self-guided walk takes about two hours. It starts at Rådhuspladsen (City Hall Square) and heads along the pedestrian street, the Strøget, through the old city, onto the island of Slotsholmen (home of Christiansborg Palace), along the harbor promenade, and through Nyhavn, the sailors' quarter with the city's iconic canal-front houses. The walk officially ends at Kongens Nytorv ("King's New Square"), though you can continue another 10 minutes to Amalienborg Palace and then another 15 minutes beyond that to *The Little Mermaid*.

❶ Rådhuspladsen

Start from Rådhuspladsen, the bustling heart of Copenhagen, dominated by the tower of the City Hall. For 700 years, Co-

penhagen was contained within its city walls, and this square was its fortified west end. By the mid-1800s, 140,000 people were packed inside. The overcrowding led to hygiene problems. (A cholera outbreak killed 5,000.) It was clear: The walls needed to come down...and they did. Those formidable town walls survive today only in echoes—a circular series of roads and the remnants of moats, which are now people-friendly city lakes (see the sidebar on page 42).

• *Stand 50 yards in front of City Hall and turn clockwise for a...*

Rådhuspladsen Spin-Tour: The **City Hall**, or Rådhus, is worth a visit (described on page 73). Old **Hans Christian Andersen** sits to the right of City Hall, almost begging to be in another photo (as he used to in real life). Climb onto his well-worn knee. (While up there, you might take off your shirt for a racy photo, as many Danes enjoy doing.)

He's looking at ❷ **Tivoli Gardens** (across the street), which

Copenhagen City Walk

① Rådhuspladsen
② Tivoli Gardens
③ Weather Girls
④ Strøget
⑤ St. Peter's Church
⑥ Cathedral of Our Lady
⑦ Copenhagen University
⑧ Gammeltorv & Nytorv
⑨ Amagertorv
⑩ Gråbrødretorv
⑪ Royal Copenhagen Store & Illums Bolighus
⑫ Bishop Absalon Statue
⑬ Christiansborg Palace Chapel
⑭ Frederik VII Statue
⑮ Børsen
⑯ Havnegade Promenade
⑰ Inderhavnsbroen Sliding Bridge
⑱ View of Nyhavn
⑲ Kongens Nytorv
⑳ Hviids Vinstue
㉑ Amalienborg Palace & Square
㉒ To Little Mermaid

he loved and which inspired him. Tivoli Gardens was founded in 1843, when magazine publisher Georg Carstensen convinced the king to let him build a pleasure garden outside the walls of crowded Copenhagen. The king quickly agreed, knowing that happy people care less about fighting for democracy. Tivoli became Europe's first great public amusement park. When the train lines came, the station was placed just beyond Tivoli.

The big, glassy building with the *DI* sign is filled with the offices of Danish Industry—a collection of Danish companies whose logos you can see in the windows (plus the Irma grocery store at street level).

The big, broad boulevard is **Vesterbrogade** ("Western Way"), which led to the western gate of the medieval city (behind you, where the pedestrian boulevard begins). Here, in the traffic hub of this huge city, you'll notice...not many cars. Denmark's high tax on car purchases makes the bus, Metro, or bike a sweeter option.

Down Vesterbrogade towers the **Radisson Blu Royal Hotel**, Copenhagen's only skyscraper. Locals say it seems so tall because the clouds hang so low. When it was built in 1960, Copenhageners took one look and decided—that's enough of a skyline. Notice there are no other buildings taller than the five-story limit in the old center.

The golden ❸ **weather girls** (on the corner, high above Vesterbrogade) indicate the weather: on a bike (fair weather) or with an umbrella (foul). These two have been called the only women in Copenhagen you can trust, but for years they've been stuck in the almost-sunny mode...with the bike just peeking out. Notice that the red temperature dots max out at 28° Celsius (that's 82° Fahrenheit...a good memory aid: transpose 28 to get 82).

To the right, just down the street, is the Tiger Store (a popular local "dollar store"...nearly everything is super affordable). The next street (once the local Fleet Street, with the big newspapers) still has the offices for *Politiken* (the leading Danish newspaper) and the best bookstore in town, Boghallen.

As you spin farther right, three fast-food joints stand at the entry to the Strøget, Copenhagen's grand pedestrian boulevard—where we're heading next. Just beyond that and the Art Deco-style Palace Hotel (with a tower to serve as a sister to the City Hall) is the **Lur Blowers sculpture,** which honors the earliest warrior Danes. The *lur* is a curvy, trombone-sounding horn that was used to call soldiers to battle or to accompany pagan religious processions. The earliest bronze *lurs* date as far back as 3,500 years ago. Later, the Vikings used a wood version of the *lur*. The ancient originals, which still play, are displayed in the National Museum.

• *Now head down the pedestrian boulevard (pickpocket alert).*

❹ The Strøget

The American trio of Burger King, 7-Eleven, and KFC marks the start of this otherwise charming pedestrian street. Finished in 1962, Copenhagen's experimental, tremendously successful, and much-copied pedestrian shopping mall is a string of lively (and individually named) streets and lovely squares that bunny-hop through the old town from City Hall to the Nyhavn quarter, a 20-minute stroll away. Though the Strøget has become hamburgerized, historic bits and attractive pieces of old Copenhagen are just off this commercial can-can.

As you wander down this street, remember that the commercial focus of a historic street like the Strøget drives up the land value, which generally trashes the charm and tears down the old buildings. Look above the modern window displays and street-level advertising to discover bits of 19th-century character that still survive. This end of the Strøget is young and cheap, while the far

end has the high-end de-signer shops. Along the way, wonderfully quiet and laid-back areas are just a block or two away on either side.

After one block (at Kattesundet), make a side trip three blocks left into Copenhagen's color-ful **university district** (Latin Quarter). Formerly the old brothel neighborhood, later the heart of Copenhagen's hippie community in the 1960s, today this student area is SoHo chic. Enjoy the colorful string of artsy shops and cafés. Because the old town was densely populated and built of wood, very little survived its many fires. After half-timbered and thatched buildings kept burning down, the city finally mandated that new construction be made of stone. But because stone was so expensive, many people built half-timbered structures, then disguised their facades with stucco, which made them look like stone. Exposed half-timbered structures are seen in courtyards and from the back sides. At Sankt Peders Stræde, turn right and walk to the end of the street. Notice the old guild signs (a baker, a key maker, and so on) identifying the original businesses here.

Along the way, look for large mansions that once circled expansive **courtyards.** As the population grew, the city walls constricted Copenhagen's physical size. The courtyards were gradually filled with higgledy-piggledy secondary buildings. Today throughout the old center, you can step off a busy pedestrian mall and back in time in these characteristic, half-timbered, time-warp courtyards. Replace the parked car with a tired horse and the bikes with a line of outhouses, and you're in 19th-century Copenhagen. If you see an open courtyard door, you're welcome to discreetly wander in and look around.

You'll also pass funky shops and the big brick ❺ **St. Peter's Church** (Sankt Petri Kirke)—the old German merchant community's church, which still holds services in German. Its fine 17th-century brick funerary chapel (filling a ground-floor building out back due to the boggy nature of the soil) is filled with fancy German tombs (typically open to visitors Wed-Sat 11:00-15:00).

• *When Sankt Peders Stræde intersects with Nørregade, look right to find the big, Neoclassical...*

❻ Cathedral of Our Lady (Vor Frue Kirke)

The obelisk-like **Reformation Memorial** across the street from the cathedral celebrates Denmark's break from the Roman Catholic Church to become Lutheran in 1536. Walk around and study the reliefs of great Danish reformers protesting from their pulpits. The relief facing the church shows King Christian III presiding over the pivotal town council meeting when they decided to break away from Rome. As a young man, Prince Christian had traveled to Germany, where he was influenced by Martin Luther. He returned to take the Danish throne by force, despite Catholic opposition. Realizing the advantages of being the head of his own state church, Christian confiscated church property and established the state Lutheran Church. King Christian was crowned inside this cathedral. Be-

cause of the reforms of 1536, there's no Mary in the Cathedral of Our Lady. The other reliefs show the popular religious uprising, with people taking control of the word of God by translating the Bible from Latin into their own language.

Like much of this part of town, the church burned down in the 1807 British bombardment of the city during the Napoleanic Wars. Rebuilt in the Neoclassical style, the cathedral's **facade** looks like a Greek temple. (Two blocks to the right, in the distance, notice more Neoclassicism—the law courts.) You can see why Golden Age Copenhagen (early 1800s) fancied itself a Nordic Athens. Old Testament figures (King David and Moses) flank the cathedral's entryway. Above, John the Baptist stands where you'd expect to see Greek gods. He invites you in...into the New Testament.

The **interior** is a world of Neoclassical serenity (free, open Mon-Sat 8:00-17:00, Sun 12:00-16:30). It feels like a pagan temple that now houses Christianity. The nave is lined by the 12 apostles, clad in classical robes—masterpieces by the great Danish sculptor Bertel Thorvaldsen (see sidebar, page 82). Each strikes a meditative pose, carrying his identifying symbol: Peter with keys, Andrew with the X-shaped cross of his execution,

Matthew and John writing their books, and so on. They lead to a statue of the *Risen Christ* (see photo), standing where the statue of Zeus would have been: inside a temple-like niche, flanked by

columns and topped with a pediment. Rather than wearing a royal robe, Jesus wears his burial shroud, opens his arms wide, and says, "Come to me." (Mormons will recognize this statue—a replica stands in the visitors center at Salt Lake City's Temple Square and is often reproduced in church publications.) The marvelous acoustics are demonstrated in free organ concerts Saturdays in July and August at noon. Notice how, in good Protestant style, only the front half of the pews are "reversible," allowing the congregation to flip around and face the pulpit (in the middle of the church) to better hear the sermon.

• *Head back outside. If you face the church's facade and look to the left (across the square called Frue Plads), you'll see...*

❼ Copenhagen University

Now home to nearly 40,000 students, this university was founded by the king in the 15th century to stop the Danish brain drain to Paris. Today tuition is free (but room, board, and beer are not). Locals say it's easy to get in, but given the wonderful student lifestyle, very hard to get out.

Step up the middle steps of the university's big building; if the doors are open, enter a colorful lobby, starring Athena and Apollo. The frescoes celebrate high thinking, with themes such as the triumph of wisdom over barbarism. Notice how harmoniously the architecture, sculpture, and painting work together.

Outside, busts honor great minds from the faculty, including (at the end) Niels Bohr, a professor who won the 1922 Nobel Prize for theoretical physics. He evaded the clutches of the Nazi science labs by fleeing to America in 1943, where he helped develop the atomic bomb.

• *Rejoin the Strøget (one block downhill from the Reformation Memorial to the black-and-gold fountain) at the twin squares called...*

❽ Gammeltorv and Nytorv

This was the old town center. In Gammeltorv ("Old Square"), the

Fountain of Charity (Caritas) is named for the figure of Charity on top. It has provided drinking water to locals since the early 1600s. Featuring a pregnant woman squirting water from her breasts next to a boy urinating, this was just too much for people of the Victorian Age. They corked both figures and raised the statue to what they hoped would be out of view. The exotic-looking kiosk was one of the city's first community telephone centers from the days before phones were privately owned. Look at the reliefs ringing its top: an airplane with bird wings (c. 1900) and two women talking on a newfangled telephonic device. (It was thought business would popularize the telephone, but actually it was women.)

While Gammeltorv was a place of happiness and merriment, Nytorv ("New Square") was a place of severity and judgment. Walk to the small raised area 20 yards in front of the old ancient-Greek-style former City Hall and courthouse. Do a 360. The square is Neoclassical (built mostly after the 1807 British bombardment). Read the old Danish on the City Hall facade: "With Law Shall Man Build the Land." Look down at the pave-

ment and read the plaque: "Here stood the town's *Kag* (whipping post) until 1780."

• *Now walk down the next stretch of the Strøget—called Nygade—to reach...*

❾ Amagertorv

This is prime real estate for talented street entertainers. Walk to the stately brick Holy Ghost Church (Helligåndskirken). The fine spire is typical of old Danish churches. Under the stepped gable was a medieval hospital run by monks (one of the oldest buildings in town, dating from the 12th century). Today the hospital is an antiques hall. In summer the pleasant courtyard is shared by a group of charities selling light bites and coffee.

Walk behind the church, down Valkendorfsgade—the street just before the church—and through a passage under the reddish-colored building at #32 (if locked, loop back and go down Klosterstræde); here you'll find the leafy and beer-stained ❿ **Gråbrødretorv.** Surrounded by fine old buildings, this "Grey Friars' Square"—a monastic square until the Reformation made it a people's square—is a popular place for an outdoor meal or drink in the summer. At the end of the square, the street called Niels Hemmingsens Gade returns (past the recommended music venue Alice, a good place for live jazz) to the Strøget.

Once back on busy Strøget, turn left and continue down Amagertorv, with its fine inlaid Italian granite stonework, to the next square with the "stork" fountain (actually three herons). The Victorian WCs here (free, steps down from fountain) are a delight.

This square, Amagertorv, is a highlight for shoppers, with the ⓫ **Royal Copenhagen store**—stacked with three floors of porcelain—and **Illums Bolighus**—a fine place to ogle modern Danish design (see "Shopping in Copenhagen," later). A block toward the canal—running parallel to the Strøget—starts Strædet, which is a "second Strøget" featuring cafés and antique shops.

North of Amagertorv, a broad pedestrian mall called **Købmagergade** leads past a fine modern bakery (Holm's) to Christian IV's Round Tower and the Latin Quarter (university district). The recommended Café Norden overlooks the fountain—a good place for a meal or coffee with a view. The second floor offers the best vantage point.

• *Looking downhill from the fountain, about halfway to an imposing palace in the distance, you'll see a great man on a horse. Walk here to view this statue of Copenhagen's founder, ⓬ Bishop Absalon, shown in his Warrior Absalon get-up.*

From the bishop, you'll continue across a bridge toward the palace and the next statue—a king on a horse. As you cross the bridge, look right to see the City Hall tower, where this walk started. (A couple of the city's competing sightseeing boat tours depart from near here—see page 53.)

Christiansborg Palace and the Birthplace of Copenhagen

You're stepping onto the island of Slotsholmen ("Castle Island"), the easy-to-defend birthplace of Copenhagen in the 12th century. It's dominated by the royal palace complex. Christiansborg Palace (with its "three crowns" spire)—the imposing former residence of kings—is now the parliament building.

Ahead of you, the Neoclassical Lutheran church with the low dome is the ⓭ **Christiansborg Palace Chapel**, site of 350 years of royal weddings and funerals (free, only open Sun 10:00-17:00 except open daily in July).

Walk to the next green copper equestrian statue. ⓮ **Frederik VII** was crowned in 1848, just months before Denmark got its constitution on June 5, 1849. (Constitution Day is celebrated with typical Danish understatement—stores are closed and workers get the day off.) Frederik, who then ruled as a constitutional monarch, stands in front of **Christiansborg Palace,** which Denmark's royal family now shares with its people's assembly (queen's wing on right, parliament on left; for information on visiting the palace, see page 79). This palace, the seat of Danish government today, is considered the birthplace of Copenhagen. It stands upon the ruins of Absalon's 12th-century castle (literally under your feet). The big stones between the statue and the street were put in for security after the 2011 terror attacks in Norway. While Danes strive to keep government accessible, security measures like this are today's reality.

This is Denmark's power island, with the Folketing (Danish parliament), Supreme Court, Ministry of Finance (to the left), and

❶ **Børsen**—the historic stock exchange (farther to the left, with the fanciful dragon-tail spire; not open to tourists). The eye-catching red-brick stock exchange was inspired by the Dutch Renaissance, like much of 17th-century Copenhagen. Built to promote the mercantile ambitions of Denmark in the 1600s, it was the "World Trade Center" of Scandinavia. The facade reads, "For the profitable use of buyer and seller." The dragon-tail spire with three crowns represents the Danish aspiration to rule a united Scandinavia—or at least be its commercial capital.

Notice Copenhagen's distinctive green copper spires all around you. Beyond the old stock exchange lies the island of **Christianshavn,** with its own distinct spire. It tops the Church of Our Savior and features an external spiral staircase winding to the top for an amazing view. While political power resided here on Slotsholmen, commercial power was in the merchant's district, Christianshavn (neighborhood and church described later, under "Sights in Copenhagen"). The Børsen symbolically connected Christianshavn with the rest of the city, in an age when trade was a very big deal.

• *Walk along the old stock exchange toward Christianshavn, but turn left at the crosswalk with the signal before you reach the end of the building. After crossing the street, go over the canal and turn right to walk along the harborfront promenade, enjoying views of Christianshavn across the water.*

❶ Havnegade Promenade

The Havnegade promenade to Nyhavn is a delightful people zone with trampolines, an ice-cream-licking ambience, and harborview benches (a good place to stop, look across the water, and ponder the trendy apartments and old warehouses turned into modern-office blocks). From here, stroll several more blocks toward the

⓱ Inderhavnsbroen sliding bridge for pedestrians and bikes. This "kissing bridge" (it's called that because the two sliding, or retractable, sections "kiss" when they come together) links the town center with Christianshavn and makes the modern Opera House

(ahead on the right, across the water) more accessible to downtown. Walk until you hit the Nyhavn canal.

Across the way, at the end of the canal, stands the glassy Royal Danish Theatre's Playhouse. While this walk finishes on Kongens Nytorv, the square at the head of this canal, you could extend it by continuing north along the harbor from the playhouse.
• *For now, turn left and walk to the center of the bridge over the canal for a...*

⓲ View of Nyhavn

Established in the 1670s along with Kongens Nytorv, Nyhavn ("New Harbor") is a recently gentrified sailors' quarter. (Hong

Kong is the last of the nasty bars from the rough old days.) With its trendy cafés, jazz clubs, and tattoo shops (pop into Tattoo Ole at #17—fun photos, very traditional), Nyhavn is a wonderful place to hang out. The canal is filled with glamorous old sailboats of all sizes. Historic sloops are welcome to moor here in Copenhagen's ever-changing boat museum. Hans Christian Andersen lived and wrote his first stories here (in the red double-gabled building at #20).

From the bridge, take a few steps left to the cheap **beer kiosk** (on Holbergsgade, open daily until late). At this minimarket, let friendly manager Nagib give you a little lesson in Danish beer, and then buy a bottle or can. Choose from Carlsberg (standard lager, 4.6 percent alcohol), Carlsberg Elephant (strong, 7.2 percent), Tuborg Grøn (standard lager, 4.6 percent), Tuborg Gold (stronger, 5.8 percent), and Tuborg Classic (dark beer, 4.6 percent). The cost? About 15 DKK, depending on the alcohol level. Take your beer out to the canal and feel like a local. A note about all the public beer-drinking here: There's no more beer consumption here than in the US; it's just out in public. Many young Danes can't afford to drink in a bar, so they "picnic drink" their beers in squares and along canals, at a quarter of the price for a bottle.

If you crave **ice cream** instead, cross the bridge, where facing the canal you'll find Vaffelbageren, a popular place with freshly made waffle cones.

Now wander the quay, enjoying the frat-party parade of tattoos (hotter weather reveals more tattoos). Celtic and Nordic mythological designs are in (as is bodybuilding, by the looks of things). The place thrives—with the cheap-beer drinkers dockside and the richer and older ones looking on from comfier cafés.

• *Make your way to the head of the canal, where you'll find a minuscule amber museum, above the House of Amber (see "Shopping in Copenhagen," page 102). Just beyond the head of Nyhavn canal sprawls the huge and the stately …*

⑲ Kongens Nytorv

The "King's New Square" is home to the National Theater, French embassy, and venerable Hotel d'Angleterre, where VIPs and pop stars stay. In the mid-1600s the city expanded, pushing its wall farther east. The equestrian statue in the middle of the square celebrates Christian V, who made this square the city's geographical and cultural center. In 1676, King Christian rode off to reconquer the southern tip of Sweden and reclaim Denmark's

dominance. He returned empty-handed and broke. Denmark became a second-rate power, but Copenhagen prospered. In the winter this square becomes a popular ice-skating rink.

Wander into ⑳ **Hviids Vinstue,** the town's oldest wine cellar (from 1723, just beyond the Metro station, at #19, under a bar) to check out its characteristic dark and woody interior and fascinating old Copenhagen photos. It's a colorful spot for an open-face sandwich and a beer (three sandwiches and a beer for 85 DKK at lunchtime). Their wintertime *gløgg* (hot spiced wine) is legendary. Across the street, towering above the Metro station, is Magasin du Nord, the grandest old department store in town.

• *You've reached the end of this walk. But if you'd like to extend it by heading out to Amalienborg Palace and* The Little Mermaid, *retrace your steps to the far side of Nyhavn canal.*

Nyhavn to Amalienborg

Stroll along the canal to the Royal Danish Theatre's Playhouse and head left along the harborfront to a large plaza dotted with outdoor cafés and benches, and views across the harbor. Then follow a delightful waterfront promenade to the modern fountain of Amaliehaven Park, immediately across the harbor from Copenhagen's slick Opera House. The striking Opera House is bigger than it looks—of its 14 floors, five are below sea level. Completed in 2005 by architect Henning Larsen, it was a $400 million gift to the nation from an oil-shipping magnate.

• *A block inland (behind the fountain) is the orderly...*

㉑ Amalienborg Palace and Square

Queen Margrethe II lives in the mansion to your immediate left as you enter the square from the harborside. (If the flag's flying, she's home.) The mansion across the street (on the right as you enter) is where her son and heir to the throne, Crown Prince Frederik, lives with his wife, Australian businesswoman Mary Donaldson, and their four children. The royal guesthouse pal-

ace is on the far left. And the palace on the far right is the **Amalienborg Museum,** which offers an intimate look at royal living (described on page 84).

Though the guards change daily at noon, they do it with royal fanfare only when the queen is in residence (see page 85 for details). The royal guard often has a police escort when it marches through town on special occasions—leading locals to joke that theirs is "the only army in the world that needs police protection."

The equestrian statue of Frederik V is a reminder that this square was the centerpiece of a planned town he envisioned in 1750. It was named for him—Frederikstaden. During the 18th century, Denmark's population grew and the country thrived (as trade flourished and its neutrality kept it out of the costly wars impoverishing much of Europe). Frederikstaden, with its strong architectural harmony, was designed as a luxury neighborhood for the city's business elite. Nobility and other big shots moved in, but the king came here only after his other palace burned down in a 1794 fire.

Just inland, the striking Frederikskirke—better known as the **Marble Church**—was designed to fit this ritzy new quarter. If it's open, step inside to bask in its vast, serene, Pantheon-esque atmosphere (free, Mon-Thu and Sat 10:00-17:00, Fri and Sun from 12:00; dome climb—35 DKK, mid-June-Aug daily at 13:00; off-season Sat-Sun at 13:00).

COPENHAGEN

• From the square, Amaliegade leads two blocks north to...

Kastellet Park

In this park, you'll find some worthwhile sightseeing. The 1908 **Gefion Fountain** illustrates the myth of the goddess who was given one night to carve a hunk out of Sweden to make into Denmark's main island, Sjælland (or "Zealand" in English), which you're on. Gefion transformed her four sons into oxen to do the job, and the chunk she removed from Sweden is supposedly Vänern, Sweden's largest lake. If you look at a map showing Sweden

and Denmark, the island and the lake are, in fact, roughly the same shape. Next to the fountain is an Anglican church built of flint.

• Climb up the stairs by the fountain and continue along the top of the rampart about five minutes to reach the harborfront site of the overrated, overfondled, and overphotographed symbol of Copenhagen, Den Lille Havfrue, *or...*

㉒ The Little Mermaid

The Little Mermaid statue was a gift to the city of Copenhagen in 1909 from brewing magnate Carl Jacobsen (whose art collection forms the basis of the Ny Carlsberg Glyptotek). Inspired by a ballet performance of Andersen's story, Jacobsen hired the young sculptor Edvard Eriksen to immortalize the mermaid as a statue. Eriksen used his wife Eline as the model. The statue sat unappreciated for 40 years until Danny Kaye sang "Wonderful Copenhagen" in the movie *Hans Christian Andersen,* and the tourist board decided to use the mermaid as a marketing symbol for the city. For the non-Disneyfied *Little Mermaid* story—and insights into Hans Christian Andersen—see the sidebar. For more on his life, see page 52.

• This is the end of our extended wonderful, wonderful Copenhagen City Walk. From here you can get back downtown on foot, by taxi, or on bus #27 (catch it along Indiakaj, a two-minute walk north).

Sights in Copenhagen

NEAR THE TRAIN STATION

Copenhagen's great train station, the Hovedbanegården, is an interesting mesh of Scandinavian culture and transportation efficiency. From the station, delightful sights fan out into the old city. The following attractions are listed roughly in order from the train station to Slotsholmen Island.

The Little Mermaid and Hans Christian Andersen

"Far out in the ocean, where the water is as blue as a cornflower, as clear as crystal, and very, very deep..." there lived a young mermaid. So begins one of Hans Christian Andersen's best-known stories.

It goes like this: One day, a young mermaid spies a passing ship and falls in love with a handsome prince. The ship is wrecked in a storm, and she saves the prince's life. To be with the prince, the mermaid asks a sea witch to give her human legs. In exchange, she agrees to give up her voice and the chance of ever returning to the sea. And, the witch tells her, if the prince doesn't marry her, she will immediately die heartbroken and without an immortal soul. The mermaid agrees, and her fish tail becomes a pair of beautiful but painful legs. She woos the prince—who loves her in return—but he eventually marries another. Heartbroken, the mermaid prepares to die. She's given one last chance to save herself: She must kill the prince on his wedding night. She sneaks into the bedchamber with a knife...but can't bear to kill the man she loves. The mermaid throws herself into the sea to die. Suddenly, she's miraculously carried up by the mermaids of the air, who give her an immortal soul as a reward for her long-suffering love.

The tale of unrequited love mirrors Andersen's own sad love life. He had two major crushes—one of them for the famous opera singer Jenny Lind—but he was turned down both times, and he never married. He had plenty of interest in sex but likely died a virgin. He had close relationships with women but stayed single, had time to travel and write, and maintained a childlike wonder about the world to his dying days.

▲▲▲Tivoli Gardens

Copenhagen's grand amusement park—opened in 1843—is 20 acres, 110,000 lanterns, and countless ice-cream cones of fun. You

pay one admission price and find yourself lost in a wonderland of rides, restaurants, games, marching bands, roulette wheels, and funny mirrors. A roller coaster screams through the middle of a tranquil Asian food court, and the

Small World-inspired Den Flyvende Kuffert ride floats through Hans Christian Andersen fairy tales. It's a children's fantasyland midday, but it becomes more adult-oriented later on. With or without kids, this place is a true magic kingdom. Tivoli doesn't try to be Disney. It's wonderfully and happily Danish. (Many locals appreciate the lovingly tended gardens.) I find it worth the admission just to see Danes—young and old—at play.

As you stroll the grounds, imagine the place in the mid-1800s, when it was new. Built on the site of the old town fortifications (today's lake was part of the old moat), Tivoli was an attempt to introduce provincial Danes to the world (for example, with the Asian Pavilion) and to bring people of all classes together.

Cost: 135 DKK Mon-Fri, 145 DKK Sat-Sun, 60 DKK for kids under 8, free for kids under 3. To go on rides, you must buy ride tickets (from booth at entrance or from machines in the park—machines take credit card only, 30 DKK/ticket, color-coded rides cost 1-4 tickets apiece); or you can buy a multiride pass for 245 DKK. If you'll be using at least eight tickets, buy the ride pass instead. To leave and come back later, you'll have to buy a 35-DKK re-entry ticket before you exit.

Hours: Late March-mid-Sept daily 11:00-23:00, Fri-Sat until 24:00. In winter, Tivoli opens daily 11:00-22:00 from mid-Oct to early Nov for Halloween, from mid-Nov to New Year's Day for a Christmas market with *gløgg* (hot spiced wine) and ice-skating on Tivoli Lake, and during most of Feb. Dress warmly for chilly evenings any time of year. There are lockers by each entrance.

Information: +45 33 15 10 01, www.tivoli.dk.

Getting There: Tivoli is across Bernstoffsgade from the train station. If you're catching a late train, this is *the* place to spend your last Copenhagen hours.

Entertainment at Tivoli: Upon arrival (through main entrance, on left in the service center), pick up a map and look for the events schedule. Take a moment to plan your entertainment for the evening. Events are generally spread between 15:00 and 23:00; the 19:30 concert in the concert hall can be as little as 75 DKK or more than 1,000 DKK, depending on the performer (box office +45 33 15 10 01). If the Tivoli Symphony is playing, it's worth paying for. The ticket box office is outside, just to the left of the main entrance (daily 10:00-20:00; concert tickets include Tivoli admission).

Free concerts, pantomime theater, ballet, acrobats, puppets, and other shows pop up all over the park, and a well-organized visitor can enjoy an exciting evening of entertainment without spending a single krone beyond the entry fee. Friday evenings feature a (usually free) rock or pop show at 22:00. People gather around the lake 45 minutes before closing time for the "Tivoli Illuminations." Fireworks blast a few nights each summer. The park is particularly romantic at dusk, when the lights go on.

Eating at Tivoli: Inside the park, expect to pay amusement-park prices for amusement-park-quality food. Still, a meal here is part of the fun.

$$ Søcafeen serves traditional open-face sandwiches and main courses in a fun beer garden with lakeside ambience. **$$$ Mazzoli's Caffè & Trattoria,** in a circular building near the lake, serves classic Italian fare and pizza. **$$$ Wagamama,** a modern pan-Asian slurpathon from the UK, serves healthy noodle dishes (at the far back side of the park, also possible to enter from outside). **$$$ Fru Nimb** offers a large selection of open-face sandwiches in a garden setting. For cheaper fare, look for a *pølse* (sausage) stand. And if you're longing for something sweet, **Cakenhagen** serves classic Danish cakes and pastries that you can wash down with a cup of tea—or champagne.

For something more upscale, consider the complex of Nimb restaurants, in the big Taj Mahal-like pavilion near the entrance facing the train station. For dinner, **$$$$ Nimb Bar** is a definite splurge, grilling up creative international meat and seafood dishes. **$$$$ Nimb Brasserie,** sharing the same lobby, serves rustic French classics.

And if these options aren't enough, check out the eateries in the glassy Tivoli Food Hall (facing the train station) that promises "fast gourmet food."

▲City Hall (Rådhus)

This city landmark, between the train station/Tivoli and the Strøget, is free and open to the public (including a public WC). You can wander throughout the building and into the peaceful garden out back. It also offers guided tours and trips up its 345-foot-tall tower.

Cost and Hours: Free to enter building, Mon-Fri 9:00-16:00; you can usually slip in Sat 9:30-13:00 when weddings are going on, or join the Sat tour; closed Sun. Guided English-language tours—60 DKK, 45 minutes, gets you into more private, official rooms; Mon-Fri at 13:00, Sat at 10:00. Tower by escort only—40

DKK, 300 steps for the best aerial view of Copenhagen, Mon-Fri at 11:00 and 14:00, Sat at 12:00, closed Sun, +45 33 66 33 66, http://raadhus.kk.dk.

Visiting City Hall: It's draped, inside and out, in Danish symbolism. Standing over the door is the city's founder, Bishop Absalon (c. 1128-1201)—bish-op, soldier, and foreign-policy wonk. He was King Valdemar I's right-hand man. In Copen-hagen, he drove out pirates and built a fort to guard the harbor, turning a miserable fishing vil-lage into a humming Baltic sea-port. The polar bears climbing on the rooftop symbolize the

giant Danish protectorate of Greenland. Six night watchmen flank the city's gold-and-green seal under the Danish flag.

Step inside. The info desk (on the left as you enter) has racks of tourist information (city maps and other brochures). The build-ing and its huge tower were inspired by the City Hall in Siena, Italy (with the necessary bad-weather addition of a glass roof). Enormous functions fill this grand hall (the iron grate in the center of the floor is an elevator for bringing up 1,200 chairs), while the marble busts of four illustrious local boys—fairy-tale writer Hans Christian Andersen, sculptor Bertel Thorvaldsen, physicist Niels Bohr, and the building's architect, Martin Nyrop—look on. Un-derneath the floor are national archives dating back to 1275, popu-lar with Danes researching their family roots.

As you leave, pop into the amazing clock opposite the info desk. Jens Olsen's World Clock, built from 1943 to 1955, was the mother of all astronomical clocks in precision and function. And it came with something new: tracking the exact time across the world's time zones. One of its gears does a complete rotation only every 25,753 years.

▲Ny Carlsberg Glyptotek

Scandinavia's top art gallery is an impressive example of what beer money can do. Brewer Carl Jacobsen (son of J. C. Jacobsen, who funded the Museum of Na-tional History at Frederiksborg Castle) was an avid collector and patron of the arts. (Carl also donated *The Little Mermaid* statue to the city.) His namesake museum has intoxicating artifacts from the ancient world, along with some fine art from our own times. The next time you sip a Carlsberg beer, drink a toast to Carl Jacobsen and his marvelous collection. *Skål!*

Cost and Hours: 115 DKK, free on Tue; open Tue-Sun 10:00-17:00, Thu until 21:00, closed Mon; behind Tivoli at Dantes Plads 7, +45 33 41 81 41, www.glyptoteket.com. It has a classy **$$$** cafeteria under palms, as well as a rooftop terrace with snacks, drinks, and city views.

Visiting the Museum: Pick up a floor plan as you enter to help navigate the confusing layout. For a chronological swing, start with Egypt (mummy coffins and sarcophagi, a 5,000-year-old hippo statue), Greece (red-and-black painted vases, statues), the Etruscan world (Greek-looking vases), and Rome (grittily realistic statues and portrait busts).

The sober realism of 19th-century Danish Golden Age painting reflects the introspection of a once-powerful nation reduced to second-class status—and ultimately embracing what made it unique. The "French Wing" (just inside the front door) has Rodin statues. A heady, if small, exhibit of 19th-century French paintings (in a modern building within the back courtyard) shows how Realism morphed into Impressionism and Post-Impressionism, and includes a couple of canvases apiece by Géricault, Delacroix, Monet, Manet, Millet, Courbet, Degas, Pissarro, Cézanne, Van Gogh, Picasso, Renoir, and Toulouse-Lautrec. Look for art by Gauguin—from before Tahiti (when he lived in Copenhagen with his Danish wife and their five children) and after Tahiti. There's also a fine collection of modern Danish sculpture.

Linger with marble gods under the palm leaves and glass dome of the very soothing winter garden. Designers, figuring Danes would be more interested in a lush garden than in classical art, used this wonderful space as leafy bait to cleverly introduce locals to a few Greek and Roman statues. (It works for tourists, too.) One of the original *Thinker* sculptures by Rodin (wondering how to scale the Tivoli fence?) is in the museum's backyard.

Museum of Copenhagen (Københavns Museum)

This museum offers an entertaining and creative telling of the story of Copenhagen, from its origins to contemporary culture.

Cost and Hours: 90 DKK, Wed free—expect crowds; daily

9:00-18:00, Thu until 21:00; kitty-corner to the National Museum at Stormgade 18, +45 33 21 07 72, www.copenhagen.dk.

▲▲▲National Museum (Nationalmuseet)

Focus on this museum's excellent and curiously enjoyable Danish collection, which traces this civilization from its ancient beginnings. Its prehistoric collection is the best of its kind in Scandinavia. Exhibits are laid out chronologically and are eloquently described in English.

Cost and Hours: 100 DKK, Tue-Sun 10:00-17:00, Thu until 20:00, closed Mon, mandatory lockers, enter at Ny Vestergade 10, +45 33 13 44 11, www.natmus.dk. The **$$** café overlooking the entry hall serves coffee, pastries, and lunch.

Tours: Guide Richard Karpen leads private tours of the museum (price depends on number of participants, May-Sept, mobile +45 91 61 95 02, www.copenhagenwalks.com, copenhagenwalks@yahoo.com).

Visiting the Museum: Pick up the museum map as you enter, and head for the Danish history exhibit. It fills three floors, from the bottom up: prehistory, the Middle Ages and Renaissance, and modern times (1660-2000).

Danish Prehistory: Start before history did, in the Danish prehistory exhibit (on the right side of the main entrance hall). Follow the room numbers in order, working counterclockwise around the courtyard and through the millennia.

In the Stone Age section, you'll see primitive tools and still-clothed skeletons of Scandinavia's reindeer hunters. The oak coffins were originally covered by burial mounds (called "barrows"). People put valuable items into the coffins with the dead, such as a folding chair (which, back then, was a real status symbol). In the farming section, ogle the ceremonial axes and amber necklaces.

The Bronze Age galleries feature many swords crafted from the new metal. The small bronze "Chariot of the Sun"—depicting a horse pulling the sun across the sky—likely had religious significance for early Scandinavians (whose descendants continue to celebrate the solstice with fervor). In the same room are those iconic horned helmets. Contrary to popular belief (and countless tourist shops), these helmets were not worn by the Vikings, but by their predecessors—for ceremonial purposes, centuries earlier. In the next room are huge cases filled with still-playable *lur* horns (see page 60). Another room shows off a collection of well-translated rune stones proclaiming heroic deeds.

This leads to the Iron Age and an object that's neither Iron nor Danish: the 2,000-year-old Gundestrup Cauldron of art-textbook fame. This 20-pound, soup-kitchen-size bowl made of silver was found in a Danish bog, but its symbolism suggests it was originally from either Thrace (in northeast Greece) or Celtic Ireland. On the sides, hunters slay bulls, and gods cavort with

COPENHAGEN

stags, horses, dogs, and dragons. It's both mysterious and fascinating.

Prehistoric Danes were fascinated by bogs. To make iron, you need ore—and Denmark's many bogs provided that critical material in abundance, leading people to believe that the gods dwelled there. These Danes appeased the gods by sacrificing valuable items (and even people) into bogs. Fortunately for modern archaeologists, bogs happen to be an ideal environment for preserving fragile objects. One bog alone—the Nydam bog—has yielded thousands of items, including three whole ships.

No longer bogged down in prehistory, the people of Scandinavia came into contact with Roman civilization. At about this time, the Viking culture rose; you'll see the remains of an old warship. The Vikings, so feared in most of Europe, are still thought of fondly here in their homeland. You'll notice the descriptions straining to defend them: Sure, they'd pillage, rape, and plunder. But they also founded thriving, wealthy, and cultured trade towns. Love the Vikings or hate them, it's impossible to deny their massive reach—Norse Vikings even carved runes into the walls of the Hagia Sophia church (in today's Istanbul).

Middle Ages and Renaissance: Next, go upstairs and follow signs to Room 101 to start this section. You'll walk through the Middle Ages, where you'll find lots of bits and pieces of old churches, such as golden altars and *aquamaniles,* pitchers used for ritual hand-washing. The Dagmar Cross is the prototype for a popular form of crucifix worn by many Danes (Room 102, small glass display case—with colorful enamel paintings). Another cross in this case (the Roskilde Cross, studded with gemstones) was found inside the wooden head of Christ displayed high on the opposite wall. There are also exhibits on tools and trade, weapons, drinking horns, and fine, wood-carved winged altarpieces. Carry on to find a captivating room on the Norse settlers of Greenland, material on the Reformation, and an exhibit on everyday town life in the 16th and 17th centuries.

Modern Times: The next floor takes you through the last few centuries, with historic toys and a slice-of-Danish-life (1660-2000) gallery where you'll see everything from rifles and old bras to early jukeboxes. You'll learn that the Danish Golden Age (which dominates most art museums in Denmark) captured the everyday pastoral beauty of the countryside, celebrated Denmark's smallness and peace-loving nature, and mixed in some Nordic mythology. With industrialization came the labor movement and trade unions. After delving into the World Wars, Baby Boomers, creation of the postwar welfare state, and the "Depressed Decade" of the 1980s (when Denmark suffered high unemployment), the collection is capped off by a stall that, until recently, was used for selling marijuana in the squatters' community of Christiania.

The Rest of the Museum: If you're eager for more, there's plenty left to see: exhibits on the history of this building (the Prince's Palace), a large ethnology collection, antiquities, coins and medallions, temporary exhibits, and a good children's museum.

▲National Museum's Victorian Apartment (Klunkehjemmet)

The National Museum inherited an incredibly preserved Victorian apartment just around the corner. The wealthy Christensen family managed to keep its plush living quarters a 19th-century time capsule until the granddaughters passed away in 1963. Since then, it's been part of the National Museum, with all but two of its rooms looking just as they did in the late Victorian days.

Cost and Hours: 95 DKK, required one-hour tours leave from the National Museum reception desk (in English, June-Aug Sat-Sun only at 12:00; in Danish Sat-Sun at 11:00, 12:00, and 13:00 year-round).

ON SLOTSHOLMEN ISLAND

This island, where Copenhagen began in the 12th century, is a short walk from the train station and Tivoli, just across the bridge from the National Museum. It's dominated by Christiansborg Palace and several other royal and governmental buildings. Note that my Copenhagen City Walk (earlier) cuts right through Slotsholmen and covers other landmarks on the island (see page 57).

▲▲Christiansborg Palace (Christiansborg Slot)

A complex of government buildings stands on the ruins of Copenhagen's original 12th-century fortress: the parliament, Supreme

Court, prime minister's office, royal reception rooms, royal library, several museums, and royal stables. Although the current palace dates only from 1928 and the royal family moved out 200 years ago, this building—the sixth to stand here in 800 years— is rich with tradition.

Four palace sights (the reception rooms, old castle ruins, stables, and kitchen) are open to the public, giving us commoners a glimpse of the royal life.

Cost and Hours: Reception rooms-95 DKK; castle ruins, stables, and kitchen-60 DKK each or 160 DKK combo-ticket for all four. Most sights are open daily 10:00-17:00 (except Oct-April, when they're closed on Mon; may also close for royal events); stables and carriage museum open 13:30-16:00—longer hours possible in July; palace chapel open Sun 10:00-17:00 except daily in July; +45 33 92 64 92, www.christiansborg.dk.

Tours: The information-packed, hour-long English tours of the reception rooms are excellent (included with ticket, July-Aug daily at 12:00 and 15:00, rest of year at 15:00 only). Or download the free app—see website for details.

Visiting the Palace: From the equestrian statue in front, go through the wooden door; the entrance to the ruins is in the corridor on the right, and the door to the reception rooms is out in the next courtyard, also on the right.

Royal Reception Rooms: While these don't rank among Europe's best palace rooms, they're worth a look. This is still the place where Queen Margrethe II impresses visiting dignitaries. As you wander the 22 rooms in a one-way route (wearing protect-the-floor slippers), you'll gain a good feel for Danish history, royalty, and politics. Here are a few highlights:

After the Queen's Library you'll soon enter the grand Great Hall, lined with boldly colorful (almost gaudy) tapestries. The palace highlight is this dazzling set of modern tapestries—Danish-designed but Gobelin-made in Paris. This gift, given to the queen on her 60th birthday in 2000, celebrates 1,000 years of Danish history, from the Viking age to our chaotic times...and into the future. The Velvet Room is where royals privately greet VIP guests before big functions.

In the corner room on the left, don't miss the family portrait of King Christian IX, which illustrates why he's called the "father-in-law of Europe"—his children eventually became, or married into, royalty in Denmark, Russia, Greece, Britain, France, Germany, and Norway.

In the Throne Room you'll see the balcony where new monarchs are proclaimed (most recently in 1972). And at the end, in the Hall of Giants (where you take off your booties among heroic figures supporting the building), you'll see a striking painting of Queen Margrethe II from 2010 on her 70th birthday. The three playful lions, made of Norwegian silver, once guarded the throne and symbolize absolute power—long gone since 1849, when Denmark embraced the notion of a constitutional monarch.

Castle Ruins: An exhibit in the scant remains of the first fortress built by Bishop Absalon, the 12th-century founder of Copenhagen, lies under the palace. A long passage connects to another set of ruins, from the 14th-century Copenhagen Castle. There's precious little to see, but it is, um, old and well described. A video covers more recent palace history.

Royal Stables and Carriages Museum: This facility is still home to the horses that pull the queen's carriage on festive days, as well as a collection of historic carriages. While they're down from 250 horses to about a dozen, the royal stables are part of a strong tradition and, as the little video shows, will live on.

Royal Kitchen: Unless you're smitten with old ladles and shiny copper pots and pans, I'd skip this exhibit.

▲▲Thorvaldsen's Museum (Thorvaldsens Museum)

This museum tells the story and shows the monumental work of the great Danish Neoclassical sculptor Bertel Thorvaldsen (see sidebar). Considered the Italian Canova's equal among Neoclassical sculptors, Thorvaldsen spent 40 years in Rome. He was lured home to Copenhagen with the promise of a fine museum to showcase his sculptures, which opened in the revolutionary year of 1848 as Denmark's first public art gallery. Of the 500 or so sculptures Thorvaldsen completed in his life—including 90 major statues—this museum has most of them, in one form or another (the plaster model used to make the original or a copy done in marble or bronze).

Cost and Hours: 90 DKK, free on Wed, Tue-Sun 10:00-17:00, Thu until 21:00, closed Mon, includes excellent audioguide, located in Neoclassical building with colorful walls next to Christiansborg Palace, +45 33 32 15 32, www.thorvaldsensmuseum.dk.

Visiting the Museum: After buying your ticket, go straight in and pick up the included audioguide at the desk. It provides a wonderful statue-by-statue narration of the museum's key works.

The ground floor displays Thorvaldsen's statues. Start in the Great Hall, which was the original entryway of the museum. It's filled with replicas of some of the artist's biggest and grandest statues—national heroes who still stand in the prominent squares of their major cities (Munich, Warsaw, the Vatican, and others). Two great equestrian statues stare each other down from across the hall; while they both take the classic, self-assured pose of looking one way while pointing another (think Babe Ruth calling his home run), one of them (Jozef Poniatowski) is modeled after the ancient Roman general Marcus Aurelius, while the other (Bavaria's Maximilian I) wears modern garb.

Then take a spin through the smaller rooms that ring the central courtyard. Each of these is dominated by one big work—most-

ly classical subjects drawn from mythology. At the far end of the building stand the plaster models for the iconic *Risen Christ* and the 12 Apostles (the final marble versions stand in the Cathedral of Our Lady—see page 62). Peek into the central courtyard to see the planter-box tomb of Thorvaldsen himself (who died in 1844). Continue into the next row of rooms: In the far corner room look for Thorvaldsen's (very flattering) self-portrait, leaning buffly against a partially finished sculpture.

Bertel Thorvaldsen (1770-1844)

Bertel Thorvaldsen was born, raised, educated, and buried in Copenhagen, but his most productive years were spent in Rome. There he soaked up the prevailing style of the time: Neoclassical. He studied ancient Greek and Roman statues, copying their balance, grace, and impassive beauty. The simple-but-noble style suited the patriotism of the era, and Thorvaldsen got rich off it. Public squares throughout Europe are dotted with his works, celebrating local rulers, patriots, and historical figures looking like Greek heroes or Roman conquerors.

In 1819, at the height of his fame and power, Thorvaldsen returned to Copenhagen. He was asked to decorate the most important parts of the recently bombed, newly rebuilt Cathedral of Our Lady: the main altar and nave. His *Risen Christ* on the altar (along with the 12 apostles lining the nave) became his most famous and reproduced work—without even realizing it, most people imagine the caring features of Thorvaldsen's Christ when picturing what Jesus looked like.

The prolific Thorvaldsen depicted a range of subjects. His grand statues of historical figures (Copernicus in Warsaw, Maximilian I in Munich) were intended for public squares. Portrait busts of his contemporaries were usually done in the style of Roman emperors. Thorvaldsen carved the Lion Monument, depicting a weeping lion, into a cliff in Luzern, Switzerland. He did religious statues, like the *Risen Christ*. Thorvaldsen's most accessible works are from Greek mythology—*The Three Graces*, naked *Jason with the Golden Fleece*, or Ganymede crouching down to feed the eagle Jupiter.

Though many of his statues are of gleaming white marble, Thorvaldsen was not a chiseler of stone. Like Rodin and Canova, Thorvaldsen left the grunt work to others. He fashioned a life-size model in plaster, which could then be reproduced in marble or bronze by his assistants. Multiple copies were often made, even in his lifetime.

Thorvaldsen epitomized the Neoclassical style. His statues assume perfectly balanced poses—maybe even a bit stiff, say critics. They don't flail their arms dramatically or emote passionately. As you look into their faces, they seem lost in thought, as though contemplating deep spiritual truths.

In Copenhagen, catch Thorvaldsen's *Risen Christ* at the Cathedral of Our Lady, his portrait bust at City Hall, and the full range of his long career at Thorvaldsen's Museum.

Downstairs you'll find a collection of plaster casts (mostly ancient Roman statues that inspired Thorvaldsen) and a video about his career.

Upstairs, get into the mind of the artist by perusing his personal possessions and the private collection of paintings from which he drew inspiration.

Royal Library (Kongelige Bibliotek)

Copenhagen's Royal Library, dubbed the "Black Diamond" (Sorte Diamant), is a striking, modern building made of shiny black granite, leaning over the harbor at the edge of the palace complex. From the inviting lounge chairs on the Inner Harbor, you can ponder this stretch of harborfront, which serves as a showcase for architects. Inside, wander through the old and new sections, catch the fine view from the "G" level, read a magazine, and enjoy a classy—and pricey—lunch.

Cost and Hours: Free, special exhibits generally 90 DKK; Mon-Fri 8:00-21:00, Sat 9:00-19:00; July-Aug Mon-Sat 8:00-19:00, reading room hours vary, closed Sun year-round; +45 33 47 47 47, www.kb.dk.

▲Danish Jewish Museum (Dansk Jødisk Museum)

In a notable building by American architect Daniel Libeskind, this museum offers a very small but well-exhibited display of 400 years of the life and impact of Jews in Denmark.

Cost and Hours: 60 DKK; Tue-Sun 10:00-17:00; Sept-May Tue-Fri 13:00-16:00, Sat-Sun 12:00-17:00; closed Mon year-round; behind Black Diamond library at Proviantpassagen 6—enter from the courtyard behind the red-brick, ivy-covered building, +45 33 11 22 18, www.jewmus.dk.

Visiting the Museum: Frankly, the architecture overshadows the humble exhibits. Libeskind—who created the equally conceptual Jewish Museum in Berlin, and whose design was the basis for the redevelopment of the World Trade Center site in New York City—has literally written Jewish culture into this building. The floor plan, a seemingly random squiggle, is actually in the shape of the Hebrew characters for *mitzvah*, which loosely translated means "act of kindness."

Be sure to watch the two short introductory films, one about the Jews' migration to Denmark, and the other about the architect Libeskind (play continuously). As you tour the collection, the uneven floors and asymmetrical walls give you the feeling that what lies around the corner is completely unknown...much like the life and history of Danish Jews. Another interpretation might be that the uneven floors give you the sense of motion, like waves on the sea—a reminder that despite Nazi occupation in 1943, nearly 7,000 Danish Jews were ferried across the waves by fishermen to safety in neutral Sweden.

NEAR THE STRØGET
Round Tower (Rundetaarn)

Built in 1642 by Christian IV, the tower connects a church, library, and observatory (the oldest functioning observatory in Europe) with a ramp that spirals up to a fine view of Copenhagen (though the view from atop Our Savior's Church is far better—see page 94). Notice the tower's mix of red and yellow bricks; the colors are meant to convey that this is a royal structure.

Cost and Hours: 40 DKK, nothing to see inside but the ramp and the view; tower—daily 10:00-20:00, Oct-March until 18:00; observatory—summer Sun 13:00-16:00, mid-Oct-mid-March Tue-Wed 18:00-21:00, www.rundetaarn.dk; just off the Strøget on Købmagergade.

AMALIENBORG PALACE AND NEARBY

For more information on this palace and nearby attractions, including the famous *Little Mermaid* statue, see the end of my Copenhagen City Walk, earlier.

▲Amalienborg Museum (Amalienborgmuseet)

While Queen Margrethe II lives quite privately in one of the four mansions that make up the palace complex, another mansion has

been open to the public since 1994. It displays the private studies of the last four kings of the House of Glucksborg, who ruled from 1863 to 1972 (the immediate predecessors of today's queen). Your visit won't take long—you'll see six to eight rooms on each of two floors— but it affords an intimate and unique peek into Denmark's royal family. On the first floor, each of the private studies feel particularly lived-in—with cluttered pipe collections and bookcases jammed with family pictures—because they were. It's easy to imagine these blue-blooded folks just hanging out here, even today. The earliest study, Frederik VIII's (c. 1869), feels much older and more "royal"—with Renaissance gilded walls, heavy drapes, and a polar bear rug. On the second floor, you'll see the Gothic library designed for dowager Queen Caroline Amalie, the cheery gala hall (the palace's largest room) with statues by Bertel Thorvaldsen, and a hall gleaming with large gilt-bronze table decorations.

Cost and Hours: 120 DKK, 170-DKK combo-ticket includes Rosenborg Palace—available on the website or at Rosenborg only; early-July-early-Aug Tue-Sun 10:00-16:00; rest of year Tue-Sun from 11:00; closed Mon year-round except Oct; with your back to the harbor, entrance is at the far end of the square on the right; +45 33 15 32 86, www.dkks.dk.

Amalienborg Palace Changing of the Guard

This noontime event is boring in the summer, when the queen is not in residence—the guards just change places. (This goes on

for quite a long time—no need to rush here at the stroke of noon, or to crowd in during the first few minutes; you'll have plenty of good photo ops.) If the queen's at home (indicated by a flag flying above her home), the changing of the guard is accompanied by a military band.

▲▲Museum of Danish Resistance (Frihedsmuseet)

On April 9, 1940, Hitler's Nazis violated a peace treaty and invaded Denmark, overrunning the tiny nation in mere hours. This museum tells what happened next—the compelling story of Denmark's heroic Nazi-resistance struggle (1940-1945). You'll go underground and enter the occupation years in Denmark, learning how it affected the Danish population and how the resistance movement began. First-hand accounts from five characters detail the difficult choices and dilemmas they faced. Interactive exhibits let you try to print illegal magazines, tap phone conversations, and decode German messages.

Cost and Hours: 95 DKK; daily 10:00-16:00, Oct-April closed Mon; on Churchillparken between Amalienborg Palace and *The Little Mermaid* site, at Esplanaden 13; 10-minute walk from Østerport S-tog or Metro stations, or take hop-on, hop-off Harbor Bus boat #991 or #992 to Nordre Toldbod; +45 41 20 60 80, www.frihedsmuseet.dk.

ROSENBORG CASTLE AND NEARBY

▲▲▲Rosenborg Castle (Rosenborg Slot) and Treasury

This finely furnished Dutch Renaissance-style castle was built by King Christian IV in the early 1600s as a summer residence. Rosenborg was his favorite castle and where he chose to die. Open to the public since 1838, it houses the Danish crown jewels and 500 years of royal knick-knacks. While the old palace interior is a bit dark and not as immediately impressive as many of Europe's later Baroque masterpieces, it has a certain lived-in charm. It oozes the personality of the fascinating Christian IV and has one of the finest treasury collections in Europe. For more on Christian, read the sidebar.

Cost and Hours: 120 DKK, 170-DKK combo-ticket includes Amalienborg Museum; mid-June–mid-Sept daily 9:00–17:00; mid-April–mid-June and mid-Sept–Oct daily 10:00–16:00; shorter hours and generally closed Mon rest of the year; mandatory lockers take 20-DKK coin, which will be returned; Metro or S-tog: Nørreport, then 5-minute walk on Østervoldgade and through park, +45 33 15 32 86, www.dkks.dk.

Tours: For a private tour, hire guide Richard Karpen (price depends on number of participants, May–Sept, mobile +45 91 61 95 02, www.copenhagenwalks.com, copenhagenwalks@yahoo.com). Or take the following self-guided tour that I've woven together from the highlights of Richard's walk. You can also connect to the palace's free Wi-Fi to follow a step-by-step tour of the palace highlights using your phone or tablet (bring earbuds).

❷ **Self-Guided Tour:** Buy your ticket, then head back out and look for the *castle* sign. You'll tour the ground floor room by room, then climb to the third floor for the big throne room. After a quick sweep of the middle floor, finish in the basement (enter from outside) for the jewels.

• *Begin the tour on the palace's ground floor (turn right as you enter), in the Winter Room.*

Ground Floor: Here in the wood-paneled **Winter Room,** all eyes were on King Christian IV. Today, your eyes should be on him, too. Take a close look at his marble bust by the fireplace. Check this guy out—fashionable braid, hard drinker, hard lover, energetic statesman, and warrior king. Christian IV was dynamism in the flesh, wearing a toga: a true Renaissance guy. During his reign, Copenhagen doubled in size. You're surrounded by Dutch paintings (the Dutch had a huge influence on 17th-century Denmark). Note

King Christian IV: Lover and Fighter

King Christian IV (1577-1648) inherited Denmark at the peak of its power, lived his life with the exuberance of the age, and went to his grave with the country in decline. His legacy is obvious to every tourist—Rosenborg Castle, Frederiksborg Palace, the Round Tower, Christianshavn, and on and on. Look for his logo adorning many buildings: the letter "C" with a "4" inside it and a crown on top. Thanks to his place in history and his passionate personality, Danes today regard Christian IV as one of their greatest monarchs.

During his 50-year reign, Christian IV reformed the government, rebuilt the army, established a trading post in India, and tried to expand Denmark's territory. He took Kalmar from Sweden and captured strategic points in northern Germany. The king was a large man who also lived large. A skilled horseman and avid hunter, he could drink his companions under the table. He spoke several languages and gained a reputation for being outgoing and humorous. His lavish banquets were legendary, and his romantic affairs were numerous.

But Christian's appetite for war proved destructive. In 1626, Denmark again attacked northern Germany, but was beaten back. In late 1643, Sweden launched a sneak attack, and despite Christian's personal bravery (he lost an eye), the war went badly. By the end of his life, Christian was tired and bitter, and Denmark was drained.

The heroics of Christian and his sailors live on in the Danish national anthem, "King Christian Stood by the Lofty Mast."

the smaller statue of the 19-year-old king, showing him jousting jauntily on his coronation day. In another case, the golden astronomical clock—with musical works and moving figures—did everything you can imagine. Flanking the fireplace (opposite where you entered), beneath the windows, look for the panels in the tile floor that could be removed to let the music performed by the band in the basement waft in. (Who wants the actual musicians in the dining room?) The audio holes were also used to call servants.

The **study** (or "writing closet," nearest where you entered) was small (and easy to heat). Kings did a lot of corresponding. We know a lot about Christian because 3,000 of his handwritten letters survive. The painting on the right wall shows Christian at age eight.

Three years later, his father died, and little Christian technically ascended the throne, though Denmark was actually ruled by a regency until Christian was 19. A portrait of his mother hangs above the boy, and opposite is a portrait of Christian in his prime—having just conquered Sweden—standing alongside the incredible coronation crown you'll see later.

Going back through the Winter Room, head for the door to Christian's **bedroom.** Before entering, notice the little peephole in the door (used by the king to spy on those in this room—well camouflaged by the painting, and more easily seen from the other side), and the big cabinet doors for Christian's clothes and accessories, flanking the bedroom door (notice the hinges and keyholes). Heading into the bedroom, you'll see paintings showing the king as an old man... and as a dead man. (Christian died in this room.) In the case are the clothes he wore at his

finest hour. During a naval battle against Sweden (1644), Christian stood directing the action when an explosion ripped across the deck, sending him sprawling and riddling him with shrapnel. Unfazed, the 67-year-old monarch bounced right back up and kept going, inspiring his men to carry on the fight. Christian's stubborn determination during this battle is commemorated in Denmark's national anthem. Shrapnel put out Christian's eye. No problem: The warrior king with a knack for heroic publicity stunts had the shrapnel bits removed from his eye and forehead and made into earrings as a gift for his mistress. The earrings hang in the case with his blood-stained clothes (easy to miss, right side). Christian lived to be 70 and fathered 25 children (with two wives and three mistresses). Before moving on, you can peek into Christian's private bathroom—elegantly tiled with Delft porcelain.

Proceed into the **Dark Room.** Here you'll see wax casts of royal figures. This was the way famous and important people were portrayed back then. The chair is a forerunner of the whoopee cushion. When you sat on it, metal cuffs pinned your arms down, allowing the prankster to pour water down the back of the chair (see hole)—making you "wet your pants." When you stood up, the chair made embarrassing tooting sounds.

The **Marble Room** has a particularly impressive inlaid marble floor. Imagine the king meeting emissaries here in the center, with the emblems of Norway (right), Denmark (center), and Sweden (left) behind him.

The end room, called the **King's Chamber,** was used by Christian's first mistress. Notice the ceiling painting, with an orchestra looking down on you as they play.

The long **stone passage** leading to the staircase exhibits an intriguing painting (by the door to the King's Chamber) show-

ing the crowds at the coronation of Christian's son, Frederik III. After Christian's death, a weakened Denmark was invaded, occupied, and humiliated by Sweden (Treaty of Roskilde, 1658). Copenhagen alone held out through the long winter of 1658-1659 (the Siege of Copenhagen), and Sweden eventually had to withdraw from the country. During the siege, Frederik III distinguished himself with his bravery. He seized upon the resulting surge of popularity as his chance to be anointed an absolute, divinely ordained monarch (1660). This painting marks that event—study it closely for slice-of-life details. Next, near the ticket taker, a sprawling family tree makes it perfectly clear that Christian IV comes from good stock. Notice the tree is labeled in German—the second language of the realm.

• *The queen had a hand-pulled elevator, but you'll need to hike up two flights of stairs to the throne room.*

Throne Room (Third Floor): The **Long Hall**—considered one of the best-preserved Baroque rooms in Europe—was great

for banquets. The decor trumpets the accomplishments of Denmark's great kings. The four corners of the ceiling feature the four continents known at the time. (America—at the far-right end of the hall as you enter—was still considered pretty untamed; notice the decapitated head with the arrow sticking out of it.) In the center, of course, is the proud seal of the Danish Royal Family. The tapestries, designed for this room, are from the late 1600s. Effective propaganda, they show the Danes defeating their Swedish rivals on land and at sea. The king's throne—still more propaganda for two centuries of "absolute" monarchs—was made of "unicorn horn" (actually narwhal tusk from Greenland). Believed to bring protection from evil and poison, the horn was the most precious material in its day. The queen's throne is of hammered silver. The 150-pound lions are 300 years old.

The small room to the left holds a delightful **royal porcelain** display with Chinese, French, German, and Danish examples of the "white gold." For five centuries, Europeans couldn't figure out how the Chinese made this stuff. The difficulty in just getting it back to Europe in one piece made it precious. The Danish pieces, called "Flora Danica" (on the left as you enter), are from a huge royal set showing off the herbs and vegetables of the realm.

• *Heading back down, pause at the middle floor, which is worth a look.*

Middle Floor: Circling counterclockwise, you'll see more fine clocks, fancy furniture, and royal portraits. The queen enjoyed her royal lathe (with candleholders for lighting and pedals to spin it hidden away below; in the Christian VI Room). The small mirror room (up the stairs from the main hall) was where the king played Hugh Hefner—using mirrors on the floor to see what was under those hoop skirts. In hidden cupboards, he had a fold-out bed and a handy escape staircase.

• *Back outside, turn right and find the stairs leading down to the…*

Royal Danish Treasury (Castle Basement): The palace was a royal residence for a century and has been the royal vault right up until today. As you enter, first head to the right, into the **wine cellar,** with thousand-liter barrels and some fine treasury items. The first room has a vast army of tiny golden soldiers, and a wall lined with fancy rifles. Heading into the next room, you'll see fine items of amber (petrified tree resin, 30-50 million years old) and ivory. Study the large box made of amber (in a freestanding case, just to the right as you enter)—the tiny figures show a healthy interest in sex.

Now head back past the ticket taker and into the main part of the treasury, where you can browse through exquisite royal knick-knacks.

The diamond- and pearl-studded **saddles** were Christian IV's—the first for his coronation, the second for his son's wedding. When his kingdom was nearly bankrupt, Christian had these constructed lavishly—complete with solid-gold spurs—to impress visiting dignitaries and bolster Denmark's credit rating.

The next case displays **tankards.** Danes were always big drinkers, and to drink in the top style, a king had narwhal steins (#4030). Note the fancy Greenland Inuit (Eskimo) on the lid (#4023). The case is filled with exquisitely carved ivory. On the other side of that case, what's with the mooning snuffbox (#4063)? Also, check out the amorous whistle (#4064).

Drop by the case on the wall in the back-left of the room: The 17th century was the age of **brooches.** Many of these are made of freshwater pearls. Find the fancy combination toothpick and ear spoon (#4140). Look for #4146: A queen was caught having an affair after 22 years of royal marriage. Her king gave her a special present: a golden ring—showing the hand of his promiscuous queen shaking hands with a penis.

Step downstairs, away from all this silliness. Passing through the serious vault door, you come face-to-face with a big, jeweled **sword.** The tall, two-handed, 16th-century coronation sword was drawn by the new king, who cut crosses in the air in four directions, symbolically promising to defend the realm from all attacks. The cases surrounding the sword contain everyday items used by the king (all solid gold, of course). What looks like a trophy case of gold records is actually a collection of dinner plates with amber centers (#5032).

Go down the steps. In the center case is Christian IV's **coronation crown** (from 1596, seven pounds of gold and precious stones, #5124), which some con- sider to be the finest Renaissance crown in Europe. Its six tallest gables radiate symbolism. Find the symbols of justice (sword and scales), fortitude (a woman on a lion with a sword), and charity (a nursing woman—meaning the king will love God and his people as a mother loves her child). The pelican, which according to medieval legend pecks its own flesh to feed its young, symbolizes God sacrificing his son, just as the king would make great sacrifices for his people. Climb the footstool to look inside—it's as exquisite as the outside. The shields of various Danish provinces remind the king that he's surrounded by his realms.

Circling the cases along the wall (right to left), notice the fine enameled lady's goblet with traits of a good woman spelled out in Latin (#5128) and above that, an exquisite prayer book (with handwritten favorite prayers, #5134). In the fifth window, the big solid-gold baptismal basin (#5262) hangs above tiny oval silver boxes that contained the royal children's umbilical cords (handy for protection later in life, #5272); two cases over are royal writing sets with wax, seals, pens, and ink (#5320).

Go down a few more steps into the lowest level of the treasury and last room. The two **crowns** in the center cases are more modern (from 1670), lighter, and more practical—just gold and diamonds without all the symbolism. The king's crown is only four pounds, the queen's a mere two.

The cases along the walls show off the **crown jewels.** These were made in 1840 of diamonds, emeralds, rubies, and pearls from earlier royal jewelry. The saber (#5540) shows emblems of the realm's 19 provinces. The sumptuous pendant features a 19-carat diamond cut (like its neighbors) in the 58-facet "brilliant" style for maximum reflection (far-left case, #5560). Imagine these on the dance floor. The painting shows the anointing of King Christian V at the Frederiksborg Castle Chapel in 1671. The crown jewels are still worn by the queen on special occasions several times a year.

▲Rosenborg Gardens

Rosenborg Castle is surrounded by the royal pleasure gardens and, on sunny days, a minefield of sunbathing Danish beauties and picnickers. When the royal family is in residence, there's a daily changing-of-the-guard miniparade from the Royal Guard's barracks adjoining Rosenborg Castle (at 11:30) to Amalienborg Palace (at 12:00). The Queen's Rose Garden (across the moat from the palace) is a royal place for a picnic. The fine statue of Hans Christian Andersen in the park—erected while he was still alive (and approved by him)—is meant to symbolize how his stories had a message even for adults (gardens open daily 7:00-dusk).

▲National Gallery of Denmark
(Statens Museum for Kunst)

This museum fills a stately building with Danish and European paintings from the 14th century through today. It's particularly worthwhile for the chance to be immersed in great art by the Danes, and to see its good collection of French Modernists, all well described in English.

Cost and Hours: 120 DKK, Tue-Sun 10:00-18:00, Wed until 20:00, closed Mon, Sølvgade 48, +45 33 74 84 94, www.smk.dk.

Visiting the Museum: The ground floor holds special exhibits; the second floor has collections of Danish and Nordic artists from 1750 to 1900, and European art from 1300 to 1800; and the Danish and International Art after 1900 is spread between the second and third floors.

Head first to the Danish and Nordic artists section, and pick up the excellent floor plan that suggests a twisting route through the collection. Take the time to read the descriptions in each room, which put the paintings into historical context. In addition to Romantic works by prominent non-Danish artists (such as the Norwegian J. C. Dahl and the German Caspar David Friedrich),

COPENHAGEN

this is a chance to learn about some very talented Danish painters not well known outside their native land. Make a point to meet the "Skagen Painters," including Anna Ancher, Michael Ancher, Peder Severin Krøyer, and others (find them in the section called "The Modern Breakthrough I-II"). This group, with echoes of the French Impressionists, gathered in the fishing village of Skagen on the northern tip of Denmark, surrounded by the sea and strong light, and painted heroic folk-fishermen themes in the late 1800s. Also worth seeking out are the canvases of Laurits Andersen Ring, who portrayed traditional peasant scenes with modern style; and Jens Ferdinand Willumsen, who pioneered "Vitalism" (celebrating man in nature). Other exhibits are cleverly organized by theme, such as gender or the body.

In the 20th-century section, the collection of early French Modernism is particularly impressive (with works by Matisse, Picasso, Braque, and more). This is complemented with works by Danish artists, who, inspired by the French avant-garde, introduced new, radical forms and colors to Scandinavian art.

CHRISTIANSHAVN

Across the harbor from the old town, Christianshavn—the former merchant's district—is one of the most delightful neighborhoods in town to explore. It offers pleasant canalside walks and trendy restaurants, along with two things to see: Our Savior's Church (with its fanciful tower) and Christiania, a colorful alternative-living community. Before visiting, make sure to read the background on Christianshavn, which helps explain what you'll see (see sidebar).

Your first look at the island will likely be its main square. Christianshavns Torv has a Metro stop, an early Copenhagen phone kiosk (from 1896), a fine bakery across the street (Lagkagehuset), and three statues celebrating Greenland. A Danish protectorate since 1721, Greenland, with 56,000 people, is represented by two members in the Danish parliament. The square has long been a hangout for Greenlanders, who appreciate the cheap beer and long hours of the big supermarket fronting the square. For a map of Christianshavn, see page 118.

▲Our Savior's Church (Vor Frelsers Kirke)

This large Baroque church gleams inside and out. Its bright interior (1696) is shaped like a giant cube. The magnificent pipe organ is supported by elephants (a royal symbol of the prestigious Order of the Elephant). Look-ing up to the ceiling, notice elephants also sculpted into the stucco of the dome, and a little one hanging from the main chandelier. Best of all, you can climb the unique spiral spire (with an outdoor staircase winding up to its top—398 stairs in all) for great views of the city and of the Christiania commune below.

Cost and Hours: Church interior—free, open daily 11:00-15:30 but may close for special services; church tower—50 DKK, May-Sept Mon-Sat 9:30-19:00, Sun from 10:30, 35 DKK and shorter hours off-season, closed mid-Dec-Feb and in bad weather; bus #2A, #31, #37 or Metro: Christianshavn, Sankt Annægade 29, +45 41 66 63 57, www.vorfrelserskirke.dk.

◐ Spin-Tour from the Top of Our Savior's Church: Climb up until you run out of stairs. As you wind back down, look for these landmarks:

The modern windmills are a reminder that Denmark generates 47 percent of its power from wind. Below the windmills is a great aerial view of the Christiania commune. Beyond the windmills, across Øresund (the strait that separates Denmark and Sweden), stands a shuttered Swedish nuclear power plant. The lone skyscrap-er in the distance—the first and tallest skyscraper in Scandina-via—is in Malmö, Sweden. The Øresund Bridge made Malmö an easy 35-minute bus or train ride from Copenhagen (it's become a bedroom community, with much cheaper apartments making the commute worthwhile).

Farther to the right, the big red-roof zone is Amager Island. Five hundred years as the city's dumping grounds earned Amager the nickname "Crap Island." Circling on, you come to the towering Radisson Blu Royal Hotel. The area beyond it is slated to become a forest of skyscrapers—the center of Europe's biomedical industry.

Downtown Copenhagen is decorated with several striking towers and spires. The tower capped by the golden ball is a ride in Tivoli Gardens. Next is City Hall's pointy brick tower. The biggest building, with the three-crown tower, is Christiansborg Palace. The Børsen (old stock exchange) is just beyond, with its unique dragon-tail tower. Behind that is Nyhavn. Just across from that and the Royal Danish Theatre's Playhouse is the dramatic Opera House (with the flat roof and big, grassy front yard).

Christianshavn: Then and Now

Christianshavn—Copenhagen's planned port—was vital to Danish power in the 17th and 18th centuries. Denmark had always been second to Sweden when it came to possession of natural resources, so the Danes tried to make up for it by acquiring resource-rich overseas colonies. They built Christianshavn (with Amsterdam's engineering help) to run the resulting trade business—giving this neighborhood a "little Amsterdam" vibe today.

Since Denmark's economy was so dependent on trade, the port town was the natural target of enemies. When the Danes didn't support Britain against Napoleon in 1807, the Brits bombarded Christianshavn. In this "blackest year in Danish history," Christianshavn burned down. That's why today there's hardly a building here that dates from before that time.

Christianshavn remained Copenhagen's commercial center until the 1920s, when a modern harbor was built. Suddenly, Christianshavn's economy collapsed and it became a slum. Cheap prices attracted artsy types, giving it a bohemian flavor. In 1971, squatters set up shop in an old military camp in Christianshavn and created their own community called Christiania, which still survives today (see below).

Over the past few decades, Christianshavn has had a resurgence, and these days, prices are driven up by wealthy locals (who pay about 60 percent of their income in taxes) spending too much for apartments, renting them cheaply to their kids, and writing off the loss. Demand for property is huge. Today the neighborhood is inhabited mostly by rich students and young professionals, living in some of the priciest real estate in town.

COPENHAGEN

▲▲▲Christiania

In 1971, the original 700 Christianians established squatters' rights in an abandoned military barracks just a 10-minute walk from the Danish parliament building. Two generations later, this "free city" still stands—an ultra-human mishmash of idealists, hippies, potheads, nonmaterialists, and happy children (900 people, 200 cats, 200 dogs, 2 parrots, and 17 horses). There are even a handful of Willie Nelson-type seniors among the 180 remaining here from the original takeover. And an amazing thing has happened: The place has become the second-most-visited sight among tourists in Copenhagen, behind Tivoli Gardens. Move over, *Little Mermaid*.

"Pusher Street" (named for the sale of soft drugs here) is Christiania's main drag. Get beyond this touristy side of Christiania, and you'll find a fascinating, ramshackle world of moats and earthen ramparts, alternative housing, cozy tea houses, carpenter shops, hippie villas, children's playgrounds, peaceful lanes, and people who believe that "to be normal is to be in a straitjacket." A local slogan claims, *"Kun døde fisk flyder med strømmen"* ("Only dead fish swim with the current").

Hours and Tours: Christiania is open all the time but quiet (and some restaurants closed) on Mondays, which is its rest day (though "resting" from what, I'm not sure). Guided tours leave from the main entrance (60 DKK, July-Aug daily at 15:00; Sat-Sun only the rest of the year, just show up, 1-1.5 hours, in English and Danish, info +45 21 85 38 78, www.rundvisergruppen.dk). You're welcome to snap photos, except on Pusher Street (but ask residents before you photograph them).

The Community: Christiania is broken into 14 administrative neighborhoods on a former military base. Most of the land, once owned by Denmark's Ministry of Defense, has been purchased by the Christiania community; the rest of it is leased from the state (see the sidebar for details). Locals build their homes but don't own them—individuals can't buy or sell property. When someone moves out, the community decides who will be invited in to replace that person. A third of the adult population works on the outside, a third works on the inside, and a third doesn't work much at all.

There are nine rules: no cars, no hard drugs, no guns, no explosives, and so on. The Christiania flag is red and yellow because when the original hippies took over, they found a lot of red and yellow paint onsite. The three yellow dots in the flag are from the three *i*'s in "Christiania" (or, some claim, the *o*'s in "Love, Love, Love").

There's little industry within the commune; Christiania Cykler, which builds fine bikes, is an exception (www.pedersen-bike.dk). A phone chain provides a system of communal security (they have had bad experiences calling the police). Each September 26, the day the first squatters took over the barracks in 1971, Christiania has a big birthday bash.

Tourists are entirely welcome here, because they've become

Christiania

1 Carl Madsens Plads
2 Green Hall
3 Nemoland
4 Månefiskeren Café
5 Morgenstedet Vegetarian Café
6 Spiseloppen Restaurant
7 Tour Departure Point

a major part of the economy. Visitors react in very different ways to the place. Some see dogs, dirt, and dazed people. Others see a haven of peace, freedom, and no taboos. It's true that this free city isn't always pretty. But watching parents here raise their children with Christiania values makes me a believer in this social experiment. My take: Giving alternative-type people a place to be alternative is a kind of alternative beauty that deserves a place.

Christiania Documentary: For insight into Christiania, watch the one-hour 2011 documentary *Christiania: 40 Years of Occupation*. This film, produced by Seattle production company Bus No. 8, does a wonderful job of chronicling the history of Europe's oldest still-existing squatters' community. Today, this community is still going strong after 50 years—but it hasn't been easy. See www.busno8.com for details.

Visiting Christiania: The main entrance is down Prinsessegade, behind the Our Savior's Church spiral tower. Passing under the gate, take Pusher Street directly into the community. The first square—a kind of market square (souvenirs and marijuana-related stuff)—is named Carl Madsens Plads, honoring the lawyer who took the squatters' case to the Danish supreme court in 1976 and won. Beyond that is Nemoland (a food circus, on

The Fight for Christiania

Ever since several hundred squatters took over an unused military camp in 1971, Christiania has been a political hot potato. No one in the Danish establishment wanted it. And no one had the nerve to mash it.

Part of Christiania's history has been ongoing government attempts to shut the place down. At first, city officials looked the other way because back then, no one cared about the land. But skyrocketing Christianshavn land values brought pressure to open Christiania to market forces. By the 1980s, the neighborhood had become gentrified, and both the city and developers were eyeing the land Christiania's hippies were squatting on. And when Denmark's conservative government took over in 2001, they vowed to "normalize" Christiania (with pressure from the US), with police regularly conducting raids on pot sellers.

Things were looking grim for the Christianians until 2012, when the Danish government offered to sell most of the land to residents at below the market rate, and offered guaranteed loans. In exchange, Christianians had to upgrade and maintain water, sewage, and electrical services, and preserve rights of way and "rural" areas. Accepting the offer, Christianians formed a foundation—Freetown Christiania—to purchase and control the property. The parts of Christiania that were not sold are leased to residents and are still owned by the state.

For many Christianians, it's an ironic, capitalistic twist that they now own property, albeit collectively. They even sell symbolic Christiania "shares" to help pay for the land. And, every adult over age 18 now owes a monthly rent that goes toward paying off the loans and to support services. But on the flip side, this is the greatest degree of security Christiania has ever experienced in its 50 years of existence. Even so, mistrust of the establishment is by no means dead, and there are still those who wonder what the government might be up to next.

the right). A huge warehouse called the Green Hall (Den Grønne Hal) is a recycling center and hardware store (where people get most of their building materials) that does triple duty as a night-time concert hall and as a craft center for kids. If you go up the stairs between Nemoland and the Green Hall, you'll climb up to the ramparts that overlook the canal. As you wander, be careful to distinguish between real Christianians and Christiania's motley guests—drunks (mostly from other countries) who hang out here in the summer for the freedom. Part of the original charter guaranteed that the community would stay open to the public.

On the left beyond the Green Hall, a lane leads to the Månefiskeren café, and beyond that, to the Morgenstedet vegetarian restaurant (the best place for a simple, friendly meal; see "Eating in Christiania," later). Beyond these recommended restaurants, you'll find yourself lost in the totally untouristy, truly local residential parts of Christiania, where kids play in the street and the old folks sit

out on the front stoop—just like any other neighborhood. Just as St. Mark's Square isn't the "real Venice," the hippie-druggie scene on Pusher Street isn't the "real Christiania"—you can't say you've experienced Christiania until you've strolled these back streets.

A walk or bike ride through Christiania is a great way to see how this community lives. When you leave, look up—the sign above the gate says, "You are entering the EU."

Smoking Marijuana: Pusher Street was once lined with stalls selling marijuana, joints, and hash. Residents intentionally destroyed the stalls in 2004 to reduce the risk of Christiania being disbanded by the government. (One stall was spared and is on display at the National Museum.) Today, you may see tables set up with people plying their product (with others down the

street serving as "lookouts" for police who occasionally sweep the area), and you'll likely hear whispered offers of "hash" during your visit. During my last visit there was a small, pungent stretch of Pusher Street, dubbed the "Green Light District," where pot was being openly sold (signs acknowledged that this activity was still illegal, and announced three rules here: 1. Have fun; 2. No photos; and 3. No running—"because it makes people nervous"). However, purchasing and smoking may buy you more time in Denmark than you'd planned—possession of marijuana remains illegal.

About Hard Drugs: For the first few years, junkies were tolerated. But that led to violence and polluted the mellow ambience residents envisioned. In 1979, the junkies were expelled—an epic

COPENHAGEN

confrontation in the community's folk history now—and since then the symbol of a fist breaking a syringe is as prevalent as the leafy marijuana icon. Hard drugs are emphatically forbidden in Christiania.

Eating in Christiania: The people of Christiania appreciate good food and count on tourism as a big part of their economy. Consequently, there are plenty of decent eateries. Most of the restaurants are open from lunchtime until late and are closed on Monday. **Pusher Street** has a few grungy but tasty falafel stands, as well as a popular burger bar. **$ Nemoland** is the hangout zone—a fun collection of stands peddling Thai food, burgers, *shawarma,* and other fast hippie food with great, tented outdoor seating. Its stay-a-while atmosphere comes with backgammon, foosball, bakery goods, and fine views from the ramparts. **$$ Månefiskeren** ("Moonfisher Bar") looks like a modern-day Brueghel painting, with billiards, chess, snacks, and drinks. **$$ Morgenstedet** ("Morning Place") is a good, cheap vegetarian café with a mellow, woody interior and a rustic patio outside (left after Pusher Street). **$$$$ Spiseloppen** is *the* classy restaurant in the community (described on page 118). While there are lots of public concerts at the open-air Nemoland stage, for a music club experience, consider **Musik Loppen** (which has live music almost nightly, under the Spiseloppen restaurant).

GREATER COPENHAGEN
Harbor Baths

Swimming in the middle of a large city is unthinkable in most of the world, yet the enterprising Danes have made it happen. On a warm summer day there's no better way to see Copenhageners at play than to visit one of the city's Harbor Baths. The two most centrally located baths are Havnebadet Fisketorvet, next to the Fisketorvet Mall behind Kødbyen, and Islands Brygge, just south of the Langebro bridge and Christianshavn.

The baths are open to all to enjoy a refreshing saltwater dip. How refreshing? Water temperatures peak at 65 degrees in August, which should be no problem for those with Viking blood. Though the baths are located in former industrial areas, the water is monitored, and the quality is as good as what you'll find at the pristine beaches around Copenhagen. On the rare occasions it dips below acceptable levels, the baths are closed.

Cost and Hours: Free, open long hours June-Sept (lifeguards on duty 10:00-18:00), Havnebadet Fisketorvet and Islands Brygge, +45 33 66 33 70, http://svoemkbh.kk.dk/havnebade.

Getting There: Havnebadet Fisketorvet—from Kødbyen, head east on Dybbølsbro, across the train tracks to the Fisketorvet Mall. Skirt the mall to the left, following the wide promenade toward the water and you'll soon see the baths on the left. Islands Brygge—from Fisketorvet Mall, cross the Inner Harbor on the Bryggebroen pedestrian and bicycle bridge. On the other side, follow the waterside promenade north to the baths (best on a bike). Or, if coming from the main train station area, head east over Langebro bridge, then head a short distance south—you can't miss the baths. From Christianshavn, follow the ramparts west to where they meet the Inner Harbor. Pass under Langebro bridge, and you'll see the baths.

Visiting the Baths: The Havnebadet Fisketorvet is actually a huge, semisubmerged barge containing three pools: one for children, another for diving (from one-, two-, and three-meter-high boards), and an Olympic-size swimming pool. Here you'll be hemmed in on three sides by glassy modern office buildings and the Fisketorvet Mall.

The much busier Islands Brygge facility consists of five pools (two suitable for kids) and a prow-shaped diving platform offering three- and five-meter leaps into the water. The shore is one big cobbled promenade backed by a grassy area that's great for sunbathing, barbecues, and people-watching.

Carlsberg Brewery

Denmark's beloved source of legal intoxicants is Carlsberg. About 1.5 miles west of Rådhuspladsen (City Hall Square), Carlsberg

welcomes you to its visitors center for a self-guided tour, a free beer, and a small gift. Mostly, it's a ruse to ply you with a beer and get you into their substantial gift shop. The visitors center may be closed for renovation when you visit, so check the website before you go.

Cost and Hours: 100 DKK, daily 10:00-20:00, Oct-April until 17:00; half-hour guided tour—50 DKK, in English at 13:00, 14:00, and 15:00; beer tasting—75 DKK, at 12:00, 14:00, and 16:00; catch the local train to Carlsberg Station or bus #26 (get off at the Kammasvej stop and walk five minutes), or take a free shuttle from near the Vesterbrogade TI (where the hop-on, hop-off buses stop); enter at Gamle Carlsbergvej 11 around corner from brewery entrance, +45 33 27 12 82, www.visitcarlsberg.dk.

Nearby: The manicured gardens of the sprawling Frederiksberg Park (Frederiksberg Have) and adjacent Southern Field (Søndermarken) make a lovely setting for a picnic.

Open-Air Folk Museum (Frilandsmuseet)

This park, located north of Copenhagen in the suburb of Lyngby, is part of the National Museum. It's filled with traditional Danish architecture and folk culture, farm animals, and gardens. Bring a picnic or dine at the on-site restaurant.

Cost and Hours: 80 DKK; May-mid-Oct Tue-Sun 10:00-16:00, July-mid-Aug until 17:00, closed Mon and off-season; S-tog: Sorgenfri and 10-minute walk to Kongevejen 100 in Lyngby (see the "Near Copenhagen" map in the next chapter); +45 41 20 64 55, http://natmus.dk.

Bakken Amusement Park (Bakken Forlystelsespark)

Danes gather at Copenhagen's *other* great amusement park, Bakken, situated in the Dyrehaven forest about a 10-minute drive north of the city.

Cost and Hours: Free entry, 279 DKK for all-ride pass; late June-mid-Aug daily 12:00-24:00, shorter hours April-late June and mid-Aug-mid-Sept, closed mid-Sept-March except open Fri-Sun late-Nov-late-Dec; S-tog: Klampenborg, then walk 10 minutes through the woods (see the "Near Copenhagen" map in the next chapter); +45 39 63 35 44, www.bakken.dk.

Dragør Town

If you don't have time to get to the idyllic island of Ærø (see the Central Denmark chapter), consider the eight-mile trip south of Copenhagen to the cobblestoned fishing village of Dragør, near the airport (bus #250S from Nørreport or bus #35 from the Copenhagen airport). For information, see www.visit-dragoer.dk.

Shopping in Copenhagen

Shops are generally open Monday through Friday from 10:00 to 19:00 and Saturday from 9:00 to 16:00 (closed Sun). While big department stores dominate the scene, many locals favor smaller artisan shops and boutiques.

Uniquely Danish souvenirs include intricate paper cuttings with idyllic motifs of swans, flowers, or Christmas themes; mobiles with everything from bicycles to Viking ships (look for the quality Flensted brand); and the colorful artwork of Danish artist Bo Bendixen (posters, postcards, T-shirts, and more). Jewelry lovers look for amber, known as the "gold of the North." Globs of this petrified sap wash up on the shores of all the Baltic countries.

WHERE TO SHOP

Consider the following stores, markets, and neighborhoods:

For a street's worth of shops selling **"Scantiques,"** wander down Ravnsborggade from Nørrebrogade.

Copenhagen's colorful **flea markets** *(loppemarkeder)* are small but feisty and surprisingly cheap (April-Oct Sat 8:00-14:00 in Nørreport, on Nørrebrogade along the wall of the Assistens Kierkegaard Cemetery; May-Oct Fri and Sat 8:00-17:00 at Thorvaldsen's Plads, along Gammel Strand and on Kongens Nytorv). For other street markets, ask at the TI.

The city's top **department stores** (Illum at Østergade 52, and Magasin du Nord at Kongens Nytorv 13) offer a good, if expensive, look at today's Denmark. Both are on the Strøget and have fine cafeterias on their top floors. The department stores and the Politiken Bookstore on Rådhuspladsen have a good selection of maps and English travel guides.

The section of the Strøget called **Amagertorv** is a highlight for shoppers. The **Royal Copenhagen** store here sells porcelain on three floors (Mon-Fri 10:00-19:00, Sat until 18:00, Sun 11:00-17:00). The first floor up features figurines and collectibles. The second floor has a second-quality department for discounts, proving that "even the best painter can miss a stroke." Next door,

Illums Bolighus shows off three floors of modern Danish design (Mon-Fri 10:00-19:00, Sat until 18:00, Sun 11:00-16:00).

House of Amber has a shop and a tiny two-room museum with about 50 examples of prehistoric insects trapped in the amber (remember *Jurassic Park*?) under magnifying glasses. You'll also see remarkable items made of amber, from necklaces and chests to Viking ships and chess sets (museum-25 DKK, daily May-Sept 9:00-19:30, Oct-April 10:00-17:30, at the top of Nyhavn at Kongens Nytorv 2, www.houseofamber.com). If you're visiting Rosenborg Castle, you'll see the ultimate examples of amber craftsmanship in its treasury.

Nightlife in Copenhagen

For the latest event and live music listings, check at the TI and pick up the weekly *Copenhagen Post* (www.cphpost.dk).

Nightlife Neighborhoods: The **Meatpacking District,** which I've listed for its restaurants (see page 119), is also one of the city's up-and-coming des-tinations for bars and nightlife. On warm evenings, **Nyhavn** canal becomes a virtual night-club, with packs of young people hanging out along the water, sip-ping beers. **Christiania** always seems to have something musi-cal going on after dark. **Tivoli** has evening entertainment daily from mid-April through late September (see page 71).

Music Venues: Alice is a good bet for live jazz (two stages, closed Mon, Nørre Allé 7, +45 50 58 08 41, schedule at www. jazzhouse.dk. For blues, try the **Mojo Blues Bar** (nightly 20:00-late, music starts at 21:30, Løngangsstræde 21c, +45 33 11 64 53, schedule in Danish at www.mojo.dk). For locations, see the "Co-penhagen Restaurants" map later in this chapter.

Jazz Cruises: Canal Tours Copenhagen offers 1-hour jazz cruises along the canals of Copenhagen. You can bring a picnic dinner and drinks on board and enjoy a lively night on the water surrounded by Danes (175 DKK and up, late-May-mid-Sept Thu and Sun at 19:00, no tours mid-Sept-late May, departs from Canal Tours Copenhagen dock at Nyhavn, +45 32 96 30 00, www. stromma.dk). Call to reserve on July and August evenings; other-wise try arriving 20 to 30 minutes in advance.

Sleeping in Copenhagen

I've listed a few big business-class hotels, the best budget hotels in the center, and a few backpacker dorm options.

HOTELS IN CENTRAL COPENHAGEN

All of these hotels are big and modern, with elevators and non-smoking rooms.

Near Nørreport

$$$$ Ibsens Hotel is a stylish 118-room hotel with helpful staff, located in a charming neighborhood away from the main train station commotion and a short walk from the old center (consider splurging on a larger room—smaller rooms can be very tight, good rental bikes, pay parking, Vendersgade 23, S-tog and Metro: Nør-report—to find Vendersgade after surfacing from the Metro, head for the five-story brown building with the green copper dome, +45 33 13 19 13, www.arthurhotels.dk/ibsens-hotel, ibsens@arthurhotels.dk).

$$$ Hotel Jørgensen is a friendly little 30-room hotel in a great location just off Nørreport, kitty-corner from the bustling TorvehallerneKBH food market. With fresh and tidy rooms and a welcoming lounge, it's a fine option, though the halls are a narrow, tangled maze (Rømersgade 11, +45 33 13 81 86, www.hoteljorgensencopenhagen.site, hoteljoergensen@mail.dk). They also rent ¢ dorm beds.

Near Nyhavn

$$$$ 71 Nyhavn has 130 rustic but very classy rooms in a pair of beautifully restored, early-19th-century brick warehouses located at the far end of the colorful Nyhavn canal. With a professional, po-lite staff, lots of old brick and heavy timbers, and plenty of style, it's a worthwhile splurge (some rates include breakfast, air-con, rental bikes available, next to the Playhouse at Nyhavn 71, +45 33 43 62 00, www.71nyhavnhotel.dk, 71nyhavnhotel@arp-hansen.dk).

$$$ Hotel Bethel Sømandshjem ("Seamen's Home"), run by a Lutheran association, is a calm and stately former seamen's hotel facing the boisterous Nyhavn canal and offering 41 cozy rooms at the most reasonable rack rates in town. While the decor is college-dorm-inspired, the hotel boasts a kind, welcoming staff and feels surprisingly comfortable once you settle in. Plus, the colorful Ny-havn neighborhood is a great place to "come home" to after a busy day of sightseeing. Book long in advance (facing bridge over the canal at Nyhavn 22, Metro: Kongens Nytorv, +45 33 13 03 70, www.hotel-bethel.dk, info@hotel-bethel.dk).

Behind the Train Station

The area behind the train station mingles elegant old buildings, trendy nightspots, and pockets of modern sleaze. The main drag running away from the station, Istedgade, was long Copenhagen' red-light district, but this area is increasingly gentrifying and f safe (in spite of the few remaining harmless sex shops). These are also extremely handy to the Meatpacking District re zone.

$$$$ Axel Guldsmeden Hotel and **$$$$ 66 G** operated by the Guldsmeden ("Dragonfly") compa character than most—a restful spa-like ambience imported Balinese furniture, four-poster beds on sustainability and organic materials. (A 212 rooms, request a quieter back room overloo

Copenhagen Hotels

1. Ibsens Hotel
2. Hotel Jørgensen
3. 71 Nyhavn
4. Hotel Bethel Sømandshjem
5. Axel Guldsmeden Hotel
6. 66 Guldsmeden
7. Good Morning City Copenhagen Star Hotel
8. Hotel Nebo
9. Wake Up Copenhagen
10. Cabinn (5)
11. Danhostel Copenhagen City
12. Copenhagen Downtown
13. To Danhostel Copenhagen Amager

COPENHAGEN

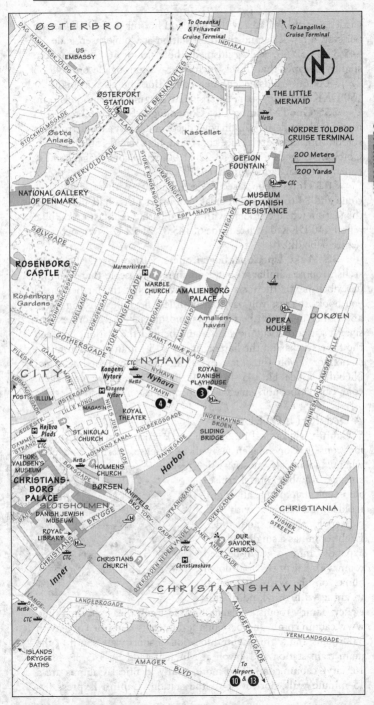

ØSTERBRO

DAG HAMMARSKJOLDS ALLE

US EMBASSY

To Oceankaj & Frihavnen Cruise Terminal

To Langelinie Cruise Terminal

INDIAKAJ

ØSTERPORT STATION

Oslo Plads

FOLKE BERNADOTTES ALLE

STOCKHOLMSGADE

Østre Anlæg

Kastellet

THE LITTLE MERMAID

Netto

STORE KONGENSGADE

GRØNNINGEN

NORDRE TOLDBOD CRUISE TERMINAL

200 Meters
200 Yards

GEFION FOUNTAIN

ØSTERVOLDGADE

SØLVGADE

NATIONAL GALLERY OF DENMARK

ESPLANADEN

AMALIEGADE

MUSEUM OF DANISH RESISTANCE

CTC

ROSENBORG CASTLE

Rosenborg Gardens

KRONPRINSESSEGADE

ADELGADE

BORGERGADE

STORE KONGENSGADE

Marmorkirken

MARBLE CHURCH

BREDGADE

AMALIENBORG PALACE

Amalien-haven

DOKØEN

OPERA HOUSE

DANSEKRØNS-SAMSØES ALLE

GOTHERSGADE

GAMMEL MONT

SANKT ANNÆ PLADS

CITY

PILESTR.

KØBMAGERGADE

POST

ILLUM

ØSTERGADE

Kongens Nytorv

Netto

NYHAVN

Nyhavn

CTC

NYHAVN

ROYAL DANISH PLAYHOUSE

3

H

Magasin

NIELS JUELS GADE

Kongens Nytorv

LILLE KONG

ROYAL THEATER

4

LÆDERSTR.

Højbro Plads

GAMMEL STRAND

CTC

ST. NIKOLAJ CHURCH

HOLBERGSGADE

HAVNEGADE

INDERHAVNS-BROEN

SLIDING BRIDGE

THOR-VALDSEN'S MUSEUM

HOLMENS KANAL

Netto

HOLMENS CHURCH

Harbor

CHRISTIANS-BORG PALACE

BØRSGADE

BØRSEN

KNIPPELS-BRO

SLOTSHOLMEN

DANISH JEWISH MUSEUM

STRANDGADE

OVERGADEN

CHRISTIANIA

"PUSHER STREET"

PRINSESSEGADE

ROYAL LIBRARY

H

CTC

CHRISTIANS

Inner

OVERGADEN NEDEN VANDET

SANKT ANNÆ GADE

CTC

OUR SAVIOR'S CHURCH

CHRISTIANS CHURCH

M

Christianshavn

CHRISTIANSHAVN

LANGE BRO

Netto

CTC

LANGEBROGADE

AMAGERBROGADE

VERMLANDSGADE

ISLANDS BRYGGE BATHS

AMAGER BLVD.

To Airport, & 13

10 & 13

garden, restful spa area with sauna and hot tub-345 DKK/person per stay, a block behind the train station at Colbjørnsensgade 14, +45 33 31 32 66, axel@guldsmedenhotels.com; **66 Guldsmeden:** slightly cheaper than Axel, 74 rooms, Vesterbrogade 66, +45 33 22 15 00, 66@guldsmedenhotels.com). Both hotels rent bikes for 150 DKK/day. They share a website: http://guldsmedenhotels.com.

$$$ Good Morning City Copenhagen Star Hotel rents 134 rooms with modern Scandinavian decor and is just a block from the station (breakfast extra, nice courtyard, bike rental-150 DKK/day, Colbjørnsensgade 13, +45 33 22 11 00, www.copenhagenstar.dk, copenhagenstar@gmorninghotels.dk).

$$$ Hotel Nebo, a secure-feeling refuge with a friendly welcome and 84 comfy if a bit creaky rooms, is just a half-block from the station (cheaper rooms with shared bath, breakfast extra, bike rental-140 DKK/day, Istedgade 6, +45 33 21 12 17, www.nebo.dk, nebo@nebo.dk).

$$ Wake Up Copenhagen offers 510 compact, slick, and stylish rooms (similar to but a notch more upscale than Cabinn, described next). The rates can range wildly, but the farther ahead you book, the less you pay (but with less flexibility). Rooms that are higher up—with better views and quieter—are more expensive. It's in a desolate no-man's-land behind the station, between the train tracks and the harbor, about a 15-minute walk from the station or Tivoli (breakfast extra, air-con, bike rental, Carsten Niebuhrs Gade 11, +45 44 80 00 00, www.wakeupcopenhagen.com, carstenniebuhrsgade@wakeupcopenhagen.dk).

A DANISH MOTEL 6

$ Cabinn is a radical innovation and a great value, with several locations in Copenhagen (as well as Odense, Aarhus, and else-where): identical, mostly col-lapsible, tiny but comfy, cruise-ship-type staterooms, all bright, molded, and shiny, with TV, coffeepot, shower, and toilet. Each room has a single bed that expands into a twin-bedded room with one or two fold-down bunks on the walls. It's tough to argue with this kind of effi-ciency (family rooms available, breakfast extra, easy pay parking, www.cabinn.com). The best of the bunch is **Cabinn City,** with 352 rooms and a great central location (a short walk south of the main train station and Tivoli at Mitchellsgade 14, +45 33 46 16 16, city@cabinn.com). Two more, nearly identical Cabinns are a 15-minute walk northwest of the station: **Cabinn Express** (86 rooms, Danasvej 32, +45 33 21 04 00, express@cabinn.com) and **Cabinn Scandinavia** (201 rooms, family rooms, Vodroffsvej 55, +45 35 36 11 11, scandinavia@cabinn.com). The largest and newest is **Cabinn Copenhagen**, a 15-minute walk southwest of the station, between the train tracks and the harbor (1,200 rooms, family rooms, small apartments, at Arni Magnussons Gade 1, +45 33 29 1900, copenhagen@cabinn.com). **Cabinn Metro,** near the Ørestad Metro station, is the farthest out (708 rooms, family rooms, on the airport side of town at Arne Jakobsens Allé 2, +45 32 46 57 00, metro@cabinn.com).

HOSTELS

¢ **Danhostel Copenhagen City,** an official HI hostel, is the hostel of the future. This huge harborside 16-story skyscraper is clean, modern, nonsmoking, and a 10-minute walk from the train station and Tivoli. Some rooms on higher floors have panoramic views over the city—book in advance. This is your best bet for a clean, basic, and inexpensive room with private baths in the city center (private rooms and family rooms available, breakfast extra, elevator, rental bikes, H. C. Andersens Boulevard 50, +45 33 11 85 85, www.danhostelcopenhagencity.dk, rec@cphhostel.dk).

¢ **Copenhagen Downtown** is beautifully located on a pleasant street right in the city center, a few steps from Slotsholmen Island and two blocks from the Strøget. Its 300 beds are a bit institutional, but it promises free dinner and comes with a guest kitchen and a colorful, fun hangout bar, which doubles as the reception (private rooms available, breakfast extra, no curfew, Vandkunsten 5, +45 70 23 21 10, www.copenhagendowntown.com, info@copenhagendowntown.com).

¢ **Danhostel Copenhagen Amager,** an official HI hostel, is on the edge of town (private rooms available, breakfast extra, family rooms, no curfew, excellent facilities, Vejlands Allé 200, Metro: Bella Center, then 10-minute walk, +45 32 52 29 08, www.danhostelcopenhagen.dk, copenhagen@danhostel.dk).

Eating in Copenhagen

CHEAP MEALS

For a quick lunch, try a *smørrebrød*, a *pølse*, or a picnic. Finish it off with a pastry.

Smørrebrød

Denmark's 300-year-old tradition of open-face sandwiches survives. Find a *smørrebrød* takeout shop and choose two or three sandwiches that look good (about 35 DKK each). They'll come wrapped and ready for a park bench. Add a cold drink, and you have a fine, quick, and very Danish lunch. Tradition calls for three sandwich courses: herring first, then meat, and then cheese.

Between Copenhagen University and Rosenborg Castle

My three favorite *smørrebrød* places are particularly handy when connecting your sightseeing between the downtown Strøget core and Rosenborg Castle.

$$$ Restaurant Schønnemann is the foodies' choice—it frequently wins awards for "Best Lunch in Copenhagen." It's a cozy cellar restaurant crammed with small tables—according to the history on the menu, people "gather here in intense togetherness." The sand on the floor evokes a bygone era when passing traders would leave their horses out on the square while they lunched here. You'll need to reserve to get a table, and you'll pay a premium for their *smørrebrød* (two lunch seatings Mon-Sat: 11:30-14:00 & 14:15-17:00, closed Sun, no dinner, Hauser Plads 16, +45 33 12 07 85).

$$ Café Halvvejen is a small mom-and-pop place serving traditional lunches and open-face sandwiches in a woody and smoke-stained café, lined with portraits of Danish royalty. You can eat inside or at an outside table in good weather (food served Mon-Sat 12:00-15:00, closed Sun, next to public library at Krystalgade 11, +45 33 11 91 12). In the evening, it becomes a hip and smoky student hangout, though no food is served.

$ Slagteren ved Kultorvet, a few blocks northwest of the university, is a small butcher shop with bowler-hatted clerks selling good, inexpensive sandwiches to go for about 45 DKK. Choose from ham, beef, or pork (Mon-Thu 8:00-17:30, Fri until 18:00, Sat until 15:00, closed Sun, sandwiches usually sell out by 13:00; just off Kultorvet square at Frederiksborggade 4, look for gold bull's head hanging outside +45 33 12 29 02).

Near Christiansborg Palace

These eateries are good choices when sightseeing on Slotsholmen.

$$ Kanal Caféen, on Frederiksholms Kanal across from Christiansborg Palace, serves lunch only and is a nice place for a traditional open-face sandwich. Inside, you'll rub elbows with locals in what feels like the cozy confines of a low-ceilinged old sailing ship; outside you can dine right above the canal and watch the tour boats go by (Mon-Fri 11:30-17:00, Sat until 15:00, closed Sun, Frederiksholms Kanal 18, +45 33 11 57 70).

$$ Café Diamanten serves open-face sandwiches, warm dishes, and salads—and pours microbrews from the tap. Take a seat inside the comfy café or under the parasols out front, with a view across the square to Thorvaldsen's Museum (Mon-Fri 9:30:-19:30, Sat-Sun 10:00-18:30, bar open Fri until 24:00, Gammel Strand 50, +45 33 93 55 45).

Burgers: $$$ Cock's & Cows is a trendy burger-and-cocktail bar with a happy, young vibe on an elegant street. Eat inside the brick-walled restaurant or in the courtyard out back (some burgers piled almost ridiculously high, daily 11:30-21:00, Gammel Strand 34, +45 69 15 79 01).

Near Gammeltorv/Nytorv

$$ Café Nytorv has a nautical theme inside and pleasant outdoor seating on Nytorv. There's a great deal on a *smørrebrød* sampler for 268 DKK—perfect for two people to share (if you smile, they'll serve it for dinner even though it's only on the lunch menu). This "Copenhagen City Plate" gives you a selection of the traditional sandwiches and extra bread on request (daily 9:00-23:00, Nytorv 15, +45 33 11 77 06).

$$ Café Sorgenfri offers a local experience in a dark, woody spot just off the Strøget—give the herring open-face sandwich a try (daily 11:00-18:00, Brolæggerstræde 8, +45 33 11 58 80).

Or duck (literally) into **$$ Kronborg Dansk Restaurant,** across the street from Café Sorgenfri, for finer-quality *smørrebrød* in a wood-beamed nautical setting (meat and fish sandwiches plus herring specialties, Sun-Wed 11:00-17:00, Thu-Sat until 22:00, Brolæggerstræde 12, +45 33 13 07 08).

Another option is **$$ Domhusets Smørrebrød** (Mon-Fri 7:00-15:00, closed Sat-Sun, off the City Hall end of the Strøget at Kattesundet 18, +45 33 15 98 98).

The *Pølse*

The famous Danish hot dog, sold in *pølsevogne* (sausage wagons) throughout the country, is another typically Danish institution that has resisted the onslaught of our global fast-food culture. Study the photo menu for variations. These are fast, cheap, tasty, and, like

COPENHAGEN

Copenhagen Restaurants

1 Restaurant Schønnemann
2 Café Halvvejen
3 Slagteren ved Kultorvet
4 Kanal Caféen
5 Café Diamanten
6 Cock's & Cows
7 Café Nytorv
8 Café Sorgenfri
9 Kronborg Dansk Rest.
10 Domhusets Smørrebrød
11 Supermarket (2)
12 Lagekagehuset Bakeries (4)
13 Nansens Bakery
14 Konditori La Glace
15 Det Lille Apotek
16 RizRaz (2)
17 Tight
18 Café Norden
19 Royal Smushi Café

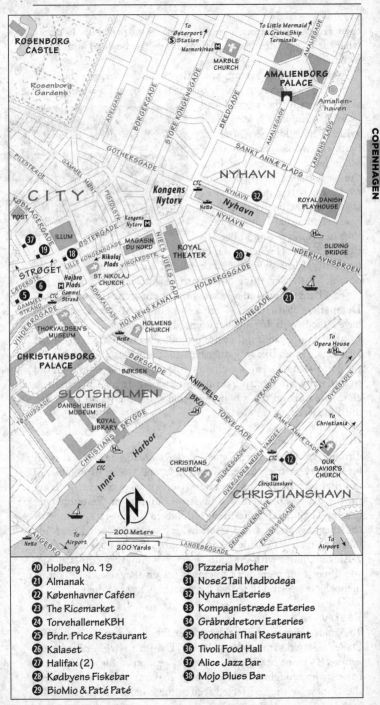

20 Holberg No. 19

21 Almanak

22 Københavner Caféen

23 The Ricemarket

24 TorvehallerneKBH

25 Brdr. Price Restaurant

26 Kalaset

27 Halifax (2)

28 Kødbyens Fiskebar

29 BioMio & Paté Paté

30 Pizzeria Mother

31 Nose2Tail Madbodega

32 Nyhavn Eateries

33 Kompagnistræde Eateries

34 Gråbrødretorv Eateries

35 Poonchai Thai Restaurant

36 Tivoli Food Hall

37 Alice Jazz Bar

38 Mojo Blues Bar

their American cousins, almost worthless nutritionally. Even so, what the locals call the "dead man's finger" is the dog Danish kids love to bite.

There's more to getting a *pølse* than simply ordering a "hot dog" (which in Copenhagen simply means a sausage with a bun on the side, generally the worst bread possible). The best is a *ristet* (or grilled) hot dog *med det hele* (with the works). Employ these other handy phrases: *rød* (red, the basic boiled weenie), *medister* (spicy, better quality), *knæk* (short, stubby, tastier than *rød*), *brød* (a bun, usually smaller than the sausage), *svøb* ("swaddled" in bacon), *Fransk* (French style, buried in a long skinny hole in the bun with sauce). *Sennep* is mustard and *ristet løg* are crispy, fried onions. Wash everything down with a *sodavand* (soda pop).

By hanging around a *pølsevogn*, you can study this institution. Denmark's "cold feet cafés" are a form of social care: People who have difficulty finding jobs are licensed to run these wiener-mobiles. As they gain seniority, they are promoted to work at more central locations. Danes like to gather here for munchies and *pølsesnak*—the local slang for empty chatter (literally, "sausage talk"). And traditionally, after getting drunk, guys stop here for a hot dog and chocolate milk on the way home—that's why the stands stay open until the wee hours.

Picnics

Throughout Copenhagen, small delis *(viktualiehandler)* sell fresh bread, tasty pastries, juice, milk, cheese, and yogurt (drinkable, in tall liter boxes). Two of the largest supermarket chains are **Irma** (in the glassy DI—Danish Industry—building on Vesterbrogade next to Tivoli) and **Super Brugsen. Netto** is a cut-rate outfit with the cheapest prices and a good bakery section (located on Rådhuspladsen at Vestergade). And, of course, there's the ever-present **7-Eleven** chain, with branches seemingly on every corner; while you'll pay a bit more here, there's a reason they're called "convenience" stores—and they also serve pastries and hot dogs.

Pastry

The golden pretzel sign hanging over the door or windows is the Danes' age-old symbol for a bakery. Danish pastries, called *wienerbrød* ("Vienna bread") in Denmark, are named for the Viennese bakers who brought the art of pastry-making to Denmark, where the Danes say they perfected it. Try these bakeries: **Lagkagehu-**

Dine with the Danes

For a unique experience and a great opportunity to meet locals in their homes, consider having this organization arrange a dinner for you with a Danish family. You get a homey two-course meal with lots of conversation. Some effort is made to match your age, interests, and occupations. Book online at least two weeks in advance (450 DKK/person, www.facebook.com/DineWithTheDanes, dinewiththedanes@msn.com). Fill out an online questionnaire, and you'll soon be contacted via Facebook or by email.

---

set (multiple locations around town; the handiest options include one in the train station, another nearby inside the Vesterbrogade TI, one along the Strøget at Frederiksborggade 21, and another on Torvegade just across from the Metro station in Christianshavn) and **Nansens** (on corner of Nansensgade and Ahlefeldtsgade, near Ibsens Hotel). **Emmerys,** an organic bakery and café, has more than 20 branches around Copenhagen, and sells good pastries and sandwiches. For a genteel bit of high-class 1870s Copenhagen, pay a lot for a coffee and a fresh Danish at **Konditori La Glace,** just off the Strøget at Skoubogade 3.

RESTAURANTS

I've listed restaurants in four areas: the downtown core, the funky Christianshavn neighborhood across the harbor, near Nørreport, and in the trendy Meatpacking District behind the main train station.

Downtown Core

$$$$ Det Lille Apotek ("The Little Pharmacy") is a candlelit place with seating spread among its four themed "parlours." It's been popular with locals for 200 years, and today it's a hit with tourists, serving open-face sandwiches at lunchtime and traditional dinners in the evening (daily 11:30-22:00, just off the Strøget, between Frue Church and Round Tower at Store Kannikestræde 15, +45 33 12 56 06, http://detlilleapotek.dk).

$$ RizRaz has two locations in Copenhagen: around the corner from the canal boat rides at Kompagnistræde 20 (+45 33 15 05 75) and across from Det Lille Apotek at Store Kannikestræde 19 (+45 42 32 68 32). At both places, you'll find a combination of burgers and meat dishes as well as vegetarian, including an all-you-can-eat Middle Eastern/Mediterranean/vegetarian buffet lunch for 99 DKK (great falafel, daily 11:30-16:00) and a bigger dinner buffet for 129 DKK (16:00-24:00). Use lots of plates and return to the buffet as many times as you like.

$$$ Tight resembles a trendy gastropub, serving an eclectic international array of food and drink (Canadian, Aussie, French, and burgers, with Danish microbrews) in a split-level maze of hip rooms that mix old timbers and brick with bright colors (daily 17:00-22:00, just off the Strøget at Hyskenstræde 10, +45 70 88 58 14).

$$$$ Café Norden, very Danish with modern "world cuisine," seasonal menus, good light meals, and fine pastries, is a big, venerable institution overlooking Amagertorv by the heron fountain. It's family-friendly, with good seats outside on the square, in the busy ground-floor interior, or with more space and better views upstairs (great people-watching from the window seats). Order at the bar—it's the same price upstairs or down (huge splittable portions, daily 9:00-24:00, Østergade 61, +45 33 11 77 91, http://cafenorden.dk).

$$$ Royal Smushi Café is a hit with dainty people who like the idea of small, gourmet, open-face sandwiches served on Royal Copenhagen porcelain. You can sit in their modern chandeliered interior or the quiet courtyard (daily 10:00-18:00, next to Royal Copenhagen porcelain store at Amagertorv 6, +45 33 12 11 22).

$$ Holberg No. 19, a cozy Mediterranean-style café with classic ambience, sits just a block off the tourist crush of the Nyhavn canal. With a loose and friendly vibe, it offers more personality and lower prices than the tourist traps along Nyhavn (no real kitchen but reasonably priced salads and sandwiches—some with an international twist, quiche, selection of wines and beers, order at the bar, Mon-Sat 8:00-22:00, Sun 10:00-20:00, Holbergsgade 19, +45 33 14 01 90).

$$$ Almanak, on the waterfront promenade near the entrance to Nyhavn, dishes artfully prepared (and tasty) open-face sandwiches and main courses in a cool and sleek restaurant and on its outdoor terrace facing the Inner Harbor. Look for the long green building on the promenade with a big sign on the roof that reads *The Standard* (Tue-Sat 12:00-22:00, Sun until 17:00, closed Mon, Havnegade 44, +45 72 14 88 08).

$$$ Københavner Caféen, cozy and old-fashioned, feels like a ship captain's dining room. The staff is enthusiastically traditional, serving local dishes and elegant open-face sandwiches for a good value. Lunch specials (139-169 DKK) are served until 17:00, when the more expensive dinner menu kicks in (daily, kitchen closes at 22:00, at Badstuestræde 10, +45 33 32 80 81).

$$$ The Ricemarket, an unpretentious Asian fusion bistro, is buried in a modern cellar between the Strøget and Rosenborg Castle. It's a casual, more affordable side-eatery of a popular local restaurant, and offers a flavorful break from Danish food (nine-dish family-style meal for 285 DKK, daily 12:00-22:00, Hauser-gade 38 near Kultorvet, +45 35 35 75 30).

$$ Illum and **Magasin du Nord** department stores serve cheery, reasonable meals in their cafeterias. At Illum, eat outside at tables along the Strøget, or head to the elegant glass-domed top floor (Østergade 52). Magasin du Nord (Kongens Nytorv 13) also has a great grocery and deli in the basement.

Also try **Café Nytorv** at Nytorv 15 or **Sorgenfri** at Brolæg-gerstræde 8 (both are described under *"Smørrebrød,"* earlier).

Christianshavn

This neighborhood is so cool, it's worth combining an evening wander with dinner. It's a 10-minute walk across the bridge from the old center, or a 3-minute ride on the Metro. Choose one of my listings (for locations, see the "Christianshavn" map on the next page), or simply wander the blocks between Christianshavns Torv, the main square, and the Christianshavn Canal—you'll find a number of lively neighborhood pubs and cafés.

$$$$ Ravelinen Restaurant, on a tiny island on the big road 100 yards south of Christianshavn, serves traditional Danish food to happy local crowds. Dine indoors or on the lovely canalside terrace (which is tented and heated, so it's comfortable even on blustery evenings). This is like Tivoli without the kitsch and tourists. They offer a shareable *koldt bord* ("cold table") meal for 308 DKK at lunch only (mid-April-late Dec daily 11:30-21:00, closed off-season, Torvegade 79, +45 32 96 20 45, http://ravelinen.dk).

$$$$ Noma, the splurge of all splurges, has for years been rated as the one of world's best restaurants. Chef René Redzepi is a pioneer in the New Nordic school of cooking, which combines modern nouvelle cuisine and molecular gastronomy techniques with locally sourced (and, in some cases, foraged) ingredients from Denmark and other Nordic lands. Reservations are hard to come by and it'll set two people back around $1,000, but for many foodies, this is at the top of the list (Tue-Fri 17:00-24:00, Sat 11:30-19:00, closed Sun-Mon, Refshalevej 96, +45 3296 3297, www.noma.dk).

$ Lagkagehuset is everybody's favorite bakery in Christianshavn. With a big selection of pastries, sandwiches, excellent fresh-baked bread, and award-winning strawberry tarts, it's a great place for breakfast or picnic fixings (takeout coffee, daily 6:00-19:00, Torvegade 45). For other locations closer to the town center, see page 114 under "Pastry."

Global Cuisine on Christianshavn's Main Drag: Torvegade, which is within a few minutes' walk of the Christianshavn Metro station, is lined with appealing and inexpensive international eateries, including Italian, cheap kebabs, Thai, Chinese, and more.

COPENHAGEN

Christianshavn

To Nyhavn

To Opera House, A

CHRISTIANS-BORG PALACE

Netto

BØRSGADE

BØRSEN

HAVNEGADE

Canal

KNIPPELS BRIDGE

PRINSESSEGADE

REFSHALEVEJ

SLOTSHOLMEN

ROYAL LIBRARY

CHRISTIANS-BRYGGE

Inner Harbor

CTC

To Train Station

CHRISTIANS CHURCH

WILDERSGADE

TORVEGADE

STRANDGADE

OVERGADEN NEDEN VANDET

OVERGADEN OVEN VANDET

BÅDSMANDSSTR.

SKT. ANNÆ GADE

CTC

Christians-havn

Christianshavns Torv

OUR SAVIOR'S CHURCH

CHRISTIANIA

CHRISTIANSHAVN

DRONNINGENSGADE

PRINSESSEGADE

AMAGERGADE

CHRISTIANSHAVNS VOLDGADE

Stadsgraven (former moat)

LANGEBROGADE

PATH

MEDIEVAL RAMPARTS

AMAGER BLVD.

To Rådhuspladsen

400 Meters

400 Yards

To Airport

1 Ravelinen Restaurant
2 To Noma
3 Lagkagehuset Bakery
4 Spicy Kitchen
5 Spiseloppen Restaurant

\$\$ Spicy Kitchen serves cheap and good Indian food—tight and cozy, it's a hit with locals (daily 17:00-22:00, Torvegade 56).

In Christiania: \$\$\$\$ Spiseloppen ("The Flea Eats") is a wonderfully classy place in Christiania. It serves great 145-DKK vegetarian meals and 190-260-DKK meaty ones by candlelight. It's gourmet anarchy—a good fit for Christiania, the free city/squatter town (Tue-Sun 17:00-22:00, kitchen closes at 21:00, closed Mon, reservations often necessary Fri-Sat; 3 blocks behind spiral spire of Our Savior's Church, on top floor of old brick warehouse, turn right just inside Christiania's main gate, enter the wildly empty warehouse, and climb the graffiti-riddled stairs; +45 32 57 95 58, http://spiseloppen.dk). Other, less-expensive Christiania eateries are listed on page 100.

Near Nørreport
\$\$\$ TorvehallerneKBH is in a pair of modern, glassy market halls right on Israels Plads. Survey both halls and the stalls on the square before settling in. In addition to produce, fish, and meat stalls, it has several inviting food counters where you can sit to eat a meal, or grab something to go. I can't think of a more enjoyable place in Copenhagen to browse for a meal than this upscale food court (pricey but fun, with quality food; Mon-Fri 10:00-19:00, Sat-Sun

until 18:00, some places open later, some closed Mon; Frederiksborggade 21, +45 70 10 60 70).

$$-$$$ Brdr. Price Restaurant—an elegant, highly re-
garded bistro serving creative Danish and international meals just
across from Rosenborg Castle—is good for a dressy splurge in their
downstairs restaurant, or for classy lighter meals in their upstairs
bistro and outdoor terrace (daily 12:00-22:00, Rosenborggade 15,
+45 38 41 10 20, www.brdr-price.dk).

$$$ Kalaset, in a funky daylight basement with mismatched
furniture, bubbles with a youthful energy and is a local favorite.
The creative, internationally inspired menu is constantly evolving,
and the decent portions are prepared "the way our grandmothers
taught us" (daily specials, outdoor seating available, daily 10:00-
late, Vendersgade 16, kitty-corner from the recommended Ibsens
Hotel, +45 33 33 00 35).

$$ Halifax, part of a small local chain, serves up "build-
your-own" burgers, where you select a patty, a side dish, and a dip-
ping sauce for your fries (Mon-Sat 11:30-22:00, Sun until 21:00,
Frederiksborggade 35, +45 82 30 43 00). They have another location just off the Strøget (at Larsbjørnsstræde 9, +45 82 30 43 01).

Meatpacking District (Kødbyen)

Literally "Meat Town," Kødbyen is an old warehouse zone huddled
up against the train tracks behind the main station. Danes raise
about 25 million pigs a year (five per person), so there's long been
lots of "meatpacking." Today, much of the meatpacking action is
diners chowing down.

There are three color-coded sectors in the district—brown,
gray, and white—and each one is a cluster of old industrial buildings. At the far end is the white zone (Den Hvide Kødby), which
has been overtaken by some of the city's most trendy and enjoyable
eateries, which mingle with the surviving offices and warehouses
of the local meatpacking industry. All of the places I list here are
within a few steps of each other (except for the Mother pizzeria, a
block away).

The curb appeal of this area is zilch (it looks like, well, a meatpacking district), but inside, these happy restaurants are bursting
with life, creativity, and flavor (and noise). They can fill up, especially on weekend evenings, when it's smart to reserve ahead.

It's a short stroll from the station: If you go south on the bridge
called Tietgens Bro, which crosses the tracks just south of the station, and carry on for about 10 minutes, you'll run right into the
area. Those sleeping in the hotels behind the station just stroll five
minutes south. Or you can ride the S-tog to the Dybbølsbro stop.

$$$$ Kødbyens Fiskebar ("Fish Bar") is one of the first and
still the most acclaimed restaurant in the Meatpacking District.

Focusing on small, thoughtfully composed plates of modern Nordic seafood, the Fiskebar has a stripped-down white interior with a big fish tank and a long cocktail bar surrounded by smaller tables. It's extremely popular (reservations are essential), and feels a bit too trendy for its own good. While the prices are high, so is the quality (in summer daily 11:00-22:00, in winter generally closed Sat-Sun; Flæsketorvet 100, +45 32 15 56 56, http://fiskebaren.dk).

$$$$ BioMio, in the old Bosch building, serves rustic Danish, vegan, and vegetarian dishes, plus meat and fish. It's 100 percent organic, and the young boss, Rune, actually serves diners (daily 17:00-22:00, Halmtorvet 19, +45 33 31 20 00, http://biomio.dk).

$$$ Paté Paté, next door to BioMio, is a tight, rollicking bistro in a former pâté factory. While a wine bar at heart—with a good selection of wines by the glass—it has a fun and accessible menu of creative modern dishes and a cozy atmosphere rare in the Meatpacking District. Ideally diners choose about three dishes per person and share (Mon-Sat 11:30-late, Sun 16:00-24:00, Slagterboderne 1, +45 39 69 55 57).

$$$ Pizzeria Mother is named for the way the sourdough for their crust must be "fed" and cared for to flourish. You can taste that care in the pizza, which has a delicious tangy crust. Out front are comfortable picnic benches, while the interior curls around the busy pizza oven with chefs working globs of dough that will soon be the basis for your pizza (daily 11:00-23:00, a block beyond the other restaurants listed here at Høkerboderne 9, +45 22 27 58 98).

$$ Nose2Tail Madbodega (*mad* means "food") prides itself on locally sourced, sustainable cooking, using the entire animal for your meal (hence the name). You'll climb down some stairs into an unpretentious white-tiled cellar (Mon-Sat 18:00-24:00, closed Sun, Flæsketorvet 13A, +45 33 93 50 45, http://nose2tail.dk).

Other Central Neighborhoods to Explore

To find a good restaurant, try simply window-shopping in one of these inviting districts.

Nyhavn's harbor canal is lined with a touristy strip of restaurants set alongside its classic sailboats. Here thriving crowds are served mediocre, overpriced food in a great setting. On any sunny day, if you want steak, fries, and a beer, this can be fun. On Friday and Saturday, the strip becomes the longest bar in the world.

Kompagnistræde is home to a changing cast of great little eateries. Running parallel to the Strøget, this street has fewer tourists and lower rent, and encourages places to compete creatively for the patronage of local diners.

Gråbrødretorv ("Grey Friars' Square") is perhaps the most popular square in the old center for a meal. It's like a food court, especially in good weather, with a variety of international dining options outside and in. The French-inspired steakhouse **$$$$ Bøf & Ost** is pricey but good, serving elegant beef and veal dishes— even pigeon—and a wide selection of French and Danish cheeses (Mon-Thu 12:00-21:30, Fri-Sat until 22:30, closed Sun, http:// boef-ost.dk). Across the

square, **$$$ Huks Fluks** enjoys a sunny location, dishing up southern European small plates, main courses, and shareable portions, and specializes in ham (Mon-Thu 11:00- 22:00, Fri-Sat until 23:00, Sun until 21:00).

Istedgade and the surrounding streets behind the train station (just above the Meatpacking District) are home to an assortment of inexpensive ethnic restaurants. You will find numerous places serving kebabs, pizza, Chinese, and Thai (including tasty meals at **$$ Poonchai Thai Restaurant**—across the street from Hotel Nebo at Istedgade 1 (daily 11:00-22:00, +45 33 22 26 06). The area can be a bit seedy, especially right behind the station, but walk a few blocks away to take your pick of inexpensive eateries frequented by locals.

Copenhagen Connections

BY PLANE
Copenhagen Airport, Kastrup

Copenhagen's international airport, about five miles south of the city, hosts a TI, baggage check, bank, ATMs, post office, shopping mall, grocery store, bakery, and more (code: CPH, www.cph. dk). The three check-in terminals are within walking distance of each other (check departures screens for your terminal). On arrival, all flights feed into one big lobby in terminal 3. When you pop out here, a TI kiosk is on your left, taxis are out the door on your right, trains are straight ahead, and shops and eateries fill the atrium above you.

Getting Between the Airport and Downtown

Your options include the Metro, trains, and taxis. There are also buses into town, but the train/Metro is generally better.

By Metro: The Metro runs directly from the airport to Christianshavn, Kongens Nytorv (near Nyhavn), and Nørreport, making it the best choice for getting into town if you're staying in any of these areas (36-DKK three-zone ticket, yellow M2 line, direction: Vanløse, 10/hour, 11 minutes to Christianshavn). The Metro station is located at the end of terminal 3 and is covered by the terminal roof.

By Train: Convenient trains also connect the airport with downtown (36-DKK three-zone ticket, covered by rail pass, 3/hour, 14 minutes). Buy your ticket from the ground-level ticket booth (look for *DSB: Tickets for Train, Metro & Bus* signs) before riding the escalator down to the tracks. Track 2 has trains going into the city (track 1 is for trains going east, to Sweden). Trains into town stop at the main train station (signed *København H;* handy if you're sleeping at my recommended hotels behind the train station), as well as the Nørreport and Østerport stations. At Nørreport, you can connect to the Metro for Kongens Nytorv (near Nyhavn) and Christianshavn.

By Bus: Bus #5C runs directly from the airport to the main train station and Nørreport station, but it's slower (45 minutes to Nørreport) with many stops along the way.

By Taxi: With the train/Metro trip being so quick, frequent, and cheap, I see no reason to take a taxi. But if you do, taxis are fast, civil, accept credit cards, and charge about 300 DKK for a ride to the town center.

BY TRAIN

DSB (Danske Statsbaner) is Denmark's national railway (+45 70 13 14 15—for English, press 1 for general information and tickets, and 2 for international trains, www.rejseplanen.dk).

When traveling to and from Copenhagen by train, keep in mind that the main station is located at the western edge of the city center. Norreport Station is more centrally located, and many trains also stop there—it's worth checking schedules carefully to determine your best final stop.

For general information on train travel in Scandinavia, see the "Transportation" section of the Practicalities chapter.

From Copenhagen by Train to: Hillerød/Frederiksborg Castle (6/hour, 40 minutes on S-tog), **Roskilde** (7/hour, 25 minutes), **Humlebæk/Louisiana Art Museum** (3/hour, 35 minutes), **Helsingør** (3/hour, 45 minutes), **Odense** (3/hour, 1.5 hours), **Ærøskøbing** (2/hour Mon-Sat, hourly on Sun, 2.5 hours to Svendborg with a transfer in Odense, then 1.25-hour ferry crossing to Ærøskøbing—see page 168 for info on ferry), **Billund/Legoland** (2/hour, 2.5 hours to Vejle, then bus #43 to Billund—see page 196), allow 3.5 hours total), **Aarhus** (2/hour, 3 hours), **Malmö** (3-5/hour, 40 minutes), **Stockholm** (almost hourly, 5-6 hours on high-speed train, some with a transfer at Malmö or Lund, reservation required; overnight service available but requires a change in Hässleholm or Lund), **Växjö** (hourly, 3 hours), **Kalmar** (about hourly, 3.5-4 hours, most direct, some with transfer), **Oslo** (4/day, 8-9 hours, transfer at Göteborg; also overnight boat option, see next page), **Hamburg** (3/day direct, 5 hours, 2 more with transfer, reservation required in summer); from Hamburg, connections run to **Berlin** (2 more hours, railway also operates 2 direct Copenhagen-Berlin buses, 7.5 hours), **Amsterdam** (5.5 more hours, change at Osnabrück), and **Frankfurt/Rhine** (hourly, 3.5 more hours).

COPENHAGEN

BY BUS

Taking the bus to **Stockholm** is cheap but time consuming (1/day, 9.5 hours, longer for overnight trips, www.flixbus.se).

BY CRUISE SHIP

More than half a million people visit Copenhagen via cruise ship each year. Most cruise ships use one of two terminals north of downtown—**Ocean-kaj,** the farther port; and **Langelinie,** about a mile closer to downtown. Another, smaller cruise port, **Nordre Toldbod,** is just south of *The Little Mermaid* and within easy walking distance (25 minutes) of Nyhavn. For

a wealth of online information for cruise-ship passengers, see CruiseCopenhagen.com. For more in-depth cruising information, pick up my *Rick Steves Scandinavian & Northern European Cruise Ports* guidebook.

BY OVERNIGHT BOAT TO OSLO

Luxurious DFDS cruise ships leave daily from Copenhagen (usually at 14:00) and arrive in Oslo about 9:00 the next morning. The 19-hour sailing includes a stop in Frederikshavn—handy for connecting that part of Denmark with Norway, but you can't ride just between the Danish ports. Boats depart from Oslo on the same schedule for the return to Copenhagen (see page 296 for Oslo departure info).

Cruise Costs: Cabins vary dramatically in price depending on the day and season (most expensive on weekends and late June-mid-Aug; cheapest on weekdays and Oct-April). You can choose from a spartan four-berth economy cabin (1,300 DKK one-way) to a luxurious double Commodore cabin higher on the ship (3,500 DKK one-way).

Onboard Services: DFDS Seaways ships offer big buffets for breakfast and dinner, gourmet restaurants—reserve a table when you book your ticket, bars, a kids' playroom, pool, hot tub, sauna, nightclubs, and tax-free shopping. All shops and restaurants accept credit cards as well as euros, dollars, and Danish, Swedish, and Norwegian currency.

Reservations: Reservations are smart in summer and on weekends. Advance bookings get the best prices. Book online (www.dfds.com), call DFDS's Copenhagen office (closed Sat-Sun, +45 33 42 38 00), or visit the **DSB Rejsebureau** at the main train station.

Port Details: The **Copenhagen Ferry Terminal** (DFDS Terminalen) is at Dampfærgevej 30, a 15-minute walk north of *The Little Mermaid*. The terminal is open daily 9:00-17:00 (luggage lockers available, coins only).

Shuttle Service: DFDS runs a shuttle between the terminal and downtown. Buy tickets (30 DKK) on the DFDS website when booking your cabin—tickets are not sold on the bus.

Getting to the Cruise Terminal: To reach the ferry terminal from the city, catch the shuttle bus marked *DFDS Terminal* near Nørreport Station at Øster Voldgade 2C. Or take the S-tog from downtown in the direction of Hellerup or Hillerød to the Nordhavn Station. Exit the station, cross under the tracks, and hike toward the water; you'll see the ship on your right.

Getting Downtown from the Cruise Terminal: Shuttle buses marked either *Banegård* or *Nørreport* meet arriving ships from Oslo. The *Banegård* bus drops you at Banegårdspladsen—in front of the main train station, near Tivoli, recommended hotels, and the start of my "Copenhagen City Walk." Buses marked *Nørreport* drop you next to Nørreport Station (near recommended hotels). From here you can ride the Metro one stop to Kongens Nytorv at Nyhavn (and more recommended hotels).

NEAR COPENHAGEN

Roskilde • Frederiksborg Castle • Louisiana Art Museum • Kronborg Castle

Copenhagen may be Denmark's star attraction, but several worthwhile sights are within an hour of the city on an island called Zealand. Public transportation makes side-tripping a joy here. Visit Roskilde's great Viking ships and cathedral with the tombs of Danish royalty. Tour Frederiksborg, Denmark's most spectacular castle, and slide along the cutting edge at the Louisiana Art Museum—a superb collection with a coastal setting as striking as its art. At Helsingør, do the dungeons of Kronborg Castle before heading on to Sweden.

PLANNING YOUR TIME

The area's essential sights are Roskilde and Frederiksborg Castle. Each destination is an easy half-day commute from Copenhagen—but in different directions (30- or 40-minute train ride, then a 20-minute walk or short bus ride). If you're really fast and well organized, you could visit both Roskilde and Frederiksborg with public transportation in a day (see "The Zealand Blitz," later).

If you're choosing between castles, Frederiksborg is a beautiful showpiece with an opulent interior, and Kronborg—darker and danker—is more typical of the way most castles really were. Both are dramatic from the outside, but Kronborg—overlooking the raging sea channel to Sweden—has a more scenic setting. Castle collectors can hit both in a day (see the two-castle day plan, later). Consider getting a Copenhagen Card (see page 43), which covers your transportation to all the destinations in this chapter, as well as admission to Roskilde Cathedral, the Roskilde Viking Ship Museum, Frederiksborg Castle, Kronborg Castle, and

Near Copenhagen

Kattegat

To Göteborg, Oslo & Kalmar

To Stockholm, Växjö & Kalmar

To Oslo

E-6

E-4

Gilleleje

KRONBORG CASTLE

Helsingborg

SWEDEN

Helsingør

Esrum Sø

205

Arresø

6

LOUISIANA ART MUSEUM

Hunde-sted

FREDENSBORG PALACE

Humle-bæk

To Rørvig

FREDERIKSBORG CASTLE

Rungsted

Øresund

Frederiks-sund

Hillerød

201

152

Ise-fjord

E-47

BAKKEN

E-6

Roskildefjord

OPEN-AIR FOLK MUSEUM

ZEALAND

Klampenborg

Ballerup

E-47

Copenhagen

See detail maps in this area

Saltholm

Lund

Roskilde

21

Høje Tåstrup

E-20

TUNNEL

Malmö

23

Lejre

Øm

14

E-20

Amager

ØRESUND

Limhamn

E-20

To Holbæk

Kastrup

Dragør

BRIDGE

To Ystad

DENMARK

Køge Bugt

10 Kilometers

To Ringsted, Odense, Ærø, Aarhus & Germany

10 Miles

---

the Louisiana Art Museum. Each train ride is just long enough for a relaxed picnic.

The Zealand Blitz—Frederiksborg Castle, Viking Ship Museum, and Roskilde Cathedral in a Day: If you have limited time and are well organized, you can see the highlights of Zealand in one exciting day. This only works in summer (June-Aug) and Monday through Saturday, when the cathedral is open until 18:00. Here's the plan (all times are rough—confirm locally before you depart, train connections take about 30-40 minutes, trains depart about every 10 minutes): Leave Copenhagen by train at 9:00, arriving in Hillerød at about 9:40. From there, walk (about 20 minutes) or catch bus #301 or #302 to Frederiksborg Castle, arriving at 10:00, just as it opens. Spend two hours touring the castle, then take the bus back to the train station for the 13:00 train back to Copenhagen (grab a picnic lunch at the station and munch it on the train). From Copenhagen, catch a 14:00 train to Roskilde, arriving just before 14:30. Take a taxi, bus #203, or walk (20-25 minutes) down to the harborfront to the Viking Ship Museum. Spend two hours touring the museum, then walk back up to the cathedral (10-15 minutes) and spend an hour there before it closes at 18:00. Wander through town back to the station and catch the 18:30 train back to Copenhagen. You'll be back at your hotel by 19:30. Or, better yet, consider having dinner in Roskilde after touring the cathedral and take a later train back to Copenhagen.

A Two-Castle Day (plus Louisiana): You can see both Frederiksborg and Kronborg castles, plus the Louisiana Art Museum, in one busy day. (This works best Tue-Fri, when Louisiana is open until 22:00.) Take the train from Copenhagen to Hillerød (leaving about 9:00), then hop on the awaiting bus to Frederiksborg Castle; you'll hear the 10:00 bells and be the first tourist inside. Linger in the sumptuous interior for a couple of hours, but get back to the station in time for a midday train (about 12:30 or 13:00) to Helsingør, a 15-minute walk from Kronborg Castle. Either munch your picnic lunch on the train, or—if it's a nice day—save it for the ramparts of Kronborg Castle. If you're castled out, skip the interior (saving the ticket price, and more time for Louisiana) and simply enjoy the Kronborg grounds and Øresund views before catching a train south toward Copenhagen. Hop off at Humlebæk for Louisiana.

GETTING AROUND

All of these sights except Roskilde are served by Copenhagen's excellent commuter-train (S-tog) system (covered by Copenhagen Card and City Pass Large—see page 48; Roskilde is on a regional train line (covered by the Copenhagen Card). All trains depart from the main station, but most also stop at other Copenhagen stations that may be closer to your hotel (for example, the Nørreport Station is near the recommended Ibsens and Jørgensen hotels). Check schedules to avoid a needless trip to the main station.

At the main train station, S-tog lines do not appear on the overhead schedule screens; simply head to tracks 9-10 to wait for your train (there's a schedule at the head of those tracks).

Roskilde

Denmark's roots, both Viking and royal, are on display in Roskilde (ROSS-killa), a pleasant town 18 miles west of Copenhagen. The town was the seat of the bishop and the residence of Danish royalty until 1450, when these shifted to Copenhagen. In its day, Roskilde was the second biggest city in the country. Today the town that introduced Christianity to Denmark in AD 980 is much smaller, except for the week of its famous rock/jazz/folk festival—northern Europe's largest—when 100,000 fans pack the place and it becomes one of Denmark's biggest cities again (late June-early July, www.roskilde-festival. dk). Wednesday and Saturday are flower/flea/produce market days (8:00-14:00).

GETTING THERE

Roskilde is an easy side trip from Copenhagen by train (7/hour, 30 minutes). Trains headed to Ringsted, Nykøbing, or Lindholm may not stop in Roskilde (which is an intermediate stop you won't see listed on departure boards)—confirm in advance. Returning to Copenhagen, hop on any train in the direction of Østerport or København H.

Orientation to Roskilde

TOURIST INFORMATION

Roskilde's helpful TI is on the main square, next to the cathedral (open Mon-Sat from 10:00, closes Mon at 15:00, Tue-Fri at 16:00, Sat at 13:00, closed Sun; Stændertorvet 1, +45 46 31 65 65, www. visitroskilde.com).

ARRIVAL IN ROSKILDE

There are no lockers at the train station (or nearby), but the TI—about a five-minute walk away—will take your bags for a few hours if you ask nicely. Free WCs are right next door to the TI.

From the train station, consider this circular route: First head to the TI, then the cathedral, and finally down to the Viking Ship Museum on the harborfront. Exit straight out from the station, and walk down to the bottom of the square. Turn left (at the Super Brugsen supermarket) on the pedestrianized shopping street, Algade (literally "the street for all"). After walking down this main drag about four blocks, you emerge into the main square, Stændertorvet, with the TI and the cathedral. After visiting the cathedral, head about 10 minutes downhill (through a pleasant park) to the Viking Ship Museum: Facing the cathedral facade, turn left and head down the tree-lined path through the park. When you emerge at the roundabout (avoiding the temptation to eat a "Viking Pizza"), continue straight through it to reach the museum.

If you want to go directly from the station to the Viking Ship Museum, you can ride a bus; see page 133.

Sights in Roskilde

▲▲Roskilde Cathedral
(Roskilde Domkirke)

Roskilde's imposing 12th-century, twin-spired cathedral houses the tombs of nearly all of the Danish kings and queens (39 royals in all; pick up the included guidebook as you enter). If you're a fan of Danish royalty or of evolving architectural styles, it's thrilling; even if you're neither, Denmark's "Westminster Abbey" is still interesting. It's a stately, modern-looking old church with great marble work, paintings, wood carvings, and an engaged congregation that makes the place feel very alive.

Cost and Hours: 60 DKK, covered by Copenhagen Card; June-Aug Mon-Sat 10:00-18:00; May and Sept Mon-Sat until

17:00; Oct-April Tue-Sat until 16:00, closed Mon; Sun 13:00-16:00 year-round; often closed for funerals and on Sat-Sun afternoons for baptisms and weddings; free organ concerts offered July-Aug Thu at 20:00; Domkirkestræde 10, +45 46 35 16 24, www.roskildedomkirke.dk.

◐ **Self-Guided Tour:** Begun in the 1170s by Bishop Absalom (and completed in 1280), Roskilde Cathedral was cleared of its side chapels and altars by the Reformation iconoclasts—leaving a blank slate for Danish royals to fill with their tombs. The highlight here is slowly strolling through a half-millennium's worth of royal chapels, representing a veritable textbook's worth of architectural styles.

• *Before entering, walk around the outside of the cathedral.*

Exterior, King's Door, and Tomb of Frederik IX: Notice the big bricks, which date from the 12th century, and how the cathedral is built on the highest ground in town. Face the towering west facade. The main King's Door (installed in 2010), depicting scenes from the ministry of Jesus, is reserved for the use of the royal family. The congregation is allowed to exit through this door only after special services.

Find the freestanding brick chapel to the left. This holds the remains of Denmark's last king, Frederik IX (1899-1972), and his wife Ingrid (parents of the current queen, born in 1940). While all of the other monarchs are inside, Frederik—who was an avid sailor in his youth—requested to be buried here, with a view of the harbor.

• *Now go around the right side, buy a ticket, and go inside. First, head to the middle of the nave to look at the...*

King's Door, from Inside: The glittering gold, highly stylized relief shows the scene after the Resurrection when Jesus breaks bread in the company of some apostles—who until this point had not recognized him (their mouths hang agape at their realization).

Glockenspiel: In the rear of the church, high on the wall, you can see the little glockenspiel that makes a racket at the top of every hour as George kills the dragon and the centuries-old bellows wail.

• *Now we'll take a clockwise spin through the interior to see the significant royal burial chapels. While this tour is not chronological, neither are the tombs. Continue through the left aisle and into the big chapel housing some of the cathedral's most recent additions (late 19th through early 20th century).*

Glücksburger Chapel: In the corner, the Glücksburger Chapel, with a plain light dome, holds the tomb of Christian IX, nicknamed the "father-in-law of Europe" for how he married his many children into royal families across the Continent. He died in 1906. The three mourning women were sculpted by Edvard Eriksen, who also produced Copenhagen's famed *Little Mermaid* statue (notice the middle woman).

St. Birgitta's Chapel: The next chapel will eventually ("Not soon," hope the Danes) have a new tenant: It has been restored to house the tomb of the current queen, Margrethe II (it was intended to hold both Margrethe and her late husband, Henrik, but he chose instead to have his remains at Fredensborg Castle—in protest for never being given the title of king). The queen teamed up with an artist to design her own tomb (there's a model on display). Her body will reside in the stepped area at the bottom, upon which stand three columns representing the far-flung Danish holdings: one made of basalt from the Faroe Islands, another of marble from Greenland, and the third of stone from Denmark proper. Topping the columns are elephants (symbols of Danish royalty) and a semitransparent glass tomb, symbolizing the unpredictability of life and how death, like a seed, is a new beginning.

St. Andrew's Chapel: The next chapel, a modern addition to the church, has a glittering mosaic over the altar. But pre-Reformation frescoes (1511) peek through the Protestant whitewash. Standing in front of this chapel, look across the nave to see the gorgeous 16th-century Baroque organ.

Christian IV Chapel: The next, larger chapel (up the stairs behind the small wooden organ) dates from the era of Christian IV, the larger-than-life 17th-century king who created modern Denmark. Christian also left his mark on Roskilde Cathedral, building the altarpiece, pulpit, distinctive twin towers...and this chapel. Walk around the stately yet humble tombs, marvel at the painting, and consider the huge personality of the greatest king in Danish history. In here you'll see a fine statue of the king, by Bertel Thorvaldsen; a large 3-D painting with Christian IV wearing his trademark eye patch, after losing his eye in battle; and his rather austere tomb (black with silver trim, surrounded by several others). Great he was...until his many wars impoverished his once-mighty country.

• *Head into the nave and climb up the stairs into the choir area.*

Nave, Choir, and High Altar: Take in the gorgeous gilded altarpiece and finely carved stalls. The three-winged altarpiece, carved in 1560 in Antwerp, shows scenes from Christ's last week. The fine carvings above the chairs in the choir feature scenes from the Old Testament on one side and the New Testament on the other.

Tomb of Margrethe I: Behind the altar is the ornately decorated tomb of Margrethe I, the Danish queen who added Norway to her holdings by marrying Norwegian King Håkon VI in 1363. Legend holds that buried in a nearby brick pilaster are the supposed remains of Harold (read the Latin: *Haraldus*) Bluetooth, who ruled more than a millennium ago (r. 958-985 or 986), made Roskilde the capital of his realm, and converted his subjects to Christianity.

• *Now explore the apse (the area behind the altar).*

Apse: Go down the stairs, walk over the well-worn tombs of 500-year-old aristocrats who had the money to buy prime tomb space, and go through the little door. Circle around the apse, noticing more fine tombs behind Margrethe's.

• *Hooking back around toward the front, dip into the many more chapels you'll pass, including...*

Frederik V's Chapel: The grand, textbook Neoclassical tomb of Frederik V has white pillars, gold trim, and mourning maidens—representing Norway and Denmark—in ancient Greek gowns. You'll also pass a room housing elaborate, canopied Baroque tombs. Imagine: Each king or queen commissioned a tomb that suited his or her time—so different, yet all so grand.

Christian I's Chapel: The next chapel, with the tomb of Christian I, has a stone column marking the heights of visiting monarchs and royalty such as Britain's Prince Charles. The *P* is for the giant Russian czar Peter the Great—clearly the tallest.

• *Leaving the cathedral, turn right and walk downhill for 10 minutes along a peaceful tree-lined lane that will eventually take you to the harbor and the Viking Ship Museum.*

▲▲▲Viking Ship Museum (Vikingeskibsmuseet)

Vik literally means "shallow inlet," and "Vikings" were the people who lived along those inlets. Roskilde—and this award-winning museum—are strategical-ly located along one such inlet. Centuries before Europe's age of explora-tion, Viking sailors navi-gated their sleek, sturdy ships as far away as the Mediterranean, the Black Sea, the Persian Gulf, and the Americas. This mu-

seum displays five different Viking ships, which were discovered in the Roskilde fjord and painstakingly excavated, preserved, and pieced back together beginning in the 1960s. The ships aren't as intact or as evocative as those in Oslo (see page 257), but this mu-seum does a better job of explaining shipbuilding. The outdoor area (on "Museum Island") continues the experience, with a chance to see modern-day Vikings creating replica ships, chat with an old-time rope maker, and learn more about the excavation. The English descriptions are excellent—it's the kind of museum where you want to read everything.

Cost and Hours: 150 DKK, covered by Copenhagen Card; daily 10:00-17:00, mid-Oct-April until 16:00, +45 46 30 02 00, www.vikingeskibsmuseet.dk.

Tours: Free 45-minute tours in English typically run mid-June-Aug daily at 12:00 and 15:00; May-mid-June and Sept Sat-Sun at 12:00; none off-season.

Boat Ride: The museum's workshop has re-created working replicas of all five of the ships on display here, plus others. For an extra 120 DKK, you can usually take a fun 50-minute sail around Roskilde's fjord in one of these replica Viking vessels (you'll row, set sail, and row again; frequent departures—up to 7/day—in sum-mer, fewer off-season, ask about schedule when you arrive or call ahead).

Eating: Café Knarr serves salads, sandwiches, and "planks" of Viking tapas with ingredients the Vikings knew (decent prices, open daily 10:00-17:00).

Getting There: It's on the harbor at Vindeboder 12. From the train station, catch bus #203 toward Boserup (24 DKK, 2/hour, 7 minutes). From the cathedral, it's a 10-minute downhill walk. The museum desk can call a taxi when you want to go back to the sta-tion, or take the bus back.

Visiting the Museum: The museum has two parts: the Viking Ship Hall, with the remains of the five ships; and, across the drawbridge, Museum Island with workshops, replica ships, a café, and more exhibits. There are ticket offices at each location; it's best to start with the Viking Ship Hall.

As you enter the **Viking Ship Hall,** check the board for the day's activities and demonstrations (including shipbuilding, weaving, blacksmithing, and minting). The 15-minute film shown in the lobby's cinema is a good introduction to your visit.

Following a one-way route, you'll first see the five ships, then go through the preservation exhibit, the kids' zone with a video about the modern voyage of the *Sea Stallion*, and finally the popular shop.

The core of the exhibit is the remains of five ships, which were deliberately sunk a thousand years ago to block an easy channel into this harbor (leaving open only the most challenging approach—virtually impossible for anyone but a local to navigate). The ships, which are named for the place where they were found (Skuldelev), represent an impressively wide range of Viking shipbuilding technology. *Skuldelev 1* is a big, sail-powered ocean-going trade ship made in Norway, with a crew of six to eight men and room for lots of cargo; it's like the ship Leif Eriksson took to America 1,000 years ago. *Skuldelev 2* is a 100-foot-long, 60-oar longship made in the Viking city of Dublin; loaded with 65 or 70 battle-hardened warriors, it struck fear into the hearts of foes. It's similar to the ones depicted in the Bayeux Tapestry in Normandy, France. *Skuldelev 3* is a modest coastal trader that stayed closer to home (wind-powered with oar backup, similar to #1 in design and also made in Norway). *Skuldelev 5* is a smaller longship—carrying about 30 warriors, it's the little sibling of #2. And *Skuldelev 6* is a small fishing vessel—a row/sail hybrid that was used for whaling and hunting seals. (There's no #4 because they originally thought #2 was two different ships...and the original names stuck.)

Exhibits in the surrounding rooms show the 25-year process of excavating and preserving the ships, explain a step-by-step attack and defense of the harbor, and give you a chance to climb aboard a couple of replica ships for a fun photo op. You'll also see displays describing the re-creation of the *Sea Stallion*, a replica of the big longship (#2) constructed by modern shipbuilders using ancient techniques. A crew of 65 rowed this ship to Dublin in 2007 and then back to Roskilde in the summer of 2008. You can watch a 20-minute film of their odyssey.

Leaving the hall, cross the drawbridge to **Museum Island.**

Replicas of all five ships—and others—bob in the harbor; you can actually climb on board the largest, the *Sea Stallion* (if in port). At the boatyard, watch modern craftsmen re-create millennium-old ships using the original methods and materials.

Poke into the various workshops, with exhibits on tools and methods. The little square called Tunet ("Gathering Place") is ringed by traditional craft shops—basket maker, rope maker, blacksmith, wood carver—which are sometimes staffed by workers doing demonstrations. In the archaeological workshop, exhibits explain how researchers excavated and preserved the precious timbers of those five ships.

Frederiksborg Castle

Frederiksborg Castle, rated ▲▲, sits on an island in the middle of a lake in the cute town of Hillerød. This grandest castle in Scandinavia is often called the "Danish Versailles." Built from 1602 to 1620, Frederiksborg was the castle of Denmark's King Christian IV. Much of it was reconstructed after an 1859 fire, with the normal Victorian over-the-top flair, by the brewer J. C. Jacobsen and his Carlsberg Foundation.

You'll still enjoy some of the magnificent spaces of the castle's heyday: the breathtaking grounds and courtyards, the sumptuous chapel, and the regalia-laden Great Hall. But most of the place was turned into a fine museum in 1878. Today it's the Museum of National History, taking you on a chronological walk through the story of Denmark from 1500 until now (the third/top floor covers modern times). The countless musty paintings are a fascinating scrapbook of Danish history—it's a veritable national portrait gallery, with images of great Danes from each historical period of the last half-millennium.

A fine path leads around the lake, with ever-changing views of the castle. The traffic-free center of Hillerød is also worth a wander.

Tourist Information: Hillerød's TI, with information on the entire North Zealand region, is in the freestanding white house next to the castle parking lot (to the left as you face the main castle gate; July-mid-Sept Mon-Sat 10:00-16:00, shorter hours in June, closed Sun and mid-Sept-May, Frederiksværksgade 2A, +45 49 21 13 33, www.visitnordsjaelland.com). Because the TI is inside an art gallery, if the TI is "closed" while the gallery is open, you can still slip inside and pick up a town map and brochures.

GETTING THERE

By Train: From Copenhagen, take the S-tog to Hillerød (line A, 6/hour, 40 minutes, bikes go free on S-tog trains).

From the Hillerød station, you can enjoy a pleasant 20-minute walk to the castle, or catch **bus #301** (direction: Ullerød) or **#302** (direction: Sophienlund). Buses are free with an S-tog ticket or Copenhagen Card. You'll find buses to the right as you exit station—ride three stops to the Frederiksborg Slot stop.

If **walking,** just follow the signs to the castle. Bear left down the busy road (Jernbanegade) until the first big intersection, where you'll turn right. After a couple of blocks, where the road curves to the left, keep going straight; from here, bear left and downhill to the pleasant square Torvet, with great views of the castle and a café pavilion. At this square, turn left and walk through the pedestrianized shopping zone directly to the castle gate.

Linking to Other Sights: If continuing directly to Helsingør (with Kronborg Castle), hop on the regional train (Lokaltog 930R, departs from track 16 at Hillerød station, Mon-Fri 2/hour, Sat-Sun 1/hour, 30 minutes). From Helsingør, it's a quick trip on the train to the town of Humlebæk (where you'll find the Louisiana Art Museum).

ORIENTATION TO FREDERIKSBORG CASTLE

Cost and Hours: 75 DKK, covered by Copenhagen Card; daily 10:00-17:00, Nov-March 11:00-15:00, +45 48 26 04 39, www.dnm.dk.

Tours: Take advantage of the free, informative, 45-minute audioguide; ask for it when you buy your ticket—it's also available as an app. Daily English-language highlights tours usually leave at 14:00 (30 minutes, included in admission).

Eating: You can picnic in the castle's moat park or enjoy the **$$-$$$ Spisestedet Leonora** at the moat's edge (*smørrebrød,* sandwiches, salads, hot dishes, open daily). Or, better, walk into the town center near the bus stop.

● SELF-GUIDED TOUR

The castle's included audio tour is excellent, and you can almost follow it in real time for a blitz of the palace's highlights. Use this self-guided tour to supplement the audioguide.

The Castle Approach

From the entrance of the castle complex, it's an appropriately regal approach to the king's residence. You can almost hear the clopping of royal hooves as you walk over the moat and through the first island (which housed the stables and small businesses needed to support a royal residence). Then walk down the winding (and therefore easy-to-defend) lane to the second island, which was home to the domestic and foreign ministries. Finally, cross over the last moat to the main palace, where the king lived.

Fountain of Neptune Courtyard

Survey the castle exterior from the Fountain of Neptune. Christian IV imported Dutch architects to create this "Christian IV style," which you'll see all over Copenhagen. The brickwork and sandstone are products of the local clay and sandy soil. The building, with its horizontal lines, triangles, and squares, is generally in Renaissance style, but notice how this is interrupted by a few token Gothic elements on the church's facade. Some say this homey touch was to let the villagers know the king was "one of them."

• *Step over the last moat, through the ornate gate, and into the castle grounds. Go in the door in the middle of the courtyard to buy your ticket, pick up your free audioguide, and put your bag in a locker (mandatory). Pick up a free floor plan; room numbers will help orient you on this tour. You'll enter the Knights' Parlor, also called The Rose, a long room decorated as it was during the palace's peak of power. Go up the stairs on the left side of this hall to the...*

Royal Chapel

Christian IV wanted to have the grandest royal chapel in Europe. For 200 years the coronation place of Danish kings, this chapel is

still used for royal weddings (and is extremely popular for commoner weddings—book long in advance). The chapel is nearly all original, dating back to 1620. As you walk around the upper level, notice the graffiti scratched on the windowpanes by the diamond rings of royal kids visiting for the summer back in the 1600s. Most of the coats of arms show off noble lineages—with a few exceptions we'll soon see. At the far end of the chapel, the wooden organ is from 1620, with its original hand-powered bellows. (Hymns play on the old carillon at the top of each hour.)

Scan the hundreds of coats of arms lining the walls. These belong to people who have received royal orders from the Danish crown (similar to Britain's knighthoods). While most are obscure princesses and dukes, a few interesting (and more familiar) names show up just past the organ. In the

first window bay after the organ, look for the distinctive red, blue, black, and green shield of South Africa—marking Nelson Mandela's coat of arms (he was awarded the highly prestigious Order of the Elephant, usually reserved for royalty). Around the side of the same column (facing the chapel interior), find the coats of arms for Dwight D. Eisenhower (with the blue anvil and the motto "Peace through understanding"), Winston Churchill (who already came from a noble line), and Field Marshal Bernard "Monty" Montgomery. Around the far side of this column is the coat of arms for France's wartime leader, Charles de Gaulle.

Leaving the chapel, you step into the king's private oratory, with evocative Neo-Romantic paintings (restored after a fire) from the mid-19th century.

• You'll emerge from the chapel into the museum collection. But before seeing that, pay a visit to the Audience Room: Go through the door in the left corner marked Audienssalen, and proceed through the little room to the long passageway (easy to miss).

Audience Room

Here, where formal meetings took place, a grand painting shows the king as a Roman emperor firmly in command (with his two sons prominent for extra political stability). This family is flanked by Christian IV (on the left) and Frederik III (on the right). Christian's military victories line the walls, and the four great continents—Europe, North America, Asia, and Africa—circle the false cupola (notice it's just an attic). Look for the odd trapdoor in one corner with a plush chair on it. This was where they could majestically lower the king to the exit.

• *Now go back to the museum section, and proceed through the numbered rooms.*

NEAR COPENHAGEN

Museum Collection

Spanning three floors and five centuries, this exhaustive collection juxtaposes portraits, paintings of historical events, furniture, and other objects from the same time period, all combining to paint a picture of a moment in Danish history. While fascinating, the collection is huge, so I've selected only the most interesting items to linger over.

First Floor: Proceed to **Room 26,** which is focused on the Reformation. The case in the middle of the room holds the first

Bible translated into Danish (from 1550—access to the word of God was a big part of the Reformation). Over the door to the next room is the image of a monk, Hans Tausen, invited by the king to preach the new thinking of the Reformation...sort of the "Danish Martin Luther." Also note the effort noble families put into legitimizing themselves with family trees and family seals.

Pass through Rooms 27, 28, and 29, and into **Room 30**—with paintings telling the story of Christian IV (for more on this dynamic Renaissance king, who built this castle and so much more, see page 87). Directly across from the door you entered is a painting of the chancellor on his deathbed, handing over the keys to the kingdom to a still-wet-behind-the-ears young Christian IV—the beginning of a long and fruitful career. On the right wall is a painting of Christian's coronation (the bearded gentleman looking out the window in the upper-left corner is Carlsberg brewer and castle benefactor J. C. Jacobsen—who, some 300 years before his birth, was probably not actually in attendance). Room 31 covers the royal family of Charles IV, while the smaller, darkened corner Room 32 displays the various Danish orders; find the most prestigious, the Order of the Elephant.

• *Hook back through Room 30, go outside on the little passage, and climb up the stairs.*

Second Floor: Go to the corner **Room 39,** which has a fascinating golden globe designed to illustrate Polish astronomer Nicolaus Copernicus' bold new heliocentric theory (that the sun, not the earth, was the center of our world). Look past the constellations to see the tiny model of the solar system at the very center, with a brass ball for the sun and little figures holding up symbols for each of the planets. The mechanical gears could actually make this model move to make the illustration more vivid.

Continue into one of the castle's most jaw-dropping rooms, the **Great Hall** (Room 38). The walls are lined with tapestries and royal portraits (including some modern ones, near the door). The remarkable wood-carved ceilings include panels illustrating vari-

ous industries. The elevated platform on the left was a gallery where musicians could play without getting in the way of the revelry.

Head back out and walk back along the left side of the hall. You can go quickly through the rooms numbered in the 40s and 50s (though pause partway down the long hallway; on the left, find the optical-illusion portrait that shows King Frederik V when viewed from one angle, and his wife when viewed from another). At the far end of this section, **Room 57** has a portrait of Hans Christian Andersen. Notice that fashion styles have gotten much more modern...suits and ties instead of tights and powdered wigs. It's time to head into the modern world.

• *Find the modern spiral staircase nearby. Downstairs are late-19th-century exhibits—which are skippable. Instead, head up to the top floor.*

Third Floor: This staircase puts you right in the middle of the modern collection. From here, the museum's focus shifts from history to art. Highlights include:

The Art Critics, showing four past-their-prime, once-rambunctious artists themselves, now happily entrenched in the art institution, leaning back to critique a younger artist's work.

A room focusing on Denmark's far-flung protectorate of Greenland, with a porcelain polar bear and portraits of explorers.

A room of distinctive Impressionist/Post-Impressionist paintings, with a Danish spin.

The *Ninth of April, 1940,* showing the (ultimately unsuccessful) Danish defense against Nazi invaders on that fateful date.

A room focusing on the royal family, with a life-size, photorealistic portrait of the beloved Queen Margrethe II. Facing her is her daughter-in-law, Mary Donaldson—who, in this portrait at least, bears a striking resemblance to another young European royal.

Peter Carlsen's *Denmark 2009*—a brilliant parody of Eugène Delacroix's famous painting *Liberty Leading the People* (a copy of the inspiration is on the facing wall). Carlsen has replaced the stirring imagery of the original with some dubious markers of contemporary Danish life: football flags, beer gut, shopping bags, tabloids, bikini babes, even a Christiania flag. It's a delightfully offbeat (and oh-so-Danish) note to end our visit to this seriously impressive palace.

NEAR THE CASTLE
Hillerød Town

While there's not much here, the pedestrianized commercial zone is pleasant enough. It's best visited from the castle. Slotsgade, the main street, leads away from the castle bus stop toward the train station and is lined with shops and cafés. An inviting Scandinavian sweater shop is right at the bus stop. And if you feel like a little (very little) cruise, a tiny ferry leaves from a pier next to the castle and stops at the castle garden across the lake (30 DKK, covered by Copenhagen Card, 2/hour, 30 minutes).

NEAR COPENHAGEN

Louisiana Art Museum

Located in the town of Humlebæk and beautifully sited on Øresund Sound, Louisiana is a holistic place that masterfully mixes art, architecture, and landscape. This was Denmark's first modern art museum, and its sculpture park is one of Europe's best.

Getting There: The museum is 18 miles north of Copenhagen. Take the train toward Helsingør, and get off at Humlebæk (3/hour, 30 minutes). It's a pleasant 10-minute walk (partly through a forest) to the museum: Exit the station and immediately go left onto Hejreskor Allé, a residential street; when the road curves right, continue straight along the narrow footpath through the trees. After you exit the trail, the museum is just ahead and across the street (at Gammel Strandvej 13).

If you're arriving by train from **Helsingør,** take the pedestrian underpass beneath the tracks, then follow the directions above. Louisiana is also connected to Helsingør by bus #388 (runs hourly, stops right at museum as well as at Humlebæk).

If you're coming from **Frederiksborg Castle,** you have two options: You can catch the Lokaltog train from Hillerød to Snekkersten, then change there to a regional train heading south to Humlebæk (1-2/hour, 30 minutes). Alternatively, you can take the S-tog toward Copenhagen and Køge, get off at Hellerup, then catch a regional train north toward Helsingør to reach Humlebæk (2/hour, 1 hour).

Cost and Hours: 130 DKK, covered by Copenhagen Card; Tue-Fri 11:00-22:00, Sat-Sun until 18:00, closed Mon; +45 49 19 07 19, www.louisiana.dk.

Cuisine Art: The $$$ cafeteria, with indoor and outdoor seating, has reasonably priced sandwiches and welcomes picnickers who buy a drink.

Visiting the Museum: Wander from famous Chagalls and Picassos to more obscure art (everything is post-1945). Poets spend days here nourishing their creative souls with new angles, ideas, and perspectives. Even those who don't think they're art lovers can get sucked into a thought-provoking exhibit and lose track of time. There's no permanent exhibit; the museum constantly organizes its substantial collection into ever-changing arrangements, augmented with borrowed and special exhibits (check the museum website for the latest). An Andy Warhol *Marilyn Monroe* you see on one visit may not be there the next. (One favorite item, French sculptor César's *The Big Thumb*—which is simply a six-foot-tall bronze thumb—isn't going anywhere, since any time they move it, patrons complain.) There's no audioguide, but everything is labeled in English.

Outside, a delightful sculpture garden sprawls through the grounds, downhill toward the sea. The views over the Øresund, one of the busiest passages in the nautical world, are nearly as inspiring as the art. The museum's floor plan is a big loop, and the seaward side is underground—so as not to block the grand views. It's fun to explore the grounds, peppered with sculptures and made accessible by bridges and steps. There are sculptures by Alexander Calder, Jean Dubuffet, Joan Miró, and others.

Taken as a whole, the museum is a joy to explore. What you see from the inside draws you out, and what you see from the outside draws you in. The place can't be rushed. Linger and enjoy.

Kronborg Castle

Kronborg Castle is located in Helsingør, a pleasant, salty Danish seaside town that's often confused with its Swedish sister, Helsingborg, just two miles across the channel. Kronborg Castle (also called Elsinore, the Anglicized version of Helsingør) is a ▲▲ sight famous for its tenuous (but profitable) ties to Shakespeare. Most of the "Hamlet" castle you'll see today—a darling

of every big-bus tour and travelogue—was built long after the historical Hamlet died (more than a thousand years ago), and Shakespeare never saw the place. But this Renaissance castle existed when a troupe of English actors performed here in Shakespeare's time (Shakespeare may have known them). These days, various Shakespearean companies from around the world perform *Hamlet* in Kronborg's courtyard each August. Among the actors who've donned tights here in the title role are Laurence Olivier, Christopher Plummer, Kenneth Branagh, and Jude Law.

To see or not to see? The castle is most impressive from the outside. The free grounds between the walls and sea are great for picnics, with a close-up view of the strait between Denmark and Sweden. If you're heading to Sweden, Kalmar Castle (described in the Southeast Sweden chapter) is a better medieval castle. And in Denmark, Frederiksborg (described earlier), which was built as an upgrade to this one, is far more opulent inside. But if Kronborg is handy to your itinerary—or you never met a castle you didn't like— it's worth a visit...even if just for a short romp across the ramparts (no ticket required). Many big-bus tours in the region stop both here and at Frederiksborg (you'll recognize some of the same fellow tourists at both places)—not a bad plan if you're a castle completist.

Tourist Information: The town of Helsingør has a TI (Mon-Fri 10:00-16:00, until 17:00 in summer, closed Sat-Sun except for short midday hours in summer; +45 49 21 13 33, www. visithelsingor.dk), a medieval center, the ferry to Sweden, and lots of Swedes who come over for the lower-priced alcohol.

GETTING THERE

Helsingør is a 45-minute train ride from Copenhagen (3/hour). Exit the station out the front door: The TI is on the little square to your left, and the castle is dead ahead along the coast (about a 15-minute walk). Between the station and the castle, you'll pass through a harborfront zone with the town's cultural center and maritime museum (described later).

ORIENTATION TO KRONBORG CASTLE

Cost and Hours: 145 DKK June-Aug, 95 DKK Sept-May, 25 percent discount with Maritime Museum ticket described later, covered by Copenhagen Card; open daily 10:00-17:00; Oct-April Tue-Sun 11:00-16:00, closed Mon; +45 33 95 42 00, www. kongeligeslotte.dk.

Tours: Free 30-minute tours in English are offered of the casements and of the royal apartments (1-2/day; call or check online for times). You can download a free audioguide to your mobile device.

VISITING THE CASTLE

Approaching the castle, pretend you're an old foe of the king, kept away by many layers of earthen ramparts and moats—just when you think you're actually at the castle, you

Øresund Region

When the Øresund (UH-ra-soond) Bridge, which connects Denmark and Sweden, opened in July 2000, it created a dynamic new metropolitan area. Almost overnight, the link forged an economic power with the 12th-largest gross domestic product in Europe. The Øresund region has surpassed Stockholm as the largest metro area in Scandinavia. Now 3.7 million Danes and Swedes—a highly trained and highly technical workforce—are within a quick commute of each other.

The bridge opens up new questions of borders. Historically, southern Sweden (the area across from Copenhagen, called Skåne) had Danish blood. It was Danish for a thousand years before Sweden took it in 1658. Notice how Copenhagen is the capital on the fringe of its realm—at one time it was in the center.

The 10-mile-long link, which has a toll motorway for cars and a two-track train line, ties together the main islands of Denmark with Europe and Sweden. The $4 billion project consisted of a 2.5-mile-long tunnel, an artificial island called Peberholm, and a 5-mile-long bridge. With speedy connecting trains, Malmö in Sweden is now an easy half-day side trip from Copenhagen (3-5/hour, 35 minutes). The train drops you at the "Malmö C" (central) station right in the heart of Malmö, and all the important sights are within a short walk.

Citing security concerns, Sweden has tightened controls at select border crossings. This means that anyone traveling from Denmark to Sweden on the Øresund Bridge needs to carry a passport, which will likely be checked by Swedish police.

find there's another gateway or waterway to pass. On the way in, you'll pass a small model of the complex to help get your bearings. On a sunny day, you could have an enjoyable visit to Kronborg just walking around these grounds and playing "king of the castle," without buying a ticket. Many do.

Follow the signs to the ticket desk, buy your ticket, stick your bag in a locker, and head upstairs. You'll pop out at the beginning of the royal apartments.

Royal Apartments

Visitors are able to walk through one-and-a-half floors of the complex. The first few rooms are filled with exhibits using touchscreens and projected videos to explain the history of the place. You'll learn how, in the 1420s, Danish King Eric of Pomerania built a fortress here to allow for the collection of "Sound Dues," levied on any passing ship hoping to enter the sound of Øresund. This proved hugely lucrative, eventually providing up to two-thirds of Den-

NEAR COPENHAGEN

mark's entire income. By the time of Shakespeare, Kronborg was well known both for its profitable ability to levy these dues, and for its famously lavish banquets—what better setting for a tale of a royal family unraveling?

Continuing into the apartments themselves, you'll find that the interior is a shadow of its former self; while the structure was

rebuilt by Christian IV after a 1629 fire, its rooms were never returned to their former grandeur, making it feel like something of an empty shell. And yet, there are still some fine pieces of furniture and art to see. Frederik II ruled Denmark from the king's chamber in the 1570s; a model shows how it likely looked back in its heyday. After passing through two smaller rooms, you come to the queen's chamber; from there, stairs lead up to the queen's gallery, custom-built for Queen Sophie to be able to quickly walk directly from her chambers to the ballroom or chapel. Follow her footsteps into the ballroom, a vast hall of epic proportions decorated by a series of paintings commissioned by Christian IV (explained by the board near the entry). At the far end, a model (enlivened by seemingly holographic figures) illustrates how this incredible space must have looked in all its original finery. Beyond the ballroom, the "Little Hall" is decorated with a fine series of tapestries depicting Danish monarchs. Then wind through several more royal halls, chambers, and bedrooms on your way back down into the courtyard. Once there, go straight across and enter the chapel. The enclosed gallery at the upper-left was the private pew of the royal family.

Casements

You'll enter the underground part of the castle through a door on the main courtyard (diagonally across from the chapel). While not particularly tight, these passages are very dark (and a good place to use your mobile phone flashlight). This extensive network of dank cellars is a double-decker substructure that once teemed with activity. The upper level, which you'll see first, was used as servants' quarters, a stable, and a storehouse. The lower level was used to train and barrack soldiers during wartime (an efficient use of so much prime, fortified space). As you explore this labyrinthine, nearly pitch-black zone (just follow the arrows), imagine the miserably claustrophobic conditions the soldiers lived in, waiting to see some action.

The most famous "resident" of the Kronborg casements was Holger Danske ("Ogier the Dane"), a mythical Viking hero revered by Danish children. The story goes that if the nation is ever in danger, this Danish superman will awaken and restore peace and security to the land (like King Arthur to the English, Barbarossa to the Germans, and Wenceslas to the Czechs). While this legend has been around for many centuries, Holger's connection to Kronborg was cemented by a Hans Christian Andersen tale, so now everybody just assumes he lives here. In one of the first rooms, you'll see a famous, giant statue of this sleeping Viking...just waiting for things to get *really* bad.

NEAR THE CASTLE
Maritime Museum of Denmark

Fans of nautical history and modern architecture should consider a visit to this museum, built within the old dry docks adjacent to the castle and designed by noted Danish firm BIG (Bjarke Ingels Group). Cutting-edge exhibits journey through Denmark's rich seafaring tradition, from the days of tall-masted sailing ships to the container-ship revolution, in which Danish shipping company Maersk is a world leader. Topics include life on board, wartime challenges, the globalization of trade, navigation, and maritime traditions (including tattoos!) in popular culture.

Cost and Hours: 120 DKK, covered by Copenhagen Card, 25 percent discount with Kronborg Castle ticket; July-Aug daily 11:00-18:00, Sept-June Tue-Sun 11:00-17:00, closed Mon; café, +45 49 21 06 85, www.mfs.dk.

CENTRAL DENMARK

Ærø • Odense

The sleepy isle of Ærø is the cuddle after the climax. It's the perfect time-passed world in which to wind down, enjoy the seagulls, and take a day off. Wander the unadulterated cobbled lanes of Denmark's best-preserved 18th-century town. Get Ærø-dynamic and pedal a rented bike into the essence of Denmark. Settle into a world of sailors, who, after the invention of steam-driven boat propellers, decided that building ships in bottles was more their style.

Between Ærø and Copenhagen, drop by bustling Odense, home of Hans Christian Andersen. Its Hans Christian Andersen Museum is excellent, and with more time, you can also enjoy its other museums (town history, trains, folk) and stroll the car-free streets of its downtown.

There's no direct ferry between Ærø and Copenhagen; it's a 2.5-hour train ride from Copenhagen to Svendborg with a transfer in Odense, then a 1.25-hour ferry crossing to Ærøskøbing (see page 168 for details).

PLANNING YOUR TIME

Allow four hours for the train-and-ferry journey between Copenhagen and Ærø (not counting a possible stopover in Odense). All trains stop in Roskilde (with its Viking Ship Museum—see previous chapter) and Odense (see the end of this chapter). On a quick trip, you can leave Copenhagen in the morning and do justice to both towns en route to Ærø.

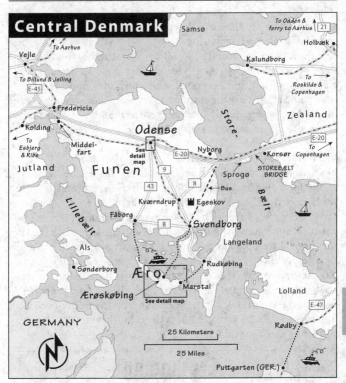

(With just one day, Odense and Roskilde together make a long but doable day trip from Copenhagen.)

While out of the way, Ærø is worth the journey. Once there, you'll want two nights and a day to properly enjoy it (for details, see "Planning Your Time" for Ærøskøbing, later).

Ærø

This small (22 by 6 miles) island on the south edge of Denmark is as salty and sleepy as can be. A typical tombstone reads: "Here lies Christian Hansen at anchor with his wife. He'll not weigh until he stands before God." It's the kind of island where baskets of strawberries sit in front of houses—for sale on the honor system.

Ærø statistics: 7,000 residents, 500,000 visitors and 80,000 boaters annually, 350 deer, seven pastors, no crosswalks, and three police officers. The three big industries are farming (wheat and dairy), shipping, and tourism—in that order. Twenty percent of the Danish fleet still resides on Ærø, in the town of Marstal. But jobs are scarce, the population is slowly dropping, and family farms are consolidating into larger units.

Ærø, home to several windmills and one of the world's largest solar power plants, is going "green." They hope to become completely wind- and solar-powered. Currently, over half the island's heat and electricity is provided by renewable sources, and most of its produce is organically grown. New technology is expected to bring Ærø closer to its goal within the next few years.

GETTING AROUND ÆRØ

On a short visit, you won't need to leave the village of Ærøskøbing, except for a countryside bike ride, if you like—everything is within walking or pedaling distance. But if you have more time or want to explore the rest of the island, you can take advantage of Ærø's **bus** network. Buses leave from a stop just above the ferry dock (leaving the ferry, walk up about a block and look right). Ærø's main bus line, Jesper Bus, is free (Mon-Fri hourly until about 20:00; fewer Sat-Sun, www.jesperbus.dk). There are two different branches— one going to Marstal at the east end of the island, and the other to Søby in the west (look for the town name on the front of the bus). The main reason to take the bus is to go to Marstal on a rainy day to visit its maritime museum.

Ærøskøbing

Ærøskøbing is Ærø's village in a bottle. It's small enough to be cute, but just big enough to feel real. The government, recognizing the value of this amazingly preserved little town, prohibits modern building anywhere in the center. It's the only town in Denmark protected in this way. Drop into the 1680s, when Ærøskøbing was the wealthy home port of a hundred windjammers. The many Danes and Germans who come here for the tranquility—washing up the cobbled main drag in waves with the landing of each boat—call it the fairy-tale town. The Danish word for "cozy," *hyggelig*, describes Ærøskøbing perfectly.

Ærøskøbing is simply a pleasant place to wander. Stubby little porthole-type houses, with their birth dates displayed in proud decorative rebar, lean on each other like drunk, sleeping sailors. Wander under flickering old-time lamps. Snoop around town. It's OK. Peek into living rooms (if people want privacy, they shut their drapes). Notice the many "snooping mirrors" on the houses—antique locals are following your every move. The harbor now caters to holiday yachts, and on midnight low tides you can almost hear the crabs playing cards.

The town economy, once rich with the windjammer trade, hit the rocks in modern times. Kids 15 to 18 years old go to a boarding school in Svendborg; many don't return. About a third of Ærø's population is over age 60. And even though young couples on the island are having more babies, it's not enough to prevent a net population decline.

PLANNING YOUR TIME

You'll regret not setting aside a minimum of two nights for your Ærøskøbing visit. In a busy day you can "do" everything you like—except relax. If ever a place was right for recreating, this is it. I'd arrive in time for an evening stroll and dinner (and, when it's running, the Night Watchman's tour—see "Nightlife in Ærøskøbing," later). The next morning, do the island bike tour, returning by midafternoon. You can see the town's three museums in less than two hours (but note that they all close early—see "Sights in Ærøskøbing," later), then browse the rest of your daylight away. Your second evening is filled with options: Stroll out to the summer huts for sunset, watch the classic sailing ships come in to moor for the evening (mostly Dutch and German boats crewed by vacationers), watch a movie in the pint-size town cinema, go bowling with local teens, or check out live music in the pub.

Note that the town can be quite dead during the off-season (basically Sept-May), but local business owners are making efforts to enliven the shorter days of fall and winter. Though several shops and restaurants close during the off-season, restaurant owners are trying to keep some dining establishments open on a rotating basis, so there should always be someplace to get a meal.

Orientation to Ærøskøbing

Ærøskøbing is tiny. Everything's just a few cobbles from the ferry landing.

TOURIST INFORMATION

The TI, which faces the ferry landing, has all the services you'd expect from a larger town's TI (late-June-mid-Aug Mon-Fri 9:00-18:00, Sat from 10:00, Sun 10:00-15:00; off-season Mon-Fri 10:00-16:00, closed Sat-Sun; +45 62 52 13 00, www.aeroe.dk).

HELPFUL HINTS

Money: The town's only ATM is at the blue building by the ferry dock, facing the TI.

CENTRAL DENMARK

Laundry: You'll find limited self-service laundry facilities at Ærøskøbing's marinas, on either side of the ferry dock.

Bike Rental: Pilebækkens Cykler rents bikes year-round at the gas station at the top of town. Manager Janne hands out free *cykel* maps so you can't get lost (7-speed bikes-80 DKK/day, 200 DKK/3 days, 400 DKK/7 days; electric bikes-200 DKK/day—book a day ahead, deposit required; Mon-Fri 9:30-16:00, Sat-Sun until 13:00; from Torvet Square, go through green door at Søndergade

end of square, past garden to next road—in the gas station at Pilebækken 7; +45 62 52 11 10). **Andelen Guesthouse** rents good bikes, too (100 DKK/day, Søndergade 28A, see "Sleeping in Ærøskøbing," later). Most people on Ærø don't bother locking up their bikes—if your rental doesn't have a lock, don't fret.

Ferries: See "Ærøskøbing Connections" on page 168.

Shopping: The town is speckled with cute little shops. Local artisans show their creations in a warehouse facing the ferry landing (daily in summer, closed Sat-Sun off-season).

Ærøskøbing Walk

This self-guided stroll, rated ▲▲▲, is ideal when the sun is low, the shadows long, and the colors rich. Start at the harbor.

Harbor: First, loiter around the harbor, where German and Dutch pleasure boaters come into port each evening. Because Ærø is only nine miles across the water from Germany, the island is popular with Germans who regularly return to this peaceful retreat on their grand old sailboats.

• *From the harbor and TI, walk up the main street a block and go left on...*

Smedegade: This is the poorest street in town, with the most architectural and higgledy-piggledy charm. Have a close look at the "street spies" on the houses— clever mirrors that let residents inside keep an eye on what's going on outside. The ship-in-a-bottle Bottle Peter Museum is on the right (described later, under "Sights in Ærøskøbing"). Notice the gutters—some protect only the doorway. Locals

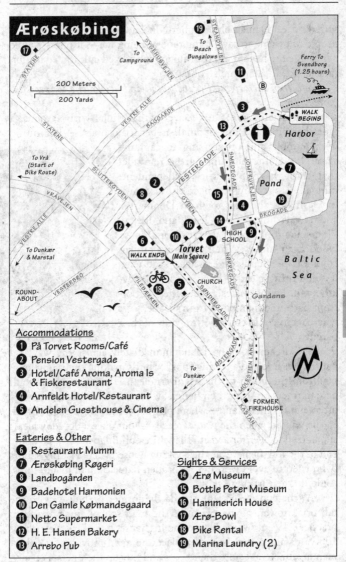

Ærøskøbing

To Campground
To Beach Bungalows
Ferry To Svendborg (1.25 hours)
WALK BEGINS
Harbor
To Vrå (Start of Bike Route)
To Dunkær & Marstal
Torvet (Main Square)
WALK ENDS
CHURCH
HIGH SCHOOL
Pond
Baltic Sea
Gardens
To Dunkær
FORMER FIREHOUSE
ROUNDABOUT
200 Meters
200 Yards

CENTRAL DENMARK

Accommodations
1. På Torvet Rooms/Café
2. Pension Vestergade
3. Hotel/Café Aroma, Aroma Is & Fiskerestaurant
4. Arnfeldt Hotel/Restaurant
5. Andelen Guesthouse & Cinema

Eateries & Other
6. Restaurant Mumm
7. Ærøskøbing Røgeri
8. Landbogården
9. Badehotel Harmonien
10. Den Gamle Købmandsgaard
11. Netto Supermarket
12. H. E. Hansen Bakery
13. Arrebo Pub

Sights & Services
14. Ærø Museum
15. Bottle Peter Museum
16. Hammerich House
17. Ærø-Bowl
18. Bike Rental
19. Marina Laundry (2)

find the rounded modern drainpipes less charming than the old-school ones with hard angles. Appreciate the finely carved old doors. Each is proudly unique—try to find two the same. Number 37 (on the left, after Arnfeldt Hotel), from the 18th century, is Ærøskøbing's cutest house. Its tiny dormer is from some old ship's poop deck. The plants above the door have a traditional purpose—to keep this part of the house damp and slow to burn in case of fire.

Smedegade ends at the Folkehøjskole (folk high school). Inspired by the Danish philosopher Nikolaj Gruntvig—who wanted people to be able to say, "I am good at being me"—it offers people of any age the benefit of government-subsidized cultural education (music, art, theater, and so on).

• *Jog left, then turn right after the school, and stroll along the peaceful, harborside...*

Molestien Lane: This gravel path is lined with gardens, a quiet beach, and a row of small-is-beautiful houses—beginning with humble and progressing to captain's class. These fine buildings are a reminder that through the centuries, independent-minded Ærøskøbing has been the last town in Germany, the first town in Denmark... and always into trade—legal and illegal. (The smuggling spirit survives in residents' blood even today. When someone returns from a trip, friends eagerly ask, "And what did you bring back?") Each garden is cleverly and lovingly designed. The harborfront path, nicknamed "Virgin's Lane," was where teens could court within view of their parents.

The dreamy-looking island immediately across the way is a nature preserve and a resting spot for birds making their long journey from the north to the Mediterranean. There's one lucky bull here (farmers raft over their heifers, who return as cows). Rainbows often end on this island—where plague victims were once buried. In the winter, when the water freezes (about once a decade), locals slip and slide over for a visit. The white building you can see at the end of the town's pier was the cooking house, where visiting sailors (who tried to avoid working with open flame on flammable ships) could do their baking.

At the end of the lane stands the former firehouse (with the tall brick tower, now a place for the high school garage band to practice). Twenty yards before the firehouse, a trail cuts left about 100 yards along the shore to a place the town provides for fishermen to launch and store their boats and tidy up their nets. A bench is strategically placed to enjoy the view.

• *Follow the rutted lane inland, back past the firehouse. Turn right and walk a block toward town. At the first intersection, take a right onto...*

Østergade: This was Ærøskøbing's east gate. In the days of German control, all island trade was legal only within the town. All who passed this point would pay various duties and taxes at a tollbooth that once stood here.

As you walk past the traditional houses, peer into living rooms. Catch snatches of Danish life. (After the bend, you can see right through the windows to the sea.) Ponder the beauty of a society with such a keen sense of civic responsibility that fishing permits entrust you "to catch only what you need." You're welcome to pick berries where you like...but "no more than what would fit in your hat."

The wood on these old houses prefers organic coverings to modern paint. Tar painted on beams as a preservative blisters in the sun. An old-fashioned paint of chalk, lime, and clay lets old houses breathe and feel more alive. (It gets darker with the rain and leaves a little color on your fingers.) Modern chemical paint has much less personality.

The first square (actually a triangle, at #55) was the old goose market. Ærøskøbing—born in the 13th century, burned in the 17th, and rebuilt in the 18th—claims (believably) to be the best-preserved town from that era in Denmark. The original plan, with 12 streets laid out by its founder, survives.

• *Leaving the square, stay left on...*

Søndergade: Look for wrought-iron girders on the walls, added to hold together bulging houses. (On the first corner, at #55, notice the nuts that could be tightened like a corset to keep the house from sagging.) Ærøskøbing's oldest houses (check out the dates)— the only ones that survived a fire during a war with Sweden—are #36 and #32. At #32, the hatch upstairs was where masts and sails were stored for the winter. These houses also have some of the finest doors in town (and in Ærøskøbing, that's saying something). The red on #32's door is the original paint job—ox blood, which, when combined with the tannin in the wood, really lasts. The courtyard behind #18 was a parking lot in pre-car days. Farmers, in town for their shopping chores, would leave their horses here. Even today, the wide-open fields are just beyond.

• *Wander down to Ærøskøbing's main square.*

Torvet Square: Notice the two hand pumps, which still work. Until 1951, townspeople came here for their water. The linden tree is the town symbol. The rocks around it celebrate the reunion of a big chunk of southern Denmark (including this island), which was ruled by

Germany from 1864 to 1920. See the town seal featuring a linden tree, over the door of the old City Hall (now the library, with computer stations in former prison cells). Read the Danish on the wall: "With law shall man a country build."

• *Our walk is over. Continue straight (popping into recommended Restaurant Mumm, the best place in town, to make a reservation for dinner). You'll return to the main street (Vestergade) and—just when you need it—the town bakery (to the left). But, if you're ready to launch right into a bike ride, instead go through the green door to the right of City Hall to reach one of the town's bike-rental places (listed earlier, under "Helpful Hints").*

Sights in Ærøskøbing

MUSEUMS

Ærøskøbing's three tiny museums cluster within a few doors of each other just off Torvet Square. While quirky and fun (and with sketchy English handouts), these museums would be much more interesting and worthwhile if they translated their Danish descriptions for the rare person on this planet who doesn't speak *Dansk*. (Your gentle encouragement might help get results.) In July, they organize daily chatty tours.

Ærø Museum (Ærøskøbing Bymuseum)

This museum fills two floors of an old house with the island's history, from seafaring to farming. Be on the lookout for household objects (such as pottery, kitchenware, and tools), paintings, a loom from 1683, an 18th-century peasant's living room with colorful furniture, and gear from a 100-year-old pharmacy. There's also a fun diorama showing an aerial view of Ærøskøbing in 1862—notice the big gardens behind nearly every house. (This museum carries on the tradition with its own garden out back—be sure to go out and explore it before you leave.)

Cost and Hours: 50 DKK; July-Aug Mon-Fri 10:00-16:00, Sat-Sun 11:00-15:00; Sept-June Mon-Sat 11:00-15:00, closed Sun; Brogade 3, +45 62 52 29 50, www.arremus.dk.

▲Bottle Peter Museum (Flaske-Peters Samling)

This fascinating house has 750 different bottled ships. Old Peter Jacobsen, who made his first bottle at 16 and his last at 85, created some 1,700 ships-in-bottles in his lifetime. He bragged that he drank the contents of each bottle...except those containing milk.

This museum opened in 1943, when the mayor of Ærøskøbing offered Peter and his wife a humble home in exchange for the right to display his works. Bottle Peter died in 1960 (and is most likely buried in a glass bottle), leaving a lifetime of elaborate little creations for visitors to squint and marvel at.

Cost and Hours: 50 DKK; July-Aug daily 10:00-16:00; April-June and Sept Mon-Sat 11:00-15:00, closed Sun; off-season call for appointment; Smedegade 22, +45 81 55 59 72.

Visiting the Museum: In two buildings facing each other across a cobbled courtyard, you'll see rack after rack of painstaking models in bottles and cigar boxes. Some are "right-handed" and some are "left-handed" (referring to the direction the bottle faced, and therefore which hand the model maker relied on to execute the fine details)—Bottle Peter could do it all.

In the entrance building, you'll see Peter's "American collection," which he sold to a Danish-American collector so he could have funds to retire. One of Peter's favorites was the "diver-bottle"—an extra-wide bottle with two separate ship models inside: One shipwreck on the "ocean floor" at the bottom of the bottle, and, above that, a second one floating on the "surface." A video shows the artist at work, and nearby you can see some of his tools.

The second building has some English panels about Peter's life (including his mischievous wit, which caused his friends great anxiety when he had an audience with the king) and the headstone he designed for his own grave: a cross embedded with seven ships-in-bottles, representing the seven seas he explored in his youth as a seaman.

Hammerich House (Hammerichs Hus)

These 12 funky rooms in three houses are filled with 200- to 300-year-old junk.

Cost and Hours: 40 DKK, July-Aug daily 10:00-13:00 with guided tours typically Wed at 11:00, otherwise ask at the Ærø Museum for access, closed off-season, Gyden 22, www.arremus.dk.

ÆRØ ISLAND BIKE RIDE (OR CAR TOUR)

This 15-mile trip shows you the best of this windmill-covered island's charms. The highest point on the island is only 180 feet above sea level, but the wind can be strong and the hills seem long and surprisingly steep.

Ærø Island Bike Ride

To Svendborg

100 KM
50 MI
DENMARK
Odense · Copa.
GER. · Ærø

To Søby

Urehoved

BEACH
BUNGALOWS

GÆSTGIVERI
BREGNINGE

CHURCH
Bregninge

Synneshøj

Borgnæs

CAMPING

Drejø

Ommels-
hoved

DIKE

Ærøskøbing
(start & end bike ride)

Vrå

Lilleø

VINDEBALLE KRO

SHORTCUTS BACK
TO ÆRØSKØBING

Vindeballe

Vodrup
Klint
(Cliffs)

Tranderup

Olde

Stokkeby

Lille
Rise

Kragnæs

TINGSTEDET
DOLMEN

BREWERY

Store
Rise

Dunkær

To Marstal
& Maritime
Museum

Baltic Sea

N

2 Kilometers

2 Miles

Vejnæs Nakke

As a bike ride, it's good exercise, though it may be more exhausting than fun if you've done only light, recreational cycling at home. You'll pay more for seven gears instead of five, but it's worth it. Rent your bike in town (see "Helpful Hints," earlier), and while my map and instructions work, a local cycle map is helpful (free loaner maps if you rent from Pilebækkens Cykler, or buy one at the TI). Bring along plenty of water, as there are few opportunities to fill up (your first good chance is at the WC at the Bregninge church; there are no real shops until downtown Bregninge).

• Leave Ærøskøbing to the west on the road to Vrå (Vråvejen, national road #N-8). From downtown, pedal up the main street (Vestergade) and turn right on Vråvejen; from the bike-rental place on Pilebækken, just turn right and pedal straight ahead—it turns into Vråvejen.

Leaving Ærøskøbing: You'll see the first of many U-shaped farmhouses, typical of Denmark. The three sides block the wind and store cows, hay, and people. *Gård* (farm) shows up in many local surnames.

At Øsemarksvej, bike along the coast in the protection of the dike built in 1856 to make the once-salty swampland to your left farmable. While the weak soil is good for hay and little else, they get the most out of it. Each winter, certain grazing areas flood with seawater. (Some locals claim this makes their cows produce fatter milk and meat.) As you roll along the dike, the land on your left is about eight feet below sea level. The little white pump house—alone in the field—is busy each spring and summer.

• *At the T-junction, go right (over the dike) toward...*

Borgnæs: The traditional old "straw house" (50 yards down, on left) is a café and shop selling fresh farm products. Just past that, a few roadside tables sell farm goodies on the honor system. Borgnæs is a cluster of modern summer houses. In spite of huge demand, a weak economy, and an aging population, development like this is no longer allowed.

• *Keep to the right (passing lots of wheat fields); at the next T-junction, turn right, following signs for Ø. Bregningemark (don't turn off for* Vindeballe*). After a secluded beach, head inland (direction: Ø. Bregninge). Pass the island's only water mill, and climb uphill over the island's 2,700-inch-high summit toward Bregninge. The tallest point on Ærø is called Synneshøj (probably means "Seems High" and it sure does—if you're even a bit out of shape, you'll feel every one of those inches).*

Gammelgård: Take a right turn marked only by a *bike route #90* sign. The road deteriorates (turns to gravel—and can be slushy if there's been heavy rain, so be careful). You'll wind scenically and some-times steeply through "Ærø's Alps," past clas-sic thatched-roofed "old farms" (hence the name of the lane—Gammelgård).

• *At the modern road, turn left (leaving bike route #90)* and pedal to the big village church. Before turning left to roll through Bregninge, visit the church.

Bregninge Church: The interior of the 12th-century Bregn-inge church is still painted in the Gothic style. Find the painter's self-portrait (behind the pulpit, right of front pew). Tradition says that if the painter wasn't happy with his pay, he'd paint a fool's

head in the church (above third pew on left). Note how the fool's mouth—the hole for a rope tied to the bell—has been worn wider and wider by centuries of ringing. (During services, the ringing bell would call those who were ill and too contagious to be allowed into the church to come for communion—distributed through the square hatches flanking the altar.)

The altarpiece—gold leaf on carved oak—is from 1528, six years before the Reformation came to Denmark. The cranium carved into the bottom indicates it's a genu-ine masterpiece by Claus Berg (from Lü-beck, Germany). This Crucifixion scene is such a commotion, it seems to cause Christ's robe to billow up. The soldiers who tra-ditionally gambled for Christ's robe have traded their dice for knives. Even the three wise men (lower right; each perhaps a Dan-ish king) made it to this Crucifixion. Notice the escaping souls of the two thieves—the one who converted on the cross being car-ried happily to heaven, and the other, with its grim-winged escort, heading straight to hell. The scene at lower left—a disciple with a bare-breasted, dark-skinned woman feed-

ing her child—symbolizes the Great Commission: "Go ye to all the world." Since this is a Catholic altarpiece, a roll call of saints lines the wings. During the restoration, the identity of the two women on the lower right was unknown, so the lettering—even in Latin—is clearly gibberish. Take a moment to study the 16th-cen-tury art on the ceiling (for example, the crucified feet ascending, leaving only footprints on earth). In the narthex, a list of pastors goes back to 1505. The current pastor (Agnes) is the first woman on the list.

• Now's the time for a bathroom break (public WC in the churchyard). If you need some food or drink, pop in to the **$$$ Gæstgiveri Bregninge** restaurant, to the right of the church as you face it (Wed-Sun 12:00-14:30 & 18:00-20:00, closed Mon-Tue except open daily in June, closed Oct-April, guest rooms available, +45 30 23 65 55, www.gaestgiveri. dk). Then roll downhill through...

Bregninge: As you bike through what is supposedly Den-mark's "second-longest village," you'll pass many more U-shaped gårds. Notice how the town is in a gully. Imagine pirates trolling along the coast, looking for church spires marking unfortified vil-lages. Ærø's 16 villages are all invisible from the sea—their church spires carefully designed not to be viewable from sea level.

• About a mile down the main road is Vindeballe. Just before the main part of the village (soon after you pass the official Vindeballe sign and the din fart sign—which tells you "your speed"), take the Vodrup Klint turnoff to the right.

Vodrup Klint: A road leads downhill (with a well-signed jog to the right) to dead-end at a rugged bluff called Vodrup Klint

(WC, picnic benches). If I were a pagan, I'd worship here for the sea, the wind, and the chilling view. Notice how the land steps in sloppy slabs down to the sea. When saturated with water, the slabs of clay that make up the land here get slick, and entire chunks can slide.

Hike down to the foamy beach (where you can pick up some flint, chalk, and wild thyme). While the wind at the top could drag a kite-flyer, the beach below can be ideal for sunbathing. Because Ærø is warmer and drier than the rest of Denmark, this island is home to plants and animals found nowhere else in the country. This southern exposure is the warmest area. Germany is dead ahead.

• *Backtrack 200 yards and follow the signs to* Tranderup. *On the way, you'll pass a lovely pond famous for its bell frogs and happy little duck houses.*

Popping out in Tranderup, you can backtrack (left) about 300 yards to get to the traditional $$$ Vindeballe Kro—a handy inn for a stop if you're hungry or thirsty (lunch served daily July–mid-Aug 12:00-14:00, dinners served Tue-Sat year-round 18:00-20:00, +45 62 52 16 13, www.vindeballekro.dk).

If you're tired or if the weather is turning bad, you can shortcut from here back to Ærøskøbing: Go down the lane across the street from the Vindeballe Kro, and you'll zip quickly downhill across the island to the dike just east of Borgnæs; turn right and retrace your steps back into town.

But there's much more to see. To continue our pedal, head on into...

Tranderup: Still following signs for *Tranderup*, stay on Tranderupgade parallel to the big road through town. You'll pass a lovely farm and a potato stand. At the main road, turn right. At the Ærøskøbing turnoff (another chance to bail out and head home), side-trip 100 yards left to the big stone (commemorating the return of the island to Denmark from Germany in 1750) and a grand island panorama. Claus Clausen's rock (in the picnic area, next to WC) is a memorial to an extremely obscure pioneer who was born in Ærø, emigrated to America, and played a role in shaping the early history of Scandinavian Lutheranism in the US.

• *Return to the big road (continuing in direction: Marstal), pass through Olde, pedal past FAF (the local wheat farmers' co-op facility), and head toward Store Rise (STOH-reh REE-zuh), the next church spire in the distance. Think of medieval travelers using spires as navigational aids.*

Store Rise Prehistoric Tomb, Church, and Brewery: Thirty yards after the Stokkeby turnoff, follow the rough, tree-lined path on the right to the Langdysse (Long Dolmen) Tingstedet, just behind the church spire. This is a 6,000-year-old **dolmen,** an early Neolithic burial place. Though Ærø once had more than 200 of these prehistoric tombs, only 13 survive. The site is a raised mound the shape and length (about 100 feet) of a Viking ship,

and archaeologists have found evidence that indicates a Viking ship may indeed have been burned and buried here.

Ting means assembly spot. Imagine a thousand years ago: Viking chiefs representing the island's various communities gathering here around their ancestors' tombs. For 6,000 years, this has been a holy spot. The stones were considered to be fertility aids: For centuries, locals in need of virility chipped off bits and took them home (the nicks in the rock nearest the information post are mine).

Tuck away your chip and carry on down the lane to the Store Rise **church.** Inside you'll find little ships hanging in the nave, a fine 12th-century altarpiece, a stick with an offering bag and a ting-a-ling bell to wake those nodding off (right of altar), double seats (so worshippers can flip to face the pulpit during sermons), and Martin Luther in the stern keeping his Protestant hand on the rudder. The list in the church allows today's pastors to trace their pastoral lineage back to Doctor Luther himself. (The current pastor, Janet, is the first woman on the list.) The churchyard is circular—a reminder of how churchyards provided a last refuge for humble communities under attack. Can you find anyone buried in the graveyard whose name doesn't end in "-sen"?

Next follow the smell of hops (or the *Rise Bryggeri* signs) to Ærø's **brewery.** Located in a historic building 400 yards beyond the Store Rise church, it welcomes visitors with free samples of its various beers. The Ærø traditional brews are available in pilsner (including the popular walnut pilsner), light ale, dark ale, a typical dark Irish-style stout, and seasonal varieties, most in both regular and organic versions (daily July-Aug 10:00-15:00; shorter hours Sept-mid-Oct, closed mid-Oct-June; +45 62 52 11 32, www.risebryggeri.dk).

• *From here, climb back to the main road and continue (direction: Marstal) on your way back home to Ærøskøbing. The three 330-foot-high modern windmills on your right are communally owned and, as they are a nonpolluting source of energy, state-subsidized. At Dunkær (3 miles from Ærøskøbing), take the small road, signed* Lille Rise, *past the topless windmill. Except for the Lille Rise, it's all downhill from here, as you coast past great sea views back home to Ærøskøbing.*

Huts at the Sunset Beach: Still rolling? Bike past the campground along the Urehoved beach (*strand* in Danish) for a look at the coziest little beach houses you'll never see back in the "big is beautiful" US. This is Europe, where small is beautiful, and the concept of sustainability is neither new nor subversive. (For more details, see "Beach Bungalow Sunset Stroll," later.)

RAINY-DAY OPTIONS

Ærø is disappointing but not unworkable in bad weather. In addition to the museums listed earlier, you could check out the evening options under "Nightlife in Ærøskøbing" (later), many of which are good in bad weather. Or hop on the free bus to Marstal to visit its maritime museum.

Marstal Maritime Museum (Marstal Søfartsmuseum)

To learn more about the island's seafaring history, visit this fine museum in the dreary town of Marstal. You'll see plenty of model ships, nautical paintings (including several scenes by acclaimed painter Carl Rasmussen), an original ship's galley, a re-created wheelhouse (with steering and navigation equipment), a collection of exotic goods brought back from faraway lands, and a children's area with a climbable mast. Designed by and for sailors, the museum presents a warts-and-all view of the hardships of the seafaring life, rather than romanticizing it.

Cost and Hours: 70 DKK; June-Aug daily 9:00-17:00; mid-April-May and Sept-Oct daily 10:00-16:00; Nov-mid-April Mon-Sat 11:00-15:00, closed Sun; Prinsensgade 1, +45 62 53 23 31, www.marmus.dk.

Getting There: Ride the free Jesper Bus (described on page 150) all the way to the harbor in Marstal, where you'll find the museum. It's about a 20-minute trip.

Nightlife in Ærøskøbing

These activities are best done in the evening, after a day of biking around the island.

▲▲Beach Bungalow Sunset Stroll

At sunset, stroll to Ærøskøbing's sand beach. Facing the ferry dock, go left, following the harbor. Upon leaving the town, you'll pass the Netto supermarket (convenient for picking up snacks, beer, or wine), a minigolf course, and a children's playground. In the rosy distance, past a wavy wheat field, is Vestre Strandvejen—a row of tiny, Monopoly-like huts facing the sunset. These beach escapes are privately owned on land rented from the town (no overnight use, WCs at each end). Each is different, but all are stained with merry memories of locals enjoying themselves Danish-style. Bring a beverage or picnic. It's perfectly acceptable—and very Danish—to borrow a porch for your sunset sit. From here, it's a fine walk out to the end of Urehoved (as this spit of land is called).

Town Walk with Night Watchman

On summer evenings from mid-May through August, the night watchman leads visitors through a 1.5-hour stroll through town. It's a fine time to be outside, meeting other travelers (40 DKK, in English Wed, starts 21:00 mid-May-July and 20:00 in Aug at Torvet Square—just show up, +45 40 46 66 75, www.aeroetours.dk).

Cinema

The cute little 30-seat Andelen Theater (in the Andelen Guesthouse—a former grain warehouse) plays movies in their original language at 19:30 (70 DKK, Danish subtitles, closed Mon and in July—when it hosts a jazz festival, new titles begin every Thu). It's run in a charming community-service kind of way. The management has installed heat, so tickets no longer come with a blanket (near Torvet Square at Søndergade 28A, +45 62 52 17 11).

Bowling

Ærø-Bowl is a six-lane alley in a modern athletic club at the edge of town. In this old-fashioned town, where no modern construction is allowed in the higgledy-piggledy center, this hip facility is a magnet for young people. One local told me, "I've never seen anyone come out of there without a smile" (hot dogs, junk food, arcade games, kids on dates; irregular hours, call to check, Statene 42A, +45 62 52 23 06).

Pub

Arrebo Pub bills itself as "probably the best bar in town." Maybe that's because it's the *only* one in town. In any case, it attracts a young crowd and is the place to go for live music and beer, but there's no food (open daily from 13:00, at the bottom of Vestergade, near ferry dock).

Sleeping in Ærøskøbing

The accommodations scene here is boom or bust. Summer weekends and all of July are packed (book long in advance). It's absolutely dead in the winter. These places come with family-run personality, and each is an easy stroll from the ferry landing.

IN ÆRØSKØBING

$$$$ På Torvet ("On the Square") is a cheery hotel/café/wine shop that brings a lively spirit to the town square. Owners Gunnar and Lili rent 11 modern, sparkling apartments, each with a private bathroom, and several with a kitchen (Torvet 7, +45 62 52 40 50, www.paatorvet.dk, info@paatorvet.dk). The recommended café serves breakfast and lunch with seating inside and out on Torvet

Square (see "Eating in Ærøskøbing," later). They also sell wine and specialty foods, and the grand piano in the dining area is ready for you to tickle its ivories.

$$$ Pension Vestergade is your best home away from home in Ærøskøbing. It's lovingly run by Susanna Greve and her daughters, Henrietta and Celia. Susanna, who's fun to talk with and is always ready with a cup of tea, has a wealth of knowledge about the town's history and takes good care of her guests. Built in 1784 for a sea captain's daughter, this creaky, sagging, and venerable eight-room place—with each room named for its particular color scheme—is on the main street in the town center. Picnic in the back garden and get to know Tillie, the live-in dog. Reserve well in advance (RS%, payment via TransferWise app or cash, cuddly hot-water bottles, half with shared bathrooms, Vestergade 44, +45 62 52 22 98, www.vestergade44.com, contact@vestergade44.com).

$$$ Hotel Aroma offers four bright, cheery, and modern rooms—two standard doubles and two large family rooms with kitchens—above the recommended Café Aroma (shared bathroom, laundry facilities, roof terrace, on Vestergade, just up the street from the ferry dock, open mid-April-Aug, closed off-season, +45 62 52 40 02, mobile +45 40 40 26 84, www.cafe-aroma.dk).

$$$ Arnfeldt Hotel was once a 19th-century captain's home. Owned by an energetic husband-and-wife team, Morten and Katrine Arnfeldt, this cozy hotel offers five clean and tidy rooms, three with shared baths (on-site restaurant serves meals Fri-Sat in June and Aug, Tue-Sat in July; Smedegade 33, +45 62 52 23 00, www.arnfeldthotel.dk mail@arnfeldthotel.dk).

$$ Andelen Guesthouse, run by Englishman Adam, is brimming with a funky nautical charm. An old warehouse that's been converted into a hotel, it has five guest rooms that share two bathrooms and one two-level family room with private bath (cash only, no breakfast—but can be purchased nearby at På Torvet Café, free entry to downstairs movie theater, nice rental bikes-100 DKK/day, pay laundry, Søndergade 28A, mobile +45 61 26 75 11, www.andelenguesthouse.com, info@andelenguesthouse.com).

OUTSIDE ÆRØSKØBING

For locations, see the "Ærø Island Bike Ride" map, earlier.

$$ Vindeballe Kro, about three miles from Ærøskøbing, is a traditional inn in Vindeballe at the island's central crossroads. Maria and Steen rent 10 straightforward, well-kept rooms (free parking; +45 62 52 16 13, www.vindeballekro.dk, mail@vindeballekro.dk). They also have a restaurant (described earlier, under "Ærø Island Bike Ride").

¢ Ærø Campground is set on a fine beach a few minutes' walk out of town. This three-star campground offers a lodge with a fireplace, campsites, and cabins (open April-Oct; facing the water, follow waterfront to the left; +45 62 52 18 54, www.aeroecamp.dk, aeroecamping@gmail.com).

Eating in Ærøskøbing

Ærøskøbing has a handful of charming and hardworking little eateries. Business is so light that chefs and owners come and go constantly, making it tough to predict the best value for the coming year. I'd spend 20 minutes enjoying the warm evening light and do a strolling survey before making a choice. I've listed only the serious kitchens. Note that almost everything closes by 21:00—don't wait too late to eat (if you'll be taking a later ferry from Svendborg to Ærø, either eat before your boat trip or call ahead to reserve a place...otherwise you're out of luck). During the winter, some of my recommended restaurants take turns staying open, so you should be able to find a decent place to eat (the TI posts a list of restaurant opening days and times).

$$$$ Restaurant Mumm is where visiting yachters go for a good and classy meal. Portions are huge, and on balmy days their garden terrace out back is a hit. Call ahead to reserve or book online (daily specials, starters, main courses, daily 18:00-21:00, shorter hours and closed Sun-Mon in off-season, near Torvet Square at Søndergade 12, +45 62 52 12 12, www.mumm.restaurant).

$$ På Torvet Café, right on Torvet Square, offers a tasty lunch menu, with hearty portions that are stylishly presented. Dine in the cozy café or out on the square (daily May-mid-Sept 12:00-15:30, shorter hours off-season, +45 30 34 46 50).

$$ Café Aroma, a reasonably priced Danish café that feels like a rustic old diner, has a big front porch filled with tables and good entrées, sandwiches, and burgers. Ask about the daily special, which will save you money and is not listed on the menu. Order at the bar (mid-April-Aug Thu-Mon 11:00-20:00, closed Tue-Wed and in off-season, on Vestergade, just up from the ferry dock, +45 62 52 40 02). They also run a delicious ice-cream shop; a high-quality, pricey fish restaurant next door (**Fiskerestaurant,** open July only); and produce gourmet handmade licorice just across the street.

$$ Ærøskøbing Røgeri serves wonderful smoked-fish meals on paper plates. With picnic tables facing the harbor, it's great for a light meal. Eat there or find a pleasant picnic site at the beach or at the park behind the fish house. A smoked-fish dinner with potato salad, bread, and a couple of cold Carlsbergs or Ærø brews are a well-earned reward after a long bike ride (daily 10:00-

21:00, April-mid-June and mid-Aug-mid-Oct 11:00-19:00, closed mid-Oct-March, Havnen 15, +45 62 52 40 07).

$$$$ Landbogården, a diner and music/event space, is run by artists Jacob and Gertrud, who pride themselves on serving "honest and special" dishes using local ingredients (meat, fish, international dishes, Tue-Sun 18:00-21:00, closed Mon and Jan, near the top of Vestergade at #54, +45 29 71 23 48, www.landbogaarden.dk).

Hotel Restaurants: Two hotels in town have dining rooms with good but expensive food; I'd eat at the restaurants I've listed above, unless they're closed. But in a pinch, try these: **$$$ Badehotel Harmonien** serves Italian dishes and wood-fired pizza, and owns the best location in town, with views of the sea from its bright and lively perch (pizza made right in the dining room, Thu-Tue 17:30-21:30, closed Wed, Brogade 1, +45 42 50 00 05). **$$$$ Arnfeldt Hotel** offers gourmet meals using local

CENTRAL DENMARK

ingredients. After stints in London and Copenhagen, chef Morten Arnfeldt is bringing upscale dining to Ærø, serving internationally inspired dishes in an inviting dining room and garden (four-course dinners, summer only, reservations required, Smedegade 33, +45 62 52 23 00, www.arnfeldthotel.dk).

SNACKS, PICNICS, AND DESSERT
Here are some places for lighter fare.

Market for Local Specialties: At **Den Gamle Købmands-gaard** ("The Old Merchants' Court") on Torvet Square you'll find a remarkable selection of mostly locally sourced and produced foods, including meat, sausage, salami, bread, fruit, honey, jam, choco-late, beer, cigars, and whiskey—which is distilled on-site (ask about tours and tastings). Grab a seat in their café for lunch or cake (daily 10:00-17:30, Torvet 5, +45 91 25 59 70).

Grocery: The **Netto** supermarket has picnic fixings and drinks, including chilled beer and wine—handy for walks to the little huts on the beach at sunset (daily 7:00-22:00, kitty-corner from ferry dock).

Bakery: Ærøskøbing's old-school **H. E. Hansen** bakery sells fresh bread and delicious pastries, plus cheese, yogurt, and drinks (Tue-Fri 7:00-17:00, Sat-Sun until 14:00, closed Mon, top of Vestergade).

Ice Cream: The ice-cream shop at Café Aroma, **Aroma Is,** serves good, flavorful ice cream—try gooseberry beer (made from Ærø stout—way better than it sounds), or the local favorite, the Ærø Special—walnut ice cream with maple syrup (daily mid-April-Aug 9:00-23:00, closed Sept-mid-April, just up from the ferry dock).

Ærøskøbing Connections

ÆRØ-SVENDBORG FERRY
The ferry ride between **Svendborg,** with connections to Copen-hagen, and **Ærøskøbing,** on the island of Ærø, is a relaxing 1.25-hour crossing. The ferry typically has plenty of room for foot pas-sengers (pay on board), but especially in July pre-booking up to one hour ahead is suggested. American credit cards with a chip work (2.50-DKK surcharge), or you can pay cash (230 DKK round-trip/person, 502 DKK round-trip/car—not including driver/passen-gers, ferry not covered by or discounted with rail pass, significant off-season discounts). You can leave the island via any of the three different Ærø ferry routes.

Drivers should reserve a spot in advance, especially on week-ends and in summer. During these busy times, reserve online at least a week in advance, if not sooner. You'll need to provide a li-cense-plate number—if you don't know it at the time you reserve, use a phone number temporarily and replace it with the license info up to one hour before boarding (see ferry website for details). Ferries depart daily in summer (roughly 10/day in each direction). Call or look online for the schedule (office open Mon-Fri 8:00-15:30, Sat-Sun 9:00-15:00, +45 62 52 40 00, www.aeroe-ferry.dk, info@aeroe-ferry.dk).

Drivers with reservations just drive on (be sure to get into the *med* reservations line). If you won't use your car in Ærø, park it in Svendborg (big, safe lot two blocks in from ferry landing, or at the far end of the harbor near the Bendix fish shop). On Ærø, parking is free.

Trains Connecting with Ærø-Svendborg Ferry

The train from **Odense** dead-ends at the Svendborg harbor (2/hour Mon-Sat, hourly on Sun, 45 minutes; don't get off at Svendborg Vest Station—wait until you get to the end of the line, called simply "Svendborg").

Arriving in Svendborg: It takes about 10 minutes to walk from the station to the dock (5 minutes if you walk briskly). Don't dawdle—the boat leaves stubbornly on time, even if trains are running late. I recommend taking a train from Odense that arrives about 30 minutes before your ferry departure to give yourself time to absorb delays and find your way. If you're cutting it close, be ready to hop off the train and walk swiftly.

To get from the Svendborg train station to the dock, turn left after exiting the train, following the sidewalk between the tracks and the station, then take a left (across the tracks) at the first street, Brogade. Head a block downhill to the harbor, make a right, and the ferry dock is ahead, across from Hotel Ærø. If you arrive early, you can head to the waiting room in the little blue building across the street from the hotel. There are several carry-out restaurants along Brogade, and a few hotels overlooking the ferry line have restaurants.

Departing from Svendborg: All Svendborg trains go to Odense (where you can connect to Copenhagen or Aarhus). A train tends to leave shortly after the ferry arrives (a tight connection—it's a good idea to buy your train ticket in advance instead of making a mad rush to use the one ticket machine at the station; the ferry office in Ærøskøbing also sells train tickets). To reach the train from the Svendborg ferry dock, pass Hotel Ærø and continue a block along the waiting lane for the ferry, turn left and go up Brogade one block, then take a right and follow the sidewalk between the tracks and the train station. Look for a train signed *Odense* waiting on the single track.

Odense

Founded in AD 988 and named after Odin (the Nordic Zeus), Odense is the main city of the big island of Funen (Fyn in Danish) and the birthplace of storyteller Hans Christian Andersen (whom the Danes call simply H. C., pronounced "hoe see"; for more on the author, see the Copenhagen chapter). Although the author was born here in poverty and left at the tender age of 14 to pursue a career in the theater scene of Copenhagen, H. C. is Odense's favorite son—you'll find his name and image all over town. He once said, "Perhaps Odense will one day become famous because of me." Today, Odense (OH-then-za) is one of Denmark's most popular tourist destinations.

Orientation to Odense

As Denmark's third-largest city, with 179,000 people, Odense is big and industrial. But its old center, tidy and neatly urbanized, re-

tains some pockets of the fairy-tale charm it had in the days of H. C. Everything is within easy walking distance, except for the open-air folk museum.

The train station sits at the north end of the town center. A few blocks south runs the main pedestrian shopping boulevard, Vestergade. Near the eastern end of this drag, and a couple of blocks up, is a tight tangle of atmospheric old lanes, where you'll find the Hans Christian Andersen Museum and Møntergården, Odense's urban history museum.

TOURIST INFORMATION

There's no permanent TI office but look for the summer mobile kiosk in front of the Town Hall (Rådhuset), the big brick palace overlooking the square at the east end of the Vestergade pedestrian street (+45 63 75 75

Odense

DANISH RAILWAY MUSEUM

THOMAS THRIGES GADE

200 Meters
200 Yards

TRAIN STATION

OLD TRAIN STN.

6 BANEGÅRD CENTER **4**

ØSTRE STATIONSVEJ

VESTRE STATIONSVEJ

JERNBANEGADE

Kongens Have

NØRREGADE

2

HANS TAUSENS GADE

3

ODENSE CASTLE

VINDEGADE

SLOTSGADE

KLOSTERVEJ

KONGENSGADE

HANS CHRISTIAN ANDERSEN BIRTH HOUSE

Fisketorvet

BANGS BODER

OVERGADE

CLAUS BERGS GADE

OVERSTRÆDE

HANS CHRISTIAN ANDERSEN MUSEUM **1**

MØNTERGÅRDEN MUSEUM & FYRTØJET

FREDERIKSGADE

9

8

VINTAPPERSTR.

GRÅBRØDRE PASSAGE

7

VESTERGADE

TOWN HALL

Skt. Knuds Plads

SKT. KNUD'S

To Route 9 (Svendborg & Ærø)

ALBANIGADE

BRANDTS KLÆDEFABRIK MALL

To **5**

VESTERGADE

HANS CHRISTIAN ANDERSEN'S CHILDHOOD HOME

KLOSTERBAKKEN

H.C. Andersen Have

Odense Å

FILOSOFGANGEN

Munkemose

JAGTVEJ

To Funen Village & E-20 Motorway (Copenhagen & Aarhus)

Accommodations
1 Comwell H.C. Andersen Hotel
2 Milling Hotel Mini 19
3 Milling Hotel Mini 11
4 Cabinn Odense
5 To Blommenslyst B&B
6 Danhostel Odense City

Restaurant Streets
7 Vestergade
8 Kongensgade
9 Vintapperstræde

CENTRAL DENMARK

20, www.visitodense.com, otb@visitodense.com). For all the information needed for a longer stop, pick up their excellent and free *Odense* guide.

ARRIVAL IN ODENSE

The train station is located in the Bånegard Center, a large shopping complex, which also holds the bus station, library, shops, eateries, and a movie theater. For a quick visit, check your luggage at the train station (pay lockers in corridor next to DSB Resjebureau office), pick up a free town map inside the ticket office, jot down the time your train departs, and hit the town (follow signs to *Odense Centrum*).

To get to the **Town Hall** (and mobile TI), turn right out of the station, cross the busy road, then cut through the Kongens Have (King's Garden) park and head down Jernabanegade. When you come to Vestergade, take a left and follow this fine pedestrian street 100 yards to the Town Hall.

Sights in Odense

A 145-DKK combo-ticket covers the Hans Christian Andersen Museum, Andersen's birthplace, his childhood home, the Fyrtøjet (Tinderbox Cultural Center for Children), and the Møntergården Museum (these sights are free for kids under 18). Get an early start if you plan to visit all five sites, as the ticket is valid for just one day. The Danish Railway Museum and Funen Village Open-Air Museum require separate tickets. Note that the Hans Christian Andersen Museum expects to move to a new location near the Fyrtøjet in 2021—inquire locally for the latest.

▲▲▲Hans Christian Andersen Museum

This centerpiece museum displays thousands of original objects illuminating Andersen's art and life, from his iconic hat to his delightful paper cut-out illustrations. The nearby home where Andersen was born and the writer's childhood home, a few blocks away at Munkemøllestrœde 3, round out the picture; both are furnished in typical Danish style.

Cost and Hours: Covered by 145-DKK combo-ticket (described above), daily 10:00-16:00, July-late-Aug until 17:00; Claus Bergs Gade 11 (next to the recommended Comwell H. C. Andersen Hotel), +45 65 51 46 01, www.hcandersensodense.dk.

Børnekulturhuset Fyrtøjet (Tinderbox Cultural Center for Children)

This fun hands-on center for children creates a fairy-tale land with giant props and sets inspired by Hans Christian Andersen's stories. Kids can dress up in costumes and get their faces painted at the "magical wardrobe," act out a fairy tale, and do arts and crafts in the "atelier." Ask about performances (generally daily at 12:00 and 14:00; some are in Danish only, but others are done without dialogue).

Cost and Hours: Covered by 145-DKK combo-ticket (described earlier), free for kids under 18; July-mid-Aug daily 10:00-

17:00; shorter hours and closed Mon-Thu off-season; at the Møntergården Museum in the Nyborgladen building, Møntestræde 1, +45 65 51 46 01, www.hcandersensodense.dk.

▲Møntergården (Urban History Museum)

This well-presented museum fills several medieval buildings with exhibits on the history of Odense. You'll time-travel from prehistoric times (lots of arrow, spear, and ax heads) through to 1660, when the king stripped the town of its independent status. The main exhibit, "Life of the City," fills a stately 17th-century, red house (Falk Gøyes Gård) with a high-tech, well-presented exhibit about Odense in medieval and Renaissance times, covering historical events as well as glimpses of everyday life. Wedged along the side of this building is a surviving medieval lane; at the far end are four minuscule houses that the city used to house widows and orphaned students who couldn't afford to provide for themselves. It's fascinating to squeeze into these humble interiors and imagine that people lived in these almshouses through 1955 (open only in summer, but at other times you can ask at the ticket desk to have them unlocked).

Cost and Hours: Covered by 145-DKK combo-ticket (described earlier), free for kids under 18; daily 10:00-17:00, Sept-May Tue-Sun 10:00-16:00, closed Mon; Møntestræde 1, +45 65 51 46 01, www.hcandersensodense.dk.

▲Danish Railway Museum (Danmarks Jernbanemuseum)

Conveniently (and appropriately) located directly behind the train station, this is an ideal place to kill time while waiting for a train—and is worth a look for anyone who enjoys seeing old locomotives and train cars. Here at Denmark's biggest (and only official) rail museum, the huge roundhouse is filled with classic trains, while upstairs you'll walk past long display cases of model

trains and enjoy good views down onto the trains. The information is in English, picnicking is encouraged, and there are lots of children's activities.

Cost and Hours: 80 DKK, more during special exhibits, daily 10:00-16:00; Dannebrogsgade 24—just exit behind the station near track 7/8 and cross the street; +45 66 13 66 30, www.jernbanemuseet.dk.

CENTRAL DENMARK

▲Funen Village Open-Air Museum (Den Fynske Landsby)

The sleepy gathering of 26 old buildings located about two miles out of town preserves the 17th- to 19th-century culture of this region. During the summer, you'll meet people dressed in period costumes who recount what life was like in 19th-century Funen as they perform their daily chores. Dozens of farm animals also bring to life the sounds—and smells—of the era. Families can enjoy tales of Hans Christian Andersen performed on an outdoor stage (mid-July-mid-Aug). Explanations in the buildings are sparse, so buy the guidebook to help make your visit meaningful.

Cost and Hours: 145 DKK, free for kids under 18; July-Aug daily 10:00-18:00 except closes at 17:00 last half of Aug; April-June and Sept-late Oct Tue-Sun 10:00-16:00 or 17:00, closed Mon; closed late Oct-March; bus #110 or #111 from Odense Station, or take train to Fruens Bøge Station and walk 15 minutes; +45 65 51 46 01, www.museum.odense.dk.

Sleeping in Odense

Demand (and prices) are higher in Odense on weekdays and in winter; in summer and on weekends, you can often get a better deal.

$$$ Comwell H. C. Andersen Hotel is big, comfortable, and impersonal, with 145 rooms near the Hans Christian Andersen sights. It's older but nicely updated (elevator, Claus Bergs Gade 7, +45 70 27 42 74, www.comwell.com, booking@comwell.com).

$$ Milling Hotel Mini 19 has 35 tidy, basic, stylish little rooms along its tiny halls. It's located on a quiet side street just a few minutes from the train station and features extra soundproofing (elevator, limited pay parking, Hans Tausensgade 19, +45 66 12 14 27, www.millinghotels.dk, mini19@millinghotels.dk). They also run **$ Milling Hotel Mini 11,** just down the street, with industrial simplicity.

$ Cabinn Odense brings its no-frills minimalist economy to town, with 201 simple, comfy, and modern rooms (breakfast extra, elevator, pay parking for small cars only, next to the station at Østre Stationsvej 7, +45 63 14 57 00, www.cabinn.com, odense@cabinn.com). For more about this chain, see page 108.

$ Blommenslyst B&B rents four rooms in two private guesthouses just outside Odense (breakfast extra, 10-minute drive from town center, Ravnebjerggyden 31, +45 65 96 81 88, www.blommenslyst.dk, ingvartsen-speth@post.tele.dk, Marethe and Poul Erik Speth).

Hostel: ¢ Danhostel Odense City is a huge, efficient hostel towering above the train station (private rooms available, elevator, reception open 8:00-12:00 & 16:00-20:00 but self-service check-in

kiosk at other times, Østre Stationsvej 31, +45 63 11 04 25, http://
odensedanhostel.dk, odensecity@danhostel.dk).

Eating in Odense

Odense's main pedestrian shopping streets, **Vestergade** and **Kongensgade,** offer the best atmosphere and most options for lunch
and dinner.

Vintapperstræde is an alleyway full of restaurants just off
Vestergade (look for the ornamental entryway). Choose from Danish, Mexican, Italian, and more. Study the menus posted outside
each restaurant to decide, then grab a table inside or join the locals
at an outdoor table.

Odense Connections

From Odense by Train to: Copenhagen (3/hour, 1.5 hours, some
go directly to the airport), **Aarhus** (2/hour, 1.5 hours), **Billund/
Legoland** (2/hour, 1-hour train to Vejle, then transfer to bus—
see page 196; allow 2 hours total), **Svendborg/Ærø ferry** (2/hour
Mon-Sat, hourly Sun, 45 minutes, to Svendborg dock; Ærø ferry—
roughly 10/day, 1.25 hours), **Roskilde** (2/hour, 1.25 hours).

CENTRAL DENMARK

JUTLAND

Jylland

Jutland (Jylland—pronounced "YEW-lan"—in Danish) is the part of Denmark that juts up from Germany. It's a land of windswept sandy beaches, inviting lakes, Lego toys, moated manor houses, and fortified old towns. In Aarhus, the lively and student-filled capital of Jutland, you can ogle the artwork in one of Denmark's best art museums, experience centuries-old Danish town life in its open-air folk museum, and meet a boggy prehistoric man. After you wander the pedestrian street, settle in for a drink along the canalside people zone. This is a particularly family-friendly region. Make a pilgrimage to the most famous land in all of Jutland: the pint-sized kids' paradise, Legoland. The nearby village of Jelling is worth a quick stop to see the ancient rune stones known as "Denmark's birth certificate."

PLANNING YOUR TIME

Aarhus makes a natural stop for drivers connecting to Norway by ferry (from Hirtshals to Kristiansand, or Frederikshavn to Oslo). Trains also link Aarhus to Hirtshals, as well as to points south, such as Odense and Copenhagen. Allow one day and an overnight to enjoy this busy port town.

Families will likely want a whole day at Legoland (near the town of Billund), while historians might consider a brief detour to Jelling, just 10 minutes off the main Billund-Vejle road. Both are best by car but doable by public transit.

Aarhus

Aarhus (OAR-hoos, sometimes spelled Århus), Denmark's second-largest city, has a population of 277,000 and calls itself the "World's Smallest Big City." I'd argue it's more like the world's biggest little town: easy to handle and easy to like. Aarhus is Jutland's capital and cultural hub. Its Viking founders settled here—where a river hit the sea—in the eighth century, calling their town Aros. Today, modern Aarhus bustles with an important university, an inviting café-lined canal, a bursting-with-life pedestrian zone (the Strøget), a collection of top-notch museums (modern art, open-air folk, and prehistory/ethnography), and an adorable Latin Quarter filled with people living very, very well. Aarhus, a pleasant three-hour train ride from Copenhagen, is well worth a stop.

Orientation to Aarhus

Aarhus lines up along a tranquil canal that runs through the middle of town down to the harbor. Canalside Åboulevarden street is lined with charming shops and eateries. The cathedral and lively Latin Quarter are directly north of the canal, while the train station is about five blocks to the south. Stretching between the cathedral and the station is a series of linked pedestrianized shopping streets called the Strøget. The main museums are scattered far and wide: The ARoS art museum is at the western edge of downtown, the Den Gamle By open-air folk museum is a bit farther to the northwest, and the Moesgård Museum (prehistory and ethnography) is in the countryside far to the south.

TOURIST INFORMATION

The Aarhus TI is in Dokk1, a library/cultural center at the Aarhus harbor (generally Mon-Thu 10:00-19:00, Fri until 17:00, Sat-Sun until 16:00, +45 87 31 50 10, www.visitaarhus.com). There are automated info screens all around town, and in summer you'll find a mobile TI branch on the main square.

ARRIVAL IN AARHUS

By Train: At Aarhus' user-friendly train station, all tracks feed into a concourse, with ticket offices (*billetsalg;* open Mon-Fri 8:00-17:00, Sat-Sun 10:00-16:45) and a waiting room between tracks 2-3 and 4-5. A side entrance (marked *Bruun's Galleri*) takes you directly into a shopping mall; the other entrance (under the clock) leads into the blocky main terminal hall, with pay lockers, fast food, and ticket machines. Near the main doors, screens show departure times for upcoming city and regional buses.

To get into town, it's a pleasant 10-minute **walk:** Exit straight ahead, cross the street, and proceed up the wide, traffic-free shopping street (Ryesgade), which takes you directly to the canal, cathedral, and start of my Aarhus Walk.

The Letbanen **light-rail/tram** links the train station to the TI (stop: Dokk 1) and cathedral (stop: Skolebakken) in minutes but runs only twice an hour; see "Getting Around Aarhus," next.

By Car or Cruise Ship: See "Aarhus Connections," later.

GETTING AROUND AARHUS

On Foot: The sights mentioned in my self-guided walk and the ARoS art museum are all within a 15-minute walk; the Den Gamle By open-air folk museum is a few minutes farther, but still walkable (or can be reached by bus—see next).

By Bus: The Moesgård Museum and Tivoli Friheden amusement park are best reached by bus #18. It leaves from in front of the blocky Town Hall, about two blocks from the train station on Park Allé.

Bus #3A to the Den Gamle By open-air folk museum leaves from a stop across the street from the train station and makes a few other stops in the city center.

Buy tickets from machines on board (a 22-DKK, 2-zone ticket covers any of my recommended sights and is good for 2 hours). To find your bus stop, look for the handy diagram at the start of the Strøget or use the route planner at www.midttrafik.dk.

By Tram: The Letbanen light-rail/tram serves the train station and redeveloped harbor area—where the Skolebakken stop drops you close to the cathedral and the start of my walk (2/hour, buy 22-DKK ticket at machine at stop before boarding, ticket good on buses too). The tram is otherwise of little use to tourists.

By Taxi: Taxis are easy to flag down but pricey (45-DKK drop fee).

HELPFUL HINTS

Sightseeing Tips: The **Aarhus Card** provides free entry to my recommended museums, free standard entry (rides extra) to the Tivoli Friheden amusement park, and free public transportation by bus or light-rail/tram. This can be a good value for busy sightseers (329 DKK/24 hours, 449 DKK/48 hours, purchase at hotels, the Dokk1 TI, or at www.visitaarhus.com).

The **Moesgård Museum** may require advance reservations for a specific entry day and time; confirm on the museum website.

Festival: The 10-day **Aarhus Festival,** which takes place in late summer (Aug-Sept), fills the city's streets and venues with music, dance, food, and kids' activities (www.aarhusfestuge.dk).

Laundry: An unstaffed, coin-op launderette *(mønt-vask)* is four short blocks south of the train station, on the square in front of St. Paul's Church (daily 7:00-21:00, M.P. Bruunsgade 64).

JUTLAND

JUTLAND

Aarhus Center

Self-Guided Walk
1. Aarhus Cathedral
2. Cathedral Square
3. Hotel Royal
4. Viking Museum
5. Aarhus Theater
6. Church of Our Lady
7. Møllestien
8. Canal & Åboulevarden

Accommodations
9. Villa Provence
10. The Mayor Hotel
11. Hotel Guldsmeden
12. Milling Hotel Ritz
13. Cabinn
14. To Danhostel Aarhus
15. City Sleep-In

Eateries & Other
16. Lecoq
17. Den Rustikke
18. Pilhkjær
19. Carlton Brasserie
20. Sota
21. Canal Eateries
22. A Hereford Beefstouw
23. Teater Bodega
24. To Launderette

To Aarhus University

Østbanetorvet

To 14

To Ferry to Sjællands Odde

NØRREPORT

SJÆLLANDSGADE

THUNØGADE

NØRREGADE

NØRRE ALLE

NØRRE ALLE

NØRGADE

PARADISGADE

STUDSGADE

MEJLGADE

KYSTVEJEN

B. JENSENS BLVD

NAVITAS BLD.

11

SMEDEGADE

BORGGADE

KLOSTERGADE

LATIN

GULD

BADSTUEGADE

GRAVEN

16

18

CHURCH OF OUR LADY

B #3A & 18

Klostertorvet

6

VESTERGADE

Lille Torv

Pustervig Torv

19

ROSENSGADE

QUARTER

17

WALK BEGINS

OCCUPATION MUSEUM

Bassin 2

Store Torv

3

2 1

CATHEDRAL

Havnepladsen

IMMERVAD

SKT. CLEMENS STR.

4

Bispe-torvet

Skolebakken

Harbor

ABOULEVARDEN

21

8

WALK ENDS

#3A & 18

B

Telefon-torvet

Skt. Clemens Torv

KANNIKEGADE

22

5

THEATER

23

SKOLE-GYDE

SKOLEBAKKEN

13

POST

BUSGADEN

"THE STRØGET"

GADE

ABOULEVARDEN

Canal

FISKERGADE

15

HAVNEGADE

Bassin 1

SEDORFS STRÆDE

SALLING DEP'T STORE

SØNDER-

ØSTERGADE

Fredens-torv

9

AMALIEGADE

FREDENSGADE

RIDDER-STRÆDE

Dokk 1

DOKK1

RYESGADE

SØNDER ALLE

EUROPAPLADS

TOLDBODGADE

MINDEGADE

MINDET

BUS STATION

NY BANEGÅRDSGADE

SPANIEN

SYDHAVNSGADE

Bassin 3

N

200 Meters

200 Yards

TRAIN STATION

To Moesgård Museum & Tivoli Friheden

JUTLAND

Aarhus Walk

This quick little self-guided walk acquaints you with the historic center. You'll begin at the cathedral, check out the modest sights in its vicinity, wander the cute Latin Quarter, take a stroll down the "most beautiful street" in Aarhus, and end at the canal (to trace this route, see the "Aarhus Center" map). After touring the impressive cathedral, the rest of the walk should take about an hour. The three big museums (modern art, prehistory, and open-air folk) are covered later, under "Sights in Aarhus."

• *Start by touring Aarhus Cathedral.*

❶ Aarhus Cathedral (Domkirke)

While Scandinavia's biggest church (330 feet long and tall and worth ▲▲) is typically stark-white inside, it also comes with some vivid decorations dating from before the Reformation.

Cost and Hours: Free entry; Mon-Sat 9:30-16:00, Oct-April 10:00-15:00, closed Sun except for services at 10:00 and 17:00; www.aarhusdomkirke.dk.

Visiting the Cathedral: The cathedral was finished in 1520 in all its Catholic glory. Imagine it with 55 side chapels, each dedicated to a different saint and wallpapered with colorful frescoes. Bad timing. Just 16 years later, in 1536, the Reformation hit this region and Protestants cleaned out the church—side altars gone, paintings whitewashed over—and added a pulpit in the middle of the nave so parishioners could hear the sermon. The front pews were even turned away from the altar to face the pulpit (a problem for weddings today).

Ironically, that Lutheran whitewash protected the fine 16th-century Catholic art. When it was peeled back in the 1920s, the frescoes were found perfectly preserved. In 1998, the surrounding whitewash was redone, making the old original paintings, which have never been restored, pop. Noble tombs that once lined the floor (worn smooth by years of traffic) now decorate the walls. The fancy text-filled wall medallions are

epitaphs, originally paired with tombs. Ships hang from the ceilings of many Danish churches (you'll find a fine example in the left transept)—in this nation of seafarers, there were invariably women praying for the safe return of their sailors.

Step into the enclosed choir area at the front of the church. The main altarpiece, dating from 1479, features the 12 apostles flanking St. Clement (the patron saint of Aarhus and sailors—his symbol is the anchor), St. Anne, and John the Baptist. On top, Jesus is crowning Mary in heaven.

Head down the stairs to the apse area behind the altar. Find the model of the altarpiece, which demonstrates how the polyptych (many-paneled altarpiece) you just saw can be flipped to different scenes throughout the church year.

Also in this area, look for the fresco in the aisle (right of altar, facing windows) that shows a three-part universe: heaven, earth (at Mass), and—under the thick black line—purgatory...an ugly land with angels and devils fighting over souls. The kid on the gallows illustrates how the medieval Church threatened even little children with ugly damnation. Notice the angels trying desperately to save the damned. Just a little more money to the Church and...I...think...we...can...pull...Grandpa... OUT.

An earlier Romanesque church—just as huge—once stood on this spot. As you exit, notice the tiny, pointy-topped window in the back-right. It survives with its circa-1320 fresco from that earlier church. Even back then—when the city had a population of 1,000—the church seated 1,200. Imagine the entire community (and their dogs) assembled here to pray and worship their way through the darkness and uncertainty of medieval life.

• *On your way out, pause at the cathedral door to survey the main square.*

❷ Cathedral Square (Domkirkeplads)

The long, triangular square is roughly the shape of the original Viking town from AD 770. Aarhus is the Viking word for "mouth of river." The Aarhus River (now contained in the canal) flows to your left to the beach, which—before modern land reclamation—was just behind the church. The green spire peeking over the buildings dead ahead is the Church of Our Lady (which we'll visit later on this walk). Fifty yards to the right, nubile caryatids by local artist Hans Krull decorate the entry to the ❸ **Hotel Royal** and town casino. (Krull's wildly decorated bar is just beyond, down the stairs at the corner.) Also nearby (around the corner from the cathedral) is the fine **Occupation Museum 1940-1945,** about the Danish resistance during World War II (described later, under "Sights in Aarhus").

• *Fifty yards to the left of the church (as you face the square), in the basement of the Nordea Bank, is the tiny...*

❹ Viking Museum (Vikingemuseet)

When excavating the site for the bank building in 1960, remains of Viking Aarhus were uncovered. Today you can ride an escalator down to the little bank-sponsored museum showing a surviving bit of the town's original boardwalk in situ (where it was found), Viking artifacts, and a murder victim (missing his head)—all well described in English (30 DKK, open Mon-Fri 10:15-18:00, Sat-Sun until 17:00).

• *Leaving the bank, walk straight ahead along the substantial length of the cathedral (brides have plenty of time to reconsider things during their procession) to the fancy building opposite.*

❺ Aarhus Theater (Aarhus Teater)

This ornate facade, with its flowery stained glass, is Danish Art Nouveau from around 1900. Under the tiny balcony is the town seal, featuring towers, the river, St. Clement with his anchor, and St. Paul with his sword. High above, on the roofline, crouches the devil. The local bishop made a stink when this "house of sin" was built facing the cathedral. The theater builders had the last say, finishing their structure

with this smart-aleck devil triumphing (a hit with the secular, modern locals).

• *Return to the square in front of the cathedral.*

Latin Quarter

The higgledy-piggledy old town encompasses the six or eight square blocks in front of the cathedral and to the right. Latin was never spoken here—the area was named in the 1960s after the cute, boutique-ish, and similarly touristy zone in Paris. Though Aarhus' canal strip is a newer trendy spot, the Latin Quarter is still great for shopping, cafés, and strolling. Explore these streets: Volden (named for the rampart), Graven (moat), and Badstuegade ("Bath Street"). In the days when fires routinely decimated towns, bathhouses—with their open fires necessary to heat the water—were located outside the walls. Back in the 15th century, finer people bathed monthly, while everyday

riff-raff took their "Christmas bath" once a year.

• *At the far end of the square, side-trip away from the cathedral to the green spire of the...*

❻ Church of Our Lady (Vor Frue Kirke)

The smart brick building you see today is in the Dutch Renaissance style from the early 16th century, but this local "Notre-Dame" is the oldest church in town (free; Mon-Fri 10:00-16:00, Sat until 14:00, closed Sun; www.aarhusvorfrue.dk). After Christianity came to Viking Denmark in 965, a tiny wooden church was built here. Step down into the crypt of today's church (below the main altar). This evocative arcaded space (c. 1060) was originally an 11th-century stone rebuild of the first church (and only discovered in 1955). Four rune stones were also discovered on this site.

Back upstairs, find the graphic crucifix, with its tangled thieves flanking Christ, which was carved and painted by a Lübeck artist in 1530. As at Aarhus Cathedral, the church's whitewashed walls are covered with fine epitaph medallions with family portraits. Step through the low door behind the rear pew (on the right with your back to the altar) into the peaceful cloister. With the Reformation, this became a hospital. Today, it's a retirement home for lucky seniors.

• *Walk west on Vestergade to the next street, Grønnegade. Turn left, then take the next right onto...*

❼ Møllestien

Locals call this quiet little cobbled lane the "most beautiful street in Aarhus." The small, pastel cottages—draped in climbing roses and hollyhock in summer—date from the 18th century. Notice the small mirrors on one of the windows. Known as "street spies," they allow people inside to inconspicuously watch what's going on outside.

• *At the end of the lane, veer left through the park (good place to picnic) toward the canal. The big, boxy building ahead of you with the rainbow ring on top is the **ARoS** art museum—consider visiting it now, or backtrack when the walk is over.*

When you reach the canal, turn left and walk about four blocks along Åboulevarden toward the cathedral spire until you get to the concrete pedestrian bridge.

❽ Canal and Åboulevarden

You're standing on the site of the original Viking bridge. The open sea was dead ahead. A protective harbor was behind you. When the town was attacked, the bridge on this spot was raised, ships were tucked safely away, and townsmen stood here to defend their fleet. Given the choice, they'd let the town burn and save their ships.

In the 1930s, the Aarhus River was covered over to make a new road—an event marked by much celebration. In the 1980s, locals reconsidered, deciding that the road cut a boring, people-mean swath through the center of their town. They removed the road, artfully canalized the river, and created a new people zone called Åboulevarden —the town's place to see and be seen. This strip of modern restaurants ensures the street stays as lively as possible even after the short summer.

• *Your walk is over. Retreating back up the canal takes you to the **ARoS** art museum, then to the **Den Gamle By** open-air folk museum. Following the canal ahead takes you past the best of the Åboulevarden canal zone that leads all the way to the harbor.*

Crossing the canal bridge and going straight (with a one-block jog left through Telefontorvet) gets you to Skt. Clemens Torv and the Strøget pedestrian area, which leads past the rooftop-view Salling department store to the train station (where you can catch a bus—either at the station or the Town Hall nearby—to Tivoli Friheden amusement park, the Den Gamle By open-air folk museum, or the Moesgård Museum).

Sights in Aarhus

I've organized these sights by distance from the center, starting with the Occupation Museum (near the cathedral) and ending with the suburban Moesgård Museum. The Aarhus Card provides free entry to these sights (see "Helpful Hints," earlier).

Occupation Museum 1940-1945 (Besættelsesmuseet)

Nazi occupiers used Aarhus' police station as their Gestapo head-quarters throughout World War II. It was the scene of tortures and executions. Today, it's a fine exhibit telling the story of the resistance and what it was like to live here under Nazi rule. You'll learn of heroic acts of sabotage, find out how guns were dropped out of British airplanes in the night, and see underground newspapers that kept occupied Danes connected and in the know (exhibit in Danish; loaner English info sheets available).

Cost and Hours: 75 DKK; Tue-Sun 11:00-17:00, closed Mon; Oct-May Wed-Sun 13:00-17:00, closed Mon-Tue; facing the cathedral, it's around to the left at Mathilde Fibigers Have 2; +45 86 18 42 77, www.besaettelsesmuseet.dk.

Salling Department Store Rooftop

Take the elevator to the store's top floor, where a modern terrace with a stunning 360-degree view over the city awaits. You'll find

locals and tourists alike enjoying a terraced seating area, an enclosed bar and café, and (for the daring) the Skywalk platform that cantilevers over the street. Venture out to the end where a glass window in the floor lets you view tiny pedestrians 80 feet below.

Cost and Hours: Free, Mon-Fri 10:00-20:00, Sat until 19:00, Sun until 18:00, Søndergade 27, +45 87 78 60 00, www.salling.dk.

▲▲ARoS Art Museum (ARoS Kunstmuseum)

ARoS is a must-see, both for the building's architecture and for its fun, accessible presentation of cutting-edge art. Square and unas-

suming from the outside, the bright white interior—with its spiral staircase winding up the museum's eight floors—is surprising. The building is divided by a vast atrium, which is free to enter if you just want to take a peek (or visit the gift shop or café). But you'll need a ticket to see the permanent collections described below as well as an impressive range of temporary exhibits.

Cost and Hours: 150 DKK; Mon-Fri 10:00-21:00, Sat-Sun until 17:00, ARoS Allé 2; +45 87 30 66 00, www.aros.dk.

Cuisine Art: The $$ lunch café on the museum's ground floor serves light meals, while the **$$$** wine and food hall on the top floor features regional specialties from local producers.

Visiting the Museum: After entering at the fourth-floor lobby, buy your ticket, pick up a museum floor plan, and walk two floors

down the spiral staircase (to floor 2) to find one of the museum's prized pieces: the squatting sculpture called *Boy* (by Australian artist Ron Mueck)—15 feet high, yet astonishingly realistic, from the wrinkly skin on his elbows to the stitching on his shorts.

Continue down to the lowest level (0). The rooms here are designated for art installations—immersive works of space, light, video, and sound that plunge the viewer into the imaginations of a roster of international artists (including Tony Oursler, Elmgreen & Dragset, and James Turrell).

Now ride the elevator all the way to the top floor (floor 8), then climb up the stairs (or ride a different elevator) to the rooftop. Here

you can experience the museum's iconic *Your Rainbow Panorama,* a 150-yard-long, 52-yard-diameter circular glass walkway in every hue of the color spectrum (by Icelandic artist Olafur Eliasson). You'll stroll through the floor-to-ceiling piece while enjoying rainbow-colored, 360-degree views over the entire city. (It's "your" panorama because you are experiencing the colors.)

For a complete change of pace, back on floor 8, examine a manageable selection of works from the museum's permanent collection. Here, paintings from the **Danish Golden Age** through the **Danish Modernist** era are arranged according to the broad themes of nature, religion, philosophy, and science. You'll see pastoral scenes of the Danish countryside, seascapes, religious subjects, aristocratic portraits, squiggly abstractions, and expressionist landscapes.

Continue down the spiral staircase, past various temporary exhibits. On floor 5, take a spin through the **classic art gallery**, featuring temporary art and multimedia installations. Like the rest of this museum, these high-concept, navel-gazing works are well presented and very accessible.

▲▲Den Gamle By (The Old Town)

This open-air folk museum has 75 half-timbered houses and craft shops. Unlike other Scandinavian open-air museums that focus on rural folk life, Den Gamle By is designed to give you a look at Danish urban life in centuries past. A fine botanical garden is next door.

Cost and Hours: 150 DKK; daily 10:00-17:00; after hours, the buildings are locked, but the peaceful park is open; +45 86 12 31 88, www.dengamleby.dk.

Getting There: Stroll 20 minutes up the canal from downtown, or catch a bus from near the train station: Bus #3A departs directly across the street from the station.

Eating: Outdoor and indoor tables are scattered around the grounds, making this a perfect place to enjoy a picnic lunch. Bring your own or order a lunch packet one day ahead by phone (weekdays—+45 86 12 31 88, weekends—+45 41 85 09 56). The cheery indoor/outdoor **$$ Gæstgivergården** is an inviting cafeteria serving affordable light meals (open year-round). In peak season, additional options include *pølse* and snack stands, a bakery, a café next to the ticket kiosk, and another café in the 1970s neighborhood.

Visiting the Museum: At the ticket desk, pick up the free map of the grounds and the flier listing what's on. Throughout the park, plaques describe each building, but the available guide-booklet (small fee) is a worthwhile investment.

The grounds reward an adventurous spirit. They're designed to be explored, so don't be too shy to open doors or poke into seemingly abandoned courtyards—you may find a chatty docent inside, telling their story, answering questions, or demonstrating an oldtimey handicraft. Follow sounds and smells to discover a whole world beyond the main streets.

The main part of the exhibit focuses on the 18th and 19th centuries. You'll start by heading up Navnløs, then hanging a right at Vestergade (passing a row house and a flower garden with samples for sale) to the canal. Head straight over the bridge and hike up the cute street lined with market stalls, shops, and a bakery until you pop out on the main square (Torvet). The building on the left side of the square, the Mayor's House (from 1597), contains a museum upstairs featuring home interiors from 1600 to 1850, including many with gorgeously painted walls. At the top of the square is the Mintmaster's Mansion, the residence of a Copenhagen noble (from 1683). Enter around back to tour the boldly colorful, 18th-century Baroque rooms. Under the heavy timbers of the attic is an exhibit about the history of this restored building.

Continuing out the far end of the square on Søndergade, you enter the 20th century. The streets and shops here evoke the year 1927, including a hardware store and (down Havbogade) a brewery where you can often buy samples (in the courtyard behind). At the end of Søndergade (on the left) is the Legetoj toy museum, with two floors of long hallways crammed with nostalgic playthings.

Walking into the next zone, you come to a street scene from 1974, with re-created apartments, a radio and TV repair shop, a hairdresser, a gynecology clinic, and a jazz bar where you can order a beer or pastry. In the Udstillinger building, you'll find the Danish Poster Museum (a delightful collection of retro posters) and the Gallery of Decorative Arts (porcelain, clocks, and silverware).

▲▲Moesgård Museum

This museum, dedicated to prehistory and ethnography, is housed in a state-of-the art venue south of Aarhus in the suburb of Højbjerg. The building juts dramatically from a hill, with grass growing on a sloping roof that visitors can walk on.

Cost and Hours: 160 DKK; may require a timed-entry slot booked online in advance—see website for details, Aarhus Card-holders can reserve as a "member"; open daily 9:00-17:00, Wed until 21:00; café, +45 87 16 10 16, www.moesmus.dk.

Getting There: The museum is located outside Aarhus at Moesgård Allé 15 in Højbjerg, in a lush, wooded park sprawling down to the sea. It's a pricey taxi trip or easy, cheap bus ride: Bus #18 leaves Aarhus from directly in front of the Town Hall on Park Allé (around the corner from the train station; 3-4/hour weekdays, 2/hour Sat-Sun, ride 20 minutes to end of line, covered by zone 2 bus ticket). Once at the museum, check what time the return bus departs (posted at the bus stop or ask at the ticket desk).

Visiting the Museum: Divided into three main periods—the Bronze Age (1800 to 500 BC), Iron Age (500 BC to AD 800), and Viking Age (AD 700 to 1050), the prehistory section features lots of real artifacts (primitive tools and pottery, plenty of spearheads and arrowheads), all well described in English, along with an impressive collection of rune stones.

The highlight is the well-preserved body of an Iron Age man. Believing that the gods dwelled in the bogs, prehistoric people threw offerings (such as spearheads) into the thick peat. The peat did a remarkable job of preserving these artifacts, many of which are now on display in the museum. The prehistoric people also sacrificed humans to the bog gods—resulting in the incredibly intact Grauballe Man, the world's best-preserved "bog-corpse." Reclining in his stately glass tomb, the more than 2,000-year-old bog man looks like a fellow half his age. He still has his skin, nails, hair, and even the slit in his throat he got at the sacrificial banquet (back in 300 BC). Spend some time with this visitor from the past. The story of his discovery (in a Jutland peat bog in 1952) and conservation is also interesting.

The Grounds: The museum sits on the pleasant grounds of the Moesgård Manor; while the manor itself is closed to the public, its grounds are fun to explore. Behind the museum, a two-mile-long circular trail stretches down to a fine beach. This "Prehistoric Trackway" runs past a few model Viking buildings, including a 12th-century stave church.

Tivoli Friheden Amusement Park
(Tivoli Friheden Forlystelsespark)

The local Tivoli, about a mile south of the Aarhus train station, offers great fun for the entire family.

Cost and Hours: 140 DKK for entry only, add 135 DKK to include rides; July-early Aug 11:30-20:00, longer hours in late July, weekends only and shorter hours most of June and Oct-Dec, closed Jan-May except for special events; bus #18 from Park Allé near Town Hall, +45 86 14 73 00, www.friheden.dk.

Sleeping in Aarhus

Aarhus has a good variety of lodgings. My recommendations range from charming hotels with personality to backpacker-friendly hostel bunks.

$$$$ Villa Provence, named for owners Steen and Annette's favorite vacation destination, is a *petit* taste of France in the center of Aarhus, and makes a very cozy and convenient home base. Its 40 fun-yet-tasteful rooms, decorated with antique furniture and old French movie posters, surround a quiet courtyard. The pub across the street can get noisy on weekends, so ask for a room facing away from the street (pay parking, 10-minute walk from station, near Åboulevarden at the end of Fredensgade, Fredens Torv 12, +45 86 18 24 00, www.villaprovence.dk, hotel@villaprovence.dk).

$$$$ The Mayor Hotel, affiliated with the Scandic chain, rents 162 sleek, well-furnished, business-class rooms 100 yards from the station (elevator, pay parking, Banegårdspladsen 14, +45 87 32 01 00, www.scandichotels.com, themayor@scandichotels.com).

$$$ Hotel Guldsmeden ("Dragonfly") is a small and welcoming hotel with 26 rooms, fluffy comforters, a delightful stay-awhile garden, and a disarmingly friendly staff. A steep staircase takes you to the best rooms, while the cheaper rooms (five rooms sharing two bathrooms) are in a ground-floor annex behind the garden (RS%, in quiet Latin Quarter at Guldsmedgade 40, +45 86 13 45 50, www.guldsmedenhotels.com, aarhus@guldsmedenhotels.com).

$$$ Milling Hotel Ritz, across the street from the station, offers 67 clean, bright rooms done in Art Deco style (elevator, Banegårdspladsen 12, +45 86 13 44 44, www.millinghotels.dk, ritz@millinghotels.dk.

$$ Cabinn, overlooking the atmospheric Åboulevarden and canal, is extremely practical. Rooms are minimalist yet comfy, and service is no-nonsense (family rooms, breakfast extra, pay parking—request when booking, rooms overlook boisterous canal or quieter courtyard, at Kannikegade 14 but main entrance on the canal at Åboulevarden 38, +45 86 75 70 00, www.cabinn.dk, aarhus@cabinn.dk). For more on this chain, see page 108.

¢ Danhostel Aarhus, an official HI hostel, is near the water two miles out of town (served by buses from the train station—see website for details; reception open daily 8:00-12:00 & 16:00-20:00, shorter hours off-season; Marienlundsvej 10, +45 86 21 21 20, www.aarhusdanhostel.dk, info@aarhusdanhostel.dk).

¢ City Sleep-In, a creative independent hostel, has a shared kitchen, fun living and games room, laundry service, and lockers. It's on a busy road facing the harbor (with thin windows—expect some street noise), a 15-minute hike from the station. It's pretty grungy, but is the only centrally located hostel option in town (breakfast extra, private rooms available, elevator, no curfew; reception open daily 8:00-11:00 & 16:00-22:00, Fri-Sat until 23:00; Havnegade 20, +45 86 19 20 55, www.citysleep-in.dk, sleep-in@citysleep-in.dk).

Eating in Aarhus

Affluent Aarhus has plenty of great little restaurants. My listings are in the old town, within a few minutes' stroll from the cathedral.

IN AND NEAR THE LATIN QUARTER

The streets of the Latin Quarter are teeming with hardworking and popular eateries. The street called Mejlgade, along the eastern edge of downtown, has a smattering of youthful, trendy restaurants that are just far enough off the tourist trail to feel local. Look for a variety of fixed-price, three-course dinners—some affordable, others a splurge.

$$$$ Lecoq chef/owner Troels Thomsen and his gang of alums from a prestigious Danish cooking school serve up a fresh twist on traditional French cuisine in an unassuming 10-table room. They pride themselves on their finely crafted presentation. Reservations are smart (daily 11:30-15:00 & 17:30-21:30, Graven 16, +45 86 19 50 74, www.cafe-lecoq.dk).

$$$$ Den Rustikke is a French-style brasserie offering mostly French dishes (including affordable fixed-price meals), either in the rollicking interior or outside, under a cozy colonnade (daily 11:30-15:00 & 17:00-21:30, Mejlgade 20, +45 86 12 00 95, www.denrustikke.dk).

$$$$ Pilhkjær is a bit more expensive and sedate, filling a cellar with elegantly casual atmosphere. The menu, which changes daily and can include fish, meat, or vegetarian offerings, is available only as a full-course meal—there's no à la carte option (Tue-Thu 17:30-22:30, Fri-Sat until 23:30, closed Sun-Mon; at the end of a long courtyard at Mejlgade 28, +45 86 18 23 30, www.pihlkjaer-restaurant.dk).

$$$ Carlton Brasserie, facing a pretty square, is a solid bet for good Danish and international food in classy (verging on stuffy) surroundings. The restaurant has tables on the square, with more formal seating in back (Mon-Thu 12:00-21:00, Fri-Sat until 22:00, closed Sun, Rosensgade 23, +45 86 20 21 22).

A few short blocks farther from the action (past the Church of Our Lady), **$$$ Sota** is a local favorite for sushi, to eat in or take away. This sleek, split-level, Tokyo-Scandinavian hybrid is in a half-timbered old house (Mon-Thu 16:00-22:00, Fri-Sat 12:00-

JUTLAND

23:00, closed Sun, reservations recommended, Vestergade 48, +45 86 47 47 88, www.sotasushibar.dk).

ALONG THE CANAL

The Åboulevarden canal zone is lined with trendy eateries—all overpriced unless you value making the scene with the locals (and all open daily until late). They have indoor and canalside seating with heaters and blankets, so diners can eat outdoors even when it's cold. Before settling in, cruise the entire strip, giving special consideration to **$$ Cross Café** (with red awnings, right at main bridge) and **$$ Ziggy,** both of which are popular for salads, sandwiches, burgers, and drinks; and **$$$ Grappa,** a classy Italian place with pastas and pizzas, as well as pricier plates. Several places along here serve basic breakfast buffets.

NEAR THE CATHEDRAL

These places, while a bit past their prime and touristy, are convenient and central.

$$$$ A Hereford Beefstouw, in the St. Clement's Brewery building facing the cathedral, is a bright, convivial, fun-loving, and woody land of happy eaters and drinkers. Choose from a hearty menu and eat amid shiny copper beer vats. If you're dropping by for a brew, they have enticing beer snacks and spicy little *ølpølse* sausages (hearty dinners such as steak, ribs, burgers, and fish; daily 17:30-23:00, Kannikegade 10, +45 86 13 53 25, www.beefstouw.com).

$$$ Teater Bodega is the venerable best bet for traditional Danish—where local men go for "food their wives won't cook." While a bit tired and old-fashioned for Aarhus' trendy young student population, it's a sentimental favorite for old-timers. Facing the theater and cathedral, it's dressy and draped in theater memorabilia (open-face sandwiches at lunch only, Mon-Sat 11:30-21:30, Sun 12:00-20:00, Skolegade 7, +45 86 12 19 17).

Aarhus Connections

BY PUBLIC TRANSPORTATION

From Aarhus by Train to: Odense (2/hour, 1.5 hours), **Copenhagen** (2/hour, 3 hours), **Ærøskøbing** (6-7/day, transfer to ferry in Svendborg, allow 5 hours total), **Billund/Legoland** (3/hour;

45-minute train to Vejle, then transfer to bus—described later), **Hamburg,** Germany (2 direct/day, more with transfers, 5 hours).

You can take the train from Aarhus to **Hirtshals,** where you can catch the **ferry to Norway** on the Color Line (www.colorline. com) or Fjordline (www.fjordline.com). Trains depart Aarhus hourly and take about 2.5 hours (to meet the Color Line ferry, transfer at Hjørring and continue to Hirtshals Havn; note that rail passes don't cover the Hjørring-Hirtshals train, but do give a 50 percent discount; buy your ticket in Hjørring or on board). Or take the same northbound train but change at Aalborg to reach **Frederikshavn** (2.5 hours) to catch the overnight DFDS ferry to **Oslo** (www.dfds.com) or 3.5-hour Stena ferry to Göteborg, **Sweden** (www.stenaline.nl). Reservations are smart for all ferries.

ROUTE TIPS FOR DRIVERS

Aarhus to Hirtshals or Fredrikshavn: It's about a two-hour drive to either ferry port. From Aarhus, head north on E-45 to Aalborg, then follow E-39 for Hirtshals or continue north on E-45 for Fredrikshavn.

Aarhus to Legoland and Jelling: From Aarhus, it's 60 miles to Billund/Legoland (go south on Skanderborg Road and get on E-45; follow signs to *Vejle, Kolding*). For **Jelling,** take the Vejle N exit and follow signs to *Vejle,* then veer right on the ring road (following signs to *Skovgade*), then follow highway 442 north. For **Legoland,** take the Vejle S exit for *Billund* (after Vejle N—it's the first exit after the dramatic Vejlefjord bridge).

Aarhus (or Legoland) to Ærø: Figure about 2.5 hours (or 2 hours from Legoland/Billund) to Svendborg and the ferry to Ærø—if you don't sightsee along the way. After heading south on E-45, take E-20 over the bridge to the island of Funen (Fyn in Danish); from Odense, take the highway south to Svendborg and the ferry dock. Cars need reservations but walk-on passengers usually don't. If you plan to bike (not drive) around Ærø, park your car in Svendborg (at the long-term lot two blocks from the dock or at the far end of the harbor near the Bendix fish shop). For ferry details, see page 168.

Legoland

Legoland is Scandinavia's top kids' sight. If you have a child (or are a child at heart), it's a fun stop. This huge park is a happy combination of rides, restaurants, trees, smiles, and 33 million Lego bricks creatively arranged into such wonders as Mount Rushmore, the Parthenon, "Mad" King Ludwig's castle, and the Statue of

Liberty. It's a Lego world here, as everything is cleverly related to this popular toy. If your time in Denmark is short, or if your family has already visited a similar Legoland park elsewhere, consider skipping the trip. But if you're in the neighborhood, a visit to the mothership of all things Lego will be a hit with kids ages two through the pre-teens.

GETTING THERE

Legoland, located in the town of Billund, is easiest to visit by car (see "Route Tips for Drivers," earlier), but doable by public transportation. The nearest train station to Billund is Vejle. Trains arrive at Vejle from **Copenhagen** (2/hour, 2.5 hours), **Odense** (2/hour, 1 hour), and **Aarhus** (3/hour, 45 minutes). At Vejle, catch bus #43 to travel the remaining 25 miles to Billund (45 minutes). For train and bus details, see www.rejseplanen.dk.

ORIENTATION TO LEGOLAND

Cost: 399 DKK for ages 3 and up, free for kids 2 and under. Advance tickets, often available at a discount, are sold online at www.legoland.dk and at many Danish locations (some stores, hotels, and TIs). Legoland generally doesn't charge in the evening (from half an hour before the rides close).

Hours: Generally April-Oct daily 10:00-18:00, later on weekends and for much of July-Aug, closed Nov-March and Wed-Fri in Sept-mid-Oct. Activities close an hour before the park, but it's basically the same place after dinner as during the day, with fewer tour groups. Confirm exact hours before heading out.

Information: +45 79 50 17 17, www.legoland.dk.

Crowd-Beating Tips: Legoland is crowded during the Danish summer school vacation, from early July through mid-August. To skip the ticket line, purchase tickets online in advance.

Money- and Time-Savers: If a one-day visit is not enough, you can pay 599 DKK for a season pass with some extra discounts. Some local hotels offer rooms bundled with a two-day park ticket. To avoid waiting in lines inside the park, consider renting a "Reserve & Ride" device, which allows you to book ahead and skip the queue for popular attractions (from 199 DKK/family plus security deposit).

Eating: Surprisingly, the park's restaurants don't serve Lego-lamb, but there are plenty of other food choices. Prices are high, so

JUTLAND

consider bringing a picnic to enjoy at one of the several spots set aside for bring-it-yourselfers.

BACKGROUND

Lego began in 1932 in the workshop of a local carpenter who named his wooden toys after the Danish phrase *leg godt* ("play well"). In 1949, the company started making the plastic interlocking building bricks for which they are world famous. Since then, Lego has continued to expand its lineup and now produces everything from Ninjago ninja warriors to motorized models, Clikits jewelry, board games, video games—many based on popular movies (*Lego Star Wars, Lego Harry Potter,* etc.)—making kids drool all around the world. *The Lego Movie,* a hit animated feature released in 2014, kicked off a series of Lego-themed films, and *Beyond the Brick: A Lego Brickumentary* looks at the toy's enduring popularity. According to the company, each person on this planet has, on average, 62 Lego blocks.

VISITING LEGOLAND

Legoland is divided into eight "worlds" with fun themes such as Adventure Land, Pirate Land, and Knight's Kingdom. Pick up a brochure at the entrance and make a plan using the colorful 3-D map. You can see it all in a day, but you'll be exhaust-

ed. The Legoredo section (filled with Wild West clichés Europeans will enjoy more than Americans) merits just a quick look, though your five-year-old might enjoy roasting a biscuit-on-a-stick around the fire with a tall, blond park employee wearing a Native American headdress.

A highlight for young and old alike is Miniland (near the entrance), where landscaped gardens are filled with carefully con-

structed Lego landscapes and cityscapes. Anyone who has ever picked up a Lego block will marvel at seeing representations of the world's famous sights, including Danish monuments, Dutch windmills, German castles, and an amazing version of the Norwegian harbor of Bergen. Children joyfully watch as tiny Lego boats ply the waters and Lego trains chug merrily along the tracks. Nearby, kids can go on mellow rides in child-size cars, trains, and boats. A highlight of Miniland is the traffic school, where drivers ages 7-13 learn the rules of the road and get a souvenir license (it's popular—make a reservation upon arrival).

More rides are scattered throughout the park. While the rides aren't thrilling by Disneyland standards, most kids will find something to enjoy (parents should check the brochure for strictly enforced height restrictions). The Falck Fire Brigade ride in Lego City invites family participation as you team up to put out a (fake) fire. The Temple is an Indiana Jones-esque Egyptian-themed treasure hunt/shoot-'em-up, and the Dragon roller coaster takes you in and around a medieval castle. Note that on a few rides (including the Pirate Splash Battle), you'll definitely get wet. Special walk-in, human-size dryers help you warm up and dry off.

The indoor museum features company history, high-tech Lego creations, a great doll collection, and a toy exhibit full of mechanical wonders from the early 1900s, many ready to jump into action with the push of a button. A Lego playroom encourages hands-on fun, and a campground is across the street if your kids refuse to move on.

Nearby: Those looking for water fun with a tropical theme can check out the Aquadome (one of Europe's largest water parks), located outside Legoland in Billund at the family resort of Lalandia (www.lalandia.dk).

SLEEPING NEAR LEGOLAND

$$$$ Legoland Hotel adjoins Legoland (family rooms and deals, +45 79 51 13 50, www.legolandconference.dk, reservation@legoland.dk).

$$$$ Legoland Holiday Village offers cabins, camping, and motel rooms that sleep up to eight people (Ellehammers Allé 2, +45 79 51 13 50, www.legoland-village.dk, reservation@legoland.dk).

$$ Hotel Svanen is close by, in Billund (Nordmarksvej 8, +45 75 33 28 33, www.hotelsvanen.dk, billund@hotelsvanen.dk).

Nearby: In a forest just outside of Billund, Erik and Mary Sort run **$ Gregersminde,** a B&B with a great setup: six double rooms (some with shared bath), plus a cottage that sleeps up to six people. Guests enjoy a huge living room, a kitchen, lots of Lego toys, and a kid-friendly yard (breakfast extra, rental bikes, leave Billund on Grindsted Road, turn right on Stilbjergvej, go a half-mile to Stilbjergvej 4B, +45 61 27 33 23, www.gregersminde.dk, info@gregersminde.dk).

Jelling

On your way to or from Legoland, consider a short side trip to the tiny village of Jelling (YELL-ing), a place of immense importance in Danish history. Here you'll find two rune stones, set next to a 900-year-old church that's flanked by two enormous, man-made burial mounds. The two stones are often called "Denmark's birth certificate"—the first written record of Denmark's status as a nation-state. An excellent (and free) museum lies just across the street.

Two hours is ample for a visit. If pressed for time, an hour is enough to see the stones and take a quick look at the museum.

Jelling is too small for a TI, but the museum staff can answer most questions. If you're here around lunchtime, Jelling is a great spot for a picnic. There are several central eateries and a café and WC inside the museum, and another WC in the parking lot near the North Mound.

Getting There: Drivers can easily find Jelling, just 10 minutes off the main Vejle-Billund road (see "Route Tips for Drivers" under "Aarhus Connections"). Train travelers coming from Copenhagen or Aarhus must change in Vejle, which is connected to Jelling by hourly trains (direction: Herning) and bus #211.

Jelling Walk

Denmark is proud of being Europe's oldest monarchy and of the fact that Queen Margrethe II, the country's current ruler, can trace her lineage back 1,300 years to Jelling. This short, self-guided walk explores this sacred place.

• *Begin your visit at the...*

Kongernes Jelling Museum: Inside this modern, light-filled building you'll find informative exhibits, historical models of the area, and replicas of the rune stones. Kids will love the room in the back on the ground level where they can write their name in the runic alphabet—and the gift shop bristling with wooden swords and Viking garb (free; daily 10:00-17:00; Nov-April Tue-Sun 10:00-16:00, closed Mon; café, +45 41 20 63 31, http://natmus.dk/kongernes-jelling).

• *Cross the street and walk through the graveyard to examine the actual...*

Rune Stones: The stones stand just south of the church. The modern bronze-and-glass structure is designed to protect the stones from the elements while allowing easy viewing.

The smaller stone was erected by King Gorm the Old (a.k.a. Gorm the Sleepy), who ruled Denmark for 40 years in the ninth century. You probably don't read runic so I'll translate: *"King Gorm made this monument in memory of Thyra, his wife, Denmark's salvation."* These are the oldest recorded words of a Danish king, and the first time that the name Denmark is used to describe a country and not just the region.

The **larger stone** was erected by Gorm's son, Harald Bluetooth, to honor his parents, commemorate the conquering of Denmark and Norway, and mark the conversion of the Danes to Christianity. (Today's Bluetooth wireless technology takes its name from Harald, who created the decidedly nonwireless connection between the Danish and Norwegian peoples.)

Harald was a shrewd politician who had practical reasons for being baptized. He knew that if he declared Denmark to be a Christian land, he could save it from possible attack by the predatory German bishops to the south. The inscription reads: *"King Harald ordered this monument made in memory of Gorm, his father, and in memory of Thyra, his mother; that Harald who won for himself all of Denmark and Norway and made the Danes Christian."*

This large stone has three sides. One side reveals an image of Jesus and a cross, while the other has a serpent wrapped around a lion. This is important imagery that speaks to the transition from Nordic paganism to Christianity. These designs carved into the rock were once brightly painted.

• *Go around the back of the church and climb the steps to the 35-foot-high, grass-covered...*

North Mound: According to tradition, Gorm was buried in a chamber inside this mound, with his queen Thyra interred in the smaller mound to the south.

But excavations in the 1940s turned up no royal remains in either mound. (In the 1970s, what is believed to be Gorm's body was discovered below the church.) Scan the horizon and mentally remove the trees. Imagine the commanding view this site had in the past. Look north to stones that trace the outline of a ship. Below you lies a graveyard with typically Danish well-manicured plots.

• *Now descend the stairs to the...*

Church: Within the sparse interior, note the ship model hanging from the ceiling, a holdover from a pre-Christian tradition seeking a safe journey for ship and crew. The church, which dates from around 1100, is decorated with restored frescoes. A zigzag motif is repeated in the modern windows and the inlaid floor. The metal "Z" in the floor marks the spot where Gorm's body lies.

More Jutland Sights

NORTHEAST OF BILLUND
Himmelbjerget and Silkeborg

If you're connecting the Billund and Jelling area with Aarhus, consider this slower but more scenic route north through the idyllic Danish Lake District. (With less time, return to Vejle and take the E-45 motorway.)

Himmelbjerget, best seen by car, lies in the middle of Jutland near the town of Silkeborg. Both are about an hour northeast of Billund (22 miles west of Aarhus). Silkeborg is accessible by train from Aarhus with a change in Skanderborg.

Denmark's landscape is vertically challenged when compared to its mountainous neighbors Norway and Sweden. If you have a hankering to ascend to one of the country's highest points, consider a visit to the 482-foot-tall **Himmelbjerget,** which translates loftily as "The Heaven Mountain." That may be overstating it, but by Danish standards the view's not bad. One can literally drive to the top, where a short trail leads to an 80-foot-tall brick tower. Climb the **tower** for a commanding view. Clouds roll by above a patchwork of green and gold fields while boats ply the blue waters of the lake below. You may see the vintage paddle steamers make the hour-long trip between Himmelbjerget and Silkeborg in season (the dock is accessed by a short hike from the tower down to the lake).

Silkeborg, in the center of the Danish Lake District, has an excellent freshwater aquarium/exhibit/nature park called **AQUA** that's worth a visit, especially if you're traveling with kids (100 DKK for kids ages 3-11, 165 DKK for adults; daily 10:00-16:00, July-early Aug until 18:00, closed mid-Dec-Jan; +45 89 21 21 89, www.visitaqua.dk). Also in Silkeborg, modern-art lovers will enjoy the **Museum Jorn Silkeborg,** featuring colorful abstract works by Asger Jorn—a prominent member of the 1960s' COBRA movement—plus other Danish and foreign art (100 DKK, daily 10:00-17:00, closed Mon off-season, +45 86 82 53 88, www.museumjorn. dk).

SOUTHWEST OF BILLUND
▲Ribe

A Viking port 1,000 years ago, Ribe, located about 30 miles southwest of Billund, is the oldest, and possibly the loveliest, town in Denmark. It's an entertaining mix of cobbled lanes and leaning medieval houses, with a fine

cathedral boasting modern paintings under Romanesque arches. The **TI** is on the main square (Torvet 3, +45 75 42 15 00, www.visitribe.com). **$ Weis Stue,** a smoky, low-ceilinged, atmospheric inn across from the church, rents primitive rooms with a shared bath and serves good meals (no breakfast, +45 75 42 07 00, www.weis-stue.dk). Take the free **Night Watchman** tour (daily May-Oct at 20:00, also at 22:00 in summer, www.visitribe.com).

WEST OF BILLUND
North Sea Coast

If beautiful beaches and WWII-era bunkers sound appealing, consider this side trip, worth ▲▲ on a nice day. Just an hour or so west from Legoland is a land of rolling dunes, wide sandy beaches and big waves. It's often windy and the water can be brisk but the Danes who flock here in the summer don't mind. You can make a strategic strike to Blåvand and back in half a day but allow a whole day to fully experience the coast. Bring your swimsuit!

Blåvand (BLOW-van) is a popular beach destination a little over an hour west of Billund (take highway 30, then highway 475 to Varde, then follow highway 471). Turn left at Oksby on Tane Hedevej to reach the **Tirpitz Museum.** This striking structure, designed by Danish "starchitect" Bjarke Ingels, is built into the dunes and connected by tunnel to a German bunker. The bunker was part of Hitler's Atlantic Wall that stretched from Norway down to Spain. Look for the exhibit on amber (the "gold of the north" washes up on local beaches) and an amazing amber model of the Sydney Opera House, which was designed by Dane Jørn Utzon (145 DKK, daily 10:00-17:00, closed Mon Dec-March, +45

75 22 07 16, http://vardemuseerne.dk/museum/tirpitz). To reach
the wide beach, backtrack through Oksby and follow Fyrvej to the
lighthouse.

Just 20 minutes north is the low-key beach town of **Ve-
jers Strand,** where the main drag dead-ends at the beach.
$$$ Klithjem Badehotel provides nice rooms just steps from the
sea (closed Oct-April, +45 40 18 17 26, www.klithjembadehotel.
dk).

The dunes along the coast hide many other bunkers. Along
with Blåvand, you'll find an easy-to-access observation post and
troop bunker at **Hvide
Sande,** a harbor town an
hour north that straddles
the entrance to a wide bay.
After crossing the bridge,
park in the lot on the right
where you'll find a TI, plus
some shops and restau-
rants. Cross the road and
climb the Troldbjerg Hill,

heading toward a large mast and a flagpole to find the sights. More
evocative and isolated are the bunkers 20 minutes further north
at Houvig Strand. Along the way you'll pass dozens of summer
houses, many with thatched roofs and Danish flags flapping in the
breeze. Turn left at the *Houvig Strand* sign, and park in the lot,
where a path leads through the dunes to the beach. One bunker
is just in front of you and several others lie a 10-minute walk to
the right. Be careful exploring these tilting concrete structures up
close, as shifting sands covering rusty metal rebar can make them
treacherous. From Houvig Strand it's a 1.5-hour drive back to Bil-
lund via Ringkøping.

JUTLAND

NORWAY

NORWAY

Norge

Norway is stacked with superlatives—it's the most mountainous, most scenic, and most prosperous of all the Scandinavian countries. It is also a land of rich harvests—timber, oil, and fish. In fact, Norway's wealth of resources is a major reason why Norwegians have voted *"nei"* to membership in the European Union. They don't want to be forced to share fishing rights with EU countries.

The country's relatively recent independence (in 1905, from Sweden) makes Norwegians notably patriotic and proud of their traditions and history. They have a reputation for insularity, and controversially have tightened immigration laws over the past several years.

Norway's Viking past (c. AD 800-1050) can still be seen today in the country's 28 remaining stave churches—with their decorative nods to Viking ship prows—and the arti-facts housed in Oslo's Viking Ship Museum. The Vikings, who also lived in present-day Denmark and Sweden, were great traders, shipbuilders, and explorers. However, they are probably best known for their infamous invasions, which terrorized much of Europe. The sight of their dragon-prowed ships on the horizon struck fear into the hearts of people from Ireland to the Black Sea.

Named for the Norse word *vik*, which means "bay" or "inlet," the Vikings sailed their sleek, seaworthy ships on extensive voyages, laden with amber and furs for trading—and weapons for fighting. They traveled up the Seine and deep into Russia, through the Mediterranean east to Constantinople, and across the Atlantic to Greenland and even "Vinland" (Canada). They touched the soil of the Americas centuries before Columbus, causing proud "ya sure ya betcha" Scandinavian immigrants in the US to display bumper stickers that boast, "Columbus used a Viking map!"

Southern Norway

History and Hollywood have painted a picture of the Vikings as fierce barbarians, an image reinforced by the colorful names of leaders like Sven Forkbeard, Erik Bloodaxe, and Harald Bluetooth. Unless you're handy with an ax, these don't sound like the kind of men you want to hoist a tankard of mead with. They kept slaves and were all-around cruel (though there is no evidence that they forced their subjects to eat lutefisk).

But the Vikings also had a gentle side. Many were farmers, fishermen, and craftsmen who created delicate works with wood and metal. Faced with a growing population constrained by a lack of arable land, they traveled south not just to pillage and plunder, but in search of greener pastures. Sometimes they stayed and colonized, as in northeast England, which was called the "Danelaw," or in northwest France, which became known as Normandy ("Land of the North-men").

Norway Almanac

Official Name: Kongeriket Norge—"The Kingdom of Norway"—or simply Norge (Norway).

Size: At 148,700 square miles, Norway is slightly larger than Montana, and has a population of 5.4 million people (about 35 per square mile)

Geography: Sharing the Scandinavian Peninsula with Sweden, Norway also has short northern borders with Finland and Russia. Its 51,575-mile coastline extends from the Barents Sea in the Arctic Ocean to the Norwegian Sea and North Sea in the North Atlantic. Shaped by glaciers, Norway has a rugged landscape of mountains, plateaus, and deep fjords. In the part of Norway that extends north of the Arctic Circle, the sun never sets at the height of summer, and never rises in the depth of winter.

Latitude and Longitude: 62°N and 10°E, similar latitude to Canada's Northwest Territories.

Biggest Cities: Norway's capital city, Oslo, has a population of 680,000; more than 1 million live in its metropolitan area. Bergen, Norway's second-largest city, has a population of about 284,000.

Economy: The Norwegian economy grows around 1.5-2 percent each year, contributing to a healthy $434 billion gross domestic product and a per capita GDP of $80,200. Its primary exports are oil and gas—Norway produces less than 5 percent of the world's oil but exports 95 percent of it; the country is second only to Russia in natural gas production. Oil and gas make Norway one of the world's richest countries. The two commodities account for more than 50 percent of the Norwegian economy. By law, the country must save a portion of its oil revenue; the fund is currently worth almost $1 trillion.

Currency: 9 Norwegian kroner (NOK) = about $1.

Government: As the leader of Norway's parliamentary constitutional monarchy, King Harald V has largely ceremonial powers. Norway's legislative body is the Stortinget (Parliament), with 169 members elected for four-year terms.

Flag: Red with a blue Scandinavian cross outlined in white.

The Average Norwegian is 39 years old, has 1.8 children, will live to be 82, and enjoys a good coffee buzz, drinking nearly four cups a day.

The Vikings worshipped many gods and had a rich tradition of mythology. Epic sagas were verbally passed down through generations or written in angular runic writing. The sagas told the heroic tales of the gods, who lived in Valhalla, the Viking heaven, presided over by Odin, the god of both wisdom and war. Like the Egyptians, the Vikings believed in life after death, and chieftains were often buried in their ships within burial mounds, along with prized possessions such as jewelry, cooking pots, food, and Hagar the Horrible cartoons.

Similar to the Greeks and Etruscans before them, the Vikings never organized on a large national scale and eventually faded away due to bigger, better-organized enemies and the powerful influence of Christianity. By 1150, the Vikings had become Christianized and assimilated into European society. But their memory lives on in Norway.

Beginning in the 14th century, Norway came under Danish rule for more than 400 years, until the Danes took the wrong side in the Napoleonic Wars. The Treaty of Kiel forced Denmark to cede Norway to Sweden in 1814. Sweden's rule of Norway lasted until 1905, when Norway voted to dissolve the union. Like many European countries, Norway was invaded by Germany during World War II. April 9, 1940, marked the start of five years of Nazi occupation, during which a strong resistance movement developed, hindering some of the Nazi war efforts.

Each year on May 17, Norwegians celebrate their idealistic 1814 constitution with fervor and plenty of flag-waving. Men and women wear folk costumes *(bunads),* each specific to a region of Norway. Parades are held throughout the country. The parade in Oslo marches past the Royal Palace, where the royal family waves to the populace from their balcony. While the king holds almost zero political power (Norway's parliament is chaired by a prime minister), the royal family is still highly revered and respected.

High taxes contribute to Norway's high standard of living. Norwegians receive cradle-to-grave social care: university education, health care, nearly yearlong paternity leave, and an annual six weeks of vacation. Norwegians feel there is no better place than home: Norway regularly shows up in first place on the annual UN Human Development Index.

Norwegians are mainly of Nordic and Germanic heritage, with a small population of indigenous Sami people in the north.

The growing immigrant population is primarily from Sweden, Poland, Lithuania, Pakistan, and Somalia, with a recent wave from Syria. And though church attendance is way down, the vast majority of Norwegian Christians consider themselves Lutheran.

Visitors enjoy the agreeable demeanor of the Norwegian people—friendly but not overbearing, organized but not uptight, and with a lust for adventure befitting their gorgeous landscape. Known for their ability to suffer any misfortune with an accepting (if a bit pessimistic) attitude, Norwegians are easy to get along with.

Norwegians are proud of their rich folk traditions—from handmade sweaters and folk costumes to the small farms that produce a sweet brown cheese called *geitost*. Less than 7 percent of the country's land is arable, resulting in numerous small farms. The government recognizes the value of farming, especially in the remote reaches of the country, and provides rich subsidies to keep this tradition alive.

With countless fjords and waterfalls, Norway is known for its pristine water. Norwegian-bottled artisanal water has an international reputation for its crisp, clean taste. Although the designer Voss water—the H2O of choice for Hollywood celebrities—comes with a high price tag, the blue-collar Olden is just as good. (Tap water here is actually wonderful, too—and much cheaper.)

While Norwegians speak a collection of mutually understandable dialects, the two official forms of Norwegian are *bokmål* (book language) and *nynorsk* (New Norse). During the centuries of Danish rule, people in Norway's cities and upper classes adopted a Danish-influenced style of speech and writing (called Dano-Norwegian), while rural language remained closer to Old Norse. After independence, Dano-Norwegian was renamed *bokmål*, and the rural dialects were formalized as *nynorsk*, as part of a nationalistic drive for a more purely Norwegian language. Despite later efforts to combine the two forms, *bokmål* remains the most common, especially in urban areas, books, newspapers, and government agencies. Some Sami- and Finnish-speaking minorities are found in the far north.

Most Norwegians also speak English, but a few words in Norwegian will serve you well. If you visit a Norwegian home, be sure to leave your shoes at the door; indoors is usually meant for stocking-feet only. At the end of a meal, it's polite to say *"Takk for maten"* (tahk for MAH-ten); "Thanks for the food"). Norwegians rarely feel their guests have eaten enough, so be prepared to say *"Nei, takk"* (nay tahk; "No, thanks"). You can always try *"Jeg er mett"* (yay ehr met; "I am full"), but be careful not to say *"Jeg er full"*—"I am drunk." See the next page for more Norwegian survival phrases.

NORWAY

Norwegian Survival Phrases

Norwegian can be pronounced quite differently from region to region. These phrases and phonetics match the mainstream Oslo dialect, but you'll notice variations. Vowels can be tricky: å sounds like "oh," æ sounds like a bright "ah" (as in "apple"), and u sounds like the German ü (purse your lips and say "u"). To pronounce the letter Ø, purse your lips together and say "uh." Certain vowels at the ends of words (such as d and t) are sometimes barely pronounced (or not at all). In some dialects, the letters sk are pronounced "sh." In the phonetics, ī sounds like the long i in "light," and bolded syllables are stressed.

Hello. (formal)	God dag.	goo dahg
Hi. / Bye. (informal)	Hei. / Ha det.	hī / hah deh
Do you speak English?	Snakker du engelsk?	**snahk**-kehr dew **eng**-ehlsk
Yes. / No.	Ja. / Nei.	yah / nī
Please.	Vær så snill.	vayr soh sneel
Thank you (very much).	(Tusen) takk.	(**tew**-sehn) tahk
You're welcome.	Vær så god.	vayr soh goo
Can I help you?	Kan jeg hjelpe deg?	kahn yī **yehl**-peh dī
Excuse me.	Unnskyld.	**ewn**-shuld
(Very) good.	(Veldig) fint.	(**vehl**-dee) feent
Goodbye.	Farvel.	fahr-**vehl**
zero / one / two	null / en / to	newl / ayn / toh
three / four	tre / fire	treh / **fee**-reh
five / six	fem / seks	fehm / sehks
seven / eight	syv / åtte	seev / **oh**-teh
nine / ten	ni / ti	nee / tee
hundred	hundre	**hewn**-dreh
thousand	tusen	**tew**-sehn
How much?	Hvor mye?	voor **mee**-yeh
local currency: (Norwegian) crown	(Norske) kroner	(**norsh**-keh) **kroh**-nehr
Where is...?	Hvor er...?	voor ehr
...the toilet	...toalettet	toh-ah-**leh**-teh
men	menn / herrer	mehn / **hehr**-rehr
women	damer	**dah**-mehr
water / coffee	vann / kaffe	vahn / **kah**-feh
beer / wine	øl / vin	uhl / veen
Cheers!	Skål!	skohl
The bill, please.	Regningen, takk.	**rī**-ning-ehn tahk

OSLO

Though Oslo is the smallest of the Scandinavian capitals, this brisk little city offers more sightseeing thrills than you might expect. Get ready to be inspired—Oslo simply has its act together.

Situated at the head of a 60-mile-long fjord, surrounded by forests, and populated by more than a half-million people, Oslo is Norway's cultural hub. For 300 years (1624-1924), the city was called Christiania, after Danish King Christian IV. With independence, it reverted to the Old Norse name of Oslo. As an important port facing the Continent, Oslo has been one of Norway's main cities for a thousand years and the de facto capital since around 1300. Still, Oslo has always been small by European standards; in 1800, Oslo had just 10,000 people—one-fiftieth the size of Paris or London.

But Oslo experienced a growth spurt with the Industrial Age, and in 50 years (from 1850 to 1900) its population exploded upward to about 250,000. Most of "old Oslo" dates from this period, when the city's many churches and grand buildings were built of stone in the Historicism styles (neo-Gothic and neo-Romanesque) of the late 19th century.

Today the city sprawls out from its historic core to encompass nearly a million people in its metropolitan area, about one in five Norwegians. Oslo's onetime industrial area, along the Akers River, has been reclaimed as a lush green zone, filled with spiffed-up brick warehouses and (on a sunny day) hundreds of sunbathing Norwegians. The city's port hums with international shipping and a sizeable cruise industry. Its waterfront, once traffic-congested and slummy, has undergone an extreme urban makeover, and today sports ultramodern yet people-friendly residential zones and the Havnepromenaden—a pedestrian walkway stretching the length of the harbor.

Sights of the Viking spirit—past and present—tell an exciting story. Prowl through the remains of ancient Viking ships, and marvel at more peaceful but equally gutsy modern boats (the *Kon-Tiki*, *Ra II*, *Fram*, and *Gjøa*). Dive into the traditional folk culture at the Norwegian open-air folk museum and get stirred up by the country's heroic spirit at the Norwegian Resistance Museum. For a look at modern Oslo, tour the striking City Hall, peek at sculptor Gustav Vigeland's people pillars, ascend the exhilarating Holmenkollen Ski Jump, wander futuristic promenades, walk all over the Opera House, and celebrate the world's greatest peacemakers at the Nobel Peace Center.

Even with all this modernization, it's delightfully easy to escape the urban downtown and harbor area to a sprawling, green, and pastoral countryside—dotted with parks and lakes, and surrounded by hills and forests. For the visitor, Oslo is an all-you-can-see smorgasbord of historic sights, nature, art, and Nordic fun.

PLANNING YOUR TIME

Oslo offers an exciting slate of sightseeing thrills. Ideally, spend two days here. Keep in mind that the Vigeland Museum (next to Vigeland Sculpture Park) is closed on Monday. The National Museum may also be closed Monday (check ahead). Spend the two days like this:

Day 1: Take my self-guided Oslo Walk. Tour the Akershus Fortress and the Norwegian Resistance Museum, then catch a free City Hall tour (likely offered June-Aug only; off-season, tour it on your own). Spend the afternoon at the National Museum (for Norwegian art, opening in 2022), Munch Museum, or Holmenkollen Ski Jump and museum (to enjoy some wilderness).

Day 2: Ferry across the harbor to Bygdøy and tour the *Fram*, *Kon-Tiki*, and Viking Ship museums. Spend the afternoon at the Norwegian Folk Museum. Finish the day at Vigeland Sculpture Park, enjoying Gustav Vigeland's statues.

With More Time: You could easily fill a third day: Slow things down, go for a lazy hike along the Akers River (and eat at the trendy Mathallen Oslo food hall), and/or head out to the islands in the Oslofjord.

In the evening, you could enjoy a pricey dinner by the harbor or near Karl Johans Gate. Or venture to the appealing, affordable,

Greater Oslo

and less touristy dining zones around Youngstorget, Mathallen, and Olaf Ryes Plass.

OSLO

Orientation to Oslo

Oslo (pop. 680,000) is easy to manage. Most sights are contained within the city center. Much of what you'll want to see clusters in three easy-to-connect zones: **downtown,** around the harbor and the main boulevard, Karl Johans Gate (with the Royal Palace at one end and the train station at the other); in the **Bygdøy** (big-duhy) district, a 10-minute ferry ride across the harbor; and **Frogner Park** (with the Vigeland Sculpture Park), about a mile behind the palace.

With more time, head out of the core to see the more colorful neighborhoods: Majorstuen and Frogner feel "uptown," with chic boutiques, elegant homes, and lots of parks. Grünerløkka and the adjacent Akers River greenbelt is hipster central, with the foodie-paradise Mathallen and plenty of bohemian cafés. Youngstorget, a quick walk north of Karl Johans Gate, is mostly residential and packed with tempting restaurants. And Grønland, behind the train station, is the multiethnic immigrants' zone.

TOURIST INFORMATION

The big, high-tech Visit Oslo office is in the Østbanehallen—the traditional-looking building next to the central train station. Standing in the square (Jernbanetorget) by the tiger statue and facing the train station, you'll find the TI's entrance in the red-painted section between the station and the Østbanehallen. You can also enter the TI from inside the train station (generally July-Aug Mon-Sat 8:00-19:00, Sun 9:00-18:00; May-June and Sept daily 9:00-18:00; slightly shorter hours Oct-April; +47 23 10 62 00, www.visitoslo.com).

At the TI, pick up these freebies: an Oslo city/transit map; the annual *Oslo Guide* (overview of museums, eating, and nightlife); *U.F.O.* (guide to current museum exhibits); and the *What's On Oslo* monthly (museum and event listings). The TI also sells the handy Oslo Pass (described later, under "Sights in Oslo"). If you're traveling beyond Oslo, you can purchase domestic train and Norway in a Nutshell tickets here. Consider picking up the *Bergen Guide* and information for the rest of Norway, including the useful, annual *Fjord Norway Travel Guide*.

ARRIVAL IN OSLO
By Train

The central train station (Oslo Sentralstasjon, or "Oslo S" for short) is slick and helpful. You'll find ATMs, two exchange desks, and luggage storage. The station is plugged into a lively modern shopping mall called Byporten (Mon-Fri 10:00-20:00, Sat until 18:00, closed Sun), where just inside the entrance you'll find a cheap Bit sandwich shop. Inside the station is a well-stocked Co-op Prix grocery store (long hours Mon-Sat, closed Sun), a small Joker supermarket (long hours daily), and a Vinmonopolet liquor store (Oslo's most central place to buy wine or liquor—which is sold only at Vinmonopolet stores, Mon-Fri 10:00-18:00, Sat until 15:00, closed Sun).

For tickets and train info, head to the station's ticket office between tracks 8 and 9 (Mon-Fri 7:30-20:00, Sat-Sun 10:00-18:00 plus summer weekends from 7:45). Here, you can buy domestic and Norway in a Nutshell tickets, get information on the Flåm and Bergen Railway (Bergensbanen), and buy international train tickets. Domestic train tickets (but not international tickets) can also be bought at ticket machines. Tickets to Sweden are available at the blue machines marked *SJ*.

By Plane or Boat

For details on arriving in Oslo by plane or boat, see the end of this chapter.

HELPFUL HINTS

Theft Alert: Pickpockets are a problem in Oslo, particularly in crowds on the street and on subways and buses. Oslo's street population loiters around the train station; you may see aggressive panhandlers there and along Karl Johans Gate.

Pharmacy: Jernbanetorgets Vitus Apotek is open 24 hours daily (across from train station on Jernbanetorget, +47 23 35 81 00).

Laundry: Billig Vask & Rens ("Cheap Wash & Clean") is near Vår Frelsers Cemetery, a half-mile north of the train station (self-serve open daily 8:00-21:00; full-serve Mon-Fri 9:00-18:00, Sat 10:00-15:00, closed Sun; on the corner of Wessels Gate and Ullevålsveien, Ullevålsveien 15, bus #37 from train station, +47 41 64 08 33).

Bike Rental: Oslo's near-complete ban on cars in the city core and the addition of bike lanes have made it an increasingly good city for cycling, despite its hills. A public bike-rental system lets you grab basic **city bikes** from locked racks at various points around town (first hour free, then 15 NOK/15 minutes; requires smartphone app, www.oslobysykkel.no). If you're traveling with a group, you can reserve bikes in advance with **Viking Biking** (no walk-up rentals, daily flat rate of 2,000 NOK for 1-10 bikes; includes helmet, lock, and map; daily 10:00-18:00, Nedre Slottsgate 4, +47 41 26 64 96, www.vikingbikingoslo.com; see "Tours in Oslo," later, for their guided bike tours).

Movies: The domed Colosseum Kino in Majorstuen, with 1,500 seats, is a fun place to catch a big-time spectacle. Originally built in 1928, this now high-tech, four-screen theater shows first-run films in their original language (Fridtjof Nansens Vei 6, a short walk west from Marjorstuen T-bane station, www.oslokino.no).

OSLO

Sightseeing by Public Transit

With a transit pass or an Oslo Pass, take full advantage of the T-bane and the trams. Spend just five minutes getting a grip on the system, and you'll be in command. Here are some handy stops and stations.

T-bane Stations

Jernbanetorget (central station, bus and tram hub, express train to airport)

Stortinget (top of Karl Johans Gate, near Akershus Fortress)

Nationaltheatret (National Theater, also a train station, express train to airport; near City Hall, National Museum, Aker Brygge, Royal Palace)

Majorstuen (walk to Vigeland Sculpture Park, trendy shops on Bogstadveien, Colosseum cinema)

Grønland (cheap and fun restaurant zone, bottom of Grünerløkka district; the underground mall in the station is a virtual trip to Istanbul)

Holmenkollen (famous ski jump, city view)

Frognerseteren (highest point in town, jumping-off point for forest walks and bike rides)

Sognsvann (idyllic lake in forest outside of town)

Tram and Bus Stops

Trams #11 and **#12** ring the city (stops at central station, fortress, harborfront, City Hall, National Museum, Aker Brygge, Vigeland Sculpture Park, Bogstadveien, and Stortorvet)

Trams #11, #12, and **#18** to Olaf Ryes Plass (center of Grünerløkka district)

Trams #13 and **#19,** and **bus #32** (south and parallel to Karl Johans Gate to central train station; stops near Opera House and Munch Museum)

Bus #30 (Olaf Ryes Plass in Grünerløkka, train station, near Karl Johans Gate, National Theater, and Bygdøy, with stops at each Bygdøy museum)

GETTING AROUND OSLO
By Public Transit

Oslo is a big city, and taxi fares are exorbitant. Take advantage of the excellent transit system, made up of buses, trams, ferries, and a subway (*Tunnelbane,* or T-bane for short; see the "Sightseeing by Public Transit" sidebar). The system is run by Ruter, which has a transit-information center below the skinny glass tower in front of the central train station (Mon-Fri 7:00-20:00, Sat-Sun 8:00-18:00, www.ruter.no).

Schedules: The system runs like clockwork, with schedules clearly posted and followed. Download the RuterReise app for schedules at your fingertips, or check reader boards at stops for the next tram's arrival time (usually every 10 minutes).

Tickets: A different app—called RuterBillett—lets you buy tickets with your mobile phone (credit card or PayPal). **Individual tickets** work on buses, trams, ferries, the T-bane, and Vy trains (within Oslo) for one hour (37 NOK via RuterBillett app and at the transit office, ticket machines, transit office, Narvesen kiosks, and convenience stores; 57 NOK from driver; note that boats to Bygdøy require a separate, more expensive ticket). Other options include a **24-hour ticket** (111 NOK; buy on RuterBillett app or at ticket machines or the transit office; good for unlimited rides in 24-hour period) and the **Oslo Pass** (free run of entire system, including Bygdøy boats; described later under "Sights in Oslo"). Validate your ticket by holding it next to the card reader when you board.

By Taxi or Uber

Taxis come with a 150-NOK drop charge (yes, that's nearly $20 just to get in the car) that covers you for three or four kilometers—about two miles (more on evenings and weekends). Taxis are a good value only if you're with a group. If you use a minibus taxi, you can negotiate an hourly rate. To get a taxi, wave one down, find a taxi stand, or call +47 22 38 80 90. Uber works in Oslo just like in the US.

Tours in Oslo

Local Guides

You can hire a private guide for around 2,000 NOK for a two- to three-hour tour. I had a good experience with **Oslo Guideservice** (2,000 NOK/2 hours, +47 22 42 70 20, www.guideservice.no); my guide, Aksel, had a passion for both history and his hometown of Oslo. The easy-to-work-with **Oslo Guidebureau** will tailor a tour to meet your interests (+47·22 42 28 18, www.osloguidebureau.no).

Bike Tours

Viking Biking gives several different guided tours in English, including a three-hour Oslo Highlights Tour that includes Bygdøy beaches and a ride up the Akers River (425 NOK, May-Sept daily at 14:00, Nedre Slottsgate 4, +47 41 26 64 96, www.vikingbikingoslo.com). They also rent bikes to groups; see "Helpful Hints," earlier. If you'd rather walk, check out their forest-to-fjord and island nature walks.

Bus Tours

While a bus tour can help you get your bearings, most of Oslo's sightseeing is concentrated in a few discrete zones and well-

OSLO

Oslo at a Glance

▲▲▲**City Hall** Oslo's artsy 20th-century government building, lined with vibrant municipal-themed murals, best visited with included tour. **Hours:** Daily 9:00-16:00, June-Aug until 18:00; generally 3 tours/day (may not run off-season). See page 235.

▲▲▲**National Museum** Norway's cultural and natural essence, captured on canvas. **Hours:** Opens in 2022; likely Tue-Fri 10:00-18:00, Thu until 19:00, Sat-Sun 11:00-17:00, closed Mon. See page 238.

▲▲▲**Vigeland Sculpture Park and ▲▲ Vigeland Museum** Set in sprawling Frogner Park, with tons of statuary by Norway's greatest sculptor, Gustav Vigeland, and the studio where he worked. **Hours:** Sculpture park—always open; Vigeland Museum—Tue-Sun 10:00-16:00, closed Mon year-round. See page 247.

▲▲▲**Fram Museum** Captivating exhibit on two Arctic exploration ships. **Hours:** Daily June-Aug 9:00-18:00, May and Sept 10:00-18:00, Oct-April until 17:00. See page 259.

▲▲**Norwegian Resistance Museum** Gripping look at Norway's tumultuous WWII experience. **Hours:** Daily 10:00-17:00; Sept-April until 16:00. See page 242.

▲▲**Norwegian Folk Museum** Norway condensed into 150 historic buildings in a large open-air museum. **Hours:** Daily 10:00-17:00—grounds open until 20:00; Sept-May park open daily 11:00-16:00, but most historical buildings closed. See page 256.

▲▲**Viking Ship Museum** Impressive trio of ninth-century Viking ships, with exhibits on the people who built them. **Hours:** Tue-Sun 10:00-16:00, closed Mon. See page 257.

▲▲**Kon-Tiki Museum** Adventures of primitive *Kon-Tiki* and *Ra II* ships built by Thor Heyerdahl. **Hours:** Daily 10:00-17:00, June-Aug from 11:00, Nov-Feb until 16:00. See page 261.

OSLO

connected by public transit. Consider my self-guided tram tour (later) instead. If a bus tour appeals, **HMK** does a daily city tour (350 NOK/3 hours, 500 NOK/4 hours, departs from the DFDS cruise terminal, Akershusstranda 31, +47 48 08 31 02, https://sightseeingoslo.com).

Oslofjord Cruises

A fascinating world of idyllic islands sprinkled with charming vacation cabins is minutes away from the Oslo harborfront. For

▲**Aker Brygge and Tjuvholmen** Oslo's harborfront promenade and nearby arty Tjuvholmen neighborhood with Astrup Fearnley Museum, upscale galleries, shops, and cafés. See page 240.

▲**Akershus Fortress Complex and Tours** Historic military base and fortified old center, with guided tours, ho-hum castle interior, and excellent Norwegian Resistance Museum (listed earlier). **Hours:** Park generally open daily 6:00-21:00—until 18:00 in winter; fortress tours run 2/day July-mid-Aug, 1/day Sat-Sun only off-season. See page 241.

▲**Oslo Opera House** Stunning performance center that's revitalized the harborfront. **Hours:** Foyer and café/restaurant open daily roughly 11:00-18:00; Opera House tours—1-2/day year-round. See page 245.

▲**Munch Museum** Works of Norway's famous Expressionistic painter. **Hours:** Daily 10:00-17:00, Oct-May until 16:00. See page 246.

▲**Norwegian Maritime Museum** Briny voyage through Norway's rich seafaring heritage. **Hours:** Daily 10:00-17:00; Oct-April 11:00-16:00. See page 263.

▲**Grünerløkka** Oslo's popular former working-class district, bustling with cafés, pubs, and shops. See page 264.

▲**Ekeberg Sculpture Park** Hilly, hikeable 63-acre forest park with striking contemporary art and city views. See page 269.

▲**Holmenkollen Ski Jump and Ski Museum** Dizzying vista and a schuss through skiing history, plus a zip line off the top. **Hours:** Daily 9:00-20:00, May and Sept 10:00-17:00, Oct-April until 16:00. See page 271.

OSLO

locals, the fjord is a handy vacation getaway. Tourists can get a glimpse of this island world by public ferry or tour boat. Cheap ferries regularly connect the nearby islands with downtown (covered by public transit tickets and Oslo Pass).

Several tour boats leave regularly from pier 3 in front of City Hall. **Båtservice** has a relaxing and scenic 1.5-hour hop-on, hop-off service, with recorded multilingual commentary. It departs from the City Hall dock (235 NOK, discount with Oslo Pass; daily at 10:15, 11:45, 13:15, and 14:45; departs 30 minutes earlier from the Opera House and 30 minutes later from Bygdøy; +47 23 35 68 90, www.boatsightseeing.com). They also offer two-hour fjord tours with dull live commentary (355 NOK, 3/day late March-mid-Oct, additional departures in summer, 2/day on winter weekends), a dinner cruise on a sailing ship (485 NOK, no narration; "shrimp buffet" is just shrimp, bread, and butter; daily mid-June-Aug 19:00-22:00), and jazz and blues-themed cruises.

Oslo Walk

This self-guided stroll, worth ▲▲, covers the tourist-friendly walking zone in the heart of Oslo—from the train station, up the main drag, and past City Hall to the harborfront. Allow a brisk 45 minutes without stops.

❶ Central Train Station: Start at the plaza just outside the main entrance of Oslo's central train station (Oslo Sentralstasjon),

near the statue of the **tiger** prowling around out front. This alludes to the town's nickname of Tigerstaden ("Tiger Town"), and commemorates the 1,000th birthday of Oslo's founding, celebrated in the year 2000. In the 1800s, Oslo was considered an urban tiger, leaving its mark on the soul of simple country folk who ventured into the wild and crazy New York City of Norway.

In the middle of the plaza, look for the tall, skinny, glass **Ruter tower** that marks the public transit office. From here, trams zip to City Hall (harbor, boat to Bygdøy), and the T-bane subway (look for the *T* sign to your right) goes to Vigeland Sculpture Park and Holmenkollen. Tram #12—described in my self-guided tram tour, earlier—leaves from directly across the street.

The green building behind the Ruter tower is a shopping mall called **Byporten** (literally, "City Gate," see big sign on rooftop), built to greet those arriving from the airport on the shuttle train. Oslo's 37-floor pointed-glass **skyscraper,** the Radisson Blu Plaza Hotel, pokes up behind that. The hotel's 34th-floor SkyBar welcomes the public with air-conditioned views and pricey drinks. The tower was built with reflective glass so that, from a distance, it almost disappears.

Oslo's Most Strollable Spots

Oslo's pulse is best felt by strolling. Three good areas are 1) along and near the central Karl Johans Gate, which runs from the train station to the palace (follow my self-guided Oslo Walk); 2) in trendy harborside Aker Brygge, a glass-and-chrome collection of sharp cafés, fine condos, and polished produce stalls (really lively at night, tram #12 from train station); and 3) along Bogstadveien, a bustling shopping street with no-nonsense modern commerce, lots of locals, and no tourists (T-bane to Majorstuen and follow this street back toward the palace and tourist zone).

While most tourists never get out of the harbor/Karl Johans Gate district, the real, down-to-earth Oslo is better seen elsewhere, in places such as Bogstadveien. The bohemian, artsy Grünerløkka district, is also good for a daytime wander. And the new Havnepromenaden stretches all the way along the harbor, from the marina at Frognerkilen to the Sørenga neighborhood to the east. The 5.5-mile pedestrian route is marked by orange towers (get info at TI or see www.visitoslo.com/en/articles/the-harbour-promenade for route).

The area behind the Radisson—the lively and colorful "Little Karachi," centered along a street called Grønland—is where many of Oslo's immigrants settled. It's become a vibrant nightspot, offering a fun contrast to the predictable Norwegian cuisine and culture.

Oslo allows hard-drug addicts and sex workers to mix and mingle in the station area. (While it's illegal to buy sex in Norway, those who sell it are not breaking the law.) The cameras near the top of the Ruter tower monitor drug deals. Signs warn that this is a "monitored area," but keep your valuables close.

• Note that you are near the Opera House and the Munch Museum, if you'd like to side-trip there now. (The Opera House is through the park to the right of the station, and the Munch Museum is just a few minutes' walk beyond that.) Otherwise, turn your back to the station. You're now looking (across the street) up Norway's main drag, called...

Karl Johans Gate: This grand boulevard leads directly from the train station to the Royal Palace. The street is named for the French general Jean-Baptiste Bernadotte, who took the Swedish name Karl Johan when he was elected the crown prince of Sweden in 1810. He ruled as a popular king (1818-1844) during the period after Sweden took Norway from Denmark. For more on Bernadotte, see page 692.

Walk three blocks up Karl Johans Gate. This people-filled stretch is crowded with street musicians, sidewalk artists, and shops greedily devouring tourists' money. Even if you're visiting in

OSLO

Oslo Walk

To ⟨20⟩
To Majorstuen & Frogner Park
T #11 & 17

N

500 Meters
500 Yards

URANIEN-BORG

Holbergs Plass

Slottsparken

⟨18⟩

St. Olavs Plass

OLAVS GATE

ROYAL PALACE

HISTORICAL MUSEUM

KRISTIAN IV's GATE

NATIONAL GALLERY

T #11 & 17

Dronningparken

OSLO UNIVERSITY

HENRIK IBSENS GATE

Nationaltheatret T

NATIONAL THEATER

US EMBASSY

⟨21⟩

NATIONAL THEATER STATION

#30 B

⟨9⟩

⟨15⟩ ⟨14⟩ ⟨22⟩ ⟨16⟩

OSLO

⟨8⟩

Eidsvolls-plass

⟨6⟩

KARL

To Bygdøy & Frogner Park

STORTINGSGATA

WC

PARL.

⟨7⟩

⟨13⟩

VIKA

T #12

NOBEL PEACE CENTER

⟨12⟩

⟨10⟩

CITY HALL

ROSENKRANTZ GATE

NEDRE VOLLGATE

AKERSGATA

#12 T

NATIONAL MUSEUM

Rådhus-plassen

T #12

RÅDHUSGATA

⟨24⟩

To Bygdøy

AKER BRYGGE MALL

⟨11⟩

WALK ENDS

#12 T

FDR STATUE

FILIPSTAD CRUISE BERTH

Pipervika

RESISTANCE MUSEUM

FORTRESS VISITORS CENTER

TJUV-HOLMEN

CHRISTIAN RADICH TALL SHIP

AKERSHUS FORTRESS

ASTRUP FEARNLEY MUSEUM

Oslofjord

SØNDRE AKERSHUSKAIA CRUISE BERTH

VIPPETANGEN (AKERSHUS) CRUISE BERTH

To Bygdøy

Oslo Walk

1. Central Train Station
2. Oslo Cathedral
3. Stortorvet (Square)
4. Crest of Karl Johans Gate
5. Freia Sign
6. Grand Hotel & Café
7. Parliament Building
8. Statue of Wergeland
9. National Theater
10. City Hall
11. Harbor View
12. Nobel Peace Center

OSLO

OSLO

the snowy winter, you'll walk on bare concrete: Most of downtown Oslo's pedestrian streets are heated.

• *Hook right around the curved old brick structure of an old market and walk to the...*

❷ **Oslo Cathedral** (Domkirke): This Lutheran church is the third cathedral Oslo has had, built in 1697 after the second one

burned down. It's where Norway commemorates its royal marriages and deaths, and national tragedies. In the grass in front of the cathedral, you may see a memorial to the victims of the 2011 bombing and mass shooting.

Look for the cathedral's cornerstone (near the base of the steeple), a thousand-year-old carving from Oslo's first and long-gone cathedral showing how the forces of good and evil tug at each of us. Look high up on the tower. The tiny square windows midway up the copper cupola were once the lookout quarters of the fire watchman.

Step inside (daily 10:00-16:00, Fri until late) beneath the red, blue, and gold seal of Oslo and under an equally colorful ceiling (late Art Deco from the 1930s). The box above on the right is for the royal family. The fine Baroque pulpit and altarpiece date from 1700. The chandeliers are from the previous cathedral (which burned in the 17th century). The colorful windows in the choir (leading up to the altar) were made in 1910 by Emanuel Vigeland (Gustav's less famous brother).

The church courtyard (to the right as you face the entrance) is lined by a circa-1850 circular row of stalls from an **old market.** Rusty meat hooks now decorate the lamps of a peaceful café, which has quaint tables around a fountain. The atmospheric **$$$$ Café Bacchus,** at the far left end of the arcade,

serves food outside and in a classy café downstairs (sandwiches, salads, full meals, good cakes, coffee, Mon-Sat 11:30-22:30, closed Sun, +47 90 51 52 64).

• *The square that faces the cathedral is called...*

❸ **Stortorvet:** In the 17th century, when Oslo's city wall was located about here, this big square was the point where farmers entered and sold their goods. Today it's still lively as a flower and produce market (Mon-Fri). The statue shows Christian IV, the Danish king who ruled Norway around 1600, dramatically gesturing at some geraniums. He named the city, rather immodestly, Christiania. (Oslo took back its old Norse name only in 1925.) Christian was serious about Norway. During his 60-year reign, he visited it 30 times (more than all other royal visits combined during 300 years of Danish rule). The big GlasMagasinet department store is a landmark on this square.

• *Return to Karl Johans Gate, and continue up the boulevard past street performers, cafés, shops, and throngs of people. At the next corner, Kongens Gate leads left, past the 17th-century grid-plan town to Akershus Fortress (described in "Sights in Oslo," later). But we'll continue hiking straight up to the crest of the hill, enjoying some of the buskers along the way.*

Pause at the wide spot in the street (near the T-bane stop) to appreciate the...

❹ **Crest of Karl Johans Gate** (Egertorget): Look back at the train station. A thousand years ago, old Oslo was located at the foot of the wooded hill behind the station. Now look ahead to the **Royal Palace** in the distance, which was built in the 1830s "with nature and God behind it and the people at its feet." If the flag flies atop the palace, the king is in the country.

Karl Johans Gate, a parade ground laid out in about 1850 from here to the palace, is now the axis of modern Oslo. Each May 17, Norway's Constitution Day, an annual children's parade turns this street into a sea of marching student bands and young costumed flag-wavers, while the royal family watches from the palace balcony. Since 1814, Norway has preferred peace. Rather than celebrating its military on the national holiday, it celebrates its children.

In the middle of the small square, the *T* sign marks a stop of the T-bane subway. W. B. Samson's bakery is a good place for a quick, affordable lunch, with a handy cafeteria line (WC in back)—duck inside and be tempted by the pastries. Two traditional favorites are *kanelboller* (cinnamon rolls) and *skolebrød* ("school bread," with an egg and cream filling).

High overhead, the big neon ❺ **Freia sign** (dating from 1911) trumpets another sweet Norwegian treat. Norway's answer to Cadbury, the Norwegian chocolatier Freia is beloved...or it was, until an American company bought it. Still, the local factory is partly operational, and nostalgic Norwegians will always think of Freia as "a little piece of Norway."

Continuing down Karl Johans Gate: People-watching is great along Karl Johans Gate. If it's summer, half of the city's population is gone—vacationing in their cabins or farther

OSLO

away—and the people you'll see in the city center are mostly visitors.

Hike two blocks farther down Karl Johans Gate. The street called **Akersgata,** on your right, kicks off a worthwhile stroll past the site of the July 2011 bombing, the national cemetery, and through a parklike river gorge to the popular Grünerløkka quarter (an hour-long walk, described later, under "Sights in Oslo").

Pass the big brick **Parliament** building (on the left, described later). On your right, seated in the square, is a bearded, tubby statue of the 19th-century painter Christian Krohg.

If you'd like to get a city view (and perhaps a pricey refreshment), enter the glass doors facing the street at #27 (not the bank entrance at the corner) and take the elevator to the eighth-floor rooftop bar, aptly named Eight.

A few doors farther down Karl Johans Gate, just past the Freia shop (selling that favorite Norwegian chocolate), the venerable **Grand Hotel** (Oslo's celebrity hotel—Nobel Peace Prize winners sleep here) overlooks the boulevard.

• *Politely ask the waiter at the Grand Café—part of the Grand Hotel— if you can pop inside for a little sightseeing (he'll generally let you).*

❻ Grand Café: This historic café was for many years the meeting place of Oslo's intellectual and creative elite (playwright Henrik Ibsen was a regular here). It still has some beautiful old artwork—including (at the far back) a wall-length **mural** showing Norway's literary and artistic clientele from a century ago enjoying this fine hangout. On the far left, find Ibsen, coming in as he did every day at 13:00. Behind the waiter on the right, Edvard Munch leans against the window, apparently dozing. Names are on the sill beneath the mural.

• *Continue to the next corner (at the intersection of Karl Johans Gate and Rosenkrantz Gate). To your left, a little park faces Norway's...*

❼ Parliament Building (Stortinget): Norway's parliament meets here (along with anyone participating in a peaceful protest outside). *Stortinget*—from an old Viking word—basically means "Big Gathering." Built in 1866, the building seems to counter the Royal Palace at the other end of Karl Johans Gate. If the flag's flying, parliament's in session. Today the king is a figurehead, and Norway is run by a unicameral parliament and a prime minister. Guided tours of the Stortinget are offered for those interested in Norwegian government (free, 1 hour, typically Sat mornings, may be more frequent in summer—check schedule at www.stortinget. no, enter on Akersgata—on the back side of the building).

• *Cross over into the long median park. On your left, notice the red, white, and blue coin-op public WCs. (Free WCs are inside the Paleet shopping mall, on the right side of the boulevard).*

Enjoying the park, stroll toward the palace, past the fountain. Pause at the...

❽ Statue of Wergeland: The poet Henrik Wergeland helped inspire the national resurgence of Norway during the 19th century. Norway won its independence from Denmark in 1814 but within a year lost its freedom to Sweden. For nearly a century, until Norway regained independence in 1905, Norwegian culture and national spirit was stoked by artistic and literary patriots like Wergeland. In the winter, the pool here is frozen and covered with children happily ice-skating.

Across the street behind Wergeland stands the **❾ National Theater** and statues of Norway's favorite playwrights: Ibsen and Bjørnstjerne Bjørnson.

Across Karl Johans Gate, the pale yellow building is the first university building in Norway, dating from 1854. A block behind that is the National Gallery building (reopening with a new collection in 2021 or later).

Take a moment here to do a 360-degree spin to notice how quiet and orderly everything is. People seem content—and, according to most surveys, Norwegians are among the happiest people on earth. If you ask them why, their hunch is that it's because they live collectively. The Vikings would famously share one large bowl of mead, passing it around the circle. Nobody—no matter how big, angry, hairy, or smelly—gulped more than his share. They all made sure that everyone got some.

In modern times, Norwegians at the dinner table are still mindful when helping themselves not to take too much: They mentally ration enough for the people who come after them. It's a very considerate—and a very Norwegian—way of thinking. (Similarly, upper midwesterners in the US are familiar with the "Minnesota Slice": The Scandinavian-American tendency to carve off a little sliver of the last slice of pie, rather than take the entire thing.)

• *Facing the theater, turn left and follow Roald Amundsens Gate to the towering brick...*

❿ City Hall (Rådhuset): Built mostly in the 1930s with contributions from Norway's leading artists, City Hall is full of great art and is worth touring (see listing later, under "Sights in Oslo"). The mayor has his office

OSLO

here (at the base of one of the two 200-foot towers), and every December 10, this building is where the Nobel Peace Prize is presented. The semicircular square facing the building, called Fridtjof Nansens Plass, was designed to evoke Il Campo, the iconic main square in Siena, Italy, that's also dominated by its City Hall.

To see the City Hall's best exterior art, step up into the U-shaped courtyard and circle it clockwise, savoring the colorful woodcuts in the arcade. Each shows a scene from Norwegian mythology, well explained in English: Thor with his billy-goat chariot, Ask and Embla (a kind of Norse Adam and Eve), Odin on his eight-legged horse guided by ravens, the swan maidens shedding their swan disguises, and so on.

Facing City Hall, circle around its right side (through a lovely garden) until you reach the front. Like all of the statues adorning the building, the **six figures** facing the waterfront—dating from a period of Labor Party rule in Norway—celebrate the nobility of the working class. Norway, a social democracy, believes in giving respect to the workers who built their society and made it what it is, and these laborers are viewed as heroes.

• Walk to the...

⓫ Harbor: Over a decade ago, you would have dodged several lanes of busy traffic to reach Oslo's harborfront. Today, the traffic passes beneath your feet in tunnels. In addition, the city has made its town center relatively quiet and pedestrian-friendly by levying a toll on every car entering town. (This system, like in other European capitals, subsidizes public transit and the city's infrastructure.)

At the water's edge, find the shiny metal plaque (just left of center) listing the contents of a sealed time capsule planted in 2000 in the little Kavringen lighthouse, straight ahead out in the harbor (to be opened in a thousand years).

Head to the end of the stubby pier (just to the right). This is the ceremonial "enter the city" point for momentous occasions. One such instance was in 1905, when Norway gained its independence from Sweden, and a Danish prince, elected by referendum, sailed in from Copenhagen to become the first modern king of Norway. Another milestone event occurred at the end of World War II, when the king returned to Norway after the country was liberated from the Nazis.

• Stand on that important pier and give the harbor a sweeping counterclockwise look.

Harborfront Spin-Tour: Oslofjord is one big playground, with 40 city-owned, parklike islands. Big cruise ships—a large part of the local tourist economy—dock just under the Akershus Fortress on the left. (The big, boxy building clinging to the top of the fortress—just under the green steeple—is the excellent Norwegian Resistance Museum.) Just this side of the fort's impressive

13th-century ramparts, a **statue of FDR** grabs the shade. He's here in gratitude for the safe refuge the US gave to members of the royal family (including the young prince, Harald, who is now Norway's king) during World War II—while the king and his government-in-exile waged Norway's fight against the Nazis from London.

The next **pier** over is the launchpad for harbor boat tours and the shuttle boat to the Bygdøy museums. At the base of this pier, the glassy box is a fish market, serving locals and tourists alike. You may see a fisherman mooring his boat near here, selling shrimp from the back. Nearby, look for a bright-orange container box—an info point for Oslo's impressive **Havnepromenaden,** the 5.5-mile promenade that runs the entire length of the city's harborfront.

Panning left, enjoy the grand view of **City Hall.** The yellow building farther to the left, formerly a train station, today houses the ⓬ **Nobel Peace Center,** which celebrates the work of Nobel Peace Prize winners. Just to the left and behind that is the new **National Museum**, with an impressive collection of Norwegian and international art within its sleek walls (opening 2022).

Turning to facing the harbor, look to the right side, where **Aker Brygge**, Oslo's thriv-ing restaurant/shopping/nightclub zone, has re-placed the shipyard build-ings that were once the heart of Norway's once-important shipbuilding industry. Just past the end of Aker Brygge is **Tjuv-holmen,** an arts district and housing development with some of Norway's most expensive real estate. With outdoor installations, water sculptures, and plenti-ful galleries, it's anchored by the Astrup Fearnley Museum, a mod-ern art complex designed by renowned architect Renzo Piano (most famous for Paris' Pompidou Center).

These flourishing urban spaces are all part of Oslo's ambitious Fjord City (Fjordbyen) urban renewal project, which kicked off years ago with Aker Brygge and Oslo's dramatic Opera House. The city has made remarkable progress in turning the formerly in-dustrial waterfront into an inviting people zone.

• From here, you can stroll out Aker Brygge and through Tjuvholmen to a tiny public beach at the far end; tour City Hall; visit the Nobel Peace Center; hike up to Akershus Fortress; take a harbor **cruise** (see "Tours in Oslo," earlier); or catch a boat across the harbor to the museums at Bygdøy (from pier 3).

OSLO

Oslo Tram Tour

Tram #12, which becomes tram #11 halfway through its loop (at Majorstuen), circles the city from the train station, lacing together many of Oslo's main sights (see

the "Oslo" map on page 220 to trace the route). Apart from the practical value of being able to hop on and off as you sightsee your way around town (trams come by at least every 10 minutes), this 40-minute trip gives you a fine look at parts of the city you wouldn't otherwise see.

This tour starts at the central train station, at the traffic-island tram stop located immediately in front of the Ruter transit office tower. The route makes almost a complete circle and finishes at Stortorvet (the cathedral square), dropping you off a three-minute walk from where you began the tour. Ongoing construction work may disrupt trams occasionally, but the route I've outlined here should still be doable.

Starting out, you want tram #12 as it leaves from the second set of tracks, going toward Majorstuen. Confirm with your driver that the particular tram #12 you're boarding becomes tram #11 and finishes at Stortorvet; some turn into tram #19 instead, which takes a different route. If yours becomes #19, simply hop out at Majorstuen and wait for the next #11.

Here's what you'll see and places where you might want to hop out:

From the **station,** you'll go through the old grid streets of 16th-century Christiania, King Christian IV's planned Renaissance town. After the city's 17th fire, in 1624, the king finally got fed up. He decreed that only brick and stone buildings would be permitted in the city center, with wide streets to serve as fire breaks.

You'll turn a corner at the **fortress** (Christiania Torv stop; get off here for the fortress and Norwegian Resistance Museum), then head for **City Hall** (Rådhus stop). Next comes the harbor and upscale **Aker Brygge** waterfront neighborhood (jump off at the Aker Brygge stop for the National Museum, harbor, and restaurant row). Passing the harbor, you'll see on the left a few old shipyard buildings that still survive. Then the tram goes uphill into a district of ugly 1960s buildings (when elegance was replaced by "functionality"). The tram then heads onto the street Norwegians renamed **Henrik Ibsens Gate** in 2006 to commemorate the centenary of Ibsen's death, honoring the man they claim is the greatest playwright since Shakespeare.

After Henrik Ibsens Gate, the tram follows Frognerveien

through the chic **Frogner neighborhood.** Behind the fine old facades are fancy shops and spendy condos. Here and there you'll see
19th-century mansions built by aristocratic families who wanted
to live near the Royal Palace; today, many of these house foreign
embassies. Turning the corner, you roll along the edge of **Frogner
Park** (which includes **Vigeland Sculpture Park**), stopping at its
grand gate (hop out at the Vigelandsparken stop).

Ahead on the left, a statue of 1930s ice queen Sonja Henie
marks the arena where she learned to skate. Turning onto Bogstadveien, the tram usually becomes #11 at the Majorstuen stop.
Bogstadveien is lined with trendy shops, restaurants, and cafés—
it's a fun place to stroll and window-shop. (You could get out here
and walk along this street all the way to the Royal Palace park and
the top of Karl Johans Gate.) The tram veers left before the palace,
passing the **Historical Museum** and stopping at the red-brick **National Gallery** building (Tullinløkka stop). As you trundle along,
you may notice that lots of roads are ripped up for construction. It's
too cold to fix the streets in winter, so, when possible, the work is
done in summer. Jump out at **Stortorvet** (the big square filled with
flower stalls and fronted by the cathedral and the big GlasMagasinet department store). From here, you're a three-minute walk from
the station, where this tour began.

Sights in Oslo

SIGHTSEEING PASS

The **Oslo Pass** covers the city's public transit, ferry boats, and entry
to nearly every major sight—all described in a useful handbook
(445 NOK/24 hours, 655 NOK/48 hours, 820 NOK/72 hours, big
discounts for kids ages 6-17 and seniors 67 and over). It's best to buy
the pass from the TI upon arrival in Oslo. Some included sights sell
the 24-hour adult pass, but they may not sell the kids or senior pass.
Students with an ISIC card may be better off without the pass.

NEAR THE HARBORFRONT
▲▲▲City Hall (Rådhuset)

City halls, rather than churches, are the dominant buildings
in Scandinavian capitals. In 1931, Oslo tore down a slum and
began constructing its richly decorated City Hall. It was finally
finished—after a WWII delay—in 1950 to celebrate the city's
900th birthday. Norway's leading artists all contributed to the
building, which was an avant-garde thrill in its day. The promi-
nence of this building on the harborfront makes sense in this
most humanistic, yet least churchgoing, northern end of the
Continent. Up here, people pay high taxes, have high expecta-

OSLO

tions, and are generally satisfied with what their governments do with their money.

Cost and Hours: Free, daily 9:00-16:00, June-Aug until 18:00, free and fine WC in basement, +47 23 46 12 00, www.oslo. kommune.no/radhuset.

Tours: Free 45-minute guided tours generally run daily at 10:00, 12:00, and 14:00. Tours may not operate Sept-May, so check ahead.

❷ **Self-Guided Tour:** For descriptions of the building's exterior features and symbolism, see the City Hall section of my Oslo Walk, earlier. This tour focuses on the interior.

The visitor entrance is on the Karl Johans Gate side (away from the harbor). You'll step into a cavernous **main hall,** which feels like a temple to good government, with its altar-like murals celebrating "work, play, and civic administration." It's decorated with 20,000 square feet of bold and colorful murals celebrating a classless society, with everyone—town folk, country folk, and people from all walks of life—working harmoniously for a better society. The huge murals take you on a voyage through the collective psyche of Norway, from its simple rural beginnings through the scar tissue of the Nazi occupation and beyond. Filled with significance and symbolism—and well described in English—the murals become even more meaningful with the excellent guided tours.

First, turn around and face the mural over the door you came in, which celebrates the **traditional industries** of Norway (from left to right): the yellow-clad fisherman (standing in his boat, glancing nervously at a flock of seagulls), the factory worker (with his heavy apron), the blue-clad sailor (he's playing with exotic beads acquired through distant trade), the farmer (in a striped dress, with a bushel under her arm), and the miner (lower right, lifting a heavy rock). Flanking these figures are portraits of two important Norwegians: On the far right is Bjørnstjerne Bjørnson (1832-1910), a prominent poet and novelist whose works pluck the patriotic heartstrings of Norwegians. And on the far left is Fridtjof Nansen (1861-1930), the famous Arctic explorer (you can learn more about him at the Fram Museum on Bygdøy). Here Nansen sheds the heavy coat of his most famous endeavor—polar exploration—as he embarks on his second act: Once retired from seafaring, he advocated for the dissolution of Norway's union with Sweden—which took place in 1905, making Norway fully independent.

Now turn 180 degrees and face the hall's main mural, which emphasizes **Oslo's youth** participating in community life—and rebuilding the country after Nazi occupation. Across the bottom, the slum that once cluttered up Oslo's harborfront is being cleared out to make way for this building. Above that, scenes show Norway's pride in its innovative health care and education systems. Left of center, near the top, Mother Norway stands next to a church—reminding viewers that the Lutheran Church of Norway (the official state religion) provides a foundation for this society. On the right, four forms represent the arts; they illustrate how creativity springs from children. And in the center, the figure of Charity is surrounded by Culture, Philosophy, and Family.

The **Mural of the Occupation** lines the east side of the hall, tucked under the balustrade. Scan it from left to right to see the

story of Norway's WWII experience: First, the German blitzkrieg overwhelms the country. Men head for the mountains to organize a resistance movement. Women huddle around the water well, traditionally where news is passed, while Quislings (traitors named after the Norwegian fascist who ruled the country as a Nazi puppet) listen in. While Germans bomb and occupy Norway, a family gathers in their living room. As a boy clenches his fist (showing determination) and a child holds the beloved Norwegian flag, the Gestapo steps in. Columns are toppled to the ground, symbolizing how Germans shut down the culture by closing newspapers and the university. Two resistance soldiers stand up against a wall—about to be executed by firing squad. A cell of resistance fighters (wearing masks and using nicknames, so if tortured they can't reveal their compatriots' identities) plan a sabotage mission. Finally, prisoners are freed, the war is over, and Norway celebrates its happiest day, May 17, 1945: the first Constitution Day after five years under Nazi control.

While gazing at these murals, keep in mind that the Nobel Peace Prize is awarded in this central hall each December (though the general Nobel Prize ceremony occurs in Stockholm's City Hall). You'll see photos of this event in the little foyer with the strollers (on the right from where you entered). You can see videos of the ceremony and acceptance speeches in the adjacent Nobel Peace Center (listed later).

At the base of the grand marble staircase is a mural of the 11th-century **St. Hallvard,** the patron saint of Oslo. Above his head, he holds his symbol—three arrows—and he rests a millstone on his knee. As the story goes, Hallvard took pity on a pregnant woman (the naked woman in front of him) who had been wrongly accused of theft by three men. They attempted to escape, but the accusers killed the woman, shot Hallvard with three arrows, tied a millstone around his neck, and tossed him into the fjord. Miraculously, he survived (or perhaps rose from the dead). This story of compassion in the face of injustice swayed Norwegians at a time when Christianity was making its bid to be the country's main religion.

In front of the mural is a **bell** from the ship that brought Norway's royal family back home after World War II—landing at the pier right in front of City Hall.

Now head up the stairs and explore several **ceremonial rooms,** each well described in English. The wood-paneled Munch Room is dominated by the artist's oil painting *Life*. Circle around the gallery to the City Council Assembly Room, where Oslo's leadership steers the agenda of this impressive city. Notice the "three arrows and millstone" motif, recalling St. Hallvard. The city council acts collectively as a virtual "mayor"—a system, originating here in Oslo in 1986, called "parliamentary metropolitan government." Notice how this room evokes the semicircular shape of the square where you entered. Out in the hall, you'll pass gifts from visiting heads of state (*gave fra* means "gift from").

Nearby: Fans of the explorer Fridtjof Nansen might enjoy breaking for a bite or drink across the street at **Fridtjof,** an atmospheric bar filled with memorabilia from Nansen's Arctic explorations. A model of his ship, the *Fram,* hangs from the ceiling, and 1894 photos and his own drawings are upstairs (Mon-Sat 12:00-late, Sun 14:00-22:00, Nansens Plass 7, +47 93 25 22 30).

▲▲▲National Museum (Nasjonalmuseet)

Just steps off the waterfront is Oslo's strikingly modern National Museum building, opening in 2022. The new museum boasts extensive collections of fine art, decorative arts and design, and contemporary art that once had been scattered across three city museums. A tour of these galleries gives travelers bound for the mountains and fjord country a chance to pack along a little of Norway's cultural soul. Don't miss the roof terrace with its dramatic views of Akershus Fortress, Rådhusplassen, and the inner Oslo fjord.

Cost and Hours: Opening in 2022—call ahead or check website for admission price and hours; café and restaurant; Brynjulf Bulls Plass 3, +47 21 98 20 00, www.nasjonalmuseet.no.

Visiting the Museum: The permanent collection is installed

Edvard Munch (1863-1944)

Edvard Munch (pronounced "moonk") is Norway's most famous and influential painter. His life was rich, complex, and sad. His father was a doctor who had a nervous breakdown. His mother and sister both died of tuberculosis. He knew suffering. And he gave us the enduring symbol of 20th-century pain, *The Scream*.

Munch was also Norway's most forward-thinking painter, a man who traveled extensively through Europe, soaking up the colors of the Post-Impressionists and the curves of Art Nouveau. Living in Germany in the years before World War I, he helped pioneer a radical new style—Expressionism—in which raw emotion was the subject. Jarring colors and wavy lines "expressed" inner turmoil and the angst of the modern world.

After a nervous breakdown in late 1908, followed by eight months of rehab in a clinic, Munch emerged less troubled—but a less powerful painter. His late works were as a colorist: big, bright, less tormented...and less noticed.

Munch painted several versions of *The Scream:* You can see the 1910 version and much more of the artist's work at the Munch Museum (see page 246); another version of *The Scream,* from 1893, is at the National Museum.

in an ambitious chronology over two floors. The collection is international in scope, but to make the most of a visit here, focus on what's uniquely Norwegian—you're sure to see plenty that showcases the harsh beauty of Norway's landscape and the resourcefulness of the Norwegian people.

Displays on the ground floor focus on design and decorative objects, including ancient Roman artifacts, imperial Chinese porcelain, the treasured medieval Baldishol Tapestry (the oldest in Norway), Norwegian glass, and contemporary crafts.

The first floor showcases art from the 15th century to the present. Highlights are 17th-century Dutch landscapes and still lifes, early 19th-century landscapes by the Norwegian Romantic painter Johan Christian Dahl, modern classics by Impressionists and international 20th-century masters, and the moody canvases of Norway's most renowned artist, Edvard Munch—including the 1893 version of his iconic *Scream*. In response to early criticism of the painting, Munch himself added a barely visible inscription to the canvas: "Could only have been painted by a madman!"

The boxy top floor of the musem is dubbed the Light Hall (Lyshallen) for its translucent, illuminated profile. This vast space is reserved for special exhibits of Norwegian and international art.

Nobel Peace Center (Nobels Fredssenter)

This museum, housed in a former train station, celebrates the 800-some past and present Nobel Peace Prize winners and poses the question, "What is the opposite of conflict?" The ground floor is dominated by temporary exhibits on themes related to the Peace Prize ideals. The permanent collection upstairs is modest:

First you'll step into the Nobel Field, a sea of lights and touchscreens profiling various past prizewinners (from Teddy Roosevelt to Mother Theresa). Next, the Nobel Chamber has a big virtual book that invites you to learn more about the life and work of Alfred Nobel, the Swedish inventor of dynamite, who initiated the prizes.

Cost and Hours: 100 NOK; daily 10:00-18:00, closed Mon Sept-mid-May; includes English guided tours at 14:00 and 15:00—off-season weekends only at 14:00; Brynjulfs Bulls Plass 1, +47 48 30 10 00, www.nobelpeacecenter.org.

▲Aker Brygge and Tjuvholmen

Oslo's harborfront was dominated by the **Aker Brygge** shipyard until it closed in 1986. In the late 2000s, it became the first finished part of the Fjordbyen (Fjord City) urban renewal project, which has converted part of Oslo's harborfront into a people-friendly park and culture zone. Today's Aker Brygge is a stretch of overpriced waterfront restaurants facing a fine promenade—just the place to join in on a Nordic stroll on a balmy summer's eve.

The far end of Aker Brygge is marked by a big black anchor from the wreck of the German warship *Blücher*, sunk by Norwegian forces near Drøbak while heading for Oslo during the Nazi invasion on April 9, 1940. From there a bridge crosses over onto **Tjuvholmen** (Thief Island, where Oslo hung thieves back in the 17th century). This planned community boasts the

costliest apartments in town, private moorings for luxury jet boats, boardwalks with built-in seating to catch the sun, elegant shops and cafés, and the striking, wood-clad, glass-roofed **Astrup Fearnley Museum of Modern Art** (good temporary exhibits, closed Mon, www.afmuseet.no). On the harbor side of the museum, find the grassy little knob of land with an appealing sculpture park. This area is well worth a wander, including the back lanes away from the water. As you stroll here, admire how, while the entire complex feels cohesive, each building has its own personality.

Eating: Dining here is appealing but be prepared to pay royally for the experience. Choose from a slew of restaurants, or picnic on a budget at one of the many public benches, tables, or lounge chairs that offer the best seats of all (grocery stores are a block away from the harborfront views). For recommendations, see "Eating in Oslo," later.

AKERSHUS FORTRESS COMPLEX

This parklike complex of sights, worth ▲, is scattered over Oslo's fortified old center. It's also a military base, and you'll see

uniformed members of the Royal Guard keeping watch over the royal mausoleum here. But the public is welcome, and as you dodge patrol guards and vans filled with soldiers, you'll see the castle, war memorials, the Norwegian Resistance Museum,

and cannon-strewn ramparts affording fine harbor views and picnic perches. Expect bumpy cobblestone lanes and steep hills.

Hours: The park is generally open daily 6:00-21:00 (until 18:00 in winter). There's an unimpressive changing of the guard—that's singular "guard," as in just one—daily at 13:30 (at the parade ground, deep in the castle complex).

Getting There: It's a sprawling complex. From the harbor, you can hike up the stairs by the FDR statue or (less steeply) from the grid of streets just east of City Hall. As you hike up toward the ramparts, go through the gate smack in the middle of the complex (rather than hooking up around to the right). You'll pop out into an inner courtyard. The visitors center (described next) is to the left, and the other sights are through the gate on the right. Heading through this gate, you'll curl up along a tree-lined lane, then pass the Norwegian Resistance Museum on your right (capping the ramparts). The entrance to the castle is dead ahead. There are terrific harbor views from the rampart alongside the Resistance Museum.

Fortress Visitors Center: Stop here to pick up the fortress trail and site map, quickly browse through a modest exhibit tracing the story of Oslo's fortifications from medieval times, use the free WCs, and consider catching a tour (daily May-Aug 10:00-17:00, shorter hours off-season, +47 23 09 39 17, www.akershusfestning. no).

Fortress Tours: Hour-long English walking tours of the grounds help you make sense of the most historic piece of real estate in Oslo (100 NOK, July-mid-Aug daily in English at 11:00 and 15:00, off-season Sat-Sun only at 13:00; departs from Fortress Visitors Center, call ahead to confirm tour is running).

▲▲Norwegian Resistance Museum (Norges Hjemmefrontmuseum)

This fascinating museum tells the story of Norway's WWII experience: appeasement, Nazi invasion (they made Akershus one of their headquarters), resistance, liberation, and, finally, the return of the king. This is an inspirational look at how the national spirit can endure total occupation by a malevolent force. While the exhibit grows a bit more old-fashioned with each passing year, for those with an appetite for WWII history and the patience to read the displays, it's both riveting and stirring. Norway had the fiercest resistance movement in Scandinavia, and this museum shows off their (hard-earned) pride.

Cost and Hours: 60 NOK; daily 10:00-17:00, Sept-April until 16:00; next to castle, overlooking harbor, +47 23 09 31 38, www.forsvaretsmuseer.no.

Visiting the Museum: It's a one-way, chronological route. As you enter the exhibit, you're transported back to 1940, greeted by an angry commotion of rifles aimed at you. A German notice proclaiming "You will submit or die" is bayonetted onto a gun in the middle. A **timeline** on the right wall traces the brief history of skirmishes between Nazi and improvised Norwegian forces following the invasion on April 9, 1940. This ends abruptly on June 10, when the Norwegian government officially capitulates.

On the left, you'll see the German ultimatum to which King Haakon VII gave an emphatic "No." A video screen nearby plays the radio address by Vidkun Quisling, the fascist Nasjonal Samling (National Union Party) politician who declared himself ruler of Norway on the day of the invasion. (Today, Quisling's name remains synonymous with "traitor"—the Norwegian version of Benedict Arnold.)

Head **downstairs** to explore the in-depth exhibits. Various displays show secret radios, transmitters, and underground newspapers. The official name for the resistance was Milorg (for "Military Organization")—but Norwegians affectionately referred to the ragtag, guerilla force as simply *gutta på skauen* ("the boys in the forest"). Look for the display case explaining wartime difficulty and austerity in Norway. Red knit caps were worn by civilians to show solidarity with the resistance—until the hats were outlawed by Nazi officials. In the same case, notice the shoes made of fish skin, and the little row of *erstatning* (ersatz, or replacement) products. With the Nazi occupation, Norway lost its trade partners, and had to improvise.

You'll also learn about the military actions against the occupation. British-trained special forces famously blew up a strategic heavy water plant (a key part of the Nazis' atomic bomb program). The event is immortalized in the not-so-accurate 1965 Kirk Douglas film *The Heroes of Telemark*. Nearby, see the case of crude but effective homemade weapons and the German machine used to locate clandestine radio stations. Exhibits explain how the country coped with 350,000 occupying troops; how airdrops equipped a home force of 40,000 so they were ready to coordinate with the Allies when liberation was imminent; and the happy day when the resistance army came out of the forest, and peace and freedom returned to Norway. Liberation day was May 8, 1945...but it took a few days to pull together the celebration, which coincided neatly with the 17th of May—Constitution Day. (That's partly why May 17 is still celebrated so fiercely today.)

Back **upstairs,** notice the propaganda posters trying to recruit Norwegians to the Nazi cause and "protect the eastern border" from the Soviets and communism. A more recent addition to the museum (downstairs) considers the many Norwegians who did choose to cooperate with (and profit from) the Nazis.

The museum is particularly poignant because many of the patriots featured inside were executed by the Germans right out-

OSLO

side the museum's front door; a **stone memorial** marks the spot. (At war's end, the traitor Vidkun Quisling was also executed at the fortress, but at a different location.)

Akershus Castle (Akershus Slott)

One of Oslo's oldest buildings, the castle overlooking the harbor, with big, empty rooms, recalls Norway's medieval poverty. Norwegians built the first fortress here in 1299; later, in 1649, the Danes made it stronger so the Danish king Christian IV would have a suitable and safe place to stay dur-

ing his many visits. When Oslo was rebuilt in the 17th century, many of the stones from the first Oslo cathedral were reused here, in the fortress walls.

Cost and Hours: 100 NOK, includes audioguide; Mon-Sat 10:00-16:00, Sun from 12:00; Sept-April Sat-Sun 12:00-17:00 only, closed Mon-Fri; +47 23 09 35 53. The castle has been closed for renovation but should reopen by the time you visit—check locally.

Visiting the Castle: From the old kitchen, where the ticket desk and gift shop are located, you'll follow a one-way circuit of rooms open to the public. Descend through a secret passage to the dungeon, crypt, and royal tomb. Emerge behind the altar in the chapel, then walk through echoing rooms including the Daredevil's Tower, Hall of Christian IV (with portraits of Danish kings of Norway on the walls), and Hall of Olav V.

Old Christiania

In the mid-1600s, the ruling Danes had the original Oslo leveled and built a more modern grid-planned city named Christiania, after their king. They located it just below the castle for easier control and defense, and built with stone so it wouldn't burn. The checkerboard neighborhood between the castle and the cathedral today—aptly called Kvadraturen—marks that original Christiania town. There's little to see, but curious tourists can wander through this sleepy zone (between the castle and Karl Johans Gate) and look for some 17th-century buildings. Bits of Christiania's original Dutch Renaissance-style buildings survive. (Norwegian builders, accustomed to working with wood, lacked skill with stone, so the

Danes imported Dutch builders.) The area's main square, Christiania Torv (near the recommended Café Skansen), is marked by a modern fountain called "The Glove." The sculpture of Christian IV's glove points as if to indicate, "This is where we'll build my city." The old City Hall, now the Gamle Raadhus restaurant, survives.

ON THE WATERFRONT, NEAR THE TRAIN STATION
▲Oslo Opera House (Operahuset Oslo)

Oslo's striking Opera House angles up from the water on the city's

eastern harbor, across from the train station. Its boxy, low-slung, glass center holds a state-of-the-art 1,400-seat main theater with a 99-piece orchestra "in the pit," which can rise to put the orchestra "on the pedestal." The season is split between opera and ballet.

Cost and Hours: Foyer and café/restaurant open daily roughly 11:00-18:00, open longer hours during performances.

Tours: Fascinating 50-minute guided tours of the stage, backstage area, and architecture run year-round (120 NOK; usually 1-2 tours/day in English—generally at 12:00 and 13:00; reserve online at www.operaen.no, +47 21 42 21 00).

Daytime Mini-Concerts: For a few weeks in the summer, the Opera House offers sporadic one-hour daytime concerts (70 NOK, many days in late July at 14:00).

Getting There: You'll find it on Bjørvika, the next harbor over from City Hall and Akershus Fortress—just below the train station.

Visiting the Opera House: Information-packed tours explain what makes this one of the greenest buildings in Europe and why Norwegian taxpayers helped foot its half-billion-dollar construction cost—to make high culture (ballet and opera) accessible to the younger generation and a stratum of society who normally wouldn't care. You'll see a workshop employing 50 people who hand-make costumes, and learn how a foundation of 700 pylons set some 150 feet deep support the jigsaw puzzle of wood, glass, and 36,000 individual pieces of marble. The construction masterfully integrates land and water, inside and outside, nature and culture.

The jutting white marble planes of the Opera House's roof double as a public plaza. You feel a need to walk all over it. The

OSLO

Opera House is part of a larger harbor-redevelopment plan that included rerouting traffic into tunnels and turning a once-derelict industrial zone into an urban park. If you hike all the way to the top of the building (watch your footing—it's slippery when wet), you can peek over the back railing to see the high-rise development known as the Barcode Project. This sleek and distinctive collection of high-rise office buildings resembles the bars in a universal product code. The new Munch Museum resides in the futuristic building on the adjacent pier.

▲Munch Museum (Munchmuseet)

The only Norwegian painter to have had a serious impact on European art, Edvard Munch (pronounced "moonk") developed an international reputation during the 16 years he lived and worked in Germany (1892-1908)—an especially prolific period during which he created many of his most well-regarded works. But a breakdown in 1908 sent him back to Oslo, where he would live out his life working quietly at his property just outside the city. At his death in 1944, he left all the artwork still in his possession—thousands of paintings, drawings, photographs, and prints—to the city of Oslo.

These collections are now stretched over the 11 galleries and 13 floors of a new modernistic building sitting on the harbor, not far from the Opera House. This is the place to appreciate in depth the emotional, disturbing, and powerfully Expressionistic work of this strange and perplexing man, including one version of his most famous painting, *The Scream* (for more on Munch, see page 239). Works by other modernist and contemporary artists round out the exhibits.

Cost and Hours: 160 NOK, daily 10:00-20:00, café and restaurant, on the harbor at Edvard Munchs Plass 1, +47 23 49 35 00, www.munchmuseet.no.

IN THE CITY CENTER
Royal Palace (Slottet)

Set at the top of Karl Johans Gate, the Neoclassical Royal Palace is home to Norway's King Harald V and Queen Sonja. Completed in 1849, it was extensively (and expensively) renovated in 2001. To quell controversy the public is now invited inside each summer with a one-hour guided tour that includes the king's Council Chamber, the Great Dining Room (seating for 220), and the palace's finest guest room, the King Haakon suite.

Cost and Hours: 135 NOK, English tours 4/day late June-mid-Aug, tickets go on sale in March and fill fast—it's smart to book in advance at www.ticketmaster.no, limited number of tickets are available at the entrance, www.kongehuset.no.

Historical Museum (Historisk Museum)

Just below the Royal Palace is a fine Art Nouveau building offering exhibits about the history of humankind—and an easy peek at Norway's history, from the Stone Age to modern times. Skip over the ancient Egypt, Greek, and Roman displays to focus on the country's top collection of Viking artifacts.

Cost and Hours: 100 NOK, same ticket covers Viking Ship Museum on Bygdøy for 48 hours; open Tue-Sun 10:00-17:00, mid-Sept-mid-May 11:00-16:00; closed Mon year-round; Frederiks Gate 2, +47 22 85 19 00, www.khm.uio.no.

Visiting the Museum: The ground floor has medieval and Viking Age artifacts from around Norway. Ogle the gorgeous carved doors with their filigreed details from stave churches. Look for the little door to the easy-to-miss Viking section, where you'll find the museum's hidden highlight: the only intact, authentic Viking helmet ever found in Scandinavia (with an eye mask; it's unceremoniously jammed into a crowded display case). Upstairs is an exhibit about life for the far northern Sami people and other Arctic cultures. It's fun to peek in the cutaway igloo for a glimpse at Inuit lifestyles. There's also a modest anthropological exhibit about indigenous peoples of the Americas. A few Egyptian mummies and Norwegian coins through the ages are tossed in for good measure.

National Gallery (Nasjonalgalleriet)

Part of the National Museum, Oslo's National Gallery is temporarily closed. When it reopens, visitors can expect art collections, workshops, and rotating exhibitions (backing up to the Historical Museum at Universitetsgata 13, +47 21 98 20 00, www.nasjonalmuseet.no).

FROGNER PARK

The sprawling Frogner Park anchors an upscale neighborhood of the same name, 1.5 miles west of the city center. Here you'll find the breathtaking Vigeland Sculpture Park, the Vigeland Museum, and the Oslo City Museum. The Frognerbadet swimming pool is nearby.

Getting There: Tram #12—which leaves from the central train station, Rådhusplassen in front of City Hall, Aker Brygge, and other points in town—drops you off right at the park gate (Vigelandsparken stop). Tram #19 (with stops along Karl Johans Gate) takes you to Majorstuen, a 10-minute walk to the gate (or you can change at Majorstuen to tram #12 and ride it two stops to Vigelandsparken).

▲▲▲Vigeland Sculpture Park (Vigelandsparken)

Within Oslo's vast Frogner Park is Vigeland Sculpture Park, containing a lifetime of work by Norway's greatest sculptor, Gustav

OSLO

Frogner Park

Note: Vigeland Sculpture Park is the shaded area within Frogner Park—from the Main Entrance Gate to the Wheel of Life

100 Meters
100 Yards

West Cemetery

WHEEL OF LIFE

TOUR ENDS

MONOLITH

MALE GATE

FEMALE GATE

VIGELAND SCULPTURE PARK

MADSERUD ALLE

FOUNTAIN

Frogner   Park

ROSE GARDEN

VIGELAND MUSEUM

Pond

ANGRY BOY →

HALVDAN SVARTES GATE

BRIDGE

FROGNER-BADET (POOL)

NOBELS GATE

OSLO CITY MUSEUM

CAFÉ

MONOLITHVEIEN

FROGNER STADIUM

MIDDELTHUNS GATE

TOUR BEGINS

VISITORS CENTER CAFETERIA & WC

Frogner #12   T   Frogner Plass

MAIN ENTRANCE GATE

THOMAS HEFTYES GATE

FROGNERVEIEN

To Oslo Center

GYLDENLOVES GATE

#12 Vigelands-parken

MUNTHES GATE

SONJA HENIE STATUE

KIRKEVEIEN

PROF DAHLS GATE

To Majorstuen

Lofotstua Restaurant

T Frogner Stadion #12

MARIES GATE

Curry and Ketchup Indian Restaurant

Vigeland Sculpture Park Tour
1. Gustav Vigeland Statue
2. Bridge
3. Fountain
4. Monolith

Eateries
5. Lofotstua Restaurant
6. Curry and Ketchup Indian Restaurant

OSLO

Vigeland (see sidebar). In 1921, he made a deal with the city. In return for a great studio and state support, he'd spend his creative life beautifying Oslo with this sculpture garden. From 1924 until his death in 1943 he worked on-site, designing 192 bronze and granite statue groupings—600 figures in all, each nude and unique. Vigeland even planned the landscaping.

Today the park is loved and respected by the people of Oslo (no police, no fences—and no graffiti). At once majestic, hands-on, entertaining, and deeply moving, I find this park to be one of Europe's top artistic sights. In summer, this is a tempting destination in the late afternoon—after the museums have closed and there's still plenty of daylight. (Note that the nearby Vigeland Museum closes at 16:00.) The sculpture park is more than great art: It's a city at play. Appreciate its urban Norwegian ambience.

Cost and Hours: The garden is always open and free. The park is safe and lit in the evening.

Visitor Information and Services: For an illustrated guide and fine souvenir, consider the 120-NOK book in the visitors center (*besøkssenter*) on your right as you enter. The modern **$$** cafeteria has sandwiches and light meals (indoor/outdoor seating, daily 9:00-20:30 in summer, shorter hours off-season), plus books, gifts, and pay WCs.

➋ Self-Guided Tour: Frogner Park is huge, but this visit to its central spine, the Vigeland Sculpture Park, is a snap. Here's a quick, four-stop, straight-line, gate-to-monolith tour.

• *Begin by entering the park through the grand gates, from Kirkeveien (with the tram stop). In front of the visitors center, look at the...*

❶ Gustav Vigeland Statue: Vigeland has his hammer and chisel in hand...and is drenched in pigeon poop. Consider his messed-up life. He lived with his many models. His marriages failed. His children entangled his artistic agenda. He didn't age gracefully. He didn't name his statues, and he refused to explain their meanings. While those who know his life story can read it clearly in the granite and bronze, I'd forget Gustav's troubles and see his art as observations on the bittersweet cycle of life in general—from a man who must have had a passion for living.

• *Now walk 100 yards toward the fountain and the pillar.*

❷ Bridge: The 300-foot-long bridge is bound by four granite columns: Three show a man fighting a lizard, and the fourth shows a woman submitting to the lizard's embrace. Hmmm. (Vigeland was familiar with medieval mythology, where dragons represent man's primal—and sinful—nature.)

But enough lizard love; the 58 bronze statues along the bridge are a general study of the human body. They capture the joys of life (and, on a sunny day, so do the Norwegians and tourists filling the park around you). Many deal with relationships between people. In the middle, on the right, find the circular statue of a man and woman going round and round—perhaps the eternal attraction and love between the sexes. But directly opposite, another circle feels

OSLO

Gustav Vigeland (1869-1943)

Gustav Vigeland's father was a carpenter in the city of Mandal, in southern Norway. Vigeland grew up carving wood and showed promise. As a young man, he went to Oslo to study sculpture, then supplemented his education with trips abroad to Europe's art capitals. Back home, he carved out a successful, critically acclaimed career feeding newly independent Norway's hunger for homegrown art.

During his youthful trips abroad, Vigeland had frequented the studio of Auguste Rodin, admiring Rodin's naked, restless, intertwined statues. Like Rodin, Vigeland explored the yin/yang relationship of men and women. Also like Rodin, Vigeland did not personally carve or cast his statues. Rather, he formed them in clay or plaster, to be executed by a workshop of assistants. Vigeland's sturdy humans capture universal themes of the cycle of life—birth, childhood, romance, struggle, child-rearing, growing old, and death.

---

like a prison—man against the world, with no refuge.

On your left, see the famous *Angry Boy (Sinnataggen),* the hot-headed little boy and a symbol of the park. (Notice his left hand is worn shiny from too many hand-holdings.) It's said Vigeland gave a boy chocolate and then took it away to get this reaction. Look below the angry toddler, to the lower terrace—with eight bronze infants circling a head-down fetus.

• *Continue through a rose garden to the earliest sculpture unit in the park.*

❸ **Fountain:** Six giants hold a fountain, symbolically toiling with the burden of life, as water—the source of life—cascades steadily around them. Twenty tree-of-life groups surround the fountain. Four clumps of trees (on each corner) show humanity's relationship to nature and the seasons of life: childhood, young love, adulthood, and winter.

Take a quick swing through life, starting on the right with youth. In the branches you'll see a swarm of children (Vigeland called them "geniuses"): A boy sits in a tree, boys actively climb while most girls stand by quietly, and a girl glides through the branches wide-eyed and ready for life...and love. Circle clockwise to the next stage: love scenes. In the third corner, life becomes more complicated: a sad woman in an animal-like tree, a lonely child, a couple plummeting

OSLO

downward (perhaps falling out of love), a man desperately clinging to his tree, and finally an angry man driving away babies. The fourth corner completes the cycle, as death melts into the branches of the tree of life and you realize new geniuses will bloom.

The 60 bronze reliefs circling the basin develop the theme further, showing man mixing with nature and geniuses giving the

carousel of life yet another spin. Speaking of another spin, circle again and follow these reliefs.

The pattern in the pavers surrounding the basin is a maze—life's long and winding road with twists, dead ends, frustrations, and, ultimately, a way out. If you have about an hour to spare, enter the labyrinth (on the side nearest the park's entrance gate, there's a single break in the black border) and follow the white granite path until (on the monolith side) you finally get out. (Tracing this path occupies older kids, affording parents a peaceful break in the park.)

• *Or you can go straight up the steps to the...*

❹ **Monolith:** The centerpiece of the park—a teeming monolith of life surrounded by 36 groups of granite statues—continues Vigeland's cycle-of-life motif. The figures are hunched and clearly earthbound, while Vigeland explores a lifetime of human relationships. At the center, 121 figures carved out of a single block of stone rocket skyward. Three stone carvers worked daily for 14 years, cutting Vigeland's full-size plaster model into the final 180-ton, 50-foot-tall erection.

Circle the plaza, once to trace the stages of life in the 36 statue groups, and a second time to enjoy how Norwegian kids relate to the art. The statues—both young and old—seem to speak to children. Note the two wrought iron gates flanking each side of the plaza with their themes of male and female.

Vigeland lived barely long enough to see his monolith raised. Covered with bodies, it seems to pick up speed as it spirals skyward. Some people seem to naturally rise. Others struggle not to fall. Some help others. Although the granite groups around the monolith are easy to understand, Vigeland left the meaning of the monolith itself open to interpretation. Like life, it can be experienced many different ways.

From this summit of the park, look a hundred yards farther, where four children and three adults are intertwined and spinning in the *Wheel of Life* sculpture. Now, look back at the entrance. If the main gate is at 12 o'clock, the studio where Vigeland lived and worked—now the Vigeland Museum—is at 2 o'clock (see the green copper tower poking above the trees). His ashes sit in the top of the tower in clear view of the monolith. If you liked the park, visit the Vigeland Museum (described next), a delightful five-minute walk away, for an intimate look at the art and how it was made.

▲▲Vigeland Museum

This palatial city-provided studio was Gustav Vigeland's home and workplace for the last two decades of his life. The high south-facing windows provided just the right light. Vigeland, who had a deeply religious upbringing, saw his art as an expression of his soul. He once said, "The road between feeling and execution should be as short as possible." Here, immersed in his work, Vigeland supervised his craftsmen like a father, from 1924 until his death in 1943.

Today it's filled with plaster casts and studies of many of the works you'll see in the adjacent park—shedding new light on that masterpiece and allowing you to see familiar pieces from new angles. It also holds a few additional works and explains Vigeland's creative (and technical) process. While his upstairs apartment is usually closed to the public, it may be open for guided tours—check the website.

Cost and Hours: 100 NOK; Tue-Sun 10:00-16:00, closed Mon year-round; bus #20 or tram #12 to Frogner Plass, Nobels Gate 32, +47 23 49 37 00, www.vigeland.museum.no.

Visiting the Museum: It's all on one floor, roughly arranged chronologically, which you'll see in an easy clockwise loop. **Rooms I-III** explain Vigeland's development, including his early focus on biblical themes. In *Accused* (1891), Cain flees with his family, including their dog. But gradually, Vigeland grew more interested in the dynamics between families, and those between men and women. In these first rooms, look for two particularly touching sculptures in marble (a medium you won't often see used by Vigeland): *Mother and Child* (1909) and *Young Man and Woman* (1906).

Room IV is a long hall of portrait busts, which Vigeland often created without payment—he considered this task an opportunity to practice. While most of the busts don't depict famous people, you will see King Oscar II and Arctic explorer Fridtjof Nansen. **Room V** continues this theme, with a few portraits (mostly full-body) of more recognizable figures: Beethoven, Ibsen, Wergeland, Bjørnson.

Room VI, with a 1942 self-portrait, explains the process by which Vigeland created his statues. See his tools displayed in a case and read the explanation: Using the "sand casting" method, Vigeland would make a small plaster model, which guided his workers in creating a metal "skeleton." Vigeland would then bring the skeleton to life with soft clay—which he enjoyed using because its pliability allowed him to be spontaneous in his creativity. Once the clay piece was finished, plaster and sand were used to create a cast, used for the final bronze piece. For his stone works, they used a "pointing machine" to painstakingly measure the exact nuances of Vigeland's contours. Examples of using both methods (including five different versions of the famous "angry baby" bronze) are displayed around the room.

Room VII holds temporary exhibits, while **Room VIII** features the full-sized plaster models for the park's bronze fountain. The large **Room IX** has more pieces from the park, including a one-fifth-scale model of the fountain (used to win the Oslo City Council's support for the project) and the four dragon statues that top the bridge's pillars (high up and difficult to see in the park, but fascinating up close).

Room X is the dramatic climax of the museum, with a model of the entire park, and the life-size plaster models for the Monolith—in three pieces, making it easy to scrutinize the details. You'll also see wrought-iron chained dragons—originally designed as a feature for the park gates—and several plaster models for the statues that surround the Monolith. Notice the many little "freckles" on these statues, left behind by the pointer used by craftsmen to replicate Vigeland's work. The museum finishes with more temporary exhibits (in Rooms XI and XII).

Oslo City Museum (Oslo Bymuseum)

This modest, hard-to-be-thrilled-about exhibit tells the story of Oslo. For a quick overview of the city, watch the 15-minute English video (90 NOK, includes audioguide, Tue-Sun 11:00-16:00,

OSLO

closed Mon, across street from the Vigeland Museum in Frogner Manor Farm, +47 23 28 41 70, www.oslomuseum.no).

Frognerbadet
Located near Vigeland Sculpture Park, the Frognerbadet has three outdoor pools, a waterslide, high dives, a cafeteria, and lots of young families (open mid-May-late Aug, closed off-season, Middelthunsgate 28, +47 23 27 54 50).

BYGDØY NEIGHBORHOOD
This thought-provoking and exciting cluster of sights, worth ▲▲, is on a parklike peninsula just across the harbor from downtown Oslo. It provides a busy and rewarding half-day (at a minimum) of sightseeing.

Here, within a short walk, are six major sights (listed in order of importance): the **Norwegian Folk Museum,** an open-air museum with traditional wooden buildings from all corners of the country, a stave church, and a collection of 20th-century urban buildings; the **Viking Ship Museum,** showing off the best-preserved Viking ships in existence; the **Fram Museum,** showcasing the modern Viking spirit with the *Fram,* the ship of Arctic-exploration fame, and the *Gjøa,* the first ship to sail through the Northwest Passage; the **Kon-Tiki Museum,** starring the *Kon-Tiki* and the *Ra II,* in which Norwegian explorer Thor Heyerdahl proved that early civilizations could have crossed the oceans; the **Norwegian Maritime Museum,** interesting mostly to old salts; and the **Norwegian Holocaust Center,** memorializing the Holocaust in Norway.

Getting to Bygdøy: Sailing from downtown to Bygdøy is fun, fast, and gets you in a seafaring mood. Ride the Bygdøy **ferry**—marked *Public Ferry Bygdøy Museums*—from pier 3 in front of City Hall (52 NOK one-way at the ticket desk, 62 NOK on board; 78 NOK round-trip at the ticket desk; covered by Oslo Pass—but not by individual Ruter transit tickets; 3/hour, 10-15 minutes; May-Sept daily 8:55-20:55, fewer sailings spring and fall, no boats off-season). Boats generally leave from downtown at :05, :25, and :45 past each hour. In summer, avoid the nearby (much more expensive) tour boats.

For a less memorable approach, you can take **bus #30** (from train station, National Theater, or in front of City Hall, direction: Bygdøy; 20-minute trip).

Returning to Oslo: Note that after 17:00, bus and boat depar-

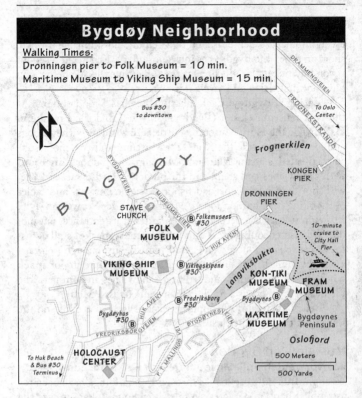

Bygdøy Neighborhood

<u>Walking Times:</u>
Dronningen pier to Folk Museum = 10 min.
Maritime Museum to Viking Ship Museum = 15 min.

tures back to downtown are sparse. If returning by ferry, get to the dock a little early—otherwise the boat is likely to be full, and you'll have to wait for the next sailing.

Getting Around Bygdøy: The Norwegian Folk and Viking Ship museums are a 10-minute walk from the ferry's first stop (Dronningen). The other boating museums (Fram, Kon-Tiki, and Maritime) are at the second ferry stop, in an area called Bygdøynes. The Holocaust Center is off Fredriksborgveien, about halfway between these two museum clusters. All Bygdøy sights are within a pleasant (when sunny) 15-minute walk of each other. The walk gives you a picturesque taste of suburban Oslo.

City bus #30 connects the sights four times hourly in this order: Norwegian Folk Museum, Viking Ship Museum, Kon-Tiki Museum, Norwegian Holocaust Center. (For the Holocaust Center, you'll use the Bygdøyhus stop a long block away; tell the bus driver you want the stop for the "HL-Senteret.") The bus turns around at its final stop (Huk), then passes the sights in reverse order on its way back to the city center.

Planning Your Day: If the weather's good, hit the folk museum first (before it gets too hot). If it's ugly out, begin with the

mostly indoor boat museums at Bygdøynes. The marginally interesting Holocaust Center is a bit of a detour, and skippable if you're
short on time. The Bygdøynes museums offer a 10 percent discount
if you buy tickets for all three at the same time; decide before you
buy your first ticket and save a few bucks.

Eating at Bygdøy: Each museum area has $ food options. At
the boat museum cluster (Bygdøynes), you'll find the **Framheim
Café** inside the Fram Museum; a little **café window** with hot dogs
and ice cream outside the Kon-Tiki Museum; and two more-sub-
stantial eateries at the Maritime Museum: the indoor **Kafe Fjord**
with sandwiches and soup, and the outdoor **Fjordterrassen Café,**
with hot dogs and deep-fried fish and veggie burgers, and tables
overlooking the harbor (open May-Aug). The Norwegian Folk
Museum houses the decent **Kafe Arkadia** at its entrance, but picnics are also encouraged. A fun little **farmers market** stall across
the street sells produce, drinks, and yogurt—just enough to forage
a healthy lunch). The Viking Ship Museum has an outdoor **snack
window** selling shrimp and salmon sandwiches in summer. The
Holocaust Center has a small **café** upstairs (closed Mon).

Beach at Bygdøy: A popular beach is located at Huk, on the
southwest tip of the peninsula.

Museums on Bygdøy

▲▲Norwegian Folk Museum (Norsk Folkemuseum)

Brought from all corners of Norway, 150 buildings have been re-
assembled here on 35 acres. While Stockholm's Skansen was the
first museum of this kind to open to the public, this collection is
a bit older, started in 1881 as the king's private collection (and the
inspiration for Skansen). The folk museum is most lively (and worth
▲▲▲) June through mid-August, when buildings are open and
staffed with attendants in period clothing (who'll happily answer
your questions). You'll also see artisans working at traditional crafts
and barnyard animals roaming about. In the off-season, the indoor
museum is fine, but the park is just a pleasant place to stroll past
lots of locked-up log cabins. Be prepared for an uphill walk to reach
the Gol stave church.

Cost and Hours: 160 NOK, daily 10:00-17:00—grounds
open until 20:00; Sept-May park open daily 11:00-16:00, but most
historical buildings closed; Museumsveien 10, bus #30 stops immediately in front, +47 22 12 37 00, www.norskfolkemuseum.no.

Tours and Activities: Upon arrival, pick up the site map and
review the list of the day's events, concerts, and guided tours (on a
video screen near the ticket desk). In summer, there are usually two
guided tours in English per day; the Telemark Farm hosts a small
daily fiddle-and-folk-dance show; and a folk music-and-dance
show is held each Sunday. If you don't take a tour, invest in a guide-

book and ask questions of the informative attendants stationed in buildings throughout the park.

Visiting the Museum: Think of the visit in three parts: the park sprinkled with old buildings, the re-created old town, and the folk-art museum. As you enter, you'll cut through the courtyard with the museum to reach the open-air sections.

The **park** is loaded with mostly log-built, sod-roofed cabins from various parts of Norway (arranged roughly geographically). Be sure to go inside the buildings. The evocative Gol stave church, at the top of a hill at the park's edge, is worth the climb. Built in 1212 in Hallingdal and painstakingly reconstructed here, it has a classic design and, inside, beautiful yet primitive wood paintings on the apse walls (c. 1452). If you won't make it to a stave church elsewhere on your trip, this is a must. (For more on stave churches, see page 318.)

Back near the entrance building, the **old town** has a variety of homes and shops that focus on urban lifestyles. It's worth exploring the tenement building, in which you can explore intimate, fully furnished apartments from various generations and lifestyles—1905, 1930, 1950, 1979, and even a Norwegian-Pakistani apartment.

In the **museum,** the ground floor beautifully presents woody, colorfully painted, and exactingly carved folk art; traditional Norwegian knitting; and weapons. Upstairs are exquisite-in-a-peasant-kind-of-way folk costumes. I'd skip the sleepy collection of Norwegian church art (in an adjoining building). But don't miss the best Sami culture exhibit I've seen in Scandinavia (across the courtyard in the green building, behind the toy exhibit). The museum's newest exhibit traces the evolution of Norway's culture and identity from 1600 to 1914.

▲▲Viking Ship Museum (Vikingskiphuset)

This impressive museum is undergoing a multiyear expansion, and exhibits will ultimately move into the new Museum of the Viking Age (scheduled to open on the same site by 2025). In the meantime, some of the ships described here may not be on display, and the building itself may be closed from time to time—check locally.

Even if the main attractions aren't on display during your visit, this museum still offers a fine look at Viking culture. You'll see finely crafted, majestic oak Viking ships dating from the 9th and 10th centuries alongside the bones of Vikings buried with these vessels and remarkable artifacts that may cause you to consider these notorious raiders in a different light. Over a thousand years ago, three things drove Vikings on their far-flung raids: hard economic times in their bleak homeland, the lure of prosperous and vulnerable communities to the south, and a mastery of the sea. There was a time when most frightened Europeans closed every prayer with, "And deliver us from the Vikings, Amen." Gazing up at the prow of one of these sleek, time-stained vessels, you can almost hear the shouts of those redheads on the rampage.

Cost and Hours: 120 NOK, ticket also covers the Historical Museum in downtown Olso for 48 hours; Tue-Sun 10:00-16:00, closed Mon; Huk Aveny 35, +47 22 85 19 00, www.khm.uio.no.

Tours: The museum doesn't offer tours, but you can use the free Wi-Fi to download an informative audioguide.

Visiting the Museum: If they're on display, focus on the two well-preserved ships, starting with the *Oseberg*, from AD 834. With its ornate carving and impressive rudder, it was likely a royal pleasure craft. It seems designed for sailing on calm inland waters during festivals, but not in the open ocean.

The *Gokstad*, from AD 950, is a practical working boat capable of sailing the high seas. A ship like this brought settlers to the west of France (Normandy was named for the Norsemen). And in such a vessel, explorers such as Erik the Red hopscotched from Norway to Iceland to Greenland and on to what they called Vinland—today's Newfoundland in Canada. Imagine 30 men hauling on long oars out at sea for weeks and months at a time. In 1892, a replica of this ship sailed from Norway to America in 44 days to celebrate the 400th anniversary of Columbus *not* discovering America.

You'll also see the ruins of a third vessel, the **Tune Ship** (c. AD 910), which saw service only briefly before being used as the tomb for an important chieftain. In this hall, every 20 minutes, the lights dim and a wrap-around film plays on the walls around the ship for five minutes—with dramatic virtual footage of the Vikings and their fleet.

The ships tend to steal the show, but don't miss the **jewelry and personal items** excavated along with the ships. The ships and related artifacts survived so well because they were buried in clay as part of a gravesite. Many of the finest items were not actually Viking art, but goodies they brought home after raiding more advanced (but less tough) people. Still, there are lots of actual Viking items, such as metal and leather goods, that give insight into their culture. Highlights are the cart and sleighs, ornately carved with scenes from Viking sagas.

▲▲▲Fram Museum (Frammuseet)

Under its distinctive A-frame roof, this museum holds the 125-foot, steam- and sail-powered ship that took modern-day Vikings Roald Amundsen and Fridtjof Nansen deep into the Arctic and Antarctic, farther north and south than any vessel had gone before. In an adjacent A-frame is Amundsen's *Gjøa*, the first ship to sail through the Northwest Passage. Together, the ex-

hibit spins a fascinating tale of adventure, scientific exploration, and human determination...all at subzero temperatures.

Cost and Hours: 120 NOK; daily June-Aug 9:00-18:00, May and Sept 10:00-18:00, Oct-April until 17:00; Bygdøynesveien 36, +47 23 28 29 50, www.frammuseum.no.

Visiting the Museum: Stepping into the museum, you're immediately bow-to-bow with the 128-foot *Fram*. Before diving in, remember that there are two parts to the museum: The *Fram*, which you're looking at, and to the left through a tunnel, the smaller *Gjøa*. I'd see the *Gjøa* first, because it's a better lead-up to the main event, and because it features a short film that's a fine introduction to the entire museum.

Crossing through the tunnel to the *Gjøa*, you'll learn about the search for the Northwest Passage (that long-sought-after trade route through the Arctic from the Atlantic to the Pacific). Exhibits tell the story of how Roald Amundsen and a crew of six used this motor- and sail-powered ship to successfully navigate the Northwest Passage (1903-1906). Exhibits describe their ordeal as well as other Arctic adventures, such as Amundsen's 1925 flight to 88 degrees north (they had to build a runway out of ice to take off and return home); and his 1926 airship (zeppelin) expedition from Oslo over the North Pole to Alaska. This section also features a 100-seat cinema showing an excellent 15-minute film about the exploration of the earth's polar regions (shows every 15 minutes).

Now return to the *Fram* and peruse the exhibits—actual artifacts and profiles of the brave explorers and their crew. The upper floor focuses on Nansen's voyages to the North Pole on the *Fram*, including an early kayak, a full-size stuffed polar bear, and a model of the ship. Here you can cross a gangway to explore the *Fram*'s claustrophobic but fascinating interior. A simulated Northern

OSLO

The Fram Museum: From Pole to Pole

The Fram Museum tells the tale of two great Norwegian explorers, Fridtjof Nansen and Roald Amundsen.

Early polar explorers focused on the Northwest Passage, believing the Arctic could hold a highly lucrative trade route between the Atlantic and the Pacific oceans. Englishman John Franklin famously led a failed expedition looking for the Northwest Passage in 1845; two ships and 129 men were never seen again. Many others attempted and failed—more than a thousand sailors were lost in the search.

A generation later, with the Northwest Passage conquered by Amundsen, explorers (inspired by tales of Franklin and his ilk) became determined to reach the North Pole.

Fridtjof Nansen (1861-1930) prepared for his North Pole expedition by crossing the inland ice of Greenland in six weeks in 1888—hand-pulling sledges all the way—and then spent the winter learning from Inuit people he met. Nansen also commissioned the *Fram,* which was purpose-built for Arctic exploration with a rounded hull, designed to withstand being stuck in ice without being crushed. (The downside was that it got tossed around in fierce waves.) It even had a windmill that could power electric lights. In the end, the *Fram* went on three major expeditions. In each one, the crew set out knowing they'd be living in subzero temperatures for three to five years.

The *Fram*'s maiden voyage was Nansen's search for the North Pole (1893-1896). He believed that, due to the natural drifting of the northern ice cap, a ship encased in ice would simply be carried by currents to the North Pole. For three years, the *Fram* drifted, trapped in the Arctic ice. While he didn't reach the North Pole, Nansen made better progress than anyone before him.

Then, **Otto Sverdrup** (1854-1930) took the helm of the *Fram* and advanced Nansen's progress (riding icebergs from 1898 until 1902), but he didn't make it all the way, either.

Finally, **Roald Amundsen** (1872-1928)—who had already successfully sailed the Northwest Passage—made plans to reach the North Pole in the *Fram* in 1910. Amundsen's crew (and financiers) believed he was heading north. But when word came that American explorer Frederick Cook had beaten him to the North Pole, Amundsen sailed the *Fram* to Antarctica instead and set out to reach the South Pole (1910-1912). Amundsen and his team were in a race to the pole with Englishman Robert Falcon Scott and his men, who had arrived aboard the ship *Terra Nova*. Amundsen beat Scott to the South Pole by about a month. And, unlike Scott, Amundsen made it home alive.

The *Fram* expeditions coincided with the nascent Norwegian independence movement and became a proud patriotic symbol of the Norwegian people.

Lights show, best viewed from the *Fram*'s main deck, is presented every 20 minutes.

Exhibits on the middle floor focus on Admundsen, who picked up where Nansen left off and explored the South Pole. You'll see an actual dogsled Admundsen's team used and a small model of the motorized sled from the rival Scott expedition. Also featured are a tent like the one Amundsen used, reconstructed shelves from his Arctic kitchen, models of the *Fram*, and a "polar simulator" plunging visitors into a 15° Fahrenheit environment.

▲▲Kon-Tiki Museum (Kon-Tiki Museet)

Next to the *Fram* is a museum housing the *Kon-Tiki* and the *Ra II*, the ships built by the larger-than-life anthropologist, seafarer, and adventurer Thor Heyerdahl (1914-2002). Heyerdahl and his crew used these ships—constructed entirely without modern technology—to undertake tropical voyages many had thought impossible. Both ships are well displayed and described in English. This museum—more lighthearted than the other boat-focused exhibits—puts you in a castaway mood.

Cost and Hours: 120 NOK, daily 10:00-17:00, June-Aug from 11:00, Nov-Feb until 16:00, Bygdøynesveien 36, +47 23 08 67 67, www.kon-tiki.no.

Background: Thor Heyerdahl believed that early South Americans could have crossed the Pacific to settle Polynesia. To prove his point, in 1947 Heyerdahl and five crewmates constructed the *Kon-Tiki* raft from balsa wood, using only premodern tools and techniques, and adorned its sail with a giant image of the sun god Kon-Tiki. They set sail from Peru on the tiny craft, surviving for 101 days on fish, coconuts, and sweet potatoes (native to Peru). About 5,000 miles later, they arrived in Polynesia. (While Heyerdahl proved that early South Americans *could* have made this trip, anthropologists doubt they did.) The *Kon-Tiki* story became a best-selling book and award-winning documentary (and helped spawn the "Tiki" culture craze in the US). Funded by the *Kon-Tiki* success, Heyerdahl went on to explore Easter Island (1955) and then turned his attention to another voyage—this time across the Atlantic. In 1970, Heyerdahl's *Ra II* made a similar 4,000-mile journey from Morocco to Barbados—on a vessel made of reeds—to prove that Africans could have populated the Americas.

Visiting the Museum: You'll see both the *Kon-Tiki* and the *Ra II* and learn about Heyerdahl's other adventures (including

OSLO

In Cold Blood

Norway likes to think of itself as a quiet, peaceful nation on the edge of Europe—after all, its legislators award the Nobel Peace Prize. So the events of July 22, 2011 had a profound effect on the country's psyche. On that day, an anti-immigration fanatic named Anders Behring Breivik set off a car bomb in Oslo, killing eight. He then traveled to a summer camp where he hunted down, shot, and killed 69 young people and counselors.

Until Breivik's attack Norway had largely escaped 21st-century terrorism. When the public learned that the man behind the violence was a native Norwegian, they reacted with a huge outpouring of grief. Bouquets flooded the square in front of Oslo Cathedral.

Arrested after the shootings, Breivik was described by police as obsessed with what he saw as the "threat" of multiculturalism and immigration to Norwegian values. It's true that Norway has a big and growing immigrant community. More than 15 percent of the population is not ethnic Norwegian, and a quarter of Oslo's residents are immigrants. These "new Norwegians" provide a much-needed and generally appreciated labor force, filling jobs that wealthy natives would rather not do.

Horrified by Breivik's actions, after the attack many Norwegians went out of their way to make immigrants feel welcome. Even though the country strengthened its immigration laws in 2014, Norway seems determined not to let the July 22 massacre poison its peaceful soul. Calls for police to start carrying weapons or to reinstate the death penalty were quickly rejected. "Breivik wanted to change Norway," an Oslo resident told me. "We're determined to keep Norway the way it was."

Easter Island and the *Ra I*, which sank partway into its journey). Everything's well-described in English and very kid-friendly. In the basement, you'll see the bottom of the *Kon-Tiki* vessel with a life-size model of a whale shark (the largest fish on earth) and other marine life that the crew observed at sea. Nearby, a small theater continuously plays a 10-minute documentary about the voyage; every day at 12:00, they show the full-length (67-minute), Oscar-winning 1950 documentary film *Kon-Tiki*.

▲Norwegian Maritime Museum (Norsk Maritimt Museum)

If you're into the sea and seafaring, this museum is a salt lick, providing a wide-ranging look at Norway's maritime heritage through exhibits, art, and a panoramic film soaring over Norway's long and varied coastline.

Cost and Hours: 120 NOK; daily 10:00-17:00, Oct-April 11:00-16:00; two cafés—one with city views; Bygdøynesveien 37, +47 22 12 37 00, www.marmuseum.no.

Visiting the Museum: The core of the museum is the Boat Hall (Båthallen), where you'll see a collection of traditional boats, fishing gear, clothing, and household goods that capture the challenges and hardships of 19th-century coastal Norway. In another display, artifacts recently recovered from some of the many shipwrecks in Oslo's old harbor illustrate international shipping, trade, and communications in the 16th and 17th centuries. The exhibit *At Sea* takes a personal look at seafarers' lives from Viking days to the present. If you appreciate maritime art, the painting collection in the gallery should float your boat. If it's still showing, watch the wrap-around, 20-minute movie *The Ocean: A Way of Life* (look for *Supervideografen* signs), which swoops you scenically over Norway's diverse coast, showing off fishing townscapes, shiplap villages, industrial harbors, and breathtaking scenery from here all the way to North Cape.

Norwegian Holocaust Center (HL-Senteret)

Located in the stately former home of Nazi collaborator Vidkun Quisling—whose name is synonymous with "complicit in atrocities"—this museum and study center offers a high-tech look at the racist ideologies that fueled the Holocaust. It's designed primarily for Norwegians, but you can borrow a tablet with English translations of the exhibits. The ground floor displays historical documents about the rise of anti-Semitism and personal effects from Holocaust victims. The exhibits continue downstairs, where the names of 760 Norwegian Jews killed by the Nazis are listed in a bright, white room. Out front, the *Innocent Questions* glass-and-neon sculpture shows an old-fashioned punch card, reminding viewers of how the Norwegian puppet government collected seemingly innocuous information before deporting its Jews.

Cost and Hours: 70 NOK; daily 10:00-17:00, mid-Sept-mid-May until 16:00; Huk Aveny 56—take bus #30 to the Bygdøyhus stop and follow brown *HL-Senteret* signs, +47 22 84 21 00, www. hlsenteret.no.

GRÜNERLØKKA AND GRØNLAND DISTRICTS

Oslo's Grünerløkka district, bisected by the Akers River, is lively, and workaday Grønland is emerging as a fun spot. You can connect it all together by following the self-guided Up Akers River and Down Grünerløkka Walk (described below).

Akers River

The source of the Akers River (and Oslo's drinking water) is the pristine Lake Maridal, situated at the edge of the Nordmarka wilderness. The idyllic recreation scenes along Lake Maridal are a favorite for nature-loving Norwegians.

Though only about five miles long, the Akers River powered Oslo's early industry: flour mills in the 1300s, sawmills in the 1500s, and Norway's Industrial Revolution in the 1800s. Today the river valley becomes a park as it winds past decent-size waterfalls and red-brick factories that now house shops and apartments. The bottom of the river —bordered by the high-rise Radisson Blu Plaza Hotel and the gritty "Little Pakistan" neighborhood of Grønland (where my walk doesn't go)—has its share of drunks and drugs, reflecting a new urban reality in Oslo.

▲Grünerløkka

The Grünerløkka district, built in the latter half of the 1800s to house the legions of workers employed at factories powered by the Akers River, has reinvented itself as a one-stop neighborhood for shopping, street life, and food. Old-style buildings have found new life as restaurants, bars, and coffeehouses. Vintage shops rub elbows with indie boutiques. Grünerløkka lies just east of the Akers River, offering welcome green spaces and urban park life.

Getting There: Grünerløkka can be reached from the center of town by a short ride on tram #11, #12, or #18, or by taking the interesting walk described next.

▲Up Akers River and Down Grünerløkka Walk

Once housing poor workers, the Grünerløkka neighborhood now attracts Norwegian hipsters and foodie tourists. This hike up the Akers River, finishing in stylish Grünerløkka, shines a different and more appealing light on Oslo than the touristy central zone. Allow about an hour at a brisk pace, including a fair bit of up and down and a 20-minute detour en route.

While there are a few sights along this walk, they're all skippable—making this a fun experience on a sunny early evening, after the museums have closed, when Oslo's young people are out enjoying their riverside park. (Several excellent dining opportunities are along or near this walk.)

Begin the walk by leaving Karl Johans Gate near where it crests (alongside the Parliament building, by the T-bane stop), and head up ❶ **Akersgata**—Oslo's "Fleet Street," lined with major newspaper companies.

After two blocks, at **Apotekergata,** you'll notice stout barriers

Grünerløkka/Grønland Area

Walk

1. Akersgata
2. July 2011 Bombing Site
3. Vår Frelsers Cemetery
4. Gamle Aker Church
5. Telthusbakken Road
6. Mathallen Oslo & Vulkan Depot
7. Åmotbrua (Bridge)
8. Big Waterfall
9. Fabrikkjentene Statue & Honse-Lovisas Hus
10. Thorvald Meyers Gate
11. Olaf Ryes Plass
12. Vaterlands Bridge

Eateries & Nightlife

13. Olaf Ryes Plass Eateries
14. Tim Wendelboe Coffee
15. Südøst Asian Crossover Rest.
16. Punjab Tandoori & Asylet
17. Istanbul & Dattera Til Hagen
18. Olympen Brown Pub

OSLO

blocking car traffic, and may see some construction work to the right. Continue into the big plaza. ❷ Behind the tall, blocky building, on Grubbegata, was where a car bomb went off on July 22, 2011 (see the "In Cold Blood" sidebar, earlier). Four buildings in the area suffered structural damage—including the long, low-lying one to the left, known as Y-Block. Locals are divided on the fate of the damaged building (and its two Picasso murals that decorated the building's facade and lobby).

Also on this square, you may see (on the right as you face the tall building) a small visitors center marked *22. juli-senteret*, with photos and information about the terror event. Along the street, notice the row of newspaper headlines under shattered glass. These were displayed in a newspaper office's window just down Akersgata, and have been preserved here—symbolizing how, for Oslo residents, time stood still on that fateful Friday morning.

Continuing straight past this somber site, you'll approach the massive brick Trefoldighets Church. Passing that, angle right onto the uphill street called **Akersveien**, along the side of the pointy-steepled St. Olav's Church. Hiking up this quiet street, you'll pass some traditional wooden houses. This is what much of "Christiania" (as Oslo was then called) looked like in the early 20th century; after World War II, most of this classic architecture was torn down in favor of modern construction.

After passing a square with a big pool, watch on the left for the entrance gate to the ❸ **Vår Frelsers (Our Savior's) Cemetery.** Stop at the big metal map just inside the gate to chart your course through the cemetery: You'll go through the light-green Æreslunden section—with the biggest plots and VIP graves (including Munch, Ibsen, Bjørnson, and many of the painters whose works you can see in the National Gallery)—

then veer right to return to Akersveien, using the exit at the far end (#13).

Once oriented, head into the cemetery and bear right into the elevated, walled area. The tall, green, canopied grave belongs to **Henrik Wergeland** (1808-1845), Norway's national poet who helped to create its May 17th celebrations (including the children's parade). Wergeland is beloved not only for his poetry, but as a champion of civil rights: He spent his life fighting a clause in the Norwegian constitution that denied the rights of citizenship to Jews. A few years after his death, it was removed.

Go up the path to the right of Wergeland, into the uppermost part of the cemetery. Bear left with the path, then turn left again. You'll pass the grave of painter Christian Krohg on your left, then reach the grave of the great Expressionist painter, **Edvard Munch** (1863-1944).

At Munch's 10 o'clock, walk under the drooping tree to the tall, obelisk-topped tomb of **Henrik Ibsen** (1828-1906), the great Norwegian playwright. Notice the hammer engraved in his tomb, an allusion to an Ibsen poem that spoke of a man chipping away inside a cave. This represents the determination of Ibsen the artist—who would walk the streets of Oslo, lost in thought, painstakingly crafting his next masterpiece in his mind.

Facing Ibsen's grave, turn left and walk toward the yellow house, exiting through the nearby gate. Turn left and walk 100 yards up Akersveien to the Romanesque ❹ **Gamle Aker Church** (from the 1100s)—the oldest building in Oslo. The church, which fell into ruins and has been impressively rebuilt, is rarely open and is pretty bare inside except for a pulpit and baptismal font from the 1700s.

On the little terrace just below the church, notice the **stone marker** indicating 639 kilometers to Nidaros Cathedral in Trondheim—the burial place of the great Norwegian king/saint, Olav II (995-1030). Olav was instrumental in Christianizing Norway, and his tomb in Trondheim was the focus of Norway's main medieval pilgrimage route. Walking half the length of Norway by foot offered forgiveness of sins. Like the Camino de Santiago in northern Spain, this pilgrimage route—long forgotten—is again in vogue, not only for spiritual reasons, but for anyone who simply wants a long walk with time to think. If you're up for a slightly longer walk than this one, the modern pilgrimage office is in the pink, half-timbered building across the street.

From the church, backtrack 20 yards, head left at the red hydrant, and go downhill on the steep ❺ **Telthusbakken** road toward the huge, gray former grain silos (now student housing). This delightful lane is lined with colorful old wooden houses, built here outside the city limits by people

OSLO

too poor to meet the no-wood fire-safety building codes within the city proper. Take a peek at the little neighborhood garden patches on the right (through the fence).

At the bottom of Telthusbakken, you'll reach busy **Maridalsveien** street. Cross it and head down to the right about 40 yards, then turn left down the driveway next to the modern **Vulkan shopping center.** Follow the driveway just in front of Vulkan as it curls around and behind the building to the recommended ❻ **Mathallen**—a foodie paradise, with more than a dozen stalls selling every kind of cuisine imaginable, and lots of outdoor tables filling an inviting plaza.

Find the **bridge** over the river at the near end of Mathallen (just follow the sound of the waterfall). You'll pop out into a beautiful little square. Turn left just before the playground and walk along the river (with the silo housing on your right). At the waterfall, look down on your left to see fish ladders—which allow salmon and sea trout to make their way upstream to spawn. Farther along, enjoy a little stretch of **boardwalk** that's cantilevered to stick out over the waterfall.

The lively **Grünerløkka** district is just to your right. But if you have 20 minutes and a little energy, detour upstream first, then hook back down. Continuing along the river, you'll pass a log bridge on your left, then a few rusty *lur* horns on your right, before you come to yet another **bridge**—this one loaded down with "love locks." Cross this bridge, turn right, and continue following the riverside path uphill.

Just above the next waterfall, cross ❼ **Åmotbrua** (Åmot Bridge), a big white springy suspension footbridge from 1852 (moved here in 1958). Keep hiking uphill along the river. At the base of the next ❽ **big waterfall,** cross over again to the large brick buildings, hiking up the stairs to the **Beyer Bridge** (above the falls) and ❾ *Fabrikkjentene,* a statue of four women laborers. They're pondering the textile factory where they and 700 others toiled long and hard. This gorge was once lined with the water mills that powered Oslo through its 19th-century Industrial Age boom.

Look back (on the side you just left) at the city's two biggest former textile factories. Once you could tell what color the fabric was being dyed each day by the color of the river. Just beyond them, between the two old factories, is a small light-gray building housing the **Labor Museum** (Arbeidermuseet, free; Wed-Sun

11:00-16:00, closed Mon-Tue; mid-Aug-late June Sat-Sun only; borrow English handout). Inside you'll see old photos that humanize the life of laborers there, and an 1899 photo exhibit by Edvard Munch's sister, Inger Munch.

The tiny red house just over and below the bridge—the **Honse-Lovisas Hus** cultural center—makes a good rest-stop (Tue-Sun 11:00-17:00, closed Mon, coffee and waffles). Continue past the red house to the red-brick Ringnes Brewery and follow ❿ **Thorvald Meyers Gate** downhill directly into the heart of Grünerløkka. First you'll go through a few blocks of modern, tidy apartment buildings. Then you'll pass a park (Birkelunden) with a tram stop and a gazebo. The next stretch of Thorvald Meyers Gate is lined with inviting bars and cafés with outdoor seating. And a few short blocks farther is Grünerløkka's main square, ⓫ **Olaf Ryes Plass**—a lively place to grab a meal or drink. Trams take you from here back to the center.

• *To continue exploring, you could keep going straight past Olaf Ryes Plass and continue walking until you reach a T-intersection with a busy road (Trondheimsveien). From there (passing the recommended Südøst Asian Crossover Restaurant) you can catch a tram back to the center, or drop down to the riverside path and follow it downstream to* ⓬ **Vaterlands bridge** *in the* **Grønland** *district. From here the train station is a five-minute walk down Stenersgata.*

Grønland

The T-bane's Grønland stop deposits you in the center of an old working-class neighborhood of Industrial Age Oslo (if you look down side streets, you'll see fine 19th-century facades). Today it's a bit shabby, like working-class and immigrant neighborhoods in other cities. But Grønland is emerging as a trendy place for eating out and after-dark fun. Locals know you'll get double the food and lots more beer for the kroner here. If you'd enjoy a whiff of Istanbul, make a point to wander through the underground commercial zone at the Grønland station (easy to visit even if you're not riding the T-bane).

SOUTHEAST OF DOWNTOWN
▲Ekeberg Sculpture Park (Ekebergparken)

In 2013, this piece of wilderness—on a forested hill over town, with grand city views—was transformed from a long-neglected public green space into a modern sculpture park. In 2013, real estate tycoon and art collector Christian Ringnes (grandson of Norwegian brewery tycoons) paid to turn the wooded area into a park. Ringnes wanted his creation to be an homage to women. To that end, the park is filled with modern and contemporary sculptures

OSLO

ranging from the ample nudes of Rodin, Renoir, and Botero to the evocative abstractions of Bourgeois, Turrell, and Holzer.

Getting There: The park, always open and free, is a 10-minute tram ride southeast of the center (at the train station, catch tram #18 from platform E, or #19 from platform C; take either one in the direction of Ljabru). Ride just a few stops to Ekebergparken, right at the park's entrance.

Background: This location (literally "Oak Hill") is historic: There's evidence that Stone Age people lived here 7,000 years ago; a spot in this park is said to be where Edvard Munch was inspired to paint *The Scream* (the viewpoint is marked *Utsiktspunkt Skrik* on maps), and in World War II, it held a Nazi military cemetery. Today the people of Oslo are embracing this lovely 63-acre mix of forest and contemporary art.

Visiting the Park: A visit here involves lots of climbing on trails through the trees. While some people come for the statues (at this point 35 in all, but with plans to expand to 80), others simply enjoy a walk in nature...and most agree that the views of Oslo's harbor scene (the Opera House, Munch Museum, and Barcode Project) may be the highlight. From the tram stop, hike up to the little cluster of buildings (including the visitors center, where you can pick up a map and join a 1.5-hour guided walk in English—see schedule at www.ekebergparken.com). In this area, you can see the first of the sculptures. For views and more art, keep heading up the hill to the restaurant...and beyond. Maps, suggesting various walking routes, are posted throughout the park.

Nearby: The faint **ruins of medieval Oslo** (free, always open) are between the harbor and Ekeberg Park—you can get a peek of them as you rumble past on the tram. History buffs can spend a few minutes wandering a park with a few scant foundations of the 11th-century town—back when it was 3,000 people huddled around a big stone cathedral, seat of the Norwegian bishop. The arcade of a 13th-century Dominican monastery still stands (office of today's Lutheran bishop). To get there, hop off at the Oslo Hospital tram stop; the ruins are across Ekebergveien street from the tram stop.

ESCAPES FROM THE CITY

Oslo is surrounded by a vast forest dotted with idyllic little lakes, huts, joggers, bikers, and sun-worshippers. One of the easiest escapes is simply to grab a beach towel and ride T-bane line #5 to its last stop, Sognsvann, and join the lakeside scene of Norwegians at play. A pleasant trail leads around the lake. To go farther afield, consider these options.

▲Holmenkollen Ski Jump and Ski Museum

The site of one of the world's oldest ski jumps (from 1892), Holmenkollen has hosted many championships, including the 1952 Winter Olympics. To win the privilege of hosting the 2011 World Ski Jump Championship, Oslo built a bigger jump to match modern ones built elsewhere—futuristic, cantilevered, and Olympic-standard. For skiers and winter-sports fans, a visit here is worth ▲▲.

Cost and Hours: 150-NOK ticket includes museum and viewing platform at top of jump; zipline-680 NOK, ski simulator-110 NOK; daily 9:00-20:00, May and Sept 10:00-17:00, Oct-April until 16:00; +47 22 92 32 64, www.skiforeningen.no.

Getting There: T-bane line #1 gets you out of the city, through the hills, forests, and mansions that surround Oslo, and to the jump (4/hour, 25 minutes, direction: Frognerseteren). From the Holmenkollen station, you'll hike steeply up the road 15 minutes to the ski jump. (Getting back down is more like 10 minutes. Note T-bane departure times before you leave.) For more details—including a slightly longer, but more scenic, approach—see "Near the Ski Jump," later.

Visiting Holmenkollen: You'll enter the complex directly under the ramp. First you'll tour the **ski museum,** which traces the evolution of the sport, from 4,000-year-old rock paintings to crude 1,500-year-old wooden sticks to the slick and quickly evolving skis of modern times, including a fun exhibit showing the royal family on skis. You'll see gear from Roald Amundsen's famous trek to the South Pole, including the stuffed remains of Obersten ("The Colonel"), one of his sled dogs. Exhibits show off lots and lots of historic skis, gear, and video clips of great moments in skiing. Kids love the downhill ski-breeze simulator...basically a superpowered fan that blasts you in the face with fierce wind.

Near the end of the museum exhibits, look for the sign up to the **ski jump.** The tilted elevator takes you up to the top (on a sunny day, you may have to wait your turn for the elevator). Stand right at the starting gate, just like an athlete, and get a feel for this daredevil sport. The jump empties into a 30,000-seat amphitheater. Climb the stairs up to the rooftop deck; when it's clear, you'll see one of the best possible views of Oslo. While the view is exciting from the top, even more thrilling is the **zip-line** ride that sends daredevils screaming (literally) down over the jump to the landing area at the very bottom in 30 heart-stopping seconds.

As you ponder the jump, consider how modern athletes continually push the boundaries of their sport. The first champion here in 1892 jumped 21 meters (nearly 69 feet). In 1930 it took a 50-meter jump to win. In 1962 it was 80 meters, and in 1980 the champ cracked 100 meters. And, most recently, a jump of 140 meters (459 feet) took first place.

To cap your Holmenkollen experience, you can step into the **simulator** (or should I say stimulator?) and fly down the ski jump and ski in a virtual downhill race. My legs were exhausted after the five-minute terror. It's located at the lower level of the complex, near the entry of the ski museum. Outside, have fun watching a candid video of those shrieking inside.

Near the Ski Jump

For an easy downhill jaunt through the Norwegian forest, with a woodsy coffee or meal break in the middle, stay on the T-bane past Holmenkollen to the end of the line at Frognerseteren. From there, follow signs five minutes downhill on the gravel path to the recommended **Frognerseteren Hovedrestaurant,** a fine traditional eatery with a sod roof, reindeer meat on the griddle, an affordable cafeteria, and a city view over more sod rooftops.

From the restaurant, head down to the little sod-roofed village and look for the *Holmenkollen 1.6* sign to the right. Follow the wide, reddish gravel path through the woods (don't be distracted by the many side-paths, which are for mountain bikers—speaking of which, keep an eye out for bicycles zipping across your path). After about 20 minutes, you'll come to a paved roller-ski course (use the gravel path alongside), then pass between the wooden Holmenkollen village church and the top of a different ski jump (Midtstubakken). Soon you'll see the glassy swoop of Holmenkollen on your right; the entrance to the jump is at the base of the ramp.

On your way back to the Holmenkollen T-bane stop, you'll pass the recommended **Holmenkollen Restaurant,** with a similar view, but without Frognerseteren's pewter-and-antlers folk theme—or pretense.

Oslofjord Island Beaches

On a hot day, the busy ferry scene at Oslo's harborfront lures locals out to the cool, green islands across the harbor where they can take a dip in the fjord, enjoy a little beach time, or simply stroll and enjoy views of the city. The larger Hovedøya offers good beaches, the ruins of a Cistercian monastery from 1147, some old cannons from the early 1800s, a marina, and a café. Little Gressholmen has good swimming, easy wandering to a pair of connected islands, and Gressholmen Kro, a rustic café dating to the 1930s.

Getting to the Islands: From Aker Brygge, catch ferry #B1, #B2, or #B3 to Hovedøya, or ferry #B4 to Gressholmen (both routes covered by city transit passes and Oslo Pass, ticket machines at dock, ferries run in summer only). For schedules and fare info, check www.ruter.no.

Beach at Bygdøy: There's also a beach at Huk on the Bygdøy peninsula; take the direct boat from pier 3 in front of City Hall or bus #30. Once there, if you head left, you'll find a clothed beach, and to the right is a nude beach.

Mountain Biking

Mountain-biking possibilities are endless (as you'll discover if you go exploring without a good map). Consider taking your bike on the T-bane (free outside of rush hour, otherwise half the normal adult fare) to the end of line #1 (Frognerseteren, 30 minutes from National Theater) to gain the most altitude possible. Then follow the gravel roads (mostly downhill but with some climbing) past several dreamy lakes to Sognsvann at the end of T-bane line #5. Farther east, from Maridalsvannet, a bike path follows the Akers River all the way back into town. Get biking details at the TI.

Amusement Parks and Wet Fun

The giant **Tusenfryd** amusement complex, just out of town, offers a world of family fun. It's sort of a combination Norwegian Disneyland/Viking Knott's Berry Farm, with more than 50 rides, plenty of entertainment, and restaurants (closed off-season, +47 64 97 66 99, www.tusenfryd.no, ride regional bus #500 from behind Oslo's train station).

Tøyenbadet, a modern indoor/outdoor pool complex with a 330-foot-long waterslide, also has a gym and sauna (northeast of downtown at Helgengate 90, +47 23 30 44 70). Oslo's free botanical gardens are nearby.

NEAR OSLO
▲Eidsvoll Manor

During the Napoleonic period, control of Norway changed from Denmark to Sweden. This ruffled the patriotic feathers of Norway's Thomas Jeffersons and Ben Franklins, and on May 17, 1814, Norway's constitution was written and signed in this stately mansion (in the town of Eidsvoll Verk, north of Oslo). While Sweden still ruled, the constitution gave Norway more autonomy. To mark the 2014 bicentennial of Norway's constitution, the manor building was restored to how it looked in 1814. A visitors center in the nearby Wergeland House uses 21st-century high-tech touches to tell the history of Norway's march to independence (the union with Sweden was dissolved in 1905). Your ticket also includes an English tour, offered daily at 12:30.

OSLO

Cost and Hours: 125 NOK; daily 10:00-17:00; Sept-April Tue-Fri 10:00-15:00, Sat-Sun 11:00-16:00; +47 63 92 22 10, www. eidsvoll1814.no.

Getting There: To get there by public transportation, take the train to the Eidsvoll Verk station (2/hour, 30 minutes). From there, ride bus #430 three stops (direction: Eidsvoll Station, 5 minutes, included with train ticket) or plan on a 20-minute walk. If you're driving from Oslo to Lillehammer and the Gudbrandsdal Valley, the manor is right on the way and worth a stop. It's a 45-minute drive from Oslo: Take road E-6 toward Trondheim, then turn right at the *Eidsvolls Bygningen* sign. Parking is free.

Drøbak

This delightful fjord town is just an hour from Oslo by bus (61 NOK, ticket covers two zones, 2/hour, bus #500 from behind the train station) or ferry from Aker Brygge (109 NOK one-way, ticket covers four zones, 2/day weekends only spring and fall, also 1/day weekdays mid-June-mid-Aug, take ferry #B21 on weekdays or #B22 on weekends, 1.25 hours, no ferry off-season, check at pier 1 or ask at Oslo TI). Consider taking the boat trip down, exploring the town, having dinner, and taking the bus back. Drøbak TI: +47 64 93 50 87, www.visitdrobak.no.

For holiday cheer year-round, stop into **Tregaarden's Julehus** Christmas shop, right off Drøbak's main square (closed Christmas-Feb, +47 64 93 41 78, http://julehus.no). Then wander out past the church and cemetery on the north side of town to a pleasant park. Looking out into the fjord, you can see the old **Oscarsborg Fortress,** where Norwegian troops fired cannons and torpedoes to sink Hitler's warship, *Blücher.* The attack bought enough time for Norway's king and parliament to escape capture and eventually set up a government-in-exile in London during the Nazi occupation of Norway (1940-1945). Nearby, a monument is dedicated to the commander of the fortress, and one of *Blücher*'s anchors rests aground (the other is at Aker Brygge in Oslo). A summer ferry shuttles visitors from the town harbor.

Eating in Drøbak: With outdoor seating, **$$$$ Restaurant Skipperstuen** is a pricey but good option for dinner overlooking the fjord and all the Oslo-bound boat traffic (Mon-Sat 12:00-22:00, Sun until 20:00; off-season closed Mon-Tue; Havnebakken 11, +47 64 93 07 03, www.skipperstuen.no).

Shopping in Oslo

Shops in Oslo are generally open 10:00-18:00 or 19:00. Many close early on Saturday and all day Sunday. Shopping centers have similar hours without the Saturday early closure. Here are a few favorite shopping suggestions (note all of these are closed on Sunday). For locations, see the "Oslo Walk" map on page 226.

Norway Designs, just outside the National Theater, shows off the country's sleek, contemporary designs in clothing, kitchenware, glass, textiles, jewelry—and high prices (Stortingsgata 12, T-bane: Nationaltheatret, +47 23 11 45 10).

Paleet is a mall in the heart of Oslo, with 30 shops on three levels and a food court in the basement (Karl Johans Gate 37, +47 23 08 08 11).

Dale of Norway, considered Norway's biggest and best maker of traditional and contemporary sweaters, offers its complete collection at their concept store in downtown Oslo (Karl Johans Gate 45, +47 97 48 12 07).

Heimen Husfliden has a superb selection of authentic Norwegian-made sweaters, *bunads* (national costumes), yarn, traditional jewelry, and colorful Norwegian folk crafts (top quality at high prices, Rosenkrantz Gate 8, +47 23 21 42 00).

GlasMagasinet is one of Oslo's oldest and fanciest department stores (top-end, good souvenir shop, near the cathedral at Stortorvet 9, +47 22 82 23 00). In the basement of the GlasMagasinet is another branch of **Heimen Husfliden** (listed earlier, +47 22 42 10 75).

The **Oslo Sweater Shop** has competitive prices for a wide range of Norwegian-made sweaters, including Dale brand (in Radisson Blu Scandinavia Hotel at Tullinsgate 5, +47 22 11 29 22).

Byporten, the big, splashy mall adjoining the central train station, is filled with youthful and hip shops, specialty stores, and eateries (Jernbanetorget 6, +47 23 36 21 60).

The street named **Bogstadveien** is considered to have the city's trendiest boutiques and chic, high-quality shops (stretches from behind the Royal Palace to Majorstuen near Vigeland Sculpture Park).

Oslo's Flea Market makes Saturday morning a happy day for those who brake for garage sales (at Vestkanttorvet, March-Nov only, two blocks east of Frogner Park at the corner of Professor Dahl's Gate and Neubergsgate).

Oslo Flaggfabrikk sells quality flags of all shapes and sizes, including the long, pennant-shaped *vimpel,* seen fluttering from flagpoles all over Norway (a 11.5-foot *vimpel* dresses up a boat or cabin wonderfully, near City Hall at Hieronymus Heyerdahlsgate

1, entrance on Tordenskioldsgate—on the other side of the block, +47 22 40 50 60).

Vinmonopolet stores are the only places where you can buy wine and spirits in Norway. The most convenient location is at the central train station. Another location, not far from Stortinget, is at Rosenkrantz Gate 11. The bottles used to be kept behind the counter, but now you can actually touch the merchandise. Locals say it went from being a jewelry store to a grocery store. (Light beer is sold in grocery stores, but strong beer is limited to Vinmonopolet shops.)

Sleeping in Oslo

Oslo's hotel rates are particularly susceptible to supply-and-demand fluctuation. You may find deals on weekends and during some parts of the summer, but even then, conventions or special meetings can cause hotel prices to double overnight.

Beyond standard hotels, Oslo is a good city for rooms in private homes and apartments offered through services such as Airbnb or www.bbnorway.com. When selecting a room, consider that sleeping downtown puts you close to the sights, but may come with noise (many loud nightclubs are in the center). The upscale area behind the Royal Palace (Frogner and Majorstuen neighborhoods) gives you a posh address. And for proximity to the trendy dining scene, look in the part of Grünerløkka near the river.

NEAR THE TRAIN STATION AND KARL JOHANS GATE

These accommodations are within a 15-minute walk of the station. While some streets near the station can feel a bit sketchy, these hotels are secure and comfortable. Parking in a central garage will run you about 250-300 NOK per day.

Thon Hotels

This chain of business-class hotels (found in big cities throughout Norway) offers little character, but provides maximum comfort per *krone* in big, modern, conveniently located buildings. Each hotel has a cheery staff and lobby, tight but well-designed rooms, Wi-Fi, free coffee in the lobby, and a big buffet breakfast. All are nonsmoking and have elevators and central air-conditioning.

Thon's **$$$$** City Hotels are a cut

above their **$$$** Budget Hotels and are generally more expensive. In Budget hotels, all rooms lack phones and minifridges.

Book by phone or online (central booking +47 21 49 69 00, www.thonhotels.no). For the best prices, check the price calendar on the Thon website. Of the more than a dozen Thon Hotels in Oslo, I find the following most convenient:

Thon City Hotel Rosenkrantz Oslo offers 152 comfortable and stylish rooms two blocks off Karl Johans Gate. Its eighth-floor lounge offers views of the Royal Palace park. They offer a free light supper every evening for guests—making this an even better value than it seems. If you want to splurge, this is the place to do it (Rosenkrantz Gate 1, +47 23 31 55 00, www.thonhotels.no/rosenkrantzoslo, rosenkrantzoslo@olavthon.no).

Thon City Hotel Terminus is similar but just a five-minute walk from the station; along with the Rosenkrantz, it offers a free light evening meal for guests (Steners Gate 10, +47 22 05 60 00, www.thonhotels.no/terminus, terminus@olavthon.no).

Thon City Hotel Cecil, ideally located near the Parliament building a block below Karl Johans Gate, has 110 efficient, comfortable rooms ringing a tall, light-filled, breakfast-room atrium (Stortingsgata 8, +47 23 31 48 00, www.thonhotels.no/cecil, cecil@olavthon.no).

Thon City Hotel Spectrum has 187 rooms just behind Oslo Spektrum concert arena. It's on a pedestrianized street, next door to a handy grocery store. Rooms facing the street can be noisy on weekends (Brugata 7; leave station out north entrance toward bus terminal, go across footbridge and down the stairs on the left, pass by tall glass Radisson Blu Plaza Hotel and walk to the other side of the park; +47 23 36 27 00, www.thonhotels.no/spectrum, spectrum@olavthon.no).

Thon Budget Hotel Astoria, with 180 rooms, has the least charm of my recommended Thon Hotels, but it's well-located and perfectly serviceable (2 blocks in front of station, 50 yards off Karl Johans Gate, Dronningens Gate 21, +47 24 14 55 50, www.thonhotels.no/astoria, astoria@olavthon.no).

Thon City Hotel Munch has 180 rooms in a location that's quiet but still relatively central, a few blocks from the National Gallery. Some rooms have hardwood floors, others have carpets. Because it recently transitioned from "Budget" to "City" class, its prices are a bit lower and a good value (Munchs Gate 5, +47 23 21 96 00, www.thonhotels.no/munch, munch@olavthon.no).

Thon City Hotel Oslo Panorama was a 15-story attempt at a downtown condominium building (the condos didn't work, so now it's a 118-room hotel). While higher rooms are more expensive, even those reserving a cheap room often get bumped up. If you request anything higher than the fourth floor, you'll likely

Oslo Center Hotels

500 Meters

500 Yards

Legend:

1. Thon City Hotel Rosenkrantz Oslo
2. Thon City Hotel Terminus
3. Thon City Hotel Cecil
4. Thon City Hotel Spectrum
5. Thon Budget Hotel Astoria
6. Thon City Hotel Munch
7. Thon City Hotel Oslo Panorama
8. Comfort Hotel Karl Johan

**Map labels:**

To Majorstuen & 13

URANIENBORG

To Majorstuen

#11 & 17

14

URANIENBORGVEIEN

HEGDE HAUGS-VEIEN

OSKARS GATE

INKOGNITOGATA

PARKVEIEN

WERGELANDSVEIEN

HOLBERGS GATE

Holbergs Plass

PILESTREDET

OLAVS GATE

KRISTIAN AUGUSTS GATE

St. Olavs Plass

6

Slottsparken

ROYAL PALACE

HISTORICAL MUSEUM

NATIONAL GALLERY

#11 & 17

KRISTIAN IVe

UNIVERSITETSGATA

OSLO UNIVERSITY

1

Dronningparken

PARKVEIEN

HENRIK IBSENS GATE

National-theatret

9

NATIONAL THEATER STATION

NATIONAL THEATER

OSLO

KARL

To Bygdøy & Frogner Park

CORT ADELERS GATE

HUITFELDTS GATE

#12

RUSELØKKVEIEN

MUNKEDAMSVEIEN

HAAKON VIIS GATE

#50 B

Eidsvolls-plass

STORTINGSGATA

WC

3

PARL.

VIKA

NATIONAL MUSEUM

NOBEL PEACE CENTER

CITY HALL

Rådhus-plassen

ROSENKRANTZ GATE

NEDRE VOLLGATE

AKERSGATA

#12

#12

T

To Bygdøy

AKER BRYGGE MALL

STRANDEN

#12

RÅDHUSGATA

FDR STATUE

ØVRE SLOTTSGATE

NEDRE SLOTTSGATE

KONGENS GATE

10

FILIPSTAD CRUISE BERTH

Pipervika

AKERSHUS-

RESISTANCE MUSEUM

FORTRESS VISITORS CENTER

TJUV-HOLMEN

CHRISTIAN RADICH TALL SHIP

STRANDA

AKERSHUS FORTRESS

Oslofjord

SØNDRE AKERSHUSKAIA CRUISE BERTH

VIPPETANGEN (AKERSHUS) CRUISE BERTH

To Bygdøy

9 Hotell Bondeheimen

10 Perminalen Hotel

11 Citybox Oslo

12 P-Hotel

13 To Saga Hotel Oslo & Villa Maria

14 Cochs Pensjonat

15 Anker Hotel

OSLO

enjoy a bigger room, perhaps with a tiny balcony and/or a kitch-enette (just off Dronningens Gate at Rådhusgata 7, about 6 blocks from station, +47 23 31 08 00, www.thonhotels.no/oslopanorama, oslopanorama@olavthon.no).

More Hotels near the Train Station

$$$$ Comfort Hotel Karl Johan fills a mod building with 181 tight rooms, across from the cathedral near the train-station end of Karl Johans Gate. It feels new, with sleek, somewhat minimalist decor and a trendy lobby that tries a little too hard to be hip and funky. Light sleepers should request a quiet room (elevator, Karl Johans Gate 12, +47 23 01 03 52, www.nordicchoicehotels.com, co.karljohan@choice.no).

$$$ Hotell Bondeheimen ("Farmer's Home") is a historic hotel run by the farmers' youth league, *Bondeungdomslaget*. It once housed the children of rural farmers attending school in Oslo. Its 145 rooms have all the comforts of a modern hotel (elevator, Rosenkrantz Gate 8, +47 23 21 41 00, www.bondeheimen.com, bookingoffice@bondeheimen.com). This almost-100-year-old building is also home to the Kaffistova cafeteria (see "Eating in Oslo") and one branch of the Heimen Husfliden shop (see "Shop-ping in Oslo").

$$ Perminalen Hotel, designed for military personnel on leave, also rents 15 rooms to tourists. It's perfectly central, spar-tan, and inexpensive. Spliced invisibly into a giant office block on a quiet street, they have the same fair prices all year—making it an excellent deal when the city is busy and rates are sky-high. All of the doubles are bunk beds (some seventh-floor rooms have tiny bal-conies, elevator, tram #12, #13, or #19 from station to Øvre Slott-sgate stop, Øvre Slottsgate 2, +47 24 00 55 00, www.perminalen. no, post.perminalen@iss.no). They also have single beds in dorms segregated by sexes (with lockers and breakfast). Its cheap mess hall is open nightly for dinner, and for lunch on weekdays.

$$ Citybox Oslo has 217 simple, basic rooms at a good price, in a nondescript urban zone a short walk from the train station. While services are minimal (self-check-in), the public areas are in-viting (breakfast extra, Prinsens Gate 6, +47 21 42 04 80, www. citybox.no, oslo@citybox.no).

$$ P-Hotel rents 93 cheaply designed, well-worn but afford-able rooms. It's a lesser value than the polished Thon hotels but may have rooms when others are full (or charging higher rates). You get a basic breakfast delivered each morning. Avoid late-night street noise by requesting a room high up or in the back (some sixth-floor rooms have balconies, Grensen 19, T-bane: Stortinget, +47 23 31 80 00, www.p-hotels.com, oslo@p-hotels.no).

OSLO

THE WEST END

This pleasant, refined-feeling residential neighborhood is a long walk or a short tram ride from downtown, tucked between the Royal Palace and Frogner Park. The busy main drag of this area is Hegdehaugsveien, lined with tram tracks, busy shops, and restaurants and cafés. The pensions listed here are affordable but are plagued by street and tram noise—try requesting a quiet room. Saga Hotel is quieter and more upscale.

$$$$ Saga Hotel Oslo feels elegant, with a trendy lobby and gold-trim furnishings. The 47 rooms are comfortable, and the location—in a posh residential area—is appealing (Eilert Sundts Gate 39, +47 22 55 44 90, www.sagahotels.no, post.oslo@sagahotels.no).

$$ Villa Marie is four blocks behind the Royal Palace. It rents several bright and cheery rooms—some with shared bathrooms and lower rates (breakfast extra, nonsmoking, tram #19 from central station to Rosenborg stop, near Uranienborg church at Holtegata 25, +47 22 60 03 59, www.villamarie.net).

$ Cochs Pensjonat is cheap and cozy, with 90 dated, simple rooms, many with kitchenettes (cheaper rooms with shared bath, discounted breakfast at nearby cafés, elevator; T-bane: Nationaltheatret, exit to Parkveien, and 10-minute walk through park; or more-convenient tram #11 to Homansbyen or #17 or #18 to Dalsbergstien; Parkveien 25, +47 23 33 24 00, www.cochs.no, booking@cochs.no, Skram family).

HOSTELS

¢ Anker Hotel, a huge student dorm open to travelers of any age, offers 250 rooms, including 34 of Oslo's best cheap doubles. The hostel also offers bunks in dorm rooms. Though it comes with the ambience of a bomb shelter, each of its rooms is spacious, simple, clean, and has a small kitchen (sheets and towels extra, elevator, no breakfast, pay parking; tram #17, or bus #30 or #31 from central station, bus and tram stop: Hausmannsgate; or 15-minute walk from station; Storgata 55, +47 22 99 72 00, www.ankerhostel.no, hostel@anker.oslo.no).

¢ Haraldsheim Youth Hostel (IYHF), a huge, modern hostel open all year, comes with a grand view, 315 beds—most of them in four-bed rooms...and a long commute (2.5 miles out of town). They also offer private rooms (sheets extra; from Oslo's central train station catch bus #31 or tram #17 to Sinsenkrysset, or T-bane lines #4 or #5 to Sinsen, then hike 5 minutes uphill to Haraldsheimveien 4; +47 22 22 29 65, www.haraldsheim.no, oslo.haraldsheim@hihostels.no). Eurailers can train to the hostel with their rail pass (2/hour, to Grefsen and walk 10 minutes).

OSLO

SLEEPING ON A TRAIN OR BOAT

Norway's trains and ferries offer ways to travel while sleeping. The eight-hour night train between Bergen and Oslo leaves at about 23:00 in each direction (nightly except Sat). An overnight cruise is another clever way to avoid a night in a hotel and to travel while you sleep, saving a day in your itinerary (see "Oslo Connections," later).

Eating in Oslo

Dining out is expensive in Oslo. How do average Norwegians afford their high-priced restaurants? They don't eat out much. This is one city in which you might want to settle for simple takeout or international food—you'll save a lot and miss little.

Splurge for a hotel that includes breakfast, or pay for it if it's optional. At around 80 NOK, a Norwegian breakfast fit for a Viking is a good deal. Picnic for lunch or dinner. Department stores often have supermarkets on the basement level, offering plenty of picnic options beyond sandwiches. The little yogurt tubs with cereal come with collapsible spoons. Wasa crackers and meat, shrimp, or cheese spread in a tube are cheap and pack well. The central station has a Joker supermarket with long hours. Some supermarkets have takeout food that is discounted just before closing—showing up just before 20:00 or so to buy some roast chicken could be your cheapest meal in Oslo. My favorite meals in Oslo are picnic dinners harborside.

You'll save by getting takeaway food from a restaurant rather than eating inside. (The tax on takeaway food is 15 percent, while the tax on dine-in food is 25 percent.) Fast-food restaurants ask if you want to take away or not before they ring up your order on the cash register. Even McDonald's has a two-tiered price list.

Oslo is awash with little budget eateries (modern, international, fast food, pizza, department-store cafeterias, and so on). **Deli de Luca,** a cheery convenience store chain that's notorious for having a store on every key corner in Oslo (including a long block off Karl Johans Gate at Universitesgata 20), is a step up from the similarly ubiquitous 7-Elevens and Narvesens. Most are open 24/7, selling sandwiches, pastries, sushi, and to-go boxes of warm pasta or Asian noodle dishes. You can fill your belly here for about 80 NOK. Some outlets have seating on the street or upstairs. Beware: This is still a *convenience* store, so not everything is well-priced.

Oslo's One-Time Grills

Norwegians are experts at completely avoiding costly restaurants. "One-time grills," or *engangsgrill*, are the rage for locals on a budget. For about 25 NOK, you get a disposable outdoor cooker consisting of an aluminum tray, easy-to-light charcoal, and a flimsy metal grill. All that's required is a sunny evening, a grassy park, and a group of friends. During balmy summer evenings, the air in Oslo's city parks is thick with the smell of disposable (and not terribly eco-friendly) grills. It's fun to see how prices for this kind of "dining" aren't that bad in the supermarket: Norwegian beer-28 NOK/half-liter, potato salad-30 NOK/tub, cooked shrimp-50 NOK/half kilo, "ready for grill" steak-two for 120 NOK, *grill pølse* hot dogs-75 NOK per dozen, *lomper* (Norwegian tortillas for wrapping hot dogs)-20 NOK per stack, and the actual grill itself (during dry spells, grill sales are sometimes halted).

Bars are also too expensive for the average Norwegian. Young night owls drink at home before *(forspiel)* and after *(nachspiel)* an evening on the town, with a couple of hours, generally around midnight, when they go out for a single drink in a public setting. A beer in a bar costs about $10 for a half-liter, while a six-pack goes for about twice that price in a grocery store.

KARL JOHANS GATE STRIP

Strangely, **Karl Johans Gate**—the most Norwegian of boulevards—is lined with a strip of American chain eateries and sports bars where you can get ribs, burgers, and pizza. **$$ Egon Restaurant** offers a daily 110-NOK all-you-can-eat pizza deal (available Tue-Sat 11:00-18:00, Sun-Mon all day)—though the rest of their menu is overpriced. Each place comes with great sidewalk seating and essentially the same prices.

$$$$ Grand Café is perhaps the most venerable place in town, with genteel decor described on page 232. They have a seasonal menu, with high-end Nordic, French, and international dishes. Reserve a window, and if you hit a time when there's no tour group, you're suddenly a posh Norwegian (Mon-Fri 11:00-23:00, Sat-Sun 12:00-23:00, Karl Johans Gate 31, +47 98 18 20 00, www.grandcafeoslo.no).

$$ Kaffebrenneriet is a good local coffeehouse chain serving quality coffee drinks and affordable sandwiches, salads, and pastries. Convenient locations include in the park along Karl Johans

OSLO

Norwegian Cuisine

Traditional Norwegian cuisine doesn't rank very high in terms of excitement. But the typical diet of meat, fish, and potatoes is evolving to incorporate more diverse products, and the food here is steadily improving. Fresh produce, colorful markets, and efficient supermarkets abound in Europe's most expensive corner.

In this land of farmers and fishermen, traditional recipes are built on ingredients like potatoes, salmon, or beef. A favorite tart-and-sweet condiment is lingonberry jam, which cuts through a heavy, salty meat dish. Some traditional places also serve *lefse*—a soft flatbread made from potatoes, milk, and flour.

Norway's national dish is *Fårikål,* a lamb or mutton stew with cabbage, peppercorns, and potatoes. This dish is so popular that the last Thursday in September is *Fårikål* day in Norway. There's really no need for a recipe, so every stew turns out differently—and every grandma claims hers is the best.

Because of its long, cold winters, Norway relies heavily on the harvesting and preservation of fish. Smoked salmon, called *røkt laks,* is prepared by salt-curing the fish and cold-smoking it, ensuring the temperature never rises above 85°F. This makes the texture smooth and almost raw. *Bacalao* is another favorite: salted and dried cod that is rehydrated and rinsed in water before cooking. You'll often find *bacalao* served with tomatoes and olives. Stockfish *(tørrfisk),* usually cod, is hung on wooden racks to air-dry (rather than salt-cure), creating a kind of "fish jerky" that goes well with beer. *Klippfisk* is yet another variation, which is partly air-dried on rocks along the shoreline, then further cured in salt.

Some Norwegians serve lutefisk around Christmas time, but you'll rarely see this salty, pungent dish on the menu. Instead, try the more pleasant *fiskekake,* a small white fish cake made with cream, eggs, milk, and flour. You can find these patties year-round.

For a break from seafood, try local specialties such as reindeer meatballs, or pork-and-ground beef meat cakes called *kjøttkaker.* True to Scandinavian cuisine, *kjøttkaker* are usually slathered in a heavy cream sauce.

Dessert and coffee after a meal are essential. *Bløtkake,* a popular delight on Norway's Constitution Day (May 17), is a layered cake drizzled with strawberry juice, covered in whipped cream, and decorated with fresh strawberries. The cloudberry *(multe),* which grows in the Scandinavian tundra, makes a unique jelly that tastes delicious on vanilla ice cream, or even whipped into a rich cream topping for heart-shaped waffles. Norwegians are proud of their breads and pastries, and you'll never be too far from a bakery that sells an almond-flavored *kringle* or a cone-shaped *krumkake* cookie filled with whipped cream.

Gate at #24, closer to the cathedral and train station at Karl Johans Gate 7, behind the cathedral at Storgata 2, facing the back of the Parliament building at Akersgata 16, and next to City Hall at Hieronymus Heyerdahls Gate 1. Most have similar hours (typically Mon-Fri 7:00-19:00, Sat 9:00-18:00, closed Sun).

$$ United Bakeries, next to the Paleet mall, is a quiet bit of Norwegian quality among sports bars, appreciated for its 80-NOK sandwiches, salads, light weekday lunches, and fresh pastries (seating inside and out, Mon-Fri 7:30-20:00, Sat 9:00-18:00, Sun 11:00-17:00).

$$$ Kaffistova, a block off the main drag, is where my thrifty Norwegian grandparents always took me. And it remains almost unchanged since the 1970s. This alcohol-free cafeteria still serves simple, hearty, and typically Norwegian meals (including big portions of Norwegian meatballs) for a good price (Mon-Fri 11:00-21:00, Sat-Sun until 19:00, Rosenkrantz Gate 8, +47 23 21 41 00).

$$$$ Theatercaféen, since 1900 the place for Norway's illuminati to see and be seen (note the celebrity portraits adorning the walls), is a swanky splurge steeped in Art Nouveau elegance (Mon-Sat 11:00-23:00, Sun 15:00-22:00, in Hotel Continental at Stortingsgata 24, across from National Theater, +47 22 82 40 50, www.theatercafeen.no).

NEAR AKERSHUS FORTRESS

$$$$ Café Skansen is a delightful spot for a quality meal—especially in good weather, when its leafy, beer garden-like terrace fills with a convivial, mostly local crowd. Or huddle in the old-time interior and dig into classic Norwegian dishes. They serve more affordable lunches until 16:00, and good salads anytime (Mon-Fri 11:00-23:00, Sat-Sun 12:00-22:00, Rådhusgata 32, +47 24 20 13 11, www.cafeskansen.no).

$$$$ Engebret Café is a classic old restaurant in a 17th-century building in the Christiania section of town below the fortress. Since 1857, it's been serving old-fashioned Norse food (reindeer is always on the menu) in a classic old Norwegian setting. In good weather, you can sit out on the delightful square with a gurgling fountain (Mon-Fri 11:30-23:00, Sat from 17:00, closed Sun and most of July, Bankplassen 1, +47 22 82 25 25, www.engebret-cafe.no).

$$$$ Solsiden ("Sunny Side"), filling a glassed-in former warehouse on the embankment just under the fortress, is a local favorite for a harborfront splurge. You'll dig into fish and seafood meals in an open, unpretentious, nautical-themed, blue-and-white interior that doesn't distract from the cooking. Think of this as a less posh-feeling alternative to the Aker Brygge scene across the harbor. Reserve ahead, and ask for a table with a view (May-mid-

OSLO

Oslo Center Restaurants

1 Egon Restaurant & United Bakeries

2 Grand Café

3 Deli de Luca

4 Kaffebrenneriet (3)

5 Kaffistova

6 Theatercaféen

7 Café Skansen

8 Engebret Café

9 Solsiden

OSLO

10 Fenaknoken Deli
11 Aker Brygge Eateries
12 Grocery (2)
13 Youngstorget Eateries
14 Illegal Burger Bar
15 Torggata North Eateries
16 Peloton
17 Torggata South Eateries
18 To Frogner Park Eateries

Sept daily 16:30-22:00, in peak times they do two dinner seatings—at 20:00 and 22:30, Akershusstranda 13, +47 22 33 36 30, www.solsiden.no).

Top-End Picnic Shopping: Near City Hall, **Fenaknoken** is a characteristic deli specializing in gourmet Norwegian products—from salmon and lefse to moose salami and dried fish. If you value authentic quality products over price, this is the place to assemble a blowout Norwegian picnic to enjoy out along the harbor (Mon-Fri 10:00-17:00, Sat until 13:30, closed Sun, Tordenskioldsgate 12, +47 22 42 34 57, www.fenaknoken.no).

HARBORSIDE DINING IN AKER BRYGGE

Aker Brygge, the harborfront development near City Hall, is popular with businesspeople and tourists. While it isn't cheap, its

inviting cafés and restaurants with outdoor tables make for a memorable waterfront meal. Before deciding where to eat, walk the entire lane (including the back side), considering both the brick-and-mortar places (some with second-floor view seating) and the various floating options. Nearly all are open for lunch and dinner.

$$$$ Lekter'n Lounge, right on the water, offers the best harbor view (rather than views of strolling people). This trendy bar has a floating dining area open only when the weather is warm. It serves hamburgers, fish-and-chips, salads, mussels, and shrimp buckets (all outdoors, Stranden 3, +47 21 52 32 31). If you go just for drinks, the sofas make you feel right at home, and a DJ adds to the ambience.

$$$$ Rorbua ("Fisherman's Cabin") is a lively yet cozy eatery tucked back into this otherwise modern stretch of restaurants. The specialty is food from Norway's north, such as whale and reindeer. Inside, it's extremely woody with a rustic charm and candlelit picnic tables surrounded by harpoons and old B&W photos. While the à la carte dinners start at around 300 NOK, a hearty daily special with coffee for 175 NOK is one of the city's best restaurant deals (daily 12:30-23:00, Stranden 71, +47 22 83 64 84, www.rorbua.as).

$$$$ Lofoten Fiskerestaurant serves fish amid a dressy yacht-club atmosphere at the end of the strip. While it's beyond the people-watching action, it's comfortable even in cold and blustery weather because of its heated atrium, which makes a meal here practically outdoor dining. Reservations are a must, especially for a harborside window table (daily 11:00-23:00, Stranden 75, +47 22 83 08 08, www.lofoten-fiskerestaurant.no).

Budget Tips: If you're on a budget, try a hot dog from a *pølse* stand or get a picnic from a nearby grocery store and grab a bench along the boardwalk. The **Co-op Mega** grocery store—in the middle of the mall a few steps behind all the fancy restaurants—has salads, warm takeaway dishes (sold by weight), and more (turn in about midway down the boardwalk, Mon-Sat 8:00-22:00, Sun 9:00-20:00). Farther down is a **Joker mini-grocery,** just over the bridge and to the right on Lille Stranden in Tjuvholmen (Mon-Sat 8:00-22:00, Sun from 11:00).

NEAR YOUNGSTORGET

Central Oslo's most appealing dining zone percolates just a 10-minute stroll north of Karl Johans Gate, around the otherwise nondescript urban square named Youngstorget. This aptly named square feels fresh and trendy, although it's tucked between all-business high-rises and Thon hotels. The square itself has several fine options, but the streets leading off it are also worth a browse—especially Torggata, lined with a couple dozen eclectic options more tempting than anything in the touristy downtown.

On Youngstorget

First, check out the hipster **food carts** that are often parked in the middle of the square, which can be a great spot for a quick, afford-able al fresco bite. But to settle in for a more serious meal, you have plenty of choices.

Three good options cluster at the base of the towering, red-brick head-quarters of the Arbei-derpartiet (Labor Party). **$$$$ Fiskeriet** started as a small fish counter (with stacks of dried cod) before expanding into a full-blown restaurant. It has a concise but tempting menu of simple fish-focused dishes, including fish-and-chips, and seating either in the tiled interior or out on the square (Mon-Fri 11:00-21:00, Sat from 12:00, closed Sun, Youngstorget 2b, +47 22 42 45 40, www.fiskeriet.com). Next door, **$$$$ Taverna'n** is an indus-trial-strength eatery with a big, rustic/trendy interior plus outdoor dining, a fun energy, and a menu of pastas, fish dishes, grill meals, and pizza—which they call "skorpe" (Mon-Fri 11:00-late, Sat from 12:00, Sun 13:00-22:00, Youngstorget 1, +47 40 01 74 37, https://tavernan.no). Rounding out the scene is **$$ Internasjonalen,** a bar with a checkerboard-tile-and-red-leather interior, a wall of lit-up liquor bottles, inviting outdoor tables on the square, and cheap sandwiches (Mon-Sat 10:00-late, Sun from 16:00, Youngstorget 2a, +47 46 82 52 40).

From any of the above, you can gaze across the square to the pinkish, crenellated former police station that was headquarters for the notorious Nazi security service during the occupation—and where traitor Vidkun Quisling surrendered to Norwegian police at war's end. Its former stables, in the arcades just below, are filled with more bars and eateries (cozy **Fyret** has a great selection of aquavit and open-face sandwiches, while **Politiker'n** has ample outdoor seating). And finally, if you were to hike up to the old police station and turn right (at the uphill corner of the square), you'd find **$$$ Illegal Burger Bar**—the best-regarded of Oslo's many trendy burger joints, with a long, creative menu of gourmet burgers (daily 14:00-late, Møllergata 23, +47 22 20 33 02).

On Torggata, North of Youngstorget

For even more options, stroll from Youngstorget up Torggata and comparison-shop menus, ignoring the American fast-food chains and keeping an eye out for these places (listed in order as you head north): A short block up Badstugata (on the left) is the high-end **$$$$ Arakataka,** serving refined New Nordic dishes in an elegant setting (650-NOK tasting *menu*, daily from 16:00, Mariboes Gate 7b, +47 23 32 83 00, www.arakataka.no). Nearby is **Tilt Bar,** a pinball-themed dive filling what used to be the old public bathhouse. On the corner of Torggata and Osterhaus Gate, at #30, **$$$ Taco República** has impressively authentic and delicious Mexican food in a tight, lively, colorful, casual setting. As servings are small, you may need several dishes to fill up (Tue-Thu 16:00-22:00, Fri 15:00-24:00, Sat from 12:00, Sun 14:00-22:00, closed Mon, +47 40 05 76 65). Just past that, at #32, **$$ Crowbar** is an industrial-mod microbrewery with an easy-to-miss self-service counter upstairs serving cheap falafel and kebabs (Sun-Fri 15:00-late, Sat from 13:00, +47 21 38 67 57). And finally, up at the corner (at #35), **$$$ Peloton** is a casual and inviting *sykkelcafe*—a bright, cheery "bicycle café" serving pizza and long list of beers, with a bike shop in the back (Mon 8:00-18:00, Tue-Fri until 24:00, Sat 10:00-24:00, Sun 12:00-23:00, +47 92 15 61 81).

On Torggata, South of Youngstorget

The stretch of Torgatta to the south, where it connects Youngstorget to Karl Johans Gate, feels less residential and more shopping-oriented. But it's also lined with a fun variety of eateries as well—most of which double as hard-partying nightspots into the wee hours. **$$$ Cafe Sør,** a few steps south of Youngstorget, has a cool ramshackle vibe and an affordable menu of salads and sandwiches. It becomes a lively dance club after hours (Mon-Sat 10:00-late, Sun from 12:00, Torggata 11, +47 23 65 46 46). Nearby, the *Strøget* sign marks the entrance to a courtyard that's jammed with lively eateries, bars, cafés, and clubs. This courtyard is a fun place to browse for a meal or drink by day, or to find a lively nightlife scene after hours. In here, **$$$$ Habibi** has an old cafeteria vibe, a menu of Palestinian mezes, and warbling Middle Eastern music. **Angst** is an achingly hip bar with brooding, atmospheric decor and a live DJ after 23:00.

DINING NEAR FROGNER PARK

These options are handy after your visit to the Vigeland Sculpture Park within sprawling Frogner Park. For locations see the "Frogner Park" map on page 248.

$$$$ Lofotstua Restaurant feels transplanted from the far northern islands it's named for. Kjell Jenssen and his son, Jan Hugo, proudly serve up fish Lofoten-style. Evangelical about fish, they will patiently explain to you the fine differences between all the local varieties, with the help of a photo-filled chart. They serve only the freshest catch, perfectly—if simply—prepared. And if you want meat, they've got it: whale or seal (Mon-Fri 15:00-21:30, closed Sat-Sun, generally closed in July, 5-minute walk from Frogner Park's main gate, tram #12, in Majorstuen at Kirkeveien 40, +47 22 46 93 96, https://lofotstua-as.business.site). This place is packed daily in winter for their famous lutefisk.

$$$ Curry and Ketchup Indian Restaurant is filled with locals enjoying hearty, decent meals for under 200 NOK. This happening place requires no reservations and feels like an Indian market, offering a flavorful meal near Vigeland's statues (daily 14:00-23:00, a 5-minute walk from Frogner Park's main gate, tram #12, in Majorstuen at Kirkeveien 51, +47 22 69 05 22).

TRENDY DINING IN GRÜNERLØKKA

For locations, see the map on page 265.

Mathallen and Vulkan

This fast-emerging zone, on the bank of the Akers River (and covered on my Akers River and Grünerløkka Walk), has recently put Oslo on the foodie map. In the appealing Akers River valley, several old brick industrial buildings and adjoining new construction house a busy hive of culinary activity that's an easy walk or tram ride from downtown (it's a 5-minute walk from the tram stop at Olaf Ryes Plass, described later).

The anchor of this area is **Mathallen Oslo**—once a 19th-century factory, now spiffed up and morphed into a riverside market with a mix of produce stalls and enticing eateries all sharing food-circus-type seating in the middle (Tue-Sat 10:00-20:00, Sun 11:00-18:00, closed Mon except in July, some restaurants open longer hours, www.mathallenoslo.no).

Inside, and ringing the perimeter, you'll find a world of options: tapas, Italian, sushi, tacos and tequila, pizza, Asian street food, Paradis gourmet ice cream, and so on. Most places have high-quality meals in the 150-200-NOK range. **$$$ Galopin** is a French wine bar with tasty light meals and cheeses. **$$$ Atelier Asian Tapas** dishes up small plates and full meals. Or browse the market vendors: **Ost & Sånt** is a high-end Norwegian farm cheese counter. **Smelt Ostesmørbrød** sells fresh breads, pastries, and sandwiches. **The Cupcake & Pie Co.** serves sweet and savory pies. Upstairs, don't miss the taco shop and the sprawling **Hitchhiker** wine bar.

More places face the outside of the hall, including—overlooking the bridge—**$$$$ Lucky Bird** fried chicken and ribs (www.luckybird.no), **$$$$ Smelteverket** ("global tapas" with wonderful views over the river, https://smelteverketoslo.no), and more. Still can't decide? For me, the winner may be **$$$$ Vulkanfisk,** with indoor and outdoor seating and a tempting menu of relatively well-priced and elegantly executed fish and seafood dishes: mussels, fish-and-chips, fish soup, garlic scampi, etc. (Mon-Sat 11:00-21:00, Sun until 20:00, +47 21 39 69 58, www.vulkanfisk.no). For just a drink, consider the sun-trap outdoor patio bar in **Dansens Hus** (the national dance theater), facing Vulkanfisk from across the street.

Just uphill is the **Vulkan Depot,** a small shopping mall with a trendy food court including Sapporo Ramen Bar, an Italian grocery store, a florist, a pharmacy, a co-working space (where independent contractors can rent a desk), and a big Rema 1000 supermarket.

Olaf Ryes Plass

Grünerløkka's main square (and the streets nearby) is lined with inviting eateries and has a relaxed, bohemian-chic vibe. To get here, hop on tram #11, #12, or #18. The top edge of the square has several pubs selling beer-centric food to a beer-centric crowd. Before choosing, simply wander and survey your options: Parkteatret (a classic café), Fontés (tapas), Eldhuset (barbecue), Skaal (sophisticated small plates), the charming little Grünerhaven café kiosk in the park itself, and perhaps the most appealing choice, **$$$ Villa Paradiso Pizzeria.** Youthful and family-friendly, it has

a rustic interior and a popular terrace overlooking the square and people scene (Olaf Ryes Plass 8, +47 22 35 40 60). Just past Villa Paradiso, a block to the west (toward the Mathallen scene described earlier), sits Oslo's most renowned coffee shop, named **Tim Wendelboe** for its celebrity-barista owner. If you're a coffee pilgrim wanting to caffeinate in style...do it here (Mon-Fri 8:30-18:00, Sat-Sun 11:00-17:00, Grüners Gate 1).

The bottom of the leafy square is more focused on nightlife. From here, it's fun to stroll south on lively Thorvald Meyers Gate back toward downtown, passing a few cheap international eateries (**Miss Gin** Vietnamese street food, **Bislett** kebab house, and **Trattoria Popolare,** with affordable pastas and sprawling outdoor seating perfectly situated to catch the sun's final rays). Eventually you'll run into the place described next.

Between Olaf Ryes Plass and Downtown: Originally a big bank, **$$$$ Südøst Asian Crossover Restaurant** now fills its vault with wine (which makes sense, given Norwegian alcohol prices). It's a fine mix of Norwegian-chic, with a woody ambience inside and a big riverside terrace outdoors with a more casual menu. Diners enjoy its setting, smart service, and creative Asian-fusion cuisine. Reservations are wise, especially on weekends. They're particularly popular on Sundays, when they offer an all-you-can-eat buffet for a relatively affordable 200 NOK (daily 11:00-24:00, at bottom of Grünerløkka, tram #11, #12, or #17 to Trondheimsveien 5, +47 23 35 30 70, https://sudost.no/hjem).

CHEAP AND SPICY IN GRØNLAND

The street called Grønland leads through this colorful immigrant neighborhood (a short walk behind the train station or T-bane: Grønland; see the map on page 265). This area is refreshingly diverse compared to the rest of the city, and whether you eat here or not, Grønland is fun to explore. You'll find plenty of street food, plus cheap and tasty *börek* (savory phyllo pastry with feta, spinach, or mushroom) sold hot and greasy to go for 25 NOK.

$$ Punjab Tandoori is friendly and serves hearty meals (lamb and chicken curry, tandoori specials). I like eating outside here with a view of the street scene (daily 11:00-23:00, Grønland 24).

$$ Istanbul Restaurant is clean and simple, with a decora-

OSLO

tive interior, outdoor seating, cheap kebabs, and affordable plates of Turkish food (Mon-Fri 10:00-24:00, Sat-Sun from 11:00, Grønland 14, +47 23 40 90 22).

$$$ Asylet is more expensive and feels like it was here long before Norway ever saw a Pakistani. This big, traditional eatery—like a Norwegian beer garden—has a rustic, cozy interior and a cobbled backyard filled with picnic tables (burgers, pub food, hearty dinner salads, daily 11:00-23:30, Grønland 28, +47 22 17 09 39).

$$$ Dattera Til Hagen feels like a college party. It's a lively scene filling a courtyard with graffiti, picnic tables, and benches under strings of colored twinkle lights. Locals like it for the tapas, burgers, salads, and Norwegian microbrews on tap (daily 11:00-late, Grønland 10, +47 22 17 18 61). On weekends after 22:00, it becomes a nightclub.

$$$$ Olympen Brown Pub is a dressy dining hall that's a blast from the past. You'll eat in a spacious, woody saloon with big dark furniture, faded paintings of circa-1920 Oslo lining the walls, and huge chandeliers. It's good for solo travelers, because sharing the long dinner tables is standard practice. They serve hearty, pricey plates and offer a huge selection of beers. Traditional Norwegian cuisine is served downstairs, while upstairs on the rooftop, the food is grilled (daily 11:00-late, Grønlandsleiret 15, +47 24 10 19 99).

NEAR THE SKI JUMP, HIGH ON THE MOUNTAIN

You can combine a trip into the forested hills surrounding the city with lunch or dinner and get a chance to see the famous Holmenkollen Ski Jump up close.

Frognerseteren Hovedrestaurant, nestled high above Oslo (and 1,387 feet above sea level), is a classy, sod-roofed old restaurant. Its packed-when-it's-sunny terrace, offering a commanding view of the city, is a popular stop for its famous apple cake and coffee. The **$$ self-service café** is affordable for hearty plates of classic Norwegian dishes, with indoor and outdoor seating (Mon-Sat 11:00-22:00, Sun 11:00-21:00). The elegant view

$$$$ restaurant is quite expensive and more formal, with reindeer specials on the menu and antler chandeliers overhead. Ideally, reserve ahead for evening dining (Mon-Fri 12:00-22:00, Sat from 13:00, Sun 13:00-21:00, +47 22 92 40 40, www.frognerseteren.no).

$$$$ Holmenkollen Restaurant, below the ski jump and a five-minute hike above the Holmenkollen T-bane stop, is a practical alternative to Frognerseteren. Woody but modern, it's slightly cheaper and also has a grand Oslofjord view, but without the folk charm and affordable self-service option. I'd eat here only if you need a solid meal near the ski jump and aren't heading up to Frognerseteren (Tue-Sat 12:00-21:00, Sun 13:00-19:00, closed Mon, Holmenkollveien 119, +47 22 13 92 00, www. holmenkollenrestaurant.no).

Oslo Connections

BY TRAIN, BUS, OR CAR

Train service in Norway is run by Vy, a government-run outfit. For train information, call +47 61 05 19 10 (press 9 for English; for international trains, press 3) or visit Vy.no. For general information about train travel in Scandinavia, see the "Transportation" section of the Practicalities chapter.

From Oslo by Train to Stockholm: The speedy X2000 train zips from downtown to downtown in about 5.5 hours, runs several times daily, and requires reservations. Ongoing construction on this line may interrupt service. Until X2000 service resumes, you can take a slower train with a change in Göteborg.

By Train to Bergen: Oslo and Bergen are linked by a spectacularly scenic train ride (at least 4/day, 7 hours, overnight possible daily except Sat). Many travelers take it as part of the **Norway in a Nutshell** route, which combines train, ferry, and bus travel in an unforgettably beautiful trip (see the Norway in a Nutshell chapter).

By Train to: Lillehammer (almost hourly, 2.25 hours), **Kristiansand** (5/day, 4.5 hours, overnight possible), **Stavanger** (5/day, 8 hours, overnight possible), **Copenhagen** (2/day, 8.5 hours, transfer at Göteborg, more with multiple changes).

By Bus to Stockholm: Taking the bus to Stockholm is cheaper but slower than the train (3/day, 8 hours, www.flixbus.se).

By Car to the Jotunheimen Mountains: See "Route Tips for Drivers" on page 365.

BY PLANE
Oslo Airport

Oslo Lufthavn, also called Gardermoen, is about 30 miles north of the city center and has a helpful 24-hour information center (code: OSL, +47 91 50 64 00, www.osl.no).

The fastest and cheapest way to get into the city center is by **train.** Exiting the baggage claim, turn left and head to the far end of the building. Here you'll see two options: local trains (Vy) take about 25 minutes to downtown (109 NOK, 2-3/hour, cheaper if you have an Oslo Pass, buy ticket at machines or pay a little extra to buy it at the counter); the private, competing Flytoget train is only a few minutes faster but costs nearly double (199 NOK, 4/hour, runs roughly 5:00-24:00, www.flytoget.no; swipe your credit card at the gate and choose your destination station). Unless you are in a big hurry or enjoy paying double, I'd stick with the Vy trains. Note that for either type of train, some departures only go as far as the central train station, while others continue—for no extra charge—to the National Theater station (closer to most recommended hotels). Unfortunately, this isn't clearly indicated on the screen; to spare yourself a transfer (or save some extra walking), ask whether your train continues to the National Theater.

Flybuss airport buses stop directly outside the arrival hall and make several downtown stops, including the central train station (199 NOK one-way, 3/hour, 40 minutes, +47 67 98 04 80)—but since it costs more than the train and takes twice as long, it's hard to justify taking the bus.

Taxis take about 45 minutes to downtown and vary in price depending on the company; figure 600-900 NOK on weekdays, more on weekends or after hours. A taxi booking machine at the information center in the arrivals hall lets you comparison-shop prices and order a cab.

Sandefjord Airport Torp

Ryanair, WizzAir, and other discount airlines use this airport 70 miles south of Oslo (code: TRF, +47 33 42 70 00, www.torp. no). You can take a bus into downtown Oslo (269 NOK, www. torpekspressen.no). Buses *to* Sandefjord depart Oslo's central bus terminal (next to the train station) about three hours before all flight departures.

BY CRUISE SHIP

Oslo has three cruise ports: Akershus, right on the harbor below Akershus Fortress; Revierkaia, around the east side of the Akershus Fortress peninsula; and Filipstad, just west of downtown. For in-depth cruising information, pick up my *Rick Steves Scandinavian & Northern European Cruise Ports* guidebook.

BY OVERNIGHT BOAT

Consider connecting Oslo and **Copenhagen** by DFDS cruise ship. The boat leaves daily from Oslo around 14:00 and arrives in Copenhagen about 9:00 the following morning (return sailing from Copenhagen follows the same schedule; about 19 hours each way). The boat leaves Oslo from the tip of the Akershus Fortress penin-

OSLO

sula (take bus #60 from the train station to the Vippetangen stop and follow signs to DFDS ticket office at Akershusstranda 31). For more specifics and sample prices, see "By Overnight Boat to Oslo" on page 123.

You can also take a DFDS cruise ship overnight from Oslo to **Frederikshavn,** on Denmark's Jutland peninsula—a great option for drivers.

Book in advance—online or by phone—for the best prices (www.dfds.com; from Norway, call DFDS's Denmark office: +45 33 42 38 00, closed Sat-Sun).

NORWAY IN A NUTSHELL

A Scenic Journey to the Sognefjord

While urban Oslo and Bergen are big draws for tourists, Norway is first and foremost a place of unforgettable natural beauty. There's a certain mystique about the "land of the midnight sun," but you'll get the most scenic travel thrills per mile, minute, and dollar by going west from Oslo rather than north.

Norway's greatest claims to scenic fame are her deep, lush fjords. Three million years ago, an ice age made this land as inhabitable as the center of Greenland. As the glaciers advanced and cut their way to the sea, they gouged out long grooves—today's fjords. The entire west coast is slashed by these stunning inlets, and the Sognefjord—Norway's longest (120 miles) and deepest (1 mile)—is tops. The seductive Sognefjord has tiny but tough ferries, towering canyons, and isolated farms and villages marinated in the mist of countless waterfalls.

A series of well-organized and spectacular bus, train, and ferry connections—appropriately nicknamed "Norway in a Nutshell"—lays Norway's beautiful fjord country before you on a scenic platter. With the Nutshell, you'll delve into two offshoots of the Sognefjord, which make an upside-down "U" route: the Aurlandsfjord and the Nærøyfjord. You'll link the ferry ride to the rest of Norway with two trains and a bus: The main train is an express route that takes you through stark and icy scenery above the tree line. To link the express train to the ferry, you'll catch the Flåmsbana train one way (passing waterfalls and forests) and a bus the other way (offering fjord views and more waterfalls). At the start of the fjord, you'll go through the town of Flåm (a transit hub), then pass briefly by the workaday town of Aurland and the hamlet of Undredal (by taking the Nutshell trip segments at your own pace, you can visit the lat-

Norway in a Nutshell

Not to Scale:
Bergen to Oslo is 300 Miles/480 KM
& 7 Hours by Rail

Atlantic

Lustrafjord

Balestrand

S o g n e fjord

Ferry

Aurland

Gudvangen

Flåm

Flåmsbana Train

Bus · Stal-heim

BERGEN   Voss   Myrdal   OSLO

ter two fjord towns on your own). All connections are designed for tourists, explained in English, convenient, and easy.

This region enjoys mild weather for its latitude, thanks to the warm Gulf Stream. (When it rains in Bergen, it just drizzles here.) But if the weather is bad, don't fret. I've often arrived to gloomy weather, only to enjoy sporadic splashes of brilliant sunshine all day long.

The Nutshell route is hugely popular. Completion of the world's longest car tunnel (the 15-mile-long Lærdal Tunnel, between Aurland and Lærdal) in 2005 rerouted the main E-16 road between Bergen and Oslo through this idyllic fjord corner. Now summer comes with a crush of crowds, dampening some of the area's magic. Unfortunately, many tourists are overcome by Nutshell tunnel-vision, and spend so much energy scurrying between boats, trains, and buses that they forget to simply enjoy the fjords. Relax—you're on vacation.

PLANNING YOUR TIME

Even the blitz tourist needs a day for the Norway in a Nutshell trip. With more time, sleep in a town along the fjord, and customize your fjord experience to include sights outside the Nutshell.

Day 1: The Nutshell works well as a single day (one-way between Oslo and Bergen, or as a long day-trip loop from either city). If you're without a

"Norway in a Nutshell" in a Nutshell

The five essential Nutshell segments are listed below (and explained in this chapter). Be sure to confirm times online or locally, as schedules can change.. Nutshell travelers originating in Bergen can do this route in reverse.

Oslo to Myrdal Train (Vy Railway): Two departures each morning—6:25 (recommended) and 8:25, 4.5-5.5 hours.

Myrdal to Flåm Train (Flåmsbana): Departures timed with Oslo train arrivals, 1 hour.

Flåm to Gudvangen Fjord Cruise: Almost hourly departures, 2 hours.

Gudvangen to Voss Bus: Departures timed with boat arrivals, 75 minutes.

Voss to Bergen Train: Hourly departures, 75 minutes.

car and want to make efficient use of your time, organize your trip so that it begins in Oslo and ends in Bergen (or vice versa).

Day 2: If you have enough time, spend the night somewhere on the Sognefjord—either along the Nutshell route itself (in Flåm or Aurland; accommodations listed later), or in another, even more appealing fjordside town (such as Balestrand or Solvorn, both described in the next chapter).

With More Time: The Sognefjord deserves more than a day. If you can spare the time, venture off the Nutshell route. You can easily connect to some non-Nutshell towns (such as Balestrand) via ferry or express boat. Drivers can improve on the Nutshell by taking a northern route: From Oslo, drive through the Gudbrandsdal Valley, go over the Jotunheimen Mountains, then along the Lustrafjord to Kaupanger; from there, you can experience the Sognefjord on a car ferry ending in Gudvangen, and drive the remainder of the Nutshell route to Bergen. (Most of these sights, and the ferry connections, are covered in the next two chapters.) For more tips, see the "Beyond the Nutshell" sidebar, later in this chapter.

Orientation to the Nutshell

The most exciting single-day trip you could make from Oslo or Bergen is this circular train/boat/bus/train jaunt through fjord country.

Local TIs (listed throughout this chapter) are well informed about your options, and sell tickets for various segments of the trip.

At TIs, train stations, and hotels, look for souvenir-worthy brochures with photos, descriptions, and exact times.

Route Overview

The basic idea is this: Take a train halfway across the mountainous spine of Norway, make your way down to the Sognefjord for a boat cruise, then climb back up out of the fjord to rejoin the main train line. Each of these steps is explained in the self-guided "Nutshell Tour" in this chapter. Transportation along the Nutshell route is carefully coordinated. If any segment of your journey is delayed, the transportation for the next segment will wait for you (because everyone on board is catching the same connection).

Doing the Nutshell one-way between Oslo and Bergen (or vice versa) is most satisfying—you'll see the whole shebang, and it's extremely efficient if you're connecting the two cities anyway. It's also possible to do most of the route in a round-trip loop from either Bergen or Oslo. Doing the round-trip from Bergen is cheaper, but it doesn't include the majestic train ride between Myrdal and Oslo. The round-trip from Oslo includes all the must-see sights but is a very long day (you'll leave Oslo at 6:25 and arrive back until around 22:30).

When to Go

The Nutshell trip is possible all year. In the summer (June-Aug), the connections are most convenient, the weather is most likely to be good...and the route is at its most crowded. Outside of this time, sights close and schedules become more challenging. Some say the Nutshell is most beautiful in winter, though schedules are severely reduced.

Nutshell Itineraries
Oslo-Bergen

You must take one of two morning departures (6:25 or 8:25) to do the entire trip from Oslo to Bergen in a day. I recommend the earlier departure to enjoy more time in Flåm (2 hours vs. 45 minutes) and generally fewer crowds. This itinerary shows typical sample times for summer travel; confirm exact times before your trip (www.vy.no for trains, https://en-tur.no for buses and ferries):

• Train from Oslo to Myrdal: 6:25-11:37
• Flåmsbana train from Myrdal to Flåm: 12:13-13:00

- Free time in Flåm: 13:00–15:00
- Boat from Flåm (Flåm kai) to Gudvangen (Gudvangen ferjekai): 15:00–17:00
- Bus from Gudvangen to Voss: 17:25–18:45
- Train from Voss to Bergen: 19:37–20:58

If you leave Oslo on the later train, you can either arrive in Bergen at the same time (with less free time in Flåm) or have more time in Flåm and Voss and arrive later (22:20).

Other Options

Here are other one-day options for doing the Nutshell in the summer. Confirm specific times before your trip.

Bergen-Oslo: Train departs Bergen-8:39, arrives Voss-9:53; bus departs Voss-10:10, arrives Gudvangen-11:20; boat departs Gudvangen-12:00, arrives Flåm-14:00; Flåmsbana train departs Flåm-16:55, arrives Myrdal-17:45; train departs Myrdal-17:53, arrives Oslo-22:35.

Day-Trip Loop from Oslo: Train departs Oslo-6:25, arrives Myrdal-11:37; Flåmsbana train departs Myrdal-12:13, arrives Flåm-13:00; boat departs Flåm-14:00, arrives Gudvangen-15:30; bus departs Gudvangen-15:40, arrives Voss-16:55; train departs Voss-17:10, arrives Oslo-22:27.

Day-Trip Loop from Bergen: Train departs Bergen-8:43, arrives Voss-9:53; bus departs Voss-10:10, arrives Gudvangen-11:20; boat departs Gudvangen-12:00, arrives Flåm-14:00; Flåmsbana train departs Flåm-14:35, arrives Myrdal-15:32; train departs Myrdal-16:47, arrives Bergen-18:56.

Buying Tickets

The easiest way to purchase Nutshell tickets is to buy a package from Fjord Tours—it will save you time and the trouble of planning your itinerary. The downside is that you're locked into their schedule and the package price can be more expensive than buying individual tickets.

On your own, you can often find discounts for the train and can choose the cheapest ferry—possibly saving up to 500 NOK. You also have more flexibility—you choose how much time you spend in Flåm and what time you arrive in Bergen or Oslo. The trade-off is that you have to plan your own itinerary and buy tickets for each leg of your journey—that's five separate tickets for a one-way trip between Oslo and Bergen.

If you have a rail pass, or if you're a student or a senior (68 or older), you'll save money by booking the Nutshell on your own.

Whether you are doing a package deal or buying tickets on your own, in summer book well in advance—four to five weeks is best. Train tickets on the Nutshell route from or back to Oslo can sell out in high season (June-Aug), as can some departures on the ferry from Flåm.

Package Deals

Fjord Tours sells the Nutshell package at train stations—including stations in Oslo and Bergen, at TIs in those two cities, and at Fjord Tours offices throughout Norway (+47 55 55 76 60, www.fjordtours.com, booking@fjordtours.com). With these packages, all your departures are fixed. You can choose between two different types of ferries: Classic, about a 2-hour ride on an old car ferry that just carries foot passengers; or Premium, 1.5 hours on a hybrid catamaran. Unless you are in a hurry (but why hurry through the fjords?), take the Classic ferry.

Here are prices (as of press time) for Nutshell packages on the Classic ferry:

- One-way from Bergen or Oslo-2,040 NOK
- Round-trip from Oslo via Voss-2,890 NOK
- Round-trip from Bergen via Myrdal-1,510 NOK

• Round-trip from Flåm–1,510 NOK

Packages on the Premium ferry cost 250-500 NOK extra. Fjord Tours also sells a Nutshell round-trip from Oslo that includes a night train, a "Sognefjord in a Nutshell" tour, and a "Sognefjord and Nærøyfjord in a Nutshell" tour.

On Your Own

Specifics on buying tickets for each leg of the Nutshell route are explained later, under the individual listings. In general, you can buy train tickets (including the Flåmsbana) at train stations in Oslo or Bergen or online at Vy.no. For the best deal, look for nonrefundable "minipris" tickets. You can buy Flåm-Gudvangen ferry tickets with one of two companies: The Fjords (more sailings, www.visitflam.com) or Lustrabaatane (cheaper prices, www.lustrabaatane.no). You can't buy tickets in advance for the Gudvangen-Voss bus; there's always room but you must pay the driver in cash. If you're a student or senior, always ask about discounts.

Rail Pass Discounts: If you have any rail pass that includes Norway, the Oslo-Bergen train is covered (plus a 59-NOK reservation fee for second class; free for first-class passholders); you also get a 30 percent discount on the Flåmsbana train. Rail-pass holders pay full fare for the boat cruise and the Gudvangen-Voss bus. Your total one-way cost between Oslo and Bergen: about 650 NOK with a first-class pass, 700 NOK with a second-class pass.

Travel Tips

Luggage: Transporting luggage on the Nutshell is no big deal, as the connections require almost no walking: At Myrdal, you just cross the platform; in Flåm, you walk 50 yards from the train to the dock; in Gudvangen, the bus meets the ferry at the dock; in Voss, the bus drops you at the train station. If you want to check your bag during your free time in Flåm, use the baggage-check cabin at the head of the train track, across the lane from the boat dock.

An alternative to carrying your luggage is **Porterservice AS.** They pick up your luggage at your hotel, transport it via train between Oslo and Bergen, and drop it off at your next hotel by 21:00 (300 NOK/piece, mobile +47 90 61 00 09, www.porterservice.no).

Eating: Options along the route aren't great—on the Nutshell I'd consider food just as a source of nutrition and forget about fine dining. You can buy some food on the fjord cruises (hot dogs, burgers, and pizza) and the Oslo-Bergen train. Depending on the timing of your layovers, Myrdal, Voss, or Flåm are your best lunch-stop options (the Myrdal and Flåm train stations have decent cafeterias, and other eateries surround the Flåm and Voss stations)—although you won't have a lot of time there if you're making the journey all in one day. Your best bet is to pack picnic meals and munch en route.

Beyond the Nutshell

The Sognefjord is the ultimate natural thrill Norway has to offer, and there's no doubt that the Nutshell route outlined in this chapter is the most efficient way to see it quickly. Unfortunately, its trains, buses, and boats are thronged with other visitors who have the same idea.

Travelers with a bit more time, and the willingness to chart their own course, often have a more rewarding Sognefjord experience. It's surprisingly easy to break out of the Nutshell and hit the northern part of the Sognefjord (for example, using the Bergen-Vik-Balestrand-Aurland-Flåm express boat, described on page 339.

In the next chapter, you'll find some tempting stopovers on the north bank of the Sognefjord, including adorable fjordside villages (such as Balestrand and Solvorn), evocative stave churches (Hopperstad and Urnes), and a chance to get up close to a glacier (at the Nigard Glacier).

Read up on your options, then be adventurous about mixing and matching the fjordside attractions that appeal to you most. Ideally, use the Nutshell as a springboard for diving into the Back Door fjords of your travel dreams.

If catching an early train in Oslo, the station has a handy grocery store open at 5:00 (6:00 on Sun).

Cruise-Ship Passengers: Tiny Flåm—in the heart of Nutshell country—is a popular destination for huge cruise ships. If arriving in Flåm by cruise ship, see my *Scandinavian & Northern European Cruise Ports* book for tips on how to approach the Nutshell during your day in port.

Nutshell Tour

If you only have one day for this region, it'll be a thrilling one—worth ▲▲▲. The following self-guided segments of the Nutshell route are narrated from Oslo to Bergen. If you're going the other way, hold the book upside down.

▲▲Oslo-Bergen Train (Via Myrdal)

The Oslo-Bergen route—called "Bergensbanen" by Norwegians—is simply the most spectacular train ride in northern Europe. The entire railway, an amazing engineering feat completed in 1909, is 300 miles long; peaks at 4,266 feet, which, at this Alaskan latitude, is far above the tree line; goes under 18 miles of snow sheds; trundles over 300 bridges; and passes through 200 tunnels in just under seven hours. To celebrate the Bergensbanen centennial in 2009, Norwegian TV mounted cameras on the outside of the train and broadcast the entire trip—and more than a million Norwegians tuned in (search for "Bergensbanen" on YouTube and you can watch it too).

Cost and Reservations: Here are the one-way fares for various segments: Oslo-Bergen-890 NOK, Oslo-Myrdal-860 NOK, Myrdal-Voss-146 NOK, Myrdal-Bergen-309 NOK, Voss-Bergen-223 NOK. You can save money on these fares if you book "minipris" tickets in advance at Vy.no. (See "On Your Own," earlier, for rail pass discounts.) If you have difficulty paying for your ticket with a US credit card online, use PayPal or call +47 61 05 19 10—press 9 for English, and you'll be given a web link where you can finish your transaction. In peak season, reserve this train four to five weeks in advance.

Schedule: The train runs three to five times per day, including two morning departures (overnight possible except Sat). The segment from Oslo to Myrdal takes about five hours; going all the way to Bergen takes seven hours.

Route Narration: The scenery crescendos as you climb over Norway's mountainous spine. After a mild three hours of deep woods and lakes, you're into the barren, windswept heaths and glaciers. Here's what you'll see traveling westward from Oslo: Leaving Oslo, you pass through a six-mile-long tunnel and stop in Drammen, Norway's fifth-largest town. The scenery stays low-key and woodsy up Hallingdal Valley until you reach Geilo, a popular ski resort. Then you enter a land of big views and tough little cabins. Finse, at about 4,000 feet, is the highest stop on the line. At several towns, the conductor may announce how many minutes the train will be stopped there. This gives you a few fun moments to get out, stretch, take a photograph, and look around.

Before Myrdal, you enter the longest high-mountain stretch of railway in Europe. Much of the line is protected by snow tunnels. The scenery gets more dramatic as you approach Myrdal (MEER-doll). Just before Myrdal, look to the right and down into the Flåm Valley, where the Flåmsbana branch line winds its way down to the fjord. Nutshell travelers get off at Myrdal.

▲▲Myrdal-Flåm Train (Flåmsbana)

The little 12-mile spur line leaves the Oslo-Bergen line at Myrdal (2,800 feet), which is nothing but a scenic high-altitude train junction with a decent cafeteria. Before boarding, pick up the free, multilingual souvenir pamphlet with lots of info on the trip (or

see www.visitflam.com/
flamsbana). Video screens
onboard and sporadic
English commentary on
the loudspeakers explain
points of interest, but
there's not much to say—
it's all about the scenery.
If you're choosing seats,
you'll enjoy slightly more
scenery if you sit on the left going down.

Cost and Reservations: 430 NOK one-way (rail-pass holders pay 301 NOK), 630 NOK round-trip. You can book one-way tickets on Vy.no; the cheapest round-trip tickets are on VisitFlam.com. You also can buy tickets onboard the train or at the Flåmsbana station in Flåm. Train staff in Oslo may tell you that the Flåmsbana is booked—don't worry, it very rarely fills. Even if it's standing-room only, you can usually squeeze in. Simply get to Myrdal and hop on the train.

However, morning trains ascending from Flåm to Myrdal (when there are several cruise ships in port) can sell out. In summer, if you want to leave Flåm in the morning, try buying your ticket the night before or right when the Flåm ticket office opens (around 7:00). The best plan is to buy your Flåmsbana ticket at the same time you buy your other train tickets.

Schedule: The train departs in each direction nearly hourly.

Route Narration: From Myrdal, the Flåmsbana train winds down to Flåm (sea level) through 20 tunnels (more than three miles' worth) in 55 thrilling minutes.

It's party time on board, and the engineer even stops the train for photos at the best waterfall, Kjosfossen. According to a Norwegian legend, Huldra (a temptress) lives behind these falls and tries to lure men to the rocks with her singing...look out for her...and keep a wary eye on your partner.

The train line is an even more impressive feat of engineering when you realize it's not a cogwheel train—it's held to the tracks only by steel wheels, though it does have five braking systems.

▲▲▲Flåm-Gudvangen Fjord Cruise

The Flåmsbana train deposits you at Flåm, a scenic, functional

NORWAY IN A NUTSHELL

transit hub at the far end of the Aurlandsfjord. If you're doing the Nutshell route nonstop, follow the crowds and hop on the sightseeing boat that'll take you to Gudvangen. With minimal English narration, the boat takes you close to the goats, sheep, waterfalls, and awesome cliffs.

Cruise Options: There are two boat companies to choose from—The Fjords (www.visitflam.com) and Lustrabaatane (www.lustrabaatane.com). The Fjords has a Classic option that takes more than two hours. It stops at Aurland, Undredal, Dyrdal, and Styvi, which is handy if you want to hop off and on along the way—though you'll need to buy separate tickets for each leg of your trip, and it'll end up costing you more (be sure to notify the ticket seller where you want to get off, to make certain they'll stop). The other option is their Premium ferry, a hybrid catamaran that's faster, silent, and more expensive. It takes about 1.5 hours nonstop between Flåm and Gudvangen.

The cheapest option is the Lustrabaatane ferry—a slow boat that takes about two hours—similar to the Classic ferry, but with no stops.

I much prefer the slower boats because the price is lower, you have more time to savor the scenery, and the bus connection in Gudvangen is immediate and reliable.

Cost and Reservations: For the Flåm-Gudvangen route, you'll pay 250-645 NOK one-way depending on the ferry (435-705 NOK round-trip). Reservations may be necessary on busy days in summer. Buy your ticket in Flåm as soon as you know which boat you want or in advance at each boat company's website. Beware: The ticket desk at the Flåm Visitors Center doubles as The Fjords boat desk, and they'll sell you a boat ticket implying theirs is the only option. Lustrabaatane tickets are sold online, at the dock in summer, and onboard.

Schedule: In summer (June-Aug), boats run multiple times daily in both directions—Classic ferry (2/day), Premium ferry (5/day), Lustrabaatane ferry (2/day). Specific departure times can vary, but generally boats leave Flåm starting at 8:00, with a last departure at 19:00. From Gudvangen, the first

The Facts on Fjords

The process that created the majestic Sognefjord began during an ice age about three million years ago. A glacier up to 6,500 feet thick slid downhill at an inch an hour, following a former river valley on its way to the sea. Rocks embedded in the glacier gouged out a steep, U-shaped valley, displacing enough rock material to form a mountain 13 miles high. When the climate warmed up, the ice age came to an end. The melting glaciers retreated and the sea level rose nearly 300 feet, flooding the valley now known as the Sognefjord. The fjord is more than a mile deep, flanked by 3,000-foot mountains—for a total relief of 9,300 feet. Waterfalls spill down the cliffs, fed by melting snow. In places, powdery sediment tinges the fjords a cloudy green, the distinct color of glacier melt.

Why are there fjords on the west coast of Norway, but not, say, on the east coast of Sweden? The creation of a fjord requires a setting of coastal mountains, a good source of moisture, and a climate cold enough for glaciers to form and advance. Due to the earth's rotation, the prevailing winds in higher latitudes blow from west to east, so chances of glaciation are ideal where there is an ocean to the west of land with coastal mountains. When the winds blow eastward over the water, they pick up a lot of moisture, then bump up against the coastal mountain range, and dump their moisture in the form of snow—which feeds the glaciers that carve valleys down to the sea.

You can find fjords along the northwest coast of Europe—including western Norway and Sweden, Denmark's Faroe Islands, Scotland's Shetland Islands, Iceland, and Greenland; the northwest coast of North America (from Puget Sound in Washington state north to Alaska); the southwest coast of South America (Chile); the west coast of New Zealand's South Island; and on the continent of Antarctica.

boat is generally at 9:30, with a last departure at 17:45. See http://en-tur.no for schedules covering both ferry lines.

Your only concern is that the Nutshell bus from Gudvangen to Voss may not meet the last departure of the day (check locally); the worst-case scenario is that you'd need to catch the regular commuter bus to Voss, which makes more stops and doesn't take the razzle-dazzle Stalheimskleiva corkscrew road.

Route Narration: You'll cruise up the lovely **Aurlandsfjord,**

motoring by the town of **Aurland** (a good home base, but only a few boats stop here), pass the towns of **Undredal, Dyrdal,** and **Styvi** (possible stops here on limited sailings by request), and hang a left at the stunning **Nærøyfjord.** The cruise ends at the apex of the Nærøyfjord, in **Gudvangen.**

The trip is breathtaking in any weather. For the last hour, as you sail down the Nærøyfjord, camera-clicking tourists scurry around struggling to get a photo that will catch the magic. Waterfalls turn the black cliffs into bridal veils, and you can nearly reach out and touch the cliffs of the Nærøyfjord. It's the world's narrowest fjord: six miles long and as little as 820 feet wide and 40 feet deep. On a sunny day, the ride is one of those fine times—like when you're high on the tip of an Alp—when a warm camaraderie spontaneously combusts between the strangers who've come together for the experience.

▲Gudvangen-Voss Bus

Nutshellers get off the boat at Gudvangen and take the 25-mile bus ride to Voss. Gudvangen offers little more than a boat dock, a giant tourist kiosk, and a re-cre-ation of a Viking village. If you want, you can browse through the grass-roofed souvenir stores and walk onto a wooden foot-bridge—then catch your bus. While some buses—designed for commuters rather than sight-seers—take the direct route to Voss, buses tied to the Nutshell

schedule take a super-scenic detour via Stalheim. If you're a water-fall junkie, sit on the left.

Cost: 115 NOK, pay on board, cash only, no rail pass discounts. Reservations are not necessary.

Schedule: Buses meet each ferry, or will show up usually within an hour. (Confirm this in advance if you plan to take the last boat of the day—the ferry crew can call ahead to be sure the bus waits for you.)

Route Narration: First the bus takes you up the **Nærøydal** and through a couple of long tunnels. Then you'll take a turnoff to drive past the landmark **Stalheim Hotel** for the first of many spectacular views back into fjord country. Though the hotel dates from 1885, there's been an inn here since about 1700, where royal mailmen would change horses. The hotel is geared for tour groups (genuine trolls sew the pewter buttons on the sweaters), but the priceless view from the backyard is free. Drivers should be sure to stop here for the view and peruse the hotel's living room to survey the art showing this perch in the 19th century.

Leaving the hotel, the bus wends its way down a road called **Stalheimskleiva,** with a corkscrew series of switchbacks flanked by a pair of dramatic waterfalls. With its 18 percent grade, it's the steepest road in Norway.

After winding your way down into the valley, you're back on the same highway. The bus goes through those same tunnels again, then continues straight on the main road through pastoral countryside to Voss. You'll pass a huge lake, then follow a crystal-clear, surging river. Just before Voss, look to the right for the wide **Tvindefossen waterfall,** tumbling down its terraced cliff. Drivers will find the grassy meadow and flat rocks at its base ideal for letting the mist fog their glasses and enjoying a drink or snack (be discreet, as "picnics are forbidden").

Voss

The Nutshell bus from Gudvangen drops you at the Voss train station, which is on the Oslo-Bergen train line. This connection is generally not as well-coordinated; you'll likely have 50 minutes or so to kill before the next train to Bergen.

Visiting Voss: A plain town in a lovely lake-and-mountain setting, Voss lacks the striking fjordside scenery of Flåm, Aurland, or Undredal, and is basically a home base for summer or winter sports (Norway's Winter Olympics teams often practice here). Voss surrounds its fine, 13th-century church with workaday streets—busy with both local shops and souvenir stores—stretching in several directions. Fans of American football may want to see the humble monument to player and coach Knute Rockne, who was born in Voss in 1888; look for the metal memorial plaque on a rock near the train station.

Voss' helpful **TI** is on the ground floor of the Gondola building, next to the train station (daily 9:00-18:00, Sat until 20:00; off-season until 16:00 and closed Sat-Sun; Skulegata 14, mobile +47 40 61 77 00, www.visitvoss.no).

Drivers should zip right through Voss, but two miles outside town, you can stop at the **Mølstertunet Folk Museum,** which has 16 buildings showing off farm life in the 17th and 18th centuries (90 NOK; daily 11:00-16:00, Sept-mid-May until 15:00 and closed Sat; Mølstervegen 143, +47 47 47 97 94, www.vossfolkemuseum. no).

▲Voss-Bergen Train

The least exciting segment of the trip—but still pleasantly scenic—this train chugs 60 miles along the valley between the midsize town of Voss and Bergen. For the best scenery, sit on the right side of the train if coming from Oslo, or the left side if coming from Bergen. Between Voss and Dale, you'll pass several scenic lakes; near Bergen, you'll go along the Veafjord.

Cost: 223 NOK, fully covered by rail passes that include Norway. Reservations aren't necessary for this leg.

Schedule: Unlike the long-distance Oslo-Bergen journey, this line is also served by more frequent commuter trains (about hourly, 75 minutes).

Voss-Oslo Train: Note that if you're doing the Nutshell round-trip loop from Oslo, you should catch the train from Voss (rather than Bergen) back to Oslo. The return trip takes 5.5 hours and costs 953 NOK; reservations are strongly recommended four to five weeks ahead in peak season.

Flåm

Flåm (pronounced "flome")—where the boat and Flåmsbana train meet, at the head of the Aurlandsfjord—feels more like a transit junction than a village. But its striking setting, easy transportation connections, and touristy bustle make it appealing as a home base for exploring the nearby area.

Orientation to Flåm

Most of Flåm's services are in a modern cluster of buildings in and around the train station, including the TI, train ticket desk, public WC, cafeteria, and souvenir shops. Just outside the station, the little red shed at the head of the tracks serves as a **left-luggage desk** (daily 8:00-19:00, on your right as you depart the train, ring bell if nobody's there), and displays a chart of the services you'll find in the station. The **boat dock** for fjord cruises is just beyond the end of the tracks. Surrounding the station are a Co-op Marked **grocery store** (with a basic pharmacy and post office inside, Mon-Fri 8:00-20:00, Sat-Sun 10:00-18:00, shorter hours off-season) and a smattering of hotels, travel agencies, and touristy restaurants. Aside from a few scattered farmhouses and some homes lining the road, there's not much of a town here. (The extremely sleepy old town center—where tourists rarely venture,

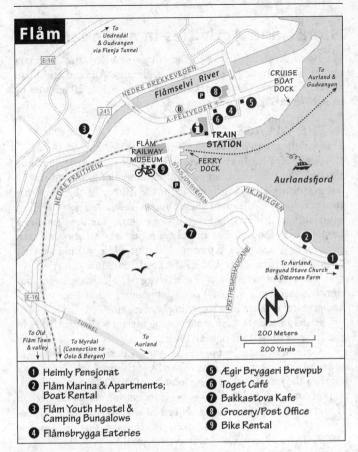

Flåm

To Undredal & Gudvangen via Flenja Tunnel

NEDRE BREKKEVEGEN

Flåmselvi River

CRUISE BOAT DOCK

To Aurland & Gudvangen

E-16

245

A-FELTVEGEN

❽

❻ ❹ ❺

❸

FLÅM RAILWAY MUSEUM

🚲 ❾

TRAIN STATION

FERRY DOCK

Aurlandsfjord

NEDRE FRETHEIM

STASJONSVEGEN

VIKJAVEGEN

❼

❷

To Aurland, Borgund Stave Church & Otternes Farm

❶

FRETHEIMSHAUGANE

N

E-16

TUNNEL

To Old Flåm Town & valley

To Myrdal (Connection to Oslo & Bergen)

To Aurland

200 Meters

200 Yards

❶ Heimly Pensjonat

❷ Flåm Marina & Apartments; Boat Rental

❸ Flåm Youth Hostel & Camping Bungalows

❹ Flåmsbrygga Eateries

❺ Ægir Bryggeri Brewpub

❻ Toget Café

❼ Bakkastova Kafe

❽ Grocery/Post Office

❾ Bike Rental

and which you'll pass on the Flåmsbana train—is a few miles up the river, in the valley.)

Tourist Information: Inside the train station you'll find the TI and the Flåm Visitors Center. The **visitors center** sells tickets for Fjord Tours packages and ferries to Gudvangen (but not the Flåm-Gudvangen boats offered by rival Lustrabaatane), the Flåmsbana train, regular train tickets, and other tours in the area (daily 7:00-19:00, shorter hours Sept-April, +47 57 63 14 00, www. visitflam.com).

At the **TI** you can purchase tickets for the express boat to Bergen, FjordSafari, Njord Seakayak Adventures, and other tours. The TI also hands out schedules for buses, boats, and trains; a diagram of the train-station area, identifying services available in each building; and information on Bergen or Oslo (daily 8:30-17:00, Oct-March 9:00-15:00, mobile +47 99 23 15 00, https:// en.sognefjord.no).

Sights and Activities in and near Flåm

I've listed several activities in the village of Flåm. But the main reason people come here is to leave it. Because Aurland and Flåm are close together (10 minutes away by car or bus, or 20 minutes by boat), I've also listed attractions near Aurland.

IN THE VILLAGE

Flåm's village activities are all along or near the pier.

The **Flåm Railway Museum** (Flåmsbana Museet), sprawling through the long old train station building alongside the tracks, has surprisingly good exhibits about the history of the train that connects Flåm to the main line up above. You'll find good English explanations, artifacts, re-creations of historic interiors (such as a humble schoolhouse), and an old train car. It's the only real museum in town and a good place to kill time while waiting for your boat or train (free, daily 9:00-17:00, until 20:00 in summer).

The pleasantly woody **Ægir Bryggeri,** a microbrewery designed to resemble an old Viking longhouse, offers beer tastings and evening meals with a matching beer menu.

The TI hands out a map suggesting several **walks and hikes** in the area, starting from right in town.

Consider renting a **boat** to go out on the peaceful waters of the fjord. You can paddle near the walls of the fjord and really get a sense of the immensity of these mountains. You can rent rowboats, motorboats, and paddleboats at the little marina across the harbor. If you'd rather have a kayak, **Njord Seakayak Adventures** does kayak tours, but won't rent you one unless you're certified (mobile +47 91 32 66 28, www.seakayaknorway.com).

FROM OR NEAR FLÅM
▲▲▲Cruising the Nærøyfjord

The most scenic fjord I've seen anywhere in Norway is about an hour from Flåm (basically the last half of the Flåm-Gudvangen trip). If you've driven to Flåm, didn't book a Nutshell tour, or are staying overnight, here are several ways to cruise it.

The Fjords Tours: This company runs several trips from Flåm; their most popular is a ferry ride to Gudvangen and a bus ride back to Flåm (435-705 NOK, 4-hour round-trip, 4/day May-Sept, fewer off-season, choose slower Classic ferry for best viewing).

In summer, they may also offer their World Heritage Cruise, a hop-on, hop-off trip up the Nærøyfjord, stopping at Bleiklindi, Bakka, Styvi, and Dyrdal—it's possible to hike about four miles between Bleiklindi and Styvi with this option. Or, consider a variation on this trip with a 45-minute stop in the village of Undredal for lunch and a goat-cheese tasting; a bus ride up to the thrilling Stegastein viewpoint; and more. These trips don't always run—check at the Flåm Visitors Center or online for details (www.visitflam.com).

FjordSafari to Nærøyfjord: FjordSafari takes little groups out onto the fjord in small, open Zodiac-type boats with an English-speaking guide. Participants wear full-body weather suits, furry hats, and spacey goggles (making everyone on the boat look like crash-test dummies). As the boat rockets across the water, you'll be thankful for the gear, no matter what the weather. Their two-hour Flåm-Gudvangen-Flåm tour focuses on the Nærøyfjord, and gets you all the fjord magnificence you can imagine (890 NOK, several departures daily). Their three-hour tour is the same but adds a stop in Undredal, where you can see goat cheese being made, sample it, and wander that sleepy village (1020 NOK, 1/day May-Aug, fewer off-season, kids get discounts, mobile +47 99 09 08 60, www.fjordsafari.com, Maylene). Skip the 1.5-hour "basic" tour, which just barely touches on the Nærøyfjord.

▲Flåm Valley Bike Ride or Hike

For the best single-day land activity from Flåm, take the Flåmsbana train to Myrdal, then hike or mountain-bike along the road (half gravel, half paved) back down to Flåm (2-3 hours by bike, gorgeous waterfalls, great mountain scenery, and a cute church with an evocative graveyard, but no fjord views).

Walkers can hike the best two hours from Myrdal to Blomheller, and catch the train from there into the valley. Or, without riding the train, you can simply walk up the valley 2.5 miles to the church and a little farther to a waterfall. Whenever you get tired hiking up or down the valley, you can hop on the next train. Pick up the helpful map with this and other hiking options (ranging from easy to strenuous) at the Flåm TI.

Bikers can rent good mountain bikes from the Flåm Bike Rental cabin next to the train station (around 180 NOK/2-hour minimum, 400 NOK/day, includes helmet; daily May-June 9:00-

18:00, July-Sept 8:00-20:00, closed off-season). You'll pay 100 NOK to take a bike to Myrdal on the train.

Otternes Farms (Otternes Bygdetun)

This humble but magical cluster of four centuries-old farms is about three miles from Flåm (easy for drivers; a decent walk or bike ride otherwise). It's a ghost vil-

lage perched high on a ridge, up a twisty gravel road midway between Flåm and Aurland. These traditional time-warp houses and barns date from the time before emigration decimated the workforce, coinage replaced barter, and industrialized margarine became more popular than butter—all of which left farmers to eke out a living relying only on their goats and the cheese they produced. Until 1919 the only road between Aurland and Flåm passed between this huddle of 27 buildings, high above the fjord. First settled in 1522, farmers lived here until the 1990s.

OVER (OR UNDER) THE MOUNTAINS, TO LÆRDAL AND BORGUND

To reach these sights, you'll first head along the fjord to Aurland (described later). Of the sights below, the Lærdal Tunnel, Stegastein viewpoint, and Aurlandsvegen "Snow Road" are best for drivers. The Borgund Stave Church can be reached by car, or by bus from Flåm or Aurland.

Lærdal Tunnel

Drivers find that this tunnel makes connecting Flåm and Lærdal a snap. It's the world's longest road-vehicle tunnel, stretching 15 miles between Aurland and Lærdal as part of the E-16 highway. It also makes the wonderful Borgund Stave Church (described later) less than an hour's drive from Aurland. The downside to the tunnel is that it goes beneath my favorite scenic drive in Norway (the Aurlandsvegen "Snow Road," described next). But with about two hours, you can drive through the tunnel to Lærdal and then return via the "Snow Road," with the Stegastein viewpoint as a finale, before dropping back into Aurland.

▲▲Stegastein Viewpoint and Aurlandsvegen "Snow Road"

With a car, clear weather, and a little nerve, consider twisting up the mountain behind Aurland on route 243 for about 20 minutes to a

magnificent view over the Aurlandsfjord. A viewpoint called Stegastein—which looks like a giant, wooden, sideways number 7—provides a platform from which you can enjoy stunning views across the fjord and straight down to Aurland. Immediately be-yond the viewpoint, you leave the fjord views and enter the beautifully desolate mountaintop world of the Aurlandsvegen "Snow Road." When this narrow ribbon of a road finally hits civilization on the other side, you're a mile from the Lærdal tunnel entrance and about 30 minutes from the fine Borgund Stave Church.

▲▲Borgund Stave Church

About 16 miles east of Lærdal, in the village of Borgund, is Norway's most-visited and one of its best-preserved stave churches.

Dating from around 1180, the interior features only a few later additions, including a 16th-century pulpit, 17th-century stone altar, painted decorations, and crossbeam reinforcements.

Cost and Hours: 100 NOK, buy tickets at mu-seum across street; open daily June-Aug 8:00-20:00, May and Sept 10:00-17:00, closed Oct-April. The museum has a shop and a fine little **$$ cafeteria** serving filling and tasty lunches, +47 57 66 81 09, www.stavechurch.com.

Getting There: It's about a 30-minute **drive** east of Lærdal, on E-16 (the road to Oslo—if coming from Aurland or Flåm, consider taking the scenic route via the Stegastein viewpoint, described earlier). There's also a convenient **bus** connection: The bus departs Flåm and Aurland around midday (direction: Lillehammer) and heads for the church, with a return bus departing Borgund in mid-afternoon (around 200-NOK round-trip, get ticket from driver, about 1 hour each way with about 1 hour at the church, bus runs daily May-Sept, tell driver you want to get off at the church, www.nor-way.no).

Stave Churches:
Norway's Wooden Wonders

Norway's most distinctive architecture is the stave church. These medieval houses of worship—tall, skinny, wooden pagodas with dragon's-head gargoyles—are distinctly Norwegian and palpably historic, transporting you right back to Viking days.

Stave churches are the finest architecture to come out of medieval Norway. Wood was plentiful and cheap, and locals had an expertise with woodworking (from all that boat-building). In 1300, there were as many as 1,000 stave churches in Norway. After a 14th-century plague, Norway's population dropped, and many churches fell into disuse or burned down. By the 19th century, only a few dozen stave churches survived. Fortunately, Norway realized their importance and protected them. Virtually all of Norway's surviving stave churches have been rebuilt or renovated, with painstaking attention to the original details.

A distinguishing feature of the "stave" design is its frame of tall, stout vertical staves (Norwegian *stav,* or "staff"). The churches typically sit on stone foundations, to keep the wooden structure off the damp ground (to prevent rot). Most stave churches were made of specially grown pine, carefully prepared before being felled for construction. As the trees grew, the tips and most of the branches were cut off, leaving the trunks just barely alive to stand in the woods for about a decade. This allowed the sap to penetrate the wood and lock in the resin, strengthening the wood while keeping it elastic. Once built, a stave church was slathered with black tar to protect it from the elements.

Stave churches are notable for their resilience and flexibility. Just as old houses creak and settle over the years, these wooden churches flex to withstand fierce winds and the march of time. When the wind shifts with the seasons, stave churches groan and moan for a couple of weeks before settling in.

Even after the Vikings stopped raiding, they ornamented the exteriors of their churches with warlike, evil spirit-fighting dragons reminiscent of their ships. Inside, the church's structure makes you feel like you're in an overturned ship's hull. Stave churches are dark, with almost no windows (aside from a few small "portholes" high up). Typical decorations include carved X-shape crossbeams, symbolizing the cross of St. Andrew (who was crucified on such a cross). Round, Romanesque arches near the tops of the staves were made from the "knees" of a tree, where the roots bend to meet the trunk. Overall, these churches are extremely vertical: the beams inside and the roofline outside lead the eye up, up, up to the heavens.

Most surviving stave churches were renovated during the Reformation (16th and 17th centuries), when they acquired more

horizontal elements such as pews, balconies, pulpits, altars, and other decorations to draw attention to the front of the church. In some (such as the churches in Lom and Urnes), the additions make the church feel almost cluttered. But the most authentic (including Hopperstad near Vik) feel truly medieval. These time-machine churches take visitors back to early Christian days: no pews (worshippers stood through the service), no pulpit, and a barrier between the congregation and the priest, to symbolically separate the physical world from the spiritual one. Incense filled the church, and the priest and congregation chanted the service back and forth to each other, creating an atmosphere that likely made worshippers feel close to God.

When traveling through Norway, you'll be encouraged to see stave church after stave church, but there's no point in visiting more than a few of them. Of Norway's 28 remaining stave churches, seven are described in this book. The easiest to see are those that have been moved to open-air museums in Oslo and Lillehammer. But I prefer to appreciate a stave church in its original fjords-and-rolling-hills setting. My two favorites are near Sognefjord: Borgund and Hopperstad. They are each delightfully situated and evocative as can be. Borgund stands in a pristine wooded valley, while Hopperstad is perched above a fjord. Borgund also comes with a good stave church museum.

Other noteworthy stave churches include the one in Lom, near the Jotunheimen Mountains, which is one of Norway's biggest and quite impressive. The Urnes church, across the Lustrafjord from Solvorn, is technically the oldest of them all—but it's been thoroughly renovated in later ages (yet still worth a visit for its exquisite carvings and the fun ferry crossing to reach it; see the More on the Sognefjord chapter). The Fantoft stave church just outside Bergen was torched by an arsonist in 1992, and the 1997 reconstruction lacks the original's magic. The stave church in Undredal (see page 324) advertises itself as the smallest (but it's also the dullest). For more on Norway's stave churches, visit StaveChurch.com.

Visiting the Church: Explore the dimly lit interior, illuminated only by the original, small, circular windows up high. The oldest and most authentic item in the church is the stone baptismal font. In medieval times, priests conducting baptisms would go outside to shoo away the evil spirits from an infant before bringing it inside the church for the ritual. (If infants died before being baptized, they couldn't be buried in the churchyard, so parents would put their bodies in little coffins and hide them under the church's floorboards to get them as close as possible to God.)

Notice the X-shaped crosses of St. Andrew (the church's patron), carvings of dragons, and medieval runes. Borgund's church also comes with one of this country's best stave-church history museums, which beautifully explains these icons of medieval Norway.

Sleeping in Flåm

My recommended accommodations are away from the tacky train-station bustle, but a close enough walk to be convenient. The first two places are located along the waterfront a quarter-mile from the station: Walk around the little harbor (with the water on your left) for about 10 minutes. It's more enjoyable to follow the level, waterfront dock than to hike up the main road.

$$$$ Heimly Pensjonat, with 22 straightforward rooms, is clean, efficient, and the best small hotel in town. Sit on the porch with new friends and watch the clouds roll down the fjord. Prices include breakfast and a three-course dinner (family rooms, doubles are mostly twins, closed off-season, +47 57 63 23 00, post@heimly.no, www.visitflam.com).

$$$ Flåm Marina and Apartments, perched right on the fjord, is ideal for families and longer stays. They offer one standard double and 10 new-feeling, self-catering apartments that each sleep 2-5 people. All units offer views of the fjord with a balcony, kitchenette, and small dining area (no breakfast, café serving lunch and dinner open during high season, boat rental, laundry facilities, next to the guest harbor just below Heimly Pensjonat, +47 57 63 35 55, www.flammarina.no, booking@flammarina.no).

¢-$$ Flåm Youth Hostel and Camping Bungalows, voted Scandinavia's most beautiful campground, is run by the friendly Håland family, who rent the cheapest beds in the area (sheets and towels included in hostel but extra in cabins, showers extra, no meals but kitchen access, laundry, apple grove, mobile +47 94 03 26 81, www.flaam-camping.no, camping@flaam-camping.no). It's a five-minute walk toward the valley from the train station: Cross the bridge and turn left up the main road; then look for the hostel on the right.

Eating in Flåm

Dining options beyond your hotel's dining room or kitchenette are expensive and touristy. Don't aim for high cuisine here—go practical. Almost all eateries are clustered near the train station complex. Hours can be unpredictable, flexing with the season, but you can expect these to be open daily in high season. Places here tend to close pretty early (especially in shoulder season)—don't wait too long for dinner.

The **Flåmsbrygga** complex, sprawling through a long building toward the fjord from the station, includes a hotel, the affordable **$$ Furukroa Caféteria** (daily 8:00-20:00 in season, sandwiches, fast-food meals, and pizzas), and the pricey **$$$$ Flåmstova Restaurant** (breakfast and lunch buffet, sit-down dinner service, www. flamsbrygga.no). Next door is their fun, Viking-longhouse-shaped brewpub, **$$$ Ægir Bryggeri** (daily 17:00-22:00, local microbrews, Viking-inspired meals). **$$ Toget Café,** with seating in old train cars, prides itself on using as many locally sourced and organic ingredients as possible. **$$ Bakkastova Kafe,** at the other end of town, feels cozier. Housed in a traditional Norwegian red cabin just above the Fretheim Hotel, with a view terrace, it serves sandwiches, salads, and authentic Norwegian fare (daily 12:00-16:00).

Aurland

A few miles north of Flåm, Aurland is more of a real town and less of a tourist depot. While it's nothing exciting (Balestrand is more lively and appealing, and Solvorn is cuter— see next chapter), it's a good, easygoing fjordside home base. And thanks to its location—on the main road and boat lines, near Flåm—it's relatively handy for those taking public transportation. For

fjord cruising options in this area, see "Cruising the Nærøyfjord," earlier.

Getting There: Aurland is an easy 10-minute drive or bus trip from Flåm. If you want to stay overnight in Aurland, note that every train (except the late-night one) arriving in Flåm connects with a bus or boat to Aurland (in summer: bus-11/day, 10 minutes, 65 NOK; ferry-4/day, 20 minutes, 195 NOK). The Flåm-

NORWAY IN A NUTSHELL

Gudvangen Classic ferry doesn't always stop at Aurland, but they will if you ask—so it's possible to continue the Nutshell route from Aurland without backtracking to Flåm. Boat tickets can be bought aboard the ferry in Aurland or at VisitFlam.com. The Bergen-Balestrand-Flåm express boat stops in Aurland (for details, see the "Express Boat Between Bergen and the Sognefjord" sidebar in the next chapter).

Orientation to Aurland

From Aurland's dingy boat dock area, walk one block up the paved street into the heart of town. On your right is the Spar supermarket (handy for picnic supplies) and Marianne Bakeri and Café (at the bridge). To your left is the Vangsgården Guest House and, behind it, Aurland Fjordhotel. To reach the TI, go straight ahead and bear right, then look behind the white church (800 years old and worth a peek). The bus stop, with buses to Flåm, is in front of the TI. For attractions near Aurland, see "Sights and Activities in and near Flåm," earlier.

Tourist Information: The TI stocks English-language brochures about hikes and day trips from the area, and sells local maps (daily 9:00-16:00, closed in off-season; behind the church—look for green-and-white *i* sign; mobile +47 91 79 41 64, https://en.sognefjord.no).

Sleeping in Aurland

$$$$ Aurland Fjordhotel is big, modern, and centrally located. While it has a business-hotel vibe, most of its 30 rooms come with gorgeous fjord-view balconies (+47 57 63 35 05, www.aurland-fjordhotel.com, post@aurland-fjordhotel.com, Steinar Kjerstein).

$$$ Vangsgården Guest House, closest to the boat landing, is a complex of old buildings dominating the old center of Aurland and run from one reception desk (Wi-Fi in main building, +47 57 63 35 80, www.vangsgaarden.no, booking@vangsgaarden.no, open all year, Astrid). The main building is a simple, old guesthouse offering basic rooms and a fine old-timey living room. Their old-fashioned **Aabelheim Pension** is Aurland's best *koselig* (cozy)-like-a-farmhouse place (same prices). And lining the waterfront are their six adorable wood **$$$$** cabins with balconies, kitchen, bathroom, and two bedrooms (sleeps 2-6 people, sheets and breakfast extra, book 2 months in advance). The owners also run the recommended Duehuset Pub and rent bikes.

NEAR AURLAND

$$ Skahjem Gard is an active farm run by Aurland's former deputy mayor, Nils Tore. He's converted his old sheep barn into seven spic-and-span family apartments with private bathrooms and kitchenettes, each sleeping up to four people (sheets and towels included, two miles up the valley—road #50, follow *Hol* signs, mobile +47 95 17 25 67, nskahjem@online.no). It's a 25-minute walk from town, but Nils will pick up and drop off travelers at the ferry. This is best for families and foursomes with cars.

¢ Winjum Huts, about a half-mile from Aurland's dock, rents 14 basic cabins on a peaceful perch overlooking the majestic fjord. The washhouse/kitchen is where you'll find the toilets and showers. Follow the road uphill past the Aurland Fjordhotel; the huts are after the first hairpin curve (apartment available, sheets extra, showers extra, no food available—just beer, mobile +47 41 47 47 51).

Eating in Aurland

$$$ Marianne Bakeri and Café is a basic little bakery/café serving the best-value food in town. It's a block from the main square, at the bridge over the river. Sit inside or on its riverside terrace (sandwiches, pizza, and quiche; daily 10:00-17:00, mobile +47 90 51 29 78).

$$$ Duehuset Pub ("The Dove's House"), run by Vangs-gården Guest House, serves up decent food in the center of town (daily 15:00-23:00, only open Fri-Sun for dinner in off-season).

The **$$$$ Aurland Fjordhotel** is your only alternative for splurges (dinner buffet, daily 19:00-22:00, shorter hours off-season, bar open later, +47 57 63 35 05, www.aurland-fjordhotel.com).

For cheap eats on dockside benches, gather a picnic at the **Spar** supermarket (Mon-Fri 9:00-20:00, Sat until 18:00, closed Sun).

Undredal

This almost impossibly remote community is home to about 80 people and 400 goats. A huge percentage of the town's former population (300 people) emigrated to the US between 1850 and 1925. Undredal was accessible only by boat until 1988, when the road from Flåm opened. There's not much in the town, which is famous for its tiny stave church and its goat cheese, but I'll never forget the picnic I had on the ferry wharf. While appealing, Undredal is quiet (some say better from the boat) and difficult to reach—you'll have to be patient to connect to other towns. For more information on the town, see www.explore-undredal.no.

Getting There: The 15-minute drive from Flåm is mostly through a tunnel. By sea, you'll sail past Undredal on the Flåm-Gudvangen boat (you can request a stop). To get the ferry to pick you up in Undredal, turn on the blinking light (though some express boats will not stop).

Visiting Undredal: Undredal has Norway's smallest still-used **stave church,** seating 40 people for services every fourth Sunday. The original church was built in 1147 (look for the four original stave pillars inside). It was later expanded, pews added, and the interior painted in the 16th century in a way that resembles the traditional Norwegian *rosemaling* style (which came later). You can get in only with a 30-minute tour (70 NOK, June-mid-Aug daily 10:00-17:00, less in shoulder season, closed Oct-April, mobile +47 95 29 76 68).

Undredal's farms exist to produce **cheese.** The beloved local cheese comes in two versions: brown and white. The brown version is unaged and slightly sweet, while the white cheese has been aged and is mild and a bit salty. For samples, visit the Undredalsbui grocery store at the harbor (Mon-Fri 9:00-16:30, Sat until 15:00, Sun 12:00-16:00, shorter hours and closed Sun off-season).

Sleeping in Undredal: $ Undredal Overnatting rents four modern, woody apartments in two fjordside cottages. The reception is at the café on the harbor, while the accommodations are at the top of town (sheets included, breakfast extra, +47 57 63 30 80, www.visitundredal.no, visit@undredal.no).

MORE ON THE SOGNEFJORD

Balestrand • Lustrafjord • Scenic Drives

Norway's world of fjords is decorated with medieval stave churches, fishing boats, cascading waterfalls, dramatic glaciers, and brightly painted shiplap villages. Travelers in a hurry zip through the fjords on the Norway in a Nutshell route (see previous chapter). Their heads spin from all the scenery, and most wish they had more time on the Sognefjord. If you can linger in fjord country, this chapter is for you.

Snuggle into the fjordside village of Balestrand, which has a variety of walking and biking options and a fun local arts scene. Balestrand is also a handy jumping-off spot for adventures great and small, including a day trip up the Fjærlandsfjord to gaze at a receding tongue of the Jostedal Glacier, or across the Sognefjord to the truly medieval-feeling Hopperstad Stave Church. Farther east is the Lustrafjord, a tranquil branch of the Sognefjord offering drivers an appealing concentration of visit-worthy sights. On the Lustrafjord, you'll enjoy enchanting hamlets with pristine fjord views (such as Solvorn), historic churches (including Norway's oldest stave church at Urnes and the humble Dale Church in the village of Luster), an opportunity to touch and even hike on a glacier (the Nigard), and more stunning fjord views.

This region is important to the people of Norway. After four centuries under Danish rule, the soul of the country was nearly lost. With partial independence and its own constitution in the early 1800s, the country experienced a resurgence of national pride. Urban Norwegians headed for the fjord country here in the west. Norway's first Romantic painters and writers were drawn to Balestrand, inspired by the unusual light and dramatic views of mountains plunging into the fjords. The Sognefjord, with its many

Sognefjord Overview

500 KM
250 MI
SWE.
FIN.
NOR.
DEN.

Breimsvatnet

Myklebust Glacier

To Utvik & Stryn

E-39

Skei

Bøya Glacier

TUNNEL

To Florø

Førdefjorden

Jølstravatnet

Grova Glacier

NORWEGIAN GLACIER MUSEUM

Førde

Fjærland (Mundal)

Haukedalsvatnet

Fjærlands-fjord

Viksdalvatnet

Lorem ipsum

Dragsvik

Hella

To Lavik & Bergen (by car and boat)

Balestrand

Vangsnes

Sognefjord

55

To Bergen (by boat)

Vik

HOPPERSTAD STAVE CHURCH

N

10 Kilometers

10 Miles

Gudvangen

Tvinde-fossen Waterfall

Vinje

BUS

STALHEIM (HOTEL & VIEW)

E-16

Voss

To Bergen

OSLO-BERGEN

branches, is featured in more Romantic paintings than any other fjord.

PLANNING YOUR TIME

If you can spare a day or two off the Norway in a Nutshell route, spend it here. Balestrand is the best home base, especially if you're relying on public transportation (it's well connected by express boat both to the Nutshell scene and to Bergen). If you have a car, consider staying in the heart of the Lustrafjord region in sweet little Solvorn (easy ferry connection to the Urnes Stave Church and a short drive to the Nigard Glacier). As fjord home bases go, Balestrand and Solvorn are both better—but less convenient—than Flåm or Aurland on the Nutshell route.

With one night in this area, you'll blitz the sights on the way between destinations; with two nights, you can slow your pace (and your pulse) to enjoy the fjord scenery and plenty of day-trip possibilities.

Balestrand

The pleasant fjord town of Balestrand (pop. 1,300) has a long history of hosting tourists, thanks to its landmark Kviknes Hotel. But it also feels real and lived-in, making Balestrand a nice mix of cuteness and convenience. The town is near, but not *too* near, the Nutshell bustle across the fjord—and yet it's an easy express-boat trip away if you'd like to dive into the Nuttiness. In short, consider Balestrand a worthwhile detour from the typical fjord visit—allowing you to dig deeper into the Sognefjord, just like the glaciers did during the last ice age.

With two nights, you can relax and consider some day trips: Cruise up the nearby Fjærlandsfjord for a peek at a distant tongue of the ever-less-mighty Jostedal Glacier, or head across the Sognefjord to the beautiful Hopperstad Stave Church in Vik. Balestrand also has outdoor activities for everyone, from dreamy fjordside strolls and strenuous mountain hikes to wildly scenic bike rides. For dinner, splurge on the memorable smorgasbord-style *koldt bord* dinner in the Kviknes Hotel dining room, then sip coffee from its balcony as you watch the sun set (or not) over the fjord.

PLANNING YOUR TIME

Balestrand's key advantage is its easy express-boat connection to Bergen, offering an alternative route to the fjord from the typical Nutshell train-bus combo. Consider zipping here on the Bergen boat, then continuing on via the Nutshell route.

One night is enough to get a taste of Balestrand. But spending two nights buys you some time for day trips. Note that the first flurry of day trips departs early, around 8:00 (includes the boat to Vik/Hopperstad Stave Church or the full-day Fjærlandsfjord glacier excursion), and the next batch departs around noon (the half-day Fjærlandsfjord glacier excursion and the last boat to Flåm). If you wait until after 12:00 to make your choice, you'll miss the boat...literally.

Balestrand pretty much shuts down from mid-September through mid-May—when most of the activities, sights, hotels, and restaurants listed here are likely closed.

Orientation to Balestrand

Most travelers arrive in Balestrand on the express boat from Bergen or Flåm. The tidy harbor area has a TI, two grocery stores, a couple of galleries, a town history museum, and a small aquarium devoted to marine life found in the fjord. The historic wooden Kviknes Hotel and its ugly modern annex dominate Balestrand's waterfront.

Even during tourist season, Balestrand is quiet. How quiet? The police station closes on weekends. And it's tiny—from the harbor to the Balestrand Hotel is a five-minute stroll, and you can walk from the aquarium to Kviknes Hotel in less time than that.

Balestrand became accessible to the wider world in 1858 when an activist minister (from the church you see across the fjord from town) brought in the first steamer service. That put Balestrand on the Grand Tour map of the Romantic Age. Even the German Kaiser chose to summer here. Today, people from around the world come here to feel the grandeur of the fjord country and connect with the essence of Norway.

TOURIST INFORMATION

At the TI, located between two supermarkets at the harbor, pick up the free, helpful *Outdoor Activities in Balestrand* brochure. The TI has numerous brochures about the Sognefjord area, including

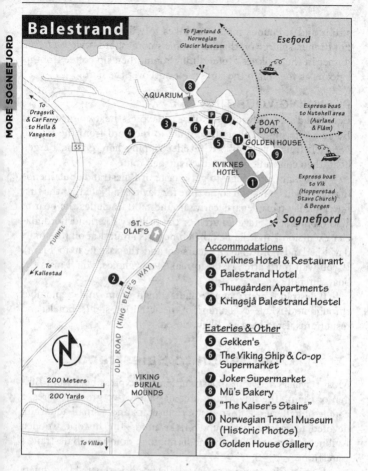

Balestrand

To Fjærland &
Norwegian
Glacier Museum

Esefjord

AQUARIUM

To
Dragsvik &
Car Ferry
to Hella &
Vangsnes

55

Express boat
to Nutshell area
(Aurland
& Flåm)

BOAT
DOCK

GOLDEN HOUSE

KVIKNES
HOTEL

Express boat
to Vik
(Hopperstad
Stave Church)
& Bergen

TUNNEL

To
Kallestad

ST.
OLAF'S

Sognefjord

OLD ROAD (KING BELE'S WAY)

200 Meters

200 Yards

VIKING
BURIAL
MOUNDS

To Villas

Accommodations
1 Kviknes Hotel & Restaurant
2 Balestrand Hotel
3 Thuegården Apartments
4 Kringsjå Balestrand Hostel

Eateries & Other
5 Gekken's
6 The Viking Ship & Co-op Supermarket
7 Joker Supermarket
8 Mü's Bakery
9 "The Kaiser's Stairs"
10 Norwegian Travel Museum (Historic Photos)
11 Golden House Gallery

many great hikes, with detailed information on the more challenging routes. It rents e-bikes (from 350 NOK) and sells tickets for the Norled ferry and various fjord, kayak, and fishing tours (daily 10:00-16:00 in summer, closed weekends in spring and fall and all of Oct-April; mobile +47 94 87 75 01—answered all year, https://en.sognefjord.no).

Local Guide: Various guides lead 1.5-hour tours around the village (www.balestrandadventure.no), or you can try **Bjørg Bjøberg,** who runs an art gallery along with her husband Arthur Adamson at the Golden House (Det Gylne Hus). She knows the town well and is happy to show visitors around (1,000-1,500 NOK/2 hours per group—gather several people and share the cost, mobile +47 91 56 28 42, bjoergfb@online.no).

Car Rental: The **Balholm Car Rental** agency usually will deliver a car to your Balestrand hotel, and pick it up, too (daily

8:00-20:00, +47 41 24 82 53, www.leigebil.no, booking@leigebil.no). The **Kviknes Hotel** can likely arrange a one-day car rental for you (+47 57 69 42 00).

Sights in Balestrand

Balestrand Harborfront Stroll

The tiny harbor stretches from the aquarium to the big, old Kviknes Hotel. Stroll its length, starting at the aquarium (described later) and little marina. Across the street, at the recommended Viking Ship shack, a German woman named Carola sells German sausages with an evangelical zeal. A couple of doors down, the Spindelvev ("Spider's Web") shop sells handicrafts made by people with physical and mental disabilities. A local home for the disabled was closed in the 1980s, but many of its former residents stayed in Balestrand because the government gave them pensions and houses in town.

Then, in the unsightly modern strip mall, you'll find the TI, Joker supermarket, and a community bulletin board with the schedule for the summer cinema (the little theater, 800 yards away, runs films nightly). On the corner is the Golden House art gallery. Behind it— built into solid rock—is the boxy home of the Norwegian Travel Museum (Norsk Reiselivsmuseum), featuring photos showing this part of Norway over the past 150 years, interactive exhibits, and souvenirs. And just beyond that is the dock where the big Bergen-Sognefjord express catamaran ties up.

Across the street is a cute white house (at #8), which used to stand at the harborfront until the big Joker supermarket and Kviknes Hotel, with its modern annex, partnered to ruin the town center. This little house was considered historic enough to be air-lifted 100 yards to this new spot. It's flanked by two other historic buildings, which house a gallery and an artisans' workshop.

Farther along, find the rust-red building that was the waiting room for the 19th-century steamer that first brought tourism to town. Walk a few steps farther and stop at the tall stone monument erected to celebrate the North Bergen Steamship Company. Its boats first connected Balestrand to the rest of the world in 1858. In front of the monument, some nondescript concrete steps lead into the water. These are "The Kaiser's Stairs," built for the German emperor, Kaiser Wilhelm II, who made his first summer visit (complete with navy convoy) in 1899 and kept returning until the outbreak of World War I.

Behind the monument stands one of the largest old wooden buildings in Norway, Kviknes Hotel. It was built in the 1870s and faces the rare little island in the fjord, which helped give the town its name: "Balestrand" means the strand or promenade in front of an island. (The island is now connected to the hotel's front yard and is part of a playground for its guests.) Hike up the black driveway that leads from the monument to the hotel's modern lobby. Go inside and find (to your left) the plush old lounge, a virtual painting gallery. All the pieces are by artists from this area, celebrating the natural wonder of the fjord country—part of the trend that helped 19th-century Norway reconnect with its heritage. (While you're here, consider making a reservation and choosing a table for a smorgasbord dinner tonight.) Leave the hotel lobby (from the door opposite to the one you entered), and head up to St. Olaf's Church. To continue this stroll, take King Bele's Way up the fjord.

Golden House (Det Gylne Hus)

This golden-colored house facing the ferry landing was built as a general store in 1928. Today it houses an art installation and a quirky museum created by local watercolorist and historian Bjørg Bjøberg, and her husband, Arthur Adamson. On the ground floor you'll find Bjørg's gallery, with her watercolors celebrating the beauty of Norway, and Arthur's paintings, celebrating the beauty of women. Upstairs is a room focusing on their local nature pilgrimage program, along with an exhibit of historical knickknacks contributed by locals wanting to preserve treasures from their families' past.

Cost and Hours: Free entry to the ground floor, 25 NOK for the second floor and the glass dome; optional private one-hour tour-50 NOK; May-Aug daily 10:00-22:00, shorter hours late April and Sept, closed in winter; mobile +47 91 56 28 42, www.detgylnehus.no.

St. Olaf's Church

This distinctive wooden church was built in 1897. Construction was started by Margaret Sophia Kvikne, the wife of Knut Kvikne (of the Kviknes Hotel family; her portrait is in the rear of the nave), but she died in 1894, before the church was finished. This devout Englishwoman wanted a church in Balestrand where English services were held...and to this day, bells ring to announce services by British clergy. Saint Olaf, who brought Christianity to Norway in the 11th century, was the country's patron saint in Catholic times. The church was built in a "Neo-stave" style, with lots of light from its windows and an altar painting inspired by the famous *Risen Christ* statue in Copenhagen's Cathedral of Our Lady. Here, Christ is flanked by fields of daisies (called "priests' collars" in Norwegian) and peace lilies. From the door of the church, enjoy a good view of the island in the fjord.

Cost and Hours: Free, open daily, services in English every Sun from late May through August.

Strolling King Bele's Way up the Fjord

For a delightful walk (or bike ride), head west out of town up the "old road"—once the main road from the harbor—for about a mile. It follows the fjord's edge, passing numerous "villas" from the late 1800s. At the time, this Swiss style was popular with some locals, who hoped to introduce a dose of Romanticism into Norwegian architecture. Look for the dragons' heads (copied from Viking-age stave churches) decorating the gables. Along the walk, you'll pass a swimming area, a campground, and two burial mounds from the Viking age, marked by a ponderous statue of the Viking King Bele. Check out the wooden shelters for the mailboxes; some give the elevation (*m.o.h.* stands for "meters over *havet*"—the sea)—not too high, are they? The walk is described in the *Outdoor Activities in Balestrand* brochure (free at the TI or your hotel).

Sognefjord Aquarium (Sognefjord Akvarium)

The tiny aquarium gives you a good look at marine life in the Sognefjord. For descriptions, borrow the English booklet at the front desk. While not thrilling, the well-explained place is a decent rainy-day option. The last room is filled with wood carvings depicting traditional everyday life in the fjordside village of Munken. The fish-filled tanks on the dock outside are also worth a look.

Cost and Hours: 70 NOK, daily 9:00-19:00, closed mid-Sept-April, +47 57 69 13 03.

Biking

You can cycle around town, or circle the scenic Esefjord (north of town, en route to the ferry landing at Dragsvik—about 6 miles each way). Or pedal west up Sognefjord along the scenic King Bele's Way (described earlier). Roads here are relatively flat. Rental bikes are usually available at the TI and through Kviknes Hotel.

Boat Tours

Balestrand Fjord Adventure specializes in Zodiac-type boat tours on the Sognefjord. Passengers wear full-body weather suits, life vests, and goggles. Join their daily round-trip cruise departing at 13:00 (800 NOK, 1.5 hours) or take the more extensive Nærøyfjord tour (1,350 NOK, 2.5 hours, 3/week, mobile +47 47 85 53 23, www.balestrandadventure.no).

NEAR BALESTRAND

These two side-trips are possible only if you've got the better part of a day in Balestrand. With a car, you can see Hopperstad Stave Church on the drive to Bergen.

▲▲Hopperstad Stave Church (Hopperstad Stavkyrkje) in Vik

The most accessible stave church in the area—and perhaps the most scenically situated in all of Norway—is located just a 20-minute express-boat ride across the Sognefjord, in the town of Vik. Hopperstad Stave Church boasts a breathtaking exterior, with several tiers of dragon heads overlooking rolling fields between fjord cliffs. The interior is notable for its emptiness. Instead of being crammed full of later additions, the church is blissfully uncluttered, as it was when it was built in the mid-12th century. (For more on stave churches, see page 318.)

Cost and Hours: 80 NOK; daily 10:00-17:00, mid-June-mid-Aug from 9:00, closed Oct-mid-May; good 30-NOK color booklet in English, +47 57 69 52 70, www. stavechurch.com/hopperstad.

Tours: Attendants will give you a free tour at your request, provided they're not too busy. (Ask where the medieval graffiti is, and they'll grab a flashlight and show you.)

Getting There: Pedestrians can ride the express passenger boat between Balestrand and Vik (98 NOK each way). The only way to get to the church and back in one day is to take the 7:50 departure from Balestrand, then return on the 11:35 departure from Vik, arriving back in Balestrand at 11:55—just in time to join a 12:00 glacier excursion (described on the next page). Because schedules can change, be sure to double-check times at the TI or www.norled.no, under "Expressboat." The church is a 20-minute walk up the valley from Vik's harbor. From the boat landing, walk up the main street from the harbor about 200 yards (past the TI, a grocery store, and hotel). Take a right at the sign for *Hopperstad Stavkyrkje*, walk 10 minutes, and you'll see the church perched on a small hill in the distance.

Since cars can't go on the express boat, **drivers** must go around the small Esefjord to the town of Dragsvik, then catch the ferry across the Sognefjord to Vangsnes (a 20-minute drive from Vik and the church).

Visiting the Church: Originally built around 1140 and retaining most of its original wood, Hopperstad was thoroughly restored and taken back to basics in the 1880s by renowned architect Peter Blix. Unlike the famous stave church at Urnes (described later), which has an interior that has been rejiggered by centuries of engineers and filled with altars and pews, the Hopperstad church looks close to the way it did when it was built. You'll see only a few added features, including the beautifully painted canopy that once covered a side altar (probably dating from around 1300), and a tombstone from 1738. There are just a few colorful illustrations and some very scant medieval "graffiti" carvings and runic inscriptions.

Notice the intact chancel screen (the only one surviving in Norway), which separates the altar area from the congregation. As with the iconostasis (panel of icons) in today's Orthodox faith, this screen gave priests privacy to do the spiritual heavy lifting. Because Hopperstad's interior lacks the typical adornments, you can really grasp the fundamentally vertical nature of stave church architecture, leading your gaze to the heavens. Follow that impulse and look up to appreciate the Viking-ship rafters. Imagine the comfort this ceiling brought the church's original parishioners, whose seafaring ancestors had once sought refuge under overturned boats. For a unique angle on this graceful structure, lay your camera on the floor and shoot the ceiling.

▲Excursion to Fjærland and the Jostedal Glacier

From Balestrand, cruise up the Fjærlandsfjord to visit the Norwegian Glacier Museum in Fjærland and to see a receding tongue of

the Jostedal Glacier (Jostedalbreen). Half-day (890 NOK) and full-day (925 NOK) excursions are sold by Balestrand's TI or onboard the boat. Reservations are smart (tours offered daily June-Aug only, +47 57 63 14 00, www.visitflam.com and follow links for "Fjærlandsfjord").

While the museum and the glacier's tongue are underwhelming, it's a pleasant excursion with a dreamy fjord cruise (1.5 hours each way). To take the all-day trip, catch the 8:00 ferry; for the shorter trip, hop on the 12:00 boat. Either way, you can return on the 15:30 boat, getting you back to Balestrand at 16:45 (just in time to catch the fast boat back to Bergen). Both tours offer the same fjord ride, museum visit, and trip to the glacier. The all-day version, however, gives you a second glacier viewing point and about 2.5 hours to hang out in the town of Fjærland. (This sleepy village, famous for its secondhand book shops, is about as exciting as Walter Mondale, the former US vice president whose ancestors came from here.)

The ferry ride (no stops, no narration) is just a scenic glide with the gulls. Bring a picnic, as there's almost no food sold on-board, and some bread to toss to the gulls (they do acrobatics to catch whatever you loft into the air). You'll be met at the ferry dock (labeled *Mundal*) by a bus—and your guide, who reads a script about the glacier as you drive up the valley for about 15 minutes. You'll stop for an hour at the **Norwegian Glacier Museum** (Norsk Bremuseum). After watching an 18-minute aerial tour of the dramatic Jostedal Glacier in the theater, you'll learn how glaciers were formed, experiment with your own hunk of glacier, weigh evidence of the woolly mammoth's existence in Norway, and learn about the effect of climate change on the fjords (way overpriced at 140 NOK, included in excursion price; daily June-Aug 10:00-19:00, April-May and Sept-Oct until 16:00, closed Nov-March; +47 57 69 32 88, www.bre.museum.no). From the museum, the bus runs you up to a café near a lake, at a spot that gives you a good look at the Bøyabreen, a tongue of the Jostedal Glacier. Marvel at how far the glacier has retreated—10 years ago, the visit was more dramatic. With global warming, glacier excursions like this become more sad than majestic. I wonder how long they'll even be able to bill this as a "glacier visit."

Considering that the fjord trip is the highlight of this journey, you could save time and money by just riding the ferry up and back (8:00-11:25). At 475 NOK for the round-trip boat ride, it's much cheaper than the tour.

Note that if you're into glaciers, a nearby arm of the Jostedal, called the **Nigard Glacier,** is a more dramatic and boots-on experience (described later, under "Sights on the Lustrafjord"). It's easy for drivers to reach; see "Orientation to Balestrand," earlier, for car-rental info.

Sleeping in Balestrand

$$$$ Kviknes Hotel is the classy grande dame of Balestrand, dominating the town and packed with tour groups. The picturesque wooden hotel—and five generations of the Kvikne family—have welcomed tourists to Balestrand since the late 19th century. The hotel has two parts: a new wing, and the historic wooden sec-

tion, with 25 older, classic rooms, and no elevator. All rooms come with balconies. The elegant Old World public spaces in the old section make you want to just sit there and sip tea all afternoon (family rooms, closed Oct-April, +47 57 69 42 00, www.
kviknes.com, booking@kviknes.no). Part of the Kviknes ritual is gorging on the *koldt bord* buffet dinner—open to nonguests, and a nice way to soak in the hotel's old-time elegance without splurging on an overnight (see "Eating in Balestrand," later; cheaper if you stay at the hotel for 2 or more nights).

$$$ Balestrand Hotel, family-run by Unni-Marie Kvikne, her California-born husband Eric Palmer, and their three children, is your best fjordside home. Open mid-May through early September, this cozy, welcoming place has 30 well-appointed, comfortable, quiet rooms; a large, modern common area with lots of English paperbacks; laundry service, balconies (in some rooms), and outdoor benches for soaking in the scenery. The waterfront yard has inviting lounge chairs and a mesmerizing view. When reserving, let them know your arrival time, and they'll pick you up at the harborfront (5-minute walk from dock, past St. Olaf's Church—or free pickup, +47 57 69 11 38, www.balestrand.com, info@balestrand.com).

$ Thuegården offers five clean, bright, modern doubles with kitchenettes, conveniently located near the ferry dock and just up the street from the Co-op grocery store. Some rooms have balconies and some come with a fjord view (discount if staying more than 3 nights, no breakfast, office inside ground-floor hair salon, +47 57 69 15 95, mobile +47 97 19 92 63, www.thuegaarden.com, thuegaarden@gmail.com).

¢-$$ Kringsjå Balestrand Hostel, a camp school for sixthgraders, rents beds and rooms to budget travelers from mid-June to mid-August. Three-quarters of their 58 beds are in doubles. All the rooms have private bathrooms and most have view balconies (private and family rooms, includes sheets and towels, game room, +47 57 69 13 03, www.kringsja.no, hotel@kringsja.no).

Eating in Balestrand

Balestrand's dining options are limited, but good.

$$$$ Kviknes Hotel offers a splendid, spendy *koldt bord* buffet dinner in a massive yet stately old dining room. For a memorable fjordside smorgasbord experience, it doesn't get any better than this. Don't rush. Consider taking a preview tour—surveying the reindeer meat, lingonberries, and fjord-caught seafood—before you dive in, so you can budget your stomach space. Get a new plate with each course and save room for dessert. Each dish is labeled in English (575 NOK/person, May-Sept daily

18:30-21:00, closed Oct-April). They also offer a four-course, locally sourced dinner for 695 NOK. After dinner, head into the rich lounge to pick up your cup of coffee or tea (included), which you'll sip sitting on classy old-fashioned furniture and basking in fjord views.

$$ Gekken's is an informal summer restaurant serving good-value meat, fish, and vegetarian dishes, along with burgers, fish-and-chips, and other fried fare. Sit in the simply decorated interior, or out on the shaded little terrace. Geir Arne "Gekken" Bale can trace his family's roots back 400 years in Balestrand. He has filled his walls with fascinating historic photos and paintings, making his dining hall an art gallery of sorts (May-Aug daily 12:00-22:00, closed Sept-April, above and behind the TI from the harbor, +47 57 69 14 14).

$ The Viking Ship, the hot-dog stand facing the harbor, is proudly run by Carola. A bratwurst missionary from Germany, she claims it took her years to get Norwegians to accept the tastier bratwurst over their beloved *pølser* weenies. Eat at her picnic tables or across the street on the harbor park (fine sausages, fish-and-chips, May-Sept daily 11:00-20:00, closed Oct-April).

Picnic: The delightful waterfront park next to the aquarium has benches and million-dollar fjord views. The Co-op and Joker **supermarkets** at the harbor have basic grocery supplies, including bread, meats, cheeses, and drinks; the Co-op is bigger and has a wider selection (both open generally Mon-Fri 8:00-20:00, shorter hours on Sat, closed Sun). **$ Mü's Bakery** offers a healthy assortment of sandwiches and fresh-baked goodies (Mon-Sat 9:30-18:00, Sun until 15:00, closed mid-Sept-early May, just inside the aquarium entrance).

Balestrand Connections

Because Balestrand is separated from the Lustrafjord by the long Fjærlandsfjord, most Balestrand connections involve a boat trip.

Express Boat Between Bergen and the Sognefjord

The made-for-tourists express boat makes it a snap to connect Bergen with Balestrand and other Sognefjord towns (for foot passengers only—no cars). In summer, the boat links Bergen, Vik, Balestrand, Aurland, and Flåm. You can also use this boat to connect towns on the Sognefjord, such as zipping from quiet Balestrand to busy Flåm, in the heart of the Nutshell action (reservations are smart—call +47 51 86 87 00 or visit www.norled.no and select "Expressboat"; discounts for students and seniors, tickets also sold on boat and at TI). The following times were good as of press time—confirm locally.

Between Bergen and the Sognefjord: The boat trip between Bergen and **Balestrand** takes four hours (760 NOK, departs Bergen May-Sept daily at 8:00 and 16:30, Oct-April Sun-Fri at 16:30, Sat at 14:15; departs Balestrand May-Sept Mon-Sat at 7:50 and 16:50, some Sun at 11:30 and 16:50, Oct-April Mon-Sat at 7:50, Sun at 16:25). In summer, the 8:00 boat from Bergen continues to Flåm.

Between Flåm and Balestrand: Going by boat between Flåm and Balestrand with the Norled ferry takes about 1.5 hours (300 NOK, departs Flåm May-Sept daily at 15:30, stops at Aurland, arrives in Balestrand at 16:50; departs Balestrand daily at 11:55 arriving Flåm at 13:25; no express boats between Flåm and Balestrand Oct-April). Another option is The Fjords express-ferry, which also stops at Leikanger, Undredal, and Aurland (300 NOK, only runs June-mid-Aug, takes 2 hours, departs Flåm Mon-Fri at 6:00, departs Balestrand at 8:30, no boats Sat-Sun, +47 57 63 14 00, www.visitflam.com). In peak season book ahead for any of the Flåm-Balestrand ferries.

From Oslo to Balestrand via the Nutshell: This variation on the standard Norway in a Nutshell route is called "Sognefjord in a Nutshell" (Oslo-Myrdal-Flåm-Balestrand-Bergen). From Oslo, you can take an early train to Flåm (no later than the 8:25 train as part of the Norway in a Nutshell route), then catch the 15:30 express boat to Balestrand and spend the night. The next day, continue on the express boat to Bergen, or return to the Nutshell route by taking the express boat to Flåm, and transferring to the next boat to Gudvangen.

BY BOAT

Express Passenger Boat: The easiest way to reach Balestrand is on the handy express boat, which connects to **Bergen, Vik** (near Hopperstad Stave Church), **Aurland,** and **Flåm** (see sidebar for schedules). Note that you can also use this boat to join the Nutshell trip in Flåm. From here, continue on the Nutshell boat down the Nærøyfjord to Gudvangen, where you'll join the crowd onward to Voss, then Bergen or Oslo. As you're making schedule and sight-seeing decisions, consider that the Balestrand-Flåm boat skips the Nærøyfjord, the most dramatic arm of the Sognefjord.

Car Ferry: Balestrand's main car-ferry dock is at the village of **Dragsvik,** a six-mile, 15-minute drive around the adorable little Esefjord. From Dragsvik, a car ferry makes the short crossing east to **Hella** (a 30-minute drive from Sogndal and the Lustrafjord), then crosses the Sognefjord south to **Vangsnes** (a 20-minute drive to Hopperstad Stave Church and onward to Bergen). The ferry goes at least once per hour (2/hour in peak times, fewer boats Sun; Dragsvik-Vangsnes, 107 NOK for car and driver; Dragsvik-Hella, 74 NOK).

Note that you can also drive through Sogndal to catch the **Kaupanger-Gudvangen** or **Mannheller-Fodnes** ferries (described under "Lustrafjord Connections," near the end of this chapter).

BY BUS

A local bus links Balestrand to **Sogndal** (5/day Mon-Fri, 3/day Sat-Sun, 1.5 hours, includes ride on Dragsvik-Hella ferry, get details at TI).

The Lustrafjord

This arm of the Sognefjord is rugged country—only 2 percent of the land is fit to build on or farm. The Lustrafjord is ringed with tiny villages where farmers sell cherries and giant raspberries. A few interesting attractions lie along the Lustrafjord: the Dale Church at Luster; the impressive Nigard Glacier (a 45-minute drive up a valley); the postcard-pretty village of Solvorn; and, across the fjord, Norway's oldest stave church at Urnes. While a bit trickier to explore by public transportation, this beautiful region is easy by car, but still feels remote. There are no ATMs between Lom and Gaupne—that's how remote this region is.

SUGGESTED ROUTE FOR DRIVERS

The Lustrafjord can be seen either coming from the north (over the Sognefjell pass from the Jotunheimen region—see next chapter) or from the south (from Balestrand or the Norway in a Nutshell route—see previous chapter). Note that public buses between Lom and Sogndal follow this same route (see "Lustrafjord Connections," later).

Here's what you'll see if you're driving from the north (if you're coming from the south, read this section backward): Descending from Sognefjell, you'll hit the fjord at the village of Skjolden (decent TI in big community center, mobile +47 99 23 15 00). Follow highway 55 along the west bank of the fjord. In the village of Luster, consider visiting the beautifully decorated Dale Church. Farther along, near the hamlet of Nes, you'll have views across the fjord of the towering Feigumfoss waterfall. Drops and dribbles come from miles around for this 650-foot tumble. Soon highway 55 veers along an inlet to the town of Gaupne, where you can choose to detour about an hour to the Nigard Glacier (up Route 604). After Gaupne, the road enters a tunnel and cuts inland, emerging at a long, fjord-like lake at the town of Hafslo. Just beyond is the turn-off for Solvorn, a town with the ferry across to Urnes and its stave church. Highway 55 continues to Sogndal, where you can choose to turn off for the Kaupanger and Mannheller ferries across the Sognefjord, or continue on highway 55 to Hella and the boat across to either Dragsvik (near Balestrand) or Vangsnes (across the Sognefjord, near Vik and Hopperstad Stave Church).

Route Timings: If you're approaching from Lom in the Gudbrandsdal Valley, figure about 1.5 hours over Sognefjell to the start of the Lustrafjord at Skjolden, then another 30 minutes to Gaupne (with the optional glacier detour: 2 hours to see it, 4 hours to hike on it). From Gaupne, figure 20 minutes to Solvorn or 30 minutes to Sogndal. Solvorn to Sogndal is about 25 minutes. Sogndal to Hella, and its boat to Balestrand, takes about one hour. These estimated times are conservative, but they don't include photo stops.

Sights on the Lustrafjord

These attractions are listed as you'll reach them driving from north to south along the fjordside highway 55. If you're sleeping in this area, you could visit all four sights in a single day (but it'd be a busy, somewhat rushed day). If you're just passing through, Dale Church and Solvorn are easy, but the other two involve major detours—choose one or skip them both.

▲Dale Church (Dale Kyrkje) in Luster

The namesake village of Luster, on the west bank of the Lustrafjord, boasts a unique 13th-century Gothic church. In a land of wooden

stave churches, this stone church, with its richly decorated interior, is worth a quick stop as you pass through town.

Cost and Hours: Free entry but donation requested, daily 10:00-20:00 but often closed for services and off-season,

good posted English info inside, just off the main road—look for red steeple, WC in graveyard, fresh goodies at bakery across the street.

Visiting the Church: The soapstone core of the church dates from about 1250, but the wooden bell tower and entry porch were

likely built around 1600. As you enter, on the left you'll see a tall, elevated platform with seating, surrounded by a wooden grill. Nick-named a "birdcage" for the feathery fashions worn by the ladies of the time, this high-profile pew—three steps higher than the pulpit—was built in the late 17th century by a wealthy parishioner. The beautifully paint-ed pulpit, decorated with faded images of the four evangelists, dates from the 13th centu-ry. In the chancel (altar area), restorers have uncovered frescoes from three different time periods: the 14th, 16th, and 17th centuries.

Most of the ones you see here were likely cre-ated around the year 1500. The crucifix high over the pews, carved around 1200, predates the church, as does the old bench (with lots of runic carvings)—making them more than eight centuries old.

▲▲Jostedal's Nigard Glacier

The Nigard Glacier (Nigardsbreen) is the most accessible branch of mainland Europe's largest glacier (the Jostedalsbreen, 185 square

miles). Hiking to or on the Nigard offers Norway's best easy opportunity for a hands-on glacier experience. It's a 45-minute detour from the Lustrafjord up Jostedal Valley. Visiting a glacier is a quintessential Norwegian experience, bringing you face-to-face

with the majesty of nature. If you can spare the time, it's worth the detour (even if you don't do a guided hike). But if glaciers don't give you tingles and you're feeling pressed, skip it.

Getting There: It's straightforward for **drivers.** When the main highway 55 along the Lustrafjord reaches Gaupne, turn onto highway 604, which you'll follow for 25 miles up the Jostedal Valley to the Breheimsenteret Glacier Information Center. Access to the glacier itself is down the toll road past the information center.

From mid-June through August, a **Glacier Bus** connects the Nigard Glacier to various home-base towns around the region (leaves Sogndal at 8:35 and 13:45, arrives at the glacier around 10:00 and 15:30, morning bus passes through Solvorn en route; departs glacier at 12:25 and 16:55, arrives back in Sogndal around 14:20 and 18:35; buses or boats from other towns, including Flåm and Aurland, may coordinate to meet this bus in Sogndal—ask at TI; combo-tickets include various glacier visits and hikes; for complete timetable, see www.visitnorway.no).

Visiting the Glacier: The architecturally striking Breheimsenteret Glacier Information Center services both Breheimen and Jostedalsbreen national parks. Drop by to confirm your glacier plans; you can also book excursions here. The center features a relaxing 15-minute film with highlights of the region, along with interactive glacier-related exhibits that explain these giant, slow-moving rivers of ice. The center also has a restaurant and gift shop (information center-free, exhibits and film-85 NOK; daily mid-June-mid-Aug 9:00-18:00, May-mid-June and mid-Aug-Sept 10:00-17:00, closed Oct-April; +47 57 68 32 50, www.jostedal.com.

The best quick visit is to walk to, but not on, the glacier. (If you want to walk *on* it, see "Hikes on the Glacier," next.) From the information center, an 80-NOK toll road continues two miles to a lake facing the actual tongue of the glacier. About 75 years ago, the glacier reached all the way to today's parking lot. (It's named for the ninth farm—*ni gard*—where it finally stopped, after crushing eight farms higher up the valley.) From the lot, you can hike all the way to the edge of today's glacier (about 45 minutes each way); or, to save about 20 minutes of walking, take a special boat to a spot that's a 20-minute hike from the glacier (40 NOK one-way, 60 NOK round-trip, 10-minute boat trip, 4/hour, mid-June-mid-Sept daily 10:00-18:00).

The walk is uneven but well-marked—follow the red *T*'s and take your time. You'll hike on stone polished smooth by the glacier, and scramble over and around boulders big and small that were deposited by it. The path takes you right up to the face of the Nigardsbreen. Respect the glacier. It's a powerful river of ice, and fatal accidents do happen. If you want to walk on the glacier, see below.

Hikes on the Glacier: Don't attempt to walk on the glacier by yourself. The Breheimsenteret Glacier Information Center has

information on local companies that offer guided, family-friendly walks that include 1-2 hours on the ice. Prices and minimum age varies by the company (470-950 NOK, from 520 NOK for kids, minimum age 4-8; I'd rate the walks PG-13 myself, book in advance, www.jostedal.com). One hour roped up with your group gives you the essential experience. You'll find yourself marveling at how well your crampons work on the 5,000-year-old-ice. Even if it's hot, wear long pants, a jacket, and your sturdiest shoes. (Think ahead. It's awkward to empty your bladder after you're roped up.)

Longer, more challenging, and much more expensive hikes get you higher views, more exercise, and real crampons. If you're adventurous, ask about even longer hikes and glacier kayaking. While it's legal to go on the glacier on your own, it's dangerous and crazy to do so without crampons.

▲▲Solvorn

On the west bank of the Lustrafjord, 10 miles northeast of Sogndal, idyllic Solvorn is a sleepy little Victorian town with colorful wooden sheds lining its waterfront. My favorite town on the Lustrafjord is tidy and quaint, well away from the bustle of the Nutshell action. Its tiny ferry crosses the fjord regularly to Urnes and its famous stave church. While not worth going far out of your way for, Solvorn is a mellow and surprisingly appealing place to kill some time waiting for the ferry...or just munching a picnic while looking across the fjord. A pensive stroll or photo shoot through the village's back lanes is a joy (look for plaques that explain historic buildings in English). Best of all, Solvorn also has a pair of excellent accommodations: a splurge (Walaker Hotel) and a budget place (Eplet Bed & Apple), described later under "Sleeping on the Lustrafjord."

Getting There: Solvorn is a steep five-minute **drive** down a switchback road from the main highway 55. The main road into town leads right to the Urnes ferry (see next listing) and dead-ends into a handy parking lot (free, 2-hour posted—but unmonitored—limit). It's a 30-minute drive or bus trip into Sogndal, where you can transfer to other **buses** (2-4 buses/day between Solvorn and Sogndal, including the Glacier Bus to the Nigard Glacier—described earlier).

▲▲Urnes Stave Church

The hamlet of Urnes (sometimes spelled "Ornes") has Norway's oldest surviving stave church, dating from 1129. While not easy to reach (it's across the Lustrafjord from other attractions), it's worth the scenic ferry ride. The exterior is smaller and simpler than most stave churches, but its interior—modified in fits and starts over the centuries—is uniquely eclectic. For more on stave churches, see page 318. If you want to pack along a bike (rentable in Solvorn), see "Bring a Bike?" at the end of this listing.

Cost and Hours: 100 NOK, includes 20-minute English tour (generally departs at :40 past the hour to coincide with ferry arrival); May-Sept daily 10:30-17:45, closed off-season, +47 57 68 39 56, www.stavechurch.com.

Getting There: Urnes is perched on the east bank of the Lustrafjord (across the fjord from highway 55 and Solvorn). Ferries generally depart Solvorn at the top of the hour and Urnes at 30 minutes past the hour (45 NOK one-way passenger fare, 121 NOK one-way for car and driver, no round-trip discount, 15-minute ride, mobile +47 91 72 17 19, www.lustrabaatane.no). You can either drive or walk onto the boat—but, since you can't drive all the way up to the church, you might as well leave your car in Solvorn. Once across, it's about a five-minute uphill walk to the main road and parking lot (where drivers must leave their cars; parking lot at the church only for disabled visitors). From here, it's a steep 15-minute walk up a switchback road to the church (follow signs for *Urnes*).

Planning Your Time: Don't dawdle on your way up to the church, as the tour is scheduled to depart at :40 past most hours, about 25 minutes after the ferry arrives (giving most visitors just enough time to make it up the hill to the church; last tour at 16:40). The first boat of the day departs Solvorn at 10:00 and the last boat at 16:50; the last boat back to Solvorn departs Urnes at 18:00. Confirm these times locally, especially the "last boat" times, and keep an eye on your watch to avoid getting stranded in Urnes.

Eating: A little café/restaurant is at the farm called Urnes Gard, across from the church (same hours as church, homemade apple cakes, +47 57 68 39 44).

Visiting the Church: Most visitors to the church take the included 20-minute tour (scheduled to begin soon after the ferry arrives—described earlier). Here are some highlights:

Buy your ticket in the white house across from the church. Visit the little museum here after you see the church, so you don't miss the tour.

Many changes were made to the exterior to modernize the church after the Reformation (the colonnaded gallery was replaced, the bell tower was added, and modern square windows were cut into the walls). Go around the left side of the church, toward the cemetery. This is the third church on this spot, but the carved doorway embedded in the wall here was inherited from the second church. Notice the two mysterious beasts— a warm-blooded predator (standing) and a cold-blooded dragon—weaving and twisting around each other, one entwining the other. Yet, as they bite each other on the neck, it's impossible to tell which one is "winning"... perhaps symbolizing the everlasting struggle of human existence. The door you see in the middle, however, has a very different message: the harmony of symmetrical figure-eights, an appropriately calming theme for those entering the church.

Now go around to the real entry door (with a wrought-iron lock and handle probably dating from the first church) and head inside. While it feels ancient and creaky, a lot of what you see in here is actually "new" compared to the 12th-century core of the church. The exquisitely carved, voluptuous, column-topping capitals are remarkably well-preserved originals. The interior was initially stark (no pews) and dark—lit not by windows (which were added much later), but by candles laid on the floor in the shape of a cross. Looking straight ahead, you see a cross with Mary on the left (where the women stood) and John the Baptist on the right (with the men). When they finally added seating, they kept things segregated: Notice the pews carved with hearts for women, crowns for men.

When a 17th-century wealthy family wanted to build a special pew for themselves, they simply sawed off some of the pinecone-topped columns to make way for it. When the church began to lean, it was reinforced with the clumsy, off-center X-shaped supports. Churchgoers learned their lesson, and never cut anything again.

The ceiling, added in the late 17th century, prevents visitors from enjoying the Viking-ship roof beams. But all of these additions have stories to tell. Experts can read various cultural influences into the church decorations, including Irish (some of the carvings) and Romanesque (the rounded arches).

Bring a Bike? To give your Lustrafjord excursion an added dimension, take a bike on the ferry to Urnes (free passage, rentable for 300 NOK/day with helmets from Eplet Bed & Apple hostel in Solvorn, where you can park your car for free). From the stave church, bike the super-scenic fjordside road nine miles—with almost no traffic—to the big Feigumfossen waterfall, and back.

Sleeping on the Lustrafjord

These accommodations are along the Lustrafjord, listed from north to south.

IN NES

$$ Nes Gard Farmhouse B&B rents 15 homey rooms, offering lots of comfort in a grand 19th-century farmhouse (includes breakfast, three-course dinner extra, discount for staying multiple days, rooms in main building more traditional, family apartment, bike rental, mobile +47 95 23 26 94, www.nesgard.no, post@nesgard. no, Månum family—Mari and Asbjørn).

¢ Viki Fjord Camping has great fjordside huts—many directly on the water, with views and balconies—located directly across from the Feigumfossen waterfall (no breakfast, sheets extra, +47 57 68 64 20, mobile +47 99 53 97 30, www.vikicamping.no, post@ vikicamping.no, Berit and Svein).

IN SOLVORN

For more on this delightful little fjordside town—my favorite home base on the Lustrafjord—see the description earlier in this chapter. While it lacks the handy boat connections of Flåm, Aurland, or Balestrand, that's part of Solvorn's charm.

$$$$ Walaker Hotel, a former inn and coach station, has

been run by the Walaker family since 1690 (that's a lot of pressure on ninth-generation owner Ole Henrik). The hotel, set right on the Lustrafjord (with a garden perfect for relaxing and, if necessary, even convalescing), is open May through September. In the main house, the halls and living rooms are filled with tradition. Notice the patriotic hymns on the piano. The 22 rooms are divided into two types: nicely appointed standard rooms in the modern annex; or recently renovated "historic" rooms with all the modern conveniences in two different old buildings: rooms with Old World elegance in the main

house, and brightly painted rooms with countryside charm in the Tingstova house next door (sea kayak rentals, +47 57 68 20 80, www.walaker.com, hotel@walaker.com). They serve excellent four-course dinners (625 NOK plus drinks, nightly at 19:30, savor your dessert with fjordside setting on the balcony). Their impressive gallery of Norwegian art is in a restored, historic farmhouse out back (free for guests; Ole Henrik leads one-hour tours of the collection, peppered with some family history, nightly after dinner).

¢ **Eplet Bed & Apple** is my kind of hostel: innovative and friendly. It's creatively run by Trond and Agnethe, whose entrepreneurial spirit and positive attitude attract enjoyable guests. With welcoming public spaces and 22 beds in seven rooms (all with views, some with decks), this place is worth considering even if you don't normally sleep at hostels (open mid-April-Sept only, private rooms, no breakfast, no elevator, pay laundry, kitchen, +47 41 64 94 69, www.eplet.net, post@eplet.net). It's about 300 yards uphill from the boat dock—look for the white house with a giant red apple painted on it. It's surrounded by a raspberry-and-apple farm (they make and sell tasty juices from both). The hostel provides free loaner bikes for guests and rents them to nonguests for 300 NOK/day (helmets available).

Eating in Solvorn: The **$$$ Linahagen Kafé**, next door to Walaker Hotel, serves good meals (June-Aug Mon-Fri 12:00-18:00, Sat until 16:00, Sun 13:00-18:00, closed Sept-May, run by Tordis and her family).

IN SOGNDAL

Sogndal is the only sizeable town in this region. While it lacks the charm of Solvorn and Balestrand, it's big enough to have a busy shopping street and a helpful **TI** (daily 9:30-23:00, inside the MIX minimart at Parkvegen 5, mobile +47 41 78 13 00).

¢ **Sogndal Youth Hostel** rents good, cheap beds (private

rooms, June-mid-Aug only, closed 10:00-17:00, near the bridge at Helgheimsvegen 9, +47 57 62 75 75, www.hihostels.no/sogndal, sogndal@hihostels.no).

Lustrafjord Connections

Sogndal is the transit hub for the Lustrafjord region.

FROM SOGNDAL BY BUS

Buses go to **Lom** over the Sognefjell pass (2/day late June-Aug only, road closed off-season, 3.5 hours, likely 1/day off-season, goes around the pass, 5 hours, change in Skei), **Solvorn** (3/day, fewer Sat-Sun, 30 minutes), **Balestrand** (5/day Mon-Fri, 3/day Sat-Sun, 2 hours, includes ride on Hella-Dragsvik ferry), **Nigard Glacier** (Glacier Bus runs 2/day mid-June-Aug only, see listing earlier for times). Most buses run less (or not at all) on weekends—check the latest at https://entur.no.

BY BOAT

Car ferry reservations are generally not necessary except for the boat to Gudvangen, and on many short rides, aren't even possible (confirm schedules at https://entur.no). From near Sogndal, various boats fan out to towns around the Sognefjord. Most leave from two towns at the southern end of the Lustrafjord: **Kaupanger** (a 15-minute drive from Sogndal) and **Mannheller** (a 5-minute drive beyond Kaupanger, 20 minutes from Sogndal).

From Kaupanger: While Kaupanger is little more than a ferry landing, the small stave-type church at the edge of town merits a look. Boats go from Kaupanger all the way down the gorgeous Nærøyfjord to **Gudvangen,** which is on the Norway in a Nutshell route (where you catch the bus to Voss). Taking this leisurely boat allows you to see the best part of the Nutshell fjord scenery (the Nærøyfjord), but misses the other half of that cruise (Aurlandsfjord). From June through August, boats leave Kaupanger daily at 9:00 and 15:00 (July-mid-Aug also at 12:00 and 18:00) for the nearly 3-hour trip; check in 15 minutes before departure (car and driver-830 NOK, adult passenger-395 NOK; reserve at least one day in advance—or longer in July-Aug; +47 57 63 14 00, www.visitflam.com—follow links to "Fjord Cruise Sognefjord"). Prices are high because this route is mainly taken by tourists, not locals. Verify schedules and prices online. Boats also connect Kaupanger to **Lærdal,** but the crossing from Mannheller to Fodnes is easier (described next).

From Mannheller: Ferries frequently make the speedy 15-minute crossing to **Fodnes** (91 NOK for a car and driver, 3/hour, no reservations possible). From Fodnes, drive through the five-mile-long tunnel to Lærdal and the main E-16 highway (near Borgund Stave Church, the long tunnel to Aurland, and the scenic overland "Snow Road" to the Stegastein fjord viewpoint—all described in the previous chapter).

To Balestrand: To reach Balestrand from the Lustrafjord, you'll take a short ferry trip (Hella-Dragsvik). For information on the car ferries to and from Balestrand, see "Balestrand Connections," earlier.

Scenic Drives from the Sognefjord

If you'll be doing a lot of driving, buy a good local map. The 1:335,000-scale *Sør-Norge nord* map by Cappelens Kart is excellent (available at local TIs and bookstores). If you are following our recommended three-week itinerary, use these directions to connect the Lustrafjord and Bergen.

▲▲From the Lustrafjord to Aurland

The drive to the pleasant fjordside town of Aurland (see previous chapter) takes you either through the world's longest car tunnel, or over an incredible mountain pass. If you aren't going as far as Lom and Jotunheimen, consider taking the pass, as the scenery here rivals the famous Sognefjell pass drive.

From Sogndal, drive 20 minutes to the Mannheller-Fodnes ferry (described earlier, under "Lustrafjord Connections"), float across the Sognefjord, then drive from Fodnes to Lærdal. From Lærdal, you have two options to Aurland: The speedy route is on E-16 through the 15-mile-long **tunnel** from Lærdal, or the Aurlandsvegen **"Snow Road"** over the pass.

The tunnel is free, and impressively nonchalant—it's signed as if it were just another of Norway's countless tunnels. But driving it is a bizarre experience: A few miles in, as you find yourself trying not to be hypnotized by the monotony, it suddenly dawns on you what it means to be driving under a mountain for 15 miles. To keep people awake, three rest chambers, each illuminated by a differently colored light, break up the drive visually. Stop and get out—if no cars are coming, test the acoustics from the center.

The second, immeasurably more scenic route is a breathtaking one-hour, 30-mile drive that winds over a pass into Aurland, cresting at over 4,000 feet and offering classic aerial fjord views (it's worth the messy pants). From the Mannheller-Fodnes ferry, take the first road to the right (to Erdal), then leave E-68 at Erdal (just west of Lærdal) for the Aurlandsvegen. This road, while well-maintained, is open only in summer, and narrow and dangerous during snowstorms (which can hit with a moment's notice, even in warm weather). Even in good weather, parts of the road can be a white-knuckle adventure, especially when meeting oncoming vehicles on the tiny, exposed hairpin turns. You'll enjoy vast and terrifying views of lakes, snowfields, and remote mountain huts and farmsteads on what feels like the top of Norway. As you begin the 12-hairpin zigzag descent to Aurland, you'll reach the sideways 7-shaped **Stegastein viewpoint**—well worth a stop. The "Snow Road" and viewpoint are both described on page 317.

▲From the Lustrafjord to Bergen, via Nærøyfjord and Gudvangen

Car ferries take tourists between Kaupanger and the Nutshell town of Gudvangen through an arm and elbow of the Sognefjord, including the staggering Nærøyfjord (for details on the ferry, see "Lustrafjord Connections," earlier). From Gudvangen, it's a 90-mile drive to Bergen via Voss (figure about one hour to Voss, then about an hour and a half into Bergen). This follows essentially the same route as the Norway in a Nutshell (Gudvangen-Voss bus, Voss-Bergen train) route. For additional commentary on the journey, see page 310.

Get off the ferry in Gudvangen and drive up the Nærøy valley past a river. You'll see the two giant falls and then go uphill through a tunnel. After the tunnel, look for a sign marked *Stalheim* and turn right. Stop for a break at the touristy Stalheim Hotel to enjoy the fabulous view down the valley. Then follow signs marked *Stalheimskleiva*. This incredible road doggedly worms its way downhill back into the depths of the valley. My brakes started overheating in a few minutes. Take it easy. As you wind down, you can view the falls from several turnouts.

The road rejoins E-16. You retrace your route through the tunnel and then continue into a mellower beauty, past lakes and farms, toward Voss. Just before you reach Voss itself, watch the right side of the road for Tvindefossen, a terraced waterfall with a handy campground/WC/kiosk picnic area that's worth a stop. Highway E-16 takes you through Voss and into Bergen. If you plan to visit Edvard Grieg's Home and the nearby Fantoft Stave Church, now is the ideal time, since you'll be driving near them—and they're a headache to reach from downtown. Both are worth a detour if you're not rushed (see the Bergen chapter).

▲▲From Balestrand to Bergen, via Vik

If you're based in Balestrand and driving to Bergen, you have two options: Take the Dragsvik-Hella ferry, drive an hour to Kaupanger (via Sogndal), and drive the route just described; or, take the following slower, twistier, more remote, and more scenic route, with a stop at the beautiful Hopperstad Stave Church. This route is slightly longer, with more time on mountain roads and less time on the boat. Take the Hella-Vangsnes ferry, then figure 15 minutes from Vangsnes to Vik, then about 1.5 hours to Voss, then another 1.5 hours into Bergen.

From Vangsnes, head into Vik on the main highway 13. In Vik, follow signs from the main road to Hopperstad Stave Church (described earlier in this chap-

ter). Then backtrack to highway 13 and follow it south, to Voss. You'll soon begin a series of switchbacks that wind you up and out of the valley. The best views are from the Storesvin-gen Fjellstove restaurant (on the left). Soon after, you'll crest the ridge, go through a tunnel, and find yourself on top of the world, in a desolate and harshly scenic landscape of scrubby mountaintops, snowbanks, lakes, and no trees, scattered with vacation cabins. After cruising atop the plateau for a while, the road twists its way down (next to a waterfall) into a very steep valley, which it meanders through the rest of the way to Voss. This is an hour-long, middle-of-nowhere journey, with few road signs—you might feel lost, but keep driving toward Voss. When highway 13 dead-ends into E-16, turn right (toward Voss and Bergen) and re-enter civilization. From here, the route follows the same roads as in the Lustrafjord-Bergen drive described earlier (including the Tvindefossen waterfall).

GUDBRANDSDAL VALLEY & JOTUNHEIMEN MOUNTAINS

Lillehammer • Lom • Drive and Hikes

Norway in a Nutshell is a great day trip (see earlier chapter), but with more time and a car, consider a scenic meander from Oslo to Bergen. You'll arc up the Gudbrandsdal Valley and over the Jotunheimen Mountains, then travel along the Lustrafjord.

After an introductory stop in Lillehammer, with its fine folk museum, you might spend the night in a log and sod farmstead-turned-hotel, tucked in a quiet valley under Norway's highest peaks. Next, Norway's highest pass takes you on an exhilarating roller-coaster ride through the heart of the myth-inspiring Jotunheimen, bristling with Norway's biggest mountains. Then the road hairpins down into Sognefjord country (covered in the previous chapter).

PLANNING YOUR TIME

While you could spend five or six days here, with two days you can cover a good slice of the region. By car, I'd spend them like this:

Day 1: Leave Oslo early, and spend midday at Lillehammer's Mai-haugen open-air folk museum for a tour and picnic. Drive up the Gud-brandsdal Valley, stopping at the stave church in Lom. Stay overnight in the Jotunheimen countryside.

Day 2: Drive the Sognefjell road over the mountains, then down along the Lustrafjord, stopping to visit the

GUDBRANDSDAL

Gudbrandsdal Valley & Jotunheimen Mountains

To Åndalsnes
To Trondheim
E-6
E-136
To Geiranger-fjord
15
Dombås
STAVE CHURCH
● Lom
PEER GYNT SETERVEIEN (TOLL ROAD)
❶ Røisheim
❹
Bøverdal
TOLL ROADS
51
Otta
Gudbrandsdal
Sognefjell
Leirdalen
❸ ❼ ❻
Glitter-tinden
Turtagrø
Kvam
Fortun
❷
TOLL ROAD
▲ Galdhøpiggen
Jotunheimen Mtns.
To Sogndal
55
Skjolden
❽
▲ Kyrkja
Vinstra
Hurrungane Range
Bessvatnet
Besseggen Ridge
Gaupne
Memurubu
Lustrafjord
Gjende ● Maurvangen
PEER GYNT VEIEN (TOLL ROAD)
❺
Tretten
Gjendesheim
51
To Hamar & Oslo
← Sognefjord
E-16
Lillehammer ●
To Myrdal, Voss & Bergen
51
Lake Mjøsa
❶ Røisheim Hotel
❷ Elvesæter Hotel
E-16
To Gjøvik & Oslo
❸ Bøverdalen Youth Hostel
❹ Strind Gard
❺ Besseggen Trailhead
30 Kilometers
❻ Spiterstulen Lodge & Trailhead
30 Miles
To Oslo
❼ Juvasshytta Lodge & Trailhead
❽ Leirvassbu Lodge & Trailhead

Dale Church and the Nigard Glacier (see previous chapter). End your day with an overnight in your choice of fjord towns, such as Solvorn, Balestrand, or Aurland (all described in previous chapters).

This plan can be condensed into one day if you skip the Nigard Glacier side trip.

The Gudbrandsdal Valley

The Gudbrandsdal Valley is the tradition-steeped country of Peer Gynt, the Norwegian Huck Finn. This romantic valley of time-worn hills, log cabins, and velvet farms has connected northern and southern Norway since ancient times. While not as striking as other parts of the Norwegian countryside, Gudbrandsdal offers a suitable first taste of the natural wonders that crescendo farther north and west (in Jotunheimen and the Sognefjord). Throughout this region, the government subsidizes small farms to keep the countryside populated and healthy.

Lillehammer

The de facto capital of the Gudbrandsdal Valley, Lillehammer is a pleasant winter and summer resort town of 27,000. It's best known for its brush with Olympic greatness as the host of the 1994 Winter Olympics.

Orientation to Lillehammer

Today Lillehammer is largely a jumping-off point for Gudbrandsdal Valley adventures, and it's the logical place to break up the long

drive between Oslo and the Jotunheimen region. If you do have time to spare here, spend it at the excellent Maihaugen open-air folk museum. The town itself has happy, old woody pedestrian zones (Gagata and Storgata) to stroll.

Tourist Information: Lillehammer's TI is inside the train station (Mon-Fri 8:00-18:00, Sat-Sun 10:00-16:00; shorter hours and closed Sun off-season; Jernbanetorget 2, +47 61 28 98 00, www.lillehammer.com).

Sights in Lillehammer

Lillehammer's two most worthwhile sights, Maihaugen and the Olympics Museum, are up the hill behind the center of town. From the train station, it's a fairly steep 15-minute walk to either sight, and the route is not well signed. To avoid this walk, consider catching the bus from in front of the train station (bus #002, #004, or #005 to Olympics Museum, 2/hour; bus #007 to Maihaugen, 1/hour; 37 NOK one-way for either bus). At the top, it's a 10-minute, mostly level walk between the two sights (follow the busy main road that connects them).

▲▲Maihaugen Open-Air Folk Museum
(Maihaugen Friluftsmuseet)

This idyllic park, full of old farmhouses and pickled slices of folk culture, provides a good introduction to what you'll see as you drive through the Gudbrandsdal Valley. Anders Sandvig, a local dentist, started the collection in 1887 (he originally displayed artifacts in his waiting room). You'll divide your time between the fine indoor museum at the entrance and the sprawling exterior exhibits.

Upon arrival, ask about special events, crafts, or musical performances. A monitor shows what's going on in the park. Summer is busy with crafts in action and people re-enacting life in the past, à la Colonial Williamsburg. There are no tours, so it's up to you to initiate conversations with the "residents." Off-season it's pretty dead, with no live crafts and most buildings locked up.

Cost and Hours: 175 NOK in summer, 135 NOK off-season; discount when combined with Olympics Museum; daily 10:00-17:00; Sept-May Tue-Sun 11:00-16:00, closed Mon; paid parking, scant English descriptions—consider purchasing the English guidebook; +47 61 28 89 00, www.maihaugen.no.

Visiting the Museum: The outdoor section, with 200 buildings from the Gudbrandsdal region, is divided into three areas: the Rural Collection, with old sod-roof log houses and a stave church; the Town Collection, with reconstructed bits of old-time Lillehammer; and the Residential Area, with 20th-century houses that look like most homes in today's Norway. The time trip can be jarring: In the 1980s house, a bubble-gum-chewing girl enthuses about her new "wireless" TV remote and plays ABBA tunes from a cassette-tape player.

The museum's excellent "We Won the Land" exhibit (at the entry) sweeps you through Norwegian history from the Ice Age to the Space Age. The Gudbrandsdal art section shows village life at its best. And you can walk through Dr. Sandvig's old dental office and the original shops of various crafts- and tradespeople.

Though the museum welcomes picnickers and has a simple cafeteria, Lillehammer's town center (a 15-minute walk below the museum) has lots of fun eateries and is better for lunch.

Norwegian Olympics Museum (Norges Olympiske Museum)

This cute museum is housed in the huge Olympic ice-hockey arena, Håkon Hall. With brief English explanations, an emphasis on Norwegians and Swedes, and an endearingly gung-ho Olympic spirit, it's worth a visit on a rainy day or for sports fans. The ground-floor exhibit traces the ancient history of the Olympics, then devotes one wall panel to each of the summer and winter Olympiads of the modern era (with special treatment for the 1952 Oslo games). Upstairs, walk the entire concourse, circling the arena seating while reviewing the highlights (and lowlights) of the 1994 games (remember Tonya Harding?). While you're up there, check out the gallery of great Norwegian athletes and the giant egg used in the Lillehammer opening ceremony.

Cost and Hours: 135 NOK, discount when combined with Maihaugen; daily 10:00-17:00; Sept-May Tue-Sun 11:00-16:00, closed Mon; +47 61 28 89 00, https://eng.ol.museum.no.

Nearby: On the hillside above Håkon Hall (a 30-minute hike or quick drive) are two ski jumps that host more Olympics sights, including a ski lift, the ski jump tower, and a bobsled ride (www.olympiaparken.no). In the summer, ski jumpers practice on the jumps, which are sprayed with water.

Sleeping and Eating in the Gudbrandsdal Valley

I prefer sleeping in the more scenic and Norwegian-feeling Jotunheimen area (described later). But if you're sleeping here, Lillehammer and the surrounding valley offer several good options. My choices for Lillehammer are near the train station; the accommodations in Kvam provide a convenient stopping point in the valley.

IN LILLEHAMMER

Sleeping: True to its name, **$$ Mølla Hotell** is situated in an old mill along the little stream running through Lillehammer. The 58 rooms blend Old World charm with modern touches. It's more cutesy-cozy and less businesslike than other Lillehammer hotels in this price range (elevator, a block below Gågata at Elvegata 12, +47 61 05 70 80, www.mollahotell.no, post@mollahotell.no).

$$ First Hotel Breiseth is a business-class hotel with 89 rooms in a handy location directly across from the train station (free parking, Jernbanegaten 1, +47 61 24 77 77, www.firsthotels.no/breiseth, breiseth@firsthotels.no).

¢ Vandrerhjem Stasjonen, Lillehammer's youth hostel, is upstairs inside the train station. With 100 beds in 33 institutional but new-feeling rooms—including 21 almost hotel-like doubles—it's a winner (elevator, Jernbanetorget 2, +47 61 26 00 24, www.stasjonen.no, lillehammer@hihostels.no).

Eating: Good restaurants are scattered around the city center, but for the widest selection, head to where the main pedestrian drag (Gågata) crosses the little stream running downhill through town. Poke a block or two up and down **Elvegata,** which stretches along the river and hosts a wide range of tempting eateries—from pubs (both rowdy and upscale) to pizza and cheap sandwich stands.

IN KVAM

Gudbrandsdal is a popular vacation valley for Norwegians, and you'll find loads of reasonable small hotels and campgrounds with huts for those who aren't quite campers (*hytter* means "cottages" or "cabins," *rom* is "private room," and *ledig* means "vacancy"). These huts normally cost about 400-600 NOK, depending on size and amenities, and can hold from four to six people. Although they are simple, you'll have a kitchenette and access to a good WC and shower. When available, sheets rent for around 60 NOK per person. Here are a couple of listings in the town of Kvam, located midway between Lillehammer and Lom.

$$ Vertshuset Sinclair has a quirky Scottish-Norwegian ambience. The 15 fine rooms are in old-fashioned motel wings. The motel was named after a Scotsman who led a band of adventurers into this valley, attempting to set up their own Scottish kingdom. They failed. All were kilt (family deals, +47 61 29 54 50, www.vertshuset-sinclair.no, post@vertshuset-sinclair.no). The motel's **$$ cafeteria,** in the main building, is handy for a quick and filling bite on the road between Lillehammer and Lom (long hours daily).

¢ Kirketeigen Ungdomssenter ("Church Youth Center"), behind the town church, welcomes travelers year-round. They have camping spots, small cabins without water, cabins with kitchen and bath, plus simple four-bed rooms in the main building (sheets and blankets extra, +47 61 21 60 90, www.kirketeigen.com, post@kirketeigen.no).

Jotunheimen Mountains

Norway's Jotunheimen ("Giants' Home") Mountains feature the country's highest peaks and some of its best hikes and drives. This national park stretches from the fjords to the glaciers. You can play roller-coaster with mountain passes, take rugged hikes, wind up scenic toll roads, get up close to a giant stave church...and sleep in a time-passed rural valley. The gateway to the mountains is the unassuming town of Lom.

Lom

Pleasant Lom—the main town between Lillehammer and Sogndal—feels like a modern ski resort village. It's home to one of Norway's most impressive stave churches. While Lom has little else to offer, the church causes the closest thing to a tour-bus traffic jam this neck of the Norwegian woods will ever see.

Orientation to Lom

Park by the stave church—you'll see its dark spire just over the bridge. The church shares a parking lot with a gift shop/church museum and some public WCs. Across the street, the sod-roofed building houses the Norwegian Mountain Museum, and over the river is the TI and Co-op Mega grocery store. If you're heading over the mountains, Lom's bank (at the Kommune building) has the last ATM before Gaupne.

Tourist Information: Lom's TI, a good source of information for hikes and drives in the Jotunheimen Mountains, is near the roundabout (Mon-Sat 9:00-21:00, Sun 10:00-18:00, +47 61 21 29 90, www.visitjotunheimen.no, info@visitjotunheimen.no).

Sights in Lom

▲▲Lom Stave Church (Lom Stavkyrkje)

Despite extensive renovations, Lom's church (from 1158) remains a striking example of a Nordic stave church. For more on these distinctive medieval churches, see page 318.

Cost and Hours: Church—90 NOK, daily 9:00-19:00 (until 17:00 last half of Aug), mid-May-mid-June and Sept 10:00-16:00, closed in winter and for funerals; museum—10 NOK, same summer hours as church, shorter hours off-season, closed Sun in winter; +47 40 43 84 86, www.lomstavechurch.no.

Tours: Try to tag along with a guided tour of the church—or, if it's not too busy, a docent can give you a quick private tour (included in ticket). Even outside of opening times—including winter—small groups can arrange a tour (60 NOK/person, 600-NOK minimum, call +47 97 07 53 97 in summer or +48 16 55 27 00 in winter).

Visiting the Church: Buy your ticket and go inside to take in the humble **interior** (still used by locals for services—notice the posted hymnal numbers). Men sat on the right, women on the left, and prisoners sat with the sheriff in the caged area in the rear. Standing in the middle of the nave, look overhead to see the earliest surviving parts of the church, such as the circle of X-shaped St. Andrew crosses and the Romanesque arches above them. High above the door (impossible to see without a flashlight—ask a docent to show you) is an old painting of a dragon- or lion-like creature—likely an old Viking symbol, possibly drawn here to smooth the forced conversion local pagans made to Christianity. When King Olav II (later to become St. Olav) swept through this valley in 1021, he gave locals an option: convert or be burned out of house and home.

On the white town flag, notice the spoon—a symbol of Lom. Because of its position nestled in the mountains, Lom gets less rainfall than other towns, so large spoons were traditionally used to spread water over the fields. The apse (behind the altar) was added in 1240, when trendy new Gothic cathedrals made an apse a must-have accessory for churches across Europe. Lepers came to the grilled window in the apse for a blessing. When the Reformation hit in 1536, the old paintings were whitewashed over. The church has changed over the years: Transepts, pews, and windows were added in the 17th century. And the circa-1720 paintings were done by a local priest's son.

Drop into the **gift shop/church museum** in the big black building in the parking lot. Its one-room exhibit celebrates 1,000 years of the stave church—interesting if you follow the loaner English descriptions. Inside you'll find a pair of beautiful model churches, headstones and other artifacts, and the only surviving stave-church dragon-head "steeple." In the display case near the early 1900s organ, find the little pencil-size stick carved with runes, dating from around 1350. It's actually a love letter from a would-be suitor. The woman rejected him, but she saved them both from embarrassment by hiding the stick under the church floorboards beneath a pew...where it was found in 1973. (Docents inside the church like to show off a replica of this stick.)

Before or after your church visit, explore the tidy, thought-provoking **graveyard** surrounding the church. Also, check out the precarious-looking little footbridge over the waterfall (the best view is from the modern road bridge into town).

Norwegian Mountain Museum (Norsk Fjellmuseum)

This worthwhile museum traces the history of the people who have lived off the land in the Jotunheimen Mountains from the Stone Age to today (and also serves as a national park office). It is one of the better museums in fjord country, with well-presented displays and plenty of actual artifacts. The exhibit, "Spellbound" (Bergtatt), explores prehistoric human and animal migrations in the surrounding mountains based on recent archaeological finds, including a 1,300-year-old ski and a 3,400-year-old shoe made of reindeer hide.

Cost and Hours: 120 NOK; daily 9:00-16:00, July-mid-Aug until 19:00, generally closed off-season; in the sod-roofed building across the road from the Lom Stave Church parking lot, +47 61 21 16 00, http://fjell.museum.no.

Sleeping near Lom

Lom itself has a handful of hotels, but the most appealing way to overnight in this area is at a rural rest stop in the countryside. All of these are on highway 55 south of Lom, toward Sognefjord—first is Strind Gard, then Bøverdalen, Røisheim, and finally Elvesæter (all within 20 minutes of Lom).

$$$$ **Røisheim,** in a marvelously remote mountain setting, is an extremely expensive storybook hotel composed of a cluster of

centuries-old, sod-roofed log farmhouses. Its posh and generous living rooms are filled with antiques. Each of the 20 rooms (in 14 buildings) is rustic but elegant, with fun "barrel bathtubs" and four-poster or canopy beds. Some rooms are in old, wooden farm buildings—*stabburs*—with low ceilings and heavy beams. The deluxe rooms are larger, with king beds and fireplaces. Call ahead so they'll be prepared for your arrival (open May-Sept; packed lunch, and an over-the-top four-course traditional dinner served at 19:30; 10 miles south of Lom on highway 55, +47 61 21 20 31, www.roisheim.no, booking@roisheim.no).

$$ **Elvesæter Hotel** has its own share of Old World romance, but is bigger, cheaper, and more modest. Delightful public spaces bunny-hop through its traditional shell, while its 200 beds sprawl through nine buildings. The Elvesæter family has done a great job of retaining the historic character of their medieval farm, even though the place is big enough to handle large tour groups. The renovated "superior" rooms are new-feeling, but have sterile modern furniture; the older, cheaper "standard" rooms are well-worn but more characteristic (open May-Sept, family rooms, good three-course dinners, swimming pool, farther up highway 55, just past Bøverdal, +47 61 21 12 10, www.topofnorway.no, elveseter@topofnorway.no). Even if you're not staying here, stop by to wander through the public spaces and pick up a flier explaining the towering Sagasøyla (Saga Column) that stands on the grounds. It was started in 1926 to celebrate the Norwegian constitution, and was to stand in front of Oslo's parliament building—but the project stalled after World War II (thanks to the artist's affinity for things

German and membership in Norway's fascist party). It was eventually finished and erected here in 1992.

¢ **Bøverdalen Youth Hostel** offers cheap but comfortable beds and a far more rugged clientele—real hikers rather than car hikers. While a bit institutional, it's well priced and well run (open late May-Sept, sheets extra, breakfast extra, hot meals, self-serve café, +47 61 21 20 64, www.hihostels.no, boverdalen@hihostels.no, Anna Berit). It's in the center of the little community of Bøverdal (store, campground, and toll road up to Galdhøpiggen area).

¢ **Strind Gard** is your very rustic option if you can't spring for Røisheim or Elvesæter, but still want the countryside-farm experience. This 150-year-old farmhouse, situated by a soothing waterfall, rents two rooms and one apartment, plus four sod-roofed log huts. The catch: Many of the buildings have no running water, so you'll use the shared facilities at the main building. While not everyone's cup of tea, this place will appeal to romantics who always wanted to sleep in a humble log cabin in the Norwegian mountains—it's downright idyllic for those who like to rough it (sheets and towels extra, no breakfast, low ceilings, farm smells, valley views, 2 miles south of Lom on highway 55, +47 61 21 12 37, www.strind-gard.no, post@strind-gard.no, Anne Jorunn and Trond Dalsegg).

Drives and Hikes in the Jotunheimen Mountains

Highway 55, which runs between Lom and the Sognefjord to the south, is the sightseeing spine of this region. From this main (and already scenic) drag, other roads spin upward into the mountains—offering even better views and exciting drives and hikes. Many of these get you up close to Norway's highest mountain, Galdhøpiggen (8,100 feet). I've listed these attractions from north to south, as you'll reach them driving from Lom to the Sognefjord; except for the first, they all branch off from highway 55. Another great high-mountain experience nearby—the hike to the Nigard Glacier near Lustrafjord—is covered in the previous chapter.

Remember that the Norwegian Mountain Museum in Lom acts as a national park office, offering excellent maps and advice for drivers and hikers—a stop here is obligatory if you're planning a jaunt into the mountains.

Besseggen Trail

This trail offers an incredible opportunity to walk between two lakes separated by a narrow ridge and a 1,000-foot cliff. It's one of Norway's most beloved hikes, which can make it crowded in the summer. To get to the trailhead, drivers detour down highway 51 after Otta south to Maurvangen. Turn right to Gjendesheim to park your car. From Gjendesheim, catch the boat to Memurubu, where the path starts at the boat dock. Hike along the ridge—with a blue lake (Bessvatnet) on one side and a green lake (Gjende) on the other—and keep your balance. The nine-mile trail loops back to Gjendesheim; plan on a seven- to eight-hour hike. Because the boat runs sporadically, time your visit to catch one (150 NOK for 20-minute ride, 3 morning departures daily, check schedules at www.gjende.no, mobile +47 91 30 67 44). This is a thrilling but potentially hazardous hike, and it's a major detour: Gjendesheim is about 1.5 hours and 50 miles from Lom.

Spiterstulen Drive and Hikes

From Røisheim, an 11-mile toll road (80 NOK) takes you from highway 55 to the Spiterstulen mountain hotel/lodge (3,600 feet) in about 30 minutes. This is the best destination for serious all-day hikes to Norway's two mightiest mountains, Glittertinden and Galdhøpiggen (a 5-hour hike up and a 3-hour hike down, doable without a guide). Or consider a guided, two-hour glacier walk (+47 61 21 94 00, www.spiterstulen.no).

Juvasshytta Drive and Glacier Hike

From Bøverdal, a private toll road (85 NOK) takes you in about 40 minutes to Juvasshytta lodge, the highest (6,040 feet) and closest you can get to Galdhøpiggen by car. From the lodge, guided, six-hour hikes go across the glacier to the summit and back (350 NOK, June-late Sept daily at 10:00, July also daily at 11:30, check in 30 minutes before, strict age limit—no kids under age 7, 4 miles each way, easy ascent but can be dangerous without a guide, hiking boots required—possible to rent from nearby ski resort). You can sleep in the updated **$$** lodge (includes breakfast, dinner optional, open June-Sept, +47 61 21 15 50, www.juvasshytta.no).

Leirvassbu Drive and Hikes

South of Elvesæter (from Bøverkinnhalsen), a scenic 11-mile toll road (50 NOK) takes you in about 30 minutes to the Leirvassbu mountain lodge at 4,600 feet, with great views and easy walks. A more serious six-mile round-trip hike goes to the lone peak, Kyrkja ("The Church", 6,600 feet), whose spire looms like a sanded-down Matterhorn on the horizon (allow 5 hours).

▲▲Sognefjell Drive to the Sognefjord

Norway's highest pass (at 4,600 feet, the highest road in northern Europe) is a thrilling drive through a cancan line of mountains, from Jotunheimen's Bøverdal Valley to the Lustrafjord (an arm of the Sognefjord). Centuries ago, the farmers of Gudbrandsdal took their horse caravans over this difficult mountain pass on treks to Bergen. Today, the road (highway 55) is still narrow, windy, and wild (and usually closed mid-Oct-May).

As you begin to ascend just beyond Elvesæter, notice the viewpoint on the left for the Leirdalen Valley—capped at the end with the Kyrkja peak (described earlier). Next you'll twist up into a lake-filled valley, then through a mild canyon with grand waterfalls. Before long, as you corkscrew up more switchbacks, you're above the tree line, enjoying a "top of the world" feeling. The best views (to the south) are of the cut-glass range called Hurrungane ("Noisy Children"). The 10 hairpin turns between Turtagrø and Fortun are exciting. Be sure to stop, get out, look around, and enjoy the lavish views. Treat each turn as if it were your last.

Just before you descend to the fjord, the terrain changes, and you reach a pullout on the right, next to a hilltop viewpoint—offering your first glimpse of the fjord. The Lustrafjord village of Skjolden is just around the bend (and down several more switchbacks). Entering Skjolden, continue following highway 55, which now traces the west bank of the Lustrafjord. For more on the sights from here on out, turn to page 342.

Gudbrandsdal and Jotunheimen Connections

BY TRAIN AND BUS

Cars are better, but if you're without wheels, here are your options: Trains run from **Oslo to Lillehammer** (almost hourly, 2.25 hours, just 1.75 hours from Oslo airport) and from **Lillehammer to Otta** (5/day, 1.5 hours). Buses meet some trains (confirm schedule at the train station in Oslo) for travelers heading from **Otta to Lom** (1-2/day, 1 hour) and onward from **Lom to Sogndal** (1-2/day late June-Aug only, road closed off-season, 3.5 hours).

ROUTE TIPS FOR DRIVERS

Use low gears and lots of patience both up (to keep the engine cool) and down (to save your brakes). Uphill traffic gets the right-of-way, but drivers, up or down, dive for the nearest fat part of the road whenever they meet. Ask backseat drivers not to scream until you've actually been hit or have left the road.

It's 2.5 hours from Oslo to Lillehammer and 3 hours after that to Lom.

From Oslo to Lillehammer: Wind out of Oslo following signs for *E-6* (not to *Drammen,* but for *Stockholm* and then to *Trondheim*). In a few minutes, you're in the wide-open pastoral countryside of eastern Norway. Norway's Constitution Hall—Eidsvoll Manor— is a five-minute detour off E-6, several miles south of Eidsvoll in Eidsvoll Verk (described on page 273; follow the signs to *Eids-voll Bygningen*). Then E-6 takes you along Norway's largest lake (Mjøsa), through the town of Hamar, and past more lake scenery into Lillehammer. Signs direct you uphill from downtown Lille-hammer to the Maihaugen open-air folk museum.

From Lillehammer to Jotunheimen: From Lillehammer, signs to *E-6/Trondheim* take you north, up the bucolic valley of

Gudbrandsdal (en route to Otta and Lom), with fine but unremarkable scenery. Along the way, a pair of toll-road side-trips (Gynt Veien and Peer Gynt Seterveien) loop off the E-6 road. While they sound romantic, they're basically windy, curvy dirt

roads over high, desolate heath and scrub-brush plateaus with fine mountain views. They're scenic, but pale in comparison with the Sognefjell road between Lom and the Lustrafjord (described ear-lier). At Otta, exit for Lom. Halfway to Lom, on the left, look for the long suspension bridge spanning the milky-blue river—a good opportunity to stretch your legs, and a scenic spot to enjoy a picnic.

BERGEN

Bergen is permanently salted with robust cobbles and a rich sea-trading heritage. Norway's capital in the 13th century, Bergen gained wealth and importance thanks to its membership in the heavyweight medieval trading club of merchant cities called the Hanseatic League. Bergen still wears her rich maritime heritage proudly—nowhere more scenically than at the picture-perfect Bryggen district, where colorful wooden warehouses line the harbor.

Protected from the open sea by a lone sheltering island, Bergen is a place of refuge from heavy winds for the giant working boats that serve the North Sea oil rigs. (Much of Norway's current affluence is funded by the oil it drills just offshore.) Bergen is also one of the most popular cruise-ship ports in northern Europe, hosting over 300 ships a year and up to five ships a day in peak season. Each morning is rush hour, as cruisers hike past the imposing Bergenhus fortress and into town.

Bergen gets an average of 80 inches of rain annually (compared to 30 inches in Oslo). A good year has 60 days of sunshine. The natives aren't apologetic about their famously lousy weather. In fact, they seem to wear it as a badge of pride. "Well, that's Bergen," they'll say matter-of-factly as they wring out their raincoats. When I complained about an all-day downpour, one resident cheerfully informed me, "There's no such thing as bad weather—just inappropriate clothing"...a local mantra that rhymes in Norwegian.

With about 280,000 people, Bergen has big-city traffic and high prices, but visitors sticking to the old center find it charming. Enjoy Bergen's salty market, then stroll the easy-on-foot old quarter, with cute lanes of delicate old wooden houses. From downtown

Bergen, a funicular zips you up a little mountain for a bird's-eye view of this sailors' town. A short foray into the countryside takes you to a variety of nearby experiences: a dramatic cable-car ride to a mountaintop perch (Ulriken643); an evocative stave church (Fantoft); and the home of Norway's most beloved composer, Edvard Grieg, at Troldhaugen.

PLANNING YOUR TIME

Bergen is worth at least one full day. It can even be enjoyed on the tail end of a day's scenic train ride from Oslo before returning on the overnight train. But that teasing taste will make you wish you had more time.

Bergen in One Day

For a busy day, you could do this:

9:00   Stroll through the Fish Market and Bryggen shops.

10:00   Take the Bryggen Walking Tour (mid-May–mid-Sept; reserve ahead), then grab lunch. Consider returning to the Bryggens Museum using your tour ticket while you're in the area.

14:00   Visit Håkon's Hall and Rosenkrantz Tower (joining a guided tour).

15:00   Stroll through Torgallmenningen square to the KODE Art Museums to see works by famous Norwegian landscape artists and Edvard Munch.

17:00   Enjoy some free time in town, or catch the bus out to Gamle Bergen.

18:00   Ride up the Fløibanen funicular (buy ticket online to avoid the line).

More Bergen Planning Tips

Although Bergen has plenty of charms of its own, it's most famous as a springboard for fjord country. You have three options: Pick up a rental car here (fjords are a 3-hour drive away); take the express boat down the Sognefjord (about 4 hours to Balestrand, 5.5 hours to Flåm/Aurland); or do "Norway in a Nutshell" as a scenic loop from Bergen. The Nutshell option also works well as a detour midway between Bergen and Oslo (hop the train from either city to Voss or Myrdal, then take a bus or spur train into the best of the Sognefjord; scenic ferry rides depart from there). While there are a million ways to enjoy the fjords, first-timers should start with this region (covered thoroughly in the Norway in a Nutshell and More on the Sognefjord chapters).

Also note that Bergen, a geographic dead-end, is an efficient place to begin or end your Scandinavian travels. Consider flying into Bergen and out of another city, such as Helsinki (or vice versa).

Orientation to Bergen

Bergen clusters around its harbor—nearly everything listed in this chapter is within a few minutes' walk. The busy Torget (the square with the Fish Market) is at the head of the harbor. As you face the sea from here, Bergen's TI is at the left end of the Fish Market. The town's historic Hanseatic Quarter, Bryggen (BRUHY-gun), lines the harbor on the right. Express boats to the Sognefjord (Balestrand and Flåm) dock at the harbor on the left.

Charming cobbled streets surround the harbor and climb the

encircling hills. Bergen's
popular Fløibanen funicu-
lar climbs high above the
city to the top of Mount
Fløyen for the best view
of the town. Surveying
the surrounding islands
and inlets, it's clear why
this city is known as the
"Gateway to the Fjords."

TOURIST INFORMATION

The centrally located TI is upstairs in the long, skinny, modern
Torghallen market building, next to the Fish Market (daily June-
Aug 8:30-22:00, May and Sept 9:00-20:00; Oct-April 9:00-16:00;
handy budget eateries downstairs and in Fish Market; +47 55 55 20
00, www.visitbergen.com).

The TI covers Bergen and western Norway, provides tour info
and tickets, has a fjord info desk, books rooms, will exchange currency, and maintains a handy events board listing today's and to-
morrow's slate of tours, concerts, and other events. Pick up this
year's edition of the free *Bergen Guide* (also likely at your hotel),
which includes a fine map. This booklet can answer most of your
sightseeing questions.

Bergen Card: You have to work hard to make this greedy
little card pay off (280 NOK/24 hours, 360 NOK/48 hours, 430
NOK/72 hours; sold at the TI, the Deli de Luca store at the Bergen
airport, and the Montana Family & Youth Hostel). It gives you free
use of the city's tram and buses, half off the Fløibanen funicular,
and free or discounted admission to many sights. For details on
what's covered, see the TI website.

ARRIVAL IN BERGEN

By Train or Bus: Bergen's train and bus stations are on Strømgat-
en, facing a park-rimmed lake. The small, manageable train station
is open long hours for booking all your travel in Norway, including
Nutshell reservations if available—and you haven't reserved ahead
(Mon-Fri 6:45-19:15, Sat-Sun 7:30-16:00). You'll find the usual
train station amenities, pay baggage lockers (daily 6:00-23:30), and
pay WCs. To get to the bus station, follow the covered walkway
behind the Narvesen newsstand via the Storsenter shopping mall.

Taxis wait to the right (with the tracks at your back); a tram
stop is to your left, just around the corner. From the train station,
it's a 10-minute walk to the TI: Cross the street (Strømgaten) in
front of the station and take Marken, a cobbled street that eventu-

Bergen

To Norwegian Fisheries Museum

SKOLTEN CRUISE TERMINAL

SKOLTEGRUNNS-KAIEN

INTERNATIONAL FERRIES

NORDNES

585

BERGENHUS FORTRESS

HÅKON'S HALL

FESTNINGS-KAIEN

TOTEM POLE

AQUARIUM

15

STRANDGATEN

C. SUNDTS GATE

HARBOR FERRIES

ROSEN-KRANTZ TOWER

POOL

HAUGEVEIEN

STRANDSIDEN

NYKIRKEN

SWIMMING BEACH

Nordnesparken

NORDNESVEIEN

C. SUNDTS GATE

STRANDGATEN

Puddefjorden

HAUGEVEIEN

HOLBERGSALLM

KLOSTERGATEN

SKOTTEGATEN

NØSTEGATEN

ENGEN

HURTIGRUTEN TERMINAL (COASTAL CRUISES)

NØSTEGATTEN

555

JEKTEVIKEN/DOKKEN CRUISE PORT

TORBORG NEDREAASGATE

Walk

1. Bergenhus Fortress
2. Bergenhus Rampart Perch
3. St. Mary's Church
4. Bryggens Museum
5. Hanseatic Quarter & Hanseatic Museum
6. Fish Market
7. Seafarers' Monument
8. Torgallmenningen (Main Square)
9. Ole Bulls Plass

Additional Sights

10. Theta Museum
11. Fløibanen Funicular
12. Cathedral
13. Leprosy Museum
14. KODE Art Museums
15. Aquarium
16. To Gamle Bergen
17. Bus to Ulriken643 Cable Car
18. Bybanen Tram to Troldhaugen, Fantoft Stave Church & Airport
19. Bus to Jekteviken/Dokken Cruise Port

BERGEN

BERGEN

ally turns into a modern retail street. Continue walking in the same direction until you reach the water.

By Plane: Bergen's sleek and modern Flesland Airport is 12 miles south of the city center (code: BGO, +47 67 03 11 00, www.avinor.no/bergen). The airport **bus** runs between the airport and downtown Bergen, stopping at the Radisson Blu Royal Hotel in Bryggen, the harborfront area near the TI (if you ask), Festplassen (in the modern part of town, near Ole Bulls Plass), and the bus station (about 120 NOK, pay driver, 6/hour at peak times, fewer in slow times, 30-minute ride). **Taxis** take up to four people and cost about 400 NOK for the 20-minute ride (depending on time of day).

The cheapest option is to take the Bybanen **tram** to the end of the line at Byparken (38 NOK, departs every 5-10 minutes, 45-minute trip, schedule at www.skyss.no). This stop—on Kaigaten, between Bergen's little lake and Ole Bulls Plass—is several blocks from most of my recommended hotels. For tram ticket details, see "Getting Around Bergen," later.

By Car: Driving is a headache in Bergen; avoid it if you can. Approaching town on E-16 (from Voss and the Sognefjord area), follow signs for *Sentrum,* which spits you out near the big, modern bus station and parking garage. Parking is difficult and costly—ask your hotelier for tips. Note that Bergen collects a congestion toll on cars entering the city (25 NOK, 51 NOK during rush hour; fee collected via transponder—your car-rental company will bill you).

By Cruise Ship: Bergen is easy for cruise passengers, regardless of which of the city's two ports your ship uses. The **Skolten** cruise terminal is on the main harborfront road, a 15-minute walk from the Fish Market and TI. On the way, you'll pass the Bergenhus fortress—the starting point for my self-guided walk. The **Jekteviken/Dokken** cruise port is farther out, south of the center. A free shuttle bus drops you off along Rasmus Meyers Allé in front of the KODE Art Museums (and near the end of my self-guided walk). For more in-depth cruising information, pick up my *Rick Steves Scandinavian & Northern European Cruise Ports* guidebook.

HELPFUL HINTS

Museum Tours: Many of Bergen's sights are barren and hard to appreciate without a guide. Fortunately, several offer wonderful and intimate guided tours. Make the most of the following sights by taking advantage of their tours: Håkon's Hall and Rosenkrantz Tower, Bryggens Museum, Hanseatic Museum (closed through 2024), Leprosy Museum, Gamle Bergen, and Edvard Grieg's Home.

Crowd Control: In high season, cruise-ship passengers mob the waterfront between 10:00 and 15:00; to avoid the crush, consider visiting an outlying sight during this time, such as Gamle Bergen or Edvard Grieg's Home.

Laundry: Drop your laundry off at **Hygienisk Vask & Rens** and pick it up clean the next day (no self-service; Mon-Fri 8:30-16:30, closed Sat-Sun; Halfdan Kjerulfsgate 8, +47 55 31 77 41).

GETTING AROUND BERGEN

Most in-town sights are no more than a 10-minute walk from the TI. But buses and trams come in handy for reaching the aquarium, Norwegian Fisheries Museum, Gamle Bergen, and farther-flung sights such as the Fantoft Stave Church, Edvard Grieg Museum at Troldhaugen, and the Ulriken643 cable car. For schedules and a travel planner, see Skyss.no.

By Bus: City buses cost 60 NOK per ride (pay driver in cash), or 39 NOK per ride if you buy a single-ride ticket from a machine or at a convenience store such as Narvesen, 7-Eleven, Rimi, and Deli de Luca. The best buses for a Bergen joyride are #6 (north along the coast) and #11 (into the hills).

By Tram: Bergen's Bybanen light-rail line is a convenient way to visit Edvard Grieg's home and the Fantoft Stave Church, or to get to Flesland Airport. The tram begins next to Byparken (on Kaigaten, between Bergen's lake and Ole Bulls Plass), then heads to the train station and continues south, ending at the airport. Buy your 39-NOK ticket from the machine before boarding (accepts credit card with PIN or coins). You can also buy single-ride tickets at convenience stores—you'll get a gray *minikort* pass. Validate the pass when you board by holding it next to the card reader (watch how other passengers do it). Ride about 20 minutes to the Paradis stop for **Fantoft** Stave Church (don't get off at the "Fantoft" stop, which is farther from the church); continue to the next stop, Hop, to hike to **Troldhaugen.**

By Ferry: The *Beffen*, a little orange ferry, chugs across the midpoint of the harbor every half-hour, from a dock near the Bryggens Museum to one near the Nykirken church (single ride-65 NOK, day pass-130 NOK, buy tickets onboard or at the dock, Mon-Fri 7:30-16:00, plus Sat May-Aug 11:00-16:00, none on Sun, 4-minute ride). Other ferries run from the Fish Market to the Norwegian Fisheries Museum and the aquarium (details in those sight listings, later). All of these "poor man's cruises" offer good harbor views.

By Taxi: For a local taxi, which can be pricey, call +47 55 99 70 00.

BERGEN

Bergen at a Glance

▲▲▲**Bryggen Walking Tour** Wonderful 1.5-hour tour of the historic Hanseatic district that covers 900 years of history and includes short visits to the Bryggens Museum, Hanseatic Assembly Rooms, Hanseatic Museum, a medieval wine cellar, plus a walk through Bryggen. **Hours:** Mid-May-mid-Sept daily at 10:00, 11:00, and 12:00. See page 374.

▲▲**Bryggens Museum** Featuring early bits of Bergen (1050-1500), found in an archaeological dig. **Hours:** Daily 9:00-16:00; mid-Sept-mid-May 11:00-15:00. See page 386.

▲▲**Hanseatic Museum and Schøtstuene** Museum highlighting Bryggen's glory days, featuring an old merchant house and a separate building housing assembly rooms—most interesting with a guided tour. **Hours:** Daily 10:00-18:00, May and Sept until 17:00, Oct-April 11:00-15:00. See page 387.

▲▲**Fløibanen Funicular** Zippy lift to top of Mount Fløyen for super views of Bergen, islands, and fjords, with picnic ops, an eatery, playground, and hiking trails. **Hours:** Daily 7:30-23:00. See page 390.

▲**Fish Market** Lively market with cheap seafood eateries and free samples. **Hours:** Daily 8:00-23:00; shorter hours Oct-April. See page 383.

▲**Bergenhus Fortress: Håkon's Hall and Rosenkrantz Tower** Fortress with a 13th-century medieval banquet hall, a climbable tower offering a history exhibit and views, and a worthwhile guided tour. **Hours:** daily 10:00-16:00; mid-Sept-mid-May daily 12:00-15:00. See page 385.

Tours in Bergen

▲▲▲Bryggen Walking Tour

This tour of the historic Hanseatic district is one of Bergen's best activities. Local guides take visitors on a 1.5-hour walk in English through 900 years of Bergen history via the old Hanseatic town. You'll spend 20 to 30 minutes at each of the following: Bryggens Museum, medieval Hanseatic Assembly Rooms

▲**St. Mary's Church** Bergen's oldest church, dating to the 12th century. **Hours:** Mon-Fri 10:00-16:00, closed mid-Sept-May. See page 391.

▲**KODE Art Museums** Collection spread among four neighboring lakeside buildings: KODE 4 (international and Norwegian artists), KODE 3 (Norwegian artists, including Munch), KODE 2 (contemporary art), and KODE 1 (decorative arts). **Hours:** Daily 10:00-17:00 (KODE 2 Thu until 20:00), closed Mon mid-Sept-mid-May. See page 392.

▲**Aquarium** Well-presented sea life, with a walk-through "shark tunnel" and feeding times at the top of most hours in summer. **Hours:** Daily 9:00-18:00, Sept-April from 10:00. See page 393.

▲**Gamle Bergen (Old Bergen)** Quaint gathering of 50 homes and shops dating from 18th-20th century, with guided tours of museum interiors at the top of the hour. **Hours:** Daily 10:00-16:00, closed Sept-mid-May. See page 393.

Near Bergen
▲▲**Edvard Grieg Museum, Troldhaugen** Home of Norway's greatest composer, with artifacts, tours, and concerts. **Hours:** Daily 9:00-18:00, Oct-April 10:00-16:00. See page 396.

▲**Ulriken643 Cable Car** A quick ride up to the summit of Ulriken, Bergen's tallest mountain, with nonstop views, a restaurant, and hiking trails. **Hours:** Daily 9:00-21:00, off-season until 17:00. See page 395.

BERGEN

(Schøtstuene), the Bryggen quarter, a medieval wine cellar, and Hanseatic Museum (when it reopens—closed until 2024). Tours leave from the Bryggens Museum (next to the Radisson Blu Royal Hotel). The tour price includes entry tickets to these sights, making it an especially good value (250 NOK; daily at 10:00, 11:00, and 12:00; no tours mid-Sept-mid-May, +47 55 30 80 30, www.bymuseet.no). While the museum visits are a bit rushed, your tour ticket allows you to re-enter the museums for the rest of the day. The tours are popular and can sell out, especially in July; to be safe, buy tickets in advance online or from the reception desk at the Bryggens Museum.

Local Guide

Sue Lindelid is a British expat who has spent more than 25 years showing visitors around Bergen (1,250 NOK/2-hour tour, 1,650 NOK/3-hour tour; mobile +47 90 78 59 52, suelin@hotmail.no).

▲Bus Tours

The TI sells tickets for various bus tours, including a 3.5-hour Grieg Lunch Concert tour that goes to Edvard Grieg's Home at Troldhaugen—a handy way to reach that distant sight (290 NOK, see the listing under "Sights Near Bergen," later). Buses are comfy, with big views and a fine recorded commentary. There are also several full-day tour options from Bergen, including bus/boat tours to nearby Hardanger and Sogne fjords. The TI is packed with brochures describing all the excursions.

Hop-On, Hop-Off Buses

Sightseeing Bergen links most of Bergen's major sights and also stops at the Skolten cruise port, but doesn't go to the Fantoft Stave Church, Troldhaugen, or Ulriken643 cable car. If your sightseeing plans don't extend beyond the walkable core of Bergen, skip this (300 NOK/24 hours, May-mid-Sept 9:00-16:00, every 30 minutes, also stops in front of Fish Market, mobile +47 97 78 18 88, www.sightseeingbergen.no).

Inflatable Boat Tour

After a scenic cruise along the Bergen harborfront, you'll zip out into the open fjord past islands and rocky skerries aboard a fast and breezy **Fjord Tours** rigid inflatable boat (RIB). Before heading out you'll don a survival suit and goggles for the thrilling high-speed part of the journey. Tours last 50 minutes and depart from near the Radisson Blue Royal Hotel (in Bryggen), at Bradbenken 2. Get tickets at the TI (595 NOK, daily at 13:10, www.fjordtours.com).

Bergen Walk

For a quick self-guided orientation stroll through Bergen, follow this walk from the city's fortress, through its old wooden Hanseatic Quarter and Fish Market, to the modern center of town. This walk is also a handy sightseeing spine, passing most of Bergen's best museums; ideally, you'll get sidetracked and take advantage of their excellent tours along the way. I've pointed out the museums you'll pass en route—all are described in greater detail later, under "Sights in Bergen." To trace the route of this walk, see the "Bergen" map, earlier.

• *Begin where Bergen did, at its historic fortress. To get there from the harborfront road, 50 yards before the stone tower with the water on your left, veer up the ramp behind the low stone wall on the right, through a gate, and into the fortress complex. Stand before the stony skyscraper.*

❶ Bergenhus Fortress

In the 13th century, Bergen became the Kingdom of Norway's first real capital. (Before then, kings would circulate, staying on royal farms.) This fortress complex—built in the 1240s and worth ▲— was a garrison, containing a tower for the king's residence (Rosenkrantz Tower) and a large hall for his banquets (Håkon's Hall).

This south end of the fortress complex is marked by **Rosenkrantz Tower,** the keep of the 13th-century castle. It was expanded in the 16th century by the Danish-Norwegian king, who wanted to exercise a little control over the German merchants who dominated his town. He was tired of the Germans making all the money without paying taxes. This tower—with its cannon trained not on external threats but toward Bryggen—while expensive, paid for itself many times over as Germans got the message and paid their taxes.

• *Find the gate 20 yards to the right of the tower, marked 1728. Head through this gate and into the courtyard of the Bergenhus Fortress. In front of you stands Håkon's Hall with its stepped gable. Tours for both the hall and the tower leave from the building to the right of Håkon's Hall.*

Pop into the museum lobby to enjoy a free exhibit about the massive 1944 explosion of the German ammunition ship in the harbor. For the best view of Håkon's Hall, walk through the gate to the left of the building and onto the grassy ramparts between the hall and the harbor.

Håkon's Hall is the largest secular medieval building in Norway. When the pope sent a cardinal to perform Håkon's coronation there was no suitable building in Norway for such a VIP. King Håkon fixed that by having this impressive banqueting hall built in the mid-1200s. When Norway's capital moved to Oslo in 1299, the hall was abandoned and eventually used for grain storage. For a century it had no roof. In the 19th century, it was appreciated and restored. It's essentially a giant, grand reception hall used today just as it was eight centuries ago: for banquets.

• *Continue walking along the rampart (climbing some steps and going about 100 yards past Håkon's Hall) to the far end of Bergenhus Fortress, where you'll find a statue of a king and a fine harbor view.*

❷ Bergenhus Rampart Perch and Statue of King Håkon VII

The cannon on the ramparts here illustrates how the fort protected this strategic harbor. The port is busy with both cruise ships and supply ships for the nearby North Sea oil rigs. Long before this modern commerce, this is where the cod fishermen of the north met the traders of Europe. Travelers in the 12th century described how there were so many trading vessels here "you could cross the harbor without getting your feet wet." Beyond the ships is an island protecting Bergen from the open sea.

Look left and right at the dangerous edge with no railing. If someone were to fall and get hurt here and then try to sue, the Norwegian judge's verdict would be: stupidity—case dismissed. Around you in the distance are Bergen's "seven mountains." One day each summer, locals race to climb each of these in rapid succession, accomplishing the feat in less than 12 hours.

The statue is of the beloved King Håkon VII (1872-1957), grandfather of today's king. While exiled in London during World War II, King Håkon kept up Norwegian spirits through radio broadcasts. The first king of modern Norway (after the country won its independence from Sweden in 1905), he was a Danish prince married to Queen Victoria's granddaughter—a savvy monarch who knew how to play the royalty game.

A few steps behind the statue (just right of tree-lined lane) is the site of Bergen's first cathedral, built in 1070. A hedge grows where its walls once stood. The statue of Mary marks the place of the altar, its pedestal etched with a list of 13th-century kings of Norway crowned and buried here.

These castle grounds (notice the natural amphitheater on the left) host cultural events and music festivals; Elton John, Paul McCartney, and Norwegian DJ Kygo have all packed this outdoor venue.

Continuing around Håkon's Hall, follow the linden tree-lined lane. On the left looms a massive concrete structure disguised by ivy. It was a German bunker built during the Nazi occupation—easier now to ignore than dismantle.

Twenty yards ahead on the right is a rare set of free public toilets. Notice they come with blue lights to discourage heroin junkies from using these WCs as a place to shoot up. The blue lights make it hard to see veins.

• *You've now returned to the tower and circled the castle grounds. Before leaving, consider taking a guided tour of the hall and tower. Otherwise, head back down the ramp, out to the main road, and continue with the harbor on your right. (After a block, history buffs could follow* Bergenhus *signs, up the street to the left, to the free and fascinating* **Fortress Museum**—*with its collection of Norwegian military history and Nazi occupation exhibits.) Proceed one more block along the harbor until you reach an open, parklike space on your left. Walk 100 yards (just past a handy Rema 1000 supermarket) to the top of this park to reach...*

❸ St. Mary's Church (Mariakirken)

Dating from the 12th century, this is Bergen's oldest preserved building. This stately church of the Hanseatic merchants has a

dour stone interior, but it's enlivened by a colorful, highly decorated pulpit.

In the park below the church, find the statue of Snorri Sturlason. In the 1200s, this Icelandic scribe and scholar wrote down the Viking sagas. Thanks to him, we have a better understanding of this Nordic era. A few steps to the right, look through the window of the big modern building at an archaeological site showing the oldest remains of Bergen—stubs of the 12th-century trading town's streets tumbling to the harbor before land reclamation pushed the harbor farther out.

• *The window is just a sneak peek at the excellent* ❹ *Bryggens Museum, which provides helpful historical context for the Hanseatic Quarter we're about to visit. The museum's outstanding* **Bryggen Walking Tour** *is your best bet for seeing this area (see "Tours in Bergen," earlier). Continue down to the busy harborfront. On the left is the most photographed sight in town, the Bryggen quarter. To get your bearings, first read the "Bryggen's History" sidebar; if it's nice out, cross the street to the wharf and look back for a fine overview of this area. (Or, in the rain, huddle under an awning.)*

❺ Bergen's Hanseatic Quarter (Bryggen)

Bergen's fragile wooden old town is its iconic front door. The long "tenements" (rows of warehouses) hide atmospheric lanes that creak and groan with history.

While we think of Bergen as "Norwegian," Bryggen was German—the territory of *Deutsch*-speaking merchants and traders. (The most popular surname in Bergen is the German name Hanson—"son of Hans.") From the front of Bryggen, look back at the Rosenkrantz Tower. The little red holes at its top mark where cannons once pointed at the German quarter, installed by Norwegian royalty who wanted a slice of all that taxable trade revenue. Their threat was countered by German grain—without which the Norwegians would've starved.

BERGEN

Bryggen's History

Pretty as Bryggen is today, it has a rough-and-tumble history. A horrific plague decimated the population and economy of Norway in 1350, killing about half of its people. A decade later, German merchants arrived and established a Hanseatic trading post.

For the next four centuries, from 1370 to 1754, the port of Bergen was essentially German territory, with German merchants controlling the city's trade. In 1550, Bergen was a Germanic city of 1,000 workaholic merchants—surrounded and supported by some 5,000 Norwegians.

This wasn't a military occupation, but a mutually beneficial economic partnership. The Norwegian fishermen of the far north shipped their dried cod to Bergen, where the Hanseatic merchants marketed it to Europe. Norwegian cod, an easy-to-preserve protein, provided much of Europe with food, and cod oil lit European lamps until about 1850.

In its earlier heyday, Bergen was one of the largest wooden cities in Europe (the original town dates from 1070). But those jammed-in wooden buildings, heated with lots of hearth fires, spelled disaster for Bergen. Over the centuries, the city suffered countless fires, with major blazes every 20 or so years. Each time the warehouses burned, the merchants would toss the refuse into the bay and rebuild. Gradually, the land crept out, and so did the buildings. Looking at the Hanseatic Quarter from the harborfront, you can see how the buildings have settled as the fire debris decomposed.

Notice that the first six houses are perfectly straight; they were built in the 1980s to block the view of a modern hotel behind. The more ramshackle stretch of 11 houses beyond date from the early 1700s. Each front hides a long line of five to ten businesses.

• *To wander into the heart of this woody medieval quarter, head down Bredsgården, the lane a couple of doors before the shop sign featuring the anatomically correct unicorn. We'll make a loop to the right: down this lane nearly all the way, under a passage into a square (with a well, a vibrant outdoor restaurant, and a big wooden cod), and then back to the harbor down a parallel lane. Read the information below, then explore, stopping at the big wooden cod.*

Bit by bit, Bryggen is being restored using medieval techniques and materials. As you explore, you may stumble upon a rebuilding project in action.

After the last big fire in 1702, the city rebuilt using more stone and brick, and suffered fewer fires thereafter. But one small wooden quarter—Bryggen—was built after the fire, in the early 1700s. To prevent future blazes, the Germans forbade all fires and candles for light or warmth except in isolated and carefully guarded communal houses behind each tenement. It was in these communal houses that apprentices studied, people dried out their soggy clothes, hot food was cooked, and the men drank and partied. When there was a big banquet, one man always stayed sober—a kind of designated fire watchman.

Flash forward to the 20th century. One of the biggest explosions of World War II occurred in Bergen's harbor on April 20, 1944. An ammunition ship loaded with 120 tons of dynamite blew up just in front of the fortress. The blast leveled entire neighborhoods on either side of the harbor (notice the ugly 1950s construction opposite the fortress) and did serious damage to Håkon's Hall and Rosenkrantz Tower. How big was the blast? There's a hut called "the anchor cabin" a couple of miles away in the mountains. That's where the ship's anchor landed. The blast is considered to have been accidental, despite the fact that April 20 happened to be Hitler's 55th birthday and the ship blew up about 100 yards away from the Nazi commander's headquarters (in the fortress).

After World War II, Bryggen was slated for destruction. Most of the locals wanted it gone—it reminded them of the Germans who had occupied Norway for the miserable war years. Then excavators discovered rune stones indicating that the area predated the Germans. This boosted Bryggen's approval rating, and the quarter was saved. Today this picturesque and historic zone is the undisputed tourist highlight of Bergen.

Strolling through Bryggen, you feel swallowed up by history. Long rows of planky buildings (medieval-style double tenements) lean haphazardly across narrow alleys. The last Hanseatic merchant moved out centuries ago, but this is still a place of (touristy) commerce. You'll find artists' galleries, T-shirt boutiques, leather workshops, atmospheric restaurants, fishing tackle shops, sweaters, sweaters, sweaters...and trolls.

Look up at the winch-and-pulley systems on the buildings. These connected ground-floor workrooms with top-floor storerooms. Notice that the overhanging storerooms upstairs were supported by timbers with an elbow created by a tree trunk and its root—considered the strongest way to make a right angle in construction back then. Turning right at the top of the lane, you enter a lively cobbled square. On the far side is that big wooden fish.

The wooden cod (next to a well) is a reminder that the economic foundation of Bergen—the biggest city in Scandinavia until 1650 and the biggest city in Norway until 1830—was this fish. The stone building behind the carved cod was one of the fireproof cookhouses serving a line of buildings that stretched to the harbor. Today it's the Hetland Gallery, filled with the entertaining work of a popular local artist famous for fun caricatures of the city. Facing the same square is the Bryggen visitors center, worth peeking into.
• *Enjoy the center and the shops. Then return downhill to the harborfront, turn left, and continue the walk.*

Half of Bryggen (the brick-and-stone stretch to your left between the old wooden facades and the head of the bay) was torn down around 1900. Today the stately buildings that replaced it— far less atmospheric than Bryggen's original wooden core—are filled with tacky trinket shops and touristy splurge restaurants. They do make a nice architectural cancan of pointy gables, each with its date of construction indicated near the top.

Head to the lone wooden red house at the end of the row, which houses the **Hanseatic Museum** (closed until 2024 for renovation). The man who owned this building recognized the value of the city's heritage and kept its 18th-century interior intact. Once considered a nutcase, today he's celebrated as a visionary, as his decision has left visitors with a fine example of an old merchant house.
• *The Fish Market is just across the street. But first, we'll circle a few blocks inland and around to the right.*

The red-brick building (with frilly white trim, stepped gable, and a Starbucks) is the old **meat market**. It was built in 1877, after the importance of hygiene was recognized and the meat was moved inside from today's Fish Market. At the intersection just beyond, look left (uphill past the meat market) to see the **Fløibanen station.** Ahead, on the right, is an unusually classy McDonald's in a 1710 building that was originally a bakery. A few steps uphill on Kong Oscars Gate, the tiny red shack flying the Norwegian flags is the popular, recommended 3-Kroneren hot-dog stand.

Turn right to wander the length of **Hollendergaten,** a cute, narrow lane of 200-year-old buildings. Its name comes from a time when the king organized foreign communities of traders into various neighborhoods; this was where the Dutch lived. The curving street marks the former harborfront—these buildings were originally right on the water.

Hooking left, you reach the end of Hollendergaten, then turn right onto Nedre Korskirkeallmenningen. You'll pass the grand, red stone **Børsen** building, once the stock exchange and now a hotel with a few trendy restaurants. Step inside to enjoy its 1920s Art Deco-style murals celebrating Bergen's fishing heritage.

• *Turn right to go back toward the harborfront, then cross the street (Torget) and immerse yourself in Bergen's beloved Fish Market.*

❻ Fish Market (Fisketorget)

A fish market has thrived here since the 1500s, when fishermen rowed in with their catch and haggled with hungry residents.

While it's now a food circus of eateries selling fishy treats to tourists—no local would come here to actually buy fish—this famous market is still worth ▲, offering lots of smelly photo fun and free morsels to taste (daily 8:00-23:00, but vendors may close earlier if they're not busy, shorter hours Oct-April). Watch your wallet: If you're going to get pickpocketed in Bergen, it'll likely be here.

Many stands sell premade smoked-salmon *(laks)* sandwiches, fish soup, and other snacks ideal for a light lunch (confirm prices before ordering). To try Norwegian jerky, pick up a bag of dried cod snacks *(tørrfisk)*. The red meat is minke (pronounced mink-ee) whale, caught off the coast of northern Norway. Norwegians, notorious for their whaling, defend it as a traditional livelihood for many of their people. They point out that they only harvest the minke whale, which is not on an endangered list. In recent years, Norway has assigned itself a quota of nearly 1,000 minke whales a year, with the actual catch coming to a bit over half of that.

• *When done exploring, with your back to the market, hike a block to the right (note the pointy church spire in the distance and the big blocky stone monument dead ahead) into the modern part of town and a huge wide square. Pause at the intersection just before crossing into the square, about 20 yards before the blocky monument. Look left to see Mount Ulriken with its TV tower. A cable car called Ulriken643 takes you to its 2,110-foot summit (shuttle buses to the cable car station leave from this corner; for summit details, see page 395.) Now, walk up to that big square monument and meet some Vikings.*

❼ Seafarers' Monument

Nicknamed "the cube of goat cheese" for its shape, this 1950 monument celebrates Bergen's contact with the sea and remembers those

BERGEN

who worked on it and died in it. Study the faces: All social classes are represented. The statues relate to the scenes depicted in the reliefs above. Each side represents a century (start with the Vikings and work clockwise): 10th century—Vikings, with a totem pole in the panel above recalling the pre-Columbian Nor-

wegian "discovery" of America; 18th century—equipping Europe's ships; 19th century—whaling; 20th century—shipping and war. For the 21st century, see the real people—a cross-section of today's Norway—sitting at the statue's base. Major department stores (Galleriet, Xhibition, and Telegrafen) are all nearby.

• *The monument marks the start of Bergen's main square...*

❽ Torgallmenningen

Allmenningen means "for all the people." Torg means "square." While this is the city's main gathering place, it was actually created as a firebreak. The residents of this wood-built city knew fires were inevitable. The street plan was designed with breaks, or open spaces like this square, to help contain the destruction. In 1916, it succeeded in stopping a fire, which is why it has a more modern feel today.

Walk the length of the square to a low angled slab of blue stone at the far end. This is a monument to King Olav V, who died in 1991, and a popular meeting point: Locals like to say, "Meet you at the Blue Stone."

• *You're at the center of a parklike swath known as...*

❾ Ole Bulls Plass

This drag leads from the National Theater (above on right) to a little lake (below on left).

Detour a few steps up for a better look at the **National Theater,** built in Art Nouveau style in 1909. Founded by violinist Ole Bull in 1850, this was the first theater to host plays in the Norwegian language. After 450 years of Danish and Swedish rule, 19th-century Norway enjoyed a cultural awakening,

and Bergen became an artistic power. Ole Bull collaborated with the playwright Henrik Ibsen. Ibsen commissioned Edvard Grieg to compose the music for his play *Peer Gynt*. These three lions of Norwegian culture all lived and worked right here in Bergen.

Head downhill on the square to a delightful fountain featuring a **statue of Ole Bull** in the shadow of trees. Ole Bull was an 1800s version of Elvis. A pop idol and heartthrob in his day, Ole Bull's bath water was bottled and sold by hotels, and women fainted when they heard him play violin. Living up to his name, he fathered over 40 children. Speaking of children, I love to hang out here watching families frolic in the pond, oblivious to the waterfall troll (see the statue with the harp below Ole Bull). According to legend, the troll bestows musical talent on anyone—like old Ole—who gives him a gift (he likes meat).

From here, the park spills farther downhill to a cast-iron pavilion given to the city by Germans in 1889, and on to the little man-made lake (Lille Lungegårdsvannet), which is circled by an enjoyable path.

• *If you're up for a lakeside stroll, now's your chance. Alongside the lake (to the right as you face it from here) is a row of buildings housing the enjoyable* **KODE Art Museums.** *And to the left of the lake are some fine residential streets (including the picturesque, cobbled Marken); within a few minutes' walk is the* **Leprosy Museum** *and the* **cathedral.**

Sights in Bergen

Several museums listed here—including the Bryggens Museum, Håkon's Hall, Rosenkrantz Tower, Leprosy Museum, and Gamle Bergen—are part of the Bergen City Museum (Bymuseet) organization. If you buy a ticket to any of them, you'll pay half-price at any of the others simply by showing your ticket. In summer, note that many of these sights are included in the recommended Byrggen Walking Tour (see "Tours in Bergen," earlier).

▲Bergenhus Fortress: Håkon's Hall and Rosenkrantz Tower

The tower and hall, sitting boldly out of place on the harbor just beyond Bryggen, are reminders of Bergen's importance as the first permanent capital of Norway. Both sights feel vacant and don't really speak for themselves; a guided tour, which provides a serious introduction to Bergen's history, is essential for grasping their significance.

Cost and Hours: Hall and tower-150 NOK for both, 100 NOK for one; open daily 10:00-16:00, mid-Sept-mid-May 12:00-15:00; free WC; +47 55 30 80 30, www.bymuseet.no.

Tours: 30 NOK extra for worthwhile guided tour that includes both buildings (mid-June-mid-Aug tours leave daily at 10:00 and 14:00 from the building to the right of Håkon's Hall).

Visiting the Hall and Tower: Dating from the 13th century, **Håkon's Hall** was built as a banqueting hall, and that's essentially what it still is today. It was restored in the early 20th century but was heavily damaged in World War II when a munitions ship exploded in the harbor, leaving nothing but the walls standing. In the 1950s it was restored with a grand wooden ceiling and roof modeled after the medieval roof on a church in northern Norway. Beneath the hall is a whitewashed cellar likely used for storage.

Rosenkrantz Tower, the keep of a 13th-century castle, is today a stack of barren rooms connected by tight spiral staircases, with a good history exhibit on the top two floors and a commanding view from its rooftop. In the 16th century, the ruling Danish-Norwegian king enlarged the tower and trained its cannon on the German-merchant district, Bryggen, to remind the merchants of the importance of paying their taxes.

Fortress Museum (Bergenhus Festningmuseum)

This humble museum (which functioned as a prison during the Nazi occupation), set back a couple of blocks from the fortress, will interest historians with its thoughtful exhibits about military history, especially Bergen's WWII experience (look for the Norwegian Nazi flag). You'll learn about the resistance movement in Bergen (including its underground newspapers), the role of women in the Norwegian military, and Norwegian troops who have served with UN forces in overseas conflicts.

Cost and Hours: Free, daily 11:00-17:00, ask to borrow a translation of the descriptions, just behind Thon Hotel Orion at Koengen, +47 55 54 63 87.

▲▲Bryggens Museum

Built over the 12th-century rubble of medieval Bergen, this modern museum displays artifacts from the ruins and explains the 1950s archaeological dig that uncovered the earliest bits of the city (1050-1500). A trove of artifacts, including ceramics, rune inscriptions, and a 1000-year-old tunic, shed light on the everyday lives of the medieval people who inhabited Bergen and western Norway.

Cost and Hours: 100 NOK; in summer, entry included with Bryggen Walking Tour (see "Tours in Bergen," earlier); open daily 9:00-16:00, mid-Sept-mid-May 11:00-15:00; inexpensive cafeteria; in big, modern building just beyond the end of Bryggen and the Radisson Blu Royal Hotel, +47 55 30 80 30, www.bymuseet.no.

Tours: It's best to visit as part of the Bryggen Walking Tour. From mid-September through mid-May, when there is no tour, consider buying the good museum guidebook to supplement the brief English explanations.

Visiting the Museum: The manageable, well-presented permanent exhibit occupies the ground floor. First up are the foundations from original wooden tenements dating back to the 12th century (displayed right where they were excavated) and a giant chunk of the hull of a 100-foot-long, 13th-century ship that was found here. Next, an exhibit (roughly shaped like the long, wooden double-tenements outside) shows off artifacts and explains lifestyles from medieval Bryggen. Behind that is a display of items you might have bought at the medieval market. You'll finish with exhibits about the church in Bergen, the town's role as a royal capital, and its status as a cultural capital.

▲▲Hanseatic Museum and Schøtstuene (Det Hanseatiske Museum og Schøtstuene)

The **Hanseatic Museum**—closed until at least 2024 for an extensive renovation—offers the best look inside the trademark wooden houses of Bergen. The creaky old rooms—with hundred-year-old cod hanging from the ceiling—offer a time-tunnel experience back to Bryggen's glory days. It's located in an atmospheric old merchant house furnished with dried fish, antique ropes, an old oxtail (used for wringing spilled cod-liver oil back into the bucket), sagging steps, and cupboard beds from the early 1700s—one sporting what some claim is a medieval pinup girl.

During the museum's closure, you can still visit the nearby Hanseatic Assembly Rooms at **Schøtstuene,** where Hanseatic merchants would cook and gather to feast, hold court, conduct ceremonies, be schooled, and get warm. The rooms are in a building near St. Mary's Church (follow Øvregaten behind Bryggen—Schøtstuene is on your left). Fires were allowed in this building only because it was separate from the other (highly flammable) Bryggen offices. A glass floor reveals medieval ruins of

The Hanseatic League, Blessed by Cod

Middlemen in trade, the clever German merchants of the Hanseatic League, or Hanse, ruled the waves of northern Europe for 500 years (c. 1250-1750). These sea traders first banded together in a merchant guild to defend themselves against pirates. As they spread out from Germany, they established trading posts in foreign lands, cut deals with local leaders for trading rights, built boats and wharves, and organized armies to protect ships and ports.

By the 15th century, these merchants had organized more than a hundred cities into the Hanseatic League, a free-trade zone that stretched from London to Russia. The league ran a profitable triangle of trade: Fish from Scandinavia was exchanged for grain from the eastern Baltic and for luxury goods from England and Flanders. Everyone benefited, and the German merchants—the middlemen—reaped the profits.

At its peak in the 15th century, the Hanseatic League was the dominant force—economic, military, and political—in northern Europe. This was a chaotic age when much of Europe was fragmented into petty kingdoms and dukedoms. Revenue-hungry kings and robber-baron lords levied extortionist tolls. Pirates plagued shipments. It was the Hanseatic League that brought the stability that allowed trade to flourish.

Bergen that predate the Hanseatic era. Until the Hanseatic Museum reopens, Schøtstuene is displaying some of the Hanseatic collection and runs a short film about the ongoing restoration project.

Cost: 130 NOK (includes Hanseatic Museum when it reopens), 50 percent discount with your Norwegian Fisheries Museum ticket (or save your Schøtstuene ticket for discount at Norwegian Fisheries Museum); in summer, entry included with Bryggen Walking Tour.

Hours: Daily 10:00-18:00, May and Sept until 17:00, Oct-April 11:00-15:00; Øvregaten 50, +47 53 00 61 10, www.museumvest.no.

Tours: Included with your ticket is a 40-minute guided tour of Schøtstuene (check online to confirm tour schedule, generally Tue-Fri at 12:00 and 14:00). If you won't make this tour, your best alternative is joining the Bryggen Walking Tour, which includes a 25-minute tour inside Schøtstuene.

Bergen's place in this Baltic economy was all about cod—a form of protein that could be dried, preserved, and shipped anywhere. Blessed with a good harbor conveniently located between the rich fishing spots of northern Norway and the markets of Europe, Bergen shipped dried cod and fish oil southward and imported grain, cloth, beer, wine, and ceramics.

Bryggen, along with London, Bruges, and Novgorod, was one of four principal Hanseatic trading posts known as "kontors." It was the last kontor opened (c. 1360), the least profitable, and the final one to close. Bryggen had warehouses, offices, and living quarters. Ships docked here were unloaded by counterpoise cranes. At its peak, as many as a thousand merchants, journeymen, and apprentices lived and worked here.

Bryggen was a self-contained German enclave within the city. The merchants came from Germany, worked a few years here, and retired back in the home country. They spoke German, wore German clothes, and attended their own churches. By law, they were forbidden to intermarry or fraternize with the Bergeners, except on business.

The Hanseatic League peaked around 1500, then slowly declined. Rising nation-states were jealous of the German merchants' power and wealth. The Reformation tore apart old alliances. Dutch and English traders broke the Hanseatic monopoly. Cities withdrew from the league and kontors closed. In 1754, Bergen's kontor was taken over by the Norwegians. When it closed its doors on December 31, 1899, a sea-trading era was over, but the city of Bergen had become rich...by the grace of cod.

Norwegian Fisheries Museum (Norges Fiskerimuseum)

Just up the coast from Bryggen is the Norwegian Fisheries Museum, located in a well-preserved wharfside warehouse with exhibits about life along and on the sea. Antique boats are displayed in the harbor just outside.

Cost and Hours: 100 NOK, 50 percent discount if you show your Schøtstuene ticket (or save your Fisheries ticket for discount at Schøtstuene); June-Aug daily 10:00-18:00, May and Sept until 17:00, Oct-April 11:00-15:00; Sandviksboder 23, +47 55 69 96 01, www.museumvest.no.

Getting There: From the Schøtstuene Assembly Rooms, it's a 15- to 20-minute walk along curving Nye Sandviksveien. From Schøtstuene, follow Øvregaten—which becomes Nye Sandviksveien—north for about 10 minutes. The street soon splits with Ladegårdsgaten—but keep straight, then turn left onto Johan Mohrs Gate. After Johan Mohrs Gate joins Sjøgaten, the museum is two minutes ahead, on the left.

You can also catch bus #3, #4, or #6 from the Bryggen stop (in front of the Radisson Blu Royal Hotel) and ride 5 minutes to the museum (stop: Sandvikstorget). Or, if it is running, cruise 20 minutes aboard the *Beffen* ferry (65 NOK one-way, 130 NOK day pass, June-Aug hourly 11:00-16:00, departs from the Bryggen side of the Fish Market).

Theta Museum

This small museum highlights Norway's resistance movement. You'll peek into the hidden world of a 10-person cell of courageous students, whose group—called Theta—housed other fighters and communicated with London during the Nazi occupation in World War II. It's located in Theta's former headquarters—a small up-stairs room in a wooden Bryggen building.

Cost and Hours: 50 NOK, June-Aug Tue, Sat, and Sun 14:00-16:00, closed Mon, Wed-Fri, and Sept-May, Enhjørningsgården.

▲▲Fløibanen Funicular

Bergen's popular funicular climbs 1,000 feet in seven minutes to the top of Mount Fløyen for the best view of the town, sur-rounding islands, and fjords all the way to the west coast. The top is the perfect picnic spot for enjoying the sunset. The **$$ Fløien Folkerestaurant,** the white building at the top of the funicular, offers affordable self-service food all day in season. Behind the station, you'll find a playground and a fun giant troll

photo op. The top is also the starting point for many peaceful hikes.

You'll buy your funicular ticket at the base of the Fløibanen (notice the photos in the entry hall of the construction of the fu-nicular and its 1918 grand opening).

Cost and Hours: 130 NOK round-trip, 65 NOK one-way, cheaper online and off-season; daily 7:30-23:00, departures 4/hour—on the quarter-hour most of the day, runs continuously if busy; +47 55 33 68 00, www.floyen.no.

Advance Tickets: While you can buy tickets on-site, there can be huge lines if cruise ships are in town. Online tickets are cheaper and let you skip the ticket-buying line at the funicular.

Hiking Down: If you plan to hike down from the top, buy a one-way ticket and ask for the Fløyen hiking map. From the top, walk behind the station and follow the signs to the city center. The top half of the 30-minute hike is a gravelly path through a forest with fine views. The bottom is a paved lane passing charming old wooden homes. It's a steep descent. To save your knees, you could ride the lift most of the way down and get off at the Promsgate stop to wander through the delightful cobbled and shiplap lanes (note that only the :00 and :30 departures stop at Promsgate—and this option requires a round-trip ticket).

▲St. Mary's Church (Mariakirken)

The oldest parish church and preserved building in Bergen dates to between 1130 and 1170 and is said to be one of the best-decorated medieval churches in Norway. For many years, St. Mary's Church was known as the "German Church," as it was used by German merchants of the Hanseatic League from 1408 to 1766. The last service in German was held in 1906. The stony interior is accented with a golden altarpiece, a Baroque pulpit of Dutch origin partly made from exotic materials (such as turtle skin), and artworks from various time periods.

Cost and Hours: 50 NOK, Mon-Fri 10:00-16:00, closed mid-Sept-May, 25-minute English guided tour (25 NOK) runs June-Aug Mon-Fri at 15:30, http://bergendomkirke.no, +47 55 59 71 75.

Bergen Cathedral (Bergen Domkirke)

Bergen's main church, dedicated to St. Olav (the patron saint of Norway), dates from 1301. Drop in to enjoy its stoic, plain interior with stuccoed stone walls and a giant wooden pulpit. Sit in a hard, straight-backed pew and just try to doze off. Like so many old Norwegian structures, its roof makes you feel like you're huddled under an overturned Viking ship. The church is oddly lopsided, with just one side aisle. Before leaving, look up to see the gorgeous wood-carved organ over the main entrance. In the entryway, you'll see portraits of each bishop dating all the way back to the Reformation.

Cost and Hours: Free, Mon-Fri 10:00-16:00, Sun 9:30-13:00, closed Sat, shorter hours mid-Aug-mid-June.

Leprosy Museum (Lepramuseet)

Leprosy is also known as "Hansen's Disease," because in the 1870s a Bergen man named Armauer Hansen did groundbreaking work in understanding the ailment. This unique museum is in St. Jørgens Hospital, a leprosarium that dates to about 1700. Until the 19th century, as much as 3 percent of Norway's population had leprosy. This hospital—once called "a graveyard for the living" (its last patient died in 1946)—has a meager exhibit in a thought-provoking dorm for the dying. It's most worthwhile if you read the translation of the exhibit (borrow a copy at the entry) or take the free tour (at the top of each hour). As you leave, if you're interested, ask if you can see the medicinal herb garden out back.

Cost and Hours: 100 NOK, daily 10:30-15:30, closed Sept-mid-May, between train station and Bryggen at Kong Oscars Gate 59, +47 55 30 80 37, www.bymuseet.no.

▲KODE Art Museums (KODE Kunstmuseer)

If you need to get out of the rain, check out this collection, filling four neighboring buildings facing the lake along Rasmus Meyers Allé. The KODE 3 branch specializes in Norwegian artists and has an especially good Munch exhibit. Many visitors focus on the KODE 4 building (which may be closed during your visit—check locally), on the far left, for its eclectic cross-section of international and Norwegian artists. The KODE 2 building has installations of contemporary art and a big bookstore on the first floor, while the KODE 1 building has decorative arts and silver crafts from Bergen.

Cost and Hours: 160 NOK, daily 10:00-17:00 (KODE 2 Thu until 20:00), closed Mon mid-Sept-mid-May, Rasmus Meyers Allé 3, +47 53 00 97 04, www.kodebergen.no.

Visiting KODE 3 and 4: KODE 3 presents one of the finest collections of work by Edvard Munch, including such masterpieces as *Jealousy, Melancholy, Woman in Three Stages,* and *Evening on Karl Johan.* Also on hand is a representative collection from Norway's golden age of painting (1880-1905), including highlights from the careers of Romantic landscape painters Hans Gude and J. C. Dahl. And don't miss the iconic troll and folktale

drawings and watercolors by Theodor Kittelsen.

When it's open, **KODE 4** features an easily digestible collection (from outside, enter through door 4). The ground floor includes an extensive display of works by Nikolai Astrup (1880-1928), who depicts Norway's fjords with bright colors and Expressionistic flair. One flight up, "Bergen and the World, 1400-1900" creates a visual history of Norway and Bergen with portraits, landscapes, genre scenes, and religious works. Look for paintings by J. C. Dahl and his students, who captured the majesty of Norway's natural wonders (don't miss Adelsteen Normann's impressive, photorealistic view of Romsdalsfjord). "Norwegian Art 1840-1900" includes works by Christian Krohg, as well as some portraits by Harriet Backer and realistic scenes of everyday life by Frits Thaulow.

Up on the third floor, things get modern. The Tower Hall (Tärnsalen) features Norwegian modernism and a large exhibit of Bergen's avant-garde art (1966-1985). The International Modernism section has four stars: Pablo Picasso (sketches, etchings, collages, and a few Cubist paintings), Paul Klee (Swiss color-theory painter), and the dynamic Norwegian duo of Edvard Munch and Ludvig Karisten. Rounding it out are a smattering of Surrealist, Abstract Expressionist, and Op Art pieces.

▲Bergen Aquarium (Akvariet i Bergen)

Small but fun, this aquarium claims to be the second most-visited sight in Bergen. It's wonderfully laid out and explained in English. Check out the view from inside the "shark tunnel" in the tropical shark exhibit.

Cost and Hours: Adults-295 NOK, kids-195 NOK; daily 9:00-18:00, Sept-April from 10:00, feeding times at the top of most hours in summer; cheery cafeteria with light sandwiches, Nordnesbakken 4, +47 55 55 71 71, www.akvariet.no.

Getting There: It's at the tip of the peninsula on the south end of the harbor—about a 20-minute walk or short ride on bus #11 from the city center. Or hop on the handy little harbor ferry that sails from the Fish Market to near the aquarium (65 NOK one-way, 130 NOK for day pass, less for kids, runs Mon-Fri 7:30-16:00, show ferry ticket for discount on aquarium entry, 2/hour, 10-minute ride, June-Aug 10:00-17:30, off-season until 16:00).

Nearby: The lovely park behind the aquarium has views of the sea and a popular swimming beach (described later, under "Activities in Bergen"). The totem pole erected here was a gift from Seattle, Bergen's sister city in the US.

▲Gamle Bergen Museum (Old Bergen Museum)

This Disney-cute open-air gathering of 50-some 18th- through 20th-century homes and shops was founded in 1946 to save them from destruction as Bergen modernized. Each wooden building was moved from elsewhere in Bergen and reconstructed here. Together, they create a virtual town that offers a cobbled look at the old life. It's free to wander through the town and park to enjoy the facades of the historic buildings, but to enter the 20 or so museum buildings, you'll have to join a tour (departing on the hour 10:00-16:00).

Cost and Hours: 120 NOK, daily 10:00-16:00, closed Sept-mid-May, +47 55 39 43 04, www.bymuseet.no.

Getting There: Take any bus heading west from Bryggen (such as #4, #5, or #6, direction: Lønborglien) to Gamle Bergen (stop: Gamle Bergen). The stop is just after the tunnel. When you get off, backtrack a few steps (toward the tunnel) before peeling left downhill. Follow the sidewalk as it curves under the highway—you should see a small sign for *Gamle Bergen*. At the fork under the highway, cross the road and turn left, then head right down the hill. When you reach the apartment building on your right, take a hairpin turn left down the small road (signs should direct you). You'll see the museum's white arch ahead of you. Any bus heading back into town takes you to the center (buses come by every few minutes).

ACTIVITIES IN BERGEN
▲Strolling

Bergen is a great town for wandering. Enjoy a little Norwegian paseo. On a balmy Norwegian summer evening, I'd stroll from the castle, along the harborfront, up the main square to Ole Bulls Plass, and around the lake.

For a slightly more strenuous yet rewarding walk, head up the zig-zagging road behind the Fløibanen funicular station to a viewpoint in front of a white building with a lookout tower. The building was once a fire station (which explains the tower). The lake next to it used to be a reservoir. Firefighters built the white houses beyond the lake on land given to them so that they could live close to the station. After enjoying the city views, you can either return to town the way you came, or follow Øvre Blekeveien down past the lake and white houses; then take any road to the left off Blekeveien back down to the harbor.

Shopping

Most shops are open Monday through Friday 9:00-17:00, Thursday until 19:00, and Saturday 9:00-15:00, and are closed Sunday. Many touristy shops along the harborfront strip are open daily—even during holidays—until 20:00 or 21:00. You'll see the same products offered at different prices, so shopping around can be a good idea.

Ting (Things) offers a fun alternative to troll shopping, with contemporary housewares and quirky gifts (daily 9:00-22:30, at Bryggen 13, a block past the Hanseatic Museum, +47 55 21 54 80).

Nilssen på Bryggen, next to the Hanseatic Museum, is one of the oldest shops in Bergen. You'll find Norwegian yarn for knitting and modern-style Sandnes wool sweaters, along with souvenirs and hand-embroidered Christmas items (Mon-Sat 10:00-18:00, closed Sun, Bryggen 3, +47 55 31 67 90).

Husfliden is popular for its handmade goodies and reliably Norwegian sweaters (fine variety and quality but expensive, just off Torget at Vågsallmenninge 3, +47 55 54 47 40).

The Galleriet Mall, a shopping center on Torgallmenningen, holds six floors of shops, cafés, and restaurants. You'll find a pharmacy, clothing, sporting goods, bookstores, mobile-phone shops, and a basement grocery store (Mon-Fri 9:00-21:00, Sat until 18:00, closed Sun).

Swimming

On a hot sunny day you'll find a great local scene at Bergen's public swimming areas. One is at the aquarium, and another is

in Gamle Bergen. **Nordnes Sjøbad,** near the aquarium, offers swimmers an outdoor heated pool and a protected area of the sea (80 NOK, kids-35 NOK, mid-May-Aug Mon-Fri 7:00-19:00, Sat 9:00-14:00, Sun 10:00-14:00, Sat-Sun until 19:00 in good weather, closed off-season, Nordnesparken 30, +47 53 03 91 90). **Sandviken Sjøbad,** at Gamle Bergen, is free and open all summer. It comes with changing rooms, a roped-off bit of the bay (no pool), a high dive, and lots of sunbathing space. And by 2023, a new waterfront park called **True Blue** will offer a beach, pool, and sauna, as well as play areas and gardens, in a modern, mile-long recreational space just south of the city center, along the shore of Store Lungegårdsvannet lake (get info at TI).

SIGHTS NEAR BERGEN
▲Ulriken643 Cable Car

It's amazingly easy and quick to zip up six minutes to the 643-meter-high (that's 2,110 feet)

summit of Ulriken, the tallest mountain near Bergen. The cable car has undergone a face lift and should reopen—with updated, more spacious gondolas—by the time you visit. Stepping out of the cable car, you enter a different world, with views stretching to the ocean. A chart clearly shows the many well-marked and easy hikes that fan out over the vast, rocky, grassy plateau above the tree line (circular walks of various lengths, a 40-minute hike down, and a 4-hour hike to the top of the Fløibanen funicular). For less exercise, you can simply sunbathe, unpack a picnic, or enjoy the Ulriken restaurant.

Cost and Hours: 125 NOK one-way, 195 NOK round-trip; about 8/hour, daily 9:00-21:00, off-season until 17:00; +47 53 64 36 43, www.ulriken643.no.

Getting There: It's about three miles southeast of Bergen. From the Fish Market, you can take a blue double-decker shuttle bus that includes the cost of the cable-car ride (285 NOK, ticket valid 24 hours, April-Sept daily 9:00-18:00, 2/hour, departs from the corner of Torgallmenningen and Strandgaten, buy ticket as you board or at TI). Alternatively, public buses #2 and #3 run from Småstrandgaten in the city center and stop 200 yards from the lift station.

▲▲Edvard Grieg Museum, Troldhaugen

Norway's greatest composer spent his last 22 summers (1885-1907) at his country home, soaking up inspirational fjord beauty and composing many of his great-est works. Grieg fused simple Norwegian folk tunes with the bombast of Europe's Roman-tic style. In a dreamy Victorian setting, Grieg's Troldhaugen ("Hill of the Trolls") is pleas-ant for anyone and essential for diehard fans. You can visit his house on your own, but it's more enjoyable if you take the included 20-minute tour. The house and adjacent museum are full of memories and artifacts, including the composer's Steinway. The walls are festooned with photos of the musical and literary superstars of his generation. When the hugely popular Grieg died in 1907, 40,000 mourners attended his funeral. His little studio hut near the water makes you want to sit down and modulate.

Cost and Hours: 130 NOK, includes guided tour in English, daily 9:00-18:00, Oct-April 10:00-16:00, café, +47 55 92 29 92, https://griegmuseum.no.

Grieg Lunch Concert: Troldhaugen offers a great guided tour/concert package that includes a shuttle bus from the Bergen TI to the doorstep of Grieg's home on the fjord (departs 11:00), an hour-long tour of the home, a half-hour concert (Grieg's greatest piano hits, at 13:00), and the ride back into town (you're back in the center by 14:30). Your guide will narrate the ride out of town as well as take you around Grieg's house (290 NOK, daily May-mid-Oct). Lunch isn't included, but there is a café, or you could bring a picnic. You can skip the return bus ride and spend more time in Troldhaugen. While the tour rarely sells out, it's wise to drop by the TI earlier that day to reserve your spot.

Evening Concerts: Ask at the TI about piano performances in the concert hall at Grieg's home—a gorgeous venue with the fjord stretching out behind the grand piano (390 NOK, concerts roughly mid-June-Sept Sun at 18:00, free round-trip shuttle bus leaves TI at 16:30, show your concert ticket).

BERGEN

Getting to Troldhaugen: It's six miles south of Bergen. The Bybanen tram drops you a long 20-minute walk away from Troldhaugen. Catch the tram in the city center at its terminus near Byparken (between the lake and Ole Bulls Plass), ride it for about 25 minutes (stop: Hop). Walk in the direction of Bergen (about 25 yards), cross at the crosswalk, and follow signs to Troldhaugen. Part of the way is on a pedestrian/bike path; you're halfway there when the path crosses over a busy highway. If you want to make the 13:00 lunchtime concert, leave Bergen at 12:00.

To avoid the long walk from the tram stop, consider the Grieg Lunch Concert package (described earlier). If you're driving into Bergen from the east (such as from the Sognefjord), you'll drive right by Troldhaugen on your way into town.

Fantoft Stave Church (Fantoft Stavkirke)

Situated in a quiet forest next to a mysterious stone cross, this replica of a huge, preserved-in-tar 12th-century stave church is bigger, though no better, than others covered in this book. But it's worth a look if you're in the neighborhood, even after-hours, for its atmospheric setting. The original wooden church burned down in 1992. It was rebuilt and reopened in 1997, but it will never be the same (for more on stave churches, see page 318).

Cost and Hours: 65 NOK, daily

10:30-18:00, interior closed mid-Sept-mid-May, no English information, +47 55 28 07 10.

Getting There: It's three miles south of Bergen on E-39 in Paradis. Take the Bybanen tram (from Byparken, between the lake and Ole Bulls Plass) or bus #83 (from Torget, by the Fish Market) to the Paradis stop (not the "Fantoft" stop). From Paradis, walk uphill to the parking lot on the left, and find the steep footpath to the church.

BERGEN NIGHTSPOTS

At such a high latitude, Bergen stays light until 23:00 in the summer. On warm evenings, people are out enjoying the soft light and the mellow scene.

For a selection of cool nightspots, visit the **Pingvinen** and **Café Opera** (both described in "Eating in Bergen," later) and explore the neighboring streets.

For something a little funkier, **Skostredet** ("Shoe Street," recalling the days when cobblers set up shop here) is emerging as the hip, bohemian-chic area. You'll sort through cafés, pubs, and retro shops. There's an American-style Rock and Roll '59er Diner. And **Folk og Røvere** ("People and Robbers") is an unpretentious bar with cheap beer (nightly until late, Skostredet 12).

For candlelit elegance, enjoy a drink at the historic **Dyvekes Wine Cellar.** Named for the mistress of King Christian II of Denmark (her portrait is on the signboard hanging above the door), the atmosphere of the ground-floor bar and the cellar downstairs is hard to beat (daily from 15:00, wine by the glass, beer on tap, Hollendergaten 7).

For live music, try **Madam Felle Nightclub** (on the Bryggen strip), which usually has musicians on the weekends (sometimes without a cover). And if you're really drunk at 3:00 in the morning and need a spicy hotdog, the **3-Kroneren** *pølse* stand is open.

Sleeping in Bergen

Busy with business travelers and popular with tourists, Bergen can be jammed any time of year. Even with this crush, proud and pricey hotels may be willing to make deals. Bergen also has some fine budget alternatives that can save you money.

HOTELS

$$$$ Hotel Havnekontoret, with 116 rooms and the best location in town, fills a grand old shipping headquarters dating from the 1920s. It's an especially fine value on weekends and in summer for those who eat the included dinner. While part of a chain, it has a friendly spirit. Guests are welcome to climb its historic tower (with a magnificent view) or enjoy its free sauna and exercise room downstairs. The room price includes virtually all your food—a fine breakfast, self-service waffles in the afternoon, fruit and coffee all day, and a light dinner buffet each evening. If you take advantage of them, these edible extras are easily worth 600 NOK per day per couple, making the cost of this fancy hotel little more than a hostel (facing the harbor across the street from the Radisson Blu Royal Hotel at Slottsgaten 1, +47 55 60 11 00, www.choicehotels. no, cc.havnekontoret@choice.no).

$$$$ Hotel Park Bergen is classy, comfortable, and in a fine residential neighborhood a 15-minute uphill walk from the town center (10 minutes from the train station). It's tinseled in Old World, lived-in charm, yet comes with all of today's amenities. The 35 rooms are split between two buildings, with 22 in the classy old-fashioned hotel and 13 in the modern annex across the street. They also offer eight fully furnished apartments (Harald Hårfagres Gate 35, +47 55 54 44 00, www.hotelpark.no, booking@hotelpark.no).

$$$$ Thon Hotel Rosenkrantz, with 129 rooms and an included light dinner, is one block behind Bryggen, between the Bryggens Museum and the Fløibanen funicular station—right in the heart of Bergen's appealing old quarter. Ask for a room with a double bed even if you're traveling alone—they go for the same price as a single (elevator, Rosenkrantzgaten 7, +47 55 30 14 00, www.thonhotels.com, rosenkrantz@olavthon.no).

$$$$ Thon Hotel Orion, beyond Bryggen near Håkon's Hall, has 219 rooms with a light dinner included. But be aware that many rooms face the fortress grounds, which sometimes host summer evening concerts. If you love music ask for a room on the concert side and enjoy the show; otherwise ask for a room on the quiet side and bring earplugs—or stay somewhere else (elevator, Bradbenken 3, +47 55 30 87 00, www.thonhotels.com, orion@olavthon.no).

$$$ P-Hotel has 114 basic rooms just up from Ole Bulls Plass. While it's not particularly charming and some rooms come with noise from the street and a ground-floor nightclub, it's in a prime location. Ask for a room facing the courtyard in the renovated wing (credit card only, box breakfast in your room, elevator, Vestre Torggate 9, +47 55 21 00 00, www.p-hotels.no, bergen@p-hotels.no).

$$$ Best Western Plus Hotel Hordaheimen is Bergen's oldest hotel, dating back to 1918. It has 88 well-priced rooms with hardwood floors and welcoming decor. The charming breakfast room is decorated with vintage Kinsarvik wood furniture, giving it a traditional feel (elevator, +47 55 33 50 00, www.hordaheimen.no, booking@hordaheimen.no).

$$ Citybox Bergen City is a unique, no-nonsense hotel concept: plain, white, clean, and practical. You'll book one of their

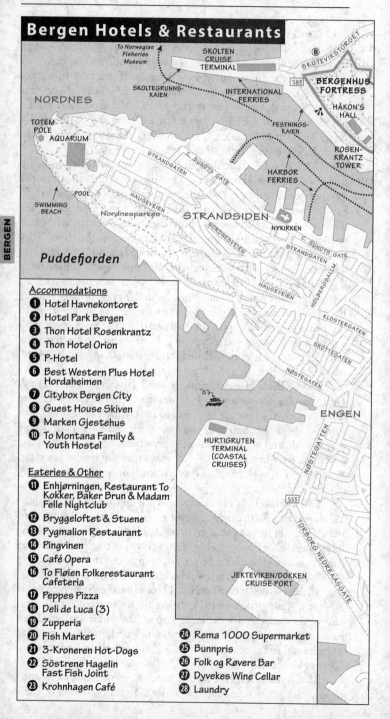

Bergen Hotels & Restaurants

Accommodations

1. Hotel Havnekontoret
2. Hotel Park Bergen
3. Thon Hotel Rosenkrantz
4. Thon Hotel Orion
5. P-Hotel
6. Best Western Plus Hotel Hordaheimen
7. Citybox Bergen City
8. Guest House Skiven
9. Marken Gjestehus
10. To Montana Family & Youth Hostel

Eateries & Other

11. Enhjørningen, Restaurant To Kokker, Baker Brun & Madam Felle Nightclub
12. Bryggeloftet & Stuene
13. Pygmalion Restaurant
14. Pingvinen
15. Café Opera
16. To Fløien Folkerestaurant Cafeteria
17. Peppes Pizza
18. Deli de Luca (3)
19. Zupperia
20. Fish Market
21. 3-Kroneren Hot-Dogs
22. Söstrene Hagelin Fast Fish Joint
23. Krohnhagen Café
24. Rema 1000 Supermarket
25. Bunnpris
26. Folk og Røvere Bar
27. Dyvekes Wine Cellar
28. Laundry

122 rooms online or by phone and receive a confirmation number. Check-in is automated—just punch in your number and get your room key card. The call-in reception is staffed 24 hours daily (family room, no breakfast, elevator, rooftop terrace, self-service laundry, just away from the bustle in a mostly residential part of town at Nygårdsgaten 31, +47 55 31 25 00, www.citybox.no, bergen@citybox.no.

$ Guest House Skiven is a humble little place beautifully situated on a steep, traffic-free cobbled lane called "the most painted street in Bergen." Alf and Elizabeth Heskja (who live upstairs) rent four bright, nonsmoking doubles. Rooms have their own sinks, but share a shower, two WCs, and a kitchen (no breakfast, 4 blocks from train station, at Skivebakken 17, mobile +47 90 05 30 30, www.skiven.no, rs@skiven.no). From the train station, go down Kong Oscars Gate, uphill on D. Krohns Gate, and up the stairs at the end of the block on the left.

DORMS AND HOSTELS

$ Marken Gjestehus is a quiet, tidy, and conveniently positioned 100-bed place between the station and the harborfront. Its rooms, while spartan, are modern and cheery. Prices can rise with demand, especially in summer (private rooms available, breakfast extra, elevator, open all year but with limited reception hours, fourth floor at Kong Oscars Gate 45, +47 55 31 44 04, www.marken-gjestehus.com, post@marken-gjestehus.com).

Away from the Center: ¢ Montana Family & Youth Hostel (IYHF), while one of Europe's best, is high-priced for a hostel and way out of town. Still, the bus connections (#12, 20 minutes from the center) and the facilities—modern rooms, classy living room, no curfew, huge free parking lot, and members' kitchen—are excellent (private rooms available; 30 Johan Blytts Vei—for location, see the "Greater Bergen" map on page 367; +47 55 20 80 70, www.montana.no, bergen.montana@hihostels.no).

Eating in Bergen

Bergen has numerous choices: restaurants with rustic, woody atmosphere, candlelight, and steep prices; trendy pubs and cafés that offer good-value meals; cafeterias, chain restaurants, and international eateries with less ambience but better value; and takeaway sandwich shops, bakeries, and cafés for a light bite.

You can always get a glass or pitcher of water at no charge, and fancy places give you free seconds on potatoes—just ask. And if you get your food to go, it's taxed at a lower rate.

SPLURGES AT BRYGGEN

You'll pay a premium to eat at these restaurants, but you'll have a memorable meal in a pleasant setting.

$$$$ Enhjørningen Restaurant ("The Unicorn") is *the* place in Bergen for fish. With thickly painted walls and no right angles, this dressy yet old-time wooden interior wins my "Bryggen Atmosphere" award. The dishes, while not hearty, are close to gourmet and beautifully presented (small plates, main dishes, multicourse meals, nightly 16:00-23:00, reservations smart, #29 on Bryggen harborfront—look for anatomically correct unicorn on the old wharf facade and dip into the alley and up the stairs, +47 55 30 69 50, www.enhjorningen.no).

$$$$ Restaurant To Kokker, down the alley from Enhjørningen (and with the same owners), serves more meat and game. The prices and quality are equivalent, but even though it's also in an elegant old wooden building, I like The Unicorn's atmosphere much better (small plates, main dishes, multicourse meals, Mon-Sat 18:00-23:00, closed Sun, +47 55 30 69 55, www.tokokker.no).

$$$ Bryggeloftet & Stuene Restaurant, in a brick building just before the wooden stretch of Bryggen, is a vast eatery serving seafood, vegetarian, and traditional meals. To dine memorably yet affordably, this is your best Bryggen bet. Upstairs feels more elegant and less touristy than the main floor—if there's a line downstairs, just head on up (lunches, dinners, Mon-Sat 11:00-23:30, Sun from 13:00, try reserving a view window upstairs—no reservations for outside seating, #11 on Bryggen harborfront, +47 55 30 20 70, www.bryggeloftet.no).

NEAR THE FISH MARKET

$$ Pygmalion Restaurant has a happy salsa vibe, with local art on the walls and a fun, healthy international menu. It's run with creativity and passion by Sissel. Her burgers are a hit, and there are always good vegetarian options, hearty salads, and pancakes (wraps, burgers, main plates, Mon-Sat 11:00-22:00, Sun 12:00-23:00, two blocks inland from the Fish Market at Nedre Korskirkealmenning 4, +47 55 31 32 60).

CHARACTERISTIC PLACES NEAR OLE BULLS PLASS

Bergen's "in" cafés are stylish, cozy, small, and open very late. Around the cinema on Neumannsgate, there are numerous Italian, Middle Eastern, and Chinese restaurants.

$$$ Pingvinen ("The Penguin") is a homey place in a charming neighborhood, serving traditional Norwegian home cooking to an enthusiastic local clientele. The pub has only indoor seating, with a long row of stools at the bar and five charming, living-room-cozy tables—a great setup for solo diners. After the kitchen closes, the place stays open very late as a pub. For Norwegian fare in an untouristy atmosphere, this is a good, affordable option. Their seasonal menu (reindeer in the fall, whale in the spring) is listed on the board (nightly until 22:00, Vaskerelven 14 near the National Theater, +47 55 60 46 46).

$$$ Café Opera, with a playful, slacker vibe and chessboards for the regulars, is the hip budget choice for its loyal, youthful following. With two floors of seating and tables out front across from the theater, it's a winner (light sandwiches until 16:00, daily 10:00-23:30, Engen 18, +47 55 23 03 15).

ATOP MOUNT FLØYEN

$$ Fløien Folkerestaurant Cafeteria, at the top of the funicular, offers meals indoors and out with a panoramic view. It's self-service, with cheap sandwiches and a soup buffet (daily 10:00-22:00, Sept-April Sat-Sun only 12:00-17:00, +47 55 33 69 99).

GOOD CHAIN RESTAURANTS

You'll find these chain restaurants in Bergen and throughout Norway. All are open long hours daily. In good weather, enjoy a takeout meal with sun-worshipping locals in Bergen's parks.

$$$ Peppes Pizza on Ole Bulls Plass has cold beer and good pizzas—consider the Thai Chicken, with satay-marinated chicken, pineapple, peanuts, and coriander (Mon-Wed 11:00-23:00, Thu-Sat until 24:00, Sun 12:00-23:00, seating inside or takeaway, Olav Kyrres Gate 11, +47 22 22 55 55).

$ Baker Brun makes 75-100-NOK sandwiches, including wonderful shrimp baguettes, and pastries such as *skillingsboller*—Bergen's version of cinnamon rolls—warm out of the oven. Their shop at Bryggen is a prime spot for a simple, inexpensive bite (open from 7:00, a little later Sat-Sun, seating inside or takeaway).

$ Deli de Luca is a cut above other takeaway joints, adding sushi, noodle dishes, and calzones to the normal lineup of sandwiches. While a bit more expensive than the others, the variety and quality are appealing (open daily 24 hours, branches in train station and near Ole Bulls Plass at Torggaten 5, branch with indoor seating on corner of Engen and Vaskerelven, +47 55 23 11 47).

$$$ Zupperia is a lively, popular chain that offers burgers, salads, Norwegian fare, and Asian dishes; their Thai soup is a local favorite. For a lighter (and cheaper) meal, order off the lunch menu any time of day (Sun-Wed 12:00-22:00, Thu-Sat until 23:30). It's near the National Theater at Vaskerelven 12.

BUDGET BETS NEAR THE FISH MARKET

The **Fish Market** has lots of stalls bursting with salmon sandwiches, fresh shrimp, fish-and-chips, and fish cakes. For a tasty, memorable, and inexpensive Bergen meal, assemble a seafood picnic here (ask for prices first; May-Sept daily 8:00-23:00, vendors may close early if they're not busy; Oct-Dec Mon-Sat 10:00-22:00, Sun from 11:00; Jan-April Sat only 9:00-15:00). Also be sure to peruse the places next door on the ground floor of the TI building, Torghallen.

$ 3-Kroneren, a classic hot-dog stand, sells a wide variety of sausages (including reindeer). The well-described English menu makes it easy to order your choice of artery-clogging guilty pleasures (open daily from 11:00 until 5:00 in the morning—you'll see the little hot-dog shack a block up Kong Oscars Gate from the harbor). Each dog comes with a free little glass of fruit punch.

$ Söstrene Hagelin Fast Fish Joint is an easygoing eatery that's cheerier than its offerings—a pale extravaganza of Norway's white cuisine. It's all fish here: fish soup, fish burgers, fish balls, fish cakes, fish wraps, and even fish pudding (Mon-Fri 9:00-19:00, Sat 10:00-17:00, closed Sun, Strandgaten 3, +47 55 90 20 13).

$ Krohnhagen Café, a humble community center next to a retirement home, is run by the church and partly staffed by volunteers. While it's designed to give Bergen's poor (and the retired) an inviting place to enjoy, everyone's welcome (it's a favorite of local guides). The dining area is bright and spacious, the staff friendly, and the menu is simple yet tasty (salad and dinner buffets, soup, waffles, cheap sandwiches, Mon-Fri 11:00-16:00, closed Sat-Sun, Kong Oscars Gate 54, +47 45 22 07 95).

PICNICS AND GROCERIES

While you'll be tempted to drop into 7-Eleven-type stores, you'll pay for the convenience. Pick up your groceries for half the price at a real supermarket. The **Rema 1000 supermarket,** just across from the Bryggens Museum and St. Mary's Church, is particularly handy (Mon-Fri 7:00-23:00, Sat 8:00-21:00, closed Sun). For groceries on a Sunday, check out **Bunnpris**—just off Ole Bulls Plass, between the National Theater and Festplassen (Mon-Sat 6:00-24:00, Sun from 8:00, Torggaten 7).

Bergen Connections

Bergen is conveniently connected to **Oslo** by plane and train (trains depart Bergen daily at 7:57, 11:57, 15:57, and 22:59—but no night train on Sat, arrive at Oslo seven scenic hours later, additional departures in summer and fall, confirm times at station, 60-NOK seat reservation with second-class rail pass required—but free with first-class rail pass, book well in advance if traveling mid-July-Aug—there may be advance purchase discounts, buy tickets at Vy website). From Bergen, you can take the Norway in a Nutshell train/bus/ferry route; for information, see the Norway in a Nutshell chapter. Train info: +47 61 05 19 10 (9 for English), Vy.no.

To get to **Stockholm** or **Copenhagen,** you'll go via Oslo (see "Oslo Connections" on page 295). Before buying a ticket for a long train trip from Bergen, look into cheap flights.

By Express Boat to Balestrand and Flåm (on Sognefjord): A handy express boat links Bergen with Balestrand (4 hours) and Flåm (5.5 hours). For details, see page 339.

By Boat to Denmark: Fjordline runs a boat from Bergen to Hirtshals, Denmark (18.5 hours; departs daily at 13:30; boat from Hirtshals departs daily at 20:00, +47 51 46 40 99, www.fjordline. com).

By Boat to the Arctic: Hurtigruten coastal cruises depart nearly daily for the seven-day trip north up the scenic west coast to Kirkenes on the Russian border.

This route was started in 1893 as a postal and cargo delivery service along the west coast of Norway. Although no longer delivering mail, their ships still fly the Norwegian postal flag by special permission and deliver people, cars, and cargo from Bergen to Kirkenes. A lifeline for remote areas, the ships call at over 30 fishing villages and cities.

For the seven-day trip to Kirkenes, allow from $1,600 and up per person based on double occupancy (includes three meals per day, taxes, and port charges). Prices vary greatly depending on the season (highest June-July), cabin, and type of ship. The fleet includes those with a bit of brass built in the 1960s, but most of the ships in service were built in the mid-1990s and later. Shorter voyages are possible (including even just a day trip to one of the villages along the route). Cabins should be booked well in advance. Ship services include a 24-hour cafeteria, a launderette on newer boats, and optional port excursions. Check online for senior and off-season (Oct-March) specials at www.hurtigruten.com or call Hurtigruten (US +1 888 645 6370, Norway +47 77 59 71 68). For most travelers, the ride makes a great one-way trip, with a flight back south as a logical last leg (rather than returning to Bergen by boat—a 12-day round-trip).

Route Tips for Drivers: For tips on connecting Bergen to Denmark via the Setesdal Valley and the Kristiansand ferry, see the South Norway chapter.

BERGEN

SOUTH NORWAY

Stavanger • Setesdal Valley • Kristiansand

South Norway is pleasant and pretty. Spend a day in the harborside town of Stavanger. Delve into the oil industry at the surprisingly interesting Norwegian Petroleum Museum. Admire the Stavanger Cathedral, window-shop in the old town, cruise the harbor, or hoof it up Pulpit Rock, an eerily flat-topped rock thrusting 2,000 feet above the Lysefjord, with an eagle's-eye view deep into the fjord. A series of time-forgotten towns stretch across the Setesdal Valley, with sod-roofed cottages and locals who practice fiddles and harmonicas, rose painting, whittling, and gold- and silverwork.

PLANNING YOUR TIME

The main draw in this part of Norway is the famous Pulpit Rock hike; poking around Stavanger, a pleasant port city and the springboard for reaching Pulpit Rock, helps round out your time here. The hike takes the better part of a day, requiring at least one overnight. Several cruises also call at Stavanger.

The Setesdal Valley—covered at the end of this chapter—is for people with ample time, a car, and a desire to explore a scenic corner of Norway. Since it's not "on the way" to much of anything (except dreary Kristiansand and the ferry to Denmark), it only makes the cut for Norway completists.

Stavanger

This waterfront burg of about 125,000 is mildly charming, its streets lined with unpretentious shiplap cottages that echo its perennial ties to the sea. Stavanger feels more cosmopolitan than most small Norwegian cities, thanks in part to its oil industry—which brings multinational workers (and their money) into the city. Known as Norway's festival city, Stavanger hosts several lively events, including jazz in May (www.maijazz.no), Scandinavia's biggest food festival in July (www.gladmat.no), and chamber music in August (www.kammermusikkfestivalen.no).

For most visitors, Stavanger functions a launch pad for side-tripping to the famous, iconic Pulpit Rock. Stavanger itself has barely enough to fill a day: The Norwegian Petroleum Museum is the only big-time sight in town, Gamle Stavanger (the "old town") offers pleasant wandering on cobbled lanes, and the city's fine cathedral is worth a peek.

Orientation to Stavanger

Stavanger is most interesting around its harbor, where you'll find the Maritime Museum, lots of shops and restaurants (particularly around the market plaza and along Kirkegata, which connects the cathedral to the Petroleum Museum), the indoor fish market, and a produce market. The artificial Lake Breiavatnet— bordered by Kongsgaten on the east and Olav V's Gate on the west—separates the train and bus stations from the harbor.

TOURIST INFORMATION

The centrally located TI can help with day trips, including logistics and tickets for reaching Pulpit Rock and other scenic hikes (June-Aug daily 8:00-18:00; Sept-May Mon-Fri 9:00-16:00, Sat until 14:00, closed Sun; Strandkaien 61, +47 51 85 92 00, www.regionstavanger.com).

ARRIVAL IN STAVANGER

Cruise liners dock right at the Vågen harbor in the very center of town. Some tie up on the west side of the harbor (called Strandkaien) next to the TI, and others put in along the east side (called Skagenkaien)—but both are an easy walk to the central market plaza. Stavanger's **train and bus stations** are a five-minute walk around Lake Breiavatnet to the inner harbor and cathedral.

Stavanger's **Sola Airport** is about nine miles outside the city (code: SVG, +47 67 03 10 00, www.avinor.no). The Flybussen airport bus connects to the train and bus stations, city center, and ferry terminal (see www.flybussen.no).

HELPFUL HINTS

Money: ATMs are on buildings facing the harbor, opposite the cathedral.

Laundry: Renseriet offers expensive drop-off service and affordable self-service (Mon-Fri 8:30-16:30, Thu until 19:00, Sat 9:00-15:00, closed Sun, Kongsgata 40, +47 51 89 56 53).

Accommodations

1. Thon Hotel Maritim
2. Hotel Victoria
3. Stavanger B&B

Eateries & Other

4. XO Mat & Vinhus
5. Renaa Xpress
6. Skagen Bageri
7. Supermarket
8. Market Plaza Eateries
9. Vågen Spiseri & Fish Market
10. N. B. Sørensen's Dampskibsexpedition
11. Sjøhuset Skagen
12. Bølgen og Moi
13. Launderette
14. Sightseeing Boats to Lysefjord & Pulpit Rock
15. Ferries to Tau & Lysebotn
16. Flybussen Stops (4)
17. Bus to Fjordline Terminal (Ferries to Hirtshals, Denmark)

Sights in and Near Stavanger

IN STAVANGER TOWN

▲Stavanger Cathedral (Stavanger Domkirke)

Stavanger's top church—which overlooks the town center on a small ridge—has a harmonious interior and a few intriguing details worth lingering over. Good English information throughout the church brings meaning to the place. Parts of the church may be closed to visitors for restoration through 2023 as it gears up to celebrate its 900th birthday in 2025.

Cost and Hours: 30 NOK, open daily 11:00-16:00, +47 51 84 04 00, www.stavangerdomkirke.no.

Visiting the Church: The cathedral, dedicated to St. Swithun (his relic, an arm, was popular with pilgrims), was originally built in 1125 in a Norman style, with basket-handle Romanesque arches. After a fire badly damaged the church in the 13th century, a new chancel was added in the pointy-arched Gothic style. You can't miss where the architecture changes about three-quarters of the way up the aisle. On the left, behind the baptismal font, notice the ivy-lined railing on the stone staircase; this pattern is part of the city's coat of arms. And nearby, appreciate the colorful, richly detailed "gristle Baroque"-style pulpit (from 1658). Notice that the whole thing is resting on Samson's stoic shoulders—even as he faces down a lion.

Stroll the church, perusing its several fine "epitaphs" (tomb markers), which are paintings in ornately decorated frames. Go on a scavenger hunt for two unique features; both are on the second columns from the back of the church. On the right, at the top facing away from the nave, notice the stone carvings of Norse mythological figures: Odin on the left, and a wolf-like beast on the right. Although the medieval Norwegians were Christians, they weren't ready to entirely abandon all of their pagan traditions. On the opposite column, circle around the base and look at ankle level, facing away from the altar. Here you see a grotesque sculpture that looks like a fish head with human hands. Notice that its head has been worn down. One interpretation is that early worshippers would ritualistically put their foot on top of it, as if to push the evil back to the underworld. Mysteriously, both of these features are one-offs—you won't find anything like them on any other column in the church.

▲▲Norwegian Petroleum Museum (Norsk Oljemuseum)

This entertaining, informative museum—dedicated to the discovery of oil in Norway's North Sea in 1969 and the industry built

up around it—offers an unapologetic look at the country's biggest money-maker. With half of Western Europe's oil reserves, the formerly poor agricultural nation of Norway is the Arabia of the North and a world-class player, producing 1.6 million barrels a day.

Cost and Hours: 150 NOK; daily 10:00-19:00; Sept-May Mon-Sat 10:00-16:00, Sun until 18:00; +47 51 93 93 00, www.norskolje.museum.no. The small museum shop sells various petroleum-based products. The museum's recommended Bølgen og Moi restaurant has an inviting terrace over the water.

Visiting the Museum: The exhibit describes how oil was formed, how it's found and produced, and what it's used for. You'll see models of oil rigs, actual drill bits, see-through cylinders that you can rotate to investigate different types of crude, and lots of explanations (in English) about various aspects of oil. Interactive exhibits cover everything from the history of the earth (4.5 billion years displayed on a large overhead globe, showing how our planet has changed—stay for the blast that killed the dinosaurs), to day-to-day life on an offshore platform, to petroleum products in our lives (though the peanut-butter-and-petroleum-jelly sandwich is a bit much). Kids enjoy climbing on the model drilling platform, trying out the emergency escape chute at the platform outside, and playing with many other hands-on exhibits.

Several included movies delve into specific aspects of oil: The main movie, *Oljeunge (Oil Kid)*, stars a fictional character who was born in 1969—the year Norway discovered oil—and shows how that discovery changed Norwegian society over the last 50 years. Other movies (in the cylindrical structures outside) highlight intrepid North Sea divers and the construction of an oil platform. Each film runs in English at least twice hourly.

Even the museum's architecture was designed to echo the foundations of the oil industry—bedrock (the stone building), slate and chalk deposits in the sea (slate floor of the main hall), and the rigs (cylindrical platforms). While the museum has its fair share of propaganda, it also has several good exhibits on the environmental toll of drilling and consuming oil.

Gamle Stavanger

Stavanger's "old town" centers on Øvre Strandgate, on the west side of the harbor. Wander the narrow, winding, cobbled back lanes, with tidy wooden houses, oasis gardens, and flower-bedecked entranceways. Peek into a workshop or gallery to find ceramics, glass, jewelry, and more. Many shops are open roughly daily 10:00-17:00.

Museum Stavanger (M.U.S.T.)

This "museum" is actually 10 different museums scattered around town (covered by a single 95-NOK combo-ticket, most closed Mon off-season, for details see www. museumstavanger.no). The various branches include the **Stavanger Museum,** featuring the history of the city and a zoological exhibit (Muségate 16); the **Maritime Museum** (Sjøfartsmuseum), near the bottom end of Vågen harbor (Nedre Strandgate 17); the **Norwegian Canning Museum** (Norsk Hermetikkmuseum—the *brisling,* or herring, is smoked the first Sunday of every month—Øvre Strandgate 88A); **Ledaal,** a royal residence and manor house (Eiganesveien 45); and **Breidablikk,** a wooden villa from the late 1800s (Eiganesveien 40A).

DAY TRIPS TO LYSEFJORD AND PULPIT ROCK

The nearby Lysefjord is an easy day trip. Those with more time (and strong legs) can hike to the top of 2,000-foot-high Pulpit Rock. The TI sells tickets for several tour companies and is a good place to confirm details before you head out.

Lysefjord Boat Tour

A boat tour here is memorable: you'll see towering mountains, waterfalls, rustic farms, and, if you're lucky, colonies of seals.

Rødne Fjord Cruise offers three-hour round-trip excursions from Stavanger to Lysefjord (including a view of Pulpit Rock—but no stops). Conveniently, boats depart from the main Vågen harbor in the heart of town (east side of the harbor, in front of Skansegata, along Skagenkaien; 580 NOK; May-Sept daily at 10:00 and 14:00, also at 12:00 July-Aug; April and Oct daily at 11:00; Jan-Feb and Nov-Dec Wed-Sun at 11:00; +47 51 89 52 70, www.rodne. no). They also offer a combined boat tour and Pulpit Rock trip (see below).

A different company, **Norled,** runs similar trips (490 NOK, July-Sept daily at 12:15, extra departures on busy days, www. norled.no). For a slower journey up the Lysefjord, it's possible to

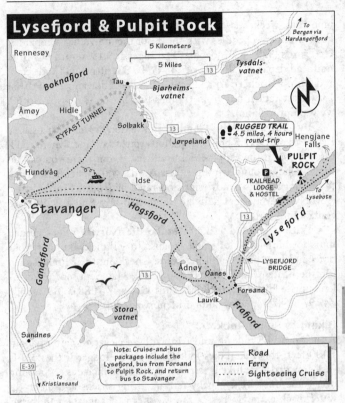

Lysefjord & Pulpit Rock

Note: Cruise-and-bus packages include the Lysefjord, bus from Forsand to Pulpit Rock, and return bus to Stavanger

Road
Ferry
Sightseeing Cruise

SOUTH NORWAY

ride on a car ferry that's part of the Stavanger-Lysebotn line (see the Ryfylke region timetable at www.kolumbus.no).

Pulpit Rock (Preikestolen)

Ascending to this dramatic 270-square-foot natural platform gives you a fantastic view of the fjord and surrounding mountains. Hiking up to the top of Pulpit Rock is a popular outing that will take the better part of a day; plan on 45 minutes travel time each way, about four hours of hiking (two hours up, two hours down), and time to linger at the top for photos. The rock has its own website with helpful advice (https://preikestolen365.com).

Getting There

By Car: From Stavanger, it's about a 45-minute drive via the nine-mile Ryfast Tunnel, which burrows under the sea at Stavanger and emerges near Solbakk on the other side (140-NOK toll). From there turn onto highway 13 and follow signs to *Preikestolen*. In summer you'll pay 250 NOK to park at the trailhead.

By Bus Tour: The trailhead is easily reached in summer with a bus tour. Trips generally go daily from hotels in Stavanger (daily

June-Aug; weekends-only March-May and Sept-Oct; none Nov-Feb). Confirm schedules with the TI or the individual companies: **Go Fjords** (329 NOK, departs Stavanger at 9:15, return bus from trailhead departs at 15:30, +47 48 06 03 33, https://gofjords.com) and **Pulpit Rock Tours** (325 NOK, departs Stavanger at 9:10 or 13:10, last return bus from trailhead at 18:00, +47 51 59 90 60, www.pulpitrock.no).

By Cruise-and-Bus Combo: This option begins with a scenic Lysefjord cruise (2.5 hours) and drops you at Forsand, where you'll catch a bus to the Pulpit Rock trailhead. From there you can do the four-hour round-trip hike; afterwards, you'll catch a bus back to Stavanger. This handy trip is operated by **Rødne Fjord Cruise** (930 NOK, May-Sept daily at 10:00, also July-Aug at 12:00, see contact info earlier).

With a Guided Hike: Outdoorlife Norway offers guided tours for individuals or small groups. They'll pick you up at your hotel and even provide hiking poles. Check out their Preikestolen Off the Beaten Track Hike (1,590 NOK, May-Sept) or Preikestolen Sunrise Hike (1,390 NOK, April-Oct, +47 51 88 03 88, mobile +47 97 65 87 04, www.outdoorlifenorway.com).

Hiking to Pulpit Rock

At just over 4.5 miles round-trip, with an elevation gain of about 1,100 feet, this hike takes four hours total—longer if the trail is very crowded. The hike is fairly strenuous and includes scrambling over sometimes tricky, rocky terrain. Bring snacks and plenty of water, pack extra clothes as the weather is changeable, and wear sturdy hiking shoes or boots. Start early or you'll be sharing the trail with dogs on long leashes, toddlers navigating boulders, and the unprepared Bermuda-shorts crowd in flip-flops.

The trail starts by the big sign at the entrance to the main parking lot. From there the path climbs steadily through forest at first and eventually into open, rocky terrain. Along the way, you can thank Nepali Sherpas—who were hired to improve sections of the route—for their fine stonework on the trail.

The farther and higher you go, the rockier and more spectacular the scenery becomes. When-ever the trail disappears onto bare rock, look for the red T's painted on stones or posts marking the route. As you near Pulpit Rock, the path tiptoes along the cliff's edge with airy views out to the Lysefjord that can only be topped by those from the rock itself.

Before you head back, scramble up the mountainside behind the rock for that iconic, tourist-brochure scene of the people-speckled Pulpit Rock soaring out over the fjord 2,000 feet below.

Sleeping at the Pulpit Rock Trailhead

The Pulpit Rock trail is usually very crowded during the middle of the day, even in bad weather. I prefer to spend the night at the trailhead, and get an early start on the trail the next morning. If you don't have a car, you can get here from Stavanger by using one of the tour options listed above.

$$$$ Preikestolen Fjellstue is a modern building with 27 bright, simple, functional rooms and a pricey restaurant with a lovely lake view (includes breakfast, free parking). Below the Fjellstue and closer to the lake, the rustic, grass-roofed **$ Preikestolhytta** hostel has rooms that sleep 2-4 and bathrooms down the hall (includes breakfast). Both are run by the Norwegian Trekking Association (+47 51 74 20 74, www.preikestolenfjellstue. no).

SOUTH NORWAY

Sleeping in Stavanger

$$$ Thon Hotel Maritim, with 140 rooms, is two blocks from the train station near the artificial Lake Breiavatnet. It can be a good deal for a big business-class hotel (elevator, Kongsgaten 32, +47 51 85 05 00, www.thonhotels.no/maritim, maritim@olavthon.no).

$$$ Hotel Victoria has 107 business-class rooms over a stately, high-ceilinged lobby facing the Skagenkaien embankment right on the harbor (elevator, Skansegata 1, +47 51 86 70 00, www.hotel-victoria.no, post@hotel-victoria.no).

$ Stavanger B&B is Stavanger's best budget option. This large red house among a sea of white houses has tidy, tiny rooms. The lodgings are basic, verging on institutional—not cozy or doily—but they're affordable and friendly. The shared toilet is down the hall; 14 rooms have their own showers, while eight share showers down the hall. Waffles, coffee, and friendly chatter are served up every evening at 21:00 (10-minute uphill walk behind train station in residential neighborhood, Vikedalsgate 1A, +47 45 41 31 60, www.stavangerbedandbreakfast.no, post@sbb.no). If you let them know in advance, they may be able to pick you up or drop you off at the boat dock or train station.

Eating in Stavanger

CASUAL DINING

$$$ XO Mat & Vinhus, in an elegant setting, serves up big portions of traditional Norwegian food and pricier contemporary fare (Mon-Wed 14:30-23:30, Thu 11:00-23:00, Fri-Sat 11:30 until late, closed Sun, a block behind main drag along harbor at Skagen 10 ved Prostebakken, mobile +47 91 00 03 07).

$$ Renaa Xpress, popular with the locals, is inside Stavanger's library and cultural center. It's a cozy café where bakers make their own bread and pastries. In addition to a variety of sandwiches, salads, and soups, they also offer sourdough pizza after 13:00 (Mon-Thu 10:00-22:00, Fri-Sat until 24:00, Sun 12:00-22:00, Sølvberggata 2, mobile +47 94 00 93 48).

$ Skagen Bageri, in a lovely, leaning wooden building dating to the 1700s, serves baked goods and traditional open-face sandwiches at reasonable prices in a cozy, rustic-elegant setting (Mon-Fri 8:00-15:00, Sat until 16:00, closed Sun; in the blue-and-white building a block off the harborfront at Skagen 18; +47 51 89 51 71).

Meny is a large supermarket with a good selection and a fine deli for super picnic shopping (Mon-Fri 7:00-20:00, Sat 9:00-18:00, closed Sun, in Straen Senteret shopping mall, Lars Hertervigs Gate 6, +47 51 50 50 10).

Market Plaza Eateries: The busy square between the cathedral and the harbor is packed with reliable Norwegian chain restaurants. If you're a fan of **Deli de Luca, Dolly Dimple's,** or **Dickens Pub,** you'll find them within a few steps of here.

DINING ALONG THE HARBOR WITH A VIEW

The harborside street of Skansegata is lined with lively restaurants and pubs, and most serve food.

$$$$ Vågen Spiseri, in the same building as the fish market, serves tasty seafood dishes based on the catch of the day (affordable lunch specials, Mon-Wed 11:00-21:00, Thu-Sat until 24:00, closed Sun, Strandkaien 37, +47 51 52 73 50, www.fisketorget-stavanger.no).

$$$$ N. B. Sørensen's Dampskibsexpedition consists of a lively pub on the first floor (pasta, fish, meat, and vegetarian dishes; Mon-Wed 16:00-24:00, Sat 11:00-late, Sun 13:00-23:00) and a fine-dining restaurant on the second floor, with tablecloths, view tables overlooking the harbor, and a pricey menu (Mon-Sat 18:00-23:00, closed Sun, Skagenkaien 26, +47 51 84 38 20, www.herlige-stavanger.no). The restaurant is named after an 1800s company that shipped from this building, among other things, Norwegians heading to the US. Passengers and cargo waited on the first floor, and the manager's office was upstairs. The place is filled with emigrant-era memorabilia.

$$$$ Sjøhuset Skagen, with a woodsy interior, invites diners to its historic building for lunch or dinner. The building, from the late 1700s, once housed a trading company. Today, you can choose from local seafood specialties with an ethnic flair, as well as plenty of meat options (Mon-Sat 11:30-24:00, Sun from 13:00, Skagenkaien 16, +47 51 89 51 80, www.skagenrestaurant.no).

$$$$ Bølgen og Moi, the restaurant at the Petroleum Museum, has great views over the harbor (good lunch specials, lunch daily 11:00-16:00; dinner Tue-Sat 18:00-20:00—reservations recommended; Kjeringholmen 748, +47 51 93 93 51, www.bolgenogmoi.no).

Stavanger Connections

From Stavanger by Train to: Kristiansand (5/day, 3 hours), **Oslo** (5/day, 8 hours, overnight possible).

By Bus to Bergen: Kystbussen operates buses between Stavanger and Bergen (hourly, 5.5 hours, +47 52 70 35 26, http://kystbussen.no).

By Boat to Denmark: Fjordline ferries sail overnight from Stavanger to Hirtshals, Denmark (12 hours, www.fjordline.com).

The Setesdal Valley

Welcome to the remote, and therefore very traditional, Setesdal Valley. Probably Norway's most authentic cranny, the valley is a mellow montage of sod-roofed water mills, ancient churches, derelict farmhouses, yellowed recipes, lovely lakes, and gentle scenery. The Setesdal Valley isn't on the way to anything (except the ferry crossing from Kristiansand to Hirtshals, in Denmark).

But that's sort of the point. Come here only if you have ample time, and really want to commune with time-passed, rural Norway.

The valley is famous for its filigree jewelry, made to adorn traditional costumes and echoing the rhythmical designs of the Viking era and Middle Ages. Each town has a weekly rotating series of hikes and activities for the regular, stay-put-for-a-week visitor. The upper valley is dead in the summer but enjoys a bustling winter.

The Setesdal Valley joined the modern age with the construction of the valley highway in the 1950s. All along the valley you'll see the unique two-story storage sheds called *stabburs* (the top floor was used for storing clothes; the bottom, food) and many sod roofs. Even the bus stops have rooftops the local goats love to munch.

In the high country, just over the Sessvatn summit (3,000 feet), you'll see herds of goats and summer farms. If you see an *ekte geitost* sign, that means genuine, homemade goat cheese is for sale. (It's sold cheaper and in more manageable sizes in grocery stores.) To some, it looks like a decade's accumulation of earwax. I think it's delicious. Remember, *ekte* means all-goat—really strong. The more popular and easier-to-eat version is made from a blend of cow and goat milk.

Without a car, the Setesdal Valley is not worth the trouble—there are no trains in the valley, and bus schedules are as sparse as the population. The sights are best for joyriding. If you're in Bergen with a car, and want to get to Denmark, this route is more interesting than repeating Oslo.

For more information on the Setesdal Valley, see www.visitsorlandet.com/setesdal.

Sights in the Setesdal Valley

I've described these roadside sights from north to south, most logically connected on a 10-hour drive from Bergen to Kristiansand. To trace this route, see the "South Norway" map at the beginning of this chapter.

From Bergen, drive about 2.5 hours, giving yourself plenty of time to catch the 9:00 Kvanndal-Utne ferry (www.norled.no). To reach **Kvanndal,** take the E-16 highway toward Voss and Oslo (signs for *Nestune, Landås, Nattland*); then, after a long tunnel, leave the Voss road and take highway 7 heading for Norheimsund, and then Kvanndal. This road, treacherous for the famed beauty of the Hardangerfjord it hugs as well as for its skinniness, is faster and safer if you beat the traffic.

The Kvanndal ferry drops you in **Utne,** where a lovely road takes you south along the Hardangerfjord. At the fjord's end, just past the huge zinc and copper industrial plant, you'll hit the industrial town of **Odda** (TI on market square at Torget 2, +47 48 07 07 77, www.visitodda.com). Odda brags that Kaiser Wilhelm came here a lot, but he's dead and I'd drive right through. If you want to visit the tongue of a glacier, drive to Buer and hike an hour to Buerbreen.

From Odda, drive into the land of boulders. The many mighty

waterfalls that line the road seem to have hurled huge rocks (with rooted trees) into the rivers and fields. Stop at the giant **double waterfall** called Låtefossen (on the left, pullout on the right, drive slowly through it if you need a car wash).

Continue over Røldalsfjellet and follow E-134 into the valley below, where the old town of **Røldal** is trying to develop some tourism (drive on by—its old church isn't worth the stop). Lakes are like frosted mirrors, making desolate huts come in pairs. Farther along on the Hardangervidda plateau is **Haukeliseter**—a group of sod-roofed buildings filled with cultural clichés and tour groups, offering light food in a lakeside setting.

At the Haukeli transportation junction, turn south on highway 9 and wind up to **Sessvatn** at 3,000 feet (toward Hovden). Enter the upper Setesdal Valley. From here, you'll follow the Otra River downhill for 140 miles south to the major port town of Kristiansand. Skip the secondary routes.

A ski resort at the top of the Setesdal Valley (2,500 feet), **Hovden** is barren in the summer and painfully in need of charm. Still, it makes a good home base if you want to explore the area and has a seasonal TI (+47 37 93 93 70, www.hovden.com). Hovden has boat rental (at Hegni Center, south edge of town, +47 37 93 93 70); a water park (Hovden Badeland, +47 37 93 93 93, www.badeland. com); the free Museum of Iron Production (Jernvinnemuseum—learn about iron production from the late Iron Age with the aid of drawings, exhibits, and recorded narration in English from a "Viking," about 100 yards behind the Hegni Center); and plenty of choices for hikes and mountain biking. Good walks offer you a chance to see reindeer, moose, arctic fox, and wabbits—so they say. Berry picking is popular in late August, when small, sweet blueberries are in season. A sporadically running chairlift sometimes takes sightseers to the top of a nearby peak, with great views in clear weather; bikers can ride the trails downhill. Hunting season starts in late August for reindeer (only in higher elevations) and later in the fall for grouse and moose (elg).

For an affordable place to sleep or eat in Hovden, consider the big, old ski chalet called ¢ **Hovden Fjellstoge.** Check out the mural in the balcony overlooking the lobby—an artistic rendition of this area's history. Behind the mural is a frightening taxidermy collection (www.hovdenfjellstoge.no).

Leaving Hovden, you enter the most scenic stretch of the drive. Nine miles south of Hovden is a two-mile side-trip to a 400-foot-high rock-pile dam, called **Dammar Vatnedalsvatn,** with great view and an impressive rockery. Sit out of the wind a few rows down the rock pile and ponder the vastness of Norwegian wood.

Farther south, the most interesting folk museum and church in Setesdal are in the teeny town of **Bykle.** The 17th-century

SOUTH NORWAY

church has two balconies—one for men and one for women (www.setesdalsmuseet.no).

On the east side of the main road (at the *Grasbrokke* sign) is an old water mill (1630). A few minutes farther south, at the sign for *Sanden Såre Camping,* exit onto a little road to stretch your legs at another old water mill with a fragile, rotten-log sluice.

In Flateland, the **Setesdal Museum** (Rygnestadtunet) offers more of what you saw at Bykle; unless you're a glutton for culture, I wouldn't do both (www.setesdalsmuseet.no). Past Flateland at **Honnevje** is a nice picnic and WC stop, with a dock along the water for swimming...for hot-weather days or polar bears.

Valle is Setesdal's prettiest village (but don't tell Bykle). In the center, you'll find fine silver- and gold-work, homemade crafts next to the TI (+47 37 93 75 29), and occasional *lefse* cooking demonstrations. The fine suspension bridge attracts kids of any age (b-b-b-b-bounce), and anyone interested in a great view over the river to strange mountains that look like polished, petrified mudslides. European rock climbers, tired of the over-climbed Alps, often entertain spectators with their sport. Is anyone climbing? To sleep in Valle, consider the basic **Valle Motell** (www.valle-motell.no).

South of Valle, the area has a lot more logging (and is less scenic). In **Nomeland,** the Sylvartun silversmith shop, whose owner Hallvard Bjørgum is also a renowned Hardanger fiddle player, sells Setesdal silver in a 17th-century, grass-roofed log cabin next to the main road.

Farther south, the road traces first the west shore of the freshwater Åraksfjord and then the east shore of the long and scenic (and also freshwater) Byglandsfjord to **Grendi,** where the Ardal Church (1827) has a rune in its yard. Three hundred yards south of the church is a 900-year-old oak tree.

A huge town by Setesdal standards (3,500 people), **Evje** is famous for its gems and mines. Fancy stones fill the shops here. Rockhounds find the nearby mines fun; for a small fee, you can hunt for gems. The **Setesdal Mineral Park** is on the main road, two miles south of town (www.mineralparken.no).

From Evje, it's about an hour's drive to this region's transportation hub, **Kristiansand.**

Kristiansand

The "capital of the south," Kristiansand has 85,000 inhabitants, a pleasant Renaissance grid-plan layout (Posebyen), a famous zoo with Norway's biggest amusement park, lots of big boats going to Denmark, and a TI (Rådhusgata 18, +47 38 07 50 00, www.visitsorlandet.com). It's the closest thing to a beach resort in Norway. Markensgate is the bustling pedestrian market street—an enjoyable place for good browsing, shopping, eating, and people-watching. Stroll along the Strand Promenaden (marina) to Christiansholm Fortress. The otherwise uninteresting harbor area has a cluster of wooden buildings called **Fiskebasaren** ("Fish Bazaar") with an indoor fish market and numerous restaurants offering a nice dinner atmosphere.

Sleeping in Kristiansand: Hotels are expensive and nondescript; consider the **$$$$ Rica Hotel Norge** (Dronningensgate 5, +47 38 17 40 00, www.hotel-norge.no) or the **$$$$ Thon Hotel Parken** (ask for quiet room, Kirkegate 15, +47 38 17 20 40, www.thonhotels.no/wergeland).

Kristiansand Connections: Trains connect to **Stavanger** (5/day, 3 hours) and **Oslo** (5/day, 4.5 hours). Kristiansand is also a hub for the **ferry to Hirtshals, Denmark,** operated by two companies: Color Line (2/day year-round, more in summer, 3.5 hours, www.colorline.com) and Fjordline (1-2/day in summer, none in winter, 2.5 hours, www.fjordline.com). Reservations are smart. You can either drive on or walk on.

SWEDEN

SWEDEN

Scandinavia's heartland, Sweden is far bigger than Denmark and far flatter than Norway. This family-friendly land is home to Ikea, Volvo, ABBA, and long summer vacations at red-painted, white-trimmed summer cottages. Its capital, Stockholm, is Scandinavia's grandest city.

Sweden is committed to its peoples' safety and security, and proud of its success in creating a society with one of the lowest poverty rates in the world. Yet Sweden has thrown in its lot with the European Union, and locals debate whether to open their economy even further.

While it's still the capital of blond, Sweden is now also home to a large immigrant population. Foreign-born and first-generation immigrants—primarily from Finland, Syria, and Iraq—make up about 20 percent of the population. Sweden is also home to about 30,000 indigenous Sami people.

Sweden used to be a Lutheran state, with the Church of Sweden as its official religion. But in the year 2000, the church and state officially separated, and Sweden no longer has a state church. Although the culture is nominally Lutheran, few people attend services regularly. While church is handy for Christmas, Easter, marriages, and burials, most Swedes are more likely to find religion in nature, such as hiking in the vast forests or fishing in one of the thousands of lakes or rivers.

Sweden is almost 80 percent wilderness, and modern legislation incorporates an ancient right of public access called *allemansrätten*, which guarantees that anyone can move freely through Sweden's natural scenery without asking landowners for permission, as long as they behave responsibly. In summer, Swedes take advantage of the long days and warm evenings for festivals such as Midsummer (in late June) and crayfish parties *(kräftskiva)* in August and September.

Many Swedes have a summer cottage—or know someone who does—where they spend countless hours swimming, soaking up the sun, and devouring boxes of juicy strawberries.

While Denmark and Norway look westward to Britain and the Atlantic, Sweden has always faced east, across the Baltic Sea. As Vikings, Norwegians went west to Iceland, Greenland, and America; Danes headed south to England, France, and the Mediterranean; and Swedes went east into Russia. (The word "Russia" has Viking roots.) In the early Middle Ages, Swedes founded the Russian cities of Nizhny Novgorod and Kiev, and even served as royal guards in Constantinople (modern-day Istanbul). During the later Middle Ages, German settlers and traders strongly influenced Sweden's culture and language. By the 17th century, Sweden was a major European power, with one of the largest naval fleets in Europe and an empire extending around the Baltic, including Finland, Estonia, Latvia, and parts of Poland, Russia, and Germany.

Sweden Almanac

Official Name: Konungariket Sverige—the Kingdom of Sweden—or simply Sweden.

Size: At 174,000 square miles, Sweden is a little bigger than California, with 10.2 million people (about 58 per square mile).

Geography: A chain of mountains divides Sweden from Norway on the Scandinavian Peninsula. Sweden's mostly forested landscape is flanked to the east by the Baltic Sea, which contributes to the temperate climate. Sweden also encompasses several islands, of which Gotland and Öland are the largest.

Latitude and Longitude: 62°N and 15°E, similar latitude to Canada's Northwest Territories.

Biggest City: Sweden's capital city, Stockholm, has a population of 974,000, with more than two million in the metropolitan area. Göteborg (581,000) and Malmö (316,000) are the next-largest cities.

Economy: Sweden has a $518 billion gross domestic product and a per capita GDP of $51,200—similar to Germany's. Manufacturing, telecommunications, automobiles, and processed foods rank among its top industries, along with timber, hydropower, and iron ore. The Swedish economy is one of the strongest in Europe, helped by its competitive high-tech businesses—and by the government's generally conservative fiscal policies. Some 71 percent of Swedish workers belong to a labor union.

Currency: 9 Swedish kronor (SEK) = about $1.

Government: King Carl XVI Gustav is the ceremonial head of Sweden's constitutional monarchy. The 349-member Swedish Parliament (Riksdag) is elected every four years and led by a prime minister, who appoints cabinet members.

Flag: The Swedish flag is blue with a yellow Scandinavian cross. The colors are derived from the Swedish coat of arms, with yellow symbolizing the generosity of the people and blue representing vigilance, truth, loyalty, perseverance, and justice.

The Average Swede is 41 years old, has 1.87 children, and will live to be 82.

SWEDEN

But by the early 19th century, Sweden's war-weary empire had shrunk. The country's current borders date from 1809.

During a massive wave of emigration from the 1860s to World War II, about a quarter of Sweden's people left for the Promised Land—America. Many emigrants were farmers from the southern region of Småland. The House of Emigrants museum in Växjö tells their story (see the Southeast Sweden chapter), as do the movies *The Emigrants* and *The New Land*, based on the books of Vilhelm Moberg.

The 20th century was good to Sweden. While other European countries were embroiled in two world wars, neutral Sweden grew stronger, finding equilibrium between the extremes of communism and the free market. In the postwar years, Sweden adopted its famous "middle way," an economic model that balanced the needs of the democratic state and the private business sector.

The Swedish model worked very well for a while, providing a booming economy and robust social services for all. But the flip side of those ambitious programs is one of the highest tax levels in the world. After a recession hit in the early 1990s, some started to criticize the middle way as unworkable. But Sweden's economy improved in the late 1990s and early 2000s, buoyed by a strong lineup of successful multinational companies. Volvo (now Chinese-owed but Sweden-based), Scania (trucks and machinery), Ikea, H&M (clothing), and Ericsson (the telecommunications giant) led the way in manufacturing, design, and technology.

The global economic downturn of 2008-2009 had its impact on Sweden's export-driven economy: Unemployment ticked upward (although it remains enviably low compared to other countries), its famously generous welfare systems felt the pressure, and its Saab car manufacturer filed for bankruptcy protection. But Sweden has rebounded since the crisis, and the country's fortunes have outpaced those of the European Union—Sweden's main export market.

Historically Sweden has had an open-door policy when it comes to accepting immigrants. Beginning in the 1960s, Sweden (like Denmark and Norway) accepted many immigrants and refugees from southeastern Europe, the Middle East, and elsewhere. This praiseworthy humanitarian

SWEDEN

policy dramatically—and sometimes painfully—diversified a formerly homogenous country. But in 2015 and 2016, with refugees flooding in from Syria, Swedish social services were tested as never before. Migration laws were tightened in 2015, and by 2019 only 5 percent of Swedish immigrants were from Syria; most were returning Swedes followed by people from India and Afghanistan.

In Sweden, the dominant language is Swedish, but most residents speak English as well. Even though communication is rarely an issue, a few Swedish words are helpful and appreciated. "Hi" is *"Hej"* (hey). "Thank you" is *"Tack"* (tack), which can also double for "please." For a longer list of Swedish survival phrases, see the next page.

Swedish Survival Phrases

Swedish pronunciation (especially the vowel sounds) can be tricky for Americans, and there's quite a bit of variation across the country; listen closely to locals and imitate, or ask for help. The most difficult Swedish sound is sj, which sounds roughly like a guttural "hw" (made in your throat); however, like many sounds, this is pronounced differently across regions—for example, Stockholmers might say it more like "shw."

Hello. (formal)	Goddag.	goh-**dahg**
Hi. / Bye. (informal)	Hej. / Hej då.	hey / hey doh
Do you speak English?	Talar du engelska?	**tah**-lar doo **eng**-ehl-skah
Yes. / No.	Ja. / Nej.	yaw / nay
Please.	Snälla. / Tack.*	**snehl**-lah / tack
Thank you (very much).	Tack (så mycket).	tack (soh **mee**-keh)
You're welcome.	Ingen orsak.	**eeng**-ehn **oor**-sahk
Can I help you?	Kan jag hjälpa dig?	kahn yaw **yehl**-pah day
Excuse me.	Ursäkta.	oor-**sehk**-tah
(Very) good.	(Mycket) bra.	(**mee**-keh) brah
Goodbye.	Adjö.	ah-**yew**
zero / one / two	noll / en / två	nohl / ehn / tvoh
three / four	tre / fyra	tree / **fee**-rah
five / six	fem / sex	fehm / sehks
seven / eight	sju / åtta	*h*woo / **oh**-tah
nine / ten	nio / tio	**nee**-oh / **tee**-oh
hundred	hundra	**hoon**-drah
thousand	tusen	**too**-sehn
How much?	Hur mycket?	hewr **mee**-keh
local currency: (Swedish) kronor	(Svenska) kronor	(**sven**-skeh) **kroh**-nor
Where is...?	Var finns...?	var feens
...the toilet	...toaletten	toh-ah-**leh**-tehn
men	män	men
women	kvinnor	**kvee**-nor
water / coffee	vatten / kaffe	**vah**-tehn / kah-**feh**
beer / wine	öl / vin	url / veen
Cheers!	Skål!	skohl
The bill, please.	Notan, tack.	**noh**-tahn tack

*Swedish has various ways to say "please," depending on the context. The simplest is *snälla,* but Swedes sometimes use the word *tack* (thank you) the way we use "please."

STOCKHOLM

If I had to call one European city home, it might be Stockholm. One-third water, one-third parks, one-third city, on the sea, surrounded by woods, bubbling with energy and history, Sweden's stunning capital is green, clean, and underrated.

The city is built on a string of islands connected by bridges. Its location midway along the Baltic Sea, behind the natural fortification of its archipelago, made it a fine port, vital to the economy and security of the Swedish peninsula. Stockholm became a political center when Gustav Vasa established the monarchy in 1523. A century later, the expansionist King Gustavus Adolphus made it an influential European capital. The Industrial Revolution brought factories and a flood of farmers from the countryside. In the 20th century, the fuming smokestacks were replaced with steel-and-glass Modernist buildings housing high-tech workers and an expanding service sector.

Today, with more than two million people in the greater metropolitan area (one in five Swedes), Stockholm is Sweden's largest city, as well as its cultural, educational, and media center. It's also the country's most ethnically diverse city. Despite its size, Stockholm is committed to limiting its environmental footprint. Development is strictly monitored, and cars must pay a toll to enter the city. The city feels wealthy, sometimes snobby, and a bit sure of itself. Stockholm rivals Oslo in expense, and beats it in pretense.

For the visitor, Stockholm offers both old and new. Crawl through Europe's best-preserved old warship and relax on a scenic harbor boat tour. Browse the cobbles and antique shops of the lantern-lit Old Town. Take a trip back in time at Skansen, Europe's first and best open-air folk museum. Marvel at Stockholm's glittering City Hall, slick shopping malls, and art museums. (Even "also ran" museums in this city rank high on the European scale.) Explore the funky vibrancy of the design-forward Södermalm district.

While progressive and sleek, Stockholm respects its heritage. In summer, military bands parade daily through the heart of town to the Royal Palace, announcing the changing of the guard and turning even the most dignified tourist into a scampering kid.

With extra time, consider one or more Stockholm side trips, including the nearby royal residence, Drottningholm Palace; the cute town of Sigtuna; or the university town of Uppsala, with its grand cathedral, Linnaeus Garden and Museum, and Iron Age mounds (see the Near Stockholm chapter). Stockholm is also an ideal home base for cruising to island destinations in the city's archipelago (see Stockholm's Archipelago chapter).

PLANNING YOUR TIME

For most visitors, Stockholm is worth at least two days. For the busiest and best plan, I'd suggest this:

Day 1

10:00	See the *Vasa* warship (movie and tour).
12:00	Tour the Skansen open-air museum and grab lunch there.
14:30	Visit the Swedish History Museum.
16:30	Follow my self-guided Modern City Walk from Kungsträdgården.
18:00	Dine at one of my recommended waterfront restaurants, or take a harbor dinner cruise.

Day 2

10:00	Ride one of the city orientation bus tours (either the hop-on, hop-off or the bus tour from the Royal Opera House), or take the City Hall tour and climb its tower.
12:15	Catch the changing of the guard at the palace (13:15 on Sun).
13:00	Have lunch on Stortorget.
14:00	Tour the Royal Armory and follow my self-guided Gamla Stan Walk. (If time and budget allow, also

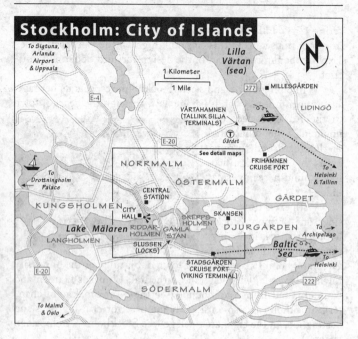

Stockholm: City of Islands

consider the Nobel Prize Museum and/or Royal
Palace sights.)

18:30   Explore Södermalm for dinner—it's just across the
locks from Gamla Stan—or take the Royal Canal
boat tour (confirm last sailing time).

Day 3

With more time, add a cruise through the scenic island archipelago
(easy to do from Stockholm), visit the royal palace at Drottningholm, take a side trip to charming Sigtuna or Uppsala (see next two
chapters), or spend more time in Stockholm (there's plenty left to
do and experience).

Orientation to Stockholm

Greater Stockholm's two million residents live on 14 islands woven
together by 54 bridges. Visitors need only concern themselves with
these districts, most of which are islands:

Norrmalm is downtown, with hotels and shopping areas, and
the combined train and bus station. **Östermalm,** to the east, is
more residential.

Kungsholmen, the mostly suburban island across from Norrmalm, is home to City Hall and inviting lakefront eateries.

Gamla Stan is the Old Town island of winding, lantern-lit
streets, antique shops, and classy cafés clustered around the Royal

Palace. The adjacent **Riddarholmen** is similarly atmospheric, but much sleepier. The locks between Lake Mälaren (to the west) and the Baltic Sea (to the east) are at a junction called **Slussen,** just south of Gamla Stan on the way to Södermalm.

Skeppsholmen is the small, central, traffic-free park/island with the Museum of Modern Art and two fine youth hostels.

Djurgården is the park-island—Stockholm's wonderful green playground, with many of the city's top sights (bike rentals just over bridge as you enter island).

Södermalm, just south of the other districts, is sometimes called "Stockholm's Brooklyn"—it's young and creative. Apart from fine views and some good eateries, this residential island may be of less interest to those on a quick visit.

TOURIST INFORMATION

Stockholm's helpful city-run TI—called **Visit Stockholm**—is downtown in the Kulturhuset, facing Sergels Torg (Mon-Fri 9:00-19:00—until 18:00 off-season, Sat until 16:00, Sun 10:00-16:00, Sergels Torg 3, T-bana: T-Centralen, +46 8 5082 8508, www.visitstockholm.com). There's also a TI at the airport in terminal 5, where most international flights arrive (daily 7:00-21:00, +46 10 109 1000, www.swedavia.se).

Around town, you'll also see the green *i* logo of **Stockholm Info,** run by a for-profit agency. While less helpful than the official TI, they hand out maps and brochures, and may be able to answer basic questions (locations include the train station's main hall and Gamla Stan). They sell the pricey **City Pass** that covers transportation and a limited number of museums (www.stockholminfo.com).

Stockholm Pass: This pass covers entry to more than 40 Stockholm sights (including the Vasa Museum and the Royal Palace) as well as unlimited City Sightseeing hop-on, hop-off bus/boat tours, including boat tours to Drottningholm Palace and Sigtuna. It's available in one-day (719 SEK) and multiday versions (up to 1,619 SEK/5-day pass), with an optional Travelcard transit add-on. The pass can save a busy sightseer time and money, but do the math to see if makes sense for your itinerary (www.stockholmpass.com).

ARRIVAL IN STOCKHOLM

For details on arriving in Stockholm by plane or boat, as well as info on taking the ferry to Tallinn or Helsinki, see "Stockholm Connections" at the end of this chapter.

By Train or Bus: Stockholm's adjacent stations for trains (Centralstation) and buses (Cityterminalen), at the southwestern edge of Norrmalm, are a hive of services (including an unofficial Stockholm Info "TI"), eateries, shops, and exchange desks. From the train station, the bus station is up the escalators from the main hall and through a glassy atrium (lined with sales desks for bus companies and cruise lines). Those sailing to Estonia or Finland with Tallink Silja (Värtahamnen port) or Viking (Stadsgården port) can catch a shuttle from the bus terminal (www.batbussarna.se). Underground is the T-Centralen subway (T-bana) station—probably the easiest way to reach your hotel. Taxi stands are outside.

The fastest way to connect the city and its airport is via the Arlanda Express shuttle train, which leaves from tracks 1 and 2 (follow *Arlanda Express/airport train* signs through the station; for details, see "Stockholm Connections—By Plane" at the end of this chapter).

By Car: Only a Swedish meatball would drive a car in Stockholm. Park it in one of the park-and-ride lots that ring the city and use public transit instead (see lot map at www.visitstockholm.com). Those sailing to Finland or Estonia should ask about long-term parking at the terminal when reserving tickets; to minimize the risk of theft and vandalism, pay extra for the most secure parking garage.

HELPFUL HINTS

Museum Admission: Entry to many of Stockholm's fine state-owned museums swings from free (when left-leaning parties control the reins of government) to fee (when center-right parties are in charge). Ask locally for the latest.

Theft Alert: Even in Stockholm, when there are crowds, there are pickpockets (such as at the Royal Palace during the changing of the guard). Too-young-to-arrest teens are hard for local police to control.

Bookstore: The aptly named **English Bookshop** sells a variety of reading materials (including Swedish-interest books) in English (Mon-Fri 10:30-18:00, Sat until 16:00, Sun 12:00-16:00, in the Södermalm district at Södermannagatan 22—see "Stockholm" map for location, +46 8 790 5510).

Pharmacy: The **C. W. Scheele** 24-hour pharmacy is near the train station at Klarabergsgatan 64 (+46 77 145 0450; see "Stockholm" map for location).

Laundry: Tvättomaten is a rare find—the only self-service independent launderette in Stockholm (48-hour full-service available; open Mon-Fri 8:30-18:30—until 17:00 in July-mid-Aug, Sat 9:30-13:00, closed Sun; across from Gustav Vasa church, Västmannagatan 61 on Odenplan—see "Stockholm" map for location, T-bana: Odenplan, +46 8 346 480, www. tvattomaten.se).

GETTING AROUND STOCKHOLM
By Public Transit

Stockholm's fine but pricey public transport network (Stockholm Transport, officially Storstockholms Lokaltrafik—but signed as *SL*) includes subway (Tun-nelbana, called "T-bana") and bus systems, and a single handy tram (#7) from the commercial center to the sights at Djurgården. The city is spread out, so most visitors will use public transport at some point. The subway is easy to fig-ure out, but many sights are better served by bus. The main lines are listed on the back of the official city map. A more detailed system map is available free from subway ticket windows, SL Centers (info desks) in main stations, and TIs (transit info +46 8 600 1000, www.sl.se).

Tickets: A single ride for subway, tram, or bus costs 38 SEK (up to 1.25 hours, including transfers); a 24-hour pass is 160 SEK, while a 72-hour pass is 315 SEK. Tickets are not sold on buses or the tram. All SL ticket sellers are clearly marked with a blue flag with the *SL* logo.

Locals and savvy tourists carry a blue **SL-Access card,** available for 20 SEK at ticket agents, subway and commuter rail stations, and SL Centers. To use the card, just touch it against the blue pad to enter the T-bana turnstile or when boarding a bus or tram. You can add value to the card at station machines or with a ticket agent.

It's still possible to buy single-journey **paper tickets** (at Press-byrån convenience stores inside almost every T-bana station, at self-service machines, and at some transit-ticket offices)—but it's not worth the hassle.

Transit App: SL also has an easy-to-use ticketing app (search "SL-Stockholm" in app stores) that works with US credit cards. Use your phone to buy tickets and to enter the public transit system (for the T-bana, hold the phone to a scanner to enter the turnstile; for the bus or tram, show it to the driver).

By Harbor Shuttle Ferry

In summer, city ferries let you make a fun, practical, and scenic

Harbor Shuttle
Other Boats

1 Bookstore
2 Pharmacy
3 Launderette

STOCKHOLM

Humle-
gården,
ROYAL
LIBRARY

To Frihamnen Port,
Värtahammen Port
& Millesgården

ÖSTER-
MALM

Karlaplan

STUREGATAN

HUMLEGÅRDS-
GATAN

Östermalmstorg

JÄRVSGATAN

SIBYLLEGATAN

NYBROGATAN

Östermalms-
torg

Östermalms-
torg

STORGATAN

NARVAVÄGEN

KARLAVÄGEN

LINNEGATAN

ARMY
MUSEUM

SWEDISH
HISTORY
MUSEUM

ECONOMY
MUSEUM

B #67

RIDDARGATAN

Nybroplan

T #7

Berzelii
Park

WC

See Djurgården detail map

Cinderella Boats
to Archipelago

STRANDVÄGEN

T #7

#7 **T**

H #80 &
Emelie

T Kungsträdgården

KUNG
STRÄDGÅRDS-
GATAN

DJURGÅRDS-
VÄGEN

GRAND
HOTEL

BLAISIE-
HOLMEN

T #7

Waxholmsbolaget
Boats to Archipelago

NATIONAL
MUSEUM

VASA
MUSEUM

NORDIC
MUSEUM

**ROYAL
PALACE**

WC

Stor-
torget

B #65

MUSEUM
OF
MODERN
ART

DJURGÅRDEN

WEST
ENTRANCE

SKANSEN

GAMLA
STAN

GERMAN
CHURCH

AF
CHAPMAN
HOSTEL

SKEPPS-
HOLMEN

H #82

Liljevalc
Gröna Lund

T #7

ABBA:
THE MUSEUM

SKANSEN
MAIN
ENTRANCE

SKEPPSBRON

SLUSSEN
(LOCKS)

H #82

*Baltic
Sea*

KASTELL-
HOLMEN

#80, 82
& Emelie **H**

GRÖNA LUND
AMUSEMENT
PARK

BECK-
HOLMEN

KATARINA
ELEVATOR

B

Mosebacke
Torg

KATARINAVÄGEN

FOTO-
GRAFISKA

STADSGÅRDSLEDEN

Emelie

To
Cruise
Port

HÖGBERGSGATAN

ÖSTGÖTAGATAN

Katerina
Cemetery

TJÄRHOVSGATAN

RENSTIERNASGATA

NYTORGSGATAN

SÖDERMANNA-
GATAN

STADSGÅRDEN
CRUISE PORT
(VIKING TERMINAL)

P

T Medborgar-
platsen

FOLKUNGAGATAN

LONDON
VIADUCT

B Londonviadukten

GÖTGATAN

SKRAPEN
MALL &
HIMLEN

KOCKSGATAN

ÅSÖGATAN

BONDEGATAN

SKÅNEGATAN

Nytorget

1

Stockholm

STOCKHOLM

Stockholm at a Glance

▲▲▲**Skansen** Europe's first and best open-air folk museum, with more than 150 old homes, churches, shops, and schools. **Hours:** Park-opens daily at 10:00, closes at 22:00 late June-Aug and progressively earlier the rest of the year; historical buildings-generally 11:00-17:00, late June-Aug some until 19:00, most closed in winter. See page 470.

▲▲▲**Vasa Museum** Ill-fated 17th-century warship dredged from the sea floor, now the showpiece of an interesting museum. **Hours:** Daily 8:30-18:00; Sept-May 10:00-17:00 except Wed until 20:00. See page 472.

▲▲**Military Parade and Changing of the Guard** Punchy pomp starting near Nybroplan and finishing at Royal Palace outer courtyard. **Hours:** Daily, Sept-late April Wed and Sat-Sun only, start time varies with season but always at midday. See page 458.

▲▲**Royal Armory** A fine collection of ceremonial medieval royal armor, historic and modern royal garments, and carriages, in the Royal Palace. **Hours:** Daily 11:00-17:00; Sept-April Tue-Sun 11:00-17:00, Thu until 20:00, closed Mon. See page 459.

▲▲**City Hall** Gilt mosaic architectural jewel of Stockholm and site of Nobel Prize banquet, with tower offering the city's best views. **Hours:** Required tours daily generally June-Aug hourly 10:00-14:00, fewer off-season. See page 462.

▲▲**Swedish History Museum** Collection of artifacts spanning Sweden's entire history, highlighted by fascinating Viking exhibit and Gold Room. **Hours:** Daily 10:00-17:00; Sept-May Tue-Sun 11:00-17:00, Wed until 20:00, closed Mon. See page 467.

▲**Kungsträdgården** Stockholm's lively central square, with life-size chess games, concerts, and perpetual action. See page 452.

▲**Sergels Torg** Modern square with underground mall. See page 454.

▲**Nobel Prize Museum** Star-studded tribute to some of the world's most accomplished scientists, artists, economists, and

shortcut across the harbor to Djurgården Island. Boat #82 leaves from the southeast end of Gamla Stan, stops near the Museum of Modern Art on Skeppsholmen, then docks near the Gröna Lund amusement park on Djurgården; boat #80 departs from Nybroplan for Djurgården (38 SEK, covered by public-transit passes, politicians. **Hours:** Daily 9:00-20:00; Sept-May Tue 11:00-20:00, Wed-Fri until 17:00, Sat-Sun 10:00-18:00, closed Mon. See page 456.

▲**Royal Palace Museums** Complex of Swedish royal museums, the two best of which are the Royal Apartments and Royal Treasury. **Hours:** Daily 10:00-16:00, July-Aug from 9:00. See page 459.

▲**Museum of Medieval Stockholm** Underground museum showing off parts of town wall King Gustav Vasa built in the 1530s. **Hours:** Tue-Sun 12:00-17:00, Wed until 20:00, closed Mon. See page 461.

▲**National Museum** Convenient, crowd-free gallery with the works of Swedish masters, along with Rembrandt, Rubens, and Impressionists. **Hours:** Tue-Sun 11:00-17:00, Fri until 21:00, closed Mon. See page 465.

▲**Nordic Museum** Danish Renaissance palace design and five fascinating centuries of traditional Swedish lifestyles. **Hours:** Daily 9:00-18:00; Sept-May 10:00-17:00, Wed until 20:00. See page 474.

▲**ABBA: The Museum** Super-commercial and wildly-popular-with-ABBA-fans experience. **Hours:** Daily 9:00-19:00; Sept-May daily 10:00-18:00, Wed until 19:00. See page 476.

▲**Thielska Galleriet** Enchanting waterside mansion with works of Scandinavian artists Larsson, Zorn, and Munch. **Hours:** Tue-Sun 12:00-17:00, closed Mon. See page 478.

▲**Fotografiska** Fun photography museum focusing on contemporary and international work, with eye-popping views from its top-floor café. **Hours:** Daily 10:00-23:00. See page 479.

▲**Millesgården** Dramatic cliffside museum and grounds featuring works of Sweden's greatest sculptor, Carl Milles. **Hours:** Tue-Sun 11:00-17:00, closed Mon. See page 480.

STOCKHOLM

3-4/hour May-late Sept, 10-minute trip, www.sl.se). The private ferry *Emelie* also makes the journey from Nybroplan to Djurgården before continuing on to the Stadsgaden cruise quay (60 SEK, buy ticket onboard—credit cards only and SL app not valid, hourly, April-Sept roughly Mon-Fri 7:50-18:20, Sat-Sun 9:50-17:20, +46

8 731 0025, www.ressel.se). While buses and trams run between the same points more frequently, the ferry is more scenic and can be faster. The hop-on, hop-off boat tour also connects many of these stops (see "Tours in Stockholm," below).

By Taxi or Uber

Stockholm is a good taxi town—provided you find a reputable cab with fair rates. Taxis are unregulated, so companies can charge whatever they like. Before hopping in a taxi, look carefully at the big yellow label that should be displayed prominently on the outside of the car (usually in the rear door window). The big number, on the right, shows the "highest unit price" *(högsta jämförpriset)* for a 10-kilometer ride that lasts 15 minutes; this number should be between 290 and 390 SEK—if it's higher, move on. (You're not obligated to take the first cab in line.) Most cabs charge a drop fee of about 45 SEK. Taxis with inflated rates tend to congregate at touristy places like the Vasa Museum or in Gamla Stan. I've been ripped off enough by cabs here to know: Take only "Taxi Stockholm 150000" cabs with the phone number (08 150 000) printed on the door. Be aware that other companies with higher rates are also called Taxi Stockholm, but you can tell them apart because of the different phone number. (Other reportedly honest companies include Taxi Kurir, +46 8 300 000, and Taxi 020, +46 8 850 0400.) Your hotel, restaurant, or museum can call a cab, which will generally arrive within minutes (no extra charge—the meter starts when you hop in).

Your Uber app works in Stockholm just as it does in the US.

Tours in Stockholm

The sightseeing company **Strömma** has a lock on most city tours, whether by bus, by boat, or on foot. Their website (www.stromma. se) details the entire program, or you can call for more information (+46 8 1200 4000). Tours can be paid for online, or simply as you board.

BY BUS

Hop-On, Hop-Off Bus Tour

Three hop-on, hop-off buses make a 1.5-hour circuit of the city, orienting riders with a recorded commentary and linking all the essential places from Skansen to City Hall; when cruises are in town, they also stop at both cruise ports (Stadsgården and Frihamnen). **Hop-On Hop-Off**'s green buses and **City Sightseeing**'s red buses both cooperate with Strömma (340 SEK/24 hours, ticket covers both buses; May-Sept 2-3/hour daily 10:00-18:00, fewer off-season, none mid-Jan-mid-Feb, www.stromma.se). **Red Sightseeing Buses** offers a similar hop-on, hop-off itinerary in open-top buses for the same price (2-5/hour, www.redbuses.se). All offer free Wi-Fi.

Quickie Orientation Bus Tour

Several different city bus tours leave from the Royal Opera House on Gustav Adolfs Torg. Strömma's Stockholm Panorama tour provides a good overview—but it costs more than the 24-hour hop-on, hop-off ticket, so I'd take this tour only if you want a quick and efficient loop with no unnecessary stops (540 SEK, 4-6/day, fewer Oct-May, 1.25 hours).

BY BOAT

▲City Boat Tours

For a good floating look at Stockholm and a pleasant break, consider a sightseeing cruise. These boat tours are pleasant at the end of the day, when the light is warm and the sights and museums are closed. The handiest are the Strömma/ Stockholm Sightseeing boats, which leave from Strömkajen, in front of the Grand Hotel, and stop at Nybroplan five minutes later. The **Royal Canal**

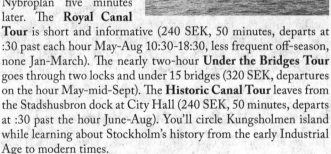

Tour is short and informative (240 SEK, 50 minutes, departs at :30 past each hour May-Aug 10:30-18:30, less frequent off-season, none Jan-March). The nearly two-hour **Under the Bridges Tour** goes through two locks and under 15 bridges (320 SEK, departures on the hour May-mid-Sept). The **Historic Canal Tour** leaves from the Stadshusbron dock at City Hall (240 SEK, 50 minutes, departs at :30 past the hour June-Aug). You'll circle Kungsholmen island while learning about Stockholm's history from the early Industrial Age to modern times.

Hop-On, Hop-Off Boat Tour

Stockholm is a city surrounded by water, making this boat option enjoyable and practical. Strömma and Red Buses offer the same small loop, stopping at key spots such as Djurgården (Skansen and Vasa Museum), Gamla Stan (near Slussen and again near Royal Palace), the Stadsgården cruise quay (with Viking Line terminal and cruise ports), and Nybroplan. Use the boat as transport from Point A to Point B, or make the whole one-hour loop and enjoy the recorded commentary (310 SEK/24 hours, 2-3/hour May-mid-Sept, pick up map for schedule and locations of boat stops, www. stromma.se or www.redbuses.se).

ON FOOT
Old Town Walk
Strömma offers a 1.25-hour Old Town walk (220 SEK, July-Aug only at 13:30, departs from ticket booth at north end of Gustav Adolfs Torg, www.stromma.se).

Local Guides
Håkan Fränden is an excellent guide who brings Stockholm to life (mobile +46 70 531 3379, hakan.franden@hotmail.com). **Marita Bergman** is a teacher and a licensed guide who enjoys showing visitors around during her school breaks (1,650 SEK/half-day tour, mobile +46 73 511 9154, bergman57.mb@gmail.com). You can also hire a private guide through the Association of Qualified Tourist Guides of Stockholm (www.guidestockholm.com). The standard rate is about 1,800 SEK for up to three hours.

BY BIKE
Stockholm is a great city to tour on two wheels. **Gamla Stan Cykel**, two blocks east of the Gamla Stan T-bana station, rents bikes year-round; reserve ahead online or by phone in summer (250 SEK/day; Mon-Fri 10:00-18:00, Sat 11:00-16:00, closed Sun; Lilla Nygatan 10—for location, see the "Gamla Stan Walk" map later, +46 8 411 1670, www.gamlastanscykel.se).

You can also rent bikes (and boats) at the **Sjöcaféet** café, next to Djurgårdsbron bridge near the Vasa Museum. It's ideally situated as a springboard for a pleasant bike ride around the parklike Djurgården island—use their free and excellent bike map/guide. For details, see page 468. For location, see the "Djurgården" map on page 469.

Walks in Stockholm

This section includes two self-guided walks to introduce you to Stockholm, both old (Gamla Stan) and new (the modern city).

GAMLA STAN WALK
Gamla Stan, Stockholm's historic island old town, is charming, photogenic, and full of antique shops, street lanterns, painted ceilings, and surprises. Until the 1600s, all of Stockholm fit in Gamla Stan. Stockholm traded with other northern ports such as Amsterdam, Lübeck, and Tallinn. German culture influenced art, building styles, and even the language, turning Old Norse into modern Swedish. With its narrow alleys and stairways, Gamla Stan mixes poorly with cars and modern economies. Today, it's been given over to the Royal Palace and to the tourists, who throng Gamla Stan's main drag, Västerlånggatan, seemingly unaware that most of Stockholm's best

Gamla Stan Walk

Walk

1 King Gustav III Statue
2 Obelisk
3 Iron Boy Statue
4 St. George Statue
5 Stortorget
6 Cathedral
7 Rune Stone
8 German Church
9 Viewpoint
10 Järntorget
11 Bridge & Lock

Other Sights

12 Nobel Prize Museum
13 Palace Tickets (2)
14 Changing of the Guard
15 Royal Armory
16 Gamla Stan Cykel
17 Museum of Medieval Stockholm

attractions are elsewhere. While you could just happily wander, this quick walk—worth ▲▲—gives meaning to Stockholm's Old Town.
• *Our walk begins along the harborfront. Start at the base of Slotts-backen (the Palace Hill esplanade) leading up to the...*

Royal Palace: Along the water, check out the ❶ **statue of King Gustav III** gazing at the palace, which was built in the 1700s on the site of Stockholm's first castle (for more about the palace, see "Sights in Stockholm," later). Gustav transformed Stockholm from a dowdy Scandinavian port into a sophisticated European capital, modeled on French culture. Gustav loved the arts, and he founded the Royal Dramatic Theater and the Royal Opera in Stockholm. Ironically, he was assassinated by a discontented nobleman, who shot Gustav in the back at a masquerade ball at the Royal Opera House in 1792 (inspiring Verdi's opera *Un Ballo in Maschera*).

Walk up the broad, cobbled boulevard alongside the palace to the crest of the hill. Stop, look back, and scan the harbor. The

grand building across the water is the National Museum, which is often mistaken for the palace. Beyond that, in the distance, is the fine row of buildings on Strandvägen street. Until the 1850s, this area was home to peasant shacks, but as Stockholm entered its grand stage, it was cleaned up and replaced by fine apartments, including some of the city's smartest addresses. A blocky gray TV tower stands tall in the distance. Turn to the palace facade on your left (finished in 1754, replacing one that burned in 1697). The niches are filled with Swedish bigwigs (literally) from the mid-18th century.

As you crest the hill, you're facing the ❷ **obelisk** that honors Stockholm's merchant class for its support in a 1788 war against Russia. In front of the obelisk are

tour buses (their drivers worried about parking cops) and a pit used for *boules*. The royal family took a liking to the French game during a Mediterranean vacation, and it's quite popular around town today.

Behind the obelisk stands Storkyrkan, Stockholm's cathedral (which we'll visit later on this walk). From this angle you can see its Baroque facade, which was added to better match the newer palace. Opposite the *boules* court and palace is the Finnish

STOCKHOLM

church (Finska Kyrkan, the deep orange building), which originated as the royal tennis hall. When the Protestant Reformation hit in 1527, church services could at last be said in the peoples' languages rather than Latin. Suddenly, each merchant community needed its own church. Finns worshipped here, the Germans built their own church (coming up on this walk), and the Swedes got the cathedral.

Stroll up the lane to the right of the Finnish church into the shady churchyard, where you'll find the fist-sized ❸ *Iron Boy,* the

tiniest public statue (out of about 600) in Stockholm. Swedish grannies knit caps for him in the winter. Local legend says the statue honors the orphans who had to transfer cargo from sea ships to lake ships before Stockholm's locks were built. Some people rub his head for good luck (which the orphans didn't have). Others, perhaps needy when it comes to this gift, rub his head for wisdom. The artist says it's simply a self-portrait of himself as a child, sitting on his bed and gazing at the moon.

• *Exit through either of the churchyard gates, turn left onto Trädgårdsgatan, then bear right with the lane to reach...*

Köpmangatan: Take a moment to explore this street from one end to the other. With its cobbles and traditional pastel facades, this is a quintessential Gamla Stan lane—and one of the oldest in town. The mellow yellow houses are predominantly from the 18th century; the reddish facades are mostly 17th century. Once merchants' homes, today these are popular with antique dealers and refined specialty shops. Back when there was comfort living within a city's walls, Gamla Stan streets like this were densely populated.

If you head left, you'll emerge on Köpmantorget square, highlighted by the breathtaking ❹ **statue of St. George** slaying the dragon, with a maiden representing Stockholm (about 10 steps to the right) looking on with thanks and admiration. If you go right,

you'll reach old Stockholm's main square, our next stop.

❺ **Stortorget:** Colorful old buildings topped with gables line this square—Stockholm's oldest. In 1400, this was the heart of medieval Stockholm (pop. 6,000). Here at the town well, many tangled lanes intersected, making it the natural center for trading. Today Stortorget is home to lots of tourists—including a steady storm of cruise groups following their guides' paddle on four-hour blitz tours of the city (typically 300 ships call here between June and September). The square also hosts concerts, occasional demonstrators, and a Christmas market in winter.

The grand building on the right is the old stock exchange, now home to the noble **Nobel Prize Museum** (described later under "Sights in Stockholm"). On the immediate left is the social-services agency **Stockholms Stadsmission** (offering the cheapest and best lunch around at the recommended Grillska Huset). If you peek into the adjacent bakery, you'll get a fine look at the richly decorated ceilings characteristic of Gamla Stan in the 17th century—the exotic flowers and animals implied that the people who lived or worked here were worldly. You'll also spy some tempting marzipan cakes (a local favorite) and *kanelbullar* (cinnamon buns). There's a cheap sandwich counter in the back and lots of picnic benches in the square.

The town well is still a popular meeting point. This square long held the town's pillory. Scan the fine old facades. The site of the **Stockholm Bloodbath** of 1520, this square has a notorious history. During a Danish power grab, many of Stockholm's movers and shakers who had challenged Danish rule—Swedish aristocracy, leading merchants, and priests—were rounded up, brought here, and beheaded. Rivers of blood were said to have flowed through the streets. Legend holds that the 80 or so white stones in the fine red facade across the square symbolize the victims. (One victim's son escaped, went into hiding, and resurfaced to lead a Swedish revolt against the Danish rulers. Three years later, the Swedes elected that rebel, Gustav Vasa, as their first king. He went on to usher in a great period in the country's history—the Swedish Renaissance.)

• *At the far end of the square (under the finest gables), turn right and follow Trångsund toward the cathedral.*

❻ **Cathedral** (Storkyrkan): Just before the painted stonework church, you'll see my personal phone booth (Rikstelefon) and the gate to the churchyard—guarded by statues of Caution and Hope. Enter the church—Stockholm's oldest, from the 14th century (60 SEK, daily 9:00-16:00). Signs explain special events, as this church is busy with tours and services in summer.

When buying your ticket, pick up the

free, worthwhile English-language flier. Exploring the cathedral's interior, you'll find many styles, ranging from medieval to modern. The front of the nave is paved with centuries-old **tombstones.** The tombstone of the Swedish reformer Olaus Petri is appropriately simple and appropriately located—under the finely carved and gilded pulpit on the left side of the nave. A witness to the Stockholm Bloodbath, Petri was nearly executed himself. He went on to befriend Gustav Vasa and guide him in Lutheranizing Sweden (and turning this cathedral from Catholic to Protestant).

Opposite the pulpit, find the **bronze plaque** in the pillar. It recalls the 1925 Swedish-led ecumenical meeting of Christian leaders that encouraged all churches to renew their efforts on behalf of peace and justice, especially given the horrific toll of World War I.

Next, the best seats in the house: the carved wood **royal boxes,** dating from 1684. This has been a royal wedding church throughout the ages. It was here, in June 2010, that Crown Princess Victoria, heir to the throne, married Daniel Westling (her personal trainer) with much pomp and ceremony.

The fine 17th-century **altar** is made of silver and ebony. Above it, the silver Christ stands like a conquering general evoking the 1650s, an era of Swedish military might.

Next to the altar is a wondrous 1489 statue, carved from oak and elk horn, of **St. George** slaying the dragon (we saw a copy of it outside a few minutes ago). To some, this symbolizes the Swedes overcoming the evil Danes (commemorating a military victory in 1471). In a broader sense, it's an inspiration to take up the struggle against even non-Danish evil. Regardless, it must be the gnarliest dragon's head in all of Europe.

Return to the back of the church to find the exit. Before leaving, just to the left of the door, notice the **painting** that depicts Stockholm in the early 1500s, showing a walled city filling today's Gamla Stan. It's a 1630 copy of the 1535 original. The church, with its black spire, dominated the town back then. The strange sun and sky predicted big changes in Sweden—and as a matter of fact, that's what happened. Gustav Vasa brought on huge reforms in religion and beyond. (The doors just to the left and right of the painting lead to a free WC.) Heading outside, you'll emerge into the kid-friendly churchyard, which was once the cemetery.

• *With your back to the church's front door, go right. At the next corner, turn left (on Storkyrkobrinken), then left again on...*

Prästgatan: Enjoy a quiet wander down this peaceful 15th-century "Priests' Lane." Västerlånggatan, the touristy drag, parallels this lane one block over. (While we'll skip it now, you can walk back up it from the end point of this walk.) As you stroll Prästgatan, look for bits of its past: hoists poking out horizontally from gables (merchants used these to lift goods into their attics), tie bolts (iron bars necessary to bind the timber beams of tall buildings together), small coal or wood hatches (for fuel delivery back in the good old days), and flaming gold phoenixes under red-crown medallions (telling firefighters

which houses paid insurance and could be saved in case of fire—for example, #46). Like other Scandinavian cities, Stockholm was plagued by fire until it was finally decreed that only stone, stucco, and brick construction (like you see here) would be allowed in the town center.

After a few blocks (at Kåkbrinken), a cannon barrel on the corner (look down) guards a Viking-age ❼ **rune stone.** In case you can't read the old Nordic script, it says: "Torsten and Frogun erected this stone in memory of their son."

• *Continue one block farther down Prästgatan to Tyska Brinken and turn left. Look up to see the powerful brick steeple of the...*

❽ **German Church** (Tyska Kyrkan): The church's carillon has played four times a day since 1666. Think of the days when German merchants worked here. Today, Germans come to Sweden not to run the economy, but to enjoy its pristine nature (which is progressively harder to find in their own crowded homeland). Sweden formally became a Lutheran country even before the northern part of Germany—making this the very first German Lutheran church (free to enter).

• *Wander through the churchyard (past a cute church café) and out the back. Exit right onto Svartmangatan and follow it to the right, ending at an iron railing overlooking Österlånggatan.*

❾ **Viewpoint:** From this perch, survey the street below to the left and right. Notice how it curves. This marks the old shoreline. In medieval times, piers stretched out like fingers into the harbor. Gradually, as land was reclaimed and developed, these piers were extended, becoming lanes leading to piers farther away. Behind you is a cute shop where elves can actually be seen making elves.

• *Walk right to Österlånggatan, and continue on to...*

❿ **Järntorget:** A customs square in medieval times, this was

Fika: Sweden's Coffee Break

Swedes drink more coffee per capita than just about any other nationality. The Swedish coffee break— or *fika*—is a ritual. *Fika* is to Sweden what teatime is to Britain. The typical *fika* is a morning or afternoon break in the workday, but can happen any time, any day. It's the perfect opportunity (and excuse) for tourists to take a break as well.

Fika fare is coffee with a snack— something sweet or savory. Your best bet is a *kanelbulle*, a Swedish cinnamon bun, although some prefer *pariserbulle*, a bun filled with vanilla cream. These can be found nearly everywhere coffee is sold, including just about any café or *konditori* (bakery) in Stockholm. A coffee and a cinnamon bun in a café will cost you about 40 SEK. (Most cafés will give you a coffee refill for free.) But at Pressbyrån, the Swedish convenience stores found all over town, you can satisfy your *fika* fix for 25 SEK by getting a coffee and bun to go. Grab a park bench or waterside perch, relax, and enjoy.

the home of Sweden's first bank back in 1680 (the yellow building with the bars on the windows). The Co-op Nära supermarket on this square offers picnic fixings. From here, Västerlånggatan— the eating, shopping, and commercial pedestrian mall of Gamla Stan—leads back across the island. You'll be there in a minute, but first finish this walk.

• *Continue from the square (opposite where you entered) down Järntorgsgatan; you'll emerge at a busy intersection and bridge. For now, things are a bit of a mess because of an enormous redevelopment project that will eventually turn this area into a green people-zone. Continue ahead, crossing onto the bridge to reach a viewpoint window (cut into the construction wall that lines the bridge).*

⓫ Bridge Overlooking Slussen: This area is called Slussen, named for the locks between the salt water of the Baltic Sea (to your left) and the fresh water of huge **Lake Mälaren** (to your right). (The locks are being rebuilt, and cranes may obstruct your view.) Stockholm exists because this is where Lake Mälaren meets the sea. Traders would sail their goods from far inland to this point, where they'd meet merchants who would ship the goods south to Europe. In the 13th century, the new kingdom of Sweden needed revenue and began levying duty taxes on all the iron, copper, and furs shipped through here.

From the bridge, you may notice a current in the water, indicating that the weir has been lowered and water is spilling from Lake Mälaren (about two feet above sea level) into the sea. Today, the locks are nicknamed "the divorce lock" because this is where captains and first mates learn to communicate under pressure and in the public eye.

Opposite Gamla Stan is the **Södermalm** neighborhood—youthful, artsy, and casual—with its popular Katarina viewing platform (see "Stockholm's Best Views" sidebar, later). Moored on the saltwater side are cruise ships, which bring thousands of visitors into town each day during high season. Many of these boats are bound for Finland. The towering white syringe is the Gröna Lund amusement park's free-fall ride. The revolving *Djurgården Färjan* sign, along the embankment to your left, marks the ferry that zips from here to Gröna Lund and Djurgården.

• *Our walk is finished, but feel free to linger longer in Gamla Stan—day or night, it's a lively place. You can backtrack along* **Västerlånggatan,** *the main commercial drag, or visit one of Gamla Stan's sights (described later, under "Sights in Stockholm").*

Another option is to walk 15 minutes to **Kungsträdgården,** *the starting point of my self-guided Modern City Walk (see next). Either walk along the embankment and take the diagonal bridge directly across to the square, or walk back through the middle of Gamla Stan, take the stately walkway past the parliament building, then turn right when you cross the bridge.*

MODERN CITY WALK

On this walk, we'll use the park called Kungsträdgården as a springboard to explore the modern center of Stockholm—a commercial zone that puts the focus not on old kings and mementos of superpower days, but on shopping.

• *Find the statue of King Karl XII, facing the waterfront at the harbor end of the park.*

❶ **Kungsträdgården:** Centuries ago, this "King's Garden" was the private kitchen garden of the king, where he grew his cabbage salad. Today, this downtown people-watching center, worth

▲, is considered Stockholm's living room, symbolizing the Swedes' freedom-loving spirit. While the name implies that the garden is a private royal domain, the giant clump of elm trees just behind the statue is a reminder that it's the people who rule now. In the 1970s, demonstrators chained themselves to these

STOCKHOLM

Modern City Walk

1. Kungsträdgården
2. Urban Shopping Zone
3. Illums Bolighus
4. Nordiska Kompaniet
5. Gallerian Mall
6. Sergels Torg
7. Kulturhuset
8. Sergelgatan
9. Hötorget

trees to stop the building of an underground train station here. They prevailed, and today, locals enjoy the peaceful, breezy ambience of a teahouse instead.

Farther on, watch for the Astroturf zone with "latte dads" and their kids, and enjoy a summer concert at the bandstand. There's always something going on. High above is a handy reference point—the revolving clock on the NK department store.

Kungsträdgården—surrounded by the harborfront and tour boats, the Royal Opera House, and shopping opportunities (including a welcoming Volvo showroom near the top-left side of the square, showing off the latest in Swedish car design)—is *the* place to feel Stockholm's pulse (but always ask first: *"Kan jag kanna på din puls?"*).

The garden also plays host to huge parties. The Taste of Stockholm festival runs for a week in early June, when restaurateurs show off and bands entertain all day. Beer flows liberally—a rare public spectacle in Sweden.

• *Stroll through Kungsträdgården, past the fountain and the Volvo store, and up to Hamngatan street. From here, we'll turn left and walk the length of the NK department store (across the street) as we wade through Stockholm's...*

❷ **Urban Shopping Zone** (Hamngatan): In just a couple of blocks, we'll pass some major landmarks of Swedish consumerism. First, anchoring the corner at the top of Kungsträdgården, is the gigantic ❸ **Illums Bolighus** design shop. (You can enter from the square and stroll all the way through it, exiting at Hamngatan on the far end.) This is a Danish institution, making its play for customers with this prime location. Across the street, notice the giant gold *NK* marking the ❹ **Nordiska Kompaniet** department store (locals joke that the NK stands for "no kronor left"). It's located in an elegant early-20th-century building that dominates the top end of Kungsträdgården. If it feels like an old-time American department store, that's because its architect was inspired by grand stores he'd seen in the US (circa 1910).

Another block down, on the left, is the sleeker, more modern ❺ **Gallerian mall.** Among this two-story world of shops, upstairs you'll find a Clas Ohlson hardware and electronics shop (most Stockholmers have a cabin that's always in need of a little DIY repair). And there are plenty of affordable little lunch bars and classy cafés for your *fika* (Swedish coffee-and-bun break). You may notice that American influence (frozen yogurt and other trendy food chains) is challenging the notion of the traditional *fika*.

• *High-end shoppers should consider heading into the streets behind NK, with exclusive designer boutiques and the chichi Mood Stockholm mall (see "Shopping in Stockholm," later). Otherwise, just beyond the Gallerian mall, you'll emerge into Sergels Torg. (Note that the handy tram #7 goes from here directly to Skansen and other important sights on Djurgården; departures every few minutes.)*

❻ **Sergels Torg:** This square, worth ▲, dominates the heart of modern Stockholm with its stark 1960s-era functionalist architecture. The glassy tower in the middle of the fountain plaza is ugly in daylight but glows at night, symbolic of Sweden's haunting northern lights.

• *Find the hulking, low-slung, glassy building overlooking the square. This is the...*

❼ **Kulturhuset:** Stockholm's "culture center," this lively public space hosts libraries, theater, a kids' zone, chessboards, fun shops, a fine art cinema, art exhibits, and a music venue (+46 8 5062 0200, http://kulturhusetstadsteatern.se).

Take the elevator to the top of the Kulturhuset and ride the escalator down, exploring each level en route. On the rooftop, the recommended Cafeteria Panorama has cheap meals with terrific city views.

Back at ground level outside, stand in front of the Kulturhuset (across from the fountain) and survey the expansive square nicknamed "Plattan" (the platter). Everything around you dates from the 1960s and 1970s, when this formerly run-down area was re-invented as an urban "space of the future." In the 1970s, with no nearby residences, the desolate Plattan became the domain of junkies. Now the city is actively revitalizing it, and the Plattan is becoming a people-friendly heart of the commercial town.

DesignTorget (enter from the lower level of Kulturhuset) showcases practical items for everyday use from established and emerging designers. Nearby are major boutiques and department stores, including, across the way, H&M and Åhléns.

• *Next head in the opposite direction from Kulturhuset to the street that leads past the five uniform white towers you see beyond the fountain. This is...*

❽ **Sergelgatan:** Walk up this thriving pedestrian and commercial street, enjoying the public art and people-watching. The office towers, so modern in the 1960s, have gone from seeming hopelessly out-of-date to "retro," and are now quite popular with young professionals.

• *Continue along Sergelgatan to reach the market at...*

❾ **Hötorget:** "Hötorget" means "Hay Market," but today its stalls feed people rather than horses. The adjacent indoor market, Hötorgshallen, is fun and fragrant. It dates from 1914 when, for hygienic reasons, the city forbade selling fish and meat outdoors (market described later, under "Eating in Stockholm; also hosts Sun flea market in summer). Carl Milles' statue of *Orpheus Emerging from the Underworld* (with seven sad Muses) stands in front of the city concert hall (which hosts the annual Nobel Prize award ceremony). The concert house, from 1926, is Swedish Art Deco (a.k.a. "Swedish Grace"). The lobby (open through much of the summer) still evokes Stockholm's Roaring Twenties. If the door's open, you're welcome to look in for free.

Popping into the Hötorget T-bana station provides a fun glimpse at local urban design. Stockholm's subway system was inaugurated in the 1950s, and many stations are modern art installations in themselves.

• *Our walk ends here. For more shopping and an enjoyable pedestrian boulevard leading back into the Old Town, cut down a block to Drottninggatan and turn left. This busy drag leads straight out of the commercial district, passes the parliament, then becomes the main street of Gamla Stan.*

Sights in Stockholm

GAMLA STAN (OLD TOWN)

The best of this island is covered in my self-guided Gamla Stan Walk, earlier. But here are a few ways to extend your time in the Old Town.

On Stortorget Square
▲Nobel Prize Museum

Opened in 2001 for the 100-year anniversary of the Nobel Prize, this wonderful little museum tells the story of the world's most prestigious prize. Pricey but high-tech and eloquent, it fills the grand old stock exchange building that dominates Gamla Stan's main square, Stortorget.

Cost and Hours: 130 SEK, free Tue after 17:00; daily 9:00-20:00; Sept-May Tue 11:00-20:00, Wed-Fri until 17:00, Sat-Sun 10:00-18:00, closed Mon; free downloadable audioguide on website, free 40-minute orientation tours in English—check website for times, +46 8 5348 1800, https://nobelprizemuseum.se.

Background: Stockholm-born Alfred Nobel was a great inventor, with more than 300 patents. His most famous invention: dynamite. Living in the late 1800s, Nobel was a man of his age. It was a time of great optimism, wild ideas, and grand projects. His dynamite enabled entire nations to blast their way into the modern age with canals, railroads, and tunnels. It made warfare much more destructive. And it also made Alfred Nobel a very wealthy man.

STOCKHOLM

Wanting to leave a legacy that celebrated and supported people with great ideas, Alfred used his fortune to fund the Nobel Prize. Every year since 1901, laureates have been honored in the fields of physics, chemistry, medicine, literature, economic sciences, and peacemaking.

Visiting the Museum: Inside, portraits of all 700-plus prize-winners hang from the ceiling—shuffling around the room like shirts at the dry cleaner's (miss your favorite, and he or she will come around again in six hours). Behind the ticket desk are monitors that represent the six Nobel Prize categories, each honoring the most recent laureate in that category.

Flanking the main hall beyond that—where touchscreens organized by decade invite you to learn more about the laureates—two rooms run a continuous video montage of quick programs (on one side, films celebrating the creative milieus that encouraged Nobel laureates past and present; on the other side, short films about their various paths to success).

To the right of the ticket desk, find "The Gallery," with a surprisingly captivating collection of items that various laureates have cited as important to their creative process, from scientific equipment to inspirational knickknacks. The randomness of the items offers a fascinating and humanizing insight into the great minds of our time.

The Viennese-style Bistro Nobel is the place to get creative with your coffee...and sample the famous Nobel ice cream. All Nobel laureates who visit the museum are asked to sign the bottom of a chair in the café. Turn yours over and see who warmed your chair. And don't miss the lockable hangers, to protect your fancy, furry winter coat. The Swedish Academy, which awards the Nobel Prize for literature each year, is upstairs.

Royal Palace Complex (Kungliga Slottet)

Although the royal family beds down at Drottningholm (see next chapter), this complex in Gamla Stan is still the official royal residence. The palace, designed in Italian Baroque style, was completed in 1754 after a fire wiped out the previous palace—a much more characteristic medieval/Renaissance complex. This blocky Baroque replacement, which houses various museums, is big and (frankly) pretty dull. For help locating different areas of the complex, see the "Gamla Stan Walk" map, earlier.

Planning Your Time: Visiting the several sights in and near the palace could fill a day, but Stockholm has far better attractions elsewhere. Prioritize.

Visitors in a rush should see the changing of the guard, enter the (free) Royal Armory, and skip the rest. Information booths in the semicircular courtyard (at the top, where the guard changes) and just inside the east entry give out a list of the day's guided tours and an explanatory brochure/map that marks the entrances to the different sights. The main entrance to the Royal Palace (including the apartments, chapel, and treasury) faces the long, angled square and obelisk (but you can cut through the palace's interior courtyard to get there).

The Royal Palace ticket includes four museums. Of these, the Royal Apartments are not much as far as palace rooms go but still worthwhile; the Royal Treasury is worth a look; the Museum of Three Crowns gets you down into the medieval cellars to learn about the more interesting earlier castle; and Gustav III's Museum of Antiquities is skippable. The chapel is nice enough (and it's free to enter).

Tours: In peak season, the main Royal Palace generally offers a full slate of English tours covering some of the sights for a small extra fee. If you're paying the hefty price for a ticket, consider adding on a tour—otherwise, you'll struggle to appreciate the place. Some tours are infrequent, so be sure to confirm times when you purchase your admission (for more on tours, see the individual listings below).

Expect Changes: Since the palace is used for state functions, it's sometimes closed to tourists. And, as the exterior is undergoing a 20-year renovation, some areas may be covered in scaffolding.

▲▲Military Parade and Changing of the Guard

Starting from the Army Museum (two blocks from Nybroplan at Riddargatan 13), Stockholm's daily military parade marches over Norrbro bridge, in front of the parliament building, and up to the Royal Palace's outer courtyard, where the band plays and the guard changes. Smaller contingents of guards spiral in from other parts of the palace complex, eventually convening in the same place.

The performance is fresh and spirited because these young soldiers—from every branch of the service and from all over Sweden—are visiting Stockholm just like you, and it's a chance for them to show their stuff in the big city. Pick your place at the palace courtyard, where the band arrives at about 12:15 (13:15 on Sun). The best spot to stand is along the wall in the inner courtyard, near the palace information and ticket office. There are columns with wide pedestals for easy perching, as well as benches that people stand on to view the ceremony (arrive

STOCKHOLM

early). Generally, after the barking and goose-stepping formalities, the band shows off for an impressive 30-minute marching concert.

Marching Band and Parade: Departs from Army Museum late April-Aug Mon-Sat at 11:45, Sun at 12:45 (11:35 and 12:35, respectively, if departing from Cavalry Barracks); Sept-Oct Wed and Sat at 11:45, Sun at 12:45; off-season departs from Mynttorget Wed and Sat at 12:09, Sun at 13:09. Royal appointments can disrupt the schedule; confirm times at TI. In summer, you might also catch the mounted guards (they don't appear on a regular schedule).

Royal Guards Ceremony at the Palace: Mon-Sat at 12:15, Sun at 13:15, about 40 minutes, in front of the Royal Palace. Find details at www.forsvarsmakten.se (click on "Activities").

▲▲Royal Armory (Livrustkammaren)

The oldest museum in Sweden is both more and less than an armory. Rather than dusty piles of swords and muskets, it focuses on royal clothing: impressive ceremonial armor (never used in battle) and other fashion through the ages (including a room of kidswear), plus a fine collection of coaches. It's an engaging slice of royal life. Everything is displayed under sturdy brick vaults, beautifully lit, and well described in English and by a good audioguide.

Cost and Hours: Free; daily 11:00-17:00, Sept-April Tue-Sun 11:00-17:00, Thu until 20:00, closed Mon; audioguide-40 SEK, information sheets in English available in most rooms; entrance at bottom of Slottsbacken at base of palace, +46 8 402 3030, www.livrustkammaren.se.

▲Royal Palace

The Royal Palace consists of a chapel (free) and four museums. Compared to many grand European palaces, it's underwhelm-ing and flooded with cruise-excursion groups who don't realize that Stockholm's best sightseeing is elsewhere.

Cost and Hours: 140-SEK combo-ticket covers all four museums; daily 10:00-16:00, July-Aug from 9:00; guided tours of various sights-30 SEK, check tour times online; +46 8 402 6130, www.royalcourt.se.

Orientation: I've listed the museums in order of sightseeing worthi-ness. But if you want to see them all with minimal backtracking, follow this plan: Begin at the entrance on Slottsbacken. Head up to the chapel for a peek, then descend to the treasury. Tour the Royal Apartments, exiting at the far side of the building—where you can head straight into the Museum of

Three Crowns. Exiting there, you'll find the final sight (Museum of Antiquities) to your right.

Royal Apartments: The stately palace exterior encloses 608 rooms (one more than Britain's Buckingham Palace) of glittering 18th-century Baroque and Rococo decor. Guided 45-minute tours in English run year-round a couple of times a day.

Clearly the palace of Scandinavia's superpower, it's steeped in royal history. You'll enter the grand main hall (cheapskates can get a free look at this first room before reaching the ticket checkpoint), then walk the long halls through four sections. On the main level are the Hall of State (with an exhibit of fancy state awards) and the lavish Bernadotte Apartments (some fine Rococo interiors and portraits of the Bernadotte dynasty); upstairs you'll find the State Apartments (with rooms dating to the 1690s—darker halls, faded tapestries, and a wannabe hall of mirrors) and the Guest Apartments (with less lavish quarters, where visiting heads of state still crash).

Royal Treasury (Skattkammaren): Refreshingly compact compared to the sprawling apartments, the treasury gives you a good, up-close look at Sweden's crown jewels. It's particularly worthwhile with an English guided tour or the included audioguide (which covers basically the same information).

Climbing down into the super-secure vault, you'll see 12 cases filled with fancy crowns, scepters, jeweled robes, the silver baptismal font of Karl XI, and plenty of glittering gold. The first room holds the crowns of princes and princesses, while the second shows off the more serious regalia of kings and queens. For more than a century, these crowns have gone unworn: The last Swedish coronation was Oskar II's in 1873; in 1907 his son and successor—out of deference for the constitution (and living in a Europe that was deep in the throes of modernism)—declined to wear the crown, so he was "enthroned" rather than "coronated." The crowns still belong to the monarchs and are present in the room on special occasions—but they are symbols rather than accessories.

Museum of Three Crowns (Museum Tre Kronor): This museum shows off bits of the palace from before a devastating 1697 fire. The models, illustrations, and artifacts are displayed in vaulted medieval cellars that are far more evocative than the run-of-the-mill interior of today's palace. But while the stroll through the cellars is atmospheric, it's basically just more old stuff, interesting only to real history buffs.

Royal Chapel: If you don't want to spring for a ticket, but would like a little taste of palace opulence, climb the stairs inside the main entrance for a peek into the chapel. It's standard-issue royal Baroque: colorful ceiling painting, bubbly altars, and a giant organ.

Gustav III's Museum of Antiquities (Gustav III's Antikmuseum): In the 1700s, Gustav III traveled through Italy and brought home an impressive gallery of classical Roman statues. These are displayed exactly as they were in the 1790s. This was a huge deal for those who had never been out of Sweden.

More Gamla Stan Sights

These first two sights sit on the Gamla Stan islet of Helgeandsholmen (just north of the Royal Palace), which is dominated by the parliament complex. Also at the edge of Gamla Stan is the stately island of Riddarholmen.

Parliament (Riksdag)

For a firsthand look at Sweden's government, tour the parliament buildings. Guides enjoy a chance to teach a little Swedish polisci along the standard tour of the building and its art. It's also possible to watch the parliament in session.

Cost and Hours: Free one-hour English tours run late June-mid-Aug, usually 4/day Mon-Fri (when parliament is not in session). The rest of the year tours run 1/day Sat-Sun only; you're also welcome to join Swedish citizens in the viewing gallery (free); enter at Riksgatan 3a, call +46 8 786 4862 from 9:00 to 11:00 to confirm tour times, www.riksdagen.se.

▲Museum of Medieval Stockholm (Medeltidsmuseet)

This modern, well-presented museum explains how Stockholm grew from a medieval village to a major city, with a focus on its interactions with fellow Hanseatic League trading cities. The museum does a particularly good job of weaving medieval citizens' personal stories within the historical context. Lots of artifacts, models, life-size dioramas, and sound and lighting effects—all displayed in a vast subterranean space—help bring the story to life.

When the government was digging a parking garage near the parliament complex in the 1970s, workers uncovered a major archaeological find: parts of the town wall that King Gustav Vasa built in the 1530s, as well as a churchyard—discoveries preserved here. You'll also see the preserved remains of a small cannon-ship from the 1520s and a reconstructed main market square from 13th-century Stockholm.

Cost and Hours: Free; Tue-Sun 12:00-17:00, Wed until 20:00, closed Mon; audioguide-30 SEK, enter museum from park in front of parliament—down below as you cross the bridge, +46 8 5083 1790, www.medeltidsmuseet.stockholm.se.

Nearby: The museum sits in **Strömparterren** park. With its café and Carl Milles statue of the *Sun Singer* greeting the day, it's a pleasant place for a sightseeing break (pay WC in park, free WC in museum).

Riddarholmen

Literally the "Knights Isle," Riddarholmen is the quiet and stately far side of Gamla Stan, with a historic church, private palaces, and a famous view. The knights referred to in its name were the nobles who built their palaces on this little island to be near the Royal Palace, just across the way. The island, cut off from the rest of Gamla Stan by a noisy highway, is pretty lifeless, with impersonal government agencies filling its old mansions. Still, a visit is worthwhile for a peek at its church and to enjoy the famous view of City Hall and Lake Mälaren from its far end.

A statue of Birger Jarl (considered the man who founded Stockholm in 1252) marks the main square. Surrounding it are 17th-century private palaces of old noble families (now government buildings). And towering high above is the spire of the Riddarholmen Church. Established in the 13th century as a Franciscan church, this has been the burial place of nearly every Swedish royal since the early 1600s. If you're looking for a Swedish Westminster Abbey, this is it (50 SEK, daily 10:00-17:00, Oct-Nov until 16:00). An inviting, shady café at the far end of the island is where people (and photographers) gather for Riddarholmen's iconic Stockholm view.

DOWNTOWN STOCKHOLM

I've organized these sights and activities in the urban core by island and/or neighborhood.

On Kungsholmen, West of Norrmalm
▲▲City Hall (Stadshuset)

The Stadshuset is an impressive mix of 8 million red bricks, 19 million chips of gilt mosaic, and lots of Stockholm pride. While churches dominate cities in southern Europe, in Scandinavian capitals, City Halls seem to be the most impressive buildings, celebrating humanism and the ideal of people working together in community. Built in 1923, this is still a functioning City Hall. The members of the city council—101 men and women representing the

850,000 citizens of Stockholm—are hobby legislators with regular day jobs. That's why they meet in the evening once a week. One of Europe's finest public buildings, the site of the annual Nobel Prize banquet, and a favorite spot for weddings (two per hour on Saturday afternoons, when some parts of the complex may be closed), City Hall is particularly enjoyable and worthwhile for its entertaining and required 50-minute tour.

Cost and Hours: 120 SEK; English tours offered daily, generally June-Aug hourly 10:00-14:00, fewer off-season; schedule can change due to special events—call to confirm; 300 yards behind the central train station—about a 15-minute walk from either the station or Gamla Stan, bus #3 or #50, cafeteria open to public at lunch Mon-Fri; +46 8 5082 9058, www.stockholm.se/stadshuset.

Visiting City Hall: On the tour, you'll see the building's sumptuous National Romantic-style interior (similar to Britain's Arts and Crafts style), celebrating Swedish architecture and craftwork, and created almost entirely with Swedish materials. Highlights include the so-called Blue Hall (the Italian piazza-inspired, brick-lined courtyard that was originally intended to be painted blue—hence the name—where the 1,300-plate Nobel banquet takes place); the City Council Chamber (with a gorgeously painted wood-beamed ceiling that resembles a Viking longhouse—or maybe an overturned Viking boat); the Gallery of the Prince (lined with frescoes executed by Prince Eugene of Sweden); and the glittering, gilded, Neo-Byzantine-style (and aptly named) Golden Hall, where the Nobel recipients cut a rug after the banquet.

In this over-the-top space, a glimmering mosaic Queen of Lake Mälaren oversees the proceedings with a welcoming but watchful eye, as East (see Istanbul's Hagia Sophia and the elephant, on the right) and West (notice the Eiffel Tower, Statue of Liberty, and skyscrapers with the American flag, on the left) meet here in Stockholm. Above the door across the hall is Sweden's patron saint, Erik, who seems to have lost his head (due to some sloppy mosaic planning). On the tour, you'll find out exactly how many

STOCKHOLM

centimeters each Nobel banquet attendee gets at the table, why the building's plans were altered at the last minute to make the tower exactly one meter taller, where the prince got the inspiration for his scenic frescoes, and how the Swedes reacted when they first saw that Golden Hall (hint: they weren't pleased).

▲City Hall Tower

This 348-foot-tall tower rewards those who make the climb with the classic Stockholm view: The old church spires on the atmospheric islands of Gamla Stan pose together, with the rest of the green and watery city spread-eagle around them.

Cost and Hours: 60 SEK, daily 9:10-17:10, May and Sept until 15:50, closed Oct-April.

Crowd-Beating Tips: Only 30 people at a time are allowed up into the tower every 40 minutes. To ascend, you'll need a timed-entry ticket, available only in person at the tower ticket office on the same day. It can be a long wait for the next available time, and tickets can sell out by midafternoon. If you're touring City Hall, head to the tower ticket window first to check time-slot availability; ideally an entry time will coincide with the end of your tour.

Visiting the Tower: A total of 365 steps lead to the top of the tower, but you can ride an elevator partway up—leaving you only 159 easy steps to the top.

First you'll climb up through the brick structure, emerging at an atmospheric hall filled with models of busts and statues that adorn City Hall and a huge, 25-foot-tall statue of St. Erik. The patron saint of Stockholm, Erik was supposed to be hoisted by cranes up through the middle of the tower to stand at its top. But plans changed, big Erik is forever parked halfway up the structure, and the tower's top is open for visitors to gather and enjoy the view.

From Erik, you'll twist gradually up ramps and a few steps at a time through the narrow, labyrinthine brick halls with peek-a-boo views of the city. Finally you'll emerge into the wooden section of the tower, where a spiral staircase brings you up to the roof terrace. Enjoy the view from there, but also take some time to look around at the building's features. Smaller statues of Erik, Klara, Maria Magdalena, and Nikolaus, all patron saints, face their respective parishes. Look up: You're in the company of the tower's nine bells. And if you listen carefully, you might hear departure-hall announcements wafting all the way up from the central train station.

On Blasieholmen and Skeppsholmen

The peninsula of Blasieholmen pokes out from downtown Stockholm and is tethered to the island of Skeppsholmen by a narrow bridge (with great views and adorned with glittering golden crowns). While not connected to the city by T-bana or tram, you can reach this area on bus #65 or the harbor shuttle ferry. Skeppsholmen offers a peaceful break from the bustling city, with glorious views of Gamla Stan on one side and Djurgården on the other.

▲National Museum (Nationalmuseum)

The National Museum's collections got their start through generations of royal collecting. Soon after Gustav Vasa was declared

king in 1523, he began assembling an art collection and creating state rooms in which to display the symbols of wealth and power that legitimized the new Swedish dynasty. Subsequent royals continued amassing artworks and founded the museum in 1792. The present Renaissance-style building on the Blasieholmen peninsula opened in 1866 as Sweden's national gallery. Today the museum showcases a wide range of fine arts from circa 1500 to 1900 and decorative arts, design, and portraiture from the Middle Ages up to the present.

Cost and Hours: Free for permanent collection, 100 SEK for special exhibits; Tue-Sun 11:00-17:00, Fri until 21:00, closed Mon; audioguide-20 SEK or download free Nationalmuseum app, café and restaurant, Södra Blasieholmshamnen, T-bana: Kungsträdgarden, +46 8 5195 4310, www.nationalmuseum.se.

Visiting the Museum: Visitors move through extensive galleries on two floors, where European and Scandinavian arts, crafts, and design are grouped by time periods and presented side by side, fostering a helpful cultural context for viewing works created in the same era. To avoid being overwhelmed by the encyclopedic displays, use the museum's good app (or audioguide) to narrow down your choices.

Highlights include several canvases by Rembrandt and Rubens, a fine group of French Impressionist works, and a sizable collection of Russian icons. But visitors new to Sweden and its arts should prioritize the 16th-century Vasa-dynasty rooms, paintings from the late-19th-century National Romantic movement (a reaction to Sweden's eventual separation from Norway in 1905), early 20th-century Swedish art glass, and iconic examples of mid-

20th-century Swedish design. Especially popular are the Arts and Crafts-style paintings and watercolors by Stockholm-born Carl Larsson (1853-1919), who chronicled the everyday life of his family and friends (and you can't miss his huge *Entry of King Gustav Vasa into Stockholm* decorating the upper stairwell of the museum's main hall).

Museum of Modern Art (Moderna Museet)

This bright, cheery gallery on Skeppsholmen island is as far out as can be. For serious art lovers, it warrants ▲▲. The impressive permanent collection includes modernist all-stars such as Picasso, Braque, Dalí, Matisse, Munch, Kokoschka, and Dix; lots of goofy Dada art (including a copy of Duchamp's urinal); Pollock, Twombly, Bacon, and other postmodernists; and plenty of excellent contemporary stuff as well (don't miss the beloved Rauschenberg *Goat with Tire*). Swedish artists of the 20th and 21st centuries are also featured. The curators draw from this substantial well of masterpieces to assemble changing exhibits.

The museum's fine collection of modern and contemporary sculpture is installed on the leafy grounds of Skeppsholmen island—perfect for a stroll even when the museum is closed. The building also houses the Architecture and Design Center, with changing exhibits (www.arkdes.se).

Cost and Hours: Free but sometimes a fee for special exhibits; Tue-Sun 11:00-18:00, closed Mon; download the excellent, free audioguide to enhance your visit, fine bookstore, good shop, harborview café; T-bana: Kungsträdgården plus 10-minute walk, or take bus #65; +46 8 5202 3500, www.modernamuseet.se.

Östermalm

What this ritzy residential area lacks in museums or sights, it makes up for in posh style. Explore its stately streets, dine in its destination restaurants, and be sure to explore the delightful, upscale Saluhall food market right on Östermalmstorg (see "Eating in Stockholm," later). Östermalm's harborfront is hemmed in by the pleasant park called Nybroplan; from here, ferries sail to various parts of the city and beyond (this is the jumping-off point for cruises into Stockholm's archipelago). If connecting to the sights in Djurgården, consider doing Östermalm by foot.

Stockholm's Best Views

For a bird's-eye perspective on this wonderful urban mix of water, parks, concrete, and people, consider these viewpoints.

City Hall Tower: Top of the tower comes with the classic city view (see listing earlier).

Katarina: This viewing platform—offering fine views over the steeples of Gamla Stan—rises up from Slussen (the busy transit zone between Gamla Stan and Södermalm; for location, see the "Stockholm" map, earlier). The elevator making this an easy destination may be under renovation during your visit, in which case, you'll have to walk up. You can get to the platform via pedestrian bridge from Mosebacke Torg, up above in Södermalm. In good summer weather, you'll have to wade through the swanky tables of Eriks restaurant to reach the (free and public) viewpoint.

Himlen: Rising above Södermalm's main drag, the Skrapan skyscraper has a free elevator to the **$$$$** Himlen restaurant, on the 25th floor. While they're hoping you'll order a meal or a 100-SEK cocktail in the lounge, it's generally fine to take a discreet peek at the 360-degree views—just march in the door at #78 and ride the elevator up to 25 (Mon-Sat 15:00-late, closed Sun, Götgatan 78—for location, see the "Stockholm" map, earlier, +46 8 660 6068, www.restauranghimlen.se).

▲▲Swedish History Museum (Historiska Museet)

The displays and artifacts in this excellent museum cover all of Swedish history, but the highlights are its fascinating Viking exhibit and impressive Gold Room. Also worth a look are sections on Scandinavian prehistory, medieval church art, and a well-realized display about the Danish invasion of 1361—the battle of Gotland—in which 1,800 ill-equipped Swedish farmers lost their lives. The Economy Museum - Royal Coin Cabinet, a separate museum, is in the same building (see next listing).

Cost and Hours: Free; daily 10:00-17:00, Sept-May Tue-Sun 11:00-17:00, Wed until 20:00, closed Mon; audioguide-30 SEK, a few blocks north of the Djurgården bridge at Narvavägen 13, bus #67 stops out front, +46 8 5195 5562, www.historiska.se. Kids' activities are available in an inner courtyard until 16:00.

Visiting the Museum: Billing itself as the world's largest Viking exhibition at over 10,000 square feet, **Viking World** probes the many stories and myths about these people. Were they peaceful traders and farmers—or brutal robbers and pillagers? With Yggdrasil—the enormous tree in Viking mythology—as the exhibit's centerpiece, visitors can explore Viking society, travel, trade, and spirituality through original artifacts and interactive environments.

The **"Gold Room"** (in the basement) dazzles with about 115 pounds of gold: spiral hair ornaments from 1500 BC; gold collars worn by fifth-century aristocrats; hoards of coins from Roman and Arab empires; once-buried treasure troves of jewelry and votive objects; and medieval jewel-encrusted reliquaries.

In all, the museum has about 3,000 finely crafted gold objects—largely thanks to Swedish legislation that has protected antiquities since the 17th century.

Economy Museum - Royal Coin Cabinet (Ekonomiska Museet - Kungliga Myntkabinettet)

Newly opened within the Swedish History Museum building, this separate museum is much more than your typical royal coin collection: It's the best money museum I've seen in Europe.

Cost and Hours: Free, may be fee for special exhibits, same hours as Swedish History Museum, +46 8 5195 5620, https:// ekonomiskamuseet.se.

Waterside Walk

Enjoy Stockholm's ever-expanding shoreline promenades. Tracing the downtown shoreline while dodging in-line skaters and ice-cream trolleys (rather than cars and buses), you can walk from Slussen across Gamla Stan, all the way to the good ship *Vasa* in Djurgården. Perhaps the best stretch is along the waterfront Strandvägen street (from Nybroplan past weather-beaten old boats and fancy facades to Djurgården). As you stroll, keep in mind that there's free fishing in central Stockholm, and the harbor waters are restocked every spring with thousands of fish. Locals tell of one lucky lad who pulled in an 80-pound salmon. The waterside lanes are extremely bike-friendly here and throughout Stockholm.

DJURGÅRDEN

Four hundred years ago, Djurgården ("Animal Garden") was the king's hunting ground. You'll see the royal gate to the island immediately after the bridge that connects it to the mainland. Now this entire lush island is Stockholm's fun center, protected as a national park. It still has a smattering of animal life among its biking paths, picnicking families, art galleries, various amusements, and museums, which are some of the best in Scandinavia.

Orientation: Of the three great sights on the island, the Vasa and Nordic museums are neighbors, and Skansen is a 10-minute walk away (or hop on any bus or tram—they come every couple of minutes). Several lesser or special-interest attractions (from the ABBA museum to an amusement park) are also nearby.

To get around more easily, consider **renting a bike** as you enter the island. You can get one at Sjöcaféet, a café just over the Djurgårdsbron bridge; they also rent boats (bikes-80 SEK/hour, 300 SEK/day; canoes-170 SEK/hour, kayaks-140 SEK/hour; open daily 9:00-21:00, closed off-season and in bad weather; handy city cycle maps, +46 8 660 5757, www.sjocafeet.se).

In the concrete building upstairs from the café, you'll find a **Djurgården visitors center,** with free maps, island bike routes, brochures, and information about the day's events (daily in summer 9:00-17:00, shorter hours off-season).

Getting There: Take tram #7 from Sergels Torg (the stop is right under the highway overpass) or Nybroplan (in front of the gilded theater building) and get off at one of these stops: Nordic Museum (use also for Vasa Museum), Liljevalc Gröna Lund (for ABBA museum), or Skansen. In summer, you can take a city ferry from the southeast end of Gamla Stan or from Nybroplan (see "Getting Around Stockholm," earlier). Walkers enjoy the harborside Strandvägen promenade, which leads from Nybroplan to the island (described under "Waterside Walk," earlier).

Major Museums on Djurgården
▲▲▲Skansen

Founded in 1891, Skansen was the first in what became a Europe-wide movement to preserve traditional architecture in open-air museums. It's a huge park gathering more than 150 historic buildings (homes, churches, shops, and schoolhouses) transplanted from all corners of Sweden. Other languages have borrowed the Swedish term "Skansen" (which originally meant "the Fort") to describe an "open-air museum." Today,

tourists enjoy exploring this Swedish-culture-on-a-lazy-Susan, seeing folk crafts in action and wonderfully furnished old interiors. Kids love Skansen, where they can ride a life-size wooden *Dala*-horse and stare down a hedgehog, visit Lill-Skansen (a children's zoo), and take a mini-train or pony ride. This is an enjoyable place to visit on summer days, when it's lively with families and tourists.

Cost and Hours: 220 SEK, kids-70 SEK, less off-season; park opens daily at 10:00, closes at 22:00 late June-Aug and progressively earlier the rest of the year; historical buildings generally open 11:00-17:00, late June-Aug some until 19:00, most closed in winter. Check their excellent online calendar for what's happening during your visit (www.skansen.se) or call +46 8 442 8000.

Music: Skansen does great music in summer. There's fiddling, folk dancing, and public dancing to live bands on Friday and Saturday nights. Confirm performance times before you go.

Visiting Skansen: Skansen isn't designed as a one-way loop; it's a sprawling network of lanes and buildings, yours to explore. For the full story, invest in the museum guidebook (sold at the info booth just after the entrance). With the book, you'll understand each building you duck into and even learn about the Nordic animals awaiting you in the zoo. While you're at the info booth, check the live crafts schedule to make a smart Skansen plan (the scale model displayed at the entrance will give you an idea of the park's size—and the need for a plan). Guides throughout the park are happy to answer your questions—but only if you ask them. The old houses come alive when you take the initiative to get information.

From the entrance, go up the stairs and bear left to find the escalator, and ride it up to **"The Town Quarter"** (Stadskvarteren), where shoemakers, potters, and glassblowers are busy doing their traditional thing (daily 10:00-17:00) in a re-created Old World Stockholm. Continuing deeper into the park—past the bakery, spice shop/grocery, hardware store, and a cute little courtyard café—you'll reach the central square, **Bollnästorget** (signed as "Central Skansen" but labeled on English maps as "Market Street"), with handy food stands. The rest of Sweden spreads out from here. Northern Swedish culture and architecture is in the north (top of park map), and southern Sweden's in the south (bottom of map). Various homesteads—each clustered protectively around an inner courtyard—are scattered around the complex.

Poke around. Follow signs—or your instincts. It's worth stepping into the old, red-wood Seglora Church (just past Bollnästorget), which aches with atmosphere under painted beams. The park has two **zoos**. Lill-Skansen is a children's petting zoo. Beyond the big brick spa tower and carnival rides sprawls the Scandinavian Animals section, with bears, wolves, moose ("elk"), seals, reindeer (near the Sami camp), and other animals.

Eating at Skansen: The park has eating options to suit every budget. The most memorable—and affordable—meals are at the small food court on the main square, **Bollnästorget,** where kiosks dish up "Sami slow food" (smoked reindeer), waffles, hot dogs, and more. There are lots of picnic benches—Skansen encourages **picnicking.** (A small grocery store is tucked away across the street and a bit to the left of the main entrance.)

For a sit-down meal, the old-time **$$$ Stora Gungan Krog,** right at the top of the escalator in the craftsmen's quarter, is a cozy inn (indoor or outdoor lunches—meat, fish, or veggie—with a salad-and-cracker bar). Another snug spot is **$$ Gubbhyllan,** on the ground floor and fine porch of an old house (at base of escalator, just past main entrance). Or consider one of three restaurants that share a less-atmospheric modern building facing the grandstand (just up the hill inside the main entrance), all with nice views over the city: the simple **$$$ Skansen Terrassen** cafeteria; **$$$ Tre Byttor Taverne,** with 18th-century pub ambience; and, upstairs, the fussy **$$$$ Solliden** restaurant, with a dated blue-and-white

STOCKHOLM

dining hall facing a wall of windows; the main reason to eat here is the big smorgasbord lunch.

Aquarium: The "aquarium"—featuring lemurs, meerkats, baboons, Gila monsters, giant anacondas, rattlesnakes, geckos, crocodiles, colorful tree frogs, and small sharks...but almost no fish—is located within Skansen, but is not covered by your Skansen ticket. Only animal lovers find it worth the steep admission price (120 SEK, July-Aug daily 10:00-19:00, closes earlier rest of year, +46 8 660 1082, www.skansen-akvariet.se).

▲▲▲Vasa Museum (Vasamuseet)

Stockholm turned a titanic flop into one of Europe's great sightseeing attractions. The glamorous but unseaworthy warship *Vasa*—

top-heavy with an extra cannon deck—sank 40 minutes into her 1628 maiden voyage when a breeze caught the sails and blew her over. After 333 years at the bottom of Stockholm's harbor, she rose again from the deep with the help of marine archaeologists. Rediscovered in 1956 and raised in 1961, this Edsel of the sea is today the best-preserved ship of its age anywhere—housed since 1990 in a brilliant museum. The masts perched atop the roof—best seen from a distance—show the actual height of the ship.

Cost and Hours: 170 SEK, includes film and tour; daily 8:30-18:00, Sept-May 10:00-17:00 except Wed until 20:00; WCs on level 3, good café; on the waterfront at Galärvarvsvägen 14 immediately behind Nordic Museum—facing the museum, walk around to the right, 10-minute walk from Skansen, tram #7 from downtown; +46 8 5195 5810, www.vasamuseet.se.

Crowd-Beating Tips: The museum ticket booths can have very long lines, but they generally move quickly—you likely won't wait more than 15-20 minutes. But to avoid the wait, buy tickets in advance online or use the ticket machines in the lobby. For generally lighter crowds, get here either right when it opens, or after about 16:00 (but note that the last tour starts at 16:30).

Tours: The free 25-minute **tour** is worthwhile. Because guides are given license to cover whatever they like, no two tours are alike—if you're fascinated by the place, consider taking two different tours to pick up new details. In summer, English tours run on the hour and half-hour (last tour at 16:30); off-season (Sept-May) tours go 3/day Mon-Fri, hourly Sat-Sun (last tour at 15:30). Listen for the announcement, or check at the info desk for the next tour.

Alternatively, you can access the **audioguide** by logging onto the museum's Wi-Fi (www.vasamuseet.se/audioguide).

Film: The excellent 17-minute film digitally re-creates *Vasa*-era Stockholm (and the colorfully painted ship itself), dramatizes its sinking, and documents the modern-day excavation and preservation of the vessel. It generally runs three times per hour; virtually all showings are either in English or with English subtitles.

Visiting the Museum: For a thorough visit, plan on spending at least an hour and a half—watch the film, take a guided tour, and linger over the exhibits (this works in any order). After buying your ticket, head inside. Sort out your film and tour options at the information desk to your right.

Upon entry, you're prow-to-prow with the great ship. The *Vasa*, while not quite the biggest ship in the world when launched in 1628, had the most firepower, with two fearsome decks of cannons. The 500 carved wooden statues draping the ship—once painted in bright colors—are all symbolic of the king's power. The 10-foot lion on the magnificent prow is a re-minder that Europe con-

sidered the Swedish King Gustavus Adolphus the "Lion from the North." With this great ship, Sweden was preparing to establish its empire and become more engaged in European power politics. Specifically, the Swedes (who already controlled much of today's Finland and Estonia) wanted to push south to dominate the whole of the Baltic Sea, in order to challenge their powerful rival, Poland.

Designed by a Dutch shipbuilder, the *Vasa* had 72 guns of the same size and type (a rarity on mix-and-match warships of the age), allowing maximum efficiency in reloading—since there was no need to keep track of different ammunition. Unfortunately, the king's unbending demands to build the ship high (172 feet tall) but skinny made it extremely unstable; no amount of ballast could weigh the ship down enough to prevent it from tipping.

Now explore the **exhibits,** which are situated on six levels around the grand hall, circling the ship itself. All displays are well described in English. You'll learn about the ship's rules (bread can't be older than eight years), why it sank (stale bread?), how it's preserved (the ship, not the bread), and so on. Best of all is the chance to do slow laps around the magnificent vessel at different levels. Now painstakingly restored, 98 percent of the *Vasa*'s wood is original (modern bits are the brighter and smoother planks).

On **level 4** (the entrance level), right next to the ship, you'll see a

1:10 scale model of the *Vasa* in its prime—vividly painted and fully rigged with sails. Farther along, models show how the *Vasa* was salvaged; a colorful children's section re-creates the time period; and a 10-minute multimedia show explains why the *Vasa* sank (alternating between English and Swedish showings). Heading behind the ship, you'll enjoy a great view of the sculpture-slathered stern of the *Vasa*. The facing wall features full-size replicas of the carvings, demonstrating how the ship was originally colorfully painted.

Several engaging displays are on **level 5.** "Life On Board" lets you walk through the gun deck and study cutaway models of the hive of activity that hummed below decks (handy, since you can't enter the actual ship). Artifacts—including fragments of clothing actually worn by the sailors—were salvaged along with the ship. "Battle!" is a small exhibit of cannons and an explanation of naval warfare.

Level 6 features "The Sailing Ship," with models demonstrating how the *Vasa* and similar vessels actually sailed. You'll see the (very scant) remains of some of the *Vasa*'s actual riggings and sails. **Level 7** gives you even higher views over the ship.

Don't miss **level 2**—all the way at the bottom (ride the handy industrial-size elevator)—with some of the most interesting exhibits. "The Ship" explains how this massive and majestic vessel was brought into being using wood from tranquil Swedish forests. Tucked under the ship's prow is a laboratory where today's scientists continue with their preservation efforts. The "Objects" exhibit shows off actual items found in the shipwreck, while "Face to Face" introduces you to some of those who perished when the *Vasa* sunk—with faces that were re-created from skeletal remains.

Nearby, you'll see some of the skeletons found in the shipwreck. Those remains have been extensively analyzed, revealing remarkable details about the ages, diets, and general health of the victims.

As you exit, you'll pass a hall of (generally excellent) temporary exhibits.

▲Nordic Museum (Nordiska Museet)

Built to look like a Danish Renaissance palace, this museum offers a fascinating peek at 500 years of traditional Swedish lifestyles. The exhibits insightfully place everyday items into their social/historical context in ways that help you really grasp various chapters of Sweden's past. It's arguably more informative than Skansen. Take time to let the excellent, included audioguide enliven the exhibits.

Cost and Hours: 140 SEK; daily 9:00-18:00, Sept-May 10:00-17:00, Wed until 20:00; Djurgårdsvägen 6, at Djurgårdsbron, tram #7 from downtown, +46 8 5195 4600, www.nordiskamuseet.se.

Visiting the Museum: Entering the museum's main hall, you'll be face-to-face with Carl Milles' huge painted-wood statue of Gustav Vasa, father of modern Sweden. Most of this floor is usually devoted to temporary exhibits.

Highlights of the permanent collection are on the top two floors. Head up the stairs, or take the elevator just to the left of Gustav. Begin on floor 4 and work your way down.

On **floor 4,** four exhibits ring the grand atrium. The **"Homes and Interiors"** section displays 400 years of home furnishings, some within room dioramas. As you travel through this parade of furniture—from dark, heavily draped historical rooms to modern living rooms, and from rustic countryside cottages to aristocratic state bedrooms—you'll learn the subtle meaning behind everyday furniture that we take for granted. For example, the advent of television didn't just change entertainment—it gave people a reason to gather each evening in the living room, which, in turn, became a more-used (and less formal) part of people's homes. You'll learn about the Swedish designers who, in the 1930s, eschewed stiff-backed traditional chairs in favor of sleek perches that merged ergonomics and looks—giving birth to functionalism.

Also on this floor, the **"Folk Art"** section shows off colorfully painted furniture and wood carvings; vibrant traditional costumes; and rustic Bible-story illustrations that adorned the walls of peasants' homes. The **"Sápmi"** exhibit tells the fascinating and often overlooked story of the indigenous Sami people (formerly called "Lapps"), who lived in the northern reaches of Norway, Sweden, Finland, and Russia centuries before Europeans created those modern nations. On display are shoes, ceremonial knives, colorful hats and clothing, and other features of Sami culture. You'll learn how their nomadic lifestyle—following their herds of grazing reindeer—allowed them to survive so far north, and how the Sami (who today number around 30,000) have had an impact on greater Swedish society. Finally, tucked behind the stairwell, the "Small

Things" collection shows off timepieces, ceramics, and tobacco pipes, among other items.

Floor 3 has several smaller exhibits. The most interesting are **"Table Settings"** (with carefully set tables from the 16th century until about 1950, representing customs and traditions around gathering to share food and drink—from an elegant tea party to a rowdy pub) and **"Traditions"** (showing and describing each old-time celebration of the Swedish year—from Christmas to Midsummer—as well as funerals, confirmations, and other life events). Also on display: 300 years of Swedish attire (including a fun video showing how complicated and time-consuming it was for a woman to dress in the 18th century); jewelry and textile exhibits; a dollhouse and toy collection; and a photo exhibition pulled from the museum's archive.

▲ABBA: The Museum

The Swedish pop group ABBA was, for a time, a bigger business than Volvo. Since bursting on the scene in 1974 by winning the Eurovision Song Contest with "Waterloo," and serenading Sweden's newly minted queen with "Dancing Queen" in 1976, they've sold more than 380 million records, and the musical based on their many hits, *Mamma Mia!*, has been enjoyed by 50 million people. It was only a matter of time before Stockholm opened an ABBA museum, which is conveniently located just across the street from Skansen and next to Gröna Lund amusement park. Like everything ABBA, it is aggressively for-profit and slickly promoted, with the steepest ticket price in town. True to its subject, it's bombastic, glitzy, and highly interactive. If you like ABBA, it's lots of fun; if you love ABBA, it's ▲▲▲ nirvana.

Cost and Hours: 260 SEK—credit cards only, cheaper online, 595 SEK family ticket covers two adults and up to four kids; daily 9:00-19:00, Sept-May 10:00-18:00 except Wed until 19:00, Djurgårdsvägen 68, tram #7 from downtown, +46 8 1213 2860, www.abbathemuseum.com.

Tours: ABBA aficionados will happily fork over 20 SEK extra for the intimate audioguide, in which Agnetha, Benny, Björn, and Anni-Frid share their memories, in their own words.

Getting In: Only 75 people are let in every 15 minutes with timed-entry tickets. The museum strongly encourages getting tickets in advance from their website or at the TI. In fact, they'll charge you 20 SEK extra per ticket to buy in person (but computers are standing by if you want to "prebook" on the spot). It can be crowded on summer weekends, in which case you may have to wait for a later time.

Visiting the Museum: The museum is high-tech, with plenty of actual ABBA artifacts, re-creations of rooms where the group did its composing and recording (including their famous "Polar

Studio" and their rustic archipelago cottage), a room full of gold and platinum records, plenty of high-waisted sequined pantsuits, and lots of high-energy video screens.

Included in the ticket is a "digital key" that lets you take advantage of several interactive stations. For example, you can record a music video karaoke-style as a fifth member of the group—with virtual ABBA members dancing around you—and share your musical debut via the museum's website. A small wing features the Swedish Music Hall of Fame, but apart from that, it's all ABBA.

Waterfront Sights

While the tram zips sightseers between the Vasa Museum and Skansen, it's a short, enjoyable, and very scenic walk along the waterfront—a delight on a nice day. You'll see food stands, boats bobbing in the harbor, and sunbathing Swedes.

You'll also pass several sights, listed here in the order you'll reach them (from the Djurgårdsbron bridge): **Junibacken** is a fairy-tale house based on the writings of Astrid Lindgren, who created *Pippi Longstocking*. While oriented toward Swedish kids, American children may enjoy it, too (www.junibacken.se). The pier directly in front of the Vasa Museum is actually part of the **Maritime Museum** (Sjöhistoriska), where historic ships are moored (typically big icebreakers from the Arctic, and sometimes military boats). About halfway along the waterfront is the **Museum of Spirits** (see next listing), offering a weird but welcome break from heavier sightseeing. Finally, you'll reach **Vikingaliv,** a small myth-busting museum about the Vikings that uses interactive displays to present them as colonizers and traders more than looters and warriors (you won't find a horned helmet in the place). A low-tech, hokey 10-minute ride tells "Ragnfrid's Saga" (the fictional story of the long-suffering wife of a voyaging husband; www.vikingaliv.se).

Museum of Spirits (Spiritmuseum)

The museum's highly conceptual permanent exhibit considers the role of alcohol—and specifically, flavored vodkas—in Swedish society. While Sweden got a reputation for its "loose morals" in the 1970s (mostly surrounding sex and nudity), at the same time it was extremely puritanical when it came to alcohol; the government actively tried to get Swedes to stop drinking (hence the liquor-store system and sky-high alcohol taxes that still exist). In the exhibit's season-themed rooms, you'll be able to smell different types of flavored liquors (orange in the spring, elderflower in the summer, and so on); upstairs, you can ace a virtual pub quiz, recline (or nap) in the boozy drunk-simulator room, and step into a garishly lit, buzzing room that simulates a hangover. The temporary exhibits here are also quite good.

Cost and Hours: 120 SEK, 250-SEK ticket adds a taster kit of flavored vodkas; Mon-Sat 10:00-17:00, Sun 12:00-16:00, shorter hours off-season; summertime beer pier opens for dining and 17 types of draft beer, Djurgårdsvägen 38, +46 8 1213 1300, www.spritmuseum.se.

Other Djurgården Sights
Gröna Lund Amusement Park

Stockholm's venerable and lowbrow Tivoli-type amusement park still packs in the local families and teens on cheap dates. It's a busy venue for local pop concerts.

Cost and Hours: 115 SEK to enter (free over 65 or under 7), then buy ride pass or coupons; daily late April-late Sept 12:00-23:00, closed off-season, www.gronalund.com.

▲Thielska Galleriet

If you liked the Larsson and Zorn art in the National Gallery, and/or if you're a Munch fan, this charming mansion on the water at the far end of the Djurgården park is worth the trip. The building was designed in the early 20th century for banker and art patron Ernest Thiel as a residence, but with skylight galleries to accommodate his extensive collection, which has hung here ever since.

Cost and Hours: 130 SEK, Tue-Sun 12:00-17:00, closed Mon, bus #67 from Odenplan, +46 8 662 5884, www.thielska-galleriet.se.

▲Biking the Garden Island

Djurgården is the most natural place in Stockholm to enjoy a bike ride. There's a good and reasonably priced bike-rental place just over the bridge as you enter the island (Sjöcaféet; see beginning of Djurgården section, earlier), and a world of parklike paths and lanes with harbor vistas to enjoy.

Ask for a free map and route tips when you rent your bike. Figure about an hour to pedal around Djurgården's waterfront perimeter; it's mostly flat, but with some short, steeper stretches that take you up and over the middle of the island. Those who venture beyond the Skansen park find themselves nearly all alone in the lush and evocative environs.

At the summit of the island you'll come upon **Rosendal's Garden,** with a bakery and café. You can sit in the greenhouse or in the delightful orchard or flower garden, where locals come to pick a bouquet and pay by the weight. (The garden is fertilized by the horse pies from adjacent Skansen.) Just beyond is **Rosendals Slott,** the cute mini-palace of Karl Johans XIV, founder of the Bernadotte dynasty. This palace, in the so-called Karl Johans style ("Empire style"), went together in prefabricated sections in the 1820s. The story is told on a board in front, and a nine-ton porphyry vase graces the backyard.

A garden café at the eastern tip of the island offers a scenic break midway through your pedal. For a longer ride, you can cross the canal to the Ladugårdsgärdet peninsula ("Gärdet" for short), a swanky, wooded residential district just to the north.

SÖDERMALM

Just south of Gamla Stan, the Södermalm district is the real-life antidote to the upscale areas where most visitors spend their time. While it has few tourist sights (aside from the Fotografiska and Stockholm City museums), Södermalm offers fine views and fun places to eat (for recommendations and more on this area, see "Södermalm Streets and Eats," later). Towering over Södermalm's main road is the Skrapan building, with the Himlen view terrace on its 25th floor (see "Stockholm's Best Views" sidebar, earlier).

▲Fotografiska (Photography Museum)

This museum, in a renovated 1906 industrial building right on the Stadsgården embankment, is fun and appealing. The focus is

on contemporary and international photography, exhibited in well-curated, thematic displays that change several times a year. It's a complete destination, with a top-floor café giving drop-dead views over the city (open until 21:00 in summer), a people-watching terrace café on the embankment, and a browse-worthy store.

Cost and Hours: 170 SEK—credit cards only, daily 10:00-23:00, at Stadsgårdshamnen 22, 10-minute walk from Slussen, hop-on, hop-off boats stop here, +46 8 5090 0500, www.fotografiska.eu.

Stockholm City Museum (Stadsmuseet)

Located in a 17th-century palace, this museum's permanent exhibit employs life-size dioramas to explore Stockholm's evolution over 500 years, from tiny northern trading town to urban Scandinavian metropolis.

Cost and Hours: Free; Tue and Thu 11:00-20:00, Wed and

Fri-Sun until 17:00, closed Mon; Ryssgården, T-bana: Slussen—use Södermalmstorg exit, +46 8 5083 1620, www.stadsmuseet.stockholm.se.

ON THE OUTSKIRTS

The home and garden of Carl Milles, Sweden's greatest sculptor, is less than an hour from the city center. For sights farther outside Stockholm (all reachable by public transportation), see the next chapter.

▲Millesgården

The villa and garden of Carl Milles is a veritable forest of statues by Sweden's greatest sculptor. Millesgården is dramatically situated on a bluff overlooking the harbor in Stock-holm's upper-class suburb of Lidingö. While the art is engaging and enjoyable, even the curators have little to say about it from an interpretive point of view—so your visit is basically without guidance. But in Milles' house, which dates from the 1920s, you can see his north-lit studio and get a sense of his creative genius.

Carl Milles spent much of his career teaching at the Cranbrook Academy of Art in Michigan. But he's buried here at his villa, where he lived and worked for 20 years, lov-ingly designing this sculpture garden for the public. Milles wanted his art to be displayed on pedestals...to be seen "as if silhouettes against the sky." His subjects—often Greek mythological figures such as Pegasus or Poseidon—stand out as if the sky were a blank paper. Yet unlike silhouettes, Milles' images can be enjoyed from many angles. And Milles liked to enliven his sculptures by incorporating water features into his figures. *Hand of God*, perhaps his most famous work, gives insight into Milles' belief that when the artist created, he was—in a way—divinely inspired.

Cost and Hours: 150 SEK, Tue-Sun 11:00-17:00, closed Mon, English booklet explains the art, free audioguide app, res-taurant and café, +46 8 446 7590, www.millesgarden.se.

Getting There: Catch the T-bana to Ropsten, then take bus #201, 202, 204, 206, 211, 212 or 221 to Torsviks Torg, then fol-low signs—about a five-minute walk; (allow about 45 minutes total each way).

STOCKHOLM

Shopping in Stockholm

Stockholm's smaller stores are open weekdays 10:00-18:00, Saturdays until 17:00, and Sundays 11:00-16:00. Some of the bigger stores (such as NK, H&M, and Åhléns) are open later on Saturdays and Sundays.

Fun Chain Stores

These chains have multiple branches around town; the most convenient are marked on the "Stockholm Hotels & Restaurants" map.

DesignTorget, dedicated to contemporary Swedish design, receives a commission for selling the unique works of local designers (generally Mon-Fri 11:00-18:00, Sat until 17:00, Sun 12:00-16:00, big branch underneath Sergels Torg—enter from basement level of Kulturhuset, other branches are around town and at the airport, www.designtorget.se).

Systembolaget is Sweden's state-run liquor store chain. A sample of each bottle of wine or liquor sits in a display case, with accompanying descriptions and suggested menu pairings. Look for the item number and order at the counter. Branches are in Hötorget underneath the movie theater complex, in Norrmalm at Vasagatan 25, and just up from Östermalmstorg at Nybrogatan 47 (Mon-Fri 10:00-19:00, Sat until 15:00, closed Sun, www.systembolaget.se).

Gudrun Sjödén is named for its fashion-designer founder, whose life's work has been creating cheery, functional clothing for Swedish women. Some might sniff at her sensible but colorful designs (some inspired by her summer garden), but they're free-spirited in a Pippi Longstocking sort of way (think aubergine and sunflower). You'll love it or hate it—all around town (at Regeringsgatan 30, Götgatan 44, and Stora Nygatan 33, daily 10:00-19:00, Sat until 17:00, Sun 12:00-16:00, www.gudrunsjoden.com).

Hamngatan

The main shopping zone between Kungsträdgården and Sergels Torg (described in my Modern City Walk, earlier) has plenty of huge department stores. At the top of Kungsträdgården, **Illums Bolighus** is a Danish design shop. Across the street, **Nordiska Kompaniet** (NK) is elegant and stately; the Swedish design (downstairs) and kitchenware sections are particularly impressive. The classy **Gallerian** mall is just up the street from NK and stretches seductively nearly to Sergels Torg. The **Åhléns** store, kitty-corner across Sergels Torg, is less expensive than NK and has two cafeterias and a supermarket. Affordable clothing chain **H&M** has a store right across the street. Tucked behind Åhléns is **Kartbutiken,** a handy map-and-guidebook shop that covers all of Sweden, Scandinavia, and beyond (daily, at Mäster Samuelsgatan 54).

Mood Stockholm

The city's most exclusive mall is a downtown block filled with big-name Swedish and international designers, plus a pricey food court and restaurants. The upscale decor and mellow music give it a Beverly Hills vibe (Mon-Fri 10:00-20:00, Sat until 18:00, Sun 11:00-17:00, Regeringsgatan 48). The mall anchors a ritzy, pedestrianized shopping zone; for more exclusive shops, browse the nearby streets Jakobsbergsgatan and Biblioteksgatan.

Södermalm

When Swedes want the latest items by local designers, they skip the downtown malls and head for funky Södermalm. **Götgatan,** the main drag that leads from Slussen up to this neighborhood, is a particularly good choice, with shop after shop of mostly Swedish designers. Boutiques along here—some of them one-offs, others belonging to Swedish chains—include Weekday (known for denim), Filippa K (high-end attire), and Tiogruppen (colorful bags and fabrics).

More intrepid shoppers will want to explore the area south of **Folkungagatan**—"SoFo," where scores of fun stores feature new and vintage clothing, housewares, and jewelry in the streets surrounding Nytorget.

Nybrogatan

This short and pleasant traffic-free street, which connects Östermalmstorg with the Nybroplan waterfront, is lined with small branches of interesting design shops, including Nordiska Galleriet (eye-catching modern furniture, at #11). It also has shoe and handbag stores, and an enticing cheese shop and bakery.

Nightlife and Entertainment in Stockholm

Bars and Music in Gamla Stan

The street called Stora Nygatan, with several lively bars, has perhaps the most accessible and reliable place for live jazz in town: Stampen. Several pubs here offer live Irish traditional music sessions or bluegrass several times each week; they tend to share musicians, who sometimes gather at one of these pubs for impromptu jam sessions (ask around, or stroll this street with your ears peeled). While it may seem odd to listen to Irish or bluegrass music in Stockholm, these venues are extremely popular with locals. For locations, see the "Gamla Stan Hotels & Restaurants" map.

STOCKHOLM

Stampen is two venues under one roof: a stone-vaulted cellar below (called Geronimo's FGT) and a fun-loving saloon-like jazz and R&B bar upstairs (check out the old instruments and antiques hanging from the ceiling). There's live music every night that Stampen is open (Tue-Sat, closed Mon, cover Fri-Sat only, Stora Gråmunkegränd 7, +46 8 205 793, www.stampen.se). Geronimo's, downstairs, is more of a nightclub/concert venue with a menu inspired by the American Southwest (open Tue-Sat, closed Sun-Mon, enter at Stora Nygatan 5).

Several other lively spots are within a couple of blocks of Stampen on Stora Nygatan. Your options include **Wirströms Pub** (live blues bands play in crowded cellar Mon-Wed 21:00-24:00, no cover, open daily, Stora Nygatan 13, www.wirstromspub.se); **O'Connells Irish Pub** (a lively expat sports bar with music—usually Tue-Sat at 21:00; open daily, Stora Nygatan 21, www.oconnells.se); and **The Liffey** (classic Irish pub with pub grub, live music Wed-Sun from 21:30; open daily, Stora Nygatan 40, www.theliffey.se).

Icebar Stockholm

If you want to put on a heavy coat and gloves and drink a fancy vodka in a modern-day igloo, consider the fun though touristy Icebar Stockholm. Everything—the bar, glasses, and even the tip jar—is made of ice—shipped down from Sweden's far north. You get your choice of vodka drinks and 45 minutes to enjoy the scene. If you go too early, it can be really dead. At busy times, crowds of people are let in every 45 minutes. That means there's a long line for drinks, and the place goes from being very crowded to almost empty as people gradually melt away. While there are now ice bars all over Europe, this was the second one to open (after the Ice Hotel in Lapland). And it really is pretty cool...a steady 23°F (online booking-199 SEK, drop-ins-215 SEK—on weekends drop-ins only allowed after 21:45, additional drinks-95 SEK, reservations smart; daily 11:15-24:00, Sept-May from 15:00; in the Nordic C Hotel adjacent to the main train station's Arlanda Express platform at Vasaplan 4, +46 8 5056 3520, www.icebarstockholm.se).

Swedish Massage, Spa, and Sauna

To treat yourself to a Swedish spa experience—maybe with an authentic "Swedish massage"—head for the elegant circa-1900 **CentralBadet Spa.** It's along downtown's main strolling street,

Drottninggatan, tucked back inside a tranquil and inviting garden courtyard. Admission includes entry to an extensive gym, "bubble-pool," sauna, steam room, "herbal/crystal sauna," and an elegant Art Nouveau pool. Most areas are mixed-gender, with men and women together, but some areas are reserved for women. If you won't make it to Finland, enjoy a sauna here. Bring your towel into the sauna—not for modesty, but for hygiene (to separate your body from the bench). The steam room is mixed; bring two towels (one for modesty and the other to sit on). The pool is more for floating than for jumping and splashing. The leafy courtyard restaurant is a relaxing place to enjoy affordable, healthy, and light meals (300 SEK, 400 SEK on Sat-Sun, towels and robes available for rent; slippers required—20 SEK to buy, 10 SEK to rent; Mon-Fri 7:00-20:30, Sat 8:00-19:30, Sun until 17:30; ages 18 and up, Drottninggatan 88, 10 minutes up from Sergels Torg, +46 8 5452 1300, reservations +46 8 218 821, www.central badet.se).

Sleeping in Stockholm

Stockholm's hotels are among Europe's best, offering good beds in unpretentious but interesting places. Each of these listings has helpful English-speaking staff, pleasant family rooms, and good facilities.

NEAR THE TRAIN STATION

$$$$ Freys Hotel is a Scan-mod, four-star place, with 127 compact, smartly designed rooms. It's well situated for train travelers, located on a dead-end pedestrian street across from the central station. While big, it works hard to be friendly and welcoming. Its cool, candlelit breakfast room becomes a bar in the evening, popular for its Belgian microbrews (air-con, Bryggargatan 12, +46 8 5062 1300, www.freyshotels.com, freys@freyshotels.com).

$$$$ Scandic No. 53 injects modernity into a classic old building a few blocks from the station. The 274 rooms are small and functional (no desk or chair in standard rooms) but comfortable. Everything surrounds a stylish, glassy atrium boasting a lounge/restaurant (live music until 24:00 most weekends), and a peaceful outdoor courtyard (air-con, elevator, Kungsgatan 53, +46 8 5173 6500, www.scandichotels.com, no53@scandichotels.com).

$$ Queen's Hotel enjoys a great location at the quiet top end of Stockholm's main pedestrian shopping street (about a 10-minute walk from the train station, or 25 minutes from Gamla Stan). The 59 rooms are well worn, but they're generally spacious and have big windows—and it's reasonably priced. Rooms facing the courtyard are quieter (RS%—if booking online enter rate code "RICKS," el-

STOCKHOLM

evator, Drottninggatan 71A, +46 8 249 460, www.queenshotel.se, info@queenshotel.se).

$$ Hotel Bema, a bit farther from the center, is a humble place that rents 12 fine rooms for some of the best prices in town (breakfast served at nearby café, reception open Mon-Fri 7:00-18:00, Sat-Sun 8:00-16:00, bus #65 from station to Upplandsgatan 13—near the top of the Drottninggatan pedestrian street, or walk about 15 minutes from the train station—exit toward *Vasagatan* and head straight up that street, +46 8 232 675, www.hotelbema. se, info@hotelbema.se).

¢ City Backpackers, with 140 beds a quarter-mile from the station, is youthful but classy (sheets extra, breakfast extra, pay laundry, tours, sauna; Upplandsgatan 2A, +46 8 206 920, www. citybackpackers.se, info@citybackpackers.se).

¢ City Lodge Hostel, on a quiet side street just a block from the central station, has 68 beds, a convivial lounge, and a kitchen with free cooking staples (sheets and towels extra, breakfast extra, no curfew, Klara Norra Kyrkogata 15, +46 8 226 630, www. citylodge.se, info@citylodge.se).

¢-$$ Generator Stockholm, a big and lively hostel, has 244 Scan-basic rooms spread across floors. The mix of dorms and private rooms all have private bathrooms. Close to the central station, it has a bar/café and restaurant on-site but no kitchen facilities (breakfast extra, family-friendly, elevator, bike rental, pay laundry; at Torsgatan 10, +46 8 5053 2370, www.generatorhostels.com, ask. stockholm@staygenerator.com).

ÖSTERMALM

These options in Norrmalm and Östermalm are in stately, elegant neighborhoods of five- and six-story turn-of-the-century apartment buildings. All are within easy reach of downtown sights and close to T-bana, tram, or bus stops. Östermalm is an appealing part of town but without many hotels—it's also worth checking Airbnb for apartment rentals here.

$$$$ Hotel Wellington, two blocks off Östermalmstorg, is in a charming part of town and convenient to the harbor and Djurgården. It's modern and bright, with hardwood floors, 60 rooms, and a friendly welcome. While pricey, it's a cut above in comfort, and its great amenities—such as a very generous buffet breakfast, free coffee all day, and free buffet dinner—add up to a good value (RS%, free sauna, lobby bar, garden terrace, T-bana: Östermalmstorg, exit to Storgatan and walk past big church to Storgatan 6; +46 8 667 0910, www.wellington.se, cc.wellington@ choice.se).

$$$$ Story Hotel Stureplan is a colorful boutique hotel with a creative vibe. Conveniently located near a trendy dining zone

Shopping

41 DesignTorget

42 Systembolaget (2)

43 Gudrun Sjödén (3)

44 Illums Bolighus

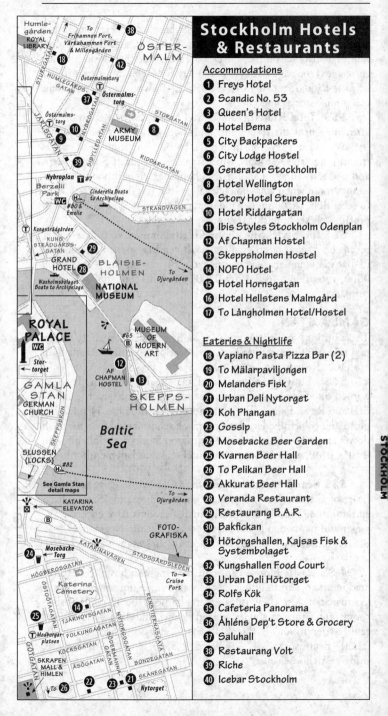

Stockholm Hotels & Restaurants

Accommodations

1. Freys Hotel
2. Scandic No. 53
3. Queen's Hotel
4. Hotel Bema
5. City Backpackers
6. City Lodge Hostel
7. Generator Stockholm
8. Hotel Wellington
9. Story Hotel Stureplan
10. Hotel Riddargatan
11. Ibis Styles Stockholm Odenplan
12. Af Chapman Hostel
13. Skeppsholmen Hostel
14. NOFO Hotel
15. Hotel Hornsgatan
16. Hotel Hellstens Malmgård
17. To Långholmen Hotel/Hostel

Eateries & Nightlife

18. Vapiano Pasta Pizza Bar (2)
19. To Mälarpaviljongen
20. Melanders Fisk
21. Urban Deli Nytorget
22. Koh Phangan
23. Gossip
24. Mosebacke Beer Garden
25. Kvarnen Beer Hall
26. To Pelikan Beer Hall
27. Akkurat Beer Hall
28. Veranda Restaurant
29. Restaurang B.A.R.
30. Bakfickan
31. Hötorgshallen, Kajsas Fisk & Systembolaget
32. Kungshallen Food Court
33. Urban Deli Hötorget
34. Rolfs Kök
35. Cafeteria Panorama
36. Åhléns Dep't Store & Grocery
37. Saluhall
38. Restaurang Volt
39. Riche
40. Icebar Stockholm

STOCKHOLM

between Östermalmstorg and the Nybroplan waterfront, it has 83 rooms above a sprawling, cleverly decorated, affordable restaurant. You'll book online, check yourself in at the kiosk, and receive a text message with your door key code (elevator, free minibar drinks, Riddargatan 6, +46 8 5450 3940, www.storyhotels.com, reception@storyhotels.com).

$$$ Hotel Riddargatan is well located on the edge of Östermalm—near the restaurants and shops on Nybrogatan and just two blocks from Nybroplan and the harbor. The front-desk staff is friendly, and the 78 rooms, while smallish, are nicely Scan-modern and perfectly functional. This is a hopping neighborhood: Ask for a quiet room when you book (elevator—but you'll climb a few steps to reception, bar/lounge, Riddargatan 14, +46 8 5557 3000, www.profilhotels.se, hotelriddargatan@profilhotels.se).

$$$ Ibis Styles Stockholm Odenplan rents 76 cookie-cutter rooms on several floors of a late-19th-century apartment building (T-bana: Odenplan, Västmannagatan 61, reservation +46 8 1209 0000, reception +46 8 1209 0300, www.ibis.com, h8774@accor.com).

GAMLA STAN

These options are in the midst of sightseeing, and a short bus or taxi ride from the train station. For locations, see the "Gamla Stan Hotels & Restaurants" map.

$$$$ Lady Hamilton Hotel, classic and romantic, is shoehorned into Gamla Stan on a quiet street a block below the cathedral and Royal Palace. The centuries-old building has 34 small but plush and colorfully decorated rooms. Each is named for a Swedish flower and is filled with antiques (elevator, Storkyrkobrinken 5, +46 8 5064 0100, www.ladyhamiltonhotel.se, info@ladyhamiltonhotel.se).

$$$ Scandic Gamla Stan offers Old World elegance in the heart of Gamla Stan (a 5-minute walk from Gamla Stan T-bana station). Its 52 nicely decorated, smallish rooms have cheery wallpaper and hardwood floors (elevator, sauna, Lilla Nygatan 25, +46 8 5173 8300, www.scandichotels.com, gamlastan@scandichotels.com).

¢-$$ Castle House Inn is an Ikea-modern hostel/hotel situated in an ancient building that's located in an untrampled part of Gamla Stan, just a few steps off the harbor. The 53 whitewashed rooms are a mix of singles, mixed dorms, standard doubles, and family-friendly quads (breakfast extra, elevator, check-in 15:00-22:00, Brunnsgränd 4, +46 8 5511 5526, www.castlehouse.se, info@castlehouse.se).

SKEPPSHOLMEN

This relaxing island—while surrounded by Stockholm—feels a world apart, both in terms of its peacefulness and its somewhat less-convenient transportation connections (you'll rely on bus #65, the harbor shuttle ferry, or your feet—it's about a 20-minute walk from the train station). For locations, see the "Stockholm Hotels & Restaurants" map.

¢-$ **Af Chapman Hostel,** a permanently moored 100-year-old schooner, is Europe's most famous youth hostel and has provided a berth for the backpacking crowd for years. Renovated from keel to stern, the old salt offers 120 bunks in four- to six-bed rooms. Reception is at the Skeppsholmen Hostel (next, same contact info).

¢-$ **Skeppsholmen Hostel** is just ashore from the *Af Chapman* (private rooms, breakfast extra, 24-hour reception, +46 8 463 2280, chapman@stfturist.se).

ON OR NEAR SÖDERMALM

Södermalm is residential and hip, with Stockholm's best café and bar scene. You'll need to take the bus or T-bana to get here from the train station, making it less than convenient for those with limited time.

$$$ **NOFO Hotel** is a boutique hotel located in a 17th-century building that faces a big courtyard in the heart of Södermalm. The 109 luxe hotel rooms are decorated with individual flair; T-bana: Medborgarplatsen or bus #53 from train station to Tjärhovsplan, then a 5-minute walk to Tjärhovsgatan 11; +46 8 5031 1200, www.nofohotel.se, info@nofo.se).

$$$ **Hotel Hornsgatan** is a tidy, welcoming, nicely decorated B&B upstairs in an old townhouse facing a busy but elegant-feeling boulevard. Four of the 17 small rooms have private baths; the others share five modern bathrooms. Thoughtfully run by Clara and Scott, this is a good value for the location (elevator, reception staffed until 22:00—make arrangements if arriving late, Hornsgatan 66B, T-bana: Mariatorget plus a short walk, 15-minute walk from Slussen/Gamla Stan, +46 8 658 2901, www.hotelhornsgatan.se, info@hotelhornsgatan.se).

$$$ **Hotel Hellstens Malmgård** is an eclectic collage of 50 rooms crammed with antiques in a circa-1770 mansion. No two rooms are alike, but all have modern baths and quirky touches such

as porcelain stoves or four-poster beds. Unwind in its secluded cobblestone courtyard, and you may forget what century you're in (elevator, T-bana: Zinkensdamm, then a 5-minute walk to Brännkyrkagatan 110; +46 8 4650 5800, www.hellstensmalmgard.se, hotel@hellstensmalmgard.se).

¢-$$$$ **Långholmen Hotel/Hostel** is on Långholmen, a small island off Södermalm that was transformed in the 1980s from Stockholm's main prison into a lovely park. Rooms are converted cells in the old prison building. You can choose between ¢ hostel-style and $$$$ hotel-standard rooms at many price levels (sheets and breakfast extra in hostel; hotel rooms include breakfast; family rooms, laundry room, kitchen, cafeteria, free parking, swimming beach and jogging paths nearby; T-bana: Hornstull, walk 10 minutes down and cross small bridge to Långholmen island, then follow hotel signs 5 minutes farther to Långholmsmuren 20; +46 8 720 8500, www.langholmen.com, info@langholmen.com).

Eating in Stockholm

To save money, eat your main meal at lunch, when cafés and restaurants have daily specials called *dagens rätt* (generally Mon-Fri only). Most museums have handy cafés with lunch deals and often with fine views. Convenience stores stock surprisingly fresh takeaway food. As anywhere, department stores and malls are eager to feed shoppers and can be a good, efficient choice. If you want culturally appropriate fast food, stop by a local hot dog stand. Picnics are

a great option—especially for dinner, when restaurant prices are highest. There are plenty of parklike, harborside spots to give your cheap picnic some class. I've also listed a few splurges—destination restaurants that offer a good sample of modern Swedish cooking.

GAMLA STAN

Most restaurants in Gamla Stan serve a weekday lunch special. Several popular places are right on the main square (Stortorget) and near the cathedral. Järntorget, at the far end, is another fun tables-in-the-square scene. Touristy places line Västerlånggatan. You'll find more romantic spots hiding on side lanes, such as the stretch of Österlånggatan that hides below Köpmantorget square (where St. George is slaying the dragon). I've listed my favorites here (for locations, see "Gamla Stan Hotels & Restaurants" map).

Gamla Stan Hotels & Restaurants

Accommodations

1. Lady Hamilton Hotel
2. Scandic Gamla Stan
3. Castle House Inn

Eateries & Nightlife

4. Grillska Huset
5. Kryp In
6. Vapiano Pasta Pizza Bar
7. Hermitage Restaurant
8. Mister French
9. Co-op Nära Grocery
10. Stampen
11. Wirströms Pub
12. O'Connells Irish Pub
13. The Liffey Irish Pub

$$ Grillska Huset is a cheap and handy cafeteria run by Stockholms Stadsmission, a charitable organization helping the poor. It's grandly situated right on the old square, with indoor and outdoor seating (tranquil garden up the stairs and out back), fine daily specials, a hearty salad bar, and a staff committed to helping others. You can feed the hungry (that's you) and help house the homeless at the same time (Tue-Sat 10:00-20:00, Sun-Mon until

19:00, Stortorget 3, +46 8 6842 3364). They also have a fine little bakery *(brödbutik)* with lots of tempting cakes and pastries (Mon-Fri 7:30-18:00, closed Sat-Sun).

$$$$ Kryp In, a small, cozy restaurant (the name means "hide away") tucked into a peaceful lane, has a stylish hardwood and candlelit interior, great sidewalk seating, and an open kitchen letting you in on Vladimir's artistry. If you dine well in Stockholm once (or twice), I'd do it here. It's gourmet without pretense. They serve delicious, modern Swedish cuisine with a 455-SEK three-course dinner. In the good-weather months, they serve weekend lunches, with specials starting at 120 SEK. Reserve ahead for dinner (275-290-SEK plates, daily 17:00-23:00, lunch Sat-Sun 12:00-16:00, a block off Stortorget at Prästgatan 17, +46 8 208 841, www.restaurangkrypin.se).

$$ Vapiano Pasta Pizza Bar, a bright, high-energy, family-oriented eatery, issues you a smart card as you enter. As you order at various stations, the card is swiped; pay the total tally as you leave. Portions are huge and easily splittable. Add flavor by picking a leaf of basil or rosemary from the potted plant on your table. Tables are often shared, making this a great place for solo travelers (daily 11:00-24:00, next to entrance to Gamla Stan T-bana station, Munkbrogatan 8, +46 8 222 940). They also have locations on Östermalm (facing Humlegården park at Sturegatan 12) and Norrmalm (near the train station at Vasagatan 16)—for these locations, see the "Stockholm Hotels & Restaurants" map.

$$ Hermitage Restaurant is a faded, hippie-feeling joint that serves a decent vegetarian buffet in a communal dining setting (daily 11:00-21:00, off-season Sat-Sun 12:00-20:00, Stora Nygatan 11, +46 8 411 9500).

Picnic Supplies in Gamla Stan: The handy and affordable **Co-op Nära** minimarket is strategically located on Järntorget, at the Slussen end of Gamla Stan; the **Munkbrohallen** supermarket downstairs in the Gamla Stan T-bana station is also very picnic-friendly (both long hours daily).

DINING ON THE WATER

In Gamla Stan: Sprawling along the harbor embankment, **$$$$ Mister French** faces a gorgeous Stockholm panorama—the main reason to eat here. The entire place opens up to the outdoors in good weather: Choose between the stylish bar (simple bar food), the full restaurant (French cuisine), or—my favorite—the lounge

Swedish Cuisine

If you don't think you'll like Swedish food, be sure to splurge at a good-quality place before you pass final judgment. Though potatoes and heavy sauces are prevalent, Sweden's meat and fish dishes can be quite tasty.

Every region of Sweden serves different specialties, but you'll always find *svenska köttbullar* on the menu (Swedish meatballs made from beef and pork in a creamy sauce). This

Swedish favorite is topped with lingonberry jam, which is served with many meat dishes across Scandinavia. Potatoes make for hearty *kroppkakor* dumplings filled with onions and minced meat. The northern variation, *pitepalt*, is filled with pork. Southern Sweden takes credit for *pytt i panna*, a medley of meat and diced potatoes that's fried and served with an egg yolk on top. And it seems every meal here includes a side of boiled, small new potatoes.

Like those of its Nordic neighbors, Sweden's extensive coastline produces some of the best seafood in the world. A light, tasty appetizer is *gravlax*, a dill-cured salmon on brown bread or crackers. You'll also likely encounter *Toast Skagen*, a spread made from shrimp, dill, mayonnaise, and Dijon mustard, eaten on buttered toast.

For a main course, the most popular seafood dish is crayfish. Though eaten only by the aristocracy in the 16th century, these shellfish have since become a nationwide delicacy; they're cooked in brine with dill and eaten cold as a finger food. Traditional crayfish parties take place outdoors on summer evenings, particularly in August. Friends and family gather around to indulge in this specialty with rye bread and a strong cheese. The Swedes also love Baltic herring; try *stekt strömming*, a specialty of the east coast, which is herring fried with butter and parsley. As usual, it's served with potatoes and lingonberry jam. Adventurous diners can have their herring pickled or fermented—or order more unusual dishes like reindeer.

Be sure to try Sweden's most popular baked good, *kanelbulle*, for a not-so-light snack. This pastry resembles a cinnamon roll, but it's made with cardamom and topped with pearl sugar. Enjoy one during *fika*, the daily Swedish coffee break so institutionalized that many locals use the term as a verb (see the *"Fika"* sidebar, earlier).

As for beer, the Swedes classify theirs by alcohol content. The higher the number, the higher the alcohol content—and the price. *Klass 1* is light beer—very low-alcohol. *Klass 2* is stronger, but still mild. And *Klass 3* has the most body, the most alcohol, and the highest price.

with comfy sofas (Tue-Sat 11:30-24:00, Sun-Mon until 17:00, smart to reserve ahead in good weather, Tullhus 2—for location, see "Gamla Stan Hotels & Restaurants" map, +46 8 202 095, www.mrfrench.se).

In Kungsholmen, Behind City Hall: On a balmy summer's eve, **$$$ Mälarpaviljongen** is a dreamy spot with hundreds of locals enjoying the perfect lakefront scene, as twinkling glasses of rosé shine like convivial lanterns. From City Hall, walk 15 minutes along Lake Mälaren (a treat in itself) to find a hundred casual outdoor tables floating on pontoons and scattered among the trees on shore. When it's cool, they have heaters and blankets (open in good weather April-Sept daily 11:00-late, easy lakeside walk or T-bana to Fridhemsplan plus a 5-minute walk to Nörr Mälarstrand 64, no reservations, +46 8 650 8701).

In Djurgården: For the location of these restaurants, see the "Djurgården" map, earlier. Just over the Djurgårdsbron bridge, **$$-$$$ Sjöcaféet** is beautifully situated and greedily soaking up the afternoon sun, filling a woody terrace stretching along the harbor. In summer, this is a fine place for a meal or just a drink before or after your Skansen or *Vasa* visit. They have affordable lunch plates (Mon-Fri 10:30-13:00 only); after 14:00, you'll pay a bit more (order at the bar, daily 8:00-20:00, often later in summer, closed off-season, bike and boat rentals, +46 8 661 4488).

$$$$ Oaxen Slip Bistro, a trendy harborfront place 200 yards below the main Skansen gate, serves creative Nordic cuisine with sturdy local ingredients in a sleek interior or on its delightfully woody terrace. Overlooking a canal in what feels like an old shipyard and filled with in-the-know locals, this place is a real treat. Reservations are smart (daily 11:30-16:00 & 17:00-23:00, Beckholmsvägen 26, +46 8 5515 3105, www.oaxen.com).

Dinner Cruises on Lake Mälaren: The big sightseeing company Strömma sells a variety of lunch and dinner cruises that allow you to enjoy the delightful waterways of Stockholm and the archipelago while you eat. Options include shorter dinner cruises to Drottningholm Palace (2.5 hours round-trip), longer ones to the outer archipelago (up to 5 hours), and *smörgåsbord* cruises around Lake Mälaren. For details and booking (and other options, including a shrimp cruise and a jazz cruise), check www.stromma.se.

SÖDERMALM STREETS AND EATS

This quickly gentrifying district, just south of Gamla Stan (steeply uphill from Slussen), has some of Stockholm's most enticing food options—especially for beer lovers. It's a bit less swanky and more affordable than some of the city's more touristy neighborhoods. Even if you don't dine in Södermalm, it's worth a stroll here just for the window-shopping fun. The most interesting areas to explore are along Götgatan and the zone south of Folkungagatan street—nicknamed "SoFo."

Götgatan and Medborgarplatsen

The neighborhood's liveliest street is Götgatan, which leads from Slussen steeply up into the heart of Södermalm. Here, mixed between the boutiques, you'll find tempting cafés and eateries.

At the top of the street, the big square called Medborgarplatsen is filled with outdoor restaurant and café tables and fronted by a big food hall (and easily reached by T-bana). This neighborhood hangout is a great scene, with almost no tourists and lots of options—especially for Swedish fast food. The recommended Kvarnen beer hall is just around the corner (described later).

$$ Melanders Fisk, inside the Söderhallarna food hall, offers table service inside or takeaway from their deli counter—but come in good weather and you can enjoy your meal outside on the square. *Skagenröra,* shrimp with mayo on toast or filling a baked potato, is the signature dish. There's also a wine bar that stays open until 22:00 (food served Mon-Sat 11:00-20:00, closed Sun, Medborgarplatsen 3, +46 8 644 4040).

Skånegatan and Nytorget

A bit farther south, these cross streets are home to fun and enticing restaurants—especially international cuisine.

$$$ Urban Deli Nytorget is half fancy artisanal delicatessen—with all manner of ingredients—and half white-subway-tile-trendy eatery, with indoor and outdoor tables filled with Stockholmers eating well. If it's busy—as it often is—they'll scrawl your name at the bottom of the long butcher-paper waiting list (no reservations). If it's full, you can grab a place at the bar and eat there—or shop in the attached upscale grocery (lots of creative boxed meals and salads to go) and picnic in the park across the street (daily 8:00-23:00, at the far end of Skånegatan at Nytorget 4, +46 8 4255 0030). Another branch is near Hörtorget (see listing later).

$$$ Koh Phangan, with an almost laughably over-the-top island atmosphere that belies its surprisingly good Thai food, has been a hit for many years. (Thailand is to Swedes what Mexico is to Americans—the sunny "south of the border" playground.) The ambience? Mix a shipwreck, Bob Marley, and a Christmas tree and you've got it (Mon-Fri 16:00-24:00, Sat-Sun from 12:00, Skånegatan 57, +46 8 642 5040).

$$ Gossip is a mellow, unpretentious hole-in-the-wall serving Bangladeshi street food (Mon-Fri 11:00-23:00, Sat-Sun from 13:00, Skånegatan 71, +46 8 640 6901).

STOCKHOLM

Beer and Pub Grub in Södermalm

Södermalm cultivates the most interesting beer scene in this beer-crazy city.

Beer Garden with a View: $$ Mosebacke, perched high above town, is a gravelly beer garden with a grand harbor view. The beer garden (open only on warm summer evenings) prides itself on its beer rather than its basic grub (read: bar snacks). It's a good place to mix with a relaxed young crowd. As each of the beer kiosks has its own specialties, survey all of them before making your choice (some open from 11:00, others later; a block inland from the top of the Katarina viewing platform, look for the triumphal arch at Mosebacke Torg 3, +46 8 5560 9890). The adjacent restaurant serves fine **$$$$** plates.

Classic Swedish Beer Halls: Two different but equally traditional Södermalm beer halls serve hearty Swedish grub in big, high-ceilinged, orange-tiled spaces with rustic wooden tables.

$$$ Kvarnen ("The Mill") is a reliable choice with a 1908 ambience. As it's the home bar for the supporters of a football club, it can be rough. Pick a classic Swedish dish from their fun and easy menu (Mon-Fri 11:00-late, Sat-Sun from 12:00, Tjärhovsgatan 4, +46 8 643 0380).

$$$$ Pelikan, an old-school beer hall, is less sloppy and has nicer food, including meatballs the size of golf balls. It's a bit deeper into Södermalm (Mon-Thu 17:00-23:00, Fri-Sun from 12:00, Blekingegatan 40, +46 8 5560 9090, www.pelikan.se).

Trendier "Craft Beer" Pub: $$$ Akkurat has a staggering variety of microbrews—both Swedish and international (on tap and bottled)—as well as whisky. It's great if you wish you were in England with a bunch of Swedes (short pub-grub menu, Mon-Fri 16:00-24:00, Sat-Sun from 13:00, Hornsgatan 18, +46 8 644 0015).

NORRMALM
At or near the Grand Hotel

$$$$ Royal Smörgåsbord: To stuff yourself with all the traditional Swedish specialties (a dozen kinds of herring, salmon, reindeer, meatballs, lingonberries, and shrimp, followed by a fine table of cheeses and desserts) with a super harbor view, consider splurging at the Grand Hotel's dressy **Veranda Restaurant.** While very touristy, this is considered the finest smorgasbord in town. The Grand Hotel, where royal guests and Nobel Prize winners stay, faces the harbor across from the palace. Pick up their English flier for a good explanation of the proper way to enjoy this grand buffet. Reservations are often necessary (595 SEK in evening, less at lunch, drinks extra, open nightly 17:00-22:00, also open for lunch Sat-Sun 12:00-16:00 year-round and Mon-Fri 11:30-17:00 in

May-Sept, no shorts after 18:00, Södra Blasieholmshamnen 8, +46 8 679 3586, www.grandhotel.se).

$$$$ Restaurang B.A.R. has a noisy, fun energy, with diners surveying meat and fish at the ice-filled counter, talking things over with the chef, and then choosing a slab or filet. Prices are on the board, and everything's grilled (Mon-Fri 11:30-14:00 & 17:00-late, Sat 16:00-late, closed Sun, behind the Grand Hotel at Blasieholmsgatan 4A, +46 8 611 5335, www.restaurangbar.se). They also have a nice (short and lower-priced) takeaway menu.

At the Royal Opera House

The Operakällaren, one of Stockholm's most exclusive restaurants, runs a little "hip pocket" restaurant called **$$$ Bakfickan,** specializing in traditional Swedish quality cooking at reasonable prices. It's ideal for someone eating out alone, or for anyone wanting an early dinner. Choose from two daily specials or order from their regular menu. Sit inside—at tiny private side tables or at the big counter with the locals—or, in good weather, grab a table on the sidewalk, facing a cheery red church (Mon-Thu 11:30-22:00, Fri-Sat until 23:00, Sun 12:00-17:00, on the inland side of Royal Opera House, +46 8 676 5808).

At or near Hötorget

Hötorget ("Hay Market"), a vibrant outdoor produce market two blocks from Sergels Torg, is a fun place to picnic-shop. The outdoor market closes at 18:00, and many merchants put their unsold produce on the push list (earlier closing and more desperate merchants on Sat).

Hötorgshallen, next to Hötorget (in the basement under the modern cinema complex), is a colorful indoor food market with an old-fashioned bustle, plenty of exotic and ethnic edibles, and—in the tradition of food markets all over Europe—some great little eateries (Mon-Fri 10:00-18:00, Sat until 16:00, closed Sun). The best is **$$ Kajsas Fisk,** hiding behind the fish stalls. They serve delicious fish soup to little Olivers who can hardly believe they're getting...more. For 125 SEK, you get a big bowl of hearty soup, a simple salad, bread and crackers—plus one soup refill. Their *stekt strömming* (traditional fried herring and potato dish) is a favorite (Mon-Thu 11:00-18:00, Fri until 19:00, Sat until 16:00, closed Sun, Hötorgshallen 3, +46 8 207 262). There's a great kebab and falafel place a few stalls away.

Kungshallen, an 800-seat indoor food court across the square from Hötorget, has more than a dozen basic eateries. What it lacks in ambience it makes up for in variety, quick service, and generally lower prices. The main floor has sit-down places, while the basement is a shopping-mall-style array of fast-food counters, including

Chinese, sushi, pizza, Greek, and Mexican (Mon-Sat 10:00-21:00, Sun until 20:00).

Just a few blocks away is a branch of **Urban Deli** (at Sveavägen 44), a good takeaway option described earlier.

On or near Drottninggatan

The pleasant, pedestrianized shopping street called Drottninggatan, which runs from the train station area up into Stockholm's suburbs, is a fine place to find a forgettable meal but with memorable people-watching. Several interchangeable eateries with sidewalk tables line the street (and don't miss the delightful, leafy park courtyard of Centralbadet, at #88, with several outdoor cafés). None merits a special detour, except the next listing.

$$$$ Rolfs Kök, a vibrant neighborhood favorite, is worth the pleasant five-minute stroll up from the end of Drottninggatan. The long bar up front fades into an open kitchen hemmed in with happy diners at counters, and tight tables fill the rest of the space before spilling out onto the sidewalk. Trendy, casual, and inviting, this bistro features international fare with a focus on Swedish classics and a good wine list. Reservations are smart (Mon-Fri 11:30-24:00, Sat-Sun from 17:00, Tegnérgatan 41, +46 8 101 696, www. rolfskok.se).

Near Sergels Torg

Kulturhuset: Handy for a simple meal with great city views, **$$ Cafeteria Panorama** offers cheap eats and inside and outside roof-terrace seating with jaw-dropping vistas (110-SEK lunch specials, Mon-Fri 11:00-20:00, Sat-Sun until 18:00, +46 8 211 035).

The many modern shopping malls and department stores around Sergels Torg all have appealing, if pricey, eateries catering to the needs of hungry local shoppers. Åhléns department store has a **Hemköp supermarket** in the basement (daily until 21:00) and two restaurants upstairs with 80-110-SEK daily lunch specials (Mon-Fri 11:00-19:30, Sat until 18:30, Sun until 17:30).

ÖSTERMALM

$$$ Saluhall, on Östermalmstorg (near recommended Hotel Wellington), is a great indoor market dating from 1888 but completely refurbished in 2019. You'll find top-quality artisanal producers and a variety of sit-down and takeout eateries. While it's nowhere near "cheap," it's one of the most pleasant market halls I've seen, oozing with upscale yet traditional Swedish class. Inside you'll find pastries and coffee, delis, juice and smoothie bars, salads and wraps, classic Scandinavian open-face sandwiches, seafood, meats and cheeses, and quality chocolates and ice cream. This is your chance to pull up a stool at a lunch counter next to well-heeled Swedes (Mon-Fri 9:30-19:00, Sat until 17:00, closed Sun).

$$$$ Restaurang Volt is a destination restaurant for those looking to splurge on New Nordic cooking: fresh, locally sourced ingredients fused into bold new recipes with fundamentally Swedish flavors. Owners Fredrik Johnsson and Peter Andersson fill their minimalist black dining room with just 31 seats, so reservations are essential (no à la carte, choose from four- or six-course tasting menus, Tue-Sat 18:00-24:00, closed Sun-Mon, Kommendörsgatan 16, +46 8 662 3400, www.restaurangvolt.se).

$$$$ Riche, a Parisian-style brasserie just a few steps off Nybroplan at Östermalm's waterfront, is a high-energy place with a youthful sophistication. They serve up pricey but nicely executed Swedish and international dishes in their winter garden, bright dining room, and white-tile and wine-glass-chandeliered bar (Mon-Sat 11:30-24:00, closed Sun, Birger Jarlsgatan 4, +46 8 5450 3560, www.riche.se).

Stockholm Connections

BY BUS

Flixbus is the largest operator of long-distance buses, which can be cheaper than trains (+46 8 5051 3750, www.flixbus.se); Vy Nettbuss also has lots of routes (www.nettbuss.com). Some bus companies offer discounts with advance purchase.

From Stockholm by Bus to: Copenhagen (about 3/day, 9 hours, longer for overnight trips), **Oslo** (4/day, 7.5 hours), **Kalmar** (4/day, fewer on weekends, 6 hours).

BY TRAIN

For Swedish train timetables and prices, consult www.sj.se, call +46 771 757 575, or use self-service ticket kiosks in stations. Remember that trains on Sweden's high-speed routes require reservations.

For general information on train travel in Sweden and Scandinavia, see the "Transportation" section of the Practicalities chapter.

From Stockholm by Train to: Uppsala (4/hour, 40 minutes; also possible on slower suburban *pendeltåg*—2/hour, 55 minutes, covered by local transit pass plus small supplement), **Växjö** (about hourly, 3.5-4.5 hours, change in Alvesta), **Kalmar** (about hourly, 4.5-5 hours, transfer in Alvesta; slower but scenic train with transfer in Linköping), **Copenhagen** (almost hourly, 5-6 hours on high-speed train, some with a transfer at Lund or Hässleholm; overnight

STOCKHOLM

train requires a change in Malmö or Lund; all trains stop at Copenhagen airport before terminating at the central train station).

By Train to Oslo: The speedy X2000 train zips from downtown Copenhagen to downtown Oslo in about 5.5 hours, runs several times daily, and requires reservations (first class often comes with a hot meal, fruit bowl, and unlimited coffee). Note that construction on this line may interrupt service. Until X2000 service resumes, you can take a slower train (6-7 hours) with a change in Göteborg.

BY BOAT
Sailing Between Stockholm and Helsinki or Tallinn

Overnight ferries connect Stockholm with Helsinki and with Tallinn (both trips take about 17 hours). In Stockholm, ports are scattered throughout the city, and terminal buildings are well organized, with cafés, lockers, and TI desks. Boats open 1.5 hours before departure, and you must be checked in 20 minutes before departure. Parking is available; ask for details when you reserve your ticket. For more on schedules, fares, and amenities for boats between Stockholm and Helsinki, see page 631; for more on the Stockholm-Tallinn ferries, see page 683.

Viking Line, with overnight boats to Helsinki, has its own terminal along the **Stadsgården** embankment on Södermalm. To get there, it's easiest to ride Viking Line's shuttle bus from the train/bus station right to the terminal (60 SEK, departs according to boat schedule, www.batbussarna.se). You can also ride public bus #53 (from the train station or Gamla Stan to the Londonviadukten stop, then walk five minutes to the terminal). A taxi from the train station is around 200 SEK.

Tallink Silja boats (which run to both Helsinki and Tallinn) leave from the **Värtahamnen** port, about three miles northeast of the city center. It's simplest to catch the Tallink Silja shuttle bus from the train/bus station (60 SEK, departs according to boat schedule, www.batbussarna.se). You can also take public transportation: Ride the T-bana to the Gärdet station, then walk 10 minutes to the harbor, or take bus #76 from downtown (leaves from several downtown locations, including Kungsträdgården; direction: Ropsten, get off at Värtahamnen Färjeterminal stop). Figure about 300 SEK for a taxi from Gamla Stan, the train station, or other downtown areas.

For Stockholm public transit information, see page 437 or visit www.sl.se.

Sailing to Other Destinations

Boats sail from Stockholm to **Turku** (daily/nightly boats, 11-12 hours). The St. Peter Line connects Stockholm to **St. Petersburg,** but the trip takes two nights—you'll sail the first night to Tallinn, then a second night to St. Petersburg; returning, you'll sail the first night to Helsinki, and the second night to Stockholm (www.stpeterline.com). Note: To visit Russia, American and Canadian citizens need a visa (arrange weeks in advance); for details, see "Connecting Helsinki and St. Petersburg" at the end of the Helsinki chapter. For connections to the islands of **Vaxholm, Grinda, Svartsö,** and **Sandhamn,** see the Stockholm's Archipelago chapter.

Visiting Stockholm by Cruise Ship

Stockholm has two cruise ports. The more central **Stadsgården** in Södermalm (described earlier) accommodates mainly ships that

are just passing through; **Frihamnen**, three miles northeast of the city center, is used primarily by ships beginning or ending a cruise in Stockholm. For many more details on Stockholm's ports, and other cruise destinations, pick up my *Rick Steves*

Scandinavian & Northern European Cruise Ports guidebook.

BY PLANE
Arlanda Airport

Stockholm's Arlanda Airport is 28 miles north of town (code: ARN, +46 10 109 1000, www.arlanda.se).

Getting Between the Airport and Downtown: The Arlanda Express **train** is the fastest way to zip between the airport and the central train station. Traveling most of the way at 125 mph, it gets you downtown in just 20 minutes—but it's not cheap (299 SEK one-way, 579 SEK round-trip, free for kids under 17 with adult, covered by rail pass, generally 4-6/hour, +46 771 720 200, www.arlandaexpress.com). Buy your ticket either at the window near the track or from a ticket machine, or pay an extra 100 SEK to buy it on board. It's worth checking the website for advance-purchase discounts and two-for-one weekend specials.

Airport shuttle buses (Flygbussarna) run between the airport and Stockholm's train/bus stations (99 SEK, 6/hour, 50 minutes, may take longer at rush hour; buy tickets online—cheapest, from station kiosks, or from 7-Eleven and Pressbyrån convenience stores at the airport and train/bus station, www.flygbussarna.se).

Taxis between the airport and the city center take 30-40 minutes (400-500 SEK, but look for price posted on side of cab). Establish the price first. Most taxis prefer credit cards.

The **cheapest airport connection** is to take bus #583 from the airport to Märsta, then switch to the *pendeltåg* #41 (suburban train, 2-3/hour), which goes to Stockholm's central train station (38 SEK, good for 1.25 hours including transfer, 1.5-hour total journey time).

Skavsta Airport

Some discount airlines use Skavsta Airport, about 60 miles south of Stockholm (code: NYO, www.skavsta.se). Flygbussarna shuttle buses connect to the city (159 SEK, cheaper online, 1-2/hour, 1.5 hours—but allow extra time for traffic, www.flygbussarna.se).

NEAR STOCKHOLM

Drottningholm Palace • Sigtuna • Uppsala

At Stockholm's doorstep are a variety of fine side-trip options—all within an hour of the capital. Drottningholm Palace, on the city's outskirts, was the summer residence—and most opulent castle—of the Swedish royal family, and has a uniquely well-preserved Baroque theater to boot. The adorable town of Sigtuna is a cutesy escape from the big city, studded with history and rune stones. Uppsala is Sweden's answer to Oxford, offering stately university facilities and museums, the home and garden of scientist Carl Linnaeus, as well as a grand cathedral and the enigmatic burial mounds of Gamla Uppsala on the outskirts of town. Note that another side-trip option is to visit a few of the islands in Stockholm's archipelago (described in the next chapter).

Drottningholm Palace

The queen's 17th-century summer castle and current royal residence has been called "Sweden's Versailles." While that's a bit of a stretch, taken as a whole the Drottningholm Palace complex is worth ▲▲. It's enjoyable to explore the place where the Swedish royals bunk and to stroll their expansive gardens. Even more worthwhile is touring the Baroque-era theater on the grounds (itself rated ▲▲), which preserves 18th-century stage sets and rare special-effects machinery. If you've seen plenty of palaces, skip the interior but enjoy the grounds and theater tour. You can likely squeeze everything in with half a day here, or linger for an entire day.

GETTING THERE

Drottingholm is an easy boat or subway-plus-bus ride from downtown Stockholm. Consider approaching by water (as the royals traditionally did) and then returning by bus and subway (as a commoner). If your heart is set on touring the palace interior, check the website before you go: It can close unexpectedly for various events.

Boats depart regularly from the Klara Malarstrand pier just across from City Hall for the relaxing hour-long trip (190 SEK one-way, 240 SEK round-trip, on the hour daily, likely additional departures in July-Aug, fewer departures Sept-April, +46 8 1200 4000, www.stromma.se). The pier is a five-minute walk from the central train station (on Vasagatan, walk toward the water, staying to the right and crossing a plaza under the freeway to reach the pier). It's worth reserving a spot in advance on weekends, or if your day plan requires a particular departure.

It's faster (30-45 minutes total) to take **public transit:** Ride the T-bana about 20 minutes to Brommaplan, where you can catch any #300-series bus for the five-minute ride to Drottningholm (as you leave the Brommaplan station, check monitors to see which bus is leaving next—usually from platform A, E, or F).

BACKGROUND

"Drottningholm" means "Queen's Island." When the original castle mysteriously burned down in 1661 immediately after a visit from Queen Hedvig Eleonora, she (quite conveniently) had already commissioned plans for a bigger, better palace.

Built over 40 years—with various rooms redecorated by centuries of later monarchs—Drottningholm has the air of overcompensating for an inferiority complex. While rarely absolute rulers, Sweden's royals long struggled with stubborn parliaments. Perhaps this made the propaganda value of the palace decor even more important. Touring the palace, you'll see art that makes the point that Sweden's royalty is divine and belongs with the gods. Portraits and prominently displayed gifts from fellow monarchs attempt to legitimize the royal family by connecting the Swedish blue bloods with Roman emperors, medieval kings, and Europe's great royal families. The portraits you'll see of France's Louis XVI and Russia's Catherine the Great are reminders that Sweden's royalty was related to or tightly networked with the European dynasties.

Of course, today's monarchs are figureheads ruled by a constitution. The royal family makes a point to be as accessible and as "normal" as royalty can be. King Carl XVI Gustaf (b. 1946)—whose main job is handing out Nobel Prizes once a year—is a car nut who talks openly about his dyslexia. He was the first Swedish king not to be crowned "by the grace of God." At his 1976 wedding to the popular Queen Silvia, ABBA serenaded his bride with "Dancing Queen." Their daughter Crown Princess Victoria is heir to the throne (she studied political science at Yale, interned with Sweden's European Union delegation, and married her personal trainer, Daniel Westling, in 2010). The king and queen still live in one wing of Drottningholm.

SIGHTS AT DROTTNINGHOLM

Drottningholm Palace (Drottningholms Slott)

While not the finest palace interior in Europe (or even in Scandinavia), Drottningholm offers a chance to stroll through a place where a monarch still lives. You'll see two floors of lavish rooms, where Sweden's royalty did their best to live in the style of Europe's divine monarchs.

Cost and Hours: Palace-140 SEK, Chinese Pavilion-100 SEK; Gardens-free; May-Sept daily 10:00-16:00, April until 15:30, rest of year open weekends only, 11:30-16:00, closed last two weeks of Dec.

Information: +46 8 402 6100, www.kungahuset.se.

Tours: You can explore the palace on your own, but with sparse posted explanations and no audioguide, it's worth the 30 SEK extra for the 30-minute English guided tour, offered several times daily (check website for current times). Alternatively, you could buy the inexpensive palace guidebook.

Services: The gift shop/café at the entrance to the grounds (near the boat dock and bus stop) acts as a visitors center; Drottningholm's only WCs are in the adjacent building. A handy Pressbyrån convenience store is also nearby (snacks, drinks, and transit tickets), and taxis are usually standing by.

Visiting Drottningholm Palace: Ascend the grand staircase (decorated with faux marble and relief-illusion paintings) and buy your ticket on the first floor. Entering the staterooms on the **first floor,** admire the craftsmanship of the walls, with gold leaf shimmering on expertly tooled leather. Then pass through the Green Cabinet and hook right into Hedvig Eleonora's State Bed Chambers. The richly colored Baroque decor here, with gold embellishments, is representative of what the entire interior once looked like. Hedvig Eleonora was a "dowager queen," mean-

ing that she was the widow of a king—her husband, King Karl X, died at age 24—after they had been married just six years. Looking around the room, you'll see symbolism of this tragic separation. For example, in the ceiling painting, Hedvig Eleonora rides a cloud, with hands joined below her—suggesting that she will be reunited with her beloved in heaven.

This room was also the residence of a later monarch, Gustav III. That's why it looks like (and was) more of a theater than a place for sleeping. In the style of the French monarchs, this is where the ceremonial tucking-in and dressing of the king would take place.

Backtrack into the golden room, then continue down the other hallway. You'll pass through a room of royal portraits with very consistent characteristics: pale skin with red cheeks; a high fore-head with gray hair (suggesting wisdom); and big eyes (windows to the soul). At the end of the hall is a grand library, which once held some 7,000 books. The small adjoining room is filled by a large model of a temple in Pompeii; Gustav III—who ordered this built—was fascinated by archaeology, and still today, there's a mu-seum of antiquities named for him at the Royal Palace in Stock-holm.

On the **second floor,** as you enter the first room, notice the faux doors, painted on the walls to create symmetry, and the hid-den doors for servants (who would scurry—unseen and unheard—through the walls to attend to the royal family). In the Blue Drawing Room is a bust of the then-king's cousin, Russian monarch Cathe-rine the Great. You'll see a gift from her in the next room, the Chi-nese Drawing Room—the (made-in-Russia) faux "Chinese" stove. This dates from a time when exotic imports from China (tea, silk, ivory, Kung Pao chicken) were exciting and new. (Around the same time, in the mid-18th century, the royals built the Chinese Pavilion on Drottningholm's grounds.) The Gobelins tapestries in this room were also a gift, from France's King Louis XVI. In the next room, the darker Oskar Room, are more tapestries—these a gift from England's King Charles I. (Sensing a trend?) You'll pass through Karl XI's Gallery (overlooking the grand staircase)—which is still used for royal functions—and into the largest room on this floor, the Hall of State. The site of royal weddings and receptions, this room boasts life-size paintings of very important Swedes in golden frames and a bombastically painted ceiling.

Drottningholm Palace Park

Like so many European "summer palaces," the Drottningholm grounds are graced with sprawling gardens—a pretty (and free) place to stroll on a fine day. Directly behind the palace is the strictly geo-metrical Baroque Garden, with angular hedges, tidy rows of trees, fountains, and outdoor "rooms" at the far end. It adjoins the more naturalistic English Garden, which Gustav III was determined to have after seeing one of the landscape gardens belonging to his cousin Catherine the Great. (It was Gustav, too, who speckled the grounds with marble statues.) At the far end of the grounds is the Chinese Pavilion, containing a fine Rococo interior with chinoiserie (separate admission).

Drottningholm Court Theater (Drottningholms Slottsteater)

This 18th-century theater has miraculously survived the ages—complete with its instruments, Baroque stage sets, and hand-operated sound-effects machines for wind, thunder, and clouds. The required guided tour is short (30 minutes), entertaining, and informative—I found it more enjoyable than the palace tour.

Cost and Hours: 110 SEK for 30-minute guided tour—buy tickets online or in the theater shop next door, English tours daily at 12:15, May-Sept, limited tours possible on weekends in April and Oct-Dec, no tours Jan-March.

Information: +46 8 556 931 00, www.dtm.se.

Performances: Check their schedule for the rare opportunity to see perfectly authentic operas (about 25 performances each summer). Tickets for this popular time-travel musical and theatrical experience cost 300-1,000 SEK and go on sale each March; purchase online (www.ticketmaster.se), at the theater shop, or by phone (from the US, call +46 77 170 7070; see theater website for details).

Background: A Swedish king built the theater in the 1760s to pacify his Prussian wife, who was appalled by the provincialism of Sweden's performing arts. This is one of two such historic theaters remaining in Europe (the other is in the Czech town of Český Krumlov). Their son, King Gustav III, loved the theater (some say more than he loved ruling Sweden): Besides ordering Stockholm's Royal Opera to be built, he also wrote, directed, and acted in several theatrical presentations (including the first-ever production in Swedish instead of French, the usual court language). He even died in a theater, assassinated at a masquerade ball in the very opera house he had built. When he died, so too did this flourishing of culture: The theater became a warehouse for storing royal bric-a-brac. The stage stayed dark until the mid-1940s, when opera and plays were once again performed here.

Visiting the Theater: On the tour, you'll see the bedrooms where famous actors and conductors would sleep while performing here, then enter the theater itself, lit only with (now simulated) candles. You'll see the extremely deep stage (with scenery peeking in from the edges), the royal boxes where the king and queen entered, and doors and curtains that were painted onto walls to achieve perfect symmetry.

It's fascinating to think that pulleys, trap doors, and contraptions that float actors in from the sky aren't so different from devices employed on stages today. Because the mechanisms are fragile, they aren't demonstrated on the tour, but you can watch a video demonstration in the theater shop next door.

Sigtuna

Sigtuna, the oldest town in Sweden (established in the 970s), is the country's cutest town as well. Worth ▲, it sits sugary sweet on Lake Mälaren, about 30 miles inland from Stockholm (reachable by train/bus or sightseeing boat). A visit here affords a relaxed look at an open-air folk museum of a town, with ruined churches, ancient rune stones, and a lane of 18th-century buildings—all with English info posts. It also offers plenty of shopping and eating options in a parklike lakeside setting. If you're looking for stereotypical Sweden and a break from the big city, Sigtuna is a fun side trip.

Getting There: By **public transport** from Stockholm, it's a one-hour trip. Take the *pendeltåg* suburban train from Stockholm to Märsta and then change to bus #570, #575, or #579. In Stockholm, you can buy all the tickets you need for a round-trip journey—just scan the ticket for each leg at the sensor before boarding each train or bus (but be alert that you can accidentally validate all at once if you stack them and scan the one on top). Guided two-hour **sightseeing cruises** run to Sigtuna on summer weekends (375 SEK round-trip, Fri-Sun morning departures from Stockholm's Stadshusbron dock at 10:00, return from Sigtuna at 16:15, www.stromma.se). If traveling by **car** to Uppsala or Oslo, Sigtuna is a short detour.

Tourist Information: The helpful TI is on the main street and eager to equip you with a town map (Mon-Fri 10:00-17:00, Sat-Sun 12:00-15:00, Storagatan 33, +46 8 5948 0650, http://destinationsigtuna.se).

NEAR STOCKHOLM

Sights in Sigtuna

Main Street: Storagatan

Sigtuna's main street provides the town's spine. Along it, besides the TI, you'll find the tiny Town Hall from 1744, with a nicely preserved interior (free, June-Aug daily 12:00-16:00), and the Sigtuna history museum, with exhibits based on area archaeological finds from the Viking and Middle ages. Pick up their free rune walk map or download it from http://sigtunamuseum.se—click "Create, play & learn" (100 SEK, free Oct-April; daily 12:00-16:00, closed Mon in Sept-June, Storagatan 55). As you stroll the street, read the historical signs posted along the way and poke into shops and cafés. The most charming place for lunch, a snack, or a drink is Tant Bruns Kaffestuga ("Auntie Brown's" Café"), tucked away just around the corner from the TI in a super-characteristic 17th-century home with a cozy garden.

Churches

Before the Reformation came along, Sigtuna was an important political and religious center, and the site of the country's archbishopric. Along with powerful monastic communities, the town had seven churches. When the Reformation hit, that was the end of the monasteries, and there was a need for only one church—the Gothic Mariakyrkan. It survived, and the rest fell into ruins. Mariakyrkan, or Mary's Church, built by the Dominicans in the 13th century, is decorated with pre-Reformation murals and is worth a look.

The stony remains of St. Olaf's Church stand in the Mary's Church cemetery. This 12th-century ruin is evocative, with stout vaults and towering walls that served the community as a place of last refuge when under attack.

Rune Stones

Sigtuna is dotted with a dozen rune stones. Literally "word stones," these memorial stones are carved with messages in an Iron Age runic language. Sigtuna has more of these than any other Swedish town. Those here generally have a cross, indicating that they are from the Christian era (11th century). Each is described in English. I like Anund's stone, which says, "Anund had this stone erected in memory of himself in his lifetime." His rune carver showed a glimpse of personality and that perhaps Anund had no friends. (It worked. Now he's in an American guidebook, and 10 centuries later, he's still remembered.)

Uppsala

Uppsala, Sweden's fourth-largest city, is a rather small town with a big history. A few blocks in front of its train station, an inviting commercial center bustles around the main square and along a scenic riverfront. Towering across the river are its historic cathedral and a venerable university. For visitors, the university features a rare 17th-century anatomical theater, an exhibit of its

prestigious academic accomplishments, and a library with literary treasures on display. Uppsala is home to the father of modern botany, Carl Linnaeus, whose garden and house—now a museum—make for a fascinating visit. And, just outside town stands Gamla Uppsala, the site of a series of majestic burial mounds where Sweden buried its royalty back in the sixth century. While Gamla Uppsala is a short bus ride away, everything else is within delightful walking distance. If you're not traveling anywhere else in Sweden other than Stockholm, Uppsala (less than an hour away) makes a pleasant day trip. While buzzing during the school year, this university town is sleepy during summer vacations.

GETTING THERE

Take the train from Stockholm's central station (3/hour, 40 minutes, 95 SEK; also possible on slower suburban *pendeltåg*—2/hour, 55 minutes, covered by local transit pass plus small supplement). Since the Uppsala station has lockers and is in the same direction from Stockholm as the airport, you could combine a quick visit here with an early arrival or late departure.

Orientation to Uppsala

TOURIST INFORMATION

You'll find helpful basic TIs (InfoPoints) scattered around town (see website for locations and hours). The most practical location is at the UL Center inside the train station (Mon-Fri 7:00-19:00, Sat 9:00-17:00, closed Sun). All locations distribute the informative *What's On Uppsala* magazine, which includes the best map of the center and a list of sights (+46 18 727 4800, www.destinationuppsala.se).

NEAR STOCKHOLM

Uppsala

LINNAEUS
GARDEN
AND MUSEUM

To
Gamla
Uppsala

STORGATAN

VÄDERKVARNSGATAN

VAKSALAGATAN

SALAGATAN

SKOLGATAN

ST. JOHANNESGATAN

SVARTBÄCKSGATAN

ST. PERSGATAN

ST. OLOFSGATAN

UPPLAND
MUSEUM

VAKSALAGATAN

KUNGSGATAN

DRAGARBRUNNSGATAN

AKADEMIGATAN

■ CATHEDRAL CAFÉ

Stora
Torget
Ⓑ #2

TRAIN
STATION

GUSTAVIANUM

CATHEDRAL

BISKOPSGATAN

BREDGRÄND

KYRKOGÅRDSGATAN

ÖVRE SLOTTSGATAN

DROTTNINGGATAN

SLOTTSGRÄND

BÄVERNS GRÄND

KUNGSÄNGSGATAN

UNIVERSITY
LIBRARY

NEDRE SLOTTSGATAN

Fyrisån River

ÖSTRA ÅGATAN

Carolina
Garden

DAG HAMMARSKJÖLDS VÄG

UPPSALA
CASTLE

Stadsträd-
gården

STRANDBODGATAN

THUNBERGSVÄGEN

200 Meters

200 Yards

ARRIVAL IN UPPSALA

From the train station (pay lockers, TI), cross the busy street and walk two blocks to Kungsängsgatan, turn right, and walk to the main square, Stora Torget. The spires of the cathedral mark two of the top three sights (the cathedral itself and the adjacent university buildings). The Linnaeus Garden and Museum is a few blocks up the river. The stop for the bus to Gamla Uppsala is on the main square.

Sights in Uppsala

▲▲Uppsala Cathedral (Uppsala Domkyrkan)

One of Scandinavia's largest, most historic cathedrals feels as vital as it does impressive. While the building was completed in 1435, the spires and interior decorations are from the late 19th century. The cathedral—with a fine Gothic interior, the relics of St. Erik, memories of countless Swedish coronations, and the tomb of King Gustav Vasa—is well worth a visit.

Cost and Hours: Free, daily 8:00-18:00; free guided English tours 1-2 times/day in season (mid-June–mid-Aug daily at

NEAR STOCKHOLM

15:00, also Mon-Fri at 10:00 and Sat-Sun at 12:30), or pick up brochure in gift shop; +46 18 430 3500, www.uppsaladomkyrka.se.

Visiting the Cathedral: Grab a seat in a pew and take in the graceful Gothic lines of the longest nave in Scandinavia (130 yards).

The gorgeously carved, gold-slathered Baroque pulpit is a reminder of the Protestant (post-Reformation) focus on preaching the word of God in the people's language. Look high above in the choir area to enjoy fine murals, restored in the 1970s. For ages, pilgrims have come here to see the relics of St. Erik. All around you are important side chapels, tombs, and memorials (each with an English description).

Near the entrance is the tomb and memorial to scientist Carl Linnaeus, the father of modern botany, who spent his career at the university here (for more on him, see the Linnaeus Garden and Museum listing, later).

In the chapel at the far east end of the church is the tomb of King Gustav Vasa and his family. This chapel was originally dedicated to the Virgin Mary. But Gustav Vasa brought the Reformation to Sweden in 1527 and usurped this prized space for his own tomb. In good Swedish style, the decision was affirmed by a vote in parliament, and bam—the country was Lutheran. (A few years later, England's King Henry VIII tried a similar religious revolution—and had a much tougher time.) Notice that in the tomb sculpture, Gustav is shown flanked by two wives—his first wife died after suffering a fall; his second wife bore him 10 children. High above are murals of Gustav's illustrious life.

Speaking of Mary, notice the modern statue of a common, rather than regal, Protestant Mary outside the chapel looking in. In keeping with the Protestant spirit here, Mary is shown not as an exalted queen, but as an everywoman, saddened by the loss of her child and seeking solace—or answers—in the church.

Cathedral Treasury: By the gift shop, you can pay to ride the elevator up to the treasury collection. Here (with the help of a loaner flashlight and English translations), you'll find medieval textiles (tapestries and vestments), swords and crowns found in Gustav's grave, and the Nobel Peace Prize won by Nathan Söderblom, an early-20th-century archbishop here (60 SEK, Mon-Sat 10:00-16:00, Sun from 12:30). In this same narthex area, notice the debit-card machine for offerings.

Eating: The **$$ Cathedral Café** (a few steps to the right as you exit the cathedral) is charming, reasonable, and handy—and your money supports the city's mission of helping the local homeless population (lunch specials, Mon-Sat 10:00-16:30, Sun 11:00-16:00). Or, survey the many eateries on or near the main square or along the river below the cathedral.

UNIVERSITY AND NEARBY

Scandinavia's first university was founded in Uppsala in 1477. Two famous grads are Carl Linnaeus (the famous botanist) and Anders Celsius (the scientist who developed the temperature scale that bears his name). The campus is scattered around the cathedral part of town, and two university buildings are particularly interesting and welcoming to visitors: the Gustavianum and the library.

▲▲Gustavianum

Facing the cathedral is the university's oldest surviving building, with a bulbous dome that doubles as a sundial (notice the gold numbers). Today it houses a well-presented museum that features an anatomical theater, a cabinet filled with miniature curiosities, and Celsius' thermometer. The collection is curiously engaging for the glimpse it gives into the mindset of 17th-century Europe, though the museum may be closed for renovation during your visit.

Cost and Hours: 50 SEK, generally Tue-Sun 10:00-16:00, Sept-May from 11:00, closed Mon year-round, Akademigatan 3, +46 18 471 7571, www.gustavianum.uu.se.

Visiting the Gustavianum: Note that renovations may result in changes in the museum's exhibits as described here.

The finely crafted **Viking artifacts** were discovered at Valsgärde, a prehistoric site near Uppsala used for burials for more than 700 years. Archaeologists have uncovered 15 boat graves here (dating from AD 600-1050—roughly one per generation), providing insight on the Viking Age.

The **anatomical theater**'s only show was human dissection. In the mid-1600s, as the enlightened ideas of the Renaissance swept far into the north of Europe, scholars began to consider dissection of the human body the ultimate scientific education. Corpses of hanged

NEAR STOCKHOLM

criminals were carefully sliced and diced here, under a dome in an almost temple-like atmosphere, demonstrating the lofty heights to which science had risen in society. Imagine 200 students standing tall all around, leaning in to view the teacher's scalpel.

Many artifacts illustrate the fascinating history of the university. The **Physics Chamber** features a collection of instruments from the 18th and 19th centuries that were used by university teachers. The Augsburg Art Cabinet takes center stage here with a dizzying array of nearly 1,000 minuscule works of art and other tidbits held in an ornately decorated oak cabinet. Built in the 1620s for a bigwig who wanted to impress his friends, the cabinet once held the items now shown in the display cases surrounding it. Find the interactive video screen, where you can take a virtual tour of the collection. Just beyond the cabinet is a thermometer that once belonged to Celsius (in his handwriting, notice how 0 and 100 were originally flip-flopped, with water boiling at 0 degrees Celsius rather than 100).

The university's **classical antiquities collection** from the Mediterranean includes ancient Greek and Roman artifacts and Egyptian sarcophagi, which were used to bring classical culture and art to students unable to travel abroad.

▲University Library (Universitetsbiblioteket)

Uppsala University's library, housed in a 19th-century building called the Carolina Rediviva, is a block uphill from the cathedral and Gustavianum. Off the entry hall (to the right) is a small but exquisite exhibit of treasured old books. Well-displayed and well-described in English, the carefully selected collection is surprisingly captivating.

Cost and Hours: Free, daily 9:00-18:00, Dag Hammarskjölds väg 1, +46 18 471 1000, www.ub.uu.se.

Visiting the Library: Display cases hold treasures like Mozart scores in the composer's hand, margin notes by Copernicus in a 13th-century astronomy book, and a 1555 map of Mexico City.

The most valuable item is the **Silver Bible,** a translation from Greek of the four Gospels into the now-extinct Gothic language. Written in Ravenna in the sixth century, Sweden's single most

precious book is so named for its silver-ink writing on purple-colored calfskin vellum. Booty from a 1648 Swedish victory in Prague, it ended up at Uppsala University in 1669.

Another rarity is the **Carta Marina,** the first more-or-less accurate map of Scandinavia, printed in Venice in 1539 from nine woodblocks. Compare this 16th-century understanding of the region with your own travels.

▲Linnaeus Garden and Museum (Linnéträdgården)

Carl Linnaeus, famous for creating the formal system for naming plant and animal species, spent his career in Uppsala as a professor. This home, office, greenhouse, and garden is the ultimate Linnaeus sight, providing a vivid look at this amazing scientist and his work.

Cost and Hours: 100 SEK for museum and garden; museum open June-Aug daily 11:00-17:00, closed Mon in May and Sept and all of Oct-April; garden open until 20:00; daily 45-minute English tours at 11:30 and 14:30; after 17:00, when the museum closes, the garden becomes a free public space—enter on Svartbäcksgatan at #27; +46 18 471 2874, www.linnaeus.uu.se.

Visiting the Garden and Museum: While Linnaeus (whose noble name was Carl von Linné) was professor of medicine and botany at the University of Uppsala, he lived and studied here. From 1743 until 1778, he ran this botanical garden and lived on site to study the plant action—day and night, year-round—of about 3,000 species. When he moved in, the university's department of medicine and botany moved in as well.

It was in this garden (the first in Sweden, originally set up in 1655) that Linnaeus developed a way to classify the plant kingdom. Wandering the garden where the most famous of all botanists did his work, you can pop into the orangery, built so temperate plants could survive the Nordic winters.

The museum, in Linnaeus' home (which he shared with his wife and seven children), is filled with the family's personal possessions and his professional gear. You'll see his insect cabinet, herbs cabinet, desk, botany tools, and notes. An included audioguide helps bring the exhibit to life.

More Sights near the University

Two free museums are within walking distance of the cathedral (both open Tue-Sun 11:00-16:00, Thu until 20:00, closed Mon). The **Uppland Museum** (Upplandsmuseet), a regional history museum with prehistoric bits and folk-art scraps, is on the river by the waterfall (+46 18 169 100, www.upplandmuseet.se). Uphill from the university library is the 16th-century Uppsala Castle, which houses **an art museum** (+46 18 727 2482, www.uppsalakonstmuseum.se).

ON THE OUTSKIRTS

▲Gamla Uppsala

This pleasant, scenic site on the outskirts of town gives historians goose bumps. Gamla Uppsala—literally, "Old Uppsala"—includes nine large royal burial mounds circled by a walking path. Fifteen hundred years ago, when the Baltic Sea was higher and it was easy to sail all the way to Uppsala, the pagan Swedish kings had their capital here. Old Uppsala is where the Swedish kingdoms came together and a nation coalesced.

Cost and Hours: The **mounds** are free and always open. The **museum** is 80 SEK and open daily 11:00-17:00 (shorter hours Sept-March—generally 10:00-16:00 and closed Tue and Thu in winter). In summer your museum admission includes a 40-minute guided English tour of the mounds (generally July-Aug daily at 12:30 and 15:30, +46 18 239 312, www.raa.se/gamlauppsala). The **church** is free and open daily 9:00-17:00, Sept-March until 16:00 (tiny church museum across the lane is free and open Sat-Sun only 12:00-15:00).

Getting There: A direct city bus stops right at the site. From Uppsala's Stora Torget, take bus #2, marked *Gamla Uppsala*, to the last stop—Kungshögarna (42 SEK if bought on board—credit cards only, otherwise buy ticket at Pressbyrån kiosk on the square; 2-4/hour, 15-minute trip). All the Gamla Uppsala sights are within 200 yards of each other, making it an easy visit.

Eating: Gamla Uppsala is great for picnics, or you can drop by the rustic and half-timbered **$ Odinsborg** café, which serves sandwiches, mead, and daily specials (daily 10:00-17:00, +46 18 323 525).

Visiting Gamla Uppsala: The highlight of a visit is to climb the evocative mounds, which you're welcome to wander. Also at the site is a small but interesting museum and a 12th-century church.

The Mounds: The focus of ritual and religious activities from the 6th through 13th century, the mounds are made meaningful with the help of English info boards posted around.

Imagine the scene over a thousand years ago, when the democratic tradition of this country helped bring the many small Swedish kingdoms together into one nation. A *ting* was a political assembly where people dealt with the issues of the day. Communities would gather here at the rock that marked their place, and then the leader, standing atop the flat mound (nearest today's café), would address the crowd as if in a natural amphitheater. It was here that Sweden became Christianized a thousand years ago.

In 2019, archaeologists unearthed two Viking-age boats underneath some modern houses in Gamla Uppsala. One of the boats included the remains of a man, horse, and dog, as well as a sword, spear, shield, and ornate comb. The find is considered especially remarkable because neither the boats nor remains had been cremated, as was the traditional practice—possibly reflecting the arrival of Christianity in the region.

Museum: Gamla Uppsala's museum gives a good overview of early Swedish history and displays items found in the mounds. While humble, it is instructive, with plenty of excavated artifacts.

Church: Likely standing upon a pagan holy site, the church dates from the 12th century and was the residence of the first Swedish archbishop. An 11th-century rune stone is embedded in the external wall. In the entryway, an iron-clad oak trunk with seven locks on it served as the church treasury back in the 12th century. In the nave, a few Catholic frescoes, whitewashed over in the 16th century with the Reformation, have been restored.

STOCKHOLM'S ARCHIPELAGO

Vaxholm • Grinda • Svartsö • Sandhamn

Some of Europe's most scenic islands stretch 80 miles out into the Baltic Sea from Stockholm. If you're cruising to or from Finland, you'll get a good look at this island beauty. If you have more time and want to immerse yourself in all that simple Swedish nature, consider spending a day or two island-hopping.

The Swedish word for "island" is simply *ö*, but the local name for this area is Skärgården—literally, "garden of skerries," which are unforested rocks sticking up from the sea. That stone is granite, carved out and deposited by glaciers. The archipelago closer to Stockholm is rockier, with bigger islands and more trees. Farther out (such as at Sandhamn), the glaciers lingered longer, slowly grinding the granite into sand and creating smaller islands.

Locals claim there are more than 30,000 of these islands, and as land here is rising slowly, more pop out every year. Some 150 are inhabited year-round, and about 100 have ferry service. There's an unwritten law of public access in the archipelago: Technically you're allowed to pitch your tent anywhere for up to two nights, provided the owner of the property can't see you from his or her house. It's polite to ask first and essential to act responsibly.

With thousands of islands to choose from, every Swede seems to have a favorite. This chapter covers four very different island destinations that offer an overview of the archipelago. Vaxholm, the gateway to the archipelago, comes with an imposing fortress, a charming fishermen's harbor, and the easiest connections to Stockholm. Rustic Grinda feels like—and used to be—a Swedish summer camp, with good hiking options. Sparsely populated Svartsö is another fine back-to-nature experience. And swanky Sandhamn thrills the sailboat set, with a lively yacht harbor, a scenic setting at the far edge of the archipelago, and (true to its name) sandy beaches.

The best way to experience the magic of the archipelago is simply to stretch out comfortably on the top deck of your ferry.

The journey truly is the destination. Enjoy the charm of lovingly painted cottages as you glide by, sitting in the sun on a sleek lounge chair positioned to catch just the right view, with the steady rhythm of the ferries lacing this world together, and people savoring quality time with each other and nature.

PLANNING YOUR TIME

On a Tour: For the best quick look, consider one of the many half- or full-day package boat trips from downtown Stockholm to the archipelago. **Strömma** runs several options, including the three-hour Archipelago Tour (1-3/day, weekends only off-season, 320 SEK), or the all-day Thousand Island Cruise (departs daily in summer at 9:30, 1,595 SEK, includes lunch and dinner; +46 8 1200 4000, www.stromma.se).

On Your Own: For more flexibility and a better dose of the local vacation scene, do it on your own. Any one of the islands in this chapter is easily doable as a single-day side trip from Stockholm. And, because all boats to and from Stockholm pass through Vaxholm, it's easy to tack on that town to any other one. For general information about the archipelago, see StockholmArchipelago.se.

For a very busy all-day itinerary that takes in the two most enjoyable island destinations (Grinda and Sandhamn), consider this plan: Catch an early boat from Stockholm to Grinda, take a quick walk around the island, then sail to Sandhamn. In Sandhamn, have lunch and enjoy the town, then take a boat back to Stockholm (maybe have dinner on board). Or you could craft a route tailored to your interests: For example, for a back-to-nature experience, try Stockholm-Grinda-Svartsö-Stockholm. For an urban mix of towns, consider Stockholm-Vaxholm-Sandhamn-Stockholm.

Overnighting on an island really lets you get away from it all and enjoy the island ambience. I've listed a few accommodations, but note that midrange options are few; most tend to be either pricey and top-end or very rustic (rented cottages with minimal plumbing).

Don't struggle too hard with the "which island?" decision. The main goal is to get well beyond Vaxholm to experience more striking scenery. I'd sail an hour or two past Vaxholm, take a short

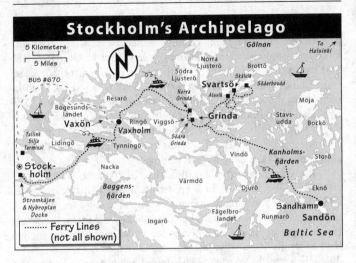

break on an island, then stop in Vaxholm on the way home. The real joy is the view from your ferry.

GETTING AROUND THE ARCHIPELAGO

A few archipelago destinations (including Vaxholm) are accessible overland, thanks to modern bridges. For other islands, you'll take a boat from downtown Stockholm: Waxholmsbolaget runs the regular public ferry service throughout the entire archipelago; Cinderella Bâtarna, part of the Stromma sightseeing company, travels to just the most popular islands. Note that tickets and passes for the Waxholmsbolaget ferries are not valid on Cinderella boats (and vice versa).

Check both companies' **online schedules** when planning your itinerary; some sailings make many more stops than others, and you might have to mix and match to make your itinerary work. While Cinderella's schedules are easy to read, the complex public ferry schedules can be confusing even to locals. You can try Waxholmsbolaget's online journey planner (in Swedish only), but if you need help, call or ask at their customer service office in Stockholm, in front of the Grand Hotel (on Strömkajen quay). Note that peak season for departures is summer (mid-June–mid-Aug); the number of boats declines off-season.

By Public Ferry (Waxholmsbolaget)

The ferries, some of them classic steamboats, depart Stockholm from the Stromkäjen quay in front of the Grand Hotel (+46 8 600 1000, www.waxholmsbolaget.se). Boats run to, among other places, these islands: **Vaxholm** (at least hourly, 1.5 hours, 93 SEK), **Grinda** (nearly hourly, 2 hours, 112 SEK), **Svartsö** (3/day, 2.5 hours, 137 SEK), and **Sandhamn** (1/day, Sat-Sun only, 3.5 hours, 165 SEK).

Tickets: Waxholmsbolaget tickets are sold on board or at the customer service center (SL-Access card or credit card only). It's smart to get to the quay early in summer.

The company offers a 1,000-SEK SL-Access "travel fund" credit for 750 SEK. Credit is splittable, making this deal worthwhile if you're traveling with a small group or doing a lot of island-hopping (buy credit on land, then use it to buy tickets on the boat). If you're staying in the archipelago for a few days, consider the Island Hopping Pass, a five-day, all-inclusive pass (525 SEK, plus a 20-SEK fee for SL-Access card—described on page 437). Buy the card at the Waxholmsbolaget office.

On Board: When you board, tell a crew member which island you're going to. Boats don't land at all of the smaller islands unless passengers have requested a stop. Hang on to your ticket, as you'll have to show it to disembark. Some boats have luggage-storage areas (ask when you board). Check the onboard monitor to see the position of your boat as it motors through the islands.

By Cinderella Boats (Strömma)

These tourist-oriented ships are generally pricier, faster, and more modern than the quainter public ferries (boats leave from near Stockholm's Nybroplan, along Strandvägen, +46 8 1200 4045, www.stromma.en-se/stockholm). Cinderella boats visit fewer islands, but they sail frequently (4/day Mon-Thu, 5/day Fri-Sun) from Stockholm to **Vaxholm** (50 minutes, 135 SEK) and **Grinda** (1.5 hours, 170 SEK). After Grinda, the line splits, going either to **Sandhamn** (from Stockholm: 1/day Mon-Thu, 2/day Fri-Sun, 2.5 hours, 190 SEK), or Finnhamn, with a stop en route at **Svartsö** (from Stockholm: 2/day, 2.5 hours, 185 SEK).

Tickets: Tickets are sold onboard, but these boats can get crowded in summer; book ahead online for the sailing you want. Otherwise, visit the Stromma ticket office in Stockholm at Södra Blasieholmshamnen 11 (near the Grand Hotel and the Waxholms-bolaget office).

Boat Tips

For the **best seat,** with less sun and nicer views, I'd go POSH: Port Out, Starboard Home (on the left side leaving Stockholm, on the right side coming back).

You can usually buy **food on board,** ranging from simple fare at snack bars to elegant sea-view dinners at fancy restaurants. If your boat has a top-deck restaurant and you want to combine your cruise with dinner, make a reservation as soon as you board or try calling ahead to reserve a table for a specific cruise (for Waxholms-bolaget, call +46 8 600 1000; for Cinderella, call +46 8 1200 4045).

HELPFUL HINTS

Tourist Information: Stockholm's TI has a free map of the archipelago, which gives a great overview to the area (for locations and hours, see page 435).

Opening Times: Any opening hours I list in this chapter are reliable only for peak season (mid-June-mid-Aug). During the rest of the tourist year, hours are flexible and completely weather-dependent; more services tend to be open on weekends than weekdays. Outside the short summer season, many places close down entirely.

Money: Bring cash. The only ATMs are in Vaxholm (though most vendors accept credit cards).

Signal for Stop: At the boat landings or jetties on small islands, you'll notice a small signal tower (a semaphore) that lets a passing boat know you want to be picked up. Pull the cord to spin the white disc and make it visible to the ship. Be sure to put it back before boarding the boat. At night, you signal with light—locals just use their mobile phones.

Local Drink: A popular drink here is *punsch*, a sweet and spicy liqueur. Stately old buildings sometimes have *punsch-verandas*, little glassed-in upstairs porches where people traditionally would imbibe and chat.

Vaxholm

The self-proclaimed gateway to the archipelago, Vaxholm is more developed and less charming than the other islands. Connected by bridge to Stockholm, it's practically a suburb, and not the place to commune with Swedish nature. But it also has an illustrious history as the anchor of Stockholm's naval defense network, and it couldn't be easier to reach (frequent buses and boats from Stockholm). While Vaxholm isn't the rustic archipelago you might be looking for, you're almost certain to pass through here at some point on your trip. If you have some extra time, hop off the boat for a visit.

Getting There: Boats constantly shuttle between Stockholm's waterfront and Vaxholm (see "Getting Around the Archipelago," earlier). **Bus #670** runs regularly from the Tekniska Högskolan T-bana stop in northern Stockholm to the center of Vaxholm (4/hour Mon-Fri, 3/hour Sat-Sun, 40 minutes, 43 SEK one-way, buy ticket in Pressbyrån convenience store across the street from station; cheaper with SL-Access card). Unless you're on a tight budget, I'd take the boat for the scenery.

Orientation to Vaxholm

Vaxholm, with about 5,000 people, is on the island of Vaxön, connected to the mainland (and Stockholm) by a series of bridges. Everything of interest is within a five-minute walk of the boat dock.

Tourist Information: Vaxholm's good TI is well stocked with brochures about Vaxholm itself, Stockholm, and the archipelago, and can help you with boat schedules (Mon-Fri 10:00-18:00, Sat-Sun until 16:00, shorter hours off-season; in the Town Hall building on Rådhustorget, +46 8 5413 1480, www.vaxholm.se).

Arrival in Vaxholm: Ferries stop at Vaxholm's south harbor (Söderhamnen). The **bus** from Stockholm arrives and departs at the bus stop called Söderhamnsplan, a few steps from the boats. To get your bearings, follow my Vaxholm Walk. Luggage lockers are in the Waxholmsbolaget building on the waterfront. The departure board is near the ticket office (*nästa avgang* means "next departure"). For more help, confirm your plans at the ticket office.

Vaxholm Walk

This 30-minute loop begins at the boat dock and takes you to the most characteristic corners of Vaxholm.

Waterfront: Dominating Vaxholm's waterfront is the big Art Nouveau Waxholms Hotell, dating from the early 20th century. Across the strait to the right is Vaxholm's stout fortress, a reminder of this town's strategic impor-

tance over the centuries.

With your back to the water, turn left and walk with the big hotel on your right. Notice the Waxholmsbolaget office building. Inside you can buy tickets, confirm boat schedules, or stow your bag in a locker. After the hamburger-and-hot-dog stand, you'll reach a roundabout. Just to your left is the stop for bus #670, connecting Vaxholm to Stockholm. Beyond that, a wooden walkway follows the seafront to the town's private boat harbor (Västerhamnen, "west harbor"), where you can count sailboats and rent a bike.

But for now, continue straight up Vaxholm's appealing, shop-lined main street, Hamngatan. After one long block (notice the handy Co-op/Konsum grocery store across the street), turn right up Rådhusgatan (following signs to *Rådhustorget*) to reach the town's main square. The TI is inside the big, yellow Town Hall building on your left. Continue kitty-corner across the square (toward the granite slope) and head downhill on a street leading to the...

Fishermen's Quarter: Norrhamnen ("north harbor") is ringed by homes formerly occupied by fishermen. Walk out to the dock and survey the charm-ing wooden cottages. In the mid-19th century, Stockholmers considered Vaxholm's herring, called *strömming*, top qual-ity. Caught fresh here, the herring could be rowed into the city in just eight hours and eaten immedi-ately; herring caught farther out had to be preserved in salt and lost its flavor.

As you look out to sea, you'll see a pale green building protrud-ing on the left. This is the charming Hembygdsgården homestead museum, with a pleasant indoor-outdoor café. It's worth heading to this little point (even if the museum is closed, as it often is): As you face the water, go left about one block, then turn right down the gravel lane called Trädgårdsgatan (also marked for *Hembygds-gården*).

Continuing down Trädgårdsgatan lane, you'll run right into the **Hembygdsgården homestead**. The big house features an en-dearing museum showing the simple, traditional fisherman's life-style (pop in if it's open; free but donation requested). Next door is a fine recommended café serving sweets and light meals with idyllic outdoor seating (both in front of and behind the museum—take wind direction into consideration as you choose your perch). This is the best spot in town for coffee or lunch. From here, look across the inlet at the tiny beach (where we're heading next).

Backtrack to the harbor, then continue straight uphill on Fiskaregatan road, and take the first left up the tiny gravel lane marked *Vallgatan*. This part of the walk takes you back in time, as you wander among old-fashioned wooden homes. At the end of the lane, head left. When you reach the water, go right along a path leading to a thriving little **sandy beach,** where you can commune with Swedes at play in good weather.

When you're done relaxing, take the wooden stairs up to the top of the rock and **Battery Park** (Batteripark)—where giant artillery helped Vaxholm flex its defensive muscles in the late 19th century. As you crest the rock and enjoy the sea views, notice (on your right) the surviving semicircular tracks from those old artillery guns. With a range of six miles, a blast from these powerful cannons could shatter glass in nearby houses. Before testing them, they'd play a bugle call to warn locals.

To head back to civilization, turn right before the embedded bunker (crossing more gun tracks and passing more fortifications on your left). As you leave the park, take a left at the fork, and the road will take you down to the embankment—just around the corner from where the boat docks (our starting point). From along this stretch of embankment, you can catch a boat across the water to Vaxholm Fortress.

Sights in Vaxholm

Vaxholm Fortress and Museum
(Vaxholms Kastell/Vaxholms Fästnings Museum)

Vaxholm's only real attraction is the fortification just across the strait. While the town feels sleepy today, for centuries it was a crucial link in Sweden's nautical defense because it presided over the most convenient passage between Stockholm and the outer archipelago (and, beyond that, the Baltic Sea, Finland, and Russia). The name "Vaxholm" means "Island of

the Signal Fire," emphasizing the burg's strategic importance. In 1548, King Gustav Vasa decided to pin his chances on this location, ordering the construction of a fortress here and literally filling in other waterways, effectively making this the only way into or out of Stockholm...which it remained for 450 years. A village sprang up across the waterway to supply the fortress, and Vaxholm was born. The town's defenses successfully held off at least two major invasions (Christian IV of Denmark in 1612, and Peter the Great of Russia in 1719). Vaxholm's might gave Sweden's kings the peace of mind they needed to expand their capital to outlying islands—which means that the pint-size powerhouse of Vaxholm is largely to thank for Stockholm's island-hopping cityscape.

Cost and Hours: 80 SEK, late June-mid-Aug daily 11:00-17:00, mid-Aug-mid-Sept Sat-Sun 11:30-15:30, closed off-season, +46 8 1200 4870, www.vaxholmsfastning.se.

Getting There: A ferry shuttles visitors back and forth from Vaxholm (50 SEK round-trip, every 15 minutes when museum is open, catch the boat just around the corner and toward the fortress from where the big ferries put in). Once on the island, hike into the castle's inner courtyard and look to the left to find the museum entrance.

Visiting the Fortress: The current, "new" fortress dates from the mid-19th century, when an older castle was torn down and replaced with this imposing granite behemoth. During the 30 years it took to complete the fortress, the tools of warfare changed. Both defensively and offensively, the new fortress was obsolete before it was even completed. The thick walls were no match for shells (rather than cannonballs), and the high hatches used for attacking tall sailing vessels were useless against new, low-lying, *Monitor*-style attack boats.

Today, the fortress welcomes guests to wander its tough little island and visit its museum. Presented chronologically on two floors (starting upstairs), the modern exhibit traces the military history of this fortress and of Sweden in general. It uses lots of models and mannequins, along with actual weaponry and artifacts, to tell the story right up to the 21st century. There's no English posted, but you can pick up good English translations as you enter.

Sleeping and Eating in Vaxholm

Since Vaxholm is so close to Stockholm, there's little reason to sleep here. But in a pinch, Waxholms is the only hotel in town.

Sleeping: $$$ Waxholms Hotell's stately Art Nouveau facade dominates the town's waterfront. Inside are 42 pleasant rooms with classy old-fashioned furnishings (loud music some nights in summer—ask what's on and request a quiet room if necessary, Hamngatan 2, +46 8 5413 0150, www.waxholmshotell.se, info@waxholmshotell.se). The hotel has a grill restaurant outside in summer and a fancy dining room inside.

Eating: Vaxholm's most tempting eatery, **$ Hembygdsgården ("Homestead Garden") Café** serves "summer lunches" (salads and sandwiches) and homemade sweets, with delightful outdoor seating around the Hembygdsgården homestead museum in the characteristic fishermen's quarter. Anette's lingonberry muffins are a treat (daily May-mid-Sept, closed off-season, +46 8 5413 1980).

$ Boulangerie Waxholm is the perfect place for a *fika* break, but also serves sandwiches, salads, and hot dishes. From the south harbor (Söderhamnen), walk to the roundabout and turn left; you'll find it at the end of the block (Mon-Fri 7:00-18:30, Sat-Sun from 8:00, +46 8 5413 1872).

Grinda

The rustic, traffic-free isle of Grinda—half retreat, half old-fashioned resort—combines back-to-nature archipelago remoteness with easy proximity to Stockholm. The forested island is an idyllic slice of Swedish nature, with walking paths, beaches, trees, and slabs of glacier-carved granite sloping into the sea. Since Grinda is a nature preserve (owned by the Stockholm Archipelago Foundation), only a few families actually live here, and there's no real town. But in the summer, Grinda becomes a magnet for day-tripping urbanites, which can make it quite crowded. It also holds nostalgia for many Stockholmers, who fondly recall when this was a summer camp island. In a way, with red-and-white cottages bunny-hopping up its gentle hills and a stately old inn anchoring its center, it retains that vibe today.

Orientation to Grinda

Grinda is small and easy to manage. It's a little wider than a mile in each direction; you can walk from end to end in a half-hour. Its main settlement—the historic **Wärdshus building** (a busy hub of tourist activities including a restaurant, bar, and conference facilities), hotel, and related amenities—sits mid-island, up the hill from its guest harbor, where private yachts and sailboats put in. A hostel and rental cabins spill over the south end of the island; a campground is a few steps away from the dock at the north end.

Major points of interest are well signposted in Swedish: *Södra Bryggan* (south dock), *Norra Bryggan* (north dock), *Värdshus* (hotel at the heart of the island), *Gästhamn* (guest harbor); *Affär* (general store); *stuga/stugby* (cottage/s); *Grindastigen* (nature trail); and *Tält-plats* (campground).

Tourist Information: The red cottage marked *Expedition/ Lilla Längan* greets arriving visitors just up the hill from the Södra Grinda ferry dock. The staff answers questions, and the cottage serves as a small shop, a place to rent kayaks or saunas, and a reception desk for the island's cottages and hostel (open daily in season; Wärdshus general info +46 8 5424 9491, www.grinda.se).

Arrival in Grinda: Public ferries use two docks at opposite ends of the island. Most sailings use Södra Grinda to the south (nearest the hostel and cottages), while a few use Norra Grinda to the north (closer to the campground). From either of these, it's about a 10- to 15-minute walk to the action.

Sights in Grinda

Grinda is made to order for strolling through the woods, taking a dip, picnicking, and communing with Swedish nature. Watch the

boats bob in the harbor and work on your Baltic tan. You can simply stick to the gravel trails connecting the island's buildings, or for more nature, take the Grindastigen trail, which loops from the Wärdshus to the southeast end of the island and back in less than an hour (signposted from near the Wärdshus).

You can rent a kayak or the private little sauna hut bobbing near the shore (inquire at the Lanthandel general store near the Wärdshus). There's no bike rental here—and the island is a bit too small to keep a serious biker busy—but you could bring one on the boat from Stockholm.

As you stroll, you might spot a few haggard-looking tents through the trees. The right to pitch a tent here was established by the Swedish government during World War II, to give the downtrodden a cheap place to sleep. Those permissions are still valid, inherited, bought, and sold, which means that Grinda has a thriving community of tent-dwelling locals who camp here all summer long (April-Oct). Once each summer they have a progressive tent-crawl bender before heading to the Wärdshus to blow a week's food budget on a fancy meal.

The island just across from the Södra Grinda dock (to the right) is Viggsö, where the members of ABBA have summer cottages and wrote many of their biggest hits.

Sleeping in Grinda

Your options are, in increasing order of rustic charm: hotel, hostel, and cottages. You can reserve any of these through the Wärdshus (+46 8 5424 9491, www.grinda.se, info@grinda.se).

Grinda is busiest in the summer, when tourists fill its hotel; in spring and fall, it mostly hosts conferences. If sleeping at the hostel or cottages, arrange arrival details (you'll probably pick up your keys at the *Expedition/Lilla Längan* shed near the south dock). The hostel and cottages charge extra for bed linens. If you have a tent, you can pitch it at the basic campsite near the north jetty for a small fee.

$$$$ Grinda Hotel rents 30 rooms (each named for a local bird or fish) in four buildings just above the Wärdshus. These are modern, comfortable, and made for relaxing, intentionally lacking distractions such as TVs or phones (cheaper if you skip breakfast; if dining at the restaurant, the "Wärdshus package" will save you a few kronor).

$ The 27 **cottages**—most near the Södra Grinda ferry dock—offer a rustic retreat (kitchenettes but no running water, shared bathroom facilities outside). From mid-June to mid-August, these require a one-week minimum rental and cost more.

¢ Grinda Hostel (Vandrarhem) is the place to sleep if you wish you'd gone to Swedish summer camp as a kid. The 44 bunks are in simple two- and four-bed cottages, surrounding a pair of firepits (great shared kitchen/dining hall). A small pebbly beach and a basic sauna are nearby.

Eating in Grinda

All your options (aside from bringing your own picnic from Stockholm) are run by the hotel, with choices in each price range.

$$$$ Grinda Wärdshus, the inn at the center of the complex, serves fine traditional Swedish meals and contemporary international dishes. Portions are small but delicious. Eat in the woody dining room or on the terrace out front (late June-Aug daily 12:00-24:00; weekends only—and some Fri—in off-season).

$$$ Grindas Framficka ("Grinda's Front Pocket") is a pleasant bistro that serves up basic but tasty food (seafood, salads, and pizza) alongside the guest harbor. Order at the counter then choose a table, or wait to be seated for a more formal atmosphere (early

June-mid-Aug daily 11:00-22:00, otherwise sporadically open in good weather—especially weekends).

The **general store and café** (Lanthandel) just below the Wärdshus is the place to rustle up some picnic fixings. You'll also find coffee, ice cream, disposable "one-time grills" for a barbecue, and kayak rentals (open long hours daily early June-mid-Aug, Fri-Sun only in shoulder season).

Svartsö

The remote and lesser-known isle of Svartsö (svert-show, literally "Black Island"), a short hop beyond Grinda, is the "Back Door" option of the bunch. Unlike Grinda, Svartsö is home to a real community; islanders have their own school and library. But with only 80 year-round residents, the old generation had to specialize. Each person learned a skill to fill a niche in the community—

one guy was a carpenter, one a plumber, one an electrician, and so on. While the island is less trampled than the others in this chapter (just one hotel and a great restaurant), it is reasonably well served by ferries. Svartsö feels remote and potentially even boring for those who aren't wowed by simply strolling through meadows. But it's ideal for those who want to slow down and immerse themselves in nature.

Svartsö hosts the school for this part of the archipelago. Because Swedish law guarantees the right to education, even kids living on remote islands are transported to class. A school boat trundles from island to island each morning to collect kids headed for the school on Svartsö. If the weather is bad, a hovercraft retrieves them. If it's really bad, and all of the snow days have been used up, a helicopter takes the kids to school.

Orientation to Svartsö: The island, about five miles long and a half-mile wide, has four docks. The main one, at the southwestern tip, is called Alsvik (with the general store and restaurant). Halfway up is Skälvik, at the northeastern end is Söderboudd, and at the northwestern end is Norra Bryggan. Most boats stop at Alsvik, but you can request a different stop (ask a crew member on board, or use the semaphore signal at the dock).

At the **Alsvik dock,** the great little general store, Svartsö Lanthandel, sells everything you could need and acts as the town TI, post office, pharmacy, and liquor store (daily mid-May-mid-Aug, sporadic hours off-season but open year-round, +46 8 5424 7325, www.svartsolanthandel.se). You can rent bikes here; in busy times, call ahead to reserve (75 SEK/hour, 200 SEK/day). The little café on the dock sells drinks and light food, and rents **$** cottages (bunk beds, shared outdoor toilets, +46 8 5424 7110).

The island has a few paved lanes and almost no traffic. Residents use three-wheeled utility motorbikes for hauling things to and from the ferry landing. The interior consists of little more than trees. With an hour or so, you can bike across the island and back, enjoying the mellow landscape and chatting with the friendly big-city people who've found their perfect escape.

Sleeping in Svartsö: Away from the crowds, **$ Svartsö Skärgårdshotel och Vandrarhem** is a five-minute uphill walk from the Norra Bryggan dock (served by both Waxholmsbolaget and Cinderella Båtarna). The rooms are basic and include breakfast (bike rental available, 15-minute ride to Alsvik harbor and Svartsö Krog restaurant, open year-round, +46 8 5424 7400, www.svartsonorra.se, info@svartsonorra.se).

Eating in Svartsö: Head right from the Alsvik dock and walk five minutes up the hill to find the excellent **$$$ Svartsö Krog** restaurant. Run by Henrik, this place specializes in dishes featuring island-grown herbs and vegetables and locally caught seafood. Choose from one of the three eating zones (each with the same menu): outside, upscale dining room, or original pub interior (an Old West-feeling tavern). Try the cod or "Svartsö-kebab" with homemade pita bread if available (daily lunch specials, three- and four-course fixed-price dinner menus, good wine and beer selection; lunch and dinner daily June-Aug; May and Sept dinner Fri-Sun, lunch Sat-Sun; closed Oct-April; +46 8 5424 7255, www.svartsokrog.se).

Sandhamn

Out on the distant fringe of the archipelago—the last stop before Finland—sits the proud village of Sandhamn (on the island of Sandön). Literally "Sand Harbor," this is where the glacier got hung up and kept on churning away, grinding stone into sand. The town has a long history as an important and posh place. In 1897, the Royal Swedish Sailing Society built its clubhouse here, putting Sandhamn on the map as the yachting center of the Baltic—Sweden's answer to Nantucket. It remains an extremely popular stop for boaters—from wealthy yachties to sailboat racers—as well as visitors simply seeking a break from the big city.

The island of Sandön feels stranded on the edge of the archipelago, rather than immersed in it. Sandhamn is on its sheltered side. Though it's far from Stockholm, Sandhamn is very popular. During the peak of summer (mid-June through late August), it's extremely crowded. Expect to stand in line, and call ahead for restaurant reservations. But even during these times, the old town is relatively peaceful and pleasant. Shoulder season is delightful in good weather, though weekends can be busy.

Orientation to Sandhamn

You'll find two halves to Sandhamn: In the shadow of that still-standing iconic yacht clubhouse is a ritzy resort/party zone throbbing with big-money nautical types. But just a few steps away, around the harbor, is an idyllic time-warp old town of colorfully painted shiplap cottages tucked between tranquil pine groves. While most tourists come here for the resort, the quieter part of Sandhamn holds the real appeal.

Sandhamn has a summer-only **TI** (open June-mid-Aug) in the harbor area (www.destinationsandhamn.se.)

Sandhamn Walk

To get your bearings from the ferry dock, take this self-guided walk. Begin by facing out to sea.

As you look out to the little point across from the dock, notice the big yellow building. In the 18th century, this was built as the **pilot house.** Because the archipelago is so treacherous to navigate—with its tens of thousands of islands and skerries, not to mention untold numbers of hidden underwater rocks—locals don't trust outsiders to bring their boats here. So passing ships unfamiliar with these waters were required to pick up a local captain (or "pilot") to take them safely all the way to Stockholm. The tradition continues today. The orange boats marked *pilot,* moored below the house, ferry loaner captains to oncoming ships. And, since this is the point of entry into Sweden, foreign ships can also be processed by customs here.

The little red shed just in front of the pilot house is home to a humble **town museum** featuring exhibits on Sandhamn's history and some seafaring tales (open sporadically in summer).

Just above the barn, look for the yellow building with the blue letters spelling **Sandhamns Värdshus.** This traditional inn, built in the late 17th century, housed sailors while they waited here to set out to sea. During that time, Stockholm had few exports, so ships that brought and unloaded cargo there came to Sandhamn to load up their holds with its abundant sand as ballast. Today the inn still serves good food (see "Eating in Sandhamn," later).

Stretching to the left of the inn are the quaint storefronts of most of Sandhamn's **eateries** (those that aren't affiliated with the big hotel)—bakery, deli, and grocery store, all of them humble but just right for a simple bite or picnic shopping. Local merchants enjoy a pleasantly symbiotic relationship. Rather than try to compete with each other, they attempt to complement what the next shop sells—each one finding just the right niche.

The area stretching beyond these storefronts is Sandhamn's **old town**—a maze of wooden cottages that's an absolute delight to explore (and easily the best activity in town). Only 50 of Sandhamn's homes (of around 450) are occupied by year-rounders. The rest are summer cottages of wealthy Stockholmers, or bunkhouses for seasonal workers in the tourist industry. Most locals live at the farthest-flung (and therefore least desirable) locations. Imagine the impact of 100,000 annual visitors on this little town.

Where the jetty meets the island, notice (on the right) the old-fashioned telephone box with the fancy *Rikstelefon* logo. Just to the right of the phone box, you can see the town's bulletin board, where locals post their classified

ads. To the left at the base of the dock is Sandhamns Kiosk, a newsstand selling local and international publications (as well as candy and *mjukglass*—soft-serve ice cream). A bit farther to the left, the giant red building with the turret on top is the **yacht clubhouse** that put Sandhamn on the map, and still entertains fun seekers today with a hotel, several restaurants, spa, minigolf course, outdoor pool, and more. You'll see its proud SSS-plus-crown logo (standing for Svenska Segelsällskapet—Swedish Sailing Society) all over town. In the 1970s, the building was owned by a notorious mobster who made meth in the basement, then smuggled it out beneath the dock to sailboats moored in the harbor.

Look for the "Bluewater Oasis" **water station** in front of the yacht clubhouse. Due to Sandhamn's low groundwater level, and the enormous increase in visitors during summer months, local authorities impose water rationing part of the year. To provide more water, a filtration system was installed that purifies water direct from the Baltic Sea. It's totally drinkable, and a good place to fill up your water bottle.

Spinning a bit farther to the left, back to where you started, survey the island across the strait (Lökholmen). Just above the trees, notice the copper dome of an **observatory** that was built by this island's eccentric German oil-magnate owner in the early 20th century. He also built a small castle (not quite visible from here) for his kids to play in.

To stroll to another fine viewpoint, walk into town and turn left along the water. After about 50 yards, a sign on the right points up a narrow lane to *Posten*. This unassuming gravel path is actually one of Sandhamn's most important streets, with the post office, police department (which handles only paperwork—real crimes are deferred to the Stockholm PD), and doctor (who visits town every second Wednesday). While Sandhamn feels remote, it's served—like other archipelago communities—by a crack emergency-response network that can dispatch a medical boat or, in extreme cases, a helicopter. With top-notch hospitals in Stockholm just a 10-minute chopper ride away, locals figure that if you have an emergency here, you might make it to the ER faster than via an ambulance navigating congested city streets. At the end of this lane, notice the giant hill of the town's namesake sand.

Continuing along the main tree-lined harborfront strip, you can't miss the signs directing yachters to the *toalett* (toilet) and *sopor* (garbage dump). Then you'll pass the Sandhamns Guiderna office, a **travel agency** where you can rent bikes, kayaks, and fishing gear (+46 7 347 4339, www.sandhamn.se). Just after that is the barn for the volunteer fire department (Brandstation). With all the wooden buildings in town, fire is a concern—one reason why Sandhamn restricts camping (and campfires).

Go beneath the skyway connecting the big red hotel to its modern annex. Then veer uphill (right) at the *Badstranden Trouville* sign, looking down at the minigolf course. After you crest the top of the hill, on the left is a big, flat expanse of rock

nicknamed Dansberget ("Dancing Rock") because it once hosted community dances with a live orchestra. Walk out to enjoy
fine **views** of the Baltic Sea—

from here, boaters can set sail
for Finland, Estonia, and St.
Petersburg, Russia. Looking
out to the horizon, notice the
three lighthouse towers poking
up from the sea, used to guide
ships to this gateway to the archipelago. The finish line for
big boat races stretches across
this gap (from the little house on the point to your left). In summer, this already busy town gets even more jammed with visitors,
thanks to the frequent sailing races that end here. The biggest
annual competition is the Götlandrunt, a round-trip from here
to the island of Götland.

Our walk is finished. You can head back into town. Or, to
hit the beach, continue another 15 minutes to Trouville beach (see
next).

Sights in Sandhamn

Beaches (Stränder)

True to its name, Sandön ("Sandy Island") has some of the archipelago's rare sandy beaches. The closest, and local favorite, is the

no-name beach tucked in a cove
just behind the old town (walk
through the community from
the main boat dock, then follow the cove around to the little
sandy stretch).

The most popular—and
crowded in summer—is Trouville beach, at the opposite end
of the island from Sandhamn
(about a 20-minute walk). To find it, walk behind the big red
hotel and take the right, uphill fork (marked with the low-profile
Badstranden Trouville sign) to the "Dancing Rock," then proceed along the road. Take a left at the fork by the tennis courts,
then walk about 10 minutes through a mysterious-feeling forest
(sometimes filled with lingonberries and blueberries), until you
reach a little settlement of red cottages. Take a right at the fork
(look up for the *Till Stranden* sign), and then, soon after, follow
the middle fork (along the plank walks) right to the beach zone:

two swathes of sand marked off by rocks, stretching toward Finland.

Kvarnberget

Just inside the old town you'll find this little hilltop with a beautiful view of the sea. From the Sandhamns Värdshus B&B, take the path leading to the left and follow it straight past the old wooden houses until you see the hill. You can simply walk up the hill to enjoy the view, or pack a picnic (beware of seagulls hovering overhead, eager to steal your lunch).

Sleeping in Sandhamn

Sandhamn has a pair of very expensive top-end hotels, a basic but comfortable B&B, and little else. If you're sleeping on Sandhamn, the B&B is the best choice.

$$$$ Sands Hotell is a stylish splurge sitting proudly at the top of town. While oriented mostly to conferences and private parties, its 19 luxurious rooms also welcome commoners in the summer (elevator, spa, +46 8 5715 3020, www.sandshotell.se, info@sandshotell.se).

$$$$ Sandhamns Seglarhotellet rents 79 nautical-themed rooms in a modern annex behind the old yacht club building (where you'll find the reception). The rooms are fine, but the prices are sky-high (loud music from disco inside the clubhouse—request a quieter back room, great gym and pool area, +46 8 5745 0400, www.sandhamn.com, reception@sandhamn.com).

$ Sandhamns Värdshus B&B rents five rustic but tasteful, classically Swedish rooms in an old mission house buried deep in the colorful old town. To melt into Sandhamn and get away from the yachties, sleep here (mostly twins, all rooms share WC and shower, tiny cottage with its own bathroom for same price, includes breakfast, reception is at the restaurant—see next, +46 8 5715 3051, www.sandhamns-vardshus.se, info@sandhamns-vardshus.se). The rooms are above a reception hall, but after 22:00, quiet time kicks in.

Eating in Sandhamn

IN THE OLD TOWN

Sandhamn's most appealing eateries are along the old town side of the harbor.

$$$$ Sandhamns Värdshus, right on the water, is the town's best eatery. They serve traditional Swedish food in three separate dining zones (which mostly share the same menu, but each also has its own specials): out on an inviting deck overlooking the water;

upstairs in a salty dining room with views; or downstairs in a simple pub (daily lunch and dinner nearly year-round, lunch specials, +46 8 5715 3051, www.sandhamns-vardshus.se).

To grab a bite or assemble a picnic, browse through these smaller eateries: **$ Monrads Deli,** behind the yacht club, is a bright shop where you can buy sandwiches and salads, meats for grilling, cheeses, cold cuts, drinks, fresh produce, and other high-quality picnic fixings (long hours daily in summer, +46 8 755 1610, www.monrads.se/butik-take-away).

In the opposite direction, **Westerbergs Livsmedel** grocery store has basic supplies (sporadic hours daily). **$$ Dykarbaren Café** serves lunches and dinners with indoor and outdoor seating (daily mid-June-mid-Aug, Wed-Sun only in shoulder season, closed off-season; +46 8 5715 3554). **$ Ankaret** has a little market (serving smoked fish and shrimp, sandwiches, and ice cream for takeaway) and outdoor seating. Just around the corner (uphill from the harbor and behind the Värdshus), **$ Sandhamns Bageriet** is a popular early-morning venue serving coffee, sweet rolls, and sandwiches (daily in summer, Sat-Sun only late-Aug-Sept).

AMONG THE YACHTIES

Sandhamn Seglarhotell has several pleasant eateries: a pricey **$$$$** restaurant with fine sea views, plus a comfy wine bar and casual outdoor terrace (+46 8 5745 0421, www.sandhamn.com).

SOUTHEAST SWEDEN

Kalmar • Öland Island • Växjö • Glass Country

The southeastern province of Småland, with dense forests and pristine lakes, is a welcome contrast to big-city Stockholm. Coastal Kalmar has a rare Old World ambience and the most magnificent medieval castle in Scandinavia. From Kalmar, hop a ferry to the beachy island of Öland, popular for its miles of bike trails, hiking paths, and sandy shores. Nestling inland is the little metropolis of Växjö, with a trio of interesting museums, including the House of Emigrants, which tells the story of Scandinavian migration to America. Lying between Kalmar and Växjö is Glass Country, a 70-mile stretch of forest sparkling with glassworks that welcome guests to tour and shop.

PLANNING YOUR TIME

Although I'm not the biggest fan of the Swedish countryside (blame my Norwegian heritage), a visit to Kalmar and Växjö provides a good dose of small-town Sweden. (I find Lund and Malmö—both popular side-trips from Copenhagen—relatively dull, and a boat trip along the much-loved Göta Canal too sleepy.) Seaside Kalmar is a natural home base for a Småland visit and a good place to break up the trip between Copenhagen and Stockholm. This two-day plan works well for those traveling by train, though you can see more if you rent a car for a day.

Day 1: In the morning, tour Kalmar Castle, getting there via my Back-Streets Walk. After lunch, laze at the town beach or explore pastoral Öland Island.

Day 2: Browse the people-friendly streets of Kalmar's town center, dropping in at the Kalmar County Museum. Depart Kalmar for Stockholm, stopping en route in Växjö (same train line;

leave luggage at Växjö train station). To have enough time to visit Växjö's glass museum and House of Emigrants, leave Kalmar by midday.

With a Car: To see even more of the region, rent a car in Kalmar on day 2 to tour the Glass Country and have more time in Växjö (sightsee there before dropping off your rental car and catching your onward train to Stockholm).

Kalmar

Kalmar feels like it used to be of strategic importance. In its heyday—back when the Sweden/Denmark border was just a few miles to the south—they called Kalmar Castle the "Key to Sweden." But today Denmark is distant, and Kalmar is a bustling small city of 64,000 (with 9,000 students in its university and maritime academy). Kalmar's salty old center, classic castle, and busy waterfront give it a wistful sailor's charm.

History students may remember Kalmar as the place where the treaty establishing the 1397 Kalmar Union was signed. This "three crowns" treaty united Norway, Sweden, and Denmark against their common enemy: German Hanseatic traders. It created a huge kingdom, dominated by Denmark, that lasted a bit more than a hundred years. But when the Swede Gustav Vasa came to power in 1523, Kalmar was rescued from the Danes, the union was dissolved...and even the European Union hasn't been able to reunify the Scandinavian Peninsula since.

Kalmar town was originally next to the castle in what's now called the Old Town (Gamla Stan). But that location put the townsfolk directly in the line of attack whenever the castle was besieged. So, after a fire decimated the town in 1647, the city fathers relocated Kalmar to the adjacent island of Kvarnholmen, encircling

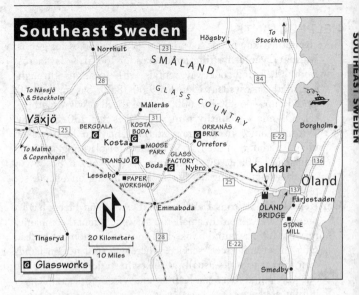

it with defensive earthworks and bastions, parts of which still survive.

The charming Old Town, Kvarnholmen town center, castle, and nearby vacation island of Öland are all enjoyable to explore, making Kalmar an appealing stop. Its boom-or-bust tourist season is busiest from mid-June through mid-August.

Orientation to Kalmar

Kalmar is easily walkable and fun by bike. The mostly pedestrianized Kvarnholmen core is walled and laid out in a grid street plan. The Old Town district is between Kvarnholmen and Kalmar Castle, which occupies a little island of its own (a 10-minute walk from Kvarnholmen). The train station and TI sit on the edge of Kvarnholmen.

Kalmar spreads out over several more island-neighborhoods, but most visitors stick to the main town center, Old Town, and castle. If your time is limited, your top priorities should be a town walk, the castle, and the public beach just beyond the castle.

TOURIST INFORMATION

The TI is in the big, modern building next to the marina (Mon-Fri 9:00-18:00, Sat-Sun 10:00-15:00, shorter hours off-season; Ölandskajen 9, +46 480 417 700, www.kalmar.com). Ask about live music and entertainment; for example, there are often free concerts on the Larmtorget town square on summer evenings.

HELPFUL HINTS

Bike Rental: Many hotels have loaner or rental bikes for guests. **Kalmar Cykeluthyrning** rents bikes for 160 SEK/day (across from TI, handy one-way rentals with locations throughout southern Sweden; Mon-Fri 9:00-18:00, Sat until 14:00, closed Sun, +46 480 010 600, reserve ahead at www.rentbike. se). **Ölands Cykeluthyrning** has bikes for 150 SEK/day. With an office in the train station and two locations on Öland Island, they are a good resource for planning an island spin (daily 9:00-19:00 in summer, +46 70 667 6280, www. olandscykeluthyrning.se). For more on biking on Öland, see page 556.

Car Rental: Major firms Europcar, Sixt, Avis, and Hertz have a presence in Kalmar. In small-town Sweden, rental companies may not have a central bricks-and-mortar location but instead offer "meet and greet" service, whereby a staff person hands over the car to you—usually at the train station. If you want a one-way rental (between Kalmar and Växjö, for example), set it up in advance.

ARRIVAL IN KALMAR

Arriving at the combined train and bus station couldn't be easier (train ticket office open Mon-Fri 6:30-18:00, Sat until 15:00, Sun 10:30-17:00; lockers available). As you walk out the front door, the town center (Kvarnholmen) is dead ahead; the TI is 100 yards to your right, across the busy street on the harbor; and Kalmar Castle and the Old Town are behind you.

Kvarnholmen Town Center Walk

Start this ▲ walk in Larmtorget, the lively, restaurant- and café-lined square a few steps uphill from the train station. This is the most inviting square in town for outdoor dining—scout your options for dinner later. It's also the nightlife center of town and the site of free summer concerts (usually Tue and Thu at 19:00; check schedule at the TI or with your hotel). The many cafés bordering the square are a reminder that this is a college town, with lots of students; and a tourist town, with lots of vacationing Swedes. The bronze fountain that dominates one side of the square depicts David standing triumphantly over the slain Goliath—a thinly veiled allusion to King Gustav Vasa, who defeated the Danes (the fountain's reliefs depict his arrival in Kalmar in 1520).

The area just to the north, up Larmgatan, is a charming old quarter with the historic Västerport gate and a restored old water tower. The tower, dating from 1900, was turned into a modern apartment building, winning an award for the architect who successfully maintained the tower's historic profile.

But for now, we'll stroll straight through town on the main pedestrian shopping street, **Storgatan** (with Ben & Jerry's on the corner). Kvarnholmen is a planned town, laid out on a regular grid plan after the 1647 fire consumed the Old Town. While a 1960s push to "modernize" stripped away much of the Old World character, surviving historic buildings and the mostly pedestrianized streets make Kvarnholmen a delight to stroll.

The first major cross-street, Kaggensgatan, leads (to the right, past a fine row of 17th-century stone houses) down to the harbor; a block to the left, on the right (at #26), is the landmark and recommended Kullzénska Caféet, whose owners refused to let this charming 18th-century merchant's house be torn down to make way for "progress." (It remains a genteel setting for *fika*.)

Continue window-shopping your way down Storgatan. On the right just after #20, admire the building marked *1667*, with the cannonballs decorating the doorway. This was the home of a war profiteer—a lucrative business in this military-minded town (now an inviting gift shop with local products, teas, chocolates, and cheese).

Storgatan leads to the town's main square, **Stortorget.** Built in the 17th century in a grand style befitting a European power, the "big square" tries a little too hard to show off—today it feels too big and too quiet (locals prefer hanging out on the cozier Larmtorget).

The **cathedral** *(domkyrkan)* dominating the square is the biggest and (some say) finest Baroque church in Sweden. Its interior,

which contains a gigantic 17th-century pulpit and bells from the earlier town cathedral, has been elegantly restored to its original glory. Its architect was inspired by the great Renaissance churches of Rome. The interior is all very high-church (for such a Lutheran country), with a fine Baroque altar, carved tombstones used for flooring, and homogeneous white walls (free, Mon-Fri 8:00-18:00, Sat-Sun from 9:00, shorter hours off-season, free noon "Lunch Music" organ concerts daily in summer—check the program on the board left of the entrance). Facing the cathedral is the decorated facade of the **Town Hall** *(rådhuset)*.

From here, go straight through the square and continue strolling down Storgatan. Notice the fine old houses, all lovingly cared for. At the end of town, the area beyond Östra Vallgatan (the old eastern wall of the city) has a pleasant **park** and small **swimming beach.** You may notice dads out with their babies—most Scandinavians get over a year of paid leave for the mom and dad to split as they like. (They're nicknamed "Latte Dads," and cafés complain that they clog their floor space with baby strollers.)

Head across the street and down the stairs toward the playground (to the left) to find, on a little pier in the water, the last remaining *klapphus*—laundry building—in Kalmar (and Scandinavia). In the mid-1800s, four of these small, wooden structures with floating floors stood here at the seaside. Washers would stand in barrels inset around the central laundry pool for a better working position. Today the *klapphus* is still occasionally used for washing rugs and carpets. The Baltic seawater is considered good for carpet health.

Across the water is the island neighborhood of Varvsholmen, which once housed an eyesore shipyard but has been converted into a modern residential develop-

ment. To the left of Varvsholmen is the sleepy island neighborhood of Ängö, traditionally home to sailors and fishermen, and now one of Kalmar's most desirable places to live. To the right stretches the Öland Bridge.

Your walk is finished. Hooking around to the right, you first reach the former city bathhouse (in a 1909 Art Nouveau building), which faces the tiny Kalmar Maritime Museum (described later). A block beyond that, the waterfront is dominated by giant red-brick buildings—steam mills once used to grind flour. Today this complex houses the fascinating Kalmar County Museum, described later.

Sights in Kalmar

THE OLD TOWN AND CASTLE

Kalmar's castle is on a small island opposite a park and the Old Town. For a guided stroll through the Old Town's back streets on your way to the castle, see page 550. Beyond the castle you'll find a pleasant beach.

▲▲Kalmar Castle (Kalmar Slott)

This moated castle is one of Europe's great medieval experiences. The imposing exterior, anchored by stout watchtowers and cuddled by a lush park, houses a Renaissance palace interior. Built in the 12th century, the castle was enlarged and further fortified by the great King Gustav Vasa (r. 1523-1560) and lived in by two of his sons, Erik XIV and Johan III. In the 1570s, Johan III redecorated the castle in the trendy Renaissance style, giving it its present shape. Kalmar Castle remained a royal hub until 1658, when the Swedish frontier shifted south and the castle lost its strategic importance. Kalmar Castle was neglected, then used as a prison, distillery, and granary. Finally, in the mid-19th century, a newfound respect for history led to the castle's renovation. Today, it's a vibrant sight giggling with kids' activities, park-like ramparts, and well-described historic rooms.

Cost and Hours: 145 SEK; daily 10:00-16:00, late June-mid-Sept until 18:00, Nov-Dec Sat-Sun only; café and restaurant, +46 480 451 490, www.kalmarslott.se. An interesting way to reach the castle is via my Back-Streets Walk route, described later.

Tours: One-hour English tours tell the goofy antics of Sweden's kings (check website for current schedule).

Visiting the Castle: There's no designated route for visitors, so consider following my tour below. You'll need a castle map to help you follow my route (castle rooms are not numbered except on the map—so the room numbers below refer to that handout). Otherwise, just read my tour in advance and then ramble, reading plaques as you go. There are good English descriptions throughout.

Approaching the castle, you'll cross a wooden drawbridge. Peering into the grassy, filled-in moat, look for sunbathers, who enjoy soaking up rays while the ramparts protect them from cool winds. To play "king of the castle," scramble along these outer ramparts.

In the central **courtyard** is the canopied Dolphin Well, a fine work of Renaissance craftsmanship.

Access to most of the rooms is from the main courtyard, but we'll use the entrance just to the right of the gift shop (unceremoniously labeled *Toalett*). Once inside, turn right to find the **Governor's Quarters** (Room 10)

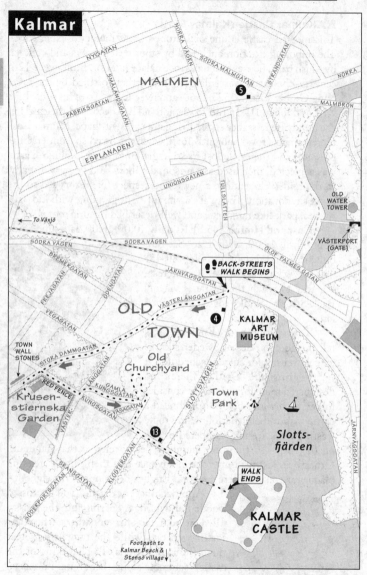

Kalmar

with a model of the early medieval castle. Notice the bulky shape of the towers before they were capped by fancy Renaissance cupolas and how the town once huddled in the shadow of the castle.

In the adjoining **Dungeon** (Room 9), you can peer down into the pit where unfortunate prisoners were held. The room was later converted into a kitchen (notice the big fireplace), and the pit became a handy place to dump food waste.

Now go through the labyrinth of rooms to the right that show

Accommodations
1. Calmar Stadshotell
2. Frimurare Hotellet
3. Kalmar Sjömanshem Vandrarhem
4. Slottshotellet
5. Hotell Hilda
6. To Hotell Svanen

Eateries & Other
7. Källaren Kronan
8. Gröna Stugan
9. Bryggan
10. Kullzénska Caféet
11. Ernesto Restaurante
12. Supermarket
13. Söderport
14. Bike Rental (2)

daily life at the castle: a reconstruction of the castle kitchen (Room 12), an excellent set of models showing the evolution of the building from medieval castle to Renaissance palace (Room 17), and an impressive copy of Erik XIV's 1561 coronation robe (Room 14, where there's also a complete rundown of the Vasa kings). In the next room (13) are similarly resplendent reproductions of royal gowns.

Now backtrack to where we entered, and climb the **Queen's**

Staircase (Room 6), up steps made of Catholic gravestones. While this simply might have been an economical way to recycle building materials, some speculate that it was a symbolic move in support of King Gustav Vasa's Reformation, after the king broke with the pope in a Henry VIII-style power struggle.

At the top of the stairs, go left through the wooden door into the **Queen's Bedroom** (Room 23). The ornate 1625 Danish bed (captured from the Danes after a battle) is the only surviving original piece of furniture in the castle. Notice the faces decorating the bed; they've had their noses chopped off, as superstitious castle-dwellers believed that potentially troublesome spirits settled in the nose. This bed could easily be disassembled ("like an Ikea bed," as my guide put it) and moved from place to place—handy for medieval kings and queens, who were forever traveling throughout their realm. Smaller servants' quarters adjoin this room.

Proceed into the **Checkered Hall** (Room 24). Examine the intricately inlaid wall panels, which make use of 17 different types of wood—each a slightly different hue. Appreciate the faded Renaissance frescoes throughout the palace.

Continue into the **dining room** (a.k.a. Gray Hall—Room 25) for the frescoes of Samson and Delilah high on the wall. The table is set for an Easter feast (based on a detailed account by a German visitor to one particular Easter meal held here). For this holiday event, the whole family was in town—including Gustav Vasa's two sons, Erik XIV and Johan III. Erik's wife, Katarzyna Jagiellonka, was a Polish Catholic (their marriage united Sweden, Poland, and Lithuania into a grand empire); for her, Easter meant an end to Lenten abstinences. Notice the diverse savories on the table, including fish patties with egg, elaborate pies, and chopped pike in the shape of pears. The giant birds are for decoration, not for eating. Logically, forks (which resembled the devil's pitchfork) were not used—just spoons, knives, and hands.

The door in the far corner with the faded sun above it leads to the **King's Chamber** (Room 26). Notice the elaborate lock on the door, installed by King Erik XIV because of constant squabbles about succession. The hunting scenes inside have been restored a bit too colorfully, but the picture of Hercules over the left window is original—likely painted by Erik himself. Examine more of the inlaid panels. To see the king's toilet, peek into the little room to the left of the fireplace, with a fine castle illustration embedded in its hidden door (if closed, ask a museum docent to open it). Also in here was a secret escape hatch the king could use in case of trouble. Perhaps King Erik XIV was right to be so paranoid; he eventually died under mysterious circumstances, perhaps poisoned by his brother Johan III, who succeeded him as king.

Backtrack through the dining room and continue into the **Golden Hall** (Room 27), with its gorgeously carved (and painstakingly restored) gilded ceiling. The entire ceiling is suspended from the true ceiling by chains. If you visually trace the lines of the ceiling, the room seems crooked—but it's actually an optical illusion to disguise the fact that it's not perfectly square. Ponder the portraits of the royal family: Gustav Vasa, one of his wives, sons Erik XIV and Johan III, and Johan's son Sigismund. Imagine the reality-show-level dysfunction that carbonated the social scene here back then.

Peek into **Agda's Chamber** (Room 28), the bedroom of Erik's consort. The replica furniture re-creates how it looked when the king's kept woman lived here. Later, the same room was used for a different type of captivity: as a prison cell for female inmates.

Cut across to the top of the King's Staircase (also made of gravestones like the Queen's Staircase, and topped by a pair of lions). The big door leads to the grand **Green Hall** (Room 31), once used for banquets and now for concerts.

At the end of this hall, the **chapel** (Room 32) is one of Sweden's most popular wedding venues (up to four ceremonies each Saturday). As reflected by the language of the posted Bible quotations, the sexes sat separately: men, on the warmer right side, were more literate and could read Latin; women, on the cooler left side, read Swedish. The fancy pews at the front were reserved for the king and queen.

Going through the door to the right of the altar, you'll enter a stairwell (Room 33), above which hangs a model ship, donated by a thankful sailor who survived a storm. In the next room (34) is Anita, a taxidermic horse who served with the Swedish military (until 1937).

The rest of the castle complex includes the vast **Burnt Hall** (Room 36), where in summer you'll likely find an interesting special art exhibit.

The Old Town

The cute, garden-filled residential zone that locals call Gamla Stan fills the parklike space between the castle and the modern town center. Destroyed by fire in 1647, the medieval village that once stood here was replaced in the 18th century by the summer homes of Kalmar's elites. This toy village of colorfully painted wooden homes, tidy yards, and perfect picket fences is worth a look.

▲Back-Streets Walk to the Castle

Consider a slight detour strolling through the Old Town on your way to the castle (see the "Kalmar" map for the route). Begin where the pleasant, tree-shaded Slottsvägen boulevard intersects with little Västerlånggatan, the cobbled street angling to the right.

Västerlånggatan: Wandering down this quaint lane, enjoy the time-passed cottages as you peek over fences into private gardens. You'll pass behind the grand mansion (now the recommended **Slottshotellet**) that belonged to the prestigious Jeansson family, who donated the parkland near the castle to the town.

Continue through the first intersection, following the path through the middle of the grassy park. As you cross the road on the far side of the park, you'll pass two lines of stones, a small surviving remnant of Kalmar's town wall (on the right).

Krusenstiernska Gården: On the left is the entrance to this relaxed, kid-friendly garden—visitors are welcome to enter any time the gates are open (generally daily 11:00-18:00 in summer). Poke inside to discover a well-preserved 19th-century garden whose charming plantings cluster around a well. The organic fruits and berries grown here are sold as jams, marmalades, and chutneys in the on-site café (along with cakes and coffee). On summer evenings, the garden is a venue for top Swedish comedy acts, which pack the place.

From the garden, backtrack to the street and follow the red fence to the right. Where the fence ends, jog left and squeeze between the yellow and red houses.

Gamla Kungsgatan and the Old Churchyard: Immerse yourself in this Swedish village world of charming cottages and flower-filled window boxes. At the bottom of the lane, on the left, watch for the Old Churchyard (Gamla Kyrkogården), dating from the 13th century and scattered with headstones. It's virtually all that remains of the original Old Town. Look for the monument topped by a statue of a man carrying a boy (St. Christopher, patron of traders and seafarers). Circling this slab, you'll see the floor plan of the original cathedral, an image looking down the cathedral's nave, and a rendering of the town before it was destroyed. The cathedral tower—which had partially survived the 1647 fire—was torn down in 1678 by the Swedes themselves, who wanted to ensure that their enemies (the Danes) couldn't use the tower to launch an attack on the castle.

About 50 yards farther into the yard, the stone slab on the pedestal (marked *Kalmarunionen 600 ar*) commemorates the 600th anniversary of the 1397 Kalmar Union, which united the Nordic states. On June 14, 1997, the contemporary leaders of those same nations—Sweden, Norway, Denmark, Finland, and Iceland—came here to honor that union. You can see their signatures etched in the stone.

Exit the churchyard the way you came in, turn right on the paved street, and take the first left (down Kungsgatan) to the main boulevard. You'll be facing the town park and the castle; on your left is the appealing, recommended Söderport café (with an inviting terrace and economical buffet lunch).

Town Park (Stadsparken): Unfurling along the waterfront between the castle and the city, this beautifully landscaped garden is Kalmar's playground and a delight to explore. With the character of a classic English park, alternately rugged and refined, it's home to many exotic plants. Locals brag that their region enjoys a milder climate than most of Sweden, and some plants here grow nowhere else in the country. The city's modern **art museum** stands in an appropriately modern building in the center of the park.

▲Kalmar Beach (Kalmarsundsbadet)

Kalmar's best beach is at the edge of the Old Town, just beyond the castle. On a hot summer day, this is a festive and happy slice of Swedish life—well worth a stroll even if you're not "going to the beach." With snack stands, showers, sand castles, wheelchair beach access, and views of the castle and the island of Öland, the beach has put Kalmar on the fun-in-the-sun map. It's quite popu-

lar with RVers and the yachting crowd. And if you enjoy people-watching, it's a combination Swedish beauty pageant and tattoo show. For some extra views and kid-leaping action, be sure to walk to the end of the long pier.

To explore more of the seafront, walk 15 minutes south of the beach to the charming little community of **Stensö**, with its own pocket-size harbor, restaurants, and charming fishing cottages.

KVARNHOLMEN TOWN CENTER

Get your bearings in downtown Kalmar with my Kvarnholmen Town Center Walk, earlier, which cuts straight through the length of the town. Then dig into its museums.

▲▲Kalmar County Museum (Kalmar Läns Museum)

This museum is worth a visit for its excellent exhibit on the royal ship *Kronan*, a 17th-century warship that capsized and sank to the bottom of the Baltic just off the island of Öland (where its hull still rests). The many salvaged artifacts preserved in the museum, well described in English, give visitors an unusually complete and intimate look at life at sea.

Cost and Hours: 150 SEK, daily 10:00-16:00, includes 45-minute English tours daily in season, usually at 13:00 (confirm locally); kid-friendly café on floor 4, Skeppsbrogatan 51, +46 480 451 300 www.kalmarlansmuseum.se.

Visiting the Museum: While the museum has plenty of exhibits, your visit will focus mostly on the third floor with the *Kronan* shipwreck artifacts.

Beyond the entry, the first floor has temporary exhibits and shows off the cannons recovered from the *Kronan* wreckage. In those days, cannons were so valuable they were prized the way a Rolls Royce would be today, so each one has its own story (described in English). In the years following the ship's sinking, these cannons were the only artifacts considered worth recovering.

From the first floor, I'd skip the temporary exhibits on Floor 2 and head directly to Floor 3, which displays salvage from the **Kronan.** Twice the size of Stockholm's famous warship *Vasa*, Kalmar's warship was a floating palace and the most heavily armed vessel in the world. But it exploded and sank about three miles beyond the island of Öland in 1676. The painted wall at the elevator shows the dramatic event: The *Kronan*'s admiral misjudged conditions and harnessed too much wind, causing the vessel to tip and its gun ports to fill with water. As the ship began to list, a fallen lantern ignited explosives in the hold, and...BLAM! The ship went right down. Its Danish and Dutch foes—who hadn't fired a shot—happily watched it sink into the deep. Of the 850 people on board, only about 40 were rescued. The wreck's whereabouts were forgotten until 1980, when it was rediscovered by amateur marine archaeologist Anders Franzén, the same man who found the *Vasa* in Stockholm's harbor in 1961.

Head into the exhibit, where you'll view a model of the ship-wreck site. You'll see a cross-section of the mighty vessel and a recovered carving of the potbellied Swedish king (one of many such carvings that decorated the ship). The small theater plays a 15-minute film about the ship.

The replica of the middle gun deck leads to the exhibit's interesting section about everyday life on board. The 850 sailors who manned the ship (about the population of a midsized town of that age) represented all walks of life, "all in the same boat." Engaging illustrations, eyewitness accounts, and actual salvage items bring the story to life. You'll see guns, musical instruments, a medicine chest, dishes, and clothing—the everyday items of the common people who worked and perished on the ship. A treasure chest contains coins from all around the known world at the time, each one carefully identified.

The final exhibit (with another short film) reminds us that the *Kronan* still rests on the sea floor, awaiting funding to be raised to the surface. You'll see a replica of the diving bell used in 1680 to retrieve the cannons and the modern diving bell from very early explorations of the site. Today a dedicated crew—including, at times, Sweden's King Carl XVI Gustav—continues to dive to recover bits and pieces.

For extra credit, head up to Floor 4 for its exhibit on **Jenny Nyström,** an early-1900s Kalmar artist who gained fame for her cute Christmas illustrations featuring elves and pixies. You'll see some of her children's books and textbooks as well as some artistic portraits with a touch of Art Nouveau flair. Ponder Nyström's status as a proto-feminist icon: She was one of the first female artists to support her family by selling her paintings.

Kalmar Maritime Museum (Kalmar Sjöfartsmuseum)

This humble, dusty little exhibit sits a long block beyond the Kalmar County Museum. It's a jumble of photos of vessels, model boats, charts, and other seafaring bric-a-brac that traces the nautical story of Kalmar up to modern times. The collection is displayed in four rooms of a former apartment, shuffled between beautiful porcelain stoves left behind by a previous owner (these were display models for his stove business). While displays are explained by an English booklet (that you can borrow or buy), volunteers are eager to show you around.

Cost and Hours: 50 SEK, daily mid-June-Aug 11:00-16:00, off-season Sun only 12:00-16:00, Södra Långgatan 81, +46 480 15875, www.kalmarsjofartsmuseum.se.

Sleeping in Kalmar

KVARNHOLMEN TOWN CENTER

$$$ Calmar Stadshotell is a 132-room fancy hotel filling its 1907 historic shell right on Kalmar's main square, Stortorget (elevator, Stortorget 14, +46 480 496 900, www.profilhotels.se, calmarstadshotell@profilhotels.se).

$$ Frimurare Hotellet, in a grand old building overlooking Larmtorget square, is just steps from the train station. Warmly run,

the place has soul and a disarmingly friendly staff. Rich public areas, wide-plank hardwood floors, and chandeliers give it a 19th-century elegance. Guests can help themselves to coffee, tea, juice, and other refreshments in the lounge anytime. The 35 rooms provide modern comfort amid period decor. Because it's squeezed between a café-packed square and a park popular for concerts, it can come with some noise (RS%, elevator, free sauna, a few loaner bikes free for Rick Steves readers, 50 yards from the train station at Larmtorget 2, +46 480 15239, www. frimurarehotellet.se, info@frimurarehotellet.se).

$ Kalmar Sjömanshem Vandrarhem, a charming green house built in 1910 for sailors and now used for student housing, opens to travelers in the summer (mid-June to mid-Aug). While its 13 rooms are very simple and bathrooms are down the hall, it has an inviting TV lounge, handy guest kitchen, and a peaceful garden behind a white picket fence facing the harbor (family rooms, sheets and towels extra, no breakfast, plenty of nearby pay parking, Ölandsgatan 45, +46 480 10810, www.kalmarsjomanshem.se, info@kalmarsjomanshem.se).

OUTSIDE THE TOWN CENTER

$$$ Slottshotellet ("Castle Hotel") is an enticing splurge in the atmospheric Old Town. It's the nicely upgraded but still homey former mansion of a local big shot. The 70 rooms—some in the mansion, others sprinkled throughout nearby buildings—sit across a leafy boulevard from Kalmar's town park, just up the street from the castle (Slottsvägen 7, +46 480 88260, www.slottshotellet.se, info@slottshotellet.se).

$$ Hotell Hilda has 12 good rooms in an updated old house, located in a modern residential zone just over the canal from the town center (elevator, limited free parking—reserve a spot when you book, Esplanaden 33, +46 480 16950, www.hotellhilda.se, info@hotellhilda.se). The ground-floor Kallskänken café, which doubles as the reception, serves good salads and sandwiches (Mon-Thu 7:00-21:00, Fri-Sat until 22:00, Sun 8:00-20:00; if checking in outside of these times, email for the door code).

¢-$$ Hotell Svanen, a 20-minute walk or short bus ride from the center, is in the Ängö neighborhood. It has a mix of nicer hotel rooms with private bath, cheaper rooms with shower down the hall, and hostel beds. Services include laundry and kitchen facilities, TV room, sauna, and rental bikes and canoes. While it's a bit institutional, you can't argue with the value (family rooms, sheets extra in hostel rooms, breakfast extra; reception daily 7:30-22:00 in summer, elevator, Rappegatan 1, +46 480 25560, www.hotellsvanen.se, info@hotellsvanen.se). Catch bus #405 at the train station to the Varvsgatan stop (2-3/hour, 5 minutes) and walk 5 minutes to the hotel, or take a taxi for about 70 SEK.

Eating in Kalmar

Kalmar has a surprising number of good dining options for a small town.

KVARNHOLMEN TOWN CENTER

$$$ Källaren Kronan, open only for dinner, is a candlelit cellar restaurant with romantic tables under low stone arches. They serve old-time Swedish dishes, including elk, as well as modern cuisine (open daily from 18:00, also open for lunch on Sat, Ölandsgatan 7, +46 480 411 400).

$$$$ Gröna Stugan ("The Green Cottage") has a great location just off the harbor. Enjoy the varied menu (burgers, short ribs, grilled fish) on their patio deck or in the light and bright dining room. Reservations are smart (Mon-Fri 11:30-14:00 & 17:00-22:00, dinner only on Sat, closed Sun, Larmgatan 1, +46 480 15858, www.gronastuganikalmar.se).

$$$ Bryggan sits inside the Baronen shopping mall, but it's poised over the harbor with view tables inside and deck seating over the water. They serve typical bistro fare, including burgers and fish-and-chips (Mon-Sat 10:00-21:00, Sun from 11:00, can close early in bad weather, Skeppsbrogatan 12, +46 480 363 626).

$$ Kullzénska Caféet, a cozy, antique-filled eatery in a historic 18th-century house, is great for a *fika* break. They serve sandwiches and homemade pastries, but locals adore the always-fresh berry cobblers (with vanilla sauce or ice cream). While it has street seating, the dining rooms upstairs are what it's all about (Mon-Fri 10:00-18:30, Sat until 17:00, Sun 12:00-16:30, on the second floor at Kaggensgatan 26, at the corner of Norra Långgatan, +46 480 28882).

$$ Ernesto Restaurante is driven by Ernesto, who came here from Naples 30 years ago. This local favorite for pasta and pizza has a high-energy feel with good indoor and outdoor seating (most menu items available for takeout, great selection of Italian wines, Mon-Fri 17:00-23:00, Sat-Sun from 13:00, Södra Långgatan 5, +46 480 24100).

Supermarket: The **Co-op** has everything you need for a good picnic, including a salad bar (daily until 21:00, in the Baronen shopping mall at the harbor, on Skeppsbrogatan).

NEAR THE CASTLE

The castle lawn cries out for a picnic (buy one at the Co-op supermarket before your visit). Or you can grab a bite in the café inside the castle itself. Otherwise, consider:

$$$$ Söderport, just across the street from the castle, offers an all-you-can-eat buffet as well as a regular menu; the dining room is pleasantly spacious but the outdoor patio has castle views (Mon-Sat 11:30-late, Sun 12:00-20:00, Slottsvägen 1, +46 480 12501). There's live music Wed-Sat evenings.

Kalmar Connections

From Kalmar by Train to: Växjö (hourly, 70 minutes), **Copenhagen** and its airport (about hourly, 3.5-4 hours, most direct, some with transfer), **Stockholm** (about hourly, 4.5-5 hours, transfer in Alvesta; slower but more scenic coastal route via Linköping).

By Bus to Stockholm: The bus to Stockholm is much cheaper but slower than the train (4/day, fewer on weekends, 6 hours).

Öland Island

Long and skinny Öland Island is a relaxed destination known for its quaint windmills, prehistoric sights, vast limestone plain, roadside produce stands on the honor system, miles of bike paths, and Swede-filled beaches. With only about 25,000 permanent residents, this castaway island attracts some 2.5 million visitors annually. It's a top vacation destination for Swedes—even the king and queen have their summer home here. Because of its relatively low rents, better weather, and easy bridge access to the mainland, Öland is also a popular bedroom community for Kalmar. If you've got good weather and some time to spare—and if the place isn't choked with summer crowds—Öland is a fine destination, especially if you don't rush it.

Dubbed the "Island of Sun and Wind," Öland enjoys a steady sea breeze and an even warmer climate than already mild Kalmar (remember, "warm" is relative in Sweden). And, because receding glaciers scraped off its top layer of soil, it has a completely different landscape than the pine-and-lake feel of mainland Sweden. The southern half of the island is an alvar, a chalky limestone plain that's broad and flat, with just a thin veneer of soil. Other island zones, with rich soil and lush vegetation, make Öland feel almost more Midwestern US than Baltic (Öland is one of Sweden's premier agricultural zones). Visitors are pleasantly surprised by the island's colorful spring wildflowers and bright sunshine, which works its magic on both holidaymakers and artists.

Centuries ago, the entire island was the king's private hunting ground. Because local famers were not allowed to fell trees (and there are fewer here than on the mainland), they made their simple houses from limestone. The island's 34 limestone churches, which were also used for defense, have few windows. Limestone walls demarcate property and contained grazing livestock.

When built in 1972, the **Öland Bridge** from Kalmar to the island was Europe's longest (3.7 miles). The channel between Kalmar and Öland is filled with underwater rocks, making passage here extremely treacherous—but ideal for the Vikings' flat-bottomed boats. (In fact, "Kalmar" comes from the phrase "stones in water.") Today, a catamaran ferry transports commuters, bicyclists, and hikers between Kalmar and the island (see details below).

GETTING THERE

By Car: The island is a breeze if you have a car and at least four hours to explore. Drivers simply head north from Kalmar a few minutes on highway 137 to the Öland Bridge. Once across, highway 136 is the island's main north-south artery.

By Ferry: A ferry runs between Kalmar and Färjestaden harbor on the island (ferry runs about hourly in summer, less frequent in spring and fall, buy 60-SEK ticket onboard, 30-minute crossing, www.ressel.se). If you want to cycle on Öland (a great way to see the island), pick up a rental bike in Kalmar and take it across on the ferry (note that bikes are not allowed on the Öland Bridge). To plan your bike trip, consult with Ölands Cykeluthyrning (shops in Kalmar and on the island at Borgholm and Mörbylånga; see listing earlier, under "Helpful Hints").

By Bus: Buses regularly connect Kalmar with the town of Borgholm (56 SEK, at least hourly in summer, 45 minutes) and, with less frequency, to other Öland destinations (check www.klt.se).

Sights on Öland

Öland is 90 miles long but only 8 miles wide. Because the bridge and the ferry deposit visitors roughly at the island's midpoint, you'll have to decide between heading north (more developed and resorty, with visitor services) or south (more remote and scenic). I've outlined a few basic ideas for each area below, but these are just the beginning—there's much more to discover on Öland.

A good first stop just after crossing the bridge is Öland's mid-island **TI** in Färjestaden—follow signs off the bridge for *turistbyrå* (Träffpunkt Öland 102, +46 485 88800, www.oland.se; there's also a branch on the main street in Borgholm). Friendly staff can help you plan a reasonable agenda to match up with your available time.

CENTRAL/NORTH ÖLAND

For a quick spin to the island, stick with the strip of Öland just north of the bridge. As you drive north along highway 136, keep an eye out for some of Öland's characteristic, old-fashioned windmills. Occasional stone churches dot the landscape (including the one in Räpplinge—just off the main road—where the royals worship when in town).

The island's main town is **Borgholm** (BOY-holm), about a 30-minute drive north of the bridge. Borgholm has a smattering of buildings preserved from the early 1800s as well as turn-of-the-century wooden villas, erected in the early 1900s when the town became a popular seaside resort. Notice that many of these have a humble shack in the garden: Locals would move into these cottages so they could rent the main villas to vacationing Stockholmers in the summer and make a killing. The traffic-free main drag, Storgatan, is lined with tacky tourist shops and ice-cream parlors (Ölandsglass, at #10, is tops). There's also a handy **TI** right on the town's main street.

A pair of interesting sights sits on the hill just above Borgholm (to reach them, you can either drive or hike—get details at TI). **Borgholm Castle** (Borgholms Slott), which looks like Kalmar Castle with its top blown off, broods on the bluff above town, as if to remind visitors of the island's onetime strategic function. Its hard-fought history has left it the empty shell you see today—impressive, but not worth the 100-SEK entry fee (www. borgholmsslott.se).

From near the castle, you can hike down to the current royal summer residence, **Solliden Palace** (Sollidens Slott). It was built

in 1906 in an Italianate style after physicians to Queen Victoria suggested the mild Öland climate might ease her ill health. The palace interior is off-limits, but its sprawling, gorgeously landscaped garden is open to us commoners. Divided into Italian (geometrical and regimented), English (wild), and Dutch (flowers) sections, the Solliden garden complex is well worth a wander (120 SEK, Mon-Sat 11:00-16:00, until 18:00 in summer, Sun until 17:00, closed off-season, on-site café, +46 485 15356, www.sollidensslott.se).

SOUTH ÖLAND

A 65-mile round-trip south of the bridge gives you a good dose of the island's more remote, windy charm.

Start by heading south on highway 136 toward the town of Karlevi. Along the way, you'll notice a beautifully preserved stone mill to your right, the **Karlevi Stenkvarn.** While its weathervane shows the year 1791, no one is really sure how old it is (it's a Dutch-type mill that was common in the 19th century). Island farmers milled flour here until the mid-1950s.

Near here, you have a few choices for checking out the **limestone plain** that covers a fifth of the island. You wouldn't know it to look at it, but this area of scrubby grass and bedrock limestone is a rare ecological environment that's treasured for its biodiversity. To get a closer look, either take the turnoff toward Stenåsa (heading east) or drive a little farther to turn toward the little settlement of Alby (you can also turn this into a loop drive). This open, agricultural landscape (quite unlike the forested mainland) was first farmed during the Stone Age, and still shows evidence of how the land was divided among farmers in medieval days. Möckelmossen, the lake on the plain, attracts all kinds of waterbirds and in winter is a favorite ice-skating site.

Gettlinge Gravfält (off the road just south of Smedby) is a wonderfully situated, boat-shaped, Iron Age graveyard with a beautiful view over the plain. It's littered with monoliths and overseen by a couple of creaky old windmills.

Farther south is the **Eketorp Fort** (Eketorps Borg), a reconstructed fifth-century stone fort that, as Iron Age forts go, is fairly interesting. Several evocative huts and buildings are designed in what someone imagined was the style back then, and the huge rock fort is surrounded by runty Linderöd pigs, a native breed that was common in Sweden 1,500 years ago. A sign reads: "For your convenience and pleasure, don't leave your children alone with the animals" (100 SEK, daily 10:00-17:00 in summer, reduced admission and hours in spring and fall, closed off-season, +46 485 662 000, www.eketorpsborg.se). It's near the southern tip of the island, on the eastern side: When you approach Grönhögen on the main road from the north, look for signs on the left.

You can push on even farther to the very southern tip of the island, home to Sweden's tallest lighthouse, the **Ottenby Nature Center** (exhibits on the nature and culture of the island), and the **Ottenby Bird Observatory,** where ornithologists monitor migratory birds that pass through this major flyway (guided tours available, see www.birdlife.se).

Växjö

A pleasant, sleepy town of almost 85,000, Växjö (locals say VEK-hwuh; Stockholmers pronounce it VEK-shuh) is in the center of Småland. An important trading town for centuries, its name loosely means "where the road meets the lake." Coming in by train or car, you'd think it might mean "buried in a vast forest." Today an enjoyable three-mile path encircles its lake, and a farmers market enlivens the otherwise quiet main square on Wednesday and Saturday mornings.

Not too big and not too small, Växjö is a cozy, quintessential Swedish town with hardly a tourist in sight. It does have a trio of worthwhile attractions: the earnest House of Emigrants, chronicling the plight of Swedes who fled to North America; the Smålands Museum, offering a convenient look at the region's famous glassware; and the cathedral, decorated with fine modern glass sculptures.

In 1996, Växjö set itself the goal of becoming a fossil-fuel-free city by the year 2050. Now a single biomass power plant provides nearly all the community's heat and hot water, half of its energy comes from renewable sources, and carbon dioxide emissions are down considerably. Växjö earned the title "Greenest City in Europe" when it received the EU's first award for sustainable development in 2007.

Orientation to Växjö

Växjö's town center is compact and pedestrian-friendly; the train station, main square, cathedral, and two important museums are all within two blocks of each other. Everything described here is little more than a 15-minute walk apart. Tourists are so rare that a polite English-speaking visitor will find locals generous, warm, and helpful.

Växjö's main attractions, clustering around the north end of its pleasant lake and the surrounding park, can be seen in three to four hours. For a delightful stopover, I'd do this loop from the station: Cross the tracks on the overpass to tour the glass and history museums. Then explore the lovely lake area, which is encircled by a path and next to a pretty park and the cathedral.

A block in front of the cathedral is the town square, Stortorget; from there stretches the main shopping street, Storgatan. Browse this orderly street before heading back to the station.

ARRIVAL IN VÄXJÖ

Växjö's modern train station faces the heart of town; walk a few steps straight ahead, and you'll be in the pedestrian shopping zone. Pick up a city map at the information desk (coin-op luggage lockers; an ATM is a block away to the right as you leave). Drivers will find several parking lots near the station.

TOURIST INFORMATION

The TI is inside the Växjö Kommun building (city hall), about a 10-minute walk from the train station(Mon-Fri 7:30-16:30, closed Sat-Sun, shorter hours off-season; pick up Glass Country map and brochures here, Västra Esplanaden 18, +46 470 430 00, www.upplev.vaxjo.se).

SOUTHEAST SWEDEN

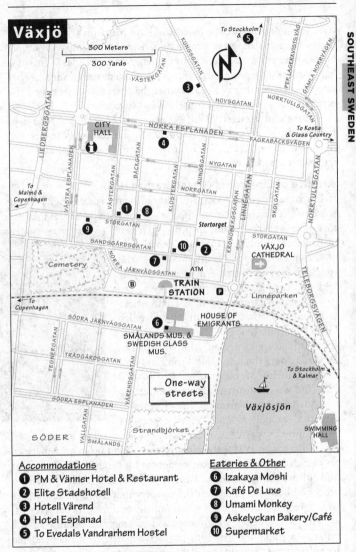

Accommodations

1. PM & Vänner Hotel & Restaurant
2. Elite Stadshotell
3. Hotell Värend
4. Hotel Esplanad
5. To Evedals Vandrarhem Hostel

Eateries & Other

6. Izakaya Moshi
7. Kafé De Luxe
8. Umami Monkey
9. Askelyckan Bakery/Café
10. Supermarket

Sights in Växjö

Smålands Museum/Swedish Glass Museum (Sveriges Glasmuseum)

These two museums share one building and one ticket (which also covers the House of Emigrants). The humble exhibits of the Smålands Museum celebrate the region's Viking-era prehistory, peasant farming past, and more recent cultural history.

The more instructive Swedish Glass Museum traces six centuries of Swedish glass production, from royal cups to simple bottles and from fine crystal to contemporary art glass. This is a handy place to learn a bit about glass if you're not headed deeper into Glass Country. Who knew that the person who designed the original Coca-Cola bottle in 1915 was a Swede?

Cost and Hours: 90-SEK combo-ticket includes House of Emigrants; June-Aug daily 10:00-17:00, shorter hours and closed Mon off-season; café, Södra Järnvägsgatan 2, +46 470 704 200, www.kulturparkensmaland.se.

▲House of Emigrants (Utvandrarnas Hus)

If you have Swedish roots, this tidy museum is exciting. Even if you don't, it's an interesting stop for anyone with immigrant ancestors. The well-presented, inspiring "Dream of America" exhibit captures the experiences of the more than one million Swedes who sought refuge in North America in the late 19th and early 20th centuries.

Cost and Hours: 90-SEK combo-ticket includes Småland Museum and Swedish Glass Museum; June-Aug daily 10:00-17:00, shorter hours and closed Mon off-season; 50 yards down the hill behind the glass museum, Vilhelm Mobergs Gata 4, +46 470 704 200, www.kulturparkensmaland.se.

Visiting the Museum: The "Dream of America" exhibit touches on all aspects of the emigrant experience. As economic woes wracked Sweden from the 1850s to the 1920s, the country was caught up in an American fever. Nearly 1.3 million mostly poor Swedes endured long voyages and culture shock to seek prosperity and freedom in the American promised land. So many left the country that Swedish authorities were forced to rethink their social policies and to institute reforms.

In part, Swedes were compelled to emigrate because of the potato—a staple food in 19th-century Sweden. With dependable (or so everyone thought) nourishment, a peacetime king, and mandatory smallpox vaccinations, the mortality rate had been dropping even among ordinary Swedes. With good (or at least better) times, families got bigger. When crops failed (especially from catastrophic freezes in 1867 and drought in 1868), it wasn't possible to feed those extra mouths, and many Swedes were forced to leave.

Swedes formed enclaves on farms and prairies across North America, from New York to Texas, and from Maine to Seattle. Displays trace immigrant lifestyles, religion, treatment in the press, women's experiences, the Swedish cultural societies that preserved

Old World traditions, and more. Homage is paid to prominent Swedish-Americans, including Charles Lindbergh and the second man on the moon, Buzz Aldrin. Rounding out the exhibits is a presentation from the museum's archive and research department.

Don't miss the display about the *Titanic:* Swedes (after Americans) were the second-largest group to perish on that ill-fated vessel. On view are a few items that went to the bottom of the Atlantic with one of the Swedish passengers.

The Moberg Room celebrates local writer Vilhelm Moberg (1898-1973), who put the Swedish immigrant experience on the map with his four-novel series *The Emigrants.* (These books—and two Max von Sydow/Liv Ullmann films based on them, *The Emigrants* and *The New Land*—are essential pretrip reading and viewing for Swedish-Americans.) Here you'll see a replica of Moberg's "writer's hut," his actual desk, and some original manuscripts.

Research/Genealogy Department: The museum has a well-established research department that can help you trace your Swedish ancestry. Visitors are welcome to drop in and use databases independently for free or to reserve time in advance to get the assistance of a staff member (about 200 SEK/2 hours; book ahead online, open Mon-Fri 10:00-16:00, shorter hours off-season; they'll also answer specific genealogy questions via email—each inquiry about 400 SEK: emigrationsforskning@kulturparkensmaland.se).

Växjö Town Park (Växjö Stadspark)

Directly downhill from the House of Emigrants, you'll reach the big lake called **Växjösjön.** This is a fine place to relax with a picnic or go for a stroll. The town park features a pleasant three-mile path around the lake that takes you from manicured flower gardens through forested areas. The top part of the lake borders the inviting Linnéparken next to the cathedral (both described next).

A 10-minute walk around the top of the lake from the House of Emigrants is the town's modern **swimming hall** (*simhall*, 95-SEK base price includes sauna, 70 SEK before 15:00; extra fee to rent a towel or locker; family ticket available, call or check online for open-swim hours, +46 470 41204, www.medley.se/vaxjosimhall).

Växjö Cathedral (Växjö Domkyrka)

Växjö's striking red-orange brick church, with its distinctive double-needle steeple, features fine sacred art—in glass, of course. Its austere, bright-white interior is enlivened by gorgeous, colorful, and highly symbolic glass sculptures.

Cost and Hours: Free entry, daily 9:00-18:00.

Visiting the Cathedral: Near the entrance, pick up the brochure offering a detailed and evangelical self-guided tour. Near the back-left corner, the *Tree of Life and Knowledge* is a fantastically detailed candelabra. On one side, find Adam and Eve reaching for a very tempting apple with the clever snake egging them on from below. On the other side, Jesus and Mary welcome the faithful with arms outstretched. In similar opposition, the snake's tempting apple is suspended across from a bunch of grapes (symbolizing the wine of the Eucharist).

At the front of the church, the modern stone altar stands before a glass-decorated triptych, itself a subtle interplay of light and dark. Explore the other pieces of glass art around the church, and take in its trio of pipe organs.

Linnaeus Park (Linnéparken)

This peaceful park beside the cathedral is dedicated to the great Swedish botanist Carl von Linné (a.k.a. Carolus Linnaeus). It has an arboretum, lots of well-categorized perennials, a cactus garden, and a children's playground.

▲Storgatan

Strolling Växjö's main pedestrian shopping boulevard is a relaxing way to cap your visit. From the main square (with the TI), Storgatan stretches several blocks west. Walk the entire length of the street to observe small-town Sweden without any tourists. Imagine growing up or raising a family here in this friendly but traditional, pleasant but predictable community. A fine destination is the popular Askelyckan bakery and café, at #25 (see listing under "Eating in Växjö," later).

Sleeping in Växjö

If you're parking a car in Växjö, be sure to use the pay-and-display meters. Parking is free overnight from 18:00 until 9:00 the next morning.

$$$ PM & Vänner Hotel, with 74 stylish rooms and a recommended eatery, has a restful in-the-know vibe. Extras include free loaner bikes, a gym, and a pool, which shares the rooftop with an appealing bar/terrace (elevator, sauna, pay parking, centrally located at Västergatan 10, +46 470 759 700, www.pmhotel.se, reservations@pmhotel.se).

$$ Elite Stadshotell is a big, modern, business-class hotel with all the comforts in its 163 rooms. It's conveniently set on the town's main square and close to everything (loaner bikes, about a block from the train station at Kungsgatan 6, +46 470 13400, www.elite.se, info.vaxjo@elite.se).

$ Hotell Värend is friendly, comfortable, and inexpensive. It has 24 worn but workable rooms at the edge of a residential neighborhood six blocks from the train station along Kungsgatan (elevator, free parking, a block beyond N. Esplanaden at Kungsgatan 27, +46 470 776 700, mobile +46 76 769 0700, www.hotellvarend.se, info@hotellvarend.se).

$$ Hotel Esplanad offers 26 comfortable, fresh rooms, all with private bath (free parking, N. Esplanaden #21A, +46 470 22580, www.hotelesplanad.com, info@hotelesplanad.com). From the train station, walk five blocks up Klostergatan and turn left on N. Esplanaden.

¢ Hostel: Växjö's fine **Evedals Vandrarhem Hostel** (an old resort hotel) is near a lake three miles north of town (breakfast extra, sheets extra, confirm reception hours before you arrive, +46 470 63034, www.evedalscamping.com, info@evedalscamping.com). From Växjö's train station, catch bus #7 (about hourly, 15 minutes).

Eating in Växjö

The restaurant scene is picking up in sleepy Växjö, with a few memorable spots in the center. If you're looking to save money, or if it's a Sunday when many restaurants are closed, visit one of central Växjö's many Asian restaurants or kebab-and-pizza shops.

$$$$ PM & Vänner is a trendy eatery where a younger crowd stands in line to see and be seen. They have good international cuisine with Swedish flair, a mod black-and-white interior, and nice outdoor tables on the pedestrian mall. Their menu changes to feature seasonal and local ingredients (Mon-Sat 11:30-23:00, closed Sun, Storgatan 22 at corner of Västergatan, +46 470 759 710).

$$$$ Izakaya Moshi serves flavorful Japanese-style small plates (sushi, dumplings, salads, grilled fish, and meats) in an airy and light space. Choose from the long communal table, a cozy booth, or terrace seating when weather allows. Reservations are smart (Tue-Sat 17:00-21:00, closed Sun-Mon, immediately adjacent to the Smålands Museum at Södra Järnvägsgatan 2, +46 470 786 830, http://izakayamoshi.se).

$$$ Kafé De Luxe, about a block from the station, is a hip and funky hangout with live music many nights. They serve lunches and dinners daily—from burgers to *tarte flambée*—in a cozy Old World interior or under a happy tent outside (credit cards only, daily 11:30-24:00, Sandgärdsgatan 19, +46 470 740 409).

$$ Umami Monkey bills itself as having the "hippest burgers south of the North Pole"—and they just might be right. Their brioche-bun burgers pop with international flavors and come with great crispy fries (credit cards only, Mon-Fri 11:00-24:00, Sat from 12:00, closed Sun, Storgatan 18, +46 470 739 000).

$ Askelyckan Bakery/Café, with an inviting terrace under a tree by a fountain on the city's main commercial drag, is a delightful place for a drink, dessert, or light lunch on a sunny day (cakes, pastries, salads and sandwiches at lunch, Mon-Fri 8:00-18:00, Sat 9:00-16:30, Sun 11:00-16:00, Storgatan 25, +46 470 12311).

Groceries: Visit the **ICA supermarket** at the corner of Sandgärdsgatan and Klostergatan, one block from the train station (long hours daily).

Växjö Connections

From Växjö by Bus to: Kosta (2-4/day, 1 hour, bus #218 from Växjö bus station; for schedules see www.lanstrafikenkron.se).

By Train to: Copenhagen (hourly, 3 hours), **Stockholm** (about hourly, 3.5-4.5 hours, change in Alvesta), **Kalmar** (hourly, 70 minutes).

Glass Country

Filling the remote-feeling woods between Växjö and Kalmar with busy glassmaking workshops, Sweden's famous Glasriket ("Kingdom of Crystal") is worth ▲▲ for those with a car. There's something deeply pleasing about a visit to a glassworks *(glasbruk).* Even at the bigger places—and especially at the smaller ones—you'll feel genuine artistic energy at work as skilled craftspeople persuade glowing globs of molten glass to take shape.

The rich natural environment of this area, with inviting forests and lakes all around, has been fundamental to the glassworks (they needed a lot of wood to keep those fires going) and the region's other product, paper (small papermaking mills relied on plentiful water to wash cotton fiber to create paper pulp).

Visiting a glassworks is usually free. At most places, it's possible to walk through the hot shop *(hytta),* observe glassblowers in action, and feel the heat from glowing furnaces. Most glassworks also have a shop/gallery displaying and selling pieces produced on-site.

The glassworks listed here are a representative mix of the dozen or so you can visit in Glass Country, ranging from charming artistic workshops to big corporate factories. On the corporate side, Kosta Boda dominates; its flagship complex is the biggest of all the glassworks, and they offer guided tours. But there are many smaller, independent producers, where you can get a more intimate view of the process.

Besides the tradition of hand-crafted glass, the region sustains the only surviving hand papermaking workshop in all of Scandinavia, in the town of Lessebo. It's well worth a visit.

For a complete change of pace, check out the local moose population (you can visit them at the Moose and Farm Animal Park just outside Kosta).

PLANNING YOUR TIME

The glassworks are best reached with a car. Travelers without a car can get a taste of Glass Country at Växjö's Swedish Glass Museum or by taking a bus from Växjö to Kosta to visit the Kosta Boda complex (see "Växjö Connections," earlier).

With a car, this region is a joy—it's small (Kalmar to Växjö is 70 miles), with light traffic and endless forest-and-lake scenery punctuated by numerous glassworks. Most are clustered in the center of the region, and while it would take the better part of a day to visit them all, distances are short and roads are good. Still, it's smart to be selective. On a tight schedule, I'd visit the Glass Factory and Transjö Hytta, possibly Kosta Boda and Bergdala, and the Lessebo paper mill, skipping the rest.

Planning Tips: Pick up a map of the region and the *Glasriket/Kingdom of Crystal* magazine from the TI in Växjö or Kalmar. The region's official website (www.glasriket.se) describes the many glassworks that welcome the public.

Note that many workshops take a lunch break sometime between 11:00 and 12:00, and stop work entirely after about 15:00 or 15:30. Most glassworks are open daily in July and August—but some glassblowers take the summer off. Check ahead to be sure the shop you want to visit will be open and glassblowers will be on view. Hours are always subject to change at the smaller places, but they welcome a phone call to confirm open times.

Gas up before you head out; there are few services in Glass Country.

GLASS COUNTRY DRIVING ROUTE

Drivers coming from Kalmar can follow the plan outlined here (if you are approaching Glass Country from Copenhagen, this route can be easily reversed): Head west on highway 25, following signs for *Växjö*; the village of Boda and its Glass Factory museum *(glasmuseum)* are your first stop. From Boda, head north to Orrefors and Orranäs Bruk. From there, proceed west on highway 31 and turn left at the sign for Lessebo and Kosta. At the intersection with highway 28, you'll find the big Kosta Boda glassworks. From there, detour south to Transjö for the best of the smaller, artsy glassworks, or continue on to Lessebo and the paper workshop. It's a straight shot from there on highway 25 to Växjö; along the way, you can visit the Bergdala glassworks (look for the Bergdala turnoff sign).

Sights in Glass Country

GLASSWORKS

These are listed in the order you'll reach them traveling from Kalmar to Växjö.

▲Glass Factory

When glass producers fell on hard times in the 1980s and 1990s, many shops either folded or consolidated. The glass workshop in the little village of Boda was one such casualty, but the municipality came together to buy its glass archive, an amazing record of artistic achievement. It's now on display in the Glass Factory museum, located in the former glass production workshop. There's also a modern hot shop with regular demonstrations, a gallery of more recent Boda glass, and an affordable shop that sells glasswork from all over Scandinavia.

Cost and Hours: 80 SEK, late April-early Sept Mon-Fri 10:00-17:00, Sat-Sun from 11:00; off-season Sat-Sun only 11:00-16:00; in Boda at Storgotan 5, well-signed just off highway 25, +46 471 249 360, www.theglassfactory.se.

Orranäs Bruk

The town of Orrefors once had a major glassworks with its own proud history, but glass is no longer commercially produced there. The once sought-after Orrefors art glass is now just a stepchild of Kosta Boda and mostly machine-made abroad. With its glassworks shuttered in 2012, Orrefors became a ghost town.

But concerned locals are blowing life back into the town and its glass heritage. Starting with an **open-air hot shop** that's operating in a park near the old shop, their project is unfolding in stages over several years. They've already reintroduced art-glass production to the town and are selling it under the name Orranäs Bruk.

Meanwhile, the town's dazzling **glass museum** continues to display its historic art pieces, from early 20th-century examples with Art Nouveau flair through works from the 1940s (www.orreforsmuseum.se).

Cost and Hours: Free, hot shop and glass museum July-Aug daily 10:00-17:00, generally closed Sun-Mon rest of year; just off highway 31 in Orrefors—follow *Orrefors Park* signs; +46 735 358 358, www.orranasglasbruk.se.

▲▲Transjö Hytta

Set up in an old converted farm 10 minutes south of Kosta, this tiny, friendly glassworks creates high-quality fine-art pieces. From the main shop, a canal-like stream (enlivened with colorful glass art baubles) leads back to the hopping hot shop. Transjö—started by a pair of highly regarded glass designers—employs up-and-

coming artists as apprentices, and their youthful vigor is infectious. You can feel the art oozing out of the ovens. The hot shop closes from July through December, but even if you don't catch the artists in action here, the setting is charming.

The gift shop out front sells a fine selection of one-of-a-kind glass art and limited-run items made on-site (the *elevarbete*/apprentice works are cheaper). The shop keeps routine hours, but if you find it closed, dial the phone numbers posted on the door and someone will let you in.

Cost and Hours: Free, shop usually open early June-mid-Sept daily 9:00-17:00; hot shop hours irregular, closed July-Dec, smart to call or email ahead; +46 478 50700, www.transjohytta.com, info@transjohytta.com. To find it, look for *Transjö* signs just south of Kosta.

▲▲Kosta Boda

The village of Kosta boasts the oldest of the *glasbruks,* dating back to 1742. Today, the Kosta Boda cam-

pus includes a modern outlet mall, a factory store, a fancy new art hotel... and, of course, the glassworks.

The highlight here is watching the **glassworks** in action. Visitors are welcomed to the hot-shop floor, where a team of glassblowers rotates through a carefully choreographed routine: grabbing a glob of molten glass on the blow pipe, rolling it on a steel table into a general shape, then turning and blowing the piece into its final form. You can visit the glassworks and its gallery on your own, but it's worth calling or emailing ahead to reserve a spot on a 30-minute English tour.

Glassmaking in Sweden

In the mid-16th century, King Gustav Vasa decided he wanted more fine glass to decorate his palace, so he invited German glassmakers to train his subjects, and the trend took off. It's no surprise that glassmaking caught on here in Sweden. The resources needed for glass are abundant: vast forests to fire the ovens, and lakes with an endless supply of sand. By the difficult 19th century—when a sixth of Sweden's population emigrated to North America—the iron mills had closed, leaving behind unemployed workers who were highly skilled at working with materials at high temperatures. Glassmaking was their salvation, and by the early 1900s, this region had more than 100 glassworks.

While glassmaking was important throughout Sweden, it was in the dense forest between Växjö and Kalmar that it took hold most strongly and lasted the longest. When other materials (like paper cartons) became cheaper than glass, the industry was hit hard. It dried up in other parts of Sweden, but here in Glass Country, workers refocused their efforts, shifting from everyday items to high-quality pieces that command top kronor. An Ikea wine glass made in China costs 10 SEK, while a handmade Swedish one might cost 150 SEK—but consumers interested in quality are willing to pay that premium.

The glassmaking process is fascinating—and hasn't changed much over the centuries. If you visit a hot shop, you'll see both everyday tableware and art pieces being created. "Mass-produced" pieces, such as wine glasses, are created by small teams of glassblowers who use an assembly-line system to produce a uniform product. Art-glass pieces, however, are never the same. The region has a passel of big-name designers, each with their own aesthetic.

In the surprisingly modest **art gallery,** high-end pieces are exhibited and often offered for sale.

Cost and Hours: Free, glassworks—usually open daily 11:00-17:00 (lunch break 10:30-11:30), shorter hours off-season; gallery—daily 11:00-17:00; www.kostaboda.se.

Tours: 100 SEK, usually 3/day in English, but best to arrange ahead by phone (+46 478 34529) or email (info@kostaboda.se).

Shopping: In the Kosta **factory outlet shop,** crystal "seconds" (with tiny bubbles or sets that don't quite match) and discontinued pieces are sold at good prices. This is duty-free shopping, and they'll

Either way, the process is the same. First, a worker places the glassblowing rod into the furnace (notice the foot pedals used to open and close the doors) and grabs a blob of molten glass. Glassblowers have to move quickly—before the glass hardens too much—but deliberately, to avoid shattering the medium or burning their colleagues. After rolling the glass out to its desired shape on a heat-resistant table, they blow into the end of the rod to open a space inside. If creating a mass-produced item, they generally stick it into a mold to ensure the correct dimensions. If making a wineglass with a stem and foot, separate pieces of glass are stretched out to the appropriate shape and attached.

For this entire process, the glass is at about 2,100 degrees Fahrenheit. If it gets too hot, glassblowers cool it down with water or air; if the glass needs to be reheated, they use a blowtorch or poke it back into the furnace. Finally, the area where the glass was attached to the rod is cut with an industrial diamond, broken off, and ground and polished smooth. The finished piece is set in a special oven to cool gradually.

At the workday's end, the raw materials for the next day's glass are dumped into giant, custom-made clay pots and placed in the ovens. Overnight, these will gradually melt down to the molten medium the glassblowers will need the next morning.

Only the best pieces are deemed "first quality" (1:A Sortering)—you'll pay a premium for these flawless items. Some items, deemed "second quality" (2:A Sortering), have minor imperfections that bring the price down substantially. When shopping, pay close attention to these labels; if you don't need your glass perfect, you can save by looking for second quality.

happily mail your purchases home (daily 10:00-18:00). Don't confuse this with the big outlet mall across the street.

Sleeping and Eating: The **$ cafeteria** inside the outlet mall features thrifty lunch specials. Nearby is the pricey **$$$$ Kosta Boda Art Hotel,** designed to impress. Everything's decorated to the hilt with (of course) artistic glass, created in the hot shop across the street. With Växjö and Kalmar so close, there's little reason to sleep here (+46 478 34830, www.kostabodaarthotel. se). But if you have a few extra minutes, poke around this over-the-top, world-of-glass complex, which includes a "glass bar," a mind-bending indoor swimming pool, and a restaurant where, on most evenings, you can watch a glassblower at work while you dine.

▲Bergdala Glassworks (Bergdalahyttan)

The small, independent Bergdala glassworks, in a village of the same name, has an enjoyably artsy hot shop. Its well-stocked shop is full of its affordable trademark blue-rimmed glassware, and the engaging "museum" around back shows off a different sampling of local artists every year.

Cost and Hours: Free, gallery/shop open daily mid-May–mid-Aug 10:00-16:00, shorter hours off-season; glassblowing Mon-Fri 7:30-15:30 (lunch break 11:00-12:00); off highway #25 near Hovmantorp, +46 478 31650, www.bergdalahyttan.se.

OTHER ATTRACTIONS
▲▲Lessebo Paper Workshop (Handpappersbruket)

Tucked just outside the gates of Lessebo's industrial-scale paper mill is a smaller stone building that's well worth a visit. It's home to an artisan workshop where paper is made by hand, using strictly traditional methods (the newest piece of machinery is from the 1920s). The Lessebo workshop is a study in the way things used to be: Cotton fibers are soaked until they become pulp, packed into a frame, pressed, dried, glazed, and hand-torn into the perfect size and shape.

This paper has long been coveted throughout Sweden for special purposes: top-of-the-line stationery (for wedding invitations), impossible-to-forge embossed document paper (for certificates or important examinations), and long-lasting archival use (the cotton fibers ensure the paper will stay pristine for decades).

You can visit the excellent gift shop on your own (watercolor paper, stationery, and cards), but to see papermaking in action, plan to join one of the fascinating 45-minute English tours. It's a rare opportunity to witness a centuries-old craft up close and personal.

Cost and Hours: 95-SEK tour tickets available online and at the door; tours run May-Sept Mon-Sat at 13:00 and Sun at 15:00—confirm times before showing up; gift shop and café open daily year-round (10:00-17:00 in summer); look for *Handpappersbruk* sign on highway 25, Storgatan 79, +46 478 77 0010, https://lessebohandpappersbruk.se.

Grönåsen Moose and Farm Animal Park (Grönåsen Älg- & Lantdjurspark)

This offbeat attraction, just outside Kosta, demonstrates the love-hate relationship Swedes feel toward their moose population. A third of a million of these giant, majes-

tic beasts live in Sweden. They're popular with hunters but unpopular with drivers. At this attraction, you'll walk through the moose-happy gift shop before taking a mile-long stroll around the perimeter of a pen holding live moose. Periodic museum exhibits—life-size dioramas with stuffed moose (including one plastered to the hood of a car)—round out the attraction. You can even buy moose sausage to grill on-site. Sure it's a hokey roadside stop, and will hardly be a hit with animal-rights activists, but for many the park is an enjoyable stop.

Cost and Hours: 120 SEK, daily 11:00-16:00, July-Aug until 17:00, closed Nov-May, just outside Kosta on the road to Orrefors, +46 478 50770, www.gronasen.se.

Eating in Glass Country

You'll find a few simple eateries scattered around the area, with the most choices concentrated around the big Kosta Boda complex, where the cafeteria in the outlet mall is the perfect place for fast and cheap, Ikea-style Swedish grub.

If you'd like to linger over a more serious dinner, consider joining one of the special **hyttsill dinners** offered at various glass workshops. Traditionally, a hot shop's fires made it a popular place to convene after hours on frigid winter nights. People would huddle around the ovens and be entertained by wandering minstrel-type entertainers called *luffar*. The food was nothing special (*hyttsill* literally means "hot-shop herring," usually served with crispy pork, potatoes, and other stick-to-your-ribs fare), but it was a nice opportunity for a convivial rural community to get together. Today modern glassworks carry on the tradition, inviting tourists on several nights through the summer. They usually have live music and glassblowers working while you dine (figure around 400 SEK per person; for more information, see www.glasriket.se).

FINLAND

FINLAND

Suomi

Finland is a fun, fascinating, overlooked corner of Europe, with a small population filling a sprawling, rocky, forested land that shares a long border with Russia. The Finns have often been overshadowed by their powerful neighbors, the Swedes and the Russians. And yet, they've persevered magnificently, with good humor, a zest for architecture and design, a deep love of saunas, and an understandable pride in things that are uniquely Finnish.

Technically Finland is Nordic, rather than Scandinavian. The Scandinavian countries—Denmark, Sweden, and Norway—are constitutional monarchies with closely related languages. Add Iceland and Finland—republics that are former Danish or Swedish colonies—and you have the Nordic countries.

For much of their history, the Finns embraced a simple agrarian and fishing lifestyle. They built not cities, but villages—easy pickings for their more ambitious neighbors. From medieval times to 1809, Finland was part of Sweden; today it still has a sizeable Swedish-speaking minority, bilingual street signs, and close cultural ties to Sweden.

In 1809, Sweden lost Finland to Russia. Under the next century of relatively benign Russian rule, the Grand Duchy of Finland began to industrialize, and Helsinki grew into a fine and elegant city. Still, at the beginning of the 1900s, the rest of Finland was mostly dirt-poor and agricultural, and its people were eagerly emigrating to northern Minnesota. (Read Toivo Pekkanen's *My Childhood* to learn about the life of a Finnish peasant in the early 1900s.)

Finland and the Baltic states (Estonia, Latvia, and Lithuania) won their independence from Russia in 1917; this was followed by brief but vicious civil wars against domestic pro-Russian factions. After this period, Finland enjoyed two decades of prosperity...until the

FINLAND

secret Nazi-Soviet pact of August 1939 assigned it to the Soviet sphere of influence. When the Red Army invaded, white-camouflaged Finnish ski troops fought back, winning the Winter War (1939-1940). They then held off the Soviets in what's called the Continuation War from 1941 until 1944, when the exhausted and outgunned Finns finally agreed to a ceasefire.

After World War II, Finland was made to suffer for having allied itself for a time with Nazi Germany and for having fought against one of the Allied Powers. As reparations, the Finns ceded Karelia (eastern Finland) and part of Lapland to the USSR, accepted a Soviet naval base on Finnish territory, and paid huge sums to the Soviet government.

In the ensuing Cold War era, Finland maintained a position of friendly neutrality toward its powerful neighbor to the east. Still, Finland's bold, trendsetting modern design and architecture blossomed, and it built up successful timber, paper, and electronics industries. All through the Cold War, Finland teetered between the West and the Soviet Union, trying to be part of Western Europe's strong economy while making nice with the Soviets.

The collapse of the Soviet Union freed Finland from Moscow's menace, but took with it 20 percent of Finland's trade. After a few years of adjustment, Finland bounced back strongly, joining the European Union and adopting the euro currency. In earlier years, Finns would move to Sweden (where they are still the biggest immigrant group), looking for better jobs. But now Finland is among

FINLAND

Finland Almanac

Official Name: Republic of Finland.

Size: At 130,558 square miles, Finland is about the size of Washington state and Oregon combined. It's home to 5.5 million people (42 per square mile).

Geography: Finland is bordered by Russia to the east, Sweden and Norway to the north, the Baltic Sea to the west, and Estonia (across the Gulf of Finland) to the south. Much of Finland is flat and covered with forests, with the Lapland region extending north of the Arctic Circle. Finland is home to 187,800 lakes and 179,500 islands.

Latitude and Longitude: 64°N and 26°E, similar latitude to Nome, Alaska.

Biggest City: The capital city, Helsinki, has a population of 648,000; 1.3 million people—about one in four Finns—live in the Helsinki urban area.

Economy: Finland's gross domestic product is $270 billion and its per-capita GDP is $48,685. Manufacturing, timber, engineering, electronics, and telecommunications are its chief industries.

Currency: €0.85 = about $1.

Government: Finland is a parliamentary republic. It has both a president, responsible for foreign policy, and a prime minister, who, along with the 200-member Parliament (Eduskunta), is responsible for domestic legislation. Members of Parliament sit for four-year terms.

Flag: White with a blue Scandinavian cross, representing winter snow and lakes.

The Average Finn is 43 years old, has 1.75 children, will live to be 81, and drinks a lot of *kahvi*—Finland leads the world in per-capita coffee consumption nearly every year.

the most technologically advanced countries in Europe (it's the headquarters of the giant telecommunications company Nokia), and its talented young people are more likely to seek their fortunes at home.

Ninety percent of Finland's population is of Finnish descent. Other ethnicities include Swedish (5 percent), Russian, Estonian, Roma, and Sami. The country is about 70 percent Lutheran, 1 percent Orthodox, 2 percent other Christian, and 27 percent unaffiliated.

When it comes to gender equality, Finland is a pioneer. In 1906, Finnish women were the first in Europe to vote. The country named its first female president in 2000 and its first female prime minister in 2003. As of 2019, Finnish government was well represented by women: Sanna Marin became prime minister at the age of 34, and nearly 50 percent of its parliament was composed of women.

Finland is officially bilingual; while 87 percent of residents speak Finnish, about 5 percent speak Swedish as a first language (and small minorities speak Sami and Russian). You'll notice that Helsinki is called *Helsingfors* in Swedish. Helsinki's street signs list places in both Finnish and Swedish. Nearly every educated young person speaks effortless English—the language barrier is just a speed bump.

Finnish is a difficult-to-learn language whose only relatives in Europe are Estonian (close) and Hungarian (distant). The only essential word needed for a quick visit is *kiitos* (KEE-tohs)—that's "thank you," and locals love to hear it. *Hei* (hey) means "hi" and *hei hei* (hey hey) means "goodbye." *Kippis* (KIHP-pihs) is what you say before you down a shot of Finnish vodka or cloudberry liqueur *(lakka)*. For more, see the Finnish survival phrases on the next page.

FINLAND

Finnish Survival Phrases

In Finnish, the emphasis always goes on the first syllable. Double vowels (e.g., ää or ii) sound similar to single vowels, but are held a bit longer. The letter y sounds like the German ü (purse your lips and say "oh"). In the phonetics, ī sounds like the long i in "light," and bolded syllables are stressed.

Good morning. (formal)	Hyvää huomenta.	**hew**-vaah **hwoh**-mehn-tah
Good day. (formal)	Hyvää päivää.	**hew**-vaah **pī**-vaah
Good evening. (formal)	Hyvää iltaa.	**hew**-vaah **eel**-taah
Hi. / Bye. (informal)	Hei. / Hei hei.	hey / hey hey
Do you speak English?	Puhutko englantia? **poo**-hoot-koh **ehn**-glahn-tee-yah	
Yes. / No.	Kyllä. / Ei.	**kewl**-lah / ay
Please.	Ole hyvä.	**oh**-leh **hew**-vah
Thank you (very much).	Kiitos (paljon).	**kee**-tohs (**pahl**-yohn)
You're welcome.	Kiitos. / Ei kestä.	**kee**-tohs / ay **kehs**-tah
Can I help you?	Voinko auttaa?	**voin**-koh **owt**-taah
Excuse me.	Anteeksi.	**ahn**-tehk-see
(Very) good.	(Oikein) hyvä.	(**oy**-kayn) **hew**-vah
Goodbye.	Näkemiin.	**nah**-keh-meen
zero / one / two	nolla / yksi / kaksi	**noh**-lah / **ewk**-see / **kahk**-see
three / four	kolme / neljä	**kohl**-meh / **nehl**-yah
five / six	viisi / kuusi	**vee**-see / **koo**-see
seven / eight	seitsemän / kahdeksan **sayt**-seh-mahn / **kah**-dehk-sahn	
nine / ten	yhdeksän / kymmenen **ew**-dehk-sahn / **kewm**-meh-nehn	
hundred	sata	**sah**-tah
thousand	tuhat	**too**-haht
How much?	Paljonko?	**pahl**-yohn-koh
local currency: euro	euro	**ay**-oo-roh
Where is...?	Missä on...?	**mee**-sah ohn
...the toilet	...WC	**vay**-say
men	miehet	**mee**-ay-heht
women	naiset	**nī**-seht
water / coffee	vesi / kahvi	**veh**-see / **kah**-vee
beer / wine	olut / viini	**oh**-luht / **vee**-nee
Cheers!	Kippis!	**kip**-pis
The bill, please.	Lasku, kiitos.	**lahs**-koo **kee**-tohs

HELSINKI

The Finnish capital (Europe's youngest) feels like an outpost of the Nordic and European worlds—it's both the northernmost capital of the EU, and a short train ride from Russia. Yet against all odds, this quirky metropolis thrives, pleasing locals and tickling tourists. While it lacks the cutesy cobbles of Copenhagen, the dramatic setting of Stockholm, or the futuristic vibe of Oslo, Helsinki holds its own among Nordic capitals with its appealing Finnish personality. It's a spruce-and-stone wonderland of stunning 19th- to 21st-century architecture, with a bustling harborfront market, a lively main boulevard, fine museums, a sophisticated design culture, dueling cathedrals (Lutheran and Orthodox), a quirky east-meets-west mélange of cultures...and a welcoming Finnish spirit that ties it all together.

Gusting winds swirl crying seagulls against a perfectly azure sky scattered with cotton-ball clouds. Rock bands and folk-dancing troupes enliven the Esplanade from the stage in front of Café Kappeli, sunny days lure coffee sippers out onto the sidewalks, and joyous festivals fill the summer (when the sky still glimmers after midnight). And in this country renowned for design, window-shopping the Design District can turn browsers into buyers of home decor, clever kitchen gadgets, handmade jewelry, and unique clothes with a Finnish accent.

While budget flights affordably connect Helsinki to the other Scandinavian capitals (and beyond), for many travelers, the next best thing to being in Helsinki is getting there on Europe's most enjoyable overnight boat. The trip from Stockholm starts with dramatic archipelago scenery, a setting sun, and a royal smorgasbord dinner. Dance until you drop and sauna until you drip. Budget travel rarely feels this hedonistic. Seventeen hours after you depart, it's "Hello Helsinki."

PLANNING YOUR TIME

Helsinki is worth at least two nights and a full day. To do the city justice, two days is ideal (or use one of the days for a side trip to Tallinn, Estonia).

For a quick one-day visit, start with the two-hour "Helsinki Panorama" orientation bus tour (see "Tours in Helsinki," later). Then follow my self-guided Helsinki Walk through the compact city center from the harbor—enjoying the ruddy harborfront market and getting goose bumps in the churches—ending near the underground Temppeliaukio Church.

With more time, explore the Design District, dive into Finnish culture in the open-air folk museum, or take a walk in Kaivopuisto Park. If the weather's good, head for Suomenlinna, the island fortress where Helsinki was born. If it's bad, go for a sauna. Make time to enjoy a cup of coffee at the landmark Café Kappeli.

For details on getting to or from Helsinki by boat from Stockholm or (more quickly) from Tallin, see "Helsinki Connections," near the end of this chapter.

Orientation to Helsinki

Helsinki (pop. 648,000) has a compact core. The city's natural gateway is South Harbor, where ships from Stockholm and Tallinn dock. At the top of the harbor is Market Square (Kauppatori), an outdoor food and souvenir bazaar. Nearby are two towering, can't-miss-them landmarks: the white Lutheran Cathedral and the red-brick Orthodox Cathedral.

Helsinki's grand pedestrian boulevard, the Esplanade, begins right at Market Square, heads up past Café Kappeli, and ends after a few blocks in the central shopping district. At the top end of the Esplanade, the broad, traffic-filled Mannerheimintie avenue veers north through town past the train and bus stations on its way

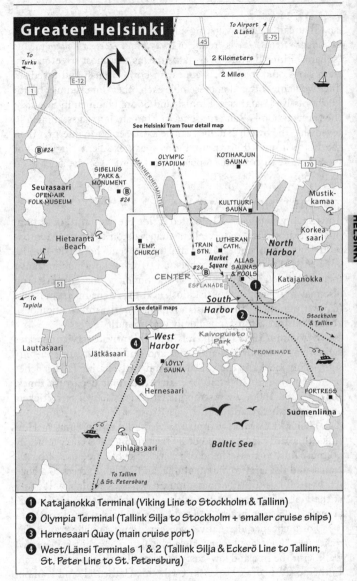

Greater Helsinki

To Airport & Lahti

To Turku

2 Kilometers
2 Miles

See Helsinki Tram Tour detail map

OLYMPIC STADIUM

KOTIHARJUN SAUNA

MANNERHEIMINTIE

Ⓑ #24

SIBELIUS PARK & MONUMENT

Seurasaari
OPEN-AIR FOLK MUSEUM

Ⓑ #24

KULTTUURI-SAUNA

Mustik-kamaa

Korkea-saari

Hietaranta Beach

TEMP. CHURCH

TRAIN STN.

LUTHERAN CATH.

North Harbor

Market Square

ALLAS SAUNAS & POOLS

Katajanokka

CENTER

Ⓑ #24

ESPLANADE

To Tapiola

See detail maps

South Harbor

To Stockholm & Tallinn

Ⓐ

Ⓑ

West Harbor

Kaivopuisto Park

PROMENADE

Lauttasaari

Jätkäsaari

LÖYLY SAUNA

FORTRESS

Ⓒ

Hernesaari

Suomenlinna

To Tallinn & St. Petersburg

Baltic Sea

Pihlajasaari

Ⓐ Katajanokka Terminal (Viking Line to Stockholm & Tallinn)
Ⓑ Olympia Terminal (Tallink Silja to Stockholm + smaller cruise ships)
Ⓒ Hernesaari Quay (main cruise port)
Ⓓ West/Länsi Terminals 1 & 2 (Tallink Silja & Eckerö Line to Tallinn; St. Peter Line to St. Petersburg)

HELSINKI

to many of Helsinki's museums and architectural landmarks. For a do-it-yourself orientation along this route, follow my Helsinki Walk, later. And for a good drive-by introduction to some sights and outlying neighborhoods that most tourists miss, hop on a tram (see my "Helsinki Tram Tour," later).

Linguistic Orientation: Finnish is completely different from the Scandinavian languages of Norwegian, Danish, and Swed-

ish. That can make navigating a bit tricky. Place names ending in
-*katu* are streets, -*tie* is "road" or "way," and -*tori* or -*aukio* means
"square." Finland's bilingual status means that most street names,
tram stops, and map labels appear in both Finnish and Swedish.
The two names often don't resemble each other (for example, South
Harbor is Eteläsatama in Finnish and Södra Hamnen in Swedish;
the train station is Rautatieasema in Finnish, Järnvägsstationen in
Swedish). The Swedish names can be a little easier to interpret than
the Finnish ones. Plus, most Finns speak excellent English. For
more help with common topographical words, see the sidebar on
page 736.

TOURIST INFORMATION

The friendly, energetic **TI,** located inside the central train station,
offers great service and excellent materials on the city (Mon-Sat
9:00-18:00, Sun until 16:00, shorter weekend hours off-season,
+358 9 3101 3300, www.myhelsinki.fi). Pick up a public-transit
map and a detailed pamphlet on the Suomenlinna Fortress. You
also may find a pop-up tourist kiosk near the Ateneum art museum
(daily in summer). There's also a regional tourist information desk
at the Helsinki airport (open daily year-round).

Strömma/Sightseeing Helsinki: This private service operates
sightseeing tours by bus and boat, and staffs small, summer-only
sightseeing kiosks on the Esplanade and by the harbor (all branches
open Mon-Sat 10:30-14:30 or matched to tour departure times,
+358 9 2288 1600, www.stromma.fi). They also sell ferry tickets
and the Helsinki Card.

Helsinki Card: If you plan to visit a lot of museums in Helsinki, this card can be a good deal. The card includes entry to nearly
30 museums, fortresses, and other major sights; free use of buses,
trams, and the ferry to Suomenlinna; and 24-hour access to a hop-
on, hop-off bus (€51/24 hours, multiday passes available). It's sold
at the Helsinki airport at the Airpro Travel Service in terminal 2,
at most downtown hotels, and online (www.helsinkicard.com).

For a cheaper alternative, you could buy a public-transit day
ticket (see "Getting Around Helsinki," later), take my self-guided
walk, visit the free and low-cost churches (Temppeliaukio Church,
Lutheran Cathedral, Uspenski Orthodox Cathedral, and Kamppi
Chapel), and stop by the free Helsinki City Museum.

ARRIVAL IN HELSINKI

By Boat: For details on arriving in Helsinki by boat, how to reach
the Old Town from the various terminals, and taking an overnight
boat to Helsinki, see "Helsinki Connections—By Boat," near the
end of this chapter.

By Train and Bus: The central train station, an architectural landmark, is near the top of the Esplanade, a 15-minute walk from Market Square. Local buses leave from both sides of the building, trams stop out front, and the Metro runs underneath. The long-distance bus station is two blocks (or one tram

stop) away, at the Kamppi shopping mall on the other side of Mannerheimintie; the ticket office and machines are on the ground floor, with bus platforms below.

By Plane: Helsinki Airport (Helsinki-Vantaa) is about 10 miles north of the city (code: HEL, www.helsinki-vantaa.fi). Local **trains** I and P run from the airport to the central rail station in about 30 minutes (€4.10, access tracks from the corridor between terminals 1 and 2; buy ticket from machines on platform—credit card only).

Several **buses** run from the airport to the train station. Consider the Finnair bus (€6.90, 3/hour, 35 minutes, www.finnair. com; stops at some downtown hotels on request; return buses leave for airport from platform 30 at Elielinaukio on west side of train station) or public bus #615 (€4.10, not covered by transit tickets or Helsinki Card, 3-6/hour, 45 minutes; buy via HSL app or HSL ticket machine, or pay driver; return buses leave for airport from platform 3 at Rautatientori on east side of train station).

Other options include Yellow Line's door-to-door shared **van service** (€35/1-3 people, €41/4-8 people, +358 10 00700, book online in advance at www.yellowline.fi) or a **taxi** (about €45).

HELPFUL HINTS

Time: Finland and Estonia are one hour ahead of Sweden and the rest of Scandinavia.

Money: Finland's currency is the euro. ATM machines are labeled *Otto.*

Pharmacy: A convenient pharmacy *(apteekki)* is **Erottajan,** on the basement level of Stockmann department store (similar hours as store, Mannerheimintie 1, +358 9 622 9930).

Laundry: On the seventh floor of the Stockmann department store, **Sol** has reasonably priced drop-off/pickup service (similar hours as store, Aleksanterinkatu 52, +358 40 779 7222).

Bike Rental: Helsinki's **HSL** transit company has bike stations throughout the city. Buy a pass and register online to receive an ID and PIN for picking up your bike from any station. Passes are sold by the day and the week, and include up to

HELSINKI

30 minutes of riding time per bike—but you can keep it and pay more for a longer ride. Convenient bike station locations include Kamppi shopping center, Market Square, the train station, and near the Esplanade (24-hour pass-€5, one-week pass-€10; bike station maps and more info at www.hsl.fi/en/citybikes).

Best View: The **Torni Tower Ateljée Bar** offers a free panorama view. Ride the elevator from the lobby of the venerable Torni Hotel (built in 1931) to the 12th floor, where you can browse around the perch or sit down for a pricey drink (daily 14:00-24:00, Yrjönkatu 26—for location, see the "Helsinki Hotels & Restaurants" map, later, tel. +358 20 123 4604).

Meet the Finns: With **Cozy Finland**'s "Meet the Finns" program, you can match your hobbies with a local—and suddenly, you're searching out classic comics at the flea market with a new Finnish friend. Their most popular service involves arranging dinner at a local host's home (around €60; www.cosyfinland.com).

What's With the Slot Machines? Finns have a love affair with lotteries and petty gambling. You'll see coin-operated games of chance everywhere, including restaurants, supermarkets, and the train station.

GETTING AROUND HELSINKI

Helsinki is compact, but public transportation can be useful for certain trips. Helsinki's **buses** and **trams** are easy—you just need the public-transit route map (available at the TI or view at www.hsl.fi). The handy **ferry** from Market Square to Suomenlinna Fortress is part of the system, as is the single **Metro** line (although the Metro is not useful for most visitors).

Tickets: Single tickets are good for 80 minutes of bus or tram travel (€2.80 on the HSL app or at HSL ticket machines at some bus and tram stops, €4 from driver—cash only). A day ticket (€8/24 hours of unlimited travel, issued on a plastic card you'll tap against a card reader when boarding the bus or tram) pays for itself if you take four or more rides; longer versions are also available (7-day maximum). Day tickets can be bought via the HSL app, at ubiquitous yellow-and-blue R-Kiosks (convenience stores), as well as at TIs, the train station, Metro stations, ticket machines at a handful of stops, and on some ferries (but not from drivers). The Helsinki Card also covers public transportation. These tickets and cards are only valid within the city of Helsinki (zones A and B), not the suburbs; for example, you'll pay separately for the public bus to the airport.

Tours in Helsinki

The big company Strömma (also called Sightseeing Helsinki) has a near monopoly on city tours, whether by bus, boat, or foot. For a fun, cheap tour, use my self-guided "Helsinki Tram Tour" (described later and rated ▲▲) to pass by many of the town's major sights in an hour.

▲▲▲Orientation Bus Tours

These two-hour "Helsinki Panorama" bus tours give an ideal city overview with a look at all of the important buildings, from the Olympic Stadium to Embassy Row. You stay on the bus the entire time, except for a 10-minute stop or two (when possible, they try to stop at the Sibelius Monument and/or Temppeliaukio Church). You'll learn strange facts, such as how Finns took down the highest steeple in town during World War II so that Soviet bombers flying

Helsinki at a Glance

Central Helsinki

▲▲▲Temppeliaukio Church Awe-inspiring, copper-topped 1969 "Church in the Rock." **Hours:** Mon-Sat 10:00-19:00, Sun 12:00-18:00, closes one hour earlier Oct-May. See page 613.

▲▲Uspenski Orthodox Cathedral Orthodoxy's most prodigious display outside of Eastern Europe. **Hours:** Tue-Fri 9:30-16:00, Sat 10:00-15:00, Sun 12:00-15:00, closed Mon. See page 607.

▲▲Lutheran Cathedral Green-domed, 19th-century Neoclassical masterpiece. **Hours:** Daily 9:00-18:00, until 24:00 in summer. See page 608.

▲Ateneum Largest collection of art in Finland, with local favorites plus works by Cézanne, Chagall, Gauguin, and Van Gogh. **Hours:** Tue and Fri 10:00-18:00, Wed-Thu until 20:00, Sat-Sun until 17:00, closed Mon. See page 609.

▲Kamppi Chapel Small, modern wooden chapel offers a moment of serenity in the city. **Hours:** Mon-Fri 8:00-20:00, Sat-Sun 10:00-18:00. See page 610.

▲National Museum of Finland The history of Finland, from prehistory through the 20th century. **Hours:** Tue-Sun 11:00-18:00, Wed until 20:00, closed Mon. See page 613.

▲Sibelius Monument Hundreds of stainless-steel organ pipes form an abstract tribute to Finnish composer Jean Sibelius. See page 614.

▲Design Museum A chronological look at Finland's impressive design pedigree, plus cutting-edge temporary exhibits. **Hours:** Daily 11:00-18:00; Sept-May Wed-Sun 11:00-18:00, Tue until 20:00, closed Mon. See page 615.

Outer Helsinki

▲▲Suomenlinna Fortress Helsinki's harbor island, sprinkled with picnic spots, museums, and military history. **Hours:** Museum daily 10:00-18:00, Oct-April until 16:00. See page 616.

▲▲Seurasaari Open-Air Folk Museum Island museum with 100 historic buildings from Finland's farthest corners. **Hours:** June-Aug daily 11:00-17:00. shorter hours May and Sept, buildings closed Oct-April. See page 619.

in from Estonia couldn't see their target. Tours get booked up, so it's wise to reserve in advance online (€32, free with Helsinki Card, daily May-Aug at 11:00 and 13:30, rest of year at 11:00 with 13:30 departures Fri-Sat only, departs from Esplanade—intersection with Fabianinkatu, +358 9 2288 1600, www.stromma.fi).

Bus Tours Departing from South Harbor: The Helsinki Panorama bus tours pick up cruise-ship passengers from the Kata-janokka terminal at 10:35 (but not during July), and from the Olympia terminal at 11:10 (tours end at the Esplanade—not back at the docks).

Hop-On, Hop-Off Bus Tours

If you'd enjoy the "Helsinki Panorama" tour described earlier, but want the chance to hop on and off, consider **City Sightseeing Helsinki** (operated by Strömma), with a 1.5-hour loop that connects downtown Helsinki, several outlying sights—including the Sibelius Monument and Olympic Stadium—as well as the Olympia cruise terminal (on cruise-ship days, the bus generally stops at Hernesaari quay—confirm in advance). Buses run every 20-40 minutes and make 19 stops (€30, €44 combo-ticket also includes harbor tour—see below, all tickets good 24 hours, May-Sept daily 10:00-16:00, www.stromma.fi). A different company, **Sightseeing City Tour** (also red buses), offers a similar route for similar prices, with fewer departures (www.citytour.fi).

Harbor Tours

Three boat companies compete for your attention along Market Square, offering snoozy cruises around the harbor and its islands roughly hourly from 10:00 to 18:00 in summer (typically 1.5 hours for €20-24; www.royalline.net, www.ihalines.fi, www.stromma. fi). The narration is slow-moving—often recorded and in as many as four languages. I'd call it an expensive nap. Here's how the companies differ: **Helsinki Sightseeing/Strömma** (yellow-and-white boats) offers the best and priciest route, going through a narrow channel in the east to reach sights that the other cruises miss. The other companies focus on the harbor itself and Suomen-linna fortress; of these, **Royal Line** (green-and-white boats) has the best food service on board, while **IHA** (blue-and-white boats) is more likely to have a live guide (half their boats have live guides, the others have recorded commentary). Taking the public ferry out to Suomenlinna and back gets you onto the water for much less money (see the "Suomenlinna Fortress" listing on page 616 for details).

SpåraKoff Pub Tram

In summer, this antique red tram makes a 45-minute loop through the city while its passengers get looped on the beer for sale on board

HELSINKI

Helsinki History

Helsinki is the only European capital with no medieval past. The Swedes founded it in the 16th century in hopes of countering Tallinn as a strategic Baltic port, but it stayed a village until the 18th century. Then, in 1746, Sweden built a huge fortress on an island outside its harbor, and Helsinki boomed as it supplied the fortress.

After the Russians took over Finland in 1809, they moved its capital and university from Turku to Helsinki—to be closer to St. Petersburg. They hired the young German architect Carl Ludvig Engel to design new public buildings in the image of St. Petersburg. This is why the oldest parts of Helsinki, around Market Square and Senate Square, feel so Russian, with pastel blue-and-yellow stone buildings with white trim and hefty columns. Hollywood even used Helsinki as a stand-in for Russia (for movies such as *Gorky Park* and *Dr. Zhivago*) during the Cold War, when filming on location wasn't possible.

Though the city was part of the Russian Empire in the 19th century, most of its residents spoke Swedish, which was the language of business and culture. In the mid-1800s, Finland began to industrialize. As Helsinki expanded, four- and five-story apartment buildings, including some Art Nouveau masterpieces, enclosed the old Russian-inspired core. Meanwhile, Finns moved from the countryside to Helsinki to take jobs as industrial laborers. The Finnish language slowly acquired equal status with Swedish, and eventually Finnish speakers became the majority in Helsinki (though Swedish remains an official language).

Downtown Helsinki didn't exist until the 1800s, when it was conscientiously designed and laid out. With its many fine Neoclassical and Art Nouveau buildings, Helsinki attracts students of urban design and planning, who enjoy exploring the Katajanokka, Kruununhaka, and Eira neighborhoods.

With a shorter history than other Nordic capitals, it helps to approach Helsinki as a city of today. Ogle its fine architecture and delve into the boutiques of the Design District for some of Scandinavia's most eye-pleasing fashion and home decor. As you browse, you'll be reminded that many recent global trends—from Marimekko's patterned fabrics to Nokia's pioneering mobile phones to Angry Birds gaming—were born right here in Helsinki.

(€12 to ride, €6/beer, May-Sept Mon-Sat 14:00-20:00, no trams Sun, leaves at the top of the hour from the Mikonkatu stop—in front of the Fennia building, across from train-station tower, www. raflaamo.fi/en/helsinki/sparakoff).

Local Guides

Helsinki Sightseeing can arrange a private guide (book at least 3 days in advance, €225/2 hours, +358 9 2288 1600, sales@stromma.

fi). **Christina Snellman** is a good, licensed guide (mobile +358 50 527 4741, chrisder@pp.inet.fi). **Archtour** offers local guides who specialize in Helsinki's architecture (+358 50 350 4700, www. archtours.com).

Helsinki Walk

This self-guided walk—worth ▲▲▲—offers a convenient spine for your Helsinki sightseeing. On a quick visit, do just the first part, focusing on the harbor, Senate Square, and the Esplanade before ending at the train station (takes about an hour). With more time, continue on with the second part of the walk, which digs deeper into the city's architectural landmarks and takes you to some of its museums (adds another 45 minutes).

HARBORFRONT, SENATE SQUARE, AND ESPLANADE

• *Start at the obelisk in the center of the harborfront market.*

❶ Market Square (Kauppatori)

This obelisk, with its double-headed eagle of imperial Russia, is the **Czarina's Stone**. It was the first public monument in Helsinki, designed by Carl Ludvig Engel and erected in 1835 to celebrate the visit by Czar Nicholas I and Czarina Alexandra. Step over the chain and climb to the top step for a clockwise spin-tour:

Begin by facing the **harbor.** The big, red Viking ship and white Silja ship are floating hotels for those making the 40-hour Stockholm-Helsinki round-trip. Farther back, a giant Ferris wheel spins over the harbor (Sky-Wheel Helsinki, www. skywheel.fi). Now pan to the right. The brick-and-tan building along the harborfront is the Old Market Hall, with some enticing, more upscale options than the basic grub at the outdoor market (for a rundown on both options, see "Eating in Helsinki," later). Between here and there, a number of harbor cruise boats vie for your business.

Farther to the right, linden trees mark the beginning of Helsinki's grand promenade, the Esplanade. Hiding in the leaves is the venerable iron-and-glass Café Kappeli. To the right of the Esplanade, a string of Neoclassical buildings lines the harbor. The

Helsinki Walk

Töölönlahti Bay

To Sibelius Monument & Seurasaari Park

FINLANDIA HALL 11

NATIONAL MUSEUM 12

MUSEOKATU

HELSINKI MUSIC CENTER 10

TEMPPELIAUKIO "ROCK" CHURCH

T #2 13

WALK ENDS

PARLIA-MENT

NATURAL HISTORY MUSEUM

KIASMA MUSEUM 9

TRAIN STATION

NATIONAL THEATER

i 7

Rautatientori

T #2 ARKADIANKATU T #2

B #24

MANN. STATUE

ATENEUM MUSEUM

Rauta-tientori

T #5

CITY CENTER MALL

KAMPPI MALL 8

Kamppi BUS STATION

KAMPPI CHAPEL

FORUM MALL

6

5

MARI-MEKKO ARTEK

STOCKMANN

ACAD.

B #24

SWEDISH THEATER

T #5

DESIGN DISTRICT

Kolmikulma Park

N

500 Meters
500 Yards

HIETALAHTI MARKET

To West Harbor Terminals

To Hernesaari Terminal

HELSINKI

blue-and-white City Hall was designed by Engel in 1833 as the town's first hotel, built to house the czar and czarina. The Lutheran Cathedral is hidden from view behind this building. Next, after the short peach-colored building, is the Swedish Embassy (flying the blue-and-yellow Swedish flag and designed to look like Stockholm's Royal Palace). Then comes the Supreme Court and, tucked back in the far corner, Finland's Presidential Palace. Finally, standing proud, and reminding Helsinki of the Russian behemoth to its east, is the Uspenski Orthodox Cathedral.

Explore the colorful **outdoor market**—part souvenirs and

1. Market Square
2. Senate Square
3. Café Kappeli
4. The Esplanade
5. Artek, Marimekko & Stockmann
6. Three Blacksmiths
7. Central Train Station
8. Kamppi Plaza & Chapel
9. Mannerheim Statue & Kiasma Museum
10. Helsinki Music Center
11. Alvar Aalto's Finlandia Hall
12. National Museum of Finland
13. Temppeliaukio (Church in the Rock)

crafts, part fruit and veggies, part fish and snacks. Sniff the stacks of trivets, made from cross-sections of juniper twigs—a fragrant, easy-to-pack gift for the folks back home (they smell even nicer when you set something hot on them).

• Done exploring? Walk to the corner of the square next to City Hall, and turn right up Sofiankatu street (City Hall has huge public WCs in the basement and free exhibits on Helsinki history). Near the end of the block, you'll pop out right in the middle of...

❷ Senate Square (Senaatintori)

This was once a simple town square with a church and City Hall—but its original buildings were burned when Russians invaded in 1808.

Later, after Finland became a grand duchy of the Russian Empire, the czar sent in architect Carl Ludvig Engel (a German who had lived and worked in St. Petersburg) to give the place some Neo-class. The result: the finest Neoclassical square in Europe. Engel represents the paradox of Helsinki: The city as we know it was built by Russia, but with an imported European architect, in a very intentionally European style. So Helsinki is, in a sense, both entirely Russian...and not Russian in the slightest.

The statue in the center of the square honors **Russian Czar Alexander II.** While he wasn't popular in Russia (he was assassinated), he was well-liked by the Finns. That's because he gave Finland more autonomy in 1863 and didn't push the Russification of Finland.

The huge **staircase** leading up to the **Lutheran Cathedral** is a popular meeting (and tanning) spot in Helsinki. Head up those stairs and survey Senate Square from the top. Scan the square from left to right. First, 90 degrees to your left is the yellow **Senate building** (now the prime minister's office). The small, blue-gray stone building with the slanted mansard roof in the far-left corner, from 1757, is one of just two pre-Russian-conquest buildings remaining in Helsinki (it's now the home of the Helsinki City Museum). **Café Engel** (opposite the cathedral at Aleksanterinkatu 26) is a fine place for a light lunch or cake and coffee. The café's winter lighting seems especially designed to boost the spirits of daylight-deprived northerners.

Facing the Senate directly across the square is its twin, the **University of Helsinki**'s main building (36,000 students, 60 percent female). Symbolically (and physically), the university and government buildings are connected via the cathedral, and both use it as a starting point for grand ceremonies.

Tucked alongside the cathedral, a line of once-grand Russian administration buildings now house the **National Library of Finland.** In czarist times, the National Library received a copy of every book printed in the Russian Empire. With all the chaos Russia suffered throughout the 20th century, a good percentage of its Slavic texts were destroyed. But Helsinki, which enjoyed relative stability, claims to have the finest collection of Slavic books in the world. This purpose-built Neoclassical building, its facade lined with Corinthian columns, is one of Engels' finest and worth a look.

HELSINKI

HELSINKI

If you'd like to visit the **cathedral interior,** now's your chance; the entrance is around the left side as you face the towering dome (for details on the interior, see the Lutheran Cathedral listing under "Sights in Helsinki," later).

• *When you're ready, head back down the stairs and angle right through the square, continuing straight down Unioninkatu.*

Along **Unioninkatu,** do a little window-shopping; this is the first of many streets we'll see lined with made-in-Finland shops (though these are more touristy than the norm). In addition to the jewelry shops and clothes boutiques, look for the Schröder sporting goods store (on the left, at #23), which shows off its famous selection of popular Finnish-made Rapala fishing lures—ideal for the fisher folk on your gift list.

At the end of this street, cross over the tram tracks to reach the fountain and female statue called *Havis Amanda.* Designed by Ville Vallgren and unveiled here in 1908, the statue has become the symbol of Helsinki, the city known as the "Daughter of the Baltic." Graduating students decorate her with a school cap every May. The voluptuous figure, modeled after the artist's Parisian mistress, was a bit too racy for the conservative town, and Vallgren had trouble getting paid. But as artists often do, Vallgren had the last laugh: For more than a hundred years now, the city budget office across the street has seen only her backside.

• *Now turn toward the Esplanade's grassy median, with the delightful...*

❸ Café Kappeli

If you've got some time, dip into this old-fashioned, gazebo-like oasis of coffee, pastry, and relaxation (get what you like at the bar inside and sit anywhere). In the

19th century, this was a popular hangout for local intellectuals and artists. Today the café offers romantic tourists waiting for their ship a great cup-of-coffee memory. The bandstand in front hosts nearly daily music and dance performances in summer.

• *Beyond Café Kappeli stretches...*

HELSINKI

❹ The Esplanade (Esplanaden)

Helsinki's top shopping boulevard sandwiches a park in the middle (another Engel design from the 1830s). The grandiose street designations—*esplanadi* and *bulevardi*—while fitting today, would have been purely aspirational in rustic little 1830s Helsinki.

The north side (on the right) is interesting for window-shopping, people-watching, and sun-worshipping. In fact, after the first block, shoppers may want to leave the park and cross over to that side of the street to browse (see "Shopping in Helsinki," later).

Otherwise, stay in the park, the green heart of the city. As you stroll, admire the mature linden trees and imagine this elegant promenade in the old days. The Esplanade was laid out in 1826 to connect the old city of the late 18th century—the established power center—with the new parts of town, where impressive new stone houses in a neo-Renaissance style were being built by the 1870s.

Notice the ornately decorated **Hotel Kämp** (on the right at #29). This city landmark is typical of the elegant hotels, shops, and restaurants that began springing up in the late 19th century as the Esplanade became a place to be seen. Today, the street's exclusive air is maintained by enterprises such as **Galleria Esplanad** (entrance at #31), a high-end fashion mall with big-name Finnish and international stores, and the recommended **Strindberg Café,** one of many tony spots along the Esplanade for a drink.

At the very top of the Esplanade, the park dead-ends at the **Swedish Theater.** Built under Russian rule to cater to Swedish residents of a Finnish city, this building encapsulates Helsinki's complex cultural mix. (The theater's recommended Teatterin deli and bar are handy for a drink or meal out in the park.)

Right across from the theater, at #39, is the huge **Academic Bookstore** (Akateeminen Kirjakauppa), designed by Modernist architect Alvar Aalto, with an extensive map and travel section, periodicals, English books, and the pricey Café Aalto (with ageless Aalto furniture) on the back mezzanine level.

• *At the end of the Esplanade, on the right, you'll reach a pedestrianized street with several landmarks of Finnish shopping and design...*

❺ Artek, Marimekko, and Stockmann

Around the corner and down the street from the Academic Bookstore is **Artek,** founded in 1935 by Alvar Aalto to showcase his practical, modern designs for furniture and housewares. And at the far corner is perhaps Finland's most famous export: **Marimekko,** the fabric designer whose bold and colorful patterns adorn everything from purses to shower curtains (more Marimekko branches are within a block of here). The other side of the street is dominated by Finland's answer to Harrods: **Stockmann,** the biggest, best, and oldest department store in town (with a great gourmet supermarket in the basement).

• *Just beyond Stockmann is Helsinki's main intersection, where the Esplanade and Mannerheimintie meet. Turn right on Mannerheimintie. At the far side of Stockmann, you'll see a landmark statue, the...*

❻ Three Blacksmiths

While there's no universally accepted meaning for this statue (from 1932), most say it celebrates human labor and cooperation and shows the solid character of the Finnish people. On the base, note the surviving bullet damage from World War II. The Soviet Union used that war as an opportunity to invade Finland—which it had lost just 20 years prior—to try to reclaim their buffer zone. In a two-part war (the Winter War, then the Continuation War), Finland held fast and emerged with its freedom—and relatively little damage.

Stockmann's entrance on Aleksanterinkatu, facing the *Three Blacksmiths,* is one of the city's most popular meeting points. Everyone in Finland knows exactly what it means when you say: "Let's meet under the Stockmann's clock." A tram stop is around the corner from the clock, on Mannerheimintie. Across the street from the clock, the Old Student Hall is decorated with legendary Finnish heroes.

• *For a shortcut to our next stop, duck through the passage (marked* City-Käytävä*) directly across the street from Stockmann's clock. This will take you through a bustling commercial zone. You'll enter—and continue straight through—the City Center shopping mall. Emerging on the far side, you're face-to-face with four granite giants guarding the...*

❼ Central Train Station (Rautatieasema)

This Helsinki landmark was designed by Eliel Saarinen (see the "Two Men Who Remade Helsinki" sidebar). The strange, huge figures on the facade, carrying illuminated globes, seem to have stepped right out of a Nordic myth. Duck into the main hall and the Eliel Restaurant inside to catch the building's early 20th-century ambience.

With your back to the train station, look to the left; diagonally across the square is the **Ateneum,** Finland's national gallery of art. It faces the **Finnish National Theater** (not visible from here)—founded to promote Finnish-speaking theater in the years Finland was dominated by Russian and Swedish speakers.

• *We've worked our way through the central part of town. If you're short on time, you can end the walk here. Or, if you're ready to explore some*

HELSINKI

more interesting buildings and monuments, continue with the second part of our walk, which delves into...

HELSINKI'S ICONIC ARCHITECTURE

Much of this walk follows the boulevard called Mannerheimintie, which serves as a showcase for much of Helsinki's signature architecture; this walk also helps you reach some of the city's farther-flung sights.

• *With your back to the station, turn right and follow the tram tracks (along Kaivokatu street) back out to Mannerheimintie. Cross the street and tracks, and continue straight ahead, toward what looks like a giant wooden bowl. You'll pop out in front of the Kamppi shopping mall.*

❽ Kamppi Plaza (Narinkkatori) and Kamppi Chapel (Kampin Kappeli)

This plaza is a Helsinki hub—both for transportation (with a Metro stop and bus station nearby) and for shopping (with the towering Kamppi Center shopping mall). Turn your attention to the round, wooden structure at the corner of the plaza nearest the Esplanade. This is one of Helsinki's most surprising bits of architecture: the **Kamppi Chapel.** Enter through the black building just to the right, and enjoy a moment or three of total serenity. (For more on the chapel, see its listing under "Sights in Helsinki," later.)

• *Leaving the chapel, cut through the middle of the big plaza, with the shopping mall on your left and the low-lying yellow building on your right. Veer right through the gap at the end of the square, and in a minute you'll see (across the busy street) an equestrian statue. Cross over to it.*

❾ Carl Gustaf Mannerheim and the Kiasma Museum of Contemporary Art

The statue depicts Finnish war hero Carl Gustaf Mannerheim, who led anti-Russian forces in the newly independent Finland's 1918 Civil War. Later, during the Winter War of 1939-1940, Mannerheim and his fellow Finns put up a stiff resistance to a massive Soviet invasion. While the Baltic States—across the Gulf of Finland—were quickly "liberated" by the Red Army, dooming them to decades under the Soviet system, the Finns managed to refuse this assistance. Mannerheim became Finland's first postwar president (the busy Mannerheimintie street is named after him). Thanks to his efforts (and those of countless others), Finland was allowed to

Two Men Who Remade Helsinki

Eliel Saarinen (1873-1950)

At the turn of the 20th century, architect Eliel Saarinen burst on the scene by pioneering the

Finnish National Romantic style. Inspired by peasant and medieval architectural traditions, his work was fundamental in creating a distinct—and modern—Finnish identity. The château-esque National Museum of Finland, designed by Saarinen and his two partners after winning a 1902 architectural competition, was his first major success. Two years later, Saarinen won the contract to construct the Helsinki train station (completed in 1919). Its design marks a transition into the Art Nouveau style of the early 1900s. The landmark station—characterized by massive male sculptures flanking its entrance, ornate glass and metalwork, and a soaring clock tower—welcomes over 300,000 travelers each day.

In the early 1920s, Saarinen and his family emigrated to the US where his son, Eero, would become the architect of such iconic projects as the Gateway Arch in St. Louis and the main terminal at Dulles International Airport near Washington, DC.

Alvar Aalto (1898-1976)

Alvar Aalto was a celebrated Finnish architect and designer working in the Modernist tradition; his buildings used abstract

forms and innovative materials without sacrificing functionality. Finlandia Hall in Helsinki is undoubtedly Aalto's most famous structure, but that's just the beginning. A Finnish Frank Lloyd Wright, Aalto concerned himself with nearly every aspect of design, from furniture to light fixtures.

Perhaps most notable of these creations was his sinuous Savoy Vase, a masterpiece of simplicity and sophistication that is emblematic of the Aalto style. His designs became so popular that in 1935 he and his wife opened Artek, a company that manufactures and sells his furniture, lamps, and textiles to this day.

chart its own democratic, capitalist course after the war. (Even so, Finland remained officially neutral through the Cold War, providing both East and West a political buffer zone.)

Mannerheim stands in front of the glassy home of the **Kiasma Museum,** with changing exhibits of contemporary art. A bit farther along and across the street from Kiasma is the Finnish **Parliament,** with its stoic row of Neoclassical columns.

From Mannerheim and Kiasma, head down into the grassy, sloping park. At the lowest point, watch out—you're crossing a busy **bicycle highway** that cuts right through the middle of the city center. Look left under the tunnel to see how a disused rail line has been turned into a subterranean pedalers' paradise.

• *The glassy building dominating the end of the park is the...*

⑩ Helsinki Music Center (Musiikkitalo)

Completed in 2011, this structure is even bigger than it looks: two-thirds of it is underground, and the entire complex houses seven separate venues. It's decorated, inside and out, with bold art (such as the gigantic pike on tiptoes that stands in the middle of the park). As you approach the bottom of the building, step into the atrium and look up to ogle the shimmering silver sculpture. While you're there, consider stopping by the ticket desk (on

the lower floor, closed Sun) to ask about performances while you're in town (the season is Sept-April). Upstairs is a music store. The interior features a lot of pine and birch accents, which warm up the space and improve the (Japanese-designed) acoustics. It didn't take long for the Music Center to become an integral part of the city's cultural life; in the first season of performances, some 400,000 people attended events here (for English tours of the facility, see "Sights in Helsinki," later).

Back outside, circle around the back side of the Music Center. Follow the straight, flat promenade that runs alongside a grassy park used for special events.

• *Crossing the street, you'll see (on the left) perhaps the most important work of Finnish architecture...*

⑪ Alvar Aalto's Finlandia Hall (Finlandia-Talo)

This big, white building can be a bit difficult for casual observers to appreciate. To get the best view of it, walk through the long parking lot all the way to the far end, and look back. The building—designed by Aalto, inside and out—opened in 1971 and immediately became a national icon. Using geometric shapes and sweeping lines, Aalto created a striking concert hall, seating up to 1,700 guests. He inclined the roofline to try to maximize the hall's acoustics—imitating the echo chamber of an old-fashioned church tower—with marginal success.

The exterior is clad in thin white marble in what appears to be a basket-weave pattern. But this effect (while beautiful) is unintentional: Not long after the hall was finished, the marble panels began bending ever so slightly. So in 1999, they were replaced at great expense—and within 10 years' time they bowed out again. The city is now planning a comprehensive renovation (scheduled to start in 2022), which includes finding a facade material that can withstand the freeze/thaw cycles of a Helsinki winter.

Turn to face shimmering **Töölönlahti Bay** (not a lake, but an inlet of the Baltic Sea)—ringed by a popular walking and jogging track. From here, you can see more Helsinki landmarks: across the lake and a bit to the left, the white tower marks the Olympic Stadium that hosted the world in 1952. And to the right are the rides of Helsinki's old-time amusement park, Linnanmäki.

• *If you'd like to extend this walk, join the natives on the waterfront path (which offers even better views of Finlandia Hall). Otherwise, consider...*

More Helsinki Sights

To reach two more major sights, go up the stairs immediately to the right of Finlandia Hall, then continue all the way up to the main road. Directly across the street stands the fine **⓬ National Museum of Finland,** which tells this country's story with lots of artifacts.

About a 10-minute walk behind the National Museum is the beautiful Church in the Rock, **⓭ Temppeliaukio.** Once inside, sit. Enjoy the music. It's a wonderful place to end this walk.

To continue on to the **Sibelius Monument,** located in a lovely park setting, take bus #24 (direction: Seurasaari) from nearby Arkadiankatu street. The same ticket is good for your return trip (within 80 minutes), or ride it to the end of the line for the bridge to Seurasaari Island and Finland's open-air folk museum. From there, bus #24 returns to the top of the Esplanade.

All three of these sights are explained in more detail later, under "Sights in Helsinki."

Helsinki Tram Tour

Of Helsinki's many trams, two convenient routes seem made-to-order for a tourist's joyride. Follow the route below to ride tram #2 and then #3, together worth ▲▲.

If you buy a single ticket, it's good for 80 minutes—just long enough for the entire circuit outlined below (€2.80 from HSL app or ticket machines at major stops, €4 from driver—cash only; trams run every 10 minutes). To hop on and off, it's best to use a day ticket (see "Getting Around Helsinki," earlier) or a Helsinki Card.

While you can hop on anywhere, it's most convenient to start your tour at Market Square.

❶ **Market Square:** Stand at the tram stop that is between the fountain and the market, and wait for one of the frequent #2 trams. Since the tracks split here briefly, it's hard to get on in the wrong direction; still, confirm that the front of the tram reads *Eläintarha*, not *Olympiaterminaali* (tram stop: Kauppatori).

❷ **Senate Square:** From Market Square, you'll first pass this proud square, with the gleaming white Lutheran Cathedral, a statue of Alexander II—Finland's favorite czar, and many of the oldest buildings in town. Then you'll head up Aleksanterinkatu street, Helsinki's Fifth Avenue-type main shopping drag (tram stop: Aleksanterinkatu).

❸ **Mannerheimintie and Museums:** A turn onto broad Mannerheimintie boulevard takes you near the contemporary Kiasma Museum and, after turning onto Arkadiankatu street (with the imposing Parliament building on the corner), to the Finnish Museum of Natural History (known as LUOMUS—on your right), home to about eight million specimens ranging from spiders to dinosaurs (tram stop: Luonnontieteellinen museo).

❹ **School of Economics and Trendy Apartments:** After passing the yellow brick buildings of the School of Economics (on your left, note facade—tram stop: Hanken), you'll enter a neighborhood with lots of desirable 1920s-era apartments. Young couples start out here, move to the suburbs when they have their kids, and return as empty-nesters. The Temppeliaukio Church (a.k.a. "Church in the Rock"), while out of sight, is just a block uphill from the next stop (Sammonkatu).

❺ **Finnish National Opera House:** Built in 1993, the National Opera House is the white, sterile, shower-tile building on the right (tram stop: Ooppera). If you're interested, the next stop (Töölön halli) is a short walk from the Sibelius Monument and its pretty park (detour along a street called Sibeliuksenkatu). Otherwise, stay onboard for a few more stops.

❻ **Sports Complex and Transfer:** The white building with the skinny tower (in the distance on the right) marks the Olym-

Helsinki Tram Tour

1 Market Square
2 Senate Square
3 Mannerheimintie & Museums
4 School of Economics & Trendy Apartments
5 Finnish National Opera House
6 Sports Complex & Transfer
7 Classic Amusement Park (Linnanmäki)
8 Working-Class District
9 National Theater/Train Station
10 Three Blacksmiths Statue
11 Design District: Funky & Artsy Shops
12 Embassy Row & End

pic Stadium, used for the 1952 summer games. (Finland's most famous Olympian is long-distance runner Paavo Nurmi, the "Flying Finn," who won five gold medals early in the 20th century.) At the **Auroran sairaala stop,** hop off and transfer to tram #3 (direction: Olympiaterminaali). On days that it's not raining, you'll see skateboarders enjoying a park of their own.

❼ Classic Amusement Park: Linnanmäki, Helsinki's low-end, Tivoli-like amusement park is by far the most-visited sight in town (on the right, free admission to park, pay per ride or for all-access wristband, open daily until late, tram stop: Linnanmäki (pohj.), www.linnanmaki.fi). Roller-coaster nuts enjoy its classics from the 1950s.

❽ Working-Class District: Next you'll enter an old working-class neighborhood. Its soccer fields (on your left) are frozen into ice rinks for hockey in the winter. You'll pass the striking granite Kallio Church (Art Nouveau, on your right) and Hakaniemi square, with a big indoor/outdoor market (on your left). Crossing a saltwater inlet, you'll pass Helsinki's Botanical Gardens (on the right).

❾ National Theater and Train Station: From here, you'll head back toward the town center, where you'll reach a big square. Fronting it is Finland's granite National Theater, in Art Nouveau style, with a statue honoring Aleksis Kivi, the father of Finnish literature. On the left is the Ateneum, Finland's national art gallery. Next, you'll pass the striking central train station, with its iconic figures stoically holding lamps (designed by the great Finnish architect Eliel Saarinen).

❿ *Three Blacksmiths* Statue: After turning left on big, busy Mannerheimintie, you'll pass the most famous statue in town, the *Three Blacksmiths* (on your left), which honors hard work and cooperation. Towering above the smiths is the Stockmann department store. Then (at the Ylioppilastalo stop), the round, white Swedish Theater marks the top of the town's graceful Esplanade park, which leads back down to the harbor (where you began this tour). From here, you'll loop through the colorful and artsy Design District.

⓫ Design District—Funky and Artsy Shops: On the right, the cemetery of the church (which dates from 1827) was cleaned out to make a park. It's called the "Plague Park," recalling a circa-1700 epidemic that killed more than half the population. Coming up, funky small boutiques, cafés, and fun shops line the streets (stops: Fredrikinkatu, Iso Roobertinkatu, and Viiskulma).

⓬ Embassy Row and the End of the Line: After the Art Deco brick church (on your right), the tram makes a hard left (at the Eiran sairaala stop, for a hospital) and enters a district with Art

Nouveau buildings. Look down streets on the right, leading to the Baltic Sea, for decorative facades and turrets.

After the Neitsytpolku stop, spy the Russian Embassy (on left), still sporting its hammer and sickle; it was built to look like London's Buckingham Palace. Across the street is the Roman Catholic church, and beyond that (on the right), a street marked "no entry" leads to the fortified US Embassy. Returning to the harbor, you'll likely see the huge Tallink Silja ship that leaves each evening for Stockholm. Its terminal (Olympiaterminaali; also the name of the tram stop) was built for the 1952 Olympics, which flooded Helsinki with visitors. The #3 tram route ends here: your choices are to transfer back to the #2 tram, which starts right here (ride it two stops to get back to **Market Square**), or walk 15 minutes back to Market Square. Along the way, you'll pass the cute brick Old Market Hall (with great little eateries).

Sights in Helsinki

Unless otherwise noted, for locations see the "Helsinki Walk" map, earlier.

NEAR THE SOUTH HARBOR

▲▲Uspenski Orthodox Cathedral (Uspenskin Katedraali)

This house of worship was built in the Katajanokka district for the

Russian military in 1868, at a time when Finland belonged to Russia (*Uspenski* is Russian for the Assumption of Mary). It hovers above Market Square and faces the Lutheran Cathedral, just as Russian culture faces Europe.

Cost and Hours: Free; Tue-Fri 9:30-16:00, Sat 10:00-15:00, Sun 12:00-15:00, closed Mon; Pormestarinrinne 1 (about a 10-minute walk beyond the harborfront Market Square).

Visiting the Cathedral: Before heading inside, view the exterior. The uppermost "onion dome" represents the sacred heart of Jesus, while the smaller ones represent his 12 apostles.

The rich imagery of the cathedral's interior is a stark contrast to the sober Lutheran Cathedral. While commonly called the "Russian church," the cathedral is actually Eastern Orthodox, answering to the patriarch in Istanbul. Today, the cathedral is the seat of the archdiocese of Helsinki, to which much of eastern Finland belongs.

The cathedral's Orthodox Mass is beautiful, with a standing congregation, candles, incense, icons in action, priests behind the iconostasis, and timeless vocal music. In the front left corner, find the icon featuring the Madonna and child, surrounded by rings and jewelry (under glass), given in thanks for prayers answered. Across from the icon, a white marble table holds memorial candles and a dish of wheat seeds, representing new life—the hope of resurrection—for the departed.

ON SENATE SQUARE

▲▲Lutheran Cathedral (Tuomiokirkkoseurakunta)

With its prominent green dome, gleaming white facade, and the 12 apostles overlooking the city and harbor, this church is the masterpiece of Carl Ludvig Engel, architect of the state buildings of the new capital city in the early 19th century.

Cost and Hours: Free; daily 9:00-18:00, until 24:00 in summer, no visits during church services or special events; www. helsinkicathedral.fi. In summer, free organ concerts are held weekly—check their website for schedule.

Visiting the Cathedral: Enter the building around the left side. Finished in 1852, the interior is pure architectural truth. Open a pew gate and sit, surrounded by the saints of Protestantism, to savor Neoclassical nirvana. Physically, this church is perfectly Protestant—austere and unadorned—with the emphasis on preaching (prominent pulpit) and music (huge organ). Statuary is limited to the local Reformation big shots: Martin Luther, Philipp Melanchthon (Luther's sidekick), and the leading Finnish reformer, Mikael Agricola. A follower of Luther at Wittenberg, Agricola brought the Reformation to Finland. He also translated the Bible into Finnish and is considered the father of the modern Finnish language. Agricola's Bible is to Finland what the Luther Bible is to Germany and the King James Bible is to the English-speaking world.

Helsinki City Museum

This interesting museum, just off Senate Square in one of the city's oldest buildings, gives an accessible overview of the city's history and culture.

Cost and Hours: Free, Mon-Fri 11:00-19:00, Sat-Sun until 17:00, Aleksanterinkatu 16, www.helsinkicitymuseum.fi.

Visiting the Museum: On the ground floor, visitors use 3-D

HELSINKI

glasses to take a trip through time, viewing the many ways the city has changed over the years (professional photographers and Helsinki citizens contributed the images used for this "time machine"). A white-board animation cleverly condenses about 350 years of the city's history into four minutes (from 1550 and Swedish rule, through the decades of Russian domination, to Finland's declaration of independence in 1917). Exhibits on the second floor take you to a typical Helsinki home in the 1950s and a local bar from the 1970s, complete with vintage soundtracks. Kids can go to school in an old-fashioned classroom, try on costumes, or jump into a horse-drawn carriage.

There's a lot to study and explore here, and it's a great place for kids or on a rainy day. Most visitors won't need to linger, but everyone leaves with a better understanding of why residents choose to call Helsinki home.

WEST OF THE ESPLANADE

These sights are scattered in the zone west of the Esplanade, listed roughly in the order you'll reach them from the city center (and in the order they appear on my self-guided walk, earlier).

▲Ateneum

The Ateneum, Finland's national art gallery, has the country's oldest and largest art collection. Come here to see Finnish artists (mid-18th to 20th century) and a fine international collection, including works by Cézanne, Chagall, Gauguin, and Van Gogh. The museum also hosts good special exhibits of Finnish and international art.

Cost and Hours: €17; Tue and Fri 10:00-18:00, Wed-Thu until 20:00, Sat-Sun until 17:00, closed Mon; near train station at Kaivokatu 2, +358 294 500 401, www.ateneum.fi.

Visiting the Museum: The permanent collection is spread over several floors in the "Stories of Finnish Art" display. The paintings—hung gallery by gallery in thematic groupings such as landscape, people, symbolism, and urban life—illustrate the development of art in Finland from 1809 until the 1970s.

You can follow the chronological display if you have the time and interest, but to see the cream of the crop, head directly up two flights of the grand entry staircase to Room 13, where classics from Finland's golden age of painting occupy every inch of wall space. In the late 19th century, Finnish artists began absorbing Parisian influences. They moved their easels outside, loosened their brushwork and handling of paint, and chose distinctly Finnish people and landscapes as their subjects. You'll see an aging grandfather walking with a young boy, country women gathered outside a church,

HELSINKI

Sauna

Finland's vaporized fountain of youth is the sauna—Scandinavia's answer to Spanx and facelifts.

A Finnish sauna is a wood-paneled room with wooden benches and a blistering-hot wood-fired stove topped with rocks. At a traditional Finnish sauna, you undress entirely before going in. Lay your towel on the bench, and sit or lie on it. Ladle water from the bucket onto the rocks to make steam. Choose a higher bench for more heat. Let yourself work up a sweat, then, just before bursting, go outside to the shower for a Niagara of liquid ice. Suddenly your shower stall becomes a Cape Canaveral launch pad, as your body scatters to every corner of the universe. A moment later you're back together and can re-enter the steam room. Repeat as necessary. The famous birch branches are always available for slapping your skin. Finns claim this enhances circulation while emitting a refreshing birch aroma that opens your sinuses. For more on the history of saunas, see www.sauna.fi.

Because many Finns have private saunas in their homes or cabins, public saunas aren't as popular as they once were. Your hotel may have one. Some saunas are semipublic (separate men's and women's hours), while others are for private use (book time slot). Some do not require you to be naked. Here are a few public saunas (for locations, see the "Greater Helsinki" map, earlier).

Kotiharjun Sauna: This good, traditional sauna has a local crowd. After stripping and steaming, cooling off is nothing fancy—just a bank of cold showers. For an extra fee, a woman in a fish-cleaner's apron will give you a wonderful full-body scrub with Brillo pad-like mitts (€12). Regulars relax with beers on the sidewalk just outside (€14, towel rental-€3, cash only; Tue-Sun 14:00-21:30, closed Mon, last entry 1.5 hours before closing; men—ground floor, women—upstairs, private sauna available; 200 yards from Sörnäinen Metro stop, Harjutorinkatu 1, +358 9 753 1535, www.kotiharjunsauna.fi).

laborers burning vegetation, pristine forests and lakes, and quietly beautiful snow.

▲Kamppi Chapel (Kampin Kappeli)

Sitting unassumingly on the busy, commercial plaza in front of the Kamppi shopping mall/bus-station complex, this restful space was opened by the city of Helsinki in 2012 to give residents and visitors a place of serenity. The wooden structure, clad in spruce and

HELSINKI

Kulttuurisauna: Sitting in a little park along the Baltic, Kulttuurisauna gives visitors a chance take a dip in the sea. Designed and operated by a husband-and-wife, Finnish-Japanese, artist-and-architect team, it's both modern and traditional. This is a *savusauna* (smoke sauna, without a chimney)—and, while the room is ventilated before bathers arrive, the smoky atmosphere lingers (€15, towel rental-€4, all nude and gender-segregated, Wed-Sun 16:00-21:00, closed Mon-Tue, last entry at 20:00, just north of downtown at Hakaniemenranta 17, nearest tram/bus stop is Hakaniemi—a 10-minute walk away, www.kulttuurisauna.fi).

Löyly: Situated on the Hernesaari peninsula, sophisticated Löyly features a sauna and a restaurant that's open to the sea. The mod-

ern building is covered in wood slats—from inside the sauna it's like looking out through Venetian blinds. There are separate dressing rooms and showers for men and women, but the saunas themselves are communal—everyone wears a bathing suit. It's possible to swim in the sea here, and in winter, there's a hole in the ice for hardy swimmers. The attached coffee bar/café/restaurant spills out onto a big view veranda and up to a rooftop terrace (€19 covers 2 hours—includes towel, seat cover, soap, and shampoo; sauna generally open Mon-Thu 16:00-22:00, Fri-Sat 13:00-23:00, Sun 12:00-18:00; $$ restaurant open Mon-Sat 11:00-22:00, Sun until 20:00; Hernesaarenranta 4, bus #14 or #18N stops outside its door, nearest tram stop—Perämiehenkatu—is a 20-minute walk; +358 9 6128 6550, www.loylyhelsinki.fi/en/). It's smart to book ahead online.

Allas: This place sits in the middle of the South Harbor action, at the edge of Market Square, with saunas that lead to a huge floating deck with three outdoor pools (fresh and sea water). Inside, there are three saunas: male, female, and mixed (€15; Mon-Fri 6:30-21:00, Sat from 9:00, Sun 10:00-20:00; café and bistro, Katajanokanlauturi 2a, www.allasseapool.fi).

with an oval footprint, encloses a 38-foot-tall, windowless cylinder of silence. Inside, indirect light seeps in around the edges of the ceiling, bathing the clean, curved, alder-wood paneling in warmth and tranquility. Does it resemble Noah's Ark? The inside of an egg? The architects intentionally left it vague—and open to each visitor's interpretation. Although it's a church, there are no services; it's open to anyone needing a reflective pause. Locals drop by between their shopping chores to sit in a pew and ponder their deity, wrestle with tough issues, or just take a break. In this peaceful spot, secular modern architecture and meditative spirituality converge beautifully.

Cost and Hours: Free, Mon-Fri 8:00-20:00, Sat-Sun 10:00-18:00, Simonkatu 7, enter through adjacent low-profile black building.

Kiasma Museum (Nykytaiteen Museo Kiasma)

Finland's museum of contemporary art, designed by American architect Steven Holl, hosts changing exhibitions of international art (there's no permanent collection). Ask at the TI or check online to find out what's showing.

Cost and Hours: €10; Tue-Fri 10:00-20:30, Sat until 18:00, Sun until 17:00, closed Mon; Mannerheiminaukio 2, near train station, +358 294 500 501, www.kiasma.fi.

Finnish Museum of Natural History (LUOMUS)

Run by the University of Helsinki, this museum has the largest natural-history collection in Finland, with display cabinets crammed with pressed plants, dried fungi, taxidermied animals, and much more. Its wide-ranging exhibits emphasize the biodiversity of Finland and the world (most with English descriptions).

Cost and Hours: €15, but free during the last three opening hours; Tue-Sun 10:00-17:00; Sept-May Tue-Fri 9:00-16:00, Sat-Sun from 10:00; closed Mon year-round; up the street behind the Parliament at Pohjoinen Rautatiekatu 13, www.luomus.fi.

Helsinki Music Center (Musiikkitalo)

This modern facility, with seven different venues, provides a home for the performing arts in Helsinki. But its biggest draw may be the park and creative contemporary art that surrounds it. You can stop in anytime it's open to look around, and in summer, the main concert hall is open for free public viewing. Music lovers can also consider taking in a performance (season runs Sept-April), and architecture fans may want to take an English tour.

Cost and Hours: Building open Mon-Fri 8:00-22:00, Sat from 10:00, Sun 10:00-20:00; concert hall open July-Aug Mon-Sat 12:00-15:00; English tours offered most days in summer for €15, check website for schedule; Mannerheimintie 13A, +358 20 707 0421, www.musiikkitalo.fi.

Finlandia Hall (Finlandia-Talo)

This 1,700-seat concert hall is Modernist designer/architect Alvar Aalto's most famous building in his native Finland. To see it from its best angle, view it from the parking lot, on the side facing Töölönlahti Bay (not from Mannerheim- intie street). Aalto was involved in every aspect of the building's design, right down to the door handles, and many fans see it as his most iconic work. Aalto

devotees or newcomers should consider a guided tour to make sense of this distinctive structure. For more about the building, see page 602 of my self-guided walk).

Cost and Hours: €16 for a tour, call ahead or visit website to check times; hall info point open Mon-Fri 9:00-19:00, closed Sat- Sun; Mannerheimintie 13e, +358 9 40241, www.finlandiatalo.fi.

HELSINKI

▲National Museum of Finland (Kansallismuseo)

This pleasant, easy-to-handle collection is in a grand building de- signed in the early 1900s by three of this country's greatest archi-

tects—including Eliel Saarinen. The museum, which recently completed a major renovation, traces the land of the Finns from prehistory to the 20th century. Highlights include Finland's largest permanent archaeological col- lection, the 1420 altarpiece dedicated to St. Birgitta (patron saint of Swe- den—which owned Finland at the time), and a reconstructed early 1800s "smoke cabin" (sauna).

Cost and Hours: €14, free on Fri from 16:00; open Tue-Sun 11:00- 18:00, Wed until 20:00, closed Mon; a 5-minute walk from Temppeliaukio Church at Mannerheimin- tie 34, +358 259 336 901, www.kansallismuseo.fi/en. The museum café has a tranquil outdoor courtyard.

▲▲▲Temppeliaukio Church

A modern example of great church architecture (from 1969), this "Church in the Rock" was blasted out of solid granite. Architect- brothers Timo and Tuomo Suomalainen won a competition to de- sign the church, which they built within a year's time. Barren of decor except for a couple of simple crosses, the church is capped with a copper-and-skylight dome; it's normally filled with live or recorded music and awestruck visitors. Grab a pew. Gawk upward at a 13-mile-long coil of copper ribbon. Look at the bull's-eye and ponder God. Forget your camera. Just sit in the middle, ignore the crowds, and be thankful for peace (under your feet is an air-raid shelter that can accommodate 6,000 people).

The church has excellent acoustics and is a popular concert venue; check at the TI for upcoming programs.

Cost and Hours: €4; generally Mon-Sat 10:00-19:00, Sun 12:00-18:00, closes one hour earlier Oct-May—but because of frequent events and church services, it's good to confirm open times by listening to the recorded message at +358 9 2340 5940; Lutherinkatu 3, +358 9 2340 6320, www.helsinginseurakunnat.fi.

Getting There: The church is at the top of a gentle hill in a residential neighborhood, about a 15-minute walk north of the bus station or a 10-minute walk from the National Museum (or take tram #2 to the Hanken or Sammonkatu stop).

▲Sibelius Monument

Six hundred stainless-steel pipes called "Love of Music"—built on solid rock, as is so much of Finland—shimmer in a park to honor Finland's greatest composer, Jean Sibelius. It's a forest of pipe-organ pipes in a forest of trees. The artist, Eila Hiltunen, was forced to add a bust of the composer's face to silence critics of her otherwise abstract work. City orientation bus tours stop here for 10 minutes—long enough.

Getting There: The monument is a few blocks from the tram stop Töölön halli (tram #2) and near the bus #24 line that also serves the Seurasaari Open-Air Folk Museum (described later). See the "Greater Helsinki" map on page 585 for general location.

DESIGN DISTRICT

Exploring Helsinki's Design District is a sightseeing highlight for many visitors. A good starting point is the Design Museum, which sits just a few blocks southwest of the Esplanade. For more on the district, see "Shopping in Helsinki," later.

▲Design Museum

Design is integral to contemporary Finnish culture, and this fine museum—with a small but insightful permanent collection and well-presented temporary exhibits—offers a good overview (all in English). Worth ▲▲▲ to those who came to Finland just for the design, it features interesting and clever installations that will appeal to just about anybody.

Cost and Hours: €12; daily 11:00-18:00; Sept-May Wed-Sun 11:00-18:00, Tue until 20:00, closed Mon; excellent (if pricey) gift shop, Korkeavuorenkatu 23, www.designmuseum.fi.

Visiting the Museum: From the ticket desk on the ground floor, turn into the permanent exhibit, called **Utopia Now: The Story of Finnish Design.** The first gallery considers the process of design—the steps from inspiration to production—and presents iconic objects of Finnish design from the 1950s (glass bowls by Alvar Aalto) as well as more recent innovations (generations of Nokia phones).

The "Icons of Design" gallery introduces viewers to the life stories of leading Finnish designers and the functional objects they've created (Aalto's iconic wooden stool, for example—a staple in classrooms around the world). The "Warehouse" collects items from different periods of the museum's collections, with a focus on "better things for everyday life," with everything from brightly colored but practical jerry cans for transporting fuel to a government-issued maternity box (a starter kit for new mothers, including clothes and sheets).

Digital applications throughout the galleries make your visit participatory: You can test how to control a Scorpion harvester (a staple of the Finnish forest industry), or you can animate a Marimekko pattern of your choosing on a wall-sized screen. A virtual headset lets you time travel to Finland's pavilion at the 1900 Paris World's Fair.

Upstairs and downstairs, you'll also find typically excellent **temporary exhibits** that allow individual Finnish designers to take center stage.

OUTER HELSINKI

A weeklong car trip up through the Finnish lakes and forests to Mikkeli and Savonlinna would be relaxing, but you can actually enjoy Finland's green trees and blue-water scenery without leaving Helsinki. Here are three great ways to get out and walk on a sunny summer day. If you have time, do at least one of them during your stay. See the "Greater Helsinki" map on page 585 for general locations.

▲▲Suomenlinna Fortress (Suomenlinnan Merilinnoitus)

The island guarding Helsinki's harbor served as a strategic fortress for three countries: Finland, Sweden, and Russia. It's now

a popular park, with delightful paths, fine views, and a visitors center. On a sunny day, it's a wonderful place to stroll among old fortifications with recreating Finns. The free Suomenlinna guide-booklet (stocked at the Helsinki TI, ferry terminal, and the visitors center) covers the island thoroughly.

The island has one good museum (the Suomenlinna Museum, at Suomenlinna Centre—described later) and several skippable ones, including a toy museum and several military museums (open summer only).

Getting There: Catch a ferry to Suomenlinna from Market Square. Walk past the high-priced excursion boats to the public HKL ferry (€2.80 one-way, covered by day ticket and Helsinki Card, 15-minute trip, 2-3/hour in May-Aug—generally at :00, :20, and :40 past the hour, but check schedule to confirm; Sept-April every 40-60 minutes). If you'll be taking at least two tram rides within 24 hours of visiting Suomenlinna, it pays to get a day ticket instead of individual tickets. If your goal is the Suomenlinna Centre and the museum, the private JT Line "water bus" gets you closer than the public ferry (€8 round-trip, 2/hour in May-Sept, departs from Market Square, +358 10 205 1880, www.jt-line.fi).

Visitor Information: The information desk at the Jetty Barracks, at the ferry landing, is open to visitors year-round (daily 10:00-18:00, Oct-April until 16:00, +358 29 533 8410, www.suomenlinna.fi). Pick up the free island map/booklet here.

Tours: The one-hour English-language island tour departs from the Suomenlinna Centre (€11, free with Helsinki Card; generally 3/day in summer, 1/day Sat-Sun only in spring and fall). The tour is fine if you're a military history buff, but it kind of misses the point of what's now essentially a giant playground for all ages.

Background: The fortress was built by the Swedes with French financial support in the mid-1700s to counter Russia's rise to power. (Russian Czar Peter the Great had built his new capital,

Suomenlinna Timeline

1748: Construction begins on the "Sweden Fortress" (Finland is part of Sweden's kingdom).

1788: The fort is a base during the Russo-Swedish War.

1808: During the Finnish War, the fortress surrenders to Russia—and remains a Russian naval base for the next 110 years.

1809: Finland becomes part of the Russian Empire.

1855: French and British navies bombard the fort during the Crimean War, inflicting heavy damage.

1917: Finland declares independence.

1918: The fort is annexed by Finland and renamed Finland Fortress (Suomenlinna).

1939: The fort serves as a base for the Finnish navy throughout World War II.

1973: The Finnish garrison moves out, the fort's administration is transferred to the Ministry of Education, and the fort is opened to the public.

St. Petersburg, on the Baltic and was eyeing the West.) Named Sveaborg ("Fortress of Sweden"), the fortress was Sweden's military pride and joy. With five miles of walls and hundreds of cannons, it was the second strongest fort of its kind in Europe after Gibraltar. Helsinki, a small community of 1,500 people before 1750, soon became a boomtown supporting this grand "Gibraltar of the North."

The fort, built by more than 10,000 workers, was a huge investment and stimulated lots of innovation. In the 1760s, it had the world's biggest and most modern dry dock. It served as a key naval base during a brief Russo-Swedish war from 1788 to 1790. But in 1808, the Russians took the "invincible" fort without a fight—by siege—as a huge and cheap military gift.

Today, Suomenlinna has 800 permanent residents, is home to Finland's Naval Academy, and is most appreciated by locals for its fine scenic strolls. The island is large—actually, it's six islands connected by bridges—and you and your imagination get free run of the fortifications and dungeon-like chambers. When it's time to eat, you'll find a half-dozen cafés and plenty of picnic opportunities.

Visiting Suomenlinna: Start your stroll of the island at the Jetty Barracks near the public ferry landing. A suggested visitors' route, marked with blue signs, runs from north to south across the fortress and will take you to all the key sights. You'll wander on cobbles past dilapidated shiplap cottages that evoke a more robust time for this once-strategic, now-leisurely island. The garrison church on your left, which was Orthodox until its 20th-century conversion to Lutheranism, doubled as a lighthouse.

A five-minute walk from the ferry brings you to the **Suomenlinna Centre,** which houses the worthwhile Suomenlinna Museum. Inside the (free) lobby, you'll find an information desk, gift shop, café, and giant model of all six islands that make up Suomenlinna—handy for orientation. The exhibits themselves are well-presented but dryly explained: fragments of old walls, cannons, period clothing, model ships, and so on; the upstairs focuses on the site's transition

from a fortress to a park. The main attraction is the fascinating 25-minute film that presents the island's complete history (€6.50 for museum and film, runs 2/hour, daily 10:00-18:00, Oct-April 10:30-16:30).

From the Suomenlinna Centre, cross the bridge—noticing the giant, rusted seaplane hall on the right, housing the Regatta Club, with a fun sailboat photo exhibition and shop. On the far side of the hall, peer into the gigantic dry dock.

Back on the main trail, climb five minutes uphill to the right into **Piper Park** (Piperin Puisto). Hike up past its elegant 19th-century café (with rocky view tables), and continue up and over the ramparts to a surreal swimming area. From here, follow the waterline—and the ramparts—to the south. You'll walk above bunkers burrowed underground, like gigantic molehills (or maybe Hobbit houses). Periodic ladders let you scramble down onto the

rocks. Imposing cannons, now used as playsets and photo-op props for kids, are still aimed ominously at the Gulf of Finland—in case, I imagine, of Russian invasion...or if they just get fed up with all of those cruise ships. Reaching the southern tip of the island, called King's Gate, peek out through the cannon holes. Then make your walk a loop by circling back to the Suomenlinna Centre and, beyond that, the ferry dock for the ride home.

Peninsula Promenade

For a breezy, salty seaside walk with island views, consider this promenade around the Kaivopuisto Park peninsula south of the center. Allow 1.5 hours at a leisurely pace. From Market Square, wander past the brick Old Market Hall and Tallink Silja terminal, and follow the shoreline pedestrian path. The first island you'll pass, Valkosaari, hosts the NJK yacht club, the largest and one of the oldest in Finland. The next island, Luoto, is home to the posh Saaristo restaurant (with shuttle boat service). During a typical winter, the bay freezes (18 inches of ice is strong enough to allow cars to drive to the islands—in the past there was even a public bus route that extended to an island during winter). The fortress island of Suomenlinna is in the distance. The hill you're circling (on the right) is a swanky neighborhood and home to several embassies; ahead, the classic Ursula Café, with its fine harbor views, is good for a coffee break (at Ehrenströmintie 3).

Around the corner, the next island, Uunisaari, is a fun destination in summer, when a little ferry connects the mainland with its sandy beach—perfect for a picnic. The island's unique plant life (much studied by local students) is believed to have hitched a ride to Finland from Siberia on the boots of Russian soldiers.

The odd-looking pier nearby is a station for washing rugs (those are not picnic tables). Saltwater brightens the rag rugs traditionally made by local grandmas. While American men put on aprons and do the barbecue, Finnish men wash the carpets. After the scrub, the rugs are sent through big mechanical wringers and hung on nearby racks to dry in the wind. The posted map shows 11 such stations scattered around Helsinki. Buy an ice cream at the nearby stand and watch the action (best in the morning).

In the distance looms Helsinki's big West Harbor port, hosting hundreds of cruise ships a year. From here you can follow Neitsytpolku street back to the town center, keeping an eye out for fun Art Nouveau buildings.

▲▲Seurasaari Open-Air Folk Museum

Located on a lovely island on the edge of town, this collection contains 100 historic buildings from every corner of Finland. It's wonderfully furnished and gives visitors an opportunity to sample the far reaches of Finland without leaving the capital city— you can see the highlights here in about an hour (if you're not taking a tour, get the map or the helpful guidebook). But it's easy to stretch out your visit with a picnic or light lunch (snacks and cakes available in the Antti farmstead at the center of the park). Off-season, when the buildings are closed, the place is empty and not worth the trouble.

Cost and Hours: Free park entry, €10 to enter buildings; June-Aug daily 11:00-17:00, shorter hours May and Sept, buildings closed Oct-April; +358 295 336 912, www.seurasaari.fi.

Tours: One-hour English tours are free with entry ticket, offered mid-June-Aug generally at 15:00 (confirm time on website).

Getting There: To reach the museum, ride bus #24 (from the top of the Esplanade, 2/hour, 25 minutes) to the last stop at Seurasaari (note departure times for your return) and walk across the quaint footbridge.

NEAR HELSINKI

Porvoo, the second-oldest town in Finland, has wooden architecture that dates from the Swedish colonial period. This coastal town can be reached from Helsinki by bus (one hour) or by summertime excursion boat from Market Square (3.5 hours; www.msjlruneberg.fi/cruises).

Turku, the historic capital of Finland, is a two-hour bus or train ride from Helsinki. Overall, Turku is a pale shadow of Helsinki, and there is little reason to make a special trip. It does have a handicraft museum in a cluster of wooden houses (the only part of town to survive a devastating fire in the early 1800s), an old castle, a fine Gothic cathedral (this was the first part of Finland to be Christianized, in the 12th century), and a market square. Viking and Tallink Silja boats sail from Turku to Stockholm every morning and evening, passing through the especially scenic Turku archipelago (see "Helsinki Connections," later, for details).

Naantali, a cute, commercial, well-preserved medieval town with a quaint harbor, is an easy 20-minute bus ride from Turku.

Shopping in Helsinki

Helsinki may be the top shopping town in the Nordic countries. Even in this region of creative design culture, Helsinki is a trendsetter; many Finnish designers are household names worldwide. The easiest place to get a taste of Finnish design is in the shops at the top end of the Esplanade, but with a little more time, it's worth delving into the nearby Design District.

Business Hours: Most shops are open all day Monday through Friday (generally 10:00 or 11:00 until 17:00 or 18:00), and have shorter hours on Saturday. Most are closed on Sundays. Shops on the Esplanade tend to stay open later and keep Sunday hours.

THE ESPLANADE AND NEARBY

Helsinki's elegant main drag, the Esplanade, is a coffee-sipper's and window-shopper's delight. Practically every big name in Finnish design has a flagship store along or near this people-pleasing strip. Here are some worth dipping into:

Marimekko, the Finnish fashion company, was founded in the early 1950s but really took off on the international stage in the 1960s, especially after Jackie Kennedy bought seven Marimekko dresses (and wore one of them on the cover of *Sports Illustrated*). You'll find the company's colorful, patterned scarves, clothes, purses, and fabrics in locations throughout central Helsinki. Their flagship store, with home decor and fashion, is just off the Esplanade (at Pohjoisesplanadi 33); other central locations include across from Stockmann department store (Aleksanterinkatu 50), and inside the Kamppi and Forum shopping centers (www.marimekko.com).

These three shops are strung along the north side of the Esplanade: **Aarikka** (#27, www.aarikka.com) has affordable and casual handmade jewelry, tableware, and home decor, most of it made from colorful spheres of wood. **Iittala** (#23, www.iittala.com) is the flagship store of a longtime Finnish glassmaker, featuring Alvar Aalto's signature wavy-mouthed vases, which haven't gone out of fashion since 1936; Oiva Toikka's iconic "dew drop"-patterned chalices and pedestal bowls from 1964; and an array of other decorative and functional glassware. **Kalevala** (#25) has been selling finely crafted, handmade-in-Finland jewelry since 1937; some pieces are modern, while others are inspired by old Scandinavian and Sami themes (www.kalevala.fi).

Finlayson, on the south side of the Esplanade, is a venerable textile design company that's been around since 1820—but their sheets, towels, rugs, and curtains are fun and modern (#14, www.finlayson.fi).

The Esplanade is capped by the enormous, eight-floor **Stockmann** department store, arguably Scandinavia's most impressive (Mon-Fri 9:00-21:00, Sat until 18:00, Sun 12:00-18:00, great basement supermarket,

Aleksanterinkatu 52B, www.stockmann.fi). Bookworms enjoy the massive **Academic Bookstore** just downhill from Stockmann (#39, same hours as Stockmann). **Artek,** Alvar and Elissa Aalto's flagship store (across from Stockmann at Keskuskatu 1B, www.artek.fi), offers fine furniture and lighting by the leading Finnish design concern.

Fans of Tove Jansson's Moomin children's stories will enjoy the **Moomin Shop,** on the second floor of the Forum shopping mall at Mannerheimintie 20, across the busy tram-lined street from Stockmann.

DESIGN DISTRICT

Helsinki's Design District is a several-block cluster of streets that's filled with design and antique shops, boutiques highlighting local fashion designers, and trendy restaurants. Explore this engaging zone to feel the creativity and uniqueness of Finnish design and urban culture. For a handy orientation to the options in this ever-changing area, visit www.designdistrict.fi (with themed walking maps) or pick up the Design District brochure from the TI.

While the Design District sprawls roughly southwest of the Esplanade nearly to the waterfront, the following zones are most worthy of exploration.

Near Kolmikulma Park: Just a block south of the Esplanade's top end (down Erottajankatu), the park called Kolmikulma (Diana Park, with its spear-throwing statue centerpiece) is a handy epicenter of Design District liveliness. Check out the following streets and shops in this area. **Uudenmaankatu** street (west from the park) has lots of good shops, including **Nounou,** which sells modern, handmade glass pieces (#2). **Momono** has well-selected examples of modern and vintage Finnish design (Yrjönkatu 1). **Formverk** features fun home decor and kitchenware (Annankatu 5). Places to eat include the recommended **Café Bar No. 9** and pedestrianized **Iso Roobertinkatu,** with lots of cheap eateries.

Fredrikinkatu, which crosses Uudenmaankatu two blocks west of the park, is one of the most engaging streets in town. Besides clothing stores, you'll find the following: **C. Hagelstam Antique Books** (#35, quaint and beautiful shop with vintage prints and books), **Chez Marius** (#26, fun kitchen gadgets and cooking gear), **Day** (kitty-corner from the Chez Marius at Bulevardi 11, quirky housewares and gifts), **Casuarina** (#30, rustic, reclaimed aesthetic home decor), **Primavera Interiors** (#41, artistic and funky home decor), and **DesiPeli** (Eerikinkatu 18, housewares including some with cool, Marimekko-type fabrics).

Near the Design Museum: The Design Museum anchors an appealing area of boutiques—and itself has a good shop with a wide range of Finnish design products (often related to current exhibits). A block south of the museum, on **Korkeavuorenkatu,** you'll find vintage shops, kitchenware, antiques, pop-up stores, clothing boutiques, hair salons, and cafés. Keep an eye out for **Pore Helsinki** (at #3), with casual fashion and accessories; and **Fasaani** (a.k.a. Helsinki Secondhand, at #5), with affordable pre-owned home-decor items just like those in galleries around town—furniture, dishes, glassware, and more (closed Sun, Korkeavuorenkatu 5, www.fasaani.fi).

OTHER SHOPPING OPTIONS

Market Square: This harborfront square is packed not only with fishmongers and producers, but also with stands selling Finnish souvenirs and more re-

fined crafts (roughly Mon-Fri 6:30-17:00, an hour later in summer, Sat until 16:00, only tourist stalls open on Sun 10:00-16:00).

Modern Shopping Malls: For less glamorous shopping needs, the **Kamppi** mall above and around the bus station is good. The **Forum** shopping center at Mannerheimintie 20 is filled with Euro fashion brands.

Flea Market: If you brake for garage sales, the outdoor **Hietalahti Market** is a 15-minute walk from the harbor or a short ride on tram #6 or #6T from Mannerheimintie to the Hietalahdentori stop (June-Aug Mon-Fri 8:00-17:00, Sat until 16:00, Sun 10:00-16:00; less action, shorter hours, and closed Sun off-season). The adjacent red-brick indoor Hietalahti Market Hall houses food stands (described later, under "Eating in Helsinki").

Sleeping in Helsinki

I've listed a wide range of accommodations in Helsinki, from fancy, well-located big hotels, to modest but cozy smaller hotels, to some unusually comfortable hostels. (And remember that some of the cheapest beds in Helsinki are on the overnight boats to Stockholm.) The hotels listed here have air-con and an elevator unless otherwise noted. Peak season is May to September, when the weather is better.

HOTELS

$$$$ Hotel Haven, with 77 elegantly appointed, comfortable rooms and a lobby that artfully mingles class and rustic comfort, owns a convenient location with good access to the harbor and the

Helsinki Hotels & Restaurants

To Sibelius Monument & Seurasaari Park

FINLANDIA HALL

NATIONAL MUSEUM

MUSEOKATU

HELSINKI MUSIC CENTER

TEMPPELIAUKIO "ROCK" CHURCH

T #2

NERVANDERKATU

MANNERHEIMINTIE

PARLIA-MENT

KIASMA MUSEUM

NATURAL HISTORY MUSEUM

NATIONAL THEATER

TRAIN STATION

RAUTATIEKATU

ARKADIANKATU

T #2 T #2

B #24

Rautatientori

MANN. STATUE

SALOMONKATU

23

T #2

24

KAIVOKATU

T

ATENEUM MUSEUM

M Rauta-tientori

CITY CENTER MALL

KESKUSKATU

POHJ. RAUTATIEKATU

ETEL.

KAMPPI MALL

Kamppi M BUS STATION

RUNEBERGINKATU

FREDRIKINKATU

KAMPPI CHAPEL

ANNANKATU

FORUM MALL

14

9

T

24

#2

MARI-MEKKO

ARTEK

STOCKMANN

26

MALMIKATU

27

#3

ACAD.

B #24

16

LAPINLAHDENKATU

KALEVANKATU

B #24

B

SWEDISH THEATER

RUOHOLAHDENKATU

EERIKINKATU

ALBERTINKATU

15

LÖNNROTINKATU

YRJÖNKATU

BULEVARDI

T #3

EROTTAJANKATU

DESIGN DISTRICT

11

Kolmikulma Park

7

#3 T

N

500 Meters

500 Yards

UUDENMAANKATU

8

To West Harbor Terminals

22

HIETALAHTI MARKET

To Hernesaari Terminal

#3 T

ISO ROOBERTINKATU

KATAJAKATU

Esplanade. "Standard" rooms face the back, with some street noise; quieter "style" rooms face the harbor (but with no views). It's worth a splurge, particularly if you can snare a deal (Unioninkatu 17, +358 9 681 930, www.hotelhaven.fi).

$$$$ GLO Hotel Kluuvi, with 184 stylish rooms, has a spa-like quality that gives you an appreciation for one (expensive) way to survive a long, dark winter. This tempting if trendy splurge, perfectly situated just north of the Esplanade, is worth considering if you prize elegance and a central location—especially if you can get a good discount (Kluuvikatu 4, +358 10 3444 400, www.glohotels. fi).

Accommodations

1. Hotel Haven
2. GLO Hotel Kluuvi
3. Hotel Rivoli Jardin
4. Hotel Fabian
5. To Hotel Katajanokka & Eurohostel
6. Scandic Grand Marina
7. GLO Hotel Art
8. Hotel Anna
9. Hotelli Finn
10. Essex Home
11. Hostel Diana Park & Café Bar No. 9

Eateries & Other

12. Market Square
13. Old Market Hall
14. Zetor
15. Lappi Restaurant
16. Teatterin Deli, Bar & Grilli
17. Strindberg
18. Savoy Restaurant
19. Spis
20. Juuri
21. Emo Restaurant & Picnic
22. Hietalahti Market Hall
23. Lasipalatsi
24. Grocery (2)
25. Café Kappeli
26. Café Aalto (in Academic Bookstore)
27. Ateljee Bar (in Torni Tower)

HELSINKI

$$$ Hotel Rivoli Jardin has a handy location, tucked away in a courtyard just off the middle of the Esplanade. Warm and personal, it has an inviting lounge and 55 rooms with classic Finnish comfort and a few classy flourishes (Kasarmikatu 40, +358 9 681 500, www.rivoli.fi, rivoli.jardin@rivoli.fi). They also rent apartments (one-week minimum).

$$$ Hotel Fabian, Hotel Haven's sister property a few blocks from the Esplanade, has 58 spacious and comfortable rooms with a black-and-white color scheme, nicely decorated public spaces, and a relaxing outdoor courtyard (Fabianinkatu 7, +358 9 6128 2000, www.hotelfabian.fi, sales@hotelfabian.fi).

$$$ Hotel Katajanokka occupies a former prison building, built in 1888, but you wouldn't know it from the chic design of this appealing four-star hotel with 106 quiet rooms. The windows no longer have bars (thanks to the local fire code), and walls have been removed so that two or three cells make a room. Check out the two original cells in the restaurant (no air-con, gym, bike rental, by Vyökatu stop of tram #4 near Katajanokka terminal, Merikasarminkatu 1A, +358 9 686 450, www.hotelkatajanokka.fi, sales@hotelkatajanokka.fi).

$$$ Scandic Grand Marina is a huge 462-room, impersonal four-star hotel filling a big, brick warehouse building near the Katajanokka terminal (Katajanokanlaituri 7, +358 9 16661, www.scandichotels.com/grandmarina, grandmarina@scandichotels.com).

$$$ GLO Hotel Art has a fine location convenient to the Design District, with 171 modern rooms behind a striking Art Nouveau facade that makes it feel like a stony medieval château has landed in the middle of Helsinki (Lönnrotinkatu 29, +358 10 3444 100, www.glohotels.fi, art@glohotels.fi).

$$ Hotel Anna is plain, conscientiously run, and feels a bit tired. Its well-worn 64 rooms in the heart of the Design District help raise funds for the Finnish Free Church (it's actually attached to a church—ask to see the shortcut to the choir loft). For more air in the rooms, ask at the desk for a key to open the larger windows (RS%, no air-con, family rooms available, 4 blocks south of the top of the Esplanade—take tram #3 from train station to Iso Roobertinkatu, Annankatu 1, +358 9 616 621, www.hotelanna.fi, info@hotelanna.fi).

$ Hotelli Finn is inexpensive and wonderfully central. Its 35 tidy rooms are stowed quietly on the sixth floor of an office building near the top of the Esplanade. It's short on amenities: tiny bathrooms, no breakfast (though a nearby bakery offers a buffet spread), and no real lobby or common space—but the price, location, and service are just right (Kalevankatu 3B, +358 9 684 4360, www.hotellifinn.fi, info@hotellifinn.fi).

$ Essex Home is a good budget alternative. Sweet Seija Lappalainen rents 13 apartments (all with kitchenettes) scattered around the residential streets of the Katajanokka peninsula (expect lots of stairs, Luotsikatu 9A, mobile +358 40 516 2714, www.essexhome.fi, info@essexhome.fi). The two "Essex Studio" rooms are a bit farther out.

HOSTELS

Helsinki's hostels are unusually comfortable, and all ages are welcome with or without a hostel membership.

¢ Eurohostel is 400 yards from the Katajanokka terminal and a 10-minute walk from Market Square. More like a budget hotel than a hostel, this modern place has a restaurant and good budget-travel information. While generally fully booked in advance, they release no-show beds at 18:00 (private and family rooms available, free morning sauna, evening sauna-€7.50, Vyökatu stop for tram #4 is around the corner, Linnankatu 9, +358 9 622 0470, www.eurohostel.eu/fi, eurohostel@eurohostel.fi).

¢ **Hostel Diana Park** is a small, friendly, centrally located hostel on the third floor of a 19th-century apartment building in the heart of the happening Design District. This is a better place to stay than Eurohostel if you're looking to meet fellow travelers in the common room and don't mind lugging your bags up the stairs (private room available, no elevator, Uudenmaankatu 9, +358 9 642 169, www.dianapark.fi, info@dianapark.fi).

Eating in Helsinki

Helsinki's many restaurants are a good value for lunch on weekdays. Finnish companies get a tax break if they distribute lunch coupons (worth €10) to their employees. It's no surprise that most downtown Helsinki restaurants offer weekday lunch specials that cost exactly the value of the coupon. These low prices evaporate in the evenings and on weekends. For locations see the "Helsinki Hotels and Restaurants Map," earlier.

FUN HARBORFRONT EATERIES

Stalls on Market Square: Helsinki's delightful and vibrant square is magnetic any time of day...but especially at lunchtime. This really is the most memorable, casual, quick-and-easy lunch place in town. A half-dozen orange tents (erected to shield diners from dive-bombing gulls) serve moose meatballs, smoked reindeer, and creamy salmon soup until 18:00. Even though you're served on paper plates, it's not unusual for the Finnish president to stop by here with visiting dignitaries. There's a crêpe place, and at the far end—my favorites—several salmon grills (€11-13 for a good meal). The only real harborside dining in this part of town is picnicking. While these places provide picnic tables, you can also have your food foil-wrapped to go and grab benches right on the water down near Uspenski Orthodox Cathedral.

Old Market Hall (Vanha Kauppahalli): Just beyond the harborside market is a cute, red-brick, indoor market hall. Its petite interior has been beautifully renovated with rich woodwork (daily 8:00-18:00, not all stalls open Sun). Today, along with produce stalls, it's a hit for its fun, inexpensive eateries. You'll find enticing coffee shops with tempting pastries; grilled, smoked, or pickled fish options; mounds of saffron-yellow paella; delectable open-face sandwiches; a handy chance to sample reindeer meat; and an array of international eateries, from Middle Eastern and Lebanese meals to Vietnamese banh mi sandwiches. In the market hall, **$ Soppakeittiö** ("Soup Kitchen") serves big bowls of filling, tasty seafood soup.

FINNISH-THEMED DINING

$$$ Zetor, a self-proclaimed "110 percent Finnish" restaurant, mercilessly lampoons Finnish rural culture and cuisine (while celebrating it deep down). Sit next to a cow-crossing sign at a tractor-turned-into-a-table, in a "Finnish Western" atmosphere. Main courses include reindeer, smoked perch pies, grilled liver, and less exotic fare. A bit touristy and tacky, this quirky place can be fun—and it gets loud after 20:00, when the dance floor gets going (daily 12:00-24:00, 200 yards north of Stockmann department store, across the street from McDonald's at Mannerheimintie 3, +358 10 766 4450).

$$$$ Lappi Restaurant is a fine place for tasty Lapp (Sami) cuisine, with an entertaining menu (including house-smoked fish, roasted elk, and reindeer shank). The snug, woody atmosphere will have you thinking you've traveled north and lashed your reindeer to the hitchin' post. Dinner reservations strongly recommended (Mon-Fri 16:00-22:30, Sat from 13:00, closed Sun, Annankatu 22, +358 9 645 550, www.lappires.com).

ESPLANADE EATERIES

Restaurants line the sunny north side of the Esplanade—offering lunch salads and light meals in their cafés (with fine sidewalk seating), plush sofas for cocktails in their bars, and fancy restaurant dining upstairs. Here are two venerable cafés, plus a fancy splurge on the south side of the Esplanade.

$$ Teatterin Deli and **Teatterin Bar** are among several interconnected eateries attached to the landmark Swedish Theater. Order a sandwich or salad from the deli counter (facing the Academic Bookstore) to eat in or take away. The long cocktail bar that faces the Esplanade is a fun space for a drink and people-watching. Whether you order a meal or a drink, you're welcome to find a seat out on the leafy Esplanade terrace (deli counter open daily until 21:00, at the top of the Esplanade, Pohjoisesplanadi 2, +358 9 6128 5000). The fancy **$$$$ Grilli** restaurant is also here.

$$$ Strindberg, near the corner of the Esplanade and Mikonkatu, oozes atmosphere and class. Downstairs is an elegant café with outdoor and indoor tables great for people-watching (sandwiches and salads). The upstairs cocktail lounge—with big sofas and bookshelves—has a den-like coziness that attracts an after-work crowd. Also upstairs, the inviting restaurant has huge main dishes with fish, meat, pasta, and vegetarian options; reserve in advance to get a window seat overlooking the Esplanade (restaurant open Mon-Sat 11:00-23:00, closed Sun; café open Mon-Sat 9:00-24:00, Sun 10:00-22:00; Pohjoisesplanadi 33, +358 9 681 2030).

Dressy Splurge Dinner: $$$$ Savoy Restaurant, where locals go for special occasions, is expensive, formal but friendly, and drenched in Alvar Aalto design. Everything in this eighth-floor view restaurant—from the chairs and lampshades to the doors—is 1937 original. The food is Continental with a Finnish touch. While the glassed-in terrace offers a great rooftop view, the elegant interior is where you'll experience a classic Finnish atmosphere. Reservations are advised for meals, but come up anytime for a drink, either inside or on the tight terrace (Mon-Fri 11:30-15:00 & 18:00-24:00, Sat dinner only, closed Sun, Eteläesplanadi 14, +358 9 6128 5300, www.savoyhelsinki.fi).

TRENDY EATERIES IN AND NEAR THE DESIGN DISTRICT

Several creative eateries cluster in the Design District, a short stroll south and west of the Esplanade, offering a fresh take on the cuisine of Finland, featuring seasonal ingredients and modern presentations.

$$$$ Spis is your best Helsinki bet for splurging on Finnish New Nordic cuisine. Reserve ahead for one of the prized tables in its tiny, peeling plaster, rustic-chic dining room (tasting menus only, Tue-Thu from 18:00, Fri-Sat from 17:30, last seating at 20:30, closed Sun-Mon, Kasarmikatu 26, mobile +358 45 305 1211, www.spis.fi).

$$$$ Juuri has a casual interior and a few outdoor tables. They serve a variety of "sapas"—small plates highlighting Finland's culinary bounty, such as herring, pike roe, and arctic char (Mon-Fri 11:30-14:30 & 17:00-23:00, Sat 12:00-23:00, Sun 16:00-23:00, Korkeavuorenkatu 27, +358 9 635 732).

$$$ Emo Restaurant is a pleasantly unpretentious wine bar in a sleepy zone just a block off of the Esplanade. They serve up €10 small plates as well as à la carte choices—cassoulet, rack of pork, rainbow trout (lunch Tue-Fri 11:30-14:30; dinner Mon-Sat 17:00-24:00, closed Sun; Kasarmikatu 44, mobile +358 10 505 0900, www.emo-ravintola.fi).

Pub Grub: A simpler choice tucked between shops in the heart of the Design District, **$$ Café Bar No. 9** attracts a loyal local following, who enjoy digging into plates of unpretentious pub food (Uudenmaankatu 9, +358 9 621 4059).

Market Hall: Hiding at the western edge of the Design District, the **$$ Hietalahti Market Hall** is a fun place to browse for a meal. Like the Old Market Hall along the South Harbor, this elegantly renovated (but less touristy) food hall is filled with a colorful variety of vendors and delightful seating upstairs (Mon-Thu 8:00-18:00, Fri-Sat until 22:00, Sun 10:00-16:00, www.hietalahdenkauppahalli.fi).

NEAR THE STATIONS

$$ Lasipalatsi, a Helsinki landmark in a 1930s functionalist building, is on Mannerheimintie between the train and bus stations. The café—with a youthful terrace on the square out back—offers a self-service buffet (€11 lunch menu available all day); there are always €5 sandwiches and cakes (Mon-Sat 8:30-20:00, closed Sun). Upstairs there's a more expensive **$$$** restaurant that's a Helsinki classic, with bird's-eye city views (Mon-Fri 11:00-24:00, closed Sat-Sun, across from the old post office building at Mannerheimintie 22, +358 9 612 6700).

PICNICS

In supermarkets, buy the semiflat bread (available dark or light) that Finns love—every slice is a heel. Finnish liquid yogurt is also a treat (sold in liter cartons). Karelian pasties, filled with rice or mashed potatoes, make a good snack. A beautiful, upscale supermarket is in the basement of the **Stockmann** department store—follow the *Delikatessen* signs downstairs (Mon-Fri until 21:00, Sat-Sun until 18:00, Aleksanterinkatu 52B). Two blocks north, **S Market** is a more workaday supermarket under the Sokos department store next to the train station (daily until 22:00).

Another option is **$ Picnic,** a casual chain offering fresh, made-to-go sandwiches, salads, and pastries. There's one just south of the midsection of the Esplanade (at Kasarmikatu 42), but you'll see them all around town, including in the Forum and Kamppi shopping centers (www.picnic.fi).

Helsinki Connections

BY BUS OR TRAIN

From Helsinki, it's easy to get to **Turku** (hourly, 2 hours by either bus or train) or **St. Petersburg, Russia** (see options later). For train info, visit www.vr.fi; for buses, consult Matkahuolto.fi.

BY BOAT
Helsinki's Ferry Terminals

Helsinki has multiple ports. Closest to the city center are the South Harbor (Eteläsatama) docks. In this area, travelers are most likely to use the **Olympia terminal** (Tallink Silja boats to Stockholm) and the **Katajanokka terminal** (Viking Line boats to Stockholm and Tallinn). Trams stop near all the South Harbor terminals (tram #5 near Katajanokka, trams #2 and #3 near Olympia).

Farther from the center (about a 40-minute walk from the train station) is **West Harbor** (Länsisatama), with two terminals serving Tallink Silja and Eckerö Line boats to Tallinn, plus departures to St. Petersburg. From there, you can reach downtown Helsinki and the central train station on trams #6T and #7 (tram stop is right outside the terminals) or by taxi (about €15-20). Terminal buildings are well organized, with cafés and other amenities. Boats open 1.5 hours before departure, and you must be checked in 20 minutes before departure. Parking is available at terminals (but space is limited); ask for details when you reserve your ticket.

For terminal locations, see the "Greater Helsinki" map at the beginning of this chapter.

Sailing Overnight Between Stockholm and Helsinki

Both Viking Line and Tallink Silja connect the capitals of Sweden and Finland. Cruises take about 17 hours. Each line offers state-of-the-art, 2,700-bed ships with luxurious smorgasbord meals, reasonable cabins, plenty of entertainment (discos, saunas, gambling), and enough duty-free shopping to sink a ship.

The boats are filled with about 45 percent Finns, 45 percent Swedes, and 10 percent cruisers from other countries. The average passenger spends as much on booze and tax-free items as on boat fare (that's why ticket prices are so reasonable—to encourage locals to spend money onboard). To maintain their tax-free status, the boats make a midnight stop in the Åland Islands—a self-governing, Swedish-speaking province of Finland that's exempt from the EU's value-added tax.

Of the two lines, Viking Line has the reputation as the party boat. Tallink Silja is considered more elegant. But both lines have their share of noisy passengers making duty-free booze runs.

Buying Tickets

Both Viking Line (www.vikingline.fi) and Tallink Silja (www.tallinksilja.com) sail nightly between Stockholm and Helsinki year-round. Boats leave (from either port) between 16:30 and 17:30, and arrive the next morning around 10:00.

Cost: Fares vary based on season, day of the week, and cabin

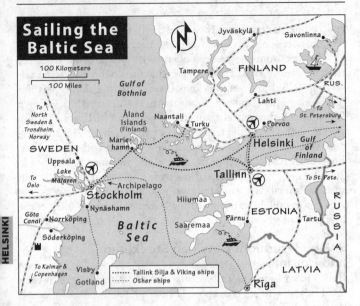

class. Mid-June to mid-August is the most expensive (and crowded), as are Friday nights. In summer, one-way tickets start at about €88 and go up from there. Travelers with rail passes that cover Sweden or Finland get discounts on both lines (cabins extra). There can be discounts for early booking, seniors, and families.

Itinerary Options: "Round-trip" fares (across and back on successive nights, giving you access to your cabin throughout the day) generally cost less than two one-way fares. The drawback is that you'll have only a few hours on land. But you may be able to get the round-trip fare on nonsuccessive nights if you book a hotel through the cruise line for the intervening night(s). If it fits your schedule, this can be a good deal.

Reservations: For summer or weekend sailings, reserve well in advance. Book online with a credit card—you'll get a reservation number and pick up your boarding card at the port. You can also book by phone or in person: **Viking Line**'s customer service line is Finnish based (+358 9 123 574). **Tallink Silja** has offices in Helsinki (Tyynenmerenkatu 9, +358 9 18041) and in Stockholm (Södra Hamnvägen 50A, Swedish +46 8 666 3330). Any travel agent in Scandinavia can also sell you a ticket (with a small booking fee).

Tips Onboard

Meals: While ships have cheap, fast cafeterias as well as classy, romantic restaurants, they are famous for their smorgasbord dinners (usually around €35-45; breakfast smorgasbord €11-15). Dinner is self-serve in two sittings, one at about 17:00, the other around 20:00. (In summer, it's best to reserve a table with your ferry booking; I prefer to have dinner at the first sitting—shortly after departure—and be on deck for sunset.) If you board without a smorgasbord reservation, go to the restaurant and make one—window seats are highly sought after and can come with a surcharge. The price includes beer, wine, soft drinks, and coffee. Note that you are not allowed to bring your own meals on board Viking ships.

Time Change: Finland is one hour ahead of Sweden. If sailing from Stockholm to Helsinki, operate on Swedish time until you're ready to go to bed, then reset your watch. Morning schedules are Finnish time, and vice versa when you return.

Money: For purchases, be prepared to primarily use credit cards while onboard. Some ships and routes may accept euros and Swedish kronor. You'll find exchange desks and/or ATMS in the terminals at each end.

Sailing to Other Destinations

Tallinn: The Estonian capital can be spliced into your itinerary as a side trip from Helsinki (or vice-versa), or as a triangle trip (Stockholm-Helsinki-Tallinn-Stockholm, must be booked as three one-ways). Tallink Silja and Eckerö Line boats to Tallinn leave from Helsinki's West Harbor while Viking Line boats use the more central Katajanokka terminal (see "Helsinki's Ferry Terminals," earlier). For more details on boat fares and schedules, see "Tallinn Connections—By Boat" on page 683.

Turku: Both Viking Line and Tallink Silja also sail from Stockholm to Turku in Finland, a shorter crossing (12 hours, departing daily at about 7:00-9:00 and 19:30-21:00). Turku, a "mini-Helsinki" with more medieval charm but less urban bustle, is two hours from Helsinki by bus or train. The cheaper boat fare saves you enough to pay for the train trip from Turku to Helsinki.

Visiting Helsinki by Cruise Ship

Cruise traffic to Helsinki is concentrated at the Hernesaari piers of the West Harbor (Länsistama); only a few cruise ships use the South Harbor (Eteläsatama). For more details on the ports, see the Port of Helsinki website (www.portofhelsinki.fi) and pick up my *Rick Steves Scandinavian & Northern European Cruise Ports* guidebook.

CONNECTING HELSINKI AND ST. PETERSBURG

Many visitors use Helsinki as a launch pad for a visit to St. Petersburg, Russia—just 240 miles east. For more details on St. Petersburg, consider my *Rick Steves Snapshot St. Petersburg, Helsinki & Tallinn*.

Visa Requirements: American and Canadian travelers to Russia need a visa, which must be arranged several weeks in advance (you must submit your passport with your visa application, so plan ahead). For details on obtaining a visa, see www.ricksteves. com/europe/russia/how-to-get-a-russian-visa.

Visa Exceptions: If you arrive in St. Petersburg **on a cruise,** the visa requirement is waived provided you contract with a local tour operator (or join one of your cruise line's excursions) for a guided visit around the city. But there is an exception that gives you time on your own in the city: If you go to St. Petersburg on a St. Peter Line ship (see below), then pay for a "shuttle service" from the dock into the city (typically €25 round-trip), you can stay up to 72 hours before returning with a St. Peter Line shuttle and boat. Although this is not a guided visit, it's treated as the "cruise exception" explained above.

Getting There by Bus or Train: The **bus** is slower and cheaper. Lux Express runs multiple buses from downtown Helsinki and the airport (runs daily including two overnight, 8 hours, about €25-30, https://luxexpress.eu/en); they also sells taxi vouchers for St. Petersburg taxis, which can be convenient. The Allegro **train,** operated by Finnish Railways, is much faster (4/day, 3.5 hours, €45-110 depending on demand, book ahead at www.vr.fi); the train arrives at St. Petersburg's Finlyandsky train station. There's also a daily overnight train to **Moscow.** Rail passes can cover the journey from Helsinki to the Russian border.

Getting There by Boat: Many Baltic Sea cruises include a stop in St. Petersburg. For those doing it on their own, **St. Peter Line** sails from Helsinki to St. Petersburg every other day, departing from West Harbor (terminal 1) in the evening. The ride takes 14 hours, and the same ship sails back to Helsinki the next day (departing 19:00). St. Peter Line also connects St. Petersburg to Tallinn about once weekly, then continues on to Stockholm. For details, see www.stpeterline.com or visit one of the Strömma/Sightseeing Helsinki kiosks for information.

ESTONIA

ESTONIA

Eesti

A crossroads between Scandinavia and Central Europe, Estonia is shaped by its eclectic past and inspired by the prospect of an ever-brighter future. In the European Union, only three microstates (Cyprus, Luxembourg, and Malta) have a smaller population than Estonia. But like its Baltic neighbors Latvia and Lithuania, Estonia has an enthusiasm for the things that make it unique—proving that you don't have to be big to have a clear cultural identity.

Estonians are related to the Finns and have a similar history—first Swedish domination, then Russian (1710-1918), and finally independence (after World War I). In 1940, Estonians were at least as affluent and as advanced as the Finns, but they could not preserve their independence from the USSR during World War II. As a result, Estonia sank into a nearly 50-year period of Soviet domination and communist stagnation.

Since regaining its independence with the collapse of the Soviet Union, the country has made great strides. It joined the EU and NATO in 2004, adopted the euro currency in 2011, and today feels pretty much as "Western" as its Nordic neighbors.

EU membership seemed like a natural step to many Estonians; they already thought of themselves as part of the Nordic world (Stockholm is just an overnight boat ride away). Language, history, religion, and frequent ferries connect Finns and Estonians. Only 50 miles separate Helsinki and Tallinn. Finns visit Tallinn to eat, drink, and shop more cheaply than at home, and the city tends to become a Finnish nightclub on summer weekends.

This "former USSR" country is anything but backward. Thanks to visionary and aggressive development policies implemented soon after independence—including the designation of internet access as a basic human right—Estonia is a global trendsetter in technology. By 1998, every school in Estonia was already online. The country has some of the fastest broadband speeds in the world, Estonians vote and file their taxes online, and the software for Skype was invented here. The multibillion-dollar windfall from

Estonia Almanac

Official Name: Eesti Vabariik—the Republic of Estonia—or simply Estonia.

Size: At 17,500 square miles, Estonia is about the size of New Hampshire and Vermont combined. It's home to over 1.2 million people (70 per square mile).

Geography: Between Latvia and Russia, Estonia borders the Baltic Sea and Gulf of Finland. It includes more than 1,500 islands and islets, and has the highest number of meteorite craters per land area in the world.

Latitude and Longitude: 59°N and 26°E, similar latitude to Juneau, Alaska.

Biggest City: The capital of Estonia, Tallinn, has about 450,000 people.

Economy: Estonia's transition to a free-market system included joining the World Trade Organization and the European Union. In recent years, it's had one of the highest per-capita income levels in Central Europe and today boasts a per-capita GDP of about $32,000. Its four major trading partners are Finland, Sweden, Russia, and Germany, and it's especially strong in electronics and telecommunications.

Currency: €0.85 = about $1.

Government: Estonia is a parliamentary democracy, with a president elected by parliament and a prime minister. The 101-member parliament (Riigikogu) is elected by popular vote every four years.

Flag: The pre-1940 Estonian flag was restored in 1990. It has three equal horizontal bands with blue at the top, black in the middle, and white on the bottom. The blue represents Estonia's lakes and sea, and the loyalty and devotion of the country to its people. The black symbolizes the homeland's rich soil and the hardships the people have suffered. The white represents hope and happiness.

The Average Estonian is 44 years old and has 1.6 children. Among the quarter-million Estonians age 65 and older, about two-thirds are women. When an Estonian sings the national anthem, it has the same tune—but different words—as that of Finland.

Skype's 2005 sale to eBay kickstarted a whole new venture-capital industry that is still paying dividends today.

This little land has a long, jagged, hauntingly beautiful coastline, over 1,000 lakes, and more than 1,500 (mostly uninhabited) islands. About 50 percent of the landscape is forest, while marshlands and bogs cover another 20 percent.

Traditional folk music buoys the national spirit—especially at the Song Festival every five years, where a significant portion of the population convenes to pour out their souls in song. Some of Estonia's traditions may strike you as quirky. Estonians snack on nearly black rye bread slathered in garlic and bury their dead in evocative pine forests. And they're among the least religious people in the world—the majority of Estonians are unaffiliated with any religion (about 10 percent are Lutheran and 16 percent are Orthodox).

Even as Estonia will always face West, across the Baltic, it also faces East, into the Russian hinterlands. While nearly seven in ten residents are of Estonian heritage, about one-quarter are of Russian descent (a legacy of Estonia's Soviet experience). Many Estonian

Russians still hold Russian passports There are smaller minorities of Ukrainians, Belarusians, and Finns. About 70 percent speak the official language—Estonian—and nearly 30 percent speak Russian.

The size of Estonia's Russian population causes some interesting challenges. After Russia vowed to "protect" Russian speakers in Ukraine and fostered a separatist revolt there, Estonians have wondered if something similar could happen here. To bridge what many see as divided loyalties, the Estonian government is working to better integrate its Russian minority, making it easier for them to acquire Estonian citizenship and addressing high unemployment in the border areas where many ethnic Russians live.

Most Estonians speak English—it's the first choice these days at school. Estonian is similar to Finnish and equally difficult; only a million people speak it worldwide. Two useful phrases to know are *Tänan* (TAH-nahn; Thank you) and *Terviseks!* (TEHR-vee-sehks; Cheers!). For more helpful words, see the Estonian survival phrases on the next page. The farther you go beyond the touristy zones, the more you see that Russian is still Estonia's second language. If you know some Russian, use it.

Estonian Survival Phrases

Estonian has a few unusual vowel sounds. The letter ä is pronounced "ah" as in "hat," but a without the umlaut sounds more like "aw" as in "hot." To make the sound ö, purse your lips and say "oh"; the letter õ is similar, but with the lips less pursed. Listen to locals and imitate. In the phonetics, ī sounds like the long i in "light," and bolded syllables are stressed.

Hello. (formal)	Tervist.	**tehr**-veest
Hi. / Bye. (informal)	Tere. / Nägemist.	**teh**-reh / **nah**-geh-meest
Do you speak English?	Kas te räägite inglise keelt? kahs teh **raah**-gee-teh **een**-glee-seh kehlt	
Yes. / No.	Jah. / Ei.	yah / ay
Please. / You're welcome.	Palun.	**pah**-lohn
Thank you (very much).	Tänan (väga).	**tah**-nahn (**vah**-gaw)
Can I help you?	Saan ma teid aidata?	saahn mah tayd ī-dah-tah
Excuse me.	Vabandust.	**vaw**-bahn-doost
(Very) good.	(Väga) hea.	(**vah**-gaw) **hey**-ah
Goodbye.	Hüvasti.	**hew**-vaw-stee
zero / one / two	null / üks / kaks	nuhl / ewks / kawks
three / four	kolm / neli	**kohlm** / **nay**-lee
five / six	viis / kuus	vees / koos
seven / eight	seitse / kaheksa	**sayt**-seh / **kaw**-hehk-sah
nine / ten	üheksa / kümme	**ew**-hehk-sah / **kew**-meh
hundred	sada	**saw**-daw
thousand	tuhat	**too**-hawt
How much?	Kui palju?	kwee **pawl**-yoo
local currency: (Estonian) crown	(Eesti) krooni (eh-stee) **kroh**-nee	
Where is...?	Kus asub...?	koos **ah**-soob
...the toilet	...tualett	**too**-ah-leht
men	mehed	**meh**-hed
women	naised	**nī**-sehd
water / coffee	vesi / kohvi	**vay**-see / **koh**-vee
beer / wine	õlu / vein	**uh**-loh / vayn
Cheers!	Terviseks!	**tehr**-vee-sehks
The bill, please.	Arve, palun.	**ahr**-veh **pah**-lohn

TALLINN

Tallinn is a rewarding detour for those who want to spice up their Scandinavian travels with a Baltic twist. Among Nordic medieval cities, there's none nearly as well preserved as Tallinn. Its mostly intact city wall includes 26 watchtowers, each topped by a pointy red roof. Baroque and choral music ring out from its old Lutheran churches. I'd guess that Tallinn (with about 450,000 people) has more restaurants, cafés, and surprises per capita and square inch than any city in this book—and the fun is comparatively cheap.

While Tallinn's Nordic Lutheran culture and language connect it with Scandinavia, two centuries of czarist Russian rule and 45 years as part of the Soviet Union left behind some Russian touches. Yet overlying all of that is the vibrancy of a free nation that's just a generation old. Estonian pride is in the air.

As a member of the merchant coalition known as the Hanseatic League, the city of Tallinn was a medieval stronghold of the Baltic trading world. Little Estonia was passed between larger powers—Germany, Denmark, Poland, and Russia—for much of its history. In the 19th and early 20th centuries, Tallinn industrialized and expanded beyond its Old Town walls. Architects put in broad streets of public buildings, low Scandinavian-style apartment buildings, and single-family wooden houses. Estonia briefly

Greater Tallinn

won its independence in 1920, but that ended in World War II, and after 1945, Soviet planners ringed the city with stands of now-crumbling concrete high-rises where many of Tallinn's Russian immigrants settled.

Since independence from the Soviet Union in 1991, Tallinn has westernized at an astounding rate. The Old Town has been scrubbed into a pristine Old World theme park—a fascinating package of pleasing towers, ramparts, facades, *striptiis* bars, churches, shops, and people-watching. Nearby, the old industrial Rotermann Quarter is an enticing mix of architectural experimentation and careful preservation.

Given its compact scale, Tallinn can easily be appreciated as a day trip from Helsinki. But the city rewards those who spend the night. More time gives you the chance to explore some of the more colorful slices of life outside the Old Town walls.

PLANNING YOUR TIME

For anyone touring Scandinavia or the Baltic, Tallinn is certainly worth a day. Many people find it works best as a full-day side trip from Helsinki. Another option is to overnight in both Helsinki and Tallinn—either as a triangular detour from Stockholm, or on the way between Stockholm and St. Petersburg. Cruise ships have discovered Tallinn, and its cobbles can be mobbed at midday.

Day-Trippers: Hit the ground running by following my self-guided walk right from the port. Enjoy a nice lunch in the Old Town. Then spend the afternoon shopping and browsing, or choose one of the outlying sights: Seaplane Harbor for boats and planes, Rotermann Quarter for new and old architecture, Estonian Open-Air Museum for folk culture, or Kumu Art Museum for Estonian art and a walk in nearby Kadriorg Park. Bring a jacket—Tallinn can be chilly or windy even on sunny summer days. And, given that locals call their cobbled streets "a free foot massage," sturdy shoes are smart, too.

With More Time: For the best orientation to the city, start your visit with my self-guided walk. But because Tallinn can be inundated midday with cruise passengers and day-trippers, you may want to save your Old Town exploration for early or late, and visit outlying sights when the center is most crowded. Check concert schedules if you'll be around for the evening.

Orientation to Tallinn

Tallinn's walled Old Town is an easy 15-minute walk from the ferry and cruise terminals, where most visitors arrive. The Old Town is divided into two parts (historically, two separate towns): the upper town (Toompea) and the lower town (with Town Hall Square). A remarkably intact medieval wall surrounds the two towns, which are themselves separated by another wall.

Town Hall Square (Raekoja Plats) marks the heart of the medieval lower town. The main TI is nearby, as are many sights and eateries. Pickpockets are a problem in the more touristy parts of the Old Town and at the viewpoints in the upper town, so keep valuables carefully stowed. The area around the Viru Keskus mall and Hotel Viru, just east of the Old Town, is useful for everyday shopping (bookstores and supermarkets), practical services (laundry), and public transport.

TOURIST INFORMATION

The hardworking and helpful TI is just a block off Town Hall Square (daily 9:00-18:00 in summer, shorter hours off-season; Niguliste 2, +372 645 7777, www.visittallinn.ee).

Tallinn Card: This card—sold at the TI, airport, train sta-

Tallinn

1 Launderette (2)
2 Travel Agency
3 Bike Rental

tion, travel agencies, ferry ports, and big hotels—covers public transit and more than 40 museums and major sights (€28/24 hours, €42/48 hours, €51/72 hours, www.tallinncard.ee). A more expensive "Plus" version includes a hop-on, hop-off bus route.

ARRIVAL IN TALLINN

For advice on taking taxis, and more details on the public transit and ticket options mentioned below, see "Getting Around Tallinn," later.

By Boat: Tallinn has three passenger/car-ferry terminals (A/B and D), and a dedicated cruise terminal. The side-by-side A/B terminals are the closest to the Old Town; the cruise terminal is just to the north; D terminal is a 10-minute walk to the east (and the farthest from Old Town). Each terminal offers baggage storage. Be sure to confirm which terminal your return boat will use.

If you have no luggage, you can **walk** 15 minutes to reach the center of town—just follow signs to the city center and set your sights on the tallest spire in the distance (or follow my self-guided walk, later). If you'd rather first visit the Seaplane Harbor, look for the Kultuurikilomeeter (Culture Kilometer) path—straight ahead as you leave the cruise port—which takes you there on a long, scenic, mostly seaside stroll (for path location, see the "Greater Tallinn" map, earlier).

If you have bags, it's best to grab a **taxi**—otherwise your rolling suitcase will take a pounding on the Old Town's cobbled streets. The taxi fare to anywhere in or near the Old Town should be less than €10; the maximum starting fare should be no more than €5.50 and posted on a yellow sticker on the right rear window. Before getting in a taxi, ask the cabbie for an estimate to avoid being overcharged.

Public **bus #2** leaves from outside the A and D terminals and runs to the A. Laikmaa stop just southeast of the Old Town—behind Hotel Viru and the Viru Keskus mall—then continues to the bus station and eventually the airport (2-3/hour; for ticket-buying details, see "Getting Around Tallinn—By Public Transportation," later).

By Plane: The Tallinn airport (Tallinna Lennujaam), three miles southeast of downtown, has a small info desk (code: TLL, www.tallinn-airport.ee, +372 605 8888). To reach the Old Town, take a **taxi** or **Uber** (generally €8-10). Another option is public **bus #2** (2-3/hour; catch from floor 0—follow bus signs down the escalator, go outside and left); the A. Laikmaa stop is near the Old Town (see bus details above).

By Train and Bus: While Tallinn has a sleepy and cute little train station (called Balti Jaam), few tourists will need to use it. The station, a five-minute walk across a busy road from the Old Town (use the pedestrian underpass), is adjacent to the big, cheap Go Hotel Shnelli and the colorful Balti Jaam Market.

Tallinn's long-distance bus station *(autobussijaam)* is midway between downtown and the airport, and served by bus #2 and trams #2 and #4.

HELPFUL HINTS

Money: Estonia uses the euro. ATMs are sometimes marked *Otto*.

Time: Estonia is one hour ahead of continental Europe, which means it's generally seven/ten hours ahead of the East/West Coasts of the US.

Laundry: The Viru Keskus mall has a handy **Top Clean** laundry drop-off service downstairs (Mon-Fri 8:00-20:00, Sat from 10:00, closed Sun; underground facing bus stalls 1 and 2, +372 610 1405, www.puhastuskeskus.ee). **Pesumaja Sol** offers self- or full-service; it's just beyond the Viru Keskus mall and Kaubamaja department store (just walkable from the Old Town, or take tram #2 or #4 to the Paberi stop, a few blocks away; Mon-Fri 7:00-20:00, Sat 8:00-16:00, closed Sun, Maakri 23, +372 677 1551).

Travel Agency: Estravel, at the corner of Suur-Karja and Müürivähe, is handy and sells boat tickets for no extra fee (Mon-Fri 9:00-18:00, closed Sat-Sun, Suur-Karja 15, +372 626 6233, www.estravel.ee).

Bike Rental: Head for **City Bike**, at the north end of the Old Town (€12/6 hours, €15/24 hours; electric bikes available; daily 10:00-18:00, Vene 33, mobile +372 511 1819, www.citybike.ee). They also do bike tours (see "Tours in Tallinn," later).

Parking: The Port of Tallinn operates several parking lots by the ferry terminals. Old Town parking is very expensive; try parking in the lot underneath Freedom Square (Vabaduse väljak), at the southern edge of the Old Town, a short walk from the TI and Town Hall Square.

GETTING AROUND TALLINN
By Public Transportation

The Old Town and surrounding areas are easy to explore on foot, but public transit is useful for reaching outlying sights (such as Kadriorg Park, Kumu Art Museum, or the Estonian Open-Air Museum). Tallinn has buses, trams, and trolley buses—note that they may reuse the same numbers (bus #2, tram #2, and trolley bus #2) but are totally different lines. Maps and schedules are posted at stops; transit maps are available at the TI or at www.visittallinn.ee. For an overview of transit stops useful to visitors, see the "Greater Tallinn" map, earlier. As you approach a station, you'll hear the name of the impending stop, then the name of the following stop—don't hop off one stop too early.

Tickets: You can buy a **single ticket** from the driver for €2 (exact change only) or a **QR ticket** for use on your phone (€1.50 for any ride up to 1 hour, can purchase up to 10 rides per ticket, shareable with other riders, purchase at Tallinn.pilet.ee or with the mobile app Pilet.ee). For longer stays, consider a **Ühiskaart smart-**

card (€2, buy at any yellow-and-blue R-Kiosk convenience store, found all over town), then load it up with credit—€1.50/ride; also available as day tickets—€4.50/24 hours, €7.50/72 hours).

By Taxi or Uber

Taxis in Tallinn are handy, but because rates are not uniform, always confirm a ballpark fare and whether it is per ride or per person before getting in. Cabbies are required to use the meter and give you a meter-printed receipt.

It's safest to order taxis by phone or ask a local to call for you—this is what Estonians usually do. **Tulika** is the largest company, with predictable, fair prices (+372 612 0000 or use their app, check latest prices at www.tulika.ee). **Tallink Takso** is another reputable option with comparable fares (+372 640 8921 or dial 1921 locally).

If you must catch a taxi off the street, go to a busy taxi stand where lots of cabs are lined up. Before you get in, take a close look at the yellow price list on the rear passenger-side door; the base fare should be no more than €5.50 and the per-kilometer charge no more than €1.10. If it's not, keep looking. A photo ID license should be attached to the middle of the dashboard. Rates must be posted by law, but are not capped or regulated, so the most common scam—unfortunately widespread and legal—is to list an inflated price on the yellow price sticker, and simply wait for a tourist to hop in without noticing.

Uber works in Tallinn like it does in the US.

Tours in Tallinn

Bus and Walking Tour

This enjoyable, narrated 2.5-hour tour of Tallinn comes in two parts: first by bus for an overview of sights outside the Old Town, such as the Song Festival Grounds and Kadriorg Park, then on foot to sights within the Old Town (€30, pay driver, in English; daily morning and early afternoon departures from ferry terminals and major hotels in city center; +372 610 8616, www.traveltoestonia. com).

Local Guides

Mati Rumessen is a top-notch guide, especially for car tours inside or outside town (€35/hour driving or walking tours, price may vary with group size and length of tour, mobile +372 509 4661, www. tourservice.ee). Other fine guides are **Antonio Villacis** (rates negotiable, mobile +372 5662 9306, antonio.villacis@gmail.com) and **Miina Puusepp** (€20/hour, mobile +372 551 7028, miinapaul@gmail.com).

Tallinn at a Glance

Central Tallinn

▲▲▲Tallinn's Old Town Well-preserved medieval center with cobblestoned lanes, gabled houses, historic churches, and turreted city walls. See page 650.

▲▲Russian Orthodox Cathedral Accessible look at the Russian Orthodox faith, with a lavish interior. **Hours:** Daily 8:00-18:00. See page 658.

▲Museum of Estonian History High-tech exhibits within the Great Guild Hall explain Estonia's national narrative. **Hours:** Daily 10:00-18:00, closed Wed off-season. See page 662.

▲Tallinn City Museum Interesting overview of Tallinn's past, from medieval times into the 20th century. **Hours:** Daily 10:30-18:00, shorter hours and closed Mon off-season. See page 663.

▲Rotermann Quarter Rejuvenated industrial zone east of the Old Town, with shopping, restaurants, and old-meets-new architecture. See page 664.

Outside the Core

▲▲Kumu Art Museum The best of contemporary Estonian art displayed in a strikingly modern building. **Hours:** Tue-Sun 11:00-18:00, Thu until 20:00, closed Mon. See page 667.

▲▲Seaplane Harbor Impressive museum of boats and planes displayed in a vast old hangar along the waterfront. **Hours:** Daily 10:00-19:00, Oct-April Tue-Sun 10:00-18:00, closed Mon. See page 669.

▲Kadriorg Park Vast, strollable oasis with the palace gardens, Kumu Art Museum, and a palace built by Czar Peter the Great. See page 666.

▲Pirita Neighborhood on the outskirts, with a popular beach, famous forest cemetery, and TV tower observation deck. See page 671.

▲Estonian Open-Air Museum Authentic farm and village buildings preserved in a forested parkland. **Hours:** Park open daily 10:00-20:00, buildings open until 18:30; in off-season park open daily 10:00-17:00 but many buildings closed. See page 672.

TALLINN

Tallinn Traveller Tours

These tours, run by well-informed locals, show you the real city. Check Traveller.ee to confirm details for their ever-changing line-up and to reserve (or call mobile +372 5837 4800). They typically offer a two-hour **Old Town Walking Tour** (€19), a **ghost walk,** and a **food tour,** as well as **bike tours** and **minibus excursions** into the Estonian countryside. All tours start from in front of the main TI.

Hop-On, Hop-Off Bus Tours

Tallinn City Tour offers three different one-hour bus tours—you can take all three (on the same day) for one price. Tours depart about once an hour. Aside from a stop near Toompea Castle, the routes are entirely outside the Old Town. But the tours do go to outlying sights such as Kadriorg Park and the towering Russalka Monument. You can catch the bus at the port terminals and at Viru Square, near the Viru Turg clothing market (€21/24 hours, +372 627 9080, www.citytour.ee). **CitySightseeing Tallinn** also runs three similar routes, with a similarly sparse frequency (€20 for all three lines, www.citysightseeing.ee).

City Bike Tours

City Bike offers a two-hour, nine-mile **Welcome to Tallinn** bike tour that takes you outside the city walls to Tallinn's more distant sights: Kadriorg Park, Song Festival Grounds, the beach at Pirita, and more (€21, daily at 11:00 in peak season, fewer in winter, departs from their office at Vene 33 in the Old Town). They can also arrange multiday, self-guided bike tours around Estonia (mobile +372 511 1819, www.citybike.ee).

Tallinn Walk

This self-guided walk, worth ▲▲▲, explores the lower and upper towns of Tallinn. The city once consisted of two feuding medieval towns separated by a wall. Toompea—the upper town on a hill—was the seat of government for Estonia. The lower town was an autonomous Hanseatic trading center filled with German, Danish, and Swedish merchants who hired Estonians to do their menial labor. Many of the Old Town's buildings are truly old, dating from the boom times of the 15th and 16th centuries. Decrepit before the 1991 fall of the Soviet Union, the Old Town has been entirely revitalized.

Two steep, narrow streets—the "Long Leg" and the "Short Leg"—connect the upper and the lower towns. This walk goes up the short leg and down the long leg. Allow about two hours for the entire walk (not counting time to enter museums along the way).

LOWER TOWN

❶ Fat Margaret Tower (Paks Margareeta) guarded the entry gate of the town in medieval times (the sea once came much closer than

it does today). Besides being a defensive outpost, the tower was made big just to impress anyone coming to town from the harbor. The relief above the gate dates from the 16th century, during Hanseatic times, when Sweden took Estonia from the German Teutonic Knights. The origin of the tower's name is a bit of a mystery. Some say it was named for a huge cannon, but others think a cook called Margaret worked in the tower long ago.

• *Once through the gate, head up Tallinn's main drag...*

❷ Pikk Street

Literally "Long Street," the medieval merchants' main drag leads from the harbor up into town. It's lined with interesting and historic buildings. Many were warehouses, complete with cranes on the gables. Strolling here, you'll feel the economic power of those early German trading days.

One short block up the street on the right, the buildings nicknamed **"Three Sisters"** (now a hotel/restaurant) are textbook examples of a merchant home/warehouse/office from the 15th-century Hanseatic Golden Age. The elaborately carved door near the corner evokes

the wealth of Tallinn's merchant class—such detailed decoration would have come with a high price tag.

After another, longer block, you'll pass the Gothic **St. Olav's Church** (Oleviste Kirik, a Baptist church today), notable for what was once the tallest spire in the land. That high spire helped approaching ships set their course—but it was also an effective lightning rod. Unfortunately, lightning strikes caused the church to burn to the ground three times. If the name didn't tip you off that this was once a Lutheran church, then the stark, whitewashed interior guaran-

Tallinn Walk

1 Fat Margaret Tower
2 Pikk Street
3 Brotherhood of the Black Heads
4 Great Guild Hall
5 Church of the Holy Ghost
6 Town Hall Square
7 Wheel Well
8 St. Nicholas Church
9 City Walls & Gardens
10 Russian Orthodox Cathedral
11 Toompea Castle & Parliament
12 Tall Hermann Tower
13 Dome Church
14 Patkuli Viewpoint
15 Kohtuotsa Viewpoint
16 Viru Gate
17 To Viru Keskus Mall

TALLINN

tees it. Climbing 234 stairs up the tower rewards you with a great view. You can enter both the church and the tower around the back side (church—free, daily 10:00-18:00; tower—€3, open April-Oct only).

While tourists see only a peaceful scene today, older locals strolling this street are reminded of dark times under Moscow's rule. The KGB used the tower at St. Olav's Church to block Finnish TV signals. The once-handsome building at Pikk #59 (the second house after the church, on the right) was, before 1991, part of a complex housing the local KGB headquarters. You can view parts of the former headquarters by visiting the **KGB Prison Cells** exhibit (described later, under "Sights in Tallinn"). "Creative interrogation methods" were used here. Locals well knew that the road of suffering started here, as Tallinn's troublemakers were sent to Siberian gulags. The ministry building was called the "tallest" building in town (because "when you're in the basement, you can already see Siberia"). Notice the bricked-up windows at steet level and the commemorative plaque (in Estonian).

• *A few short blocks farther up Pikk (after the small park), on the left at #26, is the extremely ornate doorway of the...*

❸ Brotherhood of the Black Heads

Built in 1440, this house was used as a German merchants' club for nearly 500 years (until Hitler invited Estonian Germans back

to their historical fatherland in the 1930s). Before the 19th century, many Estonians lived as serfs on the rural estates of the German nobles who dominated the economy. In Tallinn, the German big shots were part of the Great Guild (which we'll see farther up the street), while the German little shots had to make do with the Brotherhood of the Black Heads. This guild, or business fraternity, was limited to single German men. In Hanseatic towns, when a fire or battle had to be fought, bachelors were deployed first, because they had no family. Because single men were considered unattached to the community, they had no opportunity for power in the Hanseatic social structure. When a Black Head member married a local woman, he automatically gained a vested interest in the town's economy and well-being. He could then join the Great Guild, and with that status, a promising economic and political future often opened up.

Today the hall is a concert venue (and, while you can pay to tour its interior, I'd skip it—it's basically an empty shell). Its name-sake "black head" is that of St. Maurice, an early Christian soldier-martyr, beheaded in the third century AD for his refusal to honor the Roman gods. Reliefs decorating the building recall Tallinn's Hanseatic glory days.

Keep going along Pikk street. Architecture fans enjoy several **fanciful facades** along here, including the boldly Art Nouveau #18 (on the left, reminiscent of the architectural bounty of fellow Baltic capital Rīga; today this building houses one of Tallinn's leading architectural firms). Also note the colorful, eclectic building across the street (with the pointy gable).

On the left, at #16, the famous and recommended **Maiasmokk** ("Sweet Tooth") coffee shop, in business since 1864, remains a fine spot for a coffee-and-pastry break.

• *Just ahead, pause at the big yellow building on the right (at #17).*

❹ Great Guild Hall (Suurgildi Hoone)

With its wide (and therefore highly taxed) front, the Great Guild Hall was the epitome of wealth. Remember, this was the home of the most prestigious of Tallinn's Hanseatic-era guilds. Today it houses the worthwhile **Museum of Estonian History,** offering a concise and engaging survey of this country's story (for details, see "Sights in Tallinn," later).

• *Across Pikk street from the Great Guild Hall is the...*

❺ Church of the Holy Ghost (Pühavaimu Kirik)

Sporting an outdoor clock from 1633, this pretty medieval church is worth a visit. The plaque on the wall just behind the ticket desk is in Estonian and Russian, but not English; this dates from before 1991, when things were designed for "inner tourism"—within the USSR. The church retains its 14th-century design. Sometimes flying from the back pillar, the old flag of Tallinn—the same as today's red-and-white Danish flag—recalls 13th-century Danish rule. (The name "Tallinn" means "Danish Town.") The Danes sold Tallinn to the German Teutonic Knights, who lost it to the Swedes, who lost it to the Russians. The windows are mostly from the 1990s.

Cost and Hours: €1.50; Mon-Sat 12:00-16:00, closes earlier in winter, closed most of Sun to nonworshippers; English-language Lutheran services Sun at 13:00 (may be earlier in summer); Püh-avaimu 2, +372 646 4430, www.eelk.ee.

*• From here, it's a three-minute walk to the **Tallinn City Museum**— down the street to the left as you face the church (described later, under "Sights in Tallinn"). You can detour there now, or to continue this walk, follow the tiny lane leading alongside the church. This is Saiakang lane (meaning "White Bread"—bread, cakes, and pies were long sold here), which leads to...*

❻ Town Hall Square (Raekoja Plats)

A marketplace through the centuries, with a cancan of fine old buildings, this is the focal point of the Old Town. The square was the center of the autonomous lower town, a merchant city of Hanseatic traders. In medieval times here, criminals were chained to pillories for public humiliation, and knights showed off in chivalrous tournaments; today it's full of Scandinavians and Russians savoring cheap beer, children singing on the bandstand, and cruise-ship groups following numbered paddles carried high by well-scrubbed local guides.

At the passageway where you've entered the square, look left to find the **pharmacy** (Raeapteek) dating from 1422 and claiming to be Europe's oldest. With an interior that goes back to medieval times, the still-operating pharmacy welcomes visitors with painted ceiling beams, English descriptions, and long-expired aspirin. Past the functioning counter is a room of display cases with historical exhibits (closed Sun).

The 15th-century **Town Hall** (Raekoda) dominates the square; it's open to visitors in summer, and climbing its tower earns you a commanding view (for details, see "Sights in Tallinn," later).

Town Hall Square is ringed by inviting but touristy eateries. The TI is a block away (behind Town Hall).

*• Facing the Town Hall, head right up Dunkri street—lined with several more eateries—one long block to the ❼ **wheel well**, named for the "high-tech" wheel, a marvel that made fetching water easier.*

Turn left on Rataskaevu street (which soon becomes Rüütli) and walk two short blocks to...

⑧ St. Nicholas Church (Niguliste Kirik)

This 13th-century Gothic church-turned-art-museum served the German merchants and knights who lived in this neighborhood 500 years ago. On March 9, 1944, while Tallinn was in German hands, Soviet forces bombed the city, and the church and surrounding area—once a charming district, dense with medieval buildings—were burned out; only the church was rebuilt.

Cost and Hours: €6; Tue-Sun 10:00-17:00, closed Mon year-round and Tue off-season; organ or choir concerts held most weekends.

Visiting the Church: The church's interior houses a fine collection of mostly Gothic-era ecclesiastical art.

Enter the church through the modern cellar, with photos of the WWII destruction of the building (including its toppled steeple). Then make your way into the vast, open church interior. Front and center is the collection's highlight: a retable (framed altarpiece) from 1481 by Herman Rode—an exquisite example of the northern Germanic late-Gothic style. Along with scenes from the life of St. Nicholas and an array of other saints, the altarpiece shows the skyline of Lübeck, Germany (Rode's hometown, and—like Tallinn—a Hanseatic trading city). The intricate symbolism is explained by a nearby touchscreen. Also look for another work by a Lübeck master, Bernt Notke's *Danse Macabre* ("Dance of Death"). Once nearly 100 feet long, the surviving fragment shows sinister skeletons approaching people from all walks of life. This common medieval theme reminds the viewer that life is fleeting, and no matter who we are, we'll all wind up in the same place.

• *From the church, if you were to turn left and walk downhill on Rüütli street, you'd soon pass near* **Freedom Square** *(providing a taste of modern Tallinn; described later, under "Sights in Tallinn"). But for now, let's continue our walk into the upper town.*

UPPER TOWN (TOOMPEA)

• *At the corner opposite the church, climb uphill along the steep, cobbled, Lühike Jalg ("Short Leg Lane"), home to several quality craft shops. At the top of the lane, pause at the arched gateway at #9. Notice the stone tower steps leading to the arched passage and a big oak door. This is one of two gates through the wall separating the two cities. This passage is still the ritual meeting point of the mayor and prime minister whenever there is an important agreement between town and country.*

Now continue through the main gateway and climb up until you emerge into a beautiful view terrace in front of the...

❾ City Walls and Gardens

This view terrace is known as the Danish King's Garden for the ruler who gave the land to the lower town in 1311. Tallinn is fa-

mous among Danes as the birthplace of their flag. According to legend, the Danes were losing a battle here, when suddenly, a white cross fell from heaven and landed in a pool of blood. The Danes were inspired and went on to win, and to this day, their flag is

a white cross on a red background.

Once you pass through the opening in the wall (to the right after you pass through the main gate), you've officially crossed from the lower to upper town. The imposing city wall once had 46 towers, of which 26 still stand. If interested, you can climb some of the towers and ramparts (see below; note that we'll be reaching some dramatic viewpoints—overlooking different parts of town—later on this walk).

The easiest ascent is to simply scramble up the extremely steep and tight steps of the nearby **Dannebrog restaurant tower**—but you'll need to order an expensive drink to stay and enjoy the view.

The next two towers, Neitsitorn and Kiek in de Kök, have the same hours and are covered by the same ticket (€10 combo-ticket covers both towers, extra for tour of tunnels below Kiek in de Kök, Tue-Sun 10:00-17:00, Thu until 20:00, closed Mon). The **Neitsitorn** (Maiden tower), at the far end of the garden ter-

race, has a higher vantage point than Dannebrog, a few skippable exhibits, an overpriced café, and great views— particularly from the top floor, where a full glass wall reveals a panoramic townscape.

For a genuine tower climb, visit the stout, round **Kiek in de Kök tower**, with extremely tight, twisty, steep stone staircases inside (farther along the wall—cross into the upper town and follow the gravel path to the left). The fun-to-say name "Kiek in de Kök" is Low German for "Peek in the Kitch-

TALLINN

en"—so-called because the tower was situated to allow guards to literally peek into townspeople's homes. This tower is bigger than the Neitsitorn, with more impressive exhibits—not a lot of real artifacts, but plenty of cannons, mannequins, model ships, movies, and models of the castle to give you a taste of Tallinn's medieval heyday.

• *When you're finished with the towers and ramparts, head uphill into the upper town to the big, onion-domed church, circling around to the far side (facing the pink palace) to find the entrance.*

❿ Alexander Nevsky Cathedral (Aleksander Nevski Katedraal)

This Russian Orthodox cathedral—worth ▲▲—is a gorgeous building. But ever since the day it was built (in 1900), it has been a

jab in the eye for Estonians. The church went up near the end of the two centuries when Estonia was part of the Russian Empire. And, as throughout Europe in the late 19th century, Tallinn's oppressed ethnic groups—the Estonians and the Germans— were caught up in national revival movements, celebrating their own culture, language, and history rather than their Russian overlords'. So the Russians flexed their cultural muscle by building this church in this location, facing the traditional Estonian seat of power, and over the supposed grave of a legendary Estonian hero, Kalevipoeg. They also tore down a statue of Martin Luther to make room.

Cost and Hours: Free, daily 8:00-18:00, OK to visit discreetly during services (daily at 8:30 and 17:00); icon art in gift shop.

Visiting the Church: The church has been exquisitely renovated inside and out. Step inside for a sample of Russian Orthodoxy when you'll hear priests singing the liturgy in a side chapel. Typical of Russian Orthodox churches, it has glittering icons (the highest concentration fills the big screen—called an iconostasis— that shields the altar from the congregation), no pews (worshippers stand through the service), and air that's heavy with incense. All of these features combine to create a mystical, otherworldly worship experience. Notice the many candles, each representing a prayer; if there's a request or a thank-you in your heart, you're welcome to buy one at the desk by the door. Exploring this space, keep in mind that about 40 percent of Tallinn's population is ethnic Russian.

• *Across the street is the...*

❶ Toompea Castle (Toompea Loss)

The pink palace is an 18th-century Russian addition onto the medieval Toompea Castle. Today, it's the Estonian Parliament (Riigikoku) building, flying the Estonian flag—the flag of both the first (1918-1940) and second (1991-present) Estonian republics. Notice the Estonian seal: three lions for three great battles in Estonian history, and oak leaves for strength and stubbornness. Ancient pagan Estonians, who believed spirits lived in oak trees, would walk through forests of oak to toughen up. (To this day, Estonian cemeteries are in forests. Keeping some of their pagan sensibilities, they believe the spirits of the departed live on in the trees.)

• *Facing the palace, go left through the gate into the park to see the...*

❷ Tall Hermann Tower (Pikk Hermann)

This tallest tower of the castle wall is a powerful symbol for Estonians. For 50 years, while Estonian flags were hidden in cellars, the
Soviet flag flew from Tall Hermann. As the USSR was unraveling, Estonians proudly and defiantly replaced the red Soviet flag here with their own black, white, and blue flag.

• *Backtrack to the square in front of the palace, passing the Russian church on your right. Climb Toom-Kooli street to the...*

TALLINN

❸ Dome Church (Toomkirik)

Estonia is ostensibly Lutheran, but few Tallinners go to church. A recent Gallup Poll showed Estonia to be the least religious country in the European Union—only 14 percent of respondents identified
religion as an important part of their daily lives. Most churches double as concert venues or museums, but this one is still used for worship. Officially St. Mary's Church—but popularly called the Dome Church—it's a perfect example of simple Northern European Gothic, built in the 13th century during Danish rule, then rebuilt after a 1684 fire. Once the church of Tallinn's wealthy German-speaking aristocracy, it's littered with more than a hundred coats of arms, carved by local masters as memorials to the deceased and in-

scribed with German tributes. The earliest dates from the 1600s, the latest from around 1900.

Cost and Hours: Free, €5 for 140-step tower climb, daily 10:00-16:00, organ recitals Sat at 12:00, www.eelk.ee/tallinna. toom.

• *Leaving the church, turn left and hook around the back of the building. You'll pass a big, green, former noblemen's clubhouse on your right (at #1, vacated when many Germans left Estonia in the 1930s). Head down cobbled Rahukohtu lane (to the right of the yellow house with a peaked roof). Strolling the street, notice the embassy signs: Government offices and embassies have moved into these buildings and spruced up the neighborhood. Continue straight under the arch and belly up to the grand...*

⓮ Patkuli Viewpoint

Survey the scene. On the far left, the Neoclassical facade of the executive branch of Estonia's government overlooks a grand view. Below you, a bit of the old moat remains. The *Group* sign marks Tallinn's tiny train station, and the clutter of stalls behind that is the rustic Balti Jaam Market. Out on the water, ferries shuttle to and from Helsinki (just 50 miles away). Beyond the lower town's medieval wall and towers stands the green spire of St. Olav's Church, once 98 feet taller and, locals claim, the world's tallest tower in 1492. Far in the distance is the 1,000-foot-tall TV tower, the site of a standoff between Soviet paratroopers and Estonian patriots in 1991 (see page 672).

During Soviet domination, Finnish TV was even more important, as it gave Estonians their only look at Western lifestyles. Imagine: In the 1980s, many locals had never seen a banana or a pineapple—except on TV. People still talk of the day that Finland broadcast the soft-porn movie *Emmanuelle*. A historic migration of Estonians purportedly flocked from the countryside to Tallinn to get within rabbit-ear's distance of Helsinki and see all that flesh onscreen. The refurbished TV tower is now open to visitors.

• *Go back through the arch, turn immediately left down the narrow lane, turn right (onto Toom-Rüütli), take the first left, and pass through the trees to the...*

⓯ Kohtuotsa Viewpoint

Scan the view from left to right. On the far left is St. Olav's Church, then the busy cruise port and the skinny white spire of the Church of the Holy Ghost. The narrow gray spire farther to the

TALLINN

right is the 16th-century Town Hall tower. On the far right is the tower of St. Nicholas Church. Below you, trace Pikk street, Tallinn's historic main drag, which winds through the Old Town, leading from Toompea Castle down the hill (from right to left), through the gate tower, past the Church of the Holy Ghost, behind St. Olav's, and out to the harbor. Less picturesque is the clutter of Soviet-era apartment blocks on the distant horizon, but these days they're being crowded out by modern high-rises. The nearest skyscraper (white) is Hotel Viru, in Soviet times the biggest hotel in the Baltics and infamous then as a clunky, dingy slumbermill. Locals joke that Hotel Viru was built from a Soviet wonder material called "micro-concrete" (60 percent concrete, 40 percent microphones). Underneath the hotel is the modern Viru Keskus, a huge shopping mall and local transit center. To the left of Hotel Viru, between it and the ferry terminals, is the Rotermann Quarter, a former industrial area that's been revamped into a new commercial zone.

• *From the viewpoint, descend to the lower town. Go out and left down Kohtu, past the Finnish Embassy (on your left). Back at the Dome Church, turn left down Piiskopi ("Bishop's Street"). At the onion domes, turn left again and follow the old wall down Pikk Jalg ("Long Leg Lane") into the lower town. Go under the tower, then straight on Pikk street, and after two doors turn right on Voorimehe, which leads into Town Hall Square.*

⑯ Through Viru Gate

Cross through the square (to the left of the Town Hall's tower) and go downhill (passing the kitschy medieval Olde Hansa Restaurant, with its bonneted waitresses and merry men). Continue straight down Viru street toward Hotel Viru, the blocky white skyscraper in the distance. Viru street is old Tallinn's busiest and most touristy shopping street. Just past the strange and modern wood/glass/stone mall, Müürivahe street leads left along the old wall, called the **"Sweater Wall."** This is a colorful and tempting gauntlet of vendors selling knitwear (mostly machine-made). Leading left, beyond the sweaters, the picturesque **Katariina Käik** is a lane with glassblowing, weaving, and pottery shops. Back on Viru street, pass the golden arches and walk through the medieval arches— Viru Gate—that mark the end of old Tallinn. Outside the gates, opposite Viru 23, above the flower stalls, is a small park on a piece of old bastion known as the Kissing Hill (come up here after dark and you'll find out why).

• *Our walk is done. If you want to find the real world, use the crosswalk to your right to reach the* **Viru Keskus mall**, *with its basement supermarket, ticket service, bookstore, and many bus and tram stops. To explore on, cross the busy street by the complex and wander through the Rotermann Quarter (described later, under "Sights in Tallinn").*

Sights in Tallinn

IN OR NEAR THE OLD TOWN

I've covered many of Tallinn's significant Old Town sights in my Tallinn Walk, earlier. Otherwise, central Tallinn has dozens of small museums, most suitable only for those with a special interest. Following are the ones I'd visit first.

▲Museum of Estonian History (Eesti Ajaloomuuseum)

The Great Guild Hall on Pikk street houses a history museum with modern, well-presented exhibits. The museum's "Estonia 101" ap-

proach—combining actual artifacts (from prehistory to today) and high-tech interactive exhibits—is geared toward educating first-time visitors about this obscure but likeable little country.

Cost and Hours: €8, daily 10:00-18:00, closed Wed offseason, +372 696 8690, www.ajaloomuuseum.ee.

Visiting the Museum: The main display (under the whitewashed vaults) is the "Spirit of Survival" exhibit. It condenses 11,000 years of Estonian history with relative ease, while focusing on what it means to be an Estonian (Where did Estonians come from? What are their traditions?)—and outlining the important historical events that have shaped the Estonian cultural psyche (German crusaders, Danish domination, Reformation, multiple wars with Sweden, Russian occupation—to name a few). Steep steps lead down into the cellar, with an armory, ethnographic collection, items owned by historical figures, an exhibit about the Great Guild Hall itself, and a fun "time capsule" that lets you insert your face into videos illustrating episodes in local history.

Town Hall (Raekoda) and Tower

Tallinn's Town Hall opened in 1404 as a place for the city's burgomasters to meet. Now open to tourists as a museum (in summer), it has exhibits on the town's administration and history, along with an interesting bit on the story of limestone. The tower rewards those who climb its 155 steps with a wonderful city view.

Cost and Hours: Museum—€5, entrance through cellar, July-Aug Tue-Sat 11:00-16:00, closed Sept-June and Sun year-round, ask about audioguide; tower—€4, June-Aug daily 11:00-18:00, closed rest of year; +372 645 7900, www.tallinn.ee/raekoda.

▲Tallinn City Museum (Tallinna Linnamuuseum)

This humble but worthwhile museum, filling a 14th-century townhouse, features Tallinn history from 1200 to the 1950s. It's an excellent introduction to Tallinn's past, especially with the help of its good audioguide.

Cost and Hours: €6, includes audioguide, daily 10:00-17:00, shorter hours and closed Mon off-season, Vene 17, at corner of Pühavaimu, +372 615 5180, www.linnamuuseum.ee.

Visiting the Museum: Begin your visit on the first floor, passing through exhibits about Tallinn's medieval past, with an emphasis on its trading days. The Hanseatic League maintained a monopoly in the North Baltic, safeguarding the economic interests of its 100 town-members—of which Tallinn and its Black Heads Guild were major players. (For more on the Hanseatic League, see the sidebar on page 388.) You'll see exact replicas of their trading ships, made and donated to the church in gratitude after particularly safe and rewarding journeys, and a treasury room filled with precious objects of their merchant wealth. Another display draws attention to the roles Tallinn's townspeople played in support of the merchants and shippers (stonemason, blacksmith, cooper, shoemaker, etc.).

The highlight of the second floor is a model of circa-1825 Tallinn—looking much like it does today. The top floor is devoted to 20th-century life, with re-created rooms from the early 20th century and the Soviet period.

Freedom Square (Vabaduse Väljak)

Once a USSR-era parking lot at the southern tip of the Old Town, this fine public zone has been revamped by moving the cars underground. It's now a spacious plaza that invites locals (and very few tourists) to linger. Designed to host special events, it feels miles away from the cutesy cobbles just a few steps away. But it's an easy opportunity to glimpse a contrast to the tourists' Tallinn.

The towering **cross** monument facing the square (marked *Eesti Vabadussõda 1918-1920*) honors the Estonian War of Independence. Shortly after the Bolshevik Revolution set a new course for Russia, the Estonians took advantage of the post-WWI reshuffling of Europe to rise up and create—for the first time ever—an independent Estonian state. The "cross of liberty" on top of the pillar represents a military decoration from that war (and every war since). The hill behind the cross has more monuments and fragments of past fortifications.

If you're interested in learning more about Estonia's history, it's an easy five-minute walk from this square to the next sight.

Vabamu Museum of Occupations and Freedom (Okupatsioonide ja vabaduse muuseum Vabamu)

This museum tells the history of Estonia's occupation—first by the Soviets (for one year), then by the Nazis (for three years), and then again by the USSR (for nearly 50 years)—followed by periods of resistance, freedom, and recovery. The permanent collection, called "Freedom Without Borders," focuses on life under the Soviet regime, the inhumane living conditions that existed in occupied society, stories of Estonians living in exile, and finally, the movement toward independence and freedom. The included multimedia guide lets visitors explore topics at their own pace. For more about Estonia's unique Singing Revolution, see the sidebar on page 670.

Cost and Hours: €11, includes multimedia guide, €14 combo-ticket includes KGB Prison Cells (see next); daily 10:00-18:00; Oct-April Tue-Sun 11:00-18:00, closed Mon; Toompea 8, at corner of Kaarli Puiestee, +372 668 0250, www.vabamu.ee.

KGB Prison Cells (KGB Vangikongid)

Formerly a government building during the Republic of Estonia's first period of independence (1918-1939), this complex was used by the Soviets as the headquarters of the KGB secret police for nearly a half century. Prison cells and interrogation rooms house a small exhibit presented in several languages, including English.

Cost and Hours: €5, €14 combo-ticket also covers Vabamu Museum, same hours and contact info as Vabamu Museum, a 15-minute walk from Vabamu Museum at Pagari 1, look for exhibit entrance on Pikk street.

▲Rotermann Quarter (Rotermanni Kvartal)

Sprawling between Hotel Viru and the port, just east of the Old Town, this 19th-century industrial zone has been redeveloped into shopping, office, and living space. Characteristic old brick shells are being topped with visually striking glass-and-steel additions.

The Bronze Soldier

One of Tallinn's most controversial sights can't be seen in its original location, in front of the National Library (near Freedom Square). Called simply *The Bronze Soldier*, this six-foot-tall statue of a Soviet soldier marked the graves of Russians who died fighting to liberate Tallinn in 1944.

In 2007, the Estonian government exhumed those graves and moved them—along with the statue—to the Tallinn Military Cemetery, on the city's southern outskirts. Estonia's sizeable Russian minority balked at this move, and—through a series of protests and clashes—grabbed the world's attention. The Kremlin took note; furious protestors surrounded the Estonian embassy in Moscow for a week, and mysterious "cyberattacks" from Russian computers crippled Estonian governmental websites.

When the dust settled, *The Bronze Soldier* stayed in its new home—but Estonians of all stripes were confronted with a bitter reminder that even a generation after independence, tensions between ethnic Russians and ethnic Estonians have not been entirely resolved.

For those interested in the gentrification of an aging city, it's worth a quick stroll to see the cutting edge of old-meets-new Nordic architecture.

In recent years the area's former grain elevators and salt-storage warehouses have been creatively repurposed as restaurants, cafés, boutiques, and offices. To take a look around, start at Hotel Viru, cross busy Narva Maantee, and walk down Roseni street (at #7 you'll find the hard-to-resist Kalev chocolate shop). You'll also pass the Rotermanni Aatrium, where in summer, food stalls and craft tables create an open-air market in the neighborhood's central space. Fans of 20th-century architecture will want to stop by the Museum of Estonian Architecture, within a former salt-storage buildings (€6, Tue-Sun 11:00-18:00, closed Mon, Ahtri 2, www.arhitektuurimuuseum.ee).

OUTSIDE THE CORE

You can locate the following sights on the "Greater Tallinn" map, near the beginning of this chapter.

▲Kadriorg Park

This expansive seaside park, home to a summer royal residence and the Kumu Art Museum, is a five-minute tram ride or a 25-minute walk from Hotel Viru. After Russia took over Tallinn in 1710, Peter the Great built the cute, pint-sized Kadriorg Palace for Czarina Catherine (the palace's name means "Catherine's Valley"). Stately, peaceful, and crisscrossed by leafy paths, the park has a rose garden, duck-filled pond, playground and benches, and old czarist guardhouses harkening back to the days of Russian rule. It's a delightful place for a stroll or a picnic. If it's rainy, slip into one of the cafés in the park's art museums (described below).

Getting There: Ride **tram** #1 or #3 (from any tram stop in the Old Town) to the Kadriorg stop, and walk 200 yards straight ahead and up Weizenbergi, the park's main avenue. Peter's summer palace is on the left; behind it, visit the formal garden. Across from the palace is the Mikkel Museum, and at the end of the avenue is the Kumu Art Museum, the park's most important sight. A **taxi** from Hotel Viru to this area should cost €8 or less. If you're returning from here directly to the port to catch your cruise ship, ride tram #1 to the Linnahall stop, near the main cruise terminal.

Visiting Kadriorg Park: The palace's manicured **gardens** (free to enter) are a pure delight; on weekends, you'll likely see a steady parade of brides and grooms here, posing for wedding pictures. The summer palace itself is home to the **Kadriorg Art Museum** (Kadrioru Kunstimuuseum), with very modest Russian and Western European galleries (€8; Tue-Sun 10:00-18:00, Wed until 20:00, closed Mon; Weizenbergi 37, +372 606 6400, http://kadriorumuuseum.ekm.ee).

Across the road from the gardens, in the former kitchen building of the palace, is the **Mikkel Museum,** a fine little collection of Meissen porcelain (€6, same hours as Kadriorg Art Museum, http://mikkelimuuseum.ekm.ee).

The fenced-off expanse directly behind the garden is where you'll spot the local "White House" (although it's pink)—home of **Estonia's president.** Walk around to the far side to find its main entrance, with the seal of Estonia above the door, flagpoles flying both the Estonian and the EU flags, and stone-faced guards.

A five-minute walk beyond the presidential palace takes you to the Kumu Art Museum, described next. For a longer walk from here, the rugged park rolls down toward the sea.

▲▲Kumu Art Museum (Kumu Kunstimuuseum)

This main branch of the Art Museum of Estonia brings the nation's best art together in a striking modern building designed by Finnish

architect, Pekka Vapaavuori. The entire collection is accessible, well-presented, and engaging, with a particularly thought-provoking section on art from the Soviet period. The museum is well worth the trip for art lovers, or for anyone intrigued by the unique spirit of this tiny nation.

Cost and Hours: €10; Tue-Sun 11:00-18:00, Thu until 20:00, closed Mon, audioguide-€4; trendy café, +372 602 6000, http://kumu.ekm.ee.

Getting There: To reach the museum, follow the instructions for Kadriorg Park, earlier; Kumu is at the far end of the park. To get from the Old Town to Kumu directly (without walking through the park), take bus #67 or #68 (each runs every 10-15 minutes); both leave from Teatri Väljak, on the far side of the yellow National Theater, across from the Solaris shopping mall (just southeast of the Old Town). Get off at the Kumu stop, then walk up the stairs and across the bridge.

Visiting the Museum: Just off the ticket lobby (on the second floor), the **great hall** has temporary exhibits; however, the permanent collection on the third and fourth floors is Kumu's main draw. While you can rent an audioguide, the laminated gallery guides in most rooms are enough to enjoy the collection. The maze-like layout on each floor presents the art chronologically.

The **third floor** displays classics of Estonian art from the early 18th century until the end of World War II. It starts with idyllic 18th-century portraits of local aristocrats of the Biedermeier era, a time when harmo-

TALLINN

nious family life and clearly defined gender roles took precedence over all else. The exhibit then moves through 19th-century movements, including Romanticism (represented by some nice views of Tallinn, scenes of Estonian nature, and idealized images of Estonian peasant women in folk costumes). Estonian artists were slow to adopt the art trends of the early 20th century, but in time Modernist styles took hold: Pointillism (linger over the lyrical landscapes of Konrad Mägi and the recently rediscovered works of Herbert Lukk), Cubism, and Expressionism. In the 1930s, the Pallas School provided a more traditional, back-to-nature response to the wilder artistic movements of the time. With the dawn of World War II, a period soon followed by two Soviet and one German occupation, Estonian artists faced extremely difficult and dramatic circumstances. The final canvases on this floor, from the war years, convey an unmistakable melancholy and grim intensity. In the corner, one very high-ceilinged room has a wall lined with dozens of expressive busts by sculptor Villu Jaanisoo.

The **fourth-floor exhibit,** called "Conflicts and Adaptations," is a fascinating survey of Estonian art from the Soviet era (1940-1991). Soviet officials understood the role of art purely as a means to convey the ideology of the Communist Party. Estonian art, the Soviets insisted, should actively promote the communist struggle, and in the strict canon now called **Socialist Realism.** Art's primary objective was to glorify labor and the state's role in distributing its fruits.

Despite these restrictions, Estonian art in this half-century took a wide range of approaches, from syrupy images of Soviet leadership, to stern portraits of Stalin, to glorifying canvases of miners, protesters, speechifiers, metalworkers, and tractor drivers. Though some Estonian artists flirted with social commentary and the avant-garde, a few ended up in Siberia as a result. But with the condemnation of Stalinism in 1956, artists began to attempt bolder compositions and more contemporary forms of expression. Nonetheless, the social function of art continued to take precedence over personal artistic statements throughout the Soviet era.

The rest of the museum is devoted to temporary exhibits, with contemporary art on the **fifth floor** (where there's a nice view back to the Old Town from the far gallery). Don't forget to admire the **architecture** of the building, which is partly dug into the limestone hill—the facade is limestone, too (for the big picture, look for the model of the building, just inside the main doors).

▲▲Seaplane Harbor (Lennusadam)

One of Tallinn's most ambitious sights, this maritime museum fills a gigantic old hangar along the waterfront north of downtown with

everything from traditional wooden fishing boats to a submarine—all symbolic of the Estonian connection to the Baltic Sea. It has loads of hands-on activities for kids and thrills anyone interested in the sea.

Cost and Hours: €15; daily 10:00-19:00, Oct-April Tue-Sun 10:00-18:00, closed Mon; last entry one hour before closing, Vesilennuki 6, +372 620 0550, www.seaplaneharbour.com.

Getting There: It's along the waterfront, about a mile north of the Old Town. It's a long but pleasant **walk** via the Culture Kilometer (Kultuurikilomeeter) seaside path that runs from the bunker-like Linnahall building (near the cruise terminals; see the "Tallinn" map for path location). **Bus #73** stops outside the museum (Lennusadam stop); you can catch it from various stops near the Old Town, including near the Viru Keskus mall and in front of Linnahall (near the cruise terminals). A one-way **taxi** from the town center should run about €6-8. The **hop-on, hop-off buses** also stop here.

Visiting the Museum: The cavernous old **seaplane hangar** cleverly displays exhibits on three levels. The ground floor features items from below the sea (such as a salvaged 16th-century shipwreck; catwalks halfway up connect exhibits dealing with the sea surface (the impressive boat collection—from buoys to iceboats to the massive *Lembit* sub); and seaplanes are suspended overhead. The star of the show is the 195-foot-long *Lembit* submarine from 1937: Estonian-commissioned and British-built, this vessel saw fighting in World War II and later spent several decades in the service of the USSR's Red Fleet. You can climb down below decks to see how the sailors lived, peek through the periscope, and even stare down the torpedo tubes. A cool café on the top level (above the entrance) overlooks the entire huge space.

Outside, filling the old harbor, is the maritime museum's collection of **historic ships,** from old-fashioned tall ships to modern-day military boats. The highlight is the steam-powered icebreaker *Suur Tõll,* from 1914. Sometimes you can pay to go out on a brief trip on one of the sailboats (ask at the museum ticket desk).

Estonia's Singing Revolution

When you are a tiny nation lodged between two giants like Russia and Germany, simply surviving is a challenge. Having already endured 200 years of czarist Russian rule and the turmoil of World War I, little Estonia found itself annexed to the Soviet Union by the end of World War II. Their native culture was swept away: Russian replaced Estonian as the language in schools, and Russians and Ukrainians moved in, displacing Estonians. Moscow wouldn't even allow locals to wave their own flag.

But Estonians were determined to maintain their cultural identity. They had no weapons, but they created their own power by banding together and singing. Song has long been a cherished Estonian form of expression. As long ago as 1869 (during another era of Russian subjugation), Estonians gathered in massive choirs to sing and to celebrate their cultural uniqueness.

Finally, as the USSR began to crumble, the Estonians mobilized, using song to demand independence. In 1988, they gathered—300,000 strong, a third of the population—at the Song Festival Grounds outside Tallinn. The next year, the people of Latvia, Lithuania, and Estonia held hands to make the "Baltic Chain," a human chain that stretched 360 miles from Tallinn to Vilnius in Lithuania.

This so-called Singing Revolution, peaceful and nonviolent, persisted for five years, and in the end, Estonians gained their freedom. It was a remarkable achievement: One million singing Estonians succeeded against their Russian occupiers.

Even now the singing continues: Every five years, the **Song Festival Grounds** (built in 1959 and resembling an oversized Hollywood Bowl) welcomes 25,000 singers and 100,000 spectators. Singers don traditional outfits and march to the festival site from Tallinn's Freedom Square. Overlooking the grounds from the cheap seats is a statue of Gustav Ernesaks, who directed the Estonian National Male Choir for 50 years through the darkest times of Soviet rule. He was a power behind the drive for independence—and lived to see it happen. You can visit the grounds even in nonfestival years, though there's not much to see (free, open long hours; take a City Bike tour, or ride bus #1A, #5, #8, #34A, or #38 to the Lillepaviljon stop and walk 10 minutes; https://lauluvaljak.ee/et).

While the Song Festival Grounds host big pop-music acts, too, the site is a national monument for the role it played in Estonia's fight for independence. Watch the documentary film *The Singing Revolution* (www.singingrevolution.com) to draw inspiration from Estonia's valiant struggle for freedom.

▲Pirita Neighborhood

Several mildly interesting sights cluster in the Pirita neighborhood, a 15-minute drive northeast of the city. If you have a car (or a local guide with a car), or have the time to lace things together with public transportation, this can be a fun way to escape the city and see some different facets of Estonia.

Getting There: It's easy to tie these sights together. Drivers can take the waterfront Pirita Tee highway north (passing behind the Song Festival Grounds) to Pirita, then turn right to cut through the forest to the TV tower. Buses #34A and #38 follow this same route; departing from the underground bus platforms at Viru Keskus mall, they conveniently link all of the places listed here. The hop-on, hop-off bus also does a circuit that covers these sights.

Visiting Pirita: Coming from central Tallinn on Pirita Tee, you'll pass two starkly different memorials. First, as you skirt behind Kadriorg Park, watch on the left for the **Russalka Monument** (Russalka Mälestusmärk). An angel on a pedestal commemorates the 1893 sinking of the Russian warship *Russalka* ("Mermaid"). Farther along—after passing the Song Festival Grounds—look on the right for the towering **World War II Memorial** (Maarjamäe Memoriaal)—a 115-foot-tall obelisk erected to honor those who died defending the Soviet Union, and now the centerpiece of Estonia's war memorial.

Just after crossing the Pirita River and the little marina (with the yachting center built for the 1980 Olympics), watch on the right for the **ruins of St. Bridget's Convent** (Pirita Klooster; bus stop: Pirita). This early 15th-century convent, which housed both monks and nuns (in separate quarters, of course), was destroyed in 1577 by Ivan the Terrible. Its stones were quarried to build Baltic manor houses, but today you can pay a small fee to tour the evocative Gothic ruins (www.piritaklooster.ee).

Down along the water from here, **Pirita Beach** is one of the most popular in Tallinn. On a sunny summer day, Estonians are out enjoying sand, sun, and the Baltic Sea.

At the first traffic light after the convent ruins, turn right on Kloostrimetsa Tee, which cuts through a forest—and through the **Forest Cemetery** (Metsakalmistu), offering a poignant look at unique Estonian burial customs (bus stop: Metsakalmistu, then continue about 200 yards down the road, following *Teletorn* signs to the gate). Traditionally, Estonians bury the departed not in fields or parks, but in forests—thanks to a deeply rooted belief that their spirit will live on in the trees. This particular cemetery is one of Estonia's best-known, and is the eternal resting place both of commoners and of VIPs—athletes, chess champions, musicians, writers, and politicians. Exploring here, find the "Hill of Celebrities" (Kuulsuste Küngas). Among the illustrious Estonians buried here is Konstantin Päts (1847-1956), the first president of independent Estonia, who later died in a Siberian mental institution. After freedom, his remains were located and moved here to be re-interred. Lydia Koidula (1843-1886, marked by a red stone) was Estonia's premier 19th-century poet and wrote the first play in Estonian.

Just past the Forest Cemetery, the **TV tower** (Teletorn)—with its antenna topping out at 1,000 feet—was built for the 1980 Moscow Olympics (the sailing regatta took place in Tallinn). You can ride up to the 550-foot-high observation deck for sweeping views over Estonia (and, on a clear day, all the way to Finland) and the endearing "Estonian Hall of Fame," celebrating Estonian contributions to the world (www.teletorn.ee).

In front of the tower, you'll see a monument to the brave Estonians who faced off against a potential Soviet counterattack. On August 19, 1991, a coup by generals in Moscow created confusion and panic across the USSR. The next day, on August 20—still celebrated today as Estonia's national holiday—the Declaration of Independence was signed. On August 21, Russian military forces moved to take this national broadcast tower and cut off Estonian communications. But two policemen and some radio operators cleverly prevented them from entering the tower's control station, by jamming the door and threatening to engage the fire-exhaust system. Eventually a ragtag gang of Estonian civilians showed up to defend the tower and stare down the troops. By late afternoon, it became clear that Boris Yeltsin had gained control in Moscow, and the Russian troops were told to stand down. Estonia had its tower—and a few weeks later, Russia recognized this little country's right to exist.

▲Estonian Open-Air Museum (Vabaõhumuuseum)

Influenced by their ties with Nordic countries, Estonians are enthusiastic advocates of open-air museums. For this one, they salvaged farm buildings, windmills, and an old church from rural areas and transported them to a park-like setting a few miles west of the Old Town. The goal: to both save and share their heritage. Attendants are posted in many houses, but to really visualize what life was like, download the

A Look at Lasnamäe

In its attempt to bring Estonia into the Soviet fold, Moscow moved tens of thousands of Russian workers into Tallinn, using

the promise of new apartments as an incentive. Generations later, Tallinn still has a huge Russian minority (about 40 percent of the city's population) and three huge, charmless suburbs of ugly, Soviet-built apartments: Mustamäe, Õismäe, and Lasnamäe.

Today, about one of every two Tallinners lives in one of these Brezhnev-era suburbs of massive, cookie-cutter apartment blocks (many now privatized). About 80 percent of the residents who live in Lasnamäe are Russian-speaking. Some parts are poor, rough, and edgy, with blue lights in the public toilets so that junkies can't see their veins. Other sections are nicer, and by day, you can visit here without fear. You'll see carefully dressed young women, track-suited men, grass that needs mowing, cracked paving stones, grandmothers pushing strollers, and lots of new, boxy shops; a new Russian Orthodox cathedral (built with the support of Tallinn's mayor to curry favor with ethnic-Russian voters); and some modern city-owned "social apartment" buildings.

Forging Russians and Estonians into a single society, with the Estonian language dominant, was an optimistic goal after the fall of the Soviet Union. Ethnic Russians grumbled, but knew they probably had a brighter economic future in Estonia than in Russia. With a new generation of children learning both languages in school and most residents enjoying reasonable prosperity, peaceful ethnic coexistence (like between Swedes and Finns in Helsinki) may be achievable.

For a quick look at life in Lasnamäe, hop on bus #67 or #68 (each runs every 10-15 minutes); both leave from Teatri Väljak, on the far side of the yellow National Theater from the Old Town, across from the Solaris shopping mall. Ride to the last stop (about 25 minutes).

TALLINN

free NUMU app before you visit (or rent an audioguide from ticket office). The park's Kolu Tavern serves traditional dishes. You can rent a bike for a breezy roll to quiet, faraway spaces in the park.

Cost and Hours: €10, park open daily 10:00-20:00, historic buildings until 18:30; off-season: €8, park open daily 10:00-17:00 but many buildings closed; +372 654 9101, www.evm.ee.

Getting There: Take bus #21 or #21B from various stops near the Old Town (including near Viru Keskus mall, Balti Jaam Market, or Freedom Square) to the Rocca al Mare stop. Because buses back to Tallinn run infrequently, check the departure schedule as soon as you arrive, or ask staff how to find the Zoo stop, with more frequent service, a 15-minute walk away.

Lahemaa National Park (Lahemaa Rahvuspark)

This vast, flat, forested coastal preserve on the Gulf of Finland is a one-hour drive east of Tallinn. While it is a popular tour destination and the nature is pristine, the park's charms are modest. Highlights include the thick forest (including cemeteries, because Estonians bury their dead in the woods), bog walks, rich berry and mushroom picking, rebuilt manor homes, and peaceful fishing villages surrounded by the evocative ruins of Soviet occupation. Tallinn Traveller Tours organizes day trips to the national park (see listing on page 650). For hiking and cycling trail descriptions, check online (www.keskkonnaamet.ee) or stop at the park's visitor center when you arrive (open daily in summer, Mon-Fri off-season, +372 329 5555).

Shopping in Tallinn

With so many cruisers inundating Tallinn, the Old Town is full of trinkets, but it is possible to find better-quality souvenirs. Wooden goods, like butter knives and juniper-wood trivets, are a good value. Marvel at the variety of booze on sale in Tallinn's liquor stores, popular with visiting Scandinavians. Tucked into the Old Town are many craft and artisan shops where prices are lower than in Nordic countries.

Knitware and Handicrafts

The "Sweater Wall" is a fun place to browse sweaters and woolens, though few are hand-knitted by grandmothers these days. Find the

stalls under the wall on Müürivahe street (daily, near the corner of Viru street). From there, explore the picturesque **Katariina Käik,** a small alley between Müürivahe and Vene streets, which has several handicraft stores and workshops selling pieces that make nice souvenirs. (Both are located near the Viru Gate, at the end of my Tallinn Walk.)

Estonian handicrafts focus on all kinds of knitted and felted clothing: colorful sweaters, scarves, hats, socks, and mittens. Linen is also widely sold. In the Old Town, you'll find good selections at the **Estonian Handicraft House** (Pikk 27) and **Eesti Käsitöö Kodu** (Vene 12).

Books and Art

The cheery **Navitrolla Gallerii** is filled with work by the well-known Estonian artist who goes just by the name Navitrolla. His whimsical, animal-themed prints are vaguely reminiscent of *Where the Wild Things Are* (Sulevimägi 1, +372 631 3716, www.navitrolla.ee).

The **Rahva Raamat** bookstore in the Viru Keskus mall (floors 3-4) has English-language literature on the main floor and a huge wall of travel books upstairs.

Markets

Balti Jaam Market, Tallinn's bustling, recently restored market, is behind the train station. It's a great time-warp scene, fragrant with dill, berries, onions, and mushrooms. You'll hear lots of Russian and find vendors selling everything from fresh produce and street food to children's clothes and gadgets. You could easily assemble a rustic picnic here. From the train station, walk across the head of the train platforms (following *Jaama Turg* signs) and keep going (Mon-Sat 9:00-19:00, Sun until 17:00, better early).

For something tamer, the **Viru Turg outdoor market,** a block outside the Old Town's Viru Gate, has a lively, tourist-oriented collection of stalls selling mostly clothing, textiles, and flowers (daily, north of Viru street at Mere Puiestee 1).

Entertainment in Tallinn

Music

Tallinn has a dense schedule of classical music performances, especially during the annual Old Town Days, generally at the beginning of June (www.vanalinnapaevad.ee). Choral singing became a symbol of the struggle for Estonian independence after the first Estonian Song Festival in 1869 (still held every five years).

Even outside of festival times, you'll find many performances in Tallinn's churches and concert halls, advertised on posters around town or at the TI. Tickets are usually available at the door or through the Piletilevi booth in the Viru Keskus mall (daily 10:00-21:00, www.piletilevi.ee). Watch for performances by Hortus Musicus, one of Estonia's finest classical ensembles, or concerts featuring the work of Arvo Pärt, Veljo Tormis, or Erkki-Sven Tüür, who are among Estonia's best modern choral composers and arrangers.

Swimming and Fitness

The indoor water park, fitness center, 50-meter pool, and hotel at the **Kalev Spa** have long attracted Finns who travel here on fitness packages. It's centrally located, outside the Viru Gate between the Old Town and the modern shopping zone; check the website for updated hours and pricing (swimsuit rental available, Aia 18, +372 649 3370, www.kalevspa.ee).

Sleeping in Tallinn

Real hotel options are surprisingly sparse and expensive in the Old Town. You'll have more options and pay less if you're willing to stay a short walk or bus ride away, especially during the summer high-tourist season.

IN AND NEAR THE OLD TOWN

$$$$ My City Hotel fills a handsome 1950s building on the south edge of the Old Town with 68 nicely appointed rooms and a classy lobby lounge. Along with the Sõprus cinema across the street, it's done in the Stalinist Classical style—Soviet stars and sheaves of wheat still adorn the facade (air-con, elevator, pay sauna, Vana-Posti 11, +372 622 0900, www.mycityhotel.ee, booking@mycityhotel.ee).

$$$ Rija Old Town Hotel is built into the wall at the tip of the Old Town, near Fat Margaret Tower and not far from the ferry terminals (41 comfortable rooms, elevator, Lai 49, +372 614 1300, www.rijahotels.com, info.oldtownhotel@rijahotels.com).

$$ Hotel Bern, tucked at the edge of the Old Town, is a solid choice with 50 businesslike rooms in a newish brick building (air-con, elevator, Aia 10, +372 680 6630, www.tallinnhotels.ee, bern@tallinnhotels.ee).

$$ St. Barbara Hotel, an affordable choice just outside the Old Town, fills a former hospital from 1904 just beyond the ring road from Freedom Square—about a 10-minute walk from Town Hall Square. This old building is filled with 53 modern, fairly simple rooms and an atmospheric beer cellar that gives the place a Germanic vibe (elevator, free parking, Roosikrantsi 2A—just take the pedestrian underpass from Freedom Square under the busy road, +372 640 0040, www.stbarbara.ee, reservations@stbarbara.ee).

$$ Old Town Maestro's is a simple budget choice with 23 modern rooms tucked in the heart of the Old Town. While the prices are right, it comes with a catch: It sits along one of Tallinn's

Tallinn Hotels & Restaurants

To Seaplane Harbor
B #73
KALARANNA
SUUR-PATAREI
B #73
"CULTURE KILOMETER"
KALASADAMA KURSI
LINNAHALL
RAMP
To Cruise Port
RUMBI
TALL CHIMNEY
B #73
SADAMA
To A & B Terminals
#2
B
C TERM.
9
PÕHJA PUIESTEE
#1 & 2
T
NIINE
PÕHJA PUIESTEE
FAT MARGARET TOWER
2
#1 & 2
T
#21, 21B & 73
CITY WALLS
"THREE SISTERS"
FERRY MEMORIAL
RANNAMÄE TEE
MERE
KAI
Admiral Basin
To D Terminal

200 Meters
200 Yards

BALTI JAAM MARKET
T
#1 & 2
RANNAMÄE TEE
SUURTÜK
TRAIN STATION
CLIMBABLE TOWERS
8
To Open-Air Museum
PATKULI TREPP
Moat
Toompark
RAHU
UPPER
TOWN
DOME CHURCH
TOOM-KOOLI
KOHTU
PIKK JALG
ORTH. CATH.
Lossi Sq.
NEITSITORN TOWER
PARLIA-MENT & CASTLE
TALL HERMANN TOWER
KOMAN
TOOMPEA
KIEK IN DE KÖK TOWER
Harju-mägi
WISMARI
VABAMU MUSEUM
KAARLI PUIESTEE
ST. CHARLES
To Lilleküla & 10
ENDLA
NATIONAL LIBRARY
KAARLI PUIESTEE
4
FORMER LOCATION OF BRONZE SOLDIER
TALLINN-PÄRNU-IKLA
SAKALA
T
#1, 2, 3 & 4
KENTMANNI

ST. OLAV'S
PIKK
12
7
#1 & 2
T
AHTRI
ARCH. MUSEUM
KGB PRISON
17
LAI
ÕLEVIMÄGI
UUS
AIA
KAN.
KALEV SPA
ROTER-MANN QUARTER
19
AHTRI
LOWER
ESTONIAN HISTORY MUSEUM
PIKK
VENE
BLACK HEADS
CITY MUSEUM
MÜÜRIVAHE
RUSSIAN CULTURAL CTR.
ROSEN
23
HOLY GHOST
24
3
SUPER-MARKET
VIRU TURG MKT.
20
#21, 21B & 73
To Kadriorg & Kumu Art Museum
24
21
Town Hall Square
15
KAT. KÄIK
VIRU VÄRAV
VANA-VIRU
22
Viru Square
T
#1 & 2
NARVA
DOME CHURCH
11
TOWN HALL
6
14
VANA-TURG
HOTEL VIRU
VIRU KESKUS SHOPPING CTR.
18
ST. NICHOLAS
5
16
"SWEATER WALL"
TOWN
1
KISSING HILL
#1, 2, 3 & 4
B #21, 21B & 73
Tamm-saare Park
#1A, 5, 8, 34 & 58
To Bus #2 Stop
KUDRU
RÜÜTLI
HARJU
LÜHIKE
13
PÄRNU
MÜÜRIVAHE
G. OTSA
CITY WALLS
NATIONAL THEATER
ESTONIA PUIESTEE
KAUBAMAJA DEP'T STORE
RAVALA PUIESTEE
KAUKA
LAUTERI
Lembitu Park
INDEP. MEM. Freedom Square
B #73
B #73
ST. JOHN'S
T
#3 & 4
B
#21 & 21B
SOLARIS SHOPPING CTR.
B #67 & 68
To Bus Station

TALLINN

Accommodations

1. My City Hotel
2. Rija Old Town Hotel
3. Hotel Bern
4. St. Barbara Hotel
5. Old Town Maestro's
6. Villa Hortensia & Pierre Chocolaterie
7. Old House Hostel
8. Go Hotel Shnelli
9. Tallink Express Hotel
10. To Valge Villa

Eateries & Other

11. Von Krahli Aed, Vanaema Juures & Von Krahli Baar
12. Leib
13. Mekk
14. Olde Hansa & Peppersack
15. Troika
16. Pegasus
17. Hell Hunt Pub
18. Põrgu
19. Sfäär
20. Retoran Ö
21. Kompressor
22. Wok to Walk
23. Maiasmokk Café
24. Grocery (3)

rowdiest nightlife streets, so try requesting a quieter courtyard room (elevator, Suur-Karja 10, +372 626 2000, www.maestrohotel. ee, maestro@maestrohotel.ee).

$ Villa Hortensia rents six simple, creaky-floored rooms with kitchenettes above a sophisticated little café in a courtyard close to Town Hall Square. Named after the home of a group of down-and-outs in a famous Estonian novel, the hotel is creatively run by jewelry designer Jaan Pärn. It's a decent, inexpensive choice if you don't mind the ramshackle feeling and the fact that the rooms aren't serviced every day. Jaan's jewelry shop, up the stairs in the courtyard, serves as the reception (no breakfast, no elevator, 50 yards from the corner of Vene and Viru streets at Vene 6, look for *Masters' Courtyard* sign, mobile +372 504 6113, www.hoov.ee, jaan. parn@gmail.com).

¢ Old House Hostel is your cheap-and-basic option, split between two buildings on the edge of the Old Town and near the ferry terminals. There's street noise in many rooms, so bring earplugs (family rooms, breakfast extra, no lockout, shared shower and WC, kitchen facilities, unsecured free parking—reserve ahead, Uus 26, +372 641 1464, www.oldhouse.ee, info@oldhouse.ee). They also rent apartments around the Old Town.

AWAY FROM THE OLD TOWN

Near the Train Station: $ Go Hotel Shnelli, a big, high-rise "efficiency hotel" adjacent to the sleepy little train station (a 5-minute walk from the Old Town in a neighborhood that feels slightly seedy at night), rents 137 Ikea-mod rooms. It fronts a noisy street, so request a quiet room in the back—these overlook the tracks, but no trains run at night (connecting family rooms, apartment, you can save a few euros if you skip breakfast, elevator, Toompuiestee 37, +372 631 0100, www.gohotels.ee, reservations@gohotels.ee).

Near the Port: Given how compact Tallinn is (and how inexpensive honest taxis are), there's little reason to sleep near the ferry terminals—other than low prices. But if you're in a pinch, **$$ Tallink Express Hotel** is a few steps from the A/B terminals and a short walk from the Old Town. It's a modern, cheery Motel 6-type place with excellent prices and 166 comfortable, cookie-cutter rooms. The rooms can be stuffy in hot weather, as windows don't open very far and there's no air-conditioning (family rooms, elevator, free parking, Sadama 9, +372 630 0808, www.tallinkhotels. com, expresshotel@tallink.ee).

In Lilleküla, Outside the Center: Lilleküla is a quiet, green, and peaceful residential area southwest of the core with single-family houses, small Soviet-era apartment blocks, and barking dogs. For a clearer understanding of Estonian life, stay here. You'll save

TALLINN

money without sacrificing comfort. The downside: It's a 15-minute bus ride into the center.

$ Valge Villa ("White Villa") is a homey guesthouse set in a great garden. Run by Anne and Andres Vahtra and their family, who do everything right, they offer 10 spacious, wood-paneled, well-furnished rooms (family rooms, free parking, rental bikes, pay sauna, pay laundry; take bus #17 to Räägu stop, or trolley bus #2, #3, or #4 to Tedre stop; Kännu 26/2, between Rästa and Räägu streets—for location, see the "Greater Tallinn" map near the beginning of this chapter, +372 654 2302, www.white-villa.com, villa@white-villa.com). I'd take a taxi here to check in (about €15 from the ferry port), and figure out the public-transit options later.

Eating in Tallinn

Tallinn's Old Town has a wide selection of mostly tourist-oriented eateries—don't expect bargains here. For a better value (and better food), roam at least a block or two off the main drags. Some restaurants have good-value lunch specials on weekdays (look for the words *päeva praad*). As a mark of quality, watch for restaurants with an *Astu Sisse!* label in the window; this Estonian equivalent of a Michelin star is awarded to just 50 restaurants each year. Reserving ahead for dinner is a smart idea.

It's easy to find authentic Estonian food—a hearty mix of meat, potatoes, root vegetables, mushrooms, dill, garlic, bread, and soup. Pea soup is a specialty. Estonia is famous for its rye bread, called *leib*, and you usually get a few slices as a free, automatic side dish. A typical pub snack is Estonian garlic bread *(küüslauguleivad)*—deep-fried strips of dark rye bread smothered in garlic and served with a dipping sauce. Estonia's Saku beer is good, cheap, and on tap at most eateries. Try the nutty, full-bodied Tume variety.

ESTONIAN CUISINE IN THE OLD TOWN

$$ Von Krahli Aed is an elegant, almost gourmet, health-food eatery calling itself "the embassy of pure food." While not vegetarian, it is passionate about serving organic, seasonal, modern Estonian cuisine in a woody, romantic setting. Take your pick from four dining options: under old beams, in the cellar, out front on the sidewalk, or out back on the garden terrace (daily 12:00-23:00, Rataskaevu 8, +372 626 9088).

$$ Vanaema Juures ("Grandma's Place"), an eight-table cellar restaurant, serves homey, traditional Estonian meals, such as pork roast with sauerkraut and horseradish. This is a fine bet for local cuisine, and dinner reservations are strongly advised (daily 12:00-22:00, Rataskaevu 10, +372 626 9080, www.vonkrahl.ee/vanaemajuures).

$$ Leib ("Back Bread") is just outside the walls at the seaside end of the Old Town. Steps lead from the entrance into a fun garden under the medieval ramparts, and you can sit indoors or out. The classy menu—built around a passion for Baltic ingredients (spring cabbage, beets, smoked trout, sturgeon)—changes with the seasons (daily 12:00-15:00 & 18:00-23:00, Uus 31, +372 611 9026).

$$$$ Mekk is a small, fresh, upscale place, which has a name that stands for "modern Estonian cuisine." Their dinner à la carte prices are high; ask about weekday lunch specials and the chef's menu at dinner (Mon-Sat 11:00-23:00, Sun until 21:00, Suur-Karja 17, +372 680 6688).

ON AND NEAR TOWN HALL SQUARE

Tallinn's central square is a whirlpool of tacky tourism, where restaurant touts (some dressed as medieval wenches or giant *matryoshka* dolls) accost passersby to lure them in for a drink or meal. Despite being tourist traps, some of these restaurants do have good (if expensive) food.

"Medieval" Estonian Cuisine: Two well-run restaurants just below Town Hall Square specialize in re-creating medieval food (from the days before the arrival of the potato and tomato from the New World). They are each grotesquely touristy, complete with gift shops where you can buy a souvenir goblet. Sit inside to feel the atmosphere.

$$$ Olde Hansa, filling three creaky old floors and outdoor tables with tourists, candle wax, and scurrying medieval servers, has food far better than it has any right to be (daily 10:00-24:00, musicians circulate Tue-Sun after 18:00, a belch below Town Hall Square at Vana Turg 1, reserve in advance, +372 627 9020, www.oldehansa.ee).

$$$ Peppersack, across the street, tries to compete in the same price range, and feels marginally less circus-like (Vana Turg 6, +372 646 6800).

Russian Food: Right on Town Hall Square, with a folkloric-costumed waitstaff, **$$$ Troika** serves *bliny* (pancakes) and *pelmeni* (dumplings), and characteristic main dishes. Sit out on the square (reserve for dinner); in the more casual, Russian-village-themed tavern; or under a fine vault in the atmospheric cellar. A balalaika player usually strums and strolls in the evenings (daily 10:00-23:00, Raekoja Plats 15, +372 627 6245, www.troika.ee).

New Nordic near St. Nicholas Church: $$$ Pegasus, tucked into three floors of a concrete and glass building, is the perfect antidote to the kitsch on Town Hall Square. The decor and the menu are Nordic-inspired, featuring flavorful soups, risottos, fish, and salads (daily 12:00-23:00, Harju 1, +372 662 3013).

PUBS IN THE OLD TOWN

Young Estonians eat well and affordably at pubs. In some pubs, you go to the bar to order and pay before finding a table.

$$ Hell Hunt Pub ("The Gentle Wolf") was the first Western-style pub to open after 1991, and its tasty food and microbrews on tap are still attracting a mixed expat and local crowd. You can make a meal from the great pub snacks plus a salad. Choose a table in its convivial, rustic-industrial interior or on the garden terrace across the street (daily 12:00-24:00, Pikk 39, +372 681 8333).

$ Von Krahli Baar serves cheap, substantial Estonian grub—such as potato pancakes *(torud)* stuffed with mushrooms or shrimp—in a handsome stone building that doubles as a center for Estonia's alternative theater scene; there's also seating in the tiny courtyard where you enter. It started as the bar of the theater upstairs, then expanded to become a restaurant, and has a young, avant-garde vibe (daily 10:00-24:00, Rataskaevu 10, a block uphill from Town Hall Square, near Wheel Well, +372 626 9090).

$$ Põrgu ("Hell"), in a simple, uncluttered cellar, is serious about its beer. They have a wide variety of international and Estonian brews on tap—including some microbrews—and the usual range of bar snacks, salads, and main dishes (daily 12:00-24:00, Rüütli 4, +372 644 0232).

ROTERMANN QUARTER

This modern, up-and-coming district (described on page 664), just across the busy road from Tallinn's Old Town, is well worth exploring for a jolt of cutting-edge architecture and hipster edginess. It's an antidote to the central area's ye-olde aura. Consider the following choices (in a long brick building facing the Old Town), or simply explore this fast-changing scene.

$$$ Sfäär ("Sphere"), which combines an unpretentious bistro with a design shop, is a killing-two-birds look at the Rotermann Quarter. In this lively, cheery place, tables are tucked between locally designed clothes and home decor. The appealing menu features Estonian and international fare (Mon-Fri 8:00-22:00, Sat 10:00-22:00, Sun 10:00-17:00; shop open Mon-Sat 12:00-21:00, Sun until 17:00; Mere Puiestee 6E, mobile +372 5699 2200).

$$$$ Retoran Ö (Swedish for "Island"), just a few doors down in the same building, is a splurge. The dressy, trendy, retrofitted-warehouse interior feels a sophisticated world away from the Old Town's tourist traps. The seasonal menu highlights an Estonian approach to New Nordic cooking—small dishes carefully constructed with local ingredients. Reservations are smart (Mon-Sat 18:00-23:00, closed Sun, Mere Puiestee 6E—enter from the parking lot around back, +372 661 6150, www.restoran-o.ee).

BUDGET EATERIES, BREAKFAST, AND SWEETS

Pancakes at a Beer Hall: $ Kompressor, a big, open-feeling beer hall, is in all the guidebooks for its cheap, huge, and filling pancakes—savory or sweet (daily 11:00-24:00, Rataskaevu 3, +372 646 4210).

Asian: Just off Viru Square, **$ Wok to Walk** is a clean and simple spot, offering tasty made-to-order stir-fries (daily 10:00-23:00, Vana-Viru 14, +372 444 3320).

Coffee and Pastries: The **Maiasmokk** ("Sweet Tooth") café and pastry shop, founded in 1864, is the grande dame of Tallinn cafés—ideal for dessert or breakfast. Even through the Soviet days, this was *the* place for a good pastry or a glass of herby Tallinn schnapps ("Vana Tallinn"). Point to what you want from the selection of classic local pastries at the counter, and sit down for breakfast or coffee on the other side of the shop. Everything's reasonable (Mon-Fri 8:00-21:00, Sat-Sun from 9:00, Pikk 16, across from church with old clock, +372 646 4079, www.kohvikmaiasmokke.ee). They also have a pricier full-menu café upstairs and a marzipan shop (separate entrance).

Chocolates: Pierre Chocolaterie has scrumptious fresh pralines, sandwiches, and coffee in a courtyard filled with craft shops (also light meals, daily 8:30-late, Vene 6, +372 641 8061).

Supermarkets: For picnic supplies, try the **Rimi minimart,** just a block off Town Hall Square (Pikk 11) or the big **Rimi supermarket** just outside the Old Town at Aia 7, near the Viru Gate (both open daily 8:00-22:00). A larger, more upscale supermarket in the basement of the **Viru Keskus** mall (directly behind Hotel Viru) has inexpensive takeaway meals (daily 9:00-21:00).

Tallinn Connections

BY BUS OR TRAIN

The bus is usually the best way to travel by land from Tallinn (for domestic bus schedules, see www.tpilet.ee). The largest international operator, with the most departures, is Lux Express (+372 680 0909, www.luxexpress.eu); there's also Ecolines (+372 614 3600, www.ecolines.net) and Hansabuss (with onboard Wi-Fi, +372 627 9080, www.hansabuss.ee). The bus station (*autobussijaam*) is at Lastekodu 46, a short taxi ride from the Old Town, or a few stops on trams #2 or #4 to the Autobussijaam stop. Not much English is spoken at the station; reserving online is recommended.

Domestic trains are operated by Elron (www.elron.ee).

From Tallinn to: Rīga (12 buses/day, 4.5 hours, no train option; consider Tallinn Traveller Tours' "sightseeing shuttle" between these cities—a full-day, 12-hour journey with sightseeing stops en route; www.traveller.ee), **Vilnius** (5 buses/day, plus 3/day overnight, 10 hours), **St. Petersburg** (2-3 buses/week, 6.5 hours; also possible by overnight cruise—about 1/week, 18.5 hours, www.stpeterline.com; for cruise details, see page 634), **Moscow** (take the overnight train—daily departures in late afternoon, 14.5-hour trip, check current timetables at www.gorail.ee—or fly). Americans and Canadians must generally obtain a visa to travel to Russia and need to plan long in advance (for more information on current visa requirements, see www.ricksteves.com/russianvisa and confirm details at https://washington.mid.ru/en).

BY BOAT
Sailing Overnight Between Stockholm and Tallinn

Tallink Silja's overnight cruise ships between Stockholm and Tallinn leave each city in late afternoon or early evening and arrive in the other city midmorning (about 17 hours later). Ferry fares vary widely by the day and season; the highest rates are typically for Friday and Saturday nights and in summer from July to mid-August. Options range from four-person, gender-segregated dorm rooms to private cabins. The smorgasbord dinner and buffet breakfast cost extra (book these meals and reserve a table when buying your ticket). Book online (www.tallinksilja.com); booking by phone or in person may come with an extra charge (US +1 425 673 4800, Estonian +372 640 9808).

In Tallinn, Tallink Silja ships use the D terminal (see "Arrival in Tallinn," earlier). In Stockholm, boats leave from the Värtahamnen harbor (for details, see page 500).

Speeding Between Helsinki and Tallinn

Several companies offer ferries linking Helsinki and Tallinn in about two hours. Prices tend to be similar among the different operators—around €20-55 one-way; same-day round-trip tickets cost barely more (and sometimes less) than one-way fares (evening departures from Helsinki and morning departures from Tallinn tend to be cheaper; student and senior discounts available; check each company's website for schedule and prices). Advance reservations aren't essential, but usually save a little money, ensure your choice of departure, and provide peace of mind. Since price differences between operators tend to be negligible, base your choice on the most convenient departure times and ferry terminal locations. Make sure you know which terminal your boat leaves from and how to get to it (for descriptions of Helsinki's terminals, see page 630; for Tallinn's, see "Arrival in Tallinn," earlier).

Unless you're bringing a car, **Viking Line** is usually the most convenient, as in both cities it uses docks that are easy to reach by foot or public transport (Helsinki's Katajanokka terminal and Tallinn's A terminal). Viking offers a more traditional experience on a big ferry with restaurants and shops (2-5/day, 1 overnight, daytime crossing about 2 hours, www.vikingline.com).

Tallink Silja connects Helsinki's West Harbor (terminal 1 or 2) and and Tallinn's D terminal (farthest from the Old Town, but still walkable); Tallink Silja's ferries are frequent and fast (6-7/day, 2-hour crossing for most departures, some longer sailings, www.tallinksilja.com).

Eckerö Line connects Helsinki's West Harbor (terminal 2) and Tallinn's A terminal with fewer sailings (3/day, 2.25-hour crossing, www.eckeroline.com).

Slower boats have smorgasbord buffets. The slower the boat, the more likely it is to be filled with "four-legged Finns" crazy about cheap booze, slot machines, and karaoke.

By Plane

For information on Tallinn's airport, see page 646.

SCANDINAVIA: PAST & PRESENT

Throughout Scandinavia, you'll encounter reminders of the region's long and colorful history. You'll see the graves, carved rune stones, and ships of the Vikings—who worshipped Thor and Odin, and terrorized Europe with their fierceness. Evocative, wooden stave churches show how Christianity slowly seeped into the region.

You'll visit the harbors of these seafaring peoples and tour the stark castles of nobles who fought for control of Baltic trade. As modern nations emerged, absolute monarchs built luxurious palaces intended to rival Versailles. Today's streets and main squares are studded with statues and monuments honoring great kings and their battles, great patriots who lobbied for national independence, and great writers and musicians who enriched Scandinavian culture. Scandinavian museums are filled with paintings that capture the beauty of the landscape and celebrate its people. You'll hear bittersweet stories of the millions of 19th-century Scandinavians who left their homes for better lives in America. You'll learn about those who suffered under WWII Nazi occupation, and the heroes who organized resistance and sheltered Jewish people. And you'll experience the richness of Scandinavia today—its wealth, its liberal policies, and its global outlook.

Want to hear more of the Scandinavian story? Read on.

PREHISTORY AND SPEAR HUNTERS
(c. 8000 BC-AD 1)

Emerging only slowly from under glacial ice sheets, the land mass of Scandinavia was the last part of Europe to be settled. After glaciers receded at the end of the last ice age, Stone Age hunters moved north, chasing valuable deer, moose, and fish. Among these were the forebears of the Sami (Lapps) of northern Scandinavia, some of whom continue to herd reindeer and live nomadically. (For more on the indigenous Sami, visit Oslo's Historical Museum or Norwegian Folk Museum, or Stockholm's Nordic Museum.) The early Scandinavians began farming (c. 4000 BC) and eventually developed tools and weapons made of bronze (c. 1800 BC). We know these people mainly by their graves, such as the burial mounds on the island of Öland, in southeastern Sweden, or the megalithic stone dolmens on Denmark's isle of Ærø.

IRON-AGE WARRIORS (AD 1-800)

Isolated from the Continent and unconquered by the Romans, Scandinavia kept close to its prehistoric past. The more than 2,000-year-old Grauballe Man—whose corpse was preserved in a peat bog (and is now displayed at the Moesgård Museum just outside Aarhus, in Denmark's Jutland)—came from a Germanic Iron Age culture. They forged iron implements decorated with the gods of their pagan religion (such as the Gundestrup Cauldron displayed in Copenhagen's National Museum). They commemorated heroic

deeds with large stones carved with the angular alphabet known as runes (see the rune stones at Copenhagen's National Museum at Jelling, Denmark). One of their most sacred sites was at Gamla Uppsala near Stockholm, where mighty chieftains were buried along with their worldly possessions—weapons, jewels, dogs, horses, and even slaves. This distinct, pre-Christian Scandinavian culture thrived in the first centuries AD and continued even as the rest of Europe fell under the sway of Rome's Latin culture and, later, Christianity.

Though isolated, the Scandinavians made fleeting contact with Roman Europe, trading furs and amber for crucial tool-making metals from the Continent. Eventually, the Scandinavians learned to extract their own bronze and iron. With better tools, they became productive farmers and shipbuilders. The population boomed due to a warmer climate and better nutrition. The Scandinavians were soon eyeing Europe and the North Atlantic as a source for new resources and for potential expansion of their clans.

VIKINGS WITH SHIPS (800-1000)

Scandinavia's entrance onto the European stage was swift, dramatic, and unforgettable. On January 8, 793, a fleet of Scandinavian pirates came ashore on the northeast coast of England and sacked the Lindisfarne monastery, slaughtering monks, burning buildings, and plundering sacred objects. Word spread like wildfire of brutal pirates who seemed to come from nowhere, looted and pillaged with extreme prejudice, then moved on. Their victims called them *Normanni, Dani, Rus,* or worse, but the name they gave themselves came from the inlets and bays *(vik)* where they lived: the Vikings.

For the next 200 years, hardy Viking sailors plundered and explored the coasts of northern Europe. Vikings from Norway primarily went west to the British Isles and settled Iceland, Greenland, and beyond; Swedes ventured east to the Baltic states, navigated the Russian rivers, and reached Constantinople; and Danes headed south (to England, France, Spain, and Italy).

The Vikings traveled in fleets of sleek, narrow, open-topped ships a hundred feet long, called *drakkars.* (See them for yourself at the Viking Ship Museum in Oslo, or in Roskilde, near Copenhagen.) Rigged with square sails and powered by dozens of men at the oars, they could speed across the sea at 15 miles an hour and land right on the beach, where attackers would pour out, brandishing weapons.

Each Viking was decked out with a coat of mail, a small shield, and a helmet (though not one with horns as popularly thought—horns would have only gotten in the way in battle). Each warrior specialized in a particular kind of weapon: sword, spear, battle ax, or bow and arrow. At the battle's crucial moment, the Vikings might send in their secret weapon—the so-called *berserkers.* These warriors attacked with a seemingly superhuman (and possibly drug-induced) frenzy, scaring the leotards off their enemies and giving us our English word "berserk."

Despite their reputation as ruthless pirates, most Vikings were settlers who established towns, married the locals, farmed the land, hunted in the forests, and traded with their neighbors. They spread Scandinavian culture and rune stones far and wide. In northern France, the region of "Normandy" was settled by the "North-men." Erik the Red, a Norwegian Viking, was an early settler in Iceland, and his son Leif Eriksson sailed as far as the coast of North America around AD 1000.

To the dismay of Roman Catholic bishops, while the rest of Europe became Christian, the Vikings held onto their pagan gods, many of whom were, like themselves, warriors: Odin, the king of the gods (who gave us our word for Wednesday), and Thor with his hammer, the god of war (and of Thursday). Believing in an afterlife, the Vikings buried their dead ceremonially along with their possessions. Some were interred beneath large mounds of dirt (as at Gamla Uppsala near Stockholm). Others were laid to rest in ships that were buried underground, or in graves marked with stones placed upright in the shape of a full-size ship.

By the year 1000, Scandinavian society was gradually changing—unifying, Christianizing, and assimilating into European culture. Scattered Nordic peoples coalesced into kingdoms, united under the banner of Christianity. In Norway, there was King (later "Saint") Olav II (c. 1020). Among the Svea people (Sweden), King Olaf (Olof Skötkonung, c. 968-1020) unified and Christianized the land. The Danes were united by King Harald Bluetooth (c. 980), who commemorated Denmark's Christian conversion on a now-famous rune stone (located in Jelling)—although in reality, Bluetooth's "conversion" was a ploy to keep the German-Catholic bishops and missionaries at bay. Under Harald's grandson, King Canute, Denmark ruled a large empire that included parts of southern England (c. 1020).

By 1100, the last pagans were gathering at Gamla Uppsala to put on their ceremonial helmets, worship the sun, bury fallen heroes, and retell the sagas of their ancestors. Viking culture blended into the European mainstream, but we still see traces of it today—in rune stones and burial sites; in surviving tools, weapons, and jewelry; and in the dragon-prowed designs found on Christian stave churches and even on contemporary Scandinavian coins.

MEDIEVAL CHRISTIANS, BICKERING NOBLES, AND GERMAN MERCHANTS (1000-1400)

In the Middle Ages, three separate (if loosely united) kingdoms emerged: Denmark, Sweden, and Norway. They were Christian and feudal, with land worked by peasants who owed allegiance to a petty noble sworn to the king. Towns sprang up, including what would become the main cities: Oslo (1048), Copenhagen (1165), and Stockholm (1255). Rulers began flying flags featuring a cross, which eventually became the main motif in each country's national flag.

Christianity dominated. Some of the region's oldest churches (especially in Norway) are wooden stave, made with vertical planks and ornamented with dragons and other semi-pagan figures to ward off evil and ease the transition to Christianity (for more about stave churches, see the Norway in a Nutshell chapter). Devout Christians laid the cornerstones for huge cathedrals, such as the skyscraping Uppsala Cathedral in 1287, Aarhus Cathedral in 1201, and Stockholm Cathedral in 1306.

Finland entered the Scandinavian sphere when zealous Swedes launched a series of crusades to forcibly convert their pagan

Typical Castle Architecture

Castles were fortified residences for medieval nobles. Castles come in all shapes and sizes, but knowing a few general terms will help you understand them.

Barbican: Fortifed gatehouse, sometimes a standalone building located outside the main walls

Crenellation: Gap-toothed pattern of stones atop the parapet

Drawbridge: Bridge that could be raised or lowered using counterweights or a chain and winch

Great Hall: Largest room in the castle, serving as throne room, conference center, and dining hall

Hoardings (or Gallery or Brattice): Wooden huts built onto the upper parts of the stone walls; served as watchtowers, living quarters, and fighting platforms

Keep (or Donjon): High, strong stone tower in the center of the complex; the lord's home and refuge of last resort

Loopholes (or Embrasures): Narrow wall slits through which soldiers could shoot arrows

Machicolation: Stone ledge jutting out from the wall, with holes through which soldiers could drop rocks or boiling oil onto wall-scaling enemies below

Moat: Ditch encircling the wall, sometimes filled with water

Parapet: Outer railing of the wall walk

Portcullis: Iron grille that could be lowered across the entrance

Postern Gate: Small, unfortified side or rear entrance; in wartime, became a sally port used to launch surprise attacks or as an escape route

Towers: Square or round structures with crenellated tops or conical roofs serving as lookouts, chapels, living quarters, or the dungeon

Turret: Small lookout tower rising from the top of the wall

Wall Walk (or Allure): Pathway atop the wall where guards could patrol and where soldiers stood to fire at the enemy

Yard (or Bailey): Open courtyard inside the castle walls neighbors to the east, farm their lands, and fish in their lakes. They conquered and assimilated the region (c. 1200), making it a part of their own country for the next 600 years. Even today, Swedish is spoken on Finland's southern coast. Danish and German "warrior monks" fought a similar crusade against the loosely organized Estonian people, divvying up that region between themselves.

The many castles that dot Scandinavia attest to the civil warfare between nobles. A strong central government headed by a dominant king was still centuries away.

Sea trade between the Scandinavian neighbors boomed. The lucrative trade was controlled by enterprising German merchants who organized Scandinavia's ports into a free-trade zone known as the Hanseatic League (c. 1250-1750). Under German direction, Scandinavia became a powerful player in overseas commerce with the Continent. Cities such as Bergen in Norway reaped big rewards under the Hanse (as evidenced by that city's fine Håkon's Hall). German settlers emigrated to Scandinavia, influencing the culture and language. By 1370, these German traders were so rich that they wielded more actual power than any Scandinavian king. It took a queen to break them.

DOMINANT DANES, WARS, AND REFORMATION (1400-1600)

When Margrethe I of Denmark married the Norwegian king in 1363, Norway came under Danish control (where it would remain for the next 450 years). Denmark emerged as the region's main power. In 1397, Margrethe united Norway, Denmark, and Sweden with the Treaty of Kalmar, and regained control of some Scandinavian economic strongholds that had been dominated by the Hanseatic League. But after Margrethe, the union faltered. For a century, Swedish nobles chafed and occasionally rebelled against Danish domination.

In 1520, Denmark invaded Sweden and, in the notorious Stockholm Bloodbath, massacred 80 rebellious Swedish nobles in the city's main square. Gustav Vasa rallied the enraged Swedes and drove out Denmark's King Christian II (known as Christian the Tyrant in Sweden). Vasa was crowned king of Sweden on June 6, 1523 (now Sweden's flag day). He centralized the Swedish government and Protestantized the country, seizing church property to form a strong nation-state. In many ways, this was the birth of modern Sweden (and the origin of the name for Wasa flatbread).

PAST & PRESENT

By the 1500s, all of Scandinavia had converted to Lutheran-style Protestantism. They'd been primed by the influence of German Hanseatic traders and preachers. And their kings jumped at the chance to confiscate former church property and authority.

For the next century, Denmark and Sweden—the region's two powerhouses—battled for control of the Baltic's lucrative trade routes, particularly for the Øresund, the crucial strait between Denmark and Sweden that connects the Baltic with the North Sea (and is now spanned by the modern Øresund Bridge). It was during this period that much of Estonia fell under control of the Swedish empire.

SWEDISH SUPERIORITY AND ABSOLUTE MONARCHS (1600-1800)

By 1600, Denmark-Norway was still the region's superpower, but Sweden-Finland-Estonia was rising fast. Denmark's one-eyed, high-living King Christian IV was spending centuries' worth of acquired wealth building lavish castles, including Rosenborg and Frederiksborg, and putting a Renaissance face on Copenhagen and Oslo (see page 42). Meanwhile, his wars with Sweden and others were slowly sapping the country, emptying its coffers, and undermining Danish superiority. Christian IV even sold the Orkney and Shetland Islands to England to raise funds.

Sweden emerged under the inspired military leadership of King Gustavus Adolphus (1594-1632). The "Lion of the North" roared southward, conquering large chunks of Russia, Poland, Germany, and Denmark during the Thirty Years' War. The vast *Vasa* ship, which the king commissioned in 1628, trumpeted the optimism of the era—but sank ignominiously in the middle of Stockholm harbor on its maiden voyage (visit the unseaworthy vessel at the Vasa Museum in Stockholm).

Sweden's supreme moment came under Gustavus' great-grandson, Karl X Gustav (1622-1660). In 1657, Karl invaded Denmark through the back door—from the south. The winter was extremely cold, and the seas froze between several of Denmark's islands. In one of the most daring maneuvers in military history, Karl X Gustav led his armies across the ice between the islands—from Funen to Langeland to Lolland to Zealand—then sped toward Copenhagen. The astonished Danes surrendered, signing the humiliating Treaty of Roskilde (1658). The treaty gave Sweden a third of Danish territory, plus shared control of the Øresund Strait. Denmark would never again dominate, while Sweden became a major European power, with an imposing fleet and a Baltic empire that included Finland, Estonia, Latvia, and parts of Poland, Russia, and Germany.

In the 1660s, the kings of Denmark-Norway and Sweden-Finland-Estonia—following the trend set by Louis XIV in France—declared themselves to be absolute, divinely ordained monarchs. For the next 50 years, these kings scuffled with each other (and neighboring countries) for superiority in the Baltic. By 1720, the wars had drained both countries, at the very time that France and England were on the rise. Sweden ceded Estonia to the Russians, and Scandinavia sank back into relative obscurity.

For the rest of the 1700s, Denmark-Norway and Sweden-Finland mostly avoided war while trying to modernize and expand their economies. But the French Revolution (1789) and the Europe-wide wars that followed stirred up this relative peace, awakening a desire for democracy, ethnic recognition, and national independence.

PATRIOTS, ARTISTS, INDUSTRIALISTS, AND EMIGRANTS (1800s)

As Europe's monarchs ganged up on Revolutionary France under Napoleon, Scandinavia was forced to take sides. Through a series

of complicated alliances, Denmark ended up backing the loser (France), while Sweden backed the winners (Britain and others). At war's end, Denmark was forced to cede Norway to Sweden in the 1814 Treaty of Kiel. Meanwhile, Sweden had just lost Finland to Russia in 1809. Thus began the nation-building process that, a century later, would result in the five independent countries we have today.

The wars also gave Sweden (and Norway) a new king—a French soldier who was not Scandinavian and had not a drop of noble blood. But Jean-Baptiste Bernadotte, a career military man in Napoleon's army, was loved by Sweden's childless king, admired by Sweden's soldiers for his fighting prowess, and popular with the people for treating Swedish prisoners well during the wars. The bizarre choice of a French commoner was a surprise, but everyone said *oui-oui*, and Jean-Baptiste was crowned Sweden's King Karl Johan XIV (and Karl Johan III in Norway). During his reign (1818-1844), Bernadotte brought peace, prosperity, and fresh DNA, founding the royal dynasty that would produce the current monarchs of Sweden and, by intermarriage, of Norway and Denmark.

The French Revolution (and Napoleon) spread the idea throughout Europe that people should embrace their ethnic roots and demand self-rule. Norwegians—having been ruled for centuries by Danes, and now Swedes—met at Eidsvoll Manor (outside Oslo), drafted a constitution with a parliament, elected a king, and demanded independence. Though the country was still too weak to make this a political reality, the date of May 17, 1814, has become the country's Fourth of July, celebrated today with plenty of flag-waving and folk costumes by Norwegians both in and out of Norway.

Culturally, if not politically, nationalism flourished, producing artists like Johan Christian Dahl, who captured the beauty of the Norwegian countryside and the simple dignity of its people. (You can see his works at Oslo's National Museum.) Playwright Henrik Ibsen realistically portrayed the complexities of a changing Norwegian society. And composer Edvard Grieg used music to convey the majesty of the landscape near Troldhaugen, his home in Bergen.

In Denmark, nationalism inspired the German-speaking majority in the provinces of Schleswig and Holstein to call for autonomy (1848-1851). The region was finally taken by force from Denmark by Prussia (1864) and incorporated into the new state of Germany. The resulting nationwide sense of humiliation and self-critique actually spurred a cultural Golden Age. Philosopher Søren Kierkegaard captured the angst of an age when traditional certainties were crumbling. Storyteller Hans Christian Andersen (*The Ugly Duckling, The Emperor's New Clothes, The Little Mermaid,* and others) gained a Europe-wide reputation. And sculptor Bertel Thorvaldsen, who studied and worked in Rome, decorated Copenhagen with his realistic, Neoclassical statues (see them at the Cathedral of Our Lady and at Thorvaldsen's Museum).

Throughout the 1800s, Scandinavia was modernizing. The Industrial Revolution brought trains, factories, and larger cities. While some got rich, overpopulation, famine, and a changing economy forced millions of poor Scandinavian farmers to emigrate to America between 1850 and 1920 (Sweden's House of Emigrants museum in Växjö tells their story.) As in other European countries, Scandinavia saw the steady advance of democracy, parliaments, labor unions, and constitutional monarchies. The 20th century would quicken that pace.

Also during this period, Norwegian polar explorers—including Fridtjof Nansen and Roald Amundsen—began pushing the boundaries of human knowledge by going where nobody had gone

Scandi-hoovians You Might Know

Famous Danes

Hans Christian Andersen, of *Ugly Duckling* and *Little Mermaid* fame

Søren Kierkegaard, first existentialist philosopher

Bertel Thorvaldsen, Neoclassical sculptor

Karen Blixen, *Out of Africa* author (under pen name Isak Dinesen)

Niels Bohr, atomic physicist and Nobel Prize winner

Victor Borge, musical humorist

Arne Jacobsen, postwar designer and architect

Lars Ulrich, drummer for heavy metal band Metallica

Nikolaj Coster-Waldau, *Game of Thrones* actor

Carl Nielsen, symphonic composer

Lars von Trier, *enfant terrible* movie director

Morten Andersen, NFL placekicker

Famous Norwegians

Erik the Red, Viking settler in Iceland and Greenland, and father of Leif Eriksson, who sailed to North America

Edvard Grieg, Romantic-era composer

Edvard Munch, *The Scream* painter

Henrik Ibsen, playwright

Roald Amundsen, Arctic and Antarctic explorer

Gustav Vigeland, sculptor

Knute Rockne, football player/coach at University of Notre Dame

Sonja Henie, figure skater and movie actress

Thor Heyerdahl, explorer of *Kon-Tiki* fame

Jan Stenerud, NFL placekicker

Liv Ullmann, movie actress and director

before, deep into the Arctic and Antarctic (for more, visit Oslo's Fram Museum).

INDEPENDENCE AND WORLD WARS (1900-1945)

In 1905—after five and a half centuries of Danish and Swedish rule—Norway finally negotiated an end to its union with Sweden and become independent. National pride ran high, as Oslo's own Roald Amundsen became the first person to reach the South Pole (in 1911). In 1919, Finland and Estonia—after centuries of Swedish and Russian rule—won their independence while Russia was distracted by the Bolshevik Revolution.

Jo Nesbø, author of Oslo-based Harry Hole detective series
Rick Steves, travel writer

Famous Swedes

Anders Celsius, inventor of the temperature scale
Carolus Linnaeus, botanist and father of modern taxonomy
August Strindberg, playwright
Alfred Nobel, inventor of dynamite and the Nobel Peace Prize
Carl Milles, sculptor
Astrid Lindgren, children's author *(Pippi Longstocking)*
Ingmar Bergman, movie director
Ingrid Bergman, Greta Garbo, and Noomi Rapace, actresses
Max von Sydow, actor
Dag Hammarskjöld, UN secretary general
Björn Borg and Stefan Edberg, tennis players
Hans Blix, UN weapons inspector
Annika Sörenstam and Jesper Parnevik, golfers
ABBA, pop-rock supergroup
Stieg Larsson, author of the *Millennium* trilogy
Greta Thunberg, environmental activist

Famous Finns

Jean Sibelius, Romantic composer
Alvar Aalto, Modernist architect
Eliel Saarinen and son Eero, Modernist architects
Esa-Pekka Salonen, classical conductor
Tove Jansson, author of the *Moomin* books
Linus Torvalds, creator of the Linux operating system
Kimi Räikkönen and Keke Rosberg, race car drivers

The Scandinavian nations remained neutral through World War I. But when Hitler's Nazi Germany began its European conquest in World War II, it was impossible for Scandinavians—try as they might—to remain uninvolved. While officially neutral, Sweden allowed Nazi troops "on leave" to march through. Sweden's neutrality later provided a safe haven for Danish Jews and a refuge for the Danish and Norwegian resistance movements.

Germany invaded Denmark and Norway on April 9, 1940, with Operation Weserübung. Scattered fighting at the Danish border was quickly put down, and Denmark capitulated and officially cooperated with the Nazis until 1943, when the Germans took over the government. Danish resistance groups harried the Nazis and provided intelligence to the Allies. In 1943, a German diplomat informed Copenhagen's rabbi that the Jews were about to be deported. Danish citizens quickly hid and eventually evacuated all but 500 of Denmark's Jews to neutral Sweden.

Norway's army held out a few weeks longer, allowing time for King Håkon VII to flee and organize a vital resistance movement (memorialized at Oslo's Norwegian Resistance Museum). Norway spent the war chafing under a Nazi puppet government headed by Vidkun Quisling, whose surname has become synonymous with "traitor."

Denmark, Sweden, and Norway came out of the war without the horrendous damage and loss of life suffered elsewhere in Europe—in part, probably, because Hitler wanted to turn the Scandinavian countries into model states. After all, these were the people Germany was trying to emulate: tall, blond, blue-eyed symbols of the Aryan race.

Finland and Estonia's fates were more complicated. During the war, the Finns valiantly battled Russian invaders, at one point allying with Hitler against the Russians. By war's end, Finland had fought both the Soviets and the Nazis. Estonia, meanwhile, was occupied first by the Soviets and later by the Nazis.

As postwar Europe was divvied up between the communist East and the democratic West, Estonia wound up in the Soviet sphere of influence. Finland avoided this fate through a compromise policy called "Finlandization." The Finns paid lip service to Soviet authority, censored their own media, acted as a buffer against military invasion from the West, rejected rebuilding money from the US (the Marshall Plan), and avoided treaties with the West. In return, Finland remained a self-ruling capitalist democracy and a firm part of the Nordic world. They imported raw materials from the Soviets, then shipped them back as manufactured products, in a mutually beneficial trade agreement.

Meanwhile, Norway and Denmark stood with the West, joining NATO and participating in the Marshall Plan. Sweden took a more neutral approach, and Swede Dag Hammarskjöld served as the UN's Secretary General from 1953 to 1961. Estonia was subsumed into the Soviet Union as one of the 15 "republics" of the USSR, only regaining its independence with the breakup of the Soviet Union in 1991.

THE SOCIAL WELFARE STATE (1946-Present)

In the decades since World War II, the Scandinavian countries have followed a mix of free-market capitalism and enlightened socialism, and have become quite wealthy. On the high-tech edge of the global economy, the Scandinavians have made their mark with telecommunications (Nokia from Finland, Ericsson from Sweden), furniture (Sweden's Ikea), appliances (Sweden's Electrolux), health care (Novo Nordisk in Denmark), and toys (Denmark's Lego).

The Scandinavian countries make the most of their natural resources as well. In the late 1960s, Norway discovered oil in the

Little Maria...or Metallica?

Scandinavia is viewed as one of the most liberal corners of Europe, so Americans are often surprised to learn there are government restrictions on what parents can name their children. Historically, parents in Denmark, Norway, Sweden, and Finland were required to choose their child's name from a published list of acceptable monikers. Any variations had to be approved by a government board. One intent of the rules was to prevent commoners from using royal names and to ban names considered ridiculous, inappropriate, potentially harmful to the child, or just not Scandinavian enough. A Norwegian mom even spent two days in jail in the '90s for naming her son Gesher (it means "bridge" in Hebrew). But following a recent series of court rulings, Scandinavian countries are relaxing parts of their naming laws. Denmark has allowed some Legolases and Gandalfs, and in Sweden there's a girl named Metallica and a boy named Google.

Estonia took a different approach: In the 1930s it encouraged its citizens to change their Swedish-sounding names to the Estonian equivalents.

North Sea, almost instantly transforming itself into a rich nation. Denmark is blessed with rich farmland, and Sweden and Finland with lush forest. They are all rich in fish.

Citizens across Scandinavia have come to take for granted cradle-to-grave security—health care, education, unemployment benefits, welfare, and so on—all financed with high taxes. High taxes mean there's less of a gap between the very rich and the very poor, resulting in a less class-oriented society. Scandinavians are proud of this. If they seem a bit smug, you can't fault them: Statistics verify that they live longer, healthier, happier lives. In social policies, Scandinavia has often led the way in liberal attitudes toward sexuality, drug use, and LGBTQ rights.

Immigration in the late 20th century and onward has brought many citizens from non-European nations to Scandinavia. While adding diversity and contributing to the tax base, the newcomers have also threatened the homogenous fabric of a society whose roots have traditionally been white, Christian, European, democratic, and blond. The sharp influx of immigrants—many with little formal education and who speak only their native language—has challenged the public's will to extend universal benefits to those who struggle to find jobs. Far-right parties have gained support with anti-immigration platforms, and, strikingly, Denmark has introduced regulations to force immigrants to integrate into the mainstream culture. It's clear that the collectivist spirit of the Nordic model is being tested.

Today, Finland, Sweden, Denmark, and Estonia are all members of the European Union. Norway has stayed outside, though an economic agreement gives the country most of the benefits of membership. While Finland and Estonia have embraced the euro, Norway, Sweden, and Denmark have preserved their own currencies.

Complicating life for the entire globe, the coronavirus pandemic emerged in early 2020, and it remains to be seen how the Nordic countries will deal with the social and economic fallout it has caused. But as the Scandinavian people forge into the 21st century, they continue to be adamant about preserving their culture, traditions, and high standard of living while competing in a global economy.

PRACTICALITIES

This chapter covers the practical skills of European travel: how to get tourist information, pay for purchases, sightsee efficiently, find good-value accommodations, eat affordably but well, use technology wisely, and get between destinations smoothly. For more information on these topics, see RickSteves.com/travel-tips.

Tourist Information

National tourist websites can be a wealth of information. Begin your Scandinavian travel planning at VisitDenmark.com, VisitNorway.com, VisitSweden.com, VisitFinland.com, and VisitEstonia.com.

Once in Scandinavia, a good first stop in every town is generally the tourist information office (abbreviated **TI** in this book). You'll find Scandinavian TIs are usually well organized and always have an English-speaking staff. TIs are in business to help you enjoy spending money in their town—which can color their advice —but I still swing by to pick up a city map and get information on public transit, walking tours, special events, and nightlife. Some TIs have information on the entire country or at least the region, so try to pick up maps and printed information for destinations you'll be visiting later in your trip.

Travel Tips

Travel Advisories: For updated health and safety conditions, including any Covid entry restrictions for your destination, consult the US State Department's international travel website (www.travel.state.gov).

Emergency and Medical Help: In most countries in this book, dial 112 for any emergency service—ambulance, police, or fire (operators typically speak English). The exception is Norway, where you'll dial 112 for police, 110 for fire, and 113 for an ambulance. If you get sick, do as the locals do and go to a pharmacist for advice. Or ask at your hotel for help—they'll know the nearest medical and emergency services.

ETIAS Registration: The European Union may soon require US and Canadian citizens to register online with the European Travel Information and Authorization System (ETIAS) before entering Scandinavia and other Schengen Zone countries (quick and easy process). For the latest, check EtiasVisa.com.

Theft or Loss: To replace a passport, you'll need to go in person to an embassy (see next). If your credit and debit cards disappear, cancel and replace them (see "Damage Control for Lost Cards" on page 705). File a police report, either on the spot or within a day or two; you'll need it to submit an insurance claim for lost or stolen rail passes or electronics, and it can help with replacing your passport or credit and debit cards. For more information, see RickSteves.com/help.

US Embassies and Consulates: Embassies are located in all the capital cities. Passport services are by appointment. Embassies are closed on national holidays in the US and the host country.

Denmark: Dag Hammarskjölds Allé 24, Copenhagen, Mon-Thu 9:00-12:00, +45 33 41 71 00, Mon-Fri 8:30-17:00, https://dk.usembassy.gov

Norway: Morgedalsvegen 36, Oslo, Mon-Fri 8:30-17:00, +47 21 30 85 40, https://no.usembassy.gov

Sweden: Dag Hammarskjölds Väg 31, Stockholm, Mon-Fri 8:00-16:30, +46 8 783 5300, https://se.usembassy.gov

Finland: Itäinen Puistotie 14B, Helsinki, info tel. +358 40/140-5957, Mon and Wed 14:00-16:00, emergency tel. +358 9 616 250 (select 0), https://fi.usembassy.gov

Estonia: Kentmanni 20, Tallinn, Mon-Fri 9:00-12:00 & 14:00-17:00, info tel. +372 668 8100, emergency after-hours tel. +372 509 2129 or +372 668 8169, https://ee.usembassy.gov

Canadian Embassies: Canadian consular services are by appointment only. For after-hours emergencies, call Ottawa collect +1 613 996 8885.

Denmark: Kristen Bernikowsgade 1, Copenhagen, Mon-Fri 8:30-12:00 & 13:00-16:30, +45 33 48 32 00, www.denmark.gc.ca

Norway: Wergelandsveien 7, Oslo, Mon-Fri 8:30-16:30, +47 22 99 53 00, www.norway.gc.ca

Sweden: Klarabergsgatan 23 (6th floor), Stockholm, Mon-Fri 9:00-12:00, +46 8 453 3000, www.sweden.gc.ca

Finland: Pohjoisesplanadi 25B, Helsinki, Mon-Fri 8:30-11:00 & 14:00-16:30, +358 9 228 530, www.finland.gc.ca

Estonia: Toom-Kooli 13, Tallinn, Mon-Fri 8:30-17:00, +372 627 3311, https://www.international.gc.ca

Time Zones: Norway, Sweden, and Denmark, like most of continental Europe, are generally six/nine hours ahead of the East/West Coasts of the US. Finland and Estonia are one hour ahead of Norway, Sweden, and Denmark. The exceptions are the beginning and end of Daylight Saving Time: Europe "springs forward" the last Sunday in March (two weeks after most of North America) and "falls back" the last Sunday in October (one week before North America). For a handy time converter, use the world clock app on your mobile phone or download one (see www.timeanddate.com).

Business Hours: Shops generally open at 10:00 and close between 17:00 and 20:00 on weekdays; bigger stores and malls tend to stay open later, while smaller stores and shops in smaller towns may have shorter hours. On Sundays banks and most shops are closed, and public transportation options are generally fewer. Many museums in Scandinavia are closed on Mondays.

Watt's Up? Europe's electrical system is 220 volts, instead of North America's 110 volts. Most newer electronics (laptops, phones, cameras) and appliances (hair dryers, CPAP machines) convert automatically, so you won't need a converter, but you will need an adapter plug with two round prongs, sold inexpensively at travel stores in the US.

Rip up this book! Turn chapters into mini guidebooks: Break the book's spine and use a utility knife to slice apart chapters, keeping gummy edges intact. Reinforce the chapter spines with clear wide tape; use a heavy-duty stapler; or make or buy a cheap cover (see the Travel Store at RickSteves.com), swapping out chapters as you travel.

Discounts: Discounts for sights are generally not listed in this book. However, seniors (age 65 and over), youths under 18, and students and teachers with proper identification cards (obtain from www.isic.org) can get discounts at many sights—always ask. Some discounts are available only to European citizens. Note that liberal Scandinavia is Europe's most generous corner when it comes to youth discounts—children usually sightsee for half-price or free.

Online Translation Tips: Google's Chrome browser instantly translates websites; Translate.google.com and DeepL.com are also handy. The Google Translate app converts spoken or typed English into most European languages (and vice versa) and can also translate text it "reads" with your phone's camera.

Going Green: There's plenty you can do to reduce your environmental footprint when traveling. When practical, take a train instead of a flight within Europe, and use public transportation within cities. In hotels, use the "Do Not Disturb" sign to avoid daily linen and towel changes (or hang up your towels to signal you'll reuse them). Bring a reusable shopping tote and refillable water bottle (Europe's tap water is safe to drink). To find out how Rick Steves' Europe is offsetting carbon emissions with an innovative self-imposed carbon tax, go to RickSteves.com/about-us/climate-smart.

Money

Here's my basic strategy for using money in Europe:

- Upon arrival, head for an ATM at the airport and withdraw cash in the local currency, using a debit card with low international transaction fees.
- In general, pay for most expenses with a credit card with low (or no) international transaction fees. Carry cash as a back-up.
- Keep your cards and cash safe in a money belt.

PLASTIC VERSUS CASH

In Scandinavia, credit cards are widely accepted and often preferred, even for small purchases (in Stockholm, for example, you can't pay for a subway or bus ride with cash).

I use my credit card to book and pay for hotel reservations, to buy advance tickets for events or sights, and to cover most other expenses. I keep a small amount of cash on-hand, just in case.

WHAT TO BRING

I pack the following and keep it all safe in my money belt.

Debit Card: Use this at ATMs to withdraw local cash.

Credit Card: Handy for bigger transactions (at hotels, shops, restaurants, travel agencies, car-rental agencies, and so on), payment machines, and online purchases.

Backup Card: Some travelers carry a third card (debit or credit; ideally from a different bank), in case one gets lost or simply doesn't work.

A Stash of Cash: I carry $100-200 in US dollars as a cash backup, which comes in handy in an emergency (for example, if your ATM card gets eaten by the machine).

Exchange Rates

I've priced things in local currencies throughout the book. Denmark, Norway, and Sweden use crowns (*kroner* in Denmark and Norway; *kronor* in Sweden), but crowns from one country are not accepted in the next. Finland and Estonia use euros.

$1 equals about...
6 Danish kroner (DKK)
9 Norwegian kroner (NOK)
9 Swedish kronor (SEK)
0.85 euro (€)

To roughly convert Danish prices into US dollars, divide by 6 (e.g., 15 DKK = about $2.50, 100 DKK = about $16). In Sweden and Norway, divide prices by 9 (100 NOK = about $11). So, that 1,000-NOK Norwegian sweater is about $110, and your 360-SEK dinner in Stockholm is about $40. To roughly convert prices in euros to dollars, add 15 percent (€20 = about $23). Check www.oanda.com for the latest exchange rates.

What NOT to Bring: Resist the urge to buy the local currency before your trip or you'll pay the price in bad stateside exchange rates. Wait until you arrive to withdraw money. European airports have plenty of ATMs.

BEFORE YOU GO

Use this pre-trip checklist.

Know your cards. US debit cards with a Visa or MasterCard logo will work in any European ATM. As for credit cards, Visa and MasterCard are universal, American Express is less common, and Discover is unknown in Europe.

Know your PIN. Make sure you know the numeric, four-digit PIN for all of your cards, both debit and credit. Request it if you don't have one, as it may be required for some purchases in Europe (see "Using Credit Cards," later), and allow time to receive the information by mail.

Report your travel dates. Let your bank know that you'll be using your debit and credit cards in Europe, and when and where you're headed.

Adjust your ATM withdrawal limit. Find out how much you can take out daily and ask for a higher daily withdrawal limit if you want to get more cash at once. Note that European ATMs will withdraw funds only from checking accounts, not savings accounts.

Ask about fees. For any purchase or withdrawal made with a card, you may be charged a currency conversion fee (1-3 percent) and/or a Visa or MasterCard international transaction fee (less than 1 percent). If you're getting a bad deal, consider getting a new debit or credit card. Reputable no-fee cards include those from Capital One, as well as Charles Schwab debit cards. Most credit unions and some airline loyalty cards have low or no international transaction fees.

IN EUROPE
Using Cash Machines

European cash machines have English-language instructions and work just like they do at home—except they spit out local currency, calculated at the day's standard bank-to-bank rate.

In most places, ATMs are easy to locate. When possible, withdraw cash from a bank-run ATM located just outside that bank.

If your debit card doesn't work, try a lower amount—your request may have exceeded your withdrawal limit or the ATM's limit. If you still have a problem, try a different ATM or come back later.

Avoid "independent" ATMs, such as Travelex, Euronet, Moneybox, Your Cash, Cardpoint, and Cashzone. These have high fees, can be less secure, and may try to trick users with "dynamic currency conversion" (see next page).

Exchanging Cash

Minimize exchanging money in Europe; it's expensive (you'll generally lose 5 to 10 percent). Because Scandinavian countries have different currencies, avoid withdrawing more cash than you'll need; otherwise you'll likely wind up with leftover cash when leaving a country. In a pinch you can find exchange desks at major train stations or airports. Banks generally do not exchange money unless you have an account with them.

Using Credit Cards

US credit cards generally work fine in Europe—with a few exceptions.

European cards use no-signature chip-and-PIN technology; some chip cards issued in the US instead require a signature. When presented with a US card, European card readers may generate a receipt for you to sign—or prompt you to enter your PIN. At self-service payment machines (such as transit-ticket kiosks), US cards may not work. In this case, look for a cashier who can process your card manually—or pay in cash.

"Tap to pay" cards and smartphone payment apps work in Europe just as they do in the US, and sidestep chip-and-PIN compatibility issues.

Drivers Beware: Drivers may encounter automated pay points (tollbooths, parking meters, gas pumps, etc.) where US cards are not accepted. Carry cash as a back-up and be prepared to move on to the next gas station if necessary (in some countries, gas stations sell prepaid gas cards, which you should be able to purchase with any US card).

Dynamic Currency Conversion (DCC)

When paying with a credit card, you'll often be asked whether you want to pay in dollars or in the local currency. Always refuse the conversion and choose the local currency. While DCC seems convenient, it comes with a poor exchange rate, and you'll wind up losing money. Many ATMs also offer DCC—again, always select "continue without conversion."

Security Tips

Pickpockets target tourists. Keep your cash, credit cards, and passport secure in your money belt, and carry only a day's spending money in your front pocket or wallet.

Before inserting your card into an ATM, inspect the front. If anything looks crooked, loose, or damaged, it could be a sign of a card-skimming device. When entering your PIN, carefully block other people's view of the keypad.

Don't use a debit card for purchases. Because a debit card pulls funds directly from your bank account, potential charges incurred by a thief will stay on your account while the fraudulent use is investigated by your bank.

While traveling, to access your accounts online, be sure to use a secure connection (see the "Tips on Internet Security" sidebar, later).

Damage Control for Lost Cards

If you lose your credit or debit card, report the loss immediately to the respective global customer-assistance centers. With a mobile phone, call these 24-hour US numbers collect: Visa (+1 303 967 1096), MasterCard (+1 636 722 7111), and American Express (+1 336 393 1111). From a landline, you can call these US numbers collect by going through a local operator.

You'll need to provide the primary cardholder's identification-verification details (such as birth date, mother's maiden name, or Social Security number). You can generally receive a temporary card within two or three business days in Europe (see RickSteves. com/help for more).

If you report your loss within two days, you typically won't be responsible for unauthorized transactions on your account, although many banks charge a liability fee.

TIPPING

Tipping in Scandinavia isn't as automatic and generous as it is in the US. For special service, tips are appreciated, but not expected. As in the US, the proper amount depends on your resources, tipping philosophy, and the circumstances, but some general guidelines apply.

Restaurants: You don't need to tip if you order your food at a counter. At restaurants with a wait staff, it's common to tip by rounding up (about 5-10 percent) for a good meal. For details on restaurant tipping, see "Eating," later in this chapter.

Taxis: For a typical ride, round up your fare a bit (for instance, if the fare is 85 DKK, pay 90 DKK). If the cabbie hauls your bags and zips you to the airport to help you catch your flight, you might want to toss in a little more.

Services: In general, if someone in the tourism or service industry does a super job for you, a small tip of a euro or two is appropriate...but not required. If you're not sure whether (or how much) to tip, ask a local for advice.

GETTING A VAT REFUND

Wrapped into the purchase price of your Scandinavian souvenirs is a value-Added Tax (VAT) of 20-25 percent (among the highest rates in Europe). You're entitled to get most of that tax back if you purchase more than a certain amount (300 DKK in Denmark, 315 NOK in Norway, 200 SEK in Sweden, €40 in Finland, and €38 in Estonia) at a store that participates in the VAT refund scheme (look for signs in store windows—VAT is called MVA in Norway; MOMS in Denmark, Finland, and Sweden; and *käibemaks* or *km* in Estonia). Typically, you must ring up the minimum at a single retailer—you can't add up your purchases from various shops to reach the required amount. (If the store ships the goods to your US home, VAT is not assessed on your purchase.)

Getting your refund is straightforward...and worthwhile if you spend a significant amount.

At the Merchant: Have the merchant completely fill out the refund document (they'll ask for your passport; a photo of your passport usually works). Keep track of the paperwork and your original sales receipt. Note that you're not supposed to use your purchased goods before you leave Europe.

At the Border or Airport: If you've made purchases in Denmark, Sweden, Finland, and/or Estonia, process your VAT document at your last stop in the European Union (such as at the airport) with the customs agent who deals with VAT refunds. If you've shopped hard in Norway (a non-EU country), get your document(s) stamped at your point of departure from Norway.

At some airports, you'll have to go to a customs office to get your documents stamped and then to a separate VAT refund service (such as Global Blue or Planet) to process the refund. At other airports, a single VAT desk handles the whole thing. Note that refund services typically extract a 4 percent fee and can refund your money in cash immediately or credit your card. Otherwise, you'll need to mail the stamped refund documents to the address given by the merchant. Allow plenty of extra time at the airport to deal with the VAT refund process.

CUSTOMS FOR AMERICAN SHOPPERS

You can take home $800 worth of items per person duty-free, once every 31 days. Many processed and packaged foods are allowed, including cheeses, dried herbs, jams, baked goods, candy, chocolate, oil, vinegar, condiments, and honey. Fresh fruits and vegetables and most meats are not allowed, with exceptions for some canned items. As for alcohol, you can bring in one liter duty-free (it can be packed securely in your checked luggage, along with any other liquid-containing items).

To bring alcohol (or liquid-packed foods) in your carry-on bag on your flight home, buy it at a duty-free shop at the airport. You'll increase your odds of getting it onto a connecting flight if it's packaged in a "STEB"—a secure, tamper-evident bag. But stay away from liquids in opaque, ceramic, or metallic containers, which usually cannot be successfully screened (STEB or no STEB).

For details on allowable goods, customs rules, and duty rates, visit http://help.cbp.gov.

Sightseeing

Sightseeing can be hard work. Use these tips to make your visits to Scandinavia's finest sights meaningful, fun, efficient, and painless.

MAPS AND NAVIGATION TOOLS

A good map is essential for efficient navigation while sightseeing. The maps in this book are concise and simple, designed to help you locate recommended destinations, sights, hotels, and restaurants. Simple maps are generally free at TIs and hotels.

You can also use a mapping app on your mobile device, which provides turn-by-turn directions for walking, driving, and taking public transit. Google Maps, Apple Maps, and CityMaps2Go allow you to download maps for offline use; ideally, download the areas you'll need before your trip. For certain features, you'll need to be online—either using Wi-Fi or an international data plan.

For help with the Scandinavian terms you'll see on maps and signs as you travel, see the "Useful Topographical Words" sidebar on page 736.

PLAN AHEAD

Set up an itinerary that allows you to fit in all your must-see sights. For a one-stop look at opening hours in the bigger cities, see this book's "At a Glance" sidebars for major cities (Copenhagen, Oslo, Bergen, Stockholm, Helsinki, and Tallinn). Most sights keep stable hours, but you can easily confirm the latest by checking with the TI or on museum websites.

Don't put off visiting a must-see sight—you never know when a place will close unexpectedly for a holiday, strike, or restoration. Many museums are closed or have reduced hours at least a few days a year, especially on holidays such as Christmas, New Year's, and Labor Day (May 1). A list of holidays is in the appendix; check for possible closures during your trip. In summer, some sights may stay open late. Off-season hours may be shorter.

Going at the right time helps avoid crowds. This book offers tips on the best times to see specific sights. Try visiting popular sights very early or very late. Evening visits (when possible) are usually peaceful, with fewer crowds. Late morning is usually the worst time to visit a popular sight.

If you plan to hire a local guide, reserve ahead by email. Popular guides can get booked up.

Study up. To get the most out of the sight descriptions in this book, read them before your visit.

ADVANCE TICKETS AND PASSES

Given how precious your vacation time is, I recommend getting reservations for any must-see sight that offers them (check sight websites for the latest). **Advance tickets** guarantee admission at a certain time of day and allow you to skip entry lines. It's worth giving up some spontaneity to book in advance. While other tourists sweat in long ticket-buying lines—or arrive to find the sight sold out—those who've booked ahead are assured of getting in. In some cases, getting a ticket in advance simply means buying your ticket earlier on the same day. But for other sights, you may need to book weeks or even months in advance. As soon as you're ready to commit to a certain date, book it.

Some destinations offer sightseeing cards or **passes** that offer free or discounted admission to major sights and may also cover public transportation. The value of these passes often depends on how much you plan to see in a destination; do the math before you buy.

AT SIGHTS

Here's what you can typically expect:

Entering: You may not be allowed to enter if you arrive too close to closing time. And guards start ushering people out well before the actual closing time, so don't save the best for last.

Many sights have a security check. Allow extra time for these lines. Some sights require you to check daypacks and coats. (If you'd rather not check your daypack, try carrying it tucked under your arm like a purse as you enter.)

Photography: If the museum's photo policy isn't clearly posted, ask a guard. Generally, taking photos without a flash or tripod is allowed. Some sights ban selfie sticks; others ban photos altogether.

Audioguides and Apps: Many sights rent audioguides with excellent recorded descriptions in English. If you bring your own earbuds, you can often enjoy better sound. And if you don't mind being tethered to your travel partner, you'll save money by bringing a Y-jack and sharing one audioguide. Museums and sights often offer free apps that you can download to your mobile device (check their websites).

Temporary Exhibits: Museums may show special exhibits in addition to their permanent collection. Some exhibits are included in the entry price, while others come at an extra cost (which you may have to pay even if you don't want to see the exhibit).

Expect Changes: Artwork can be on tour, on loan, out sick, or shifted at the whim of the curator. Pick up a floor plan as you enter, and ask museum staff if you can't find a particular item.

Services: Important sights usually have a reasonably priced on-site café or cafeteria (handy and air-conditioned places to rejuvenate during a long visit). The WCs at sights are free and generally clean.

Before Leaving: At the gift shop, scan the postcard rack or thumb through a guidebook to be sure you haven't overlooked something that you'd like to see. Every sight or museum offers more than what is covered in this book. Use the information I provide as an introduction—not the final word.

PRACTICALITIES

Sleeping

Extensive and opinionated listings of good-value rooms are a major feature of this book's Sleeping sections. Rather than list accommodations scattered throughout a town, I choose hotels in my favorite neighborhoods that are convenient to your sightseeing.

My recommendations run the gamut, from dorm beds to fancy rooms with all the comforts. I like places that are clean, central, relatively quiet at night, reasonably priced, friendly, small enough to have a hands-on owner or manager, and run with a respect for Scandinavian traditions. I'm more impressed by a handy location and a fun-loving philosophy than flat-screen TVs and a fancy gym. Most of my recommendations fall short of perfection. But if I can find a place with most of these features, it's a keeper.

Book your accommodations as soon as your itinerary is set, especially if you want to stay at one of my top listings or if you'll be traveling during busy times. See the appendix for a list of major holidays and festivals in Scandinavia.

Some people make reservations a few days ahead as they travel. This approach fosters spontaneity, and booking sites make it easy to find available rooms, but—especially during busy times—you run the risk of settling for lesser-value accommodations.

RATES AND DEALS

I've categorized my recommended accommodations based on price, indicated with a dollar-sign rating (see sidebar). Room prices can fluctuate significantly with demand and amenities (size, views, room class, and so on), but relative price categories remain constant. Taxes, which can vary from place to place, are generally insignificant (a dollar or two per person, per night).

Room rates are especially volatile at hotels that use dynamic pricing to set rates. Prices can skyrocket during festivals and conventions, while business hotels can have deep discounts on weekends when demand plummets. Of the many hotels I recommend, it's difficult to say which will be the best value on a given day—until you do your homework.

Booking Direct: Once your dates are set, compare prices at several hotels. You can do this by checking hotel websites and booking sites such as Hotels.com or Booking.com. After you've zeroed in on your choice, book directly with the hotel itself. This increases the chances that the hotelier will be able to accommodate

Sleep Code

Hotels in this book are categorized according to the average price of a standard double with breakfast in high season.

	Denmark	Norway	Sweden	Finland	Estonia
$$$$ **Splurge**	over 1,100 DKK	over 1,500 NOK	over 2,000 SEK	over €225	over €110
$$$ **Pricier**	900-1,000 DKK	1,200-1,500 NOK	1,500-2,000 SEK	€175-225	€90-110
$$ **Moderate**	700-900 DKK	900-1,200 NOK	1,000-1,500 SEK	€125-175	€70-90
$ **Budget**	500-700 DKK	600-900 NOK	500-1,500 SEK	€75-125	€50-70
¢ **Backpacker**	under 500 DKK	under 600 NOK	under 500 SEK	under €75	under €50

Unless otherwise noted, credit cards are accepted, hotel staff speak basic English, and free Wi-Fi is available. Comparison-shop by checking prices at several hotels (on each hotel's website, on a booking site, or by email). For the best deal, *book directly with the hotel.* Ask for a discount if paying in cash; if the listing includes **RS%**, request a Rick Steves discount.

special needs or requests (such as shifting your reservation). And when you book by phone or email, the owner avoids the commission paid to booking sites, giving the hotel wiggle room to offer you a discount, a nicer room, or a free breakfast (if it's not already included).

Getting a Discount: Some hotels extend a discount to those who pay cash or stay longer than three nights. And some accommodations offer a special discount for Rick Steves readers, indicated in this guidebook by the abbreviation "**RS%.**" Discounts vary: Ask for details when you reserve. Generally, to qualify for this discount, you must book direct (not through a booking site), mention this book when you reserve, show this book upon arrival, and sometimes pay cash or stay a certain number of nights. In some cases, you may need to enter a discount code (which I've provided in the listing) in the booking form on the hotel's website. Rick Steves discounts apply to readers with either print or digital books. Understandably, discounts do not apply to promotional rates.

TYPES OF ACCOMMODATIONS

Accommodations in Scandinavia are fairly expensive, but normally very comfortable and usually come with a generous breakfast.

Using Online Services to Your Advantage

From booking services to user reviews, online businesses are playing a greater role in travelers' planning than ever before. Take advantage of their pluses—and be wise to their downsides.

Booking Sites

Booking websites such as Booking.com and Hotels.com, offer one-stop shopping for hotels. While convenient for travelers, they're both a blessing and a curse for small, independent, family-run hotels. Without a presence on these sites, small hotels become almost invisible. But to be listed, a hotel must pay a sizable commission...and promise that its own website won't undercut the price on the booking-service site.

Here's the work-around: Use the big sites to research what's out there, then book direct with the hotel by email or phone, in which case hotel owners are free to give you whatever price they like. Ask for a room without the commission mark-up (or ask for a free breakfast if not included, or a free upgrade). If you do book online, be sure to use the hotel's own website. The price will likely be the same as via a booking site, but your money goes to the hotel, not agency commissions.

As a savvy consumer, remember: When you book with an online booking service, you're adding a middleman who takes roughly 20 percent. To support small, family-run hotels whose world is more difficult than ever, book direct.

Short-Term Rental Sites

Rental juggernaut Airbnb (along with other short-term rental sites) allows travelers to rent rooms and apartments, often providing more value, space, and amenities than a cookie-cutter hotel. Airbnb fans appreciate feeling part of a real neighborhood and getting into a daily routine as "temporary Europeans." Depending on the host, Airbnb can provide an opportunity to get to know a local person, while keeping the money spent on your accommodations in the community.

When budgeting, plan on spending about $180-250 per hotel double in big cities, and $125-150 in smaller towns. Money-conscious travelers should consider doubles in hostels and rooms in simple hotels with shared baths—a respectable option in clean and wholesome Scandinavia.

Hotels

Check hotel websites for deals. When a classy, modern $200 place has a $150 special that includes two $10 buffet breakfasts, a dumpy $100 hotel room without breakfast becomes less exciting.

Some hotels can add an extra bed (for a small charge) to turn a

Critics of Airbnb see it as a threat to "traditional Europe." Landlords can make more money renting to short-stay travelers, driving rents up—and pushing local residents out to more affordable but less charming districts. When those long-term renters go, traditional businesses are replaced by ones that cater to tourists. And the character that made those neighborhoods desirable to the tourists in the first place goes too. Some cities have cracked down, requiring owners to obtain a license and to occupy rental properties part of the year (and staging disruptive "inspections" that inconvenience guests).

As a lover of Europe, I share the worry of those who see residents nudged aside by tourists. But as an advocate for travelers, I appreciate the value and cultural intimacy Airbnb provides.

User Reviews

User-generated review sites and apps such as Yelp and TripAdvisor can give you a consensus of opinions about everything from hotels and restaurants to sights and nightlife. If you scan reviews of a restaurant or hotel and see several complaints about noise or a rotten location, you've gained insight that can help in your decision-making.

But as a guidebook writer, my sense is that there is a big difference between the uncurated information on a review site and the vetted listings in a guidebook. A user-generated review is based on the limited experience of one person, who stayed at just one hotel in a given city and ate at a few restaurants there. A guidebook is the work of a trained researcher who forms a well-developed basis for comparison by visiting many restaurants and hotels year after year.

Both types of information have their place, and in many ways, they're complementary. If something is well reviewed in a guidebook and it also gets good online reviews, it's likely a winner.

double into a triple; some offer larger rooms for four or more people (I call these "family rooms" in the listings). If there's space for an extra cot, they'll cram it in for you. In general, a triple room is cheaper than the cost of a double and a single. Three or four people can economize by requesting one big room.

Some modern Scandinavian hotels offer "combi" rooms with either two narrow twin beds or one twin and a sofa that converts to a bed. These are generally cheaper than a full double.

Arrival and Check-In: Hotels and B&Bs are sometimes located on the higher floors of a multipurpose building with a secured door. In that case, look for your hotel's name on the buttons by the main entrance. When you ring the bell, you'll be buzzed in.

Hotel elevators are common, though small, and some older buildings still lack them. You may have to climb a flight of stairs to reach the elevator (if so, you can ask the front desk for help carrying your bags up).

The EU requires that hotels collect your name, nationality, and ID number. When you check in, the receptionist will normally ask for your passport and may keep it for a few hours. If you're not comfortable leaving your passport at the desk for a long time, bring a photocopy to give them instead.

If you're arriving in the morning, your room probably won't be ready. Check your bag safely at the hotel and dive right into sightseeing.

In Your Room: Most hotel rooms have a TV, telephone, and free Wi-Fi (although in old buildings with thick walls, the Wi-Fi signal might be available only in the lobby). Simpler places rarely have a room phone.

Checking Out: While it's customary to pay for your room upon departure, it can be a good idea to settle your bill the day before, when you're not in a hurry and while the manager's in.

Hotelier Help: Hoteliers can be a good source of advice. Most know their city well, and can assist you with everything from public transit and airport connections to finding a good restaurant, the nearest launderette, or a late-night pharmacy.

Hotel Hassles: Even at the best places, mechanical breakdowns occur: sinks leak, hot water turns cold, toilets gurgle and smell, the Wi-Fi goes out, or the air-conditioning dies when you need it most. Report your concerns clearly and calmly at the front desk.

If you find that night noise is a problem (if, for instance, your room is over a nightclub or facing a busy street), ask for a quieter room in the back or on an upper floor. To guard against theft in your room, keep valuables out of sight. Some rooms come with a safe, and other hotels have safes at the front desk. I've never bothered using one and in a lifetime of travel, I've never had anything stolen from my room.

For more complicated problems, don't expect instant results. Above all, keep a positive attitude. Remember, you're on vacation. If your hotel is a disappointment, spend more time out enjoying the place you came to see.

Short-Term Rentals

A short-term rental—whether an apartment, house, or room in a local's home—is an increasingly popular alternative, especially if you plan to settle in one location for several nights. For stays longer than a few days, you can usually find a rental that's comparable to—and cheaper than—a hotel room with similar amenities. Plus, you'll get a behind-the-scenes peek into how locals live.

Many places require a minimum-night stay and have strict cancellation policies. And you're generally on your own: There's no reception desk, breakfast, or daily cleaning service.

Finding Accommodations: Websites such as Airbnb, FlipKey, Booking.com, and the HomeAway family of sites (Home-Away, VRBO, and VacationRentals) let you browse a wide range of properties. Alternatively, rental agencies such as InterhomeUSA. com and RentaVilla.com can provide a more personalized service (their curated listings are also more expensive).

Before you commit, be clear on the location. I like to virtually "explore" the neighborhood using Google Street View. Also consider the proximity to public transportation, and how well-connected the property is with the rest of the city. Ask about amenities (elevator, air-conditioning, laundry, Wi-Fi, parking, etc.). Reviews from previous guests can help identify trouble spots.

Think about the kind of experience you want: Just a key and an affordable bed...or a chance to get to know a local? Some hosts offer self-check-in and minimal contact; others enjoy interacting with you. Read the description and reviews to help shape your decision.

Confirming and Paying: Many places require you to pay the entire balance before your trip, usually through the listing site. Be wary of owners who want to take your transaction offline; this gives you no recourse if things go awry. Never agree to wire money (a key indicator of a fraudulent transaction).

Apartments or Houses: If you're staying in one place for several nights, it's worth considering an apartment or rental house (shorter stays aren't worth the hassle of arranging key pickup, buying groceries, etc.). Apartment or house rentals can be especially cost-effective for groups and families. European apartments, like hotel rooms, tend to be small by US standards. But they often come with laundry facilities and small, equipped kitchens, making it easier and cheaper to dine in.

Rooms in Private Homes: Renting a room in someone's home is a good option for those traveling alone, as you're more likely to find true single rooms—with just one single bed and a price to match. These can range from air-mattress-in-living-room basic to plush-B&B-suite posh. While you can't expect your host to also be your tour guide—or even to provide you with much info—some are interested in getting to know the travelers who pass through their home.

Other Options: Swapping homes with a local works for people with an appealing place to offer (don't assume where you live is not interesting to Europeans). Good places to start are

Making Hotel Reservations

Reserve your rooms as soon as you've pinned down your travel dates. For busy national holidays, it's wise to reserve far in advance (see the appendix).

Requesting a Reservation: For family-run hotels, it's generally best to book your room directly via email or a phone call. For business-class and chain hotels, or if you'd rather book online, reserve directly through the hotel's official website (not a booking website). For complicated requests, send an email. Almost all of my recommended hotels take reservations in English.

Here's what the hotelier wants to know:

- Type(s) of room(s) you want and number of guests
- Number of nights you'll stay
- Arrival and departure dates, written European-style as day/month/year (18/06/22 or 18 June 2022)
- Special requests (en suite bathroom, cheapest room, twin beds vs. double bed, quiet room)
- Applicable discounts (such as a Rick Steves discount, cash discount, or promotional rate)

Confirming a Reservation: Most places will request a credit-card number to hold your room. If the hotel's website doesn't have a secure form where you can enter the number directly, share this info via a phone call.

Canceling a Reservation: If you must cancel, it's courteous—and smart—to do so with as much notice as possible, especially for

HomeExchange.com and LoveHomeSwap.com. To sleep for free, Couchsurfing.com is a vagabond's alternative to Airbnb. It lists millions of outgoing members, who host fellow "surfers" in their homes.

Hostels

Scandinavian hostels are among Europe's finest. A hostel provides cheap beds in dorms where you sleep alongside strangers for about $35 per night. Travelers of any age are welcome if they don't mind dorm-style accommodations and meeting other travelers. Most hostels offer kitchen facilities, guest computers, Wi-Fi, and a self-service laundry. Hostels almost always provide bedding, but the towel's up to you (though you can usually rent one). Family and private rooms are often available.

Independent hostels tend to be easygoing, colorful, and informal (no membership required; www.hostelworld.com). You may pay slightly less by booking directly with the hostel. **Official hostels** are part of Hostelling International (HI) and share an online

From: rick@ricksteves.com
Sent: Today
To: info@hotelcentral.com
Subject: Reservation request for 19-22 July

Dear Hotel Central,

I would like to stay at your hotel. Please let me know if you have a room available and the price for:
• 2 people
• Double bed and en suite bathroom in a quiet room
• Arriving 19 July, departing 22 July (3 nights)

Thank you!
Rick Steves

smaller family-run places. Cancellation policies can be strict; read the fine print before you book. Many discount deals require pre-payment and can be expensive to change or cancel.

Reconfirming a Reservation: Always call or email to reconfirm your room reservation a few days in advance. For smaller hotels and B&Bs, I call again on my arrival day to tell my host what time to expect me (especially important if arriving late—after 17:00).

Phoning: For tips on how to call hotels overseas, see page 726.

booking site (www.hihostels.com). HI hostels typically require that you be a member or else pay a bit more per night.

Camping

Scandinavian campgrounds are practical, comfortable, and economical. This is the middle-class Scandinavian family way to travel: safe, great social fun, and no reservation problems. Campgrounds are friendly, more central and convenient than rustic, and rarely full. Dedicated campers should look into the "Camping Key Europe" card (about $20), which offers discounts on stays throughout Europe. Buy the card at the first campground you visit or through CampingKeyEurope.com.

The national tourist office websites have campground listings,

but for more comprehensive guides, visit these websites: Camping.
se (Sweden), Camping.dk (Denmark), and Camping.no (Norway).
You'll find campgrounds just about everywhere you need them.

Many campgrounds also offer camping cottages *(stugor)* or
huts *(hytter)* for wannabe campers with no gear. These normally
sleep four to six in bunk beds, and come with blankets and a kitch-
enette. The toilet and shower may be in a nearby shared washhouse.
Because locals typically move in for a week or two, many campground huts are booked for summer long in advance. You can book
these ahead as well, or try your chances on the road.

Eating

For listings in this guidebook, I look for restaurants that are convenient to your hotel and sightseeing. When restaurant-hunting,
choose a spot filled with locals,
not the place with the big neon
signs boasting, "We Speak
English and Accept Credit
Cards." Venturing even a block
or two off the main drag leads
to higher-quality food for a better price.

Most Scandinavian nations
have one hard-to-appreciate sta-
ple that is cherished with a patriotic sentimentality. These dishes,
which often originated during a famine, now remind the young of
their ancestors' suffering. Norway's penitential food, lutefisk (dried
cod marinated for days in lye and water), is used for Christmas
and for jokes. Swedes and Norwegians make pickled herring the
centerpiece of any buffet (pickling was the best way to preserve the
abundant fish back in the Middle Ages). And Finns go for *kalakuk-
ko*—a fish-and-bacon hand pie, a convenient portable lunch back
in the day.

Nowadays, contemporary Scandinavian cuisine takes full advantage of its traditional local ingredients, emphasizing fresh seafood, hearty grains, seasonal berries, and sturdy root vegetables.
Using pure, fresh ingredients and innovative preparations, Scandinavia's chefs are piling up well-deserved accolades. For more on
Norwegian cuisine, see page 284; for Swedish specialties, see page
493.

RESTAURANT PRICING

I've categorized my recommended eateries based on the average
price of a typical main course, indicated with a dollar-sign rating

Restaurant Code

Eateries in this book are categorized according to the average cost of a typical main course. Drinks, desserts, and splurge items can raise the price considerably.

	Denmark	Norway	Sweden	Finland & Estonia
$$$$ Splurge	over 150 DKK	over 225 NOK	over 200 SEK	over €25
$$$ Pricier	100-150 DKK	175-225 NOK	150-200 SEK	€20-25
$$ Moderate	50-100 DKK	125-175 NOK	100-150 SEK	€15-20
$ Budget	under 50 DKK	under 125 NOK	under 100 SEK	under €15

In Scandinavia, a takeout spot is **$**; a basic sit-down café is **$$**; a casual but more upscale restaurant is **$$$**; and a swanky splurge is **$$$$**.

(see sidebar). Obviously, expensive specialties, fine wine, appetizers, and dessert can significantly increase your final bill.

The categories also indicate the personality of a place: **Budget** eateries include street food, takeaway, order-at-the-counter shops, basic cafeterias, and bakeries selling sandwiches. **Moderate** eateries are nice (but not fancy) sit-down restaurants, ideal for a straightforward, fill-the-tank meal. Most of my listings fall in this category—great for a taste of the local cuisine at a reasonable price.

Pricier eateries are a notch up, with more attention paid to the setting, presentation, and (often inventive) cuisine. **Splurge** eateries typically come with an elegant setting, polished service, and pricey and intricate cuisine. Note that in expensive Scandinavian cities, you may pay splurge prices for even more casual meals.

BREAKFAST

The vast breakfast buffet that comes with most hotel rooms is a great way to stock up on calories for a busy day of sightseeing. Plenty of local treats show up on the breakfast table: various herring dishes, hearty breads and crackers, and rich, sweet goat cheese.

You'll also find fruit, cereal, and various milks (look for words like *skummet* for skim, *let/lavt* for low-fat, *sød/hel* for whole). Grab a drinkable yogurt and go local by pouring it in the bowl and sprinkling your cereal over it. The great selection of breads and crackers comes with jam, butter *(smør)*, margarine (same word), and cheese *(ost)*. And you'll get an array of cold cuts, pickled herring, caviar paste (in a squeeze tube), and boiled eggs *(bløt/blød* is soft-boiled; *hård* is hard-boiled); use the egg cups and small spoons provided to eat your soft-boiled egg Scandinavian-style.

The brown cheese with the texture of earwax and a slightly sweet taste is called *geitost/gede ost* ("goat cheese") or *brunost* ("brown cheese"). Most common in Norway, it's not really a cheese—it's made from boiled-down, slightly sweetened whey mixed with goat or cow's milk. Give this odd but enjoyable dairy product a try—it's a tasty topping on traditional heart-shaped waffles. Swedes prefer a spreadable variety called *messmör*.

LUNCH AND DINNER

Scandinavians, not big on lunch, often just grab a sandwich and a cup of coffee at their work desk. Sandwiches are something of an art form in Scandinavia. Es-
pecially in Denmark, you'll find *smørrebrød* shops turning out tempting open-face sandwiches. These delights taste as good as they look. My favorite is the one piled high with little shrimp *(mej reje/med räkor)*. The roast beef *(roastbeef/rostbiff)* is good, too. And don't be afraid to give
herring *(sild/sill)* a try. Shops will wrap sandwiches up for a perfect picnic in a nearby park.

The largest meal of the Nordic day is dinner. At restaurants, many menus list small and large plates. Because portions tend to be large, choosing a small plate or splitting a large one makes some otherwise pricey options reasonable. Remember that taxes and the tip are included in menu prices—so a $40 Scandinavian meal is not that much more than a $30 American meal. You'll notice that even in fine restaurants, many locals just drink free tap water (for more on beverages, see next page).

The all-you-can-eat Scandinavian smorgasbord is not to be missed. For tips on navigating this epic buffet, see page 7.

Tipping: Tipping in restaurants is not an established practice in Scandinavia. A service charge is typically included in your bill, and you aren't expected to leave an additional tip. But if you enjoy great service and want to show your appreciation, round up the bill (about 5-10 percent of the total check). If you do tip, leave cash to be sure it goes to your server.

Budget Tips

Fortunately, there are plenty of strategies for stretching your food budget while on the road in expensive Scandinavia. Most towns and cities offer a range of basic eateries, and while cafeterias, street stands, and to-go meals are not high cuisine, they're undeniably cheap. Here are some tips to help you eat inexpensively.

If your hotel offers breakfast—even if they charge for it—take advantage of this option; these hotel breakfasts are often a better deal than buying breakfast around town. And while it's bad form to take freebies from the breakfast buffet to eat later, many hotels will provide you with the wrappings to pack yourself a lunch, legitimately, for $7-8. Ask for a "packed lunch"—*madpakke* (Danish) *matpakke* (Norwegian), or *packad lunch* (Swedish).

If you want to enjoy a combination of picnics and restaurant meals on your trip, you'll save money by eating in restaurants at lunch (when there's usually a special, and food is generally cheaper) and picnicking for dinner. Many restaurants offer cheap daily *(dagens)* lunch specials and buffets to entice office workers. In Sweden, for lunch, look for restaurant signs offering a *dagens rätt* or *dagens lunch*. These daily specials typically get you a main dish, salad, bread, coffee, and water.

Picnic as much as possible. Basements of big department stores have huge, first-class supermarkets with lots of alternatives

to sandwiches for picnic dinners. Or explore your options at market stalls and takeaway delis. Samples of picnic treats: *Wasa* cracker breads (the rye "Sport" flavor is my favorite), packaged meat and cheese, brown "goat cheese" *(geitost),* drinkable yogurt, smoked fish from markets, fresh fruit and vegetables, lingonberries, squeeze tubes of sandwich spreads (from mustard and mayo to shrimp and caviar), rye bread, and boxes of juice and milk. Grab a park bench or waterside perch, relax, and enjoy.

BEVERAGES

Scandinavia's heavily taxed wine, beer, and spirits can put a dent in your vacation budget. In Sweden and Norway, spirits, wine, and strong beer (more than 3.5 percent alcohol) are sold in state-run liquor stores: Systembolaget in Sweden, and Vinmonopolet in Norway. Buying a beer or glass of wine in a bar or restaurant in Sweden or Norway is particularly expensive. Therefore, many Scandinavians will have a drink or a glass of wine at home (or in their hotel room) before going out, then limit themselves to one or two glasses at the restaurant. If taking an overnight cruise during your trip, you can get a good deal on a bottle of wine or spirits in the onboard duty-free shop.

Liquor laws and prices are more relaxed in Denmark, where you can buy wine, beer, and spirits at any supermarket or corner store. Public drinking is acceptable in Denmark, while it is illegal (although often done) in Norway and Sweden. Throughout Scandinavia, drinking and driving is not tolerated.

Some local specialties are *akvavit*, a strong, vodka-like spirit distilled from grains or potatoes and infused with dill, caraway, or other herbs and spices—then drunk ice-cold (common in Norway, Sweden, and Denmark). *Lakka* is a syrupy-sweet liqueur made from cloudberries, the small orange berries grown in the Arctic (popular in Norway, Sweden, and Finland). *Salmiakka* is a nearly black, licorice-flavored liqueur (Finland, Norway, and Denmark). *Gammel Dansk* can be described as Danish bitters for the adventurous (Denmark only).

DESSERTS AND SWEETS

Scandinavians love sweets. A meal is not complete without a little treat and a cup of coffee at the end. Bakeries fill their window cases with all varieties of cakes, tarts, cookies, and pastries. The most popular ingredients are marzipan, almonds, hazelnuts, chocolate, and fresh berries. Many cakes are covered with entire sheets of solid marzipan. To find the neighborhood bakery, just look for a golden pretzel—the classic Scandinavian symbol for a bakery—hanging above the door or windows.

For a classic Danish dessert, try *rødgrød med fløde*—red berries (traditionally red currants) with cream. Swedes go for kladdkaka, a rich chocolate cake that's gooey inside but crisp on the outside. Norwegians dig into fyrstekake, a fragrant tart that sandwiches cardamon-scented almond paste in a buttery dough. The Finns make a variation on those same flavors in the cylinder-shaped *Runebergstårta*, or Runeberg torte, named for a revered Finnish poet. In Estonia, desserts often feature curd cheese, as in the popular *kohupiimakreem*, a pudding-like mix of the cheese, sugar, vanilla, and cream.

Scandinavian chocolate is some of the best in Europe. In Denmark, seek out Anthon Berg's dark chocolate and marzipan treats, as well as Toms' chocolate-covered caramels (Toms Guld are the best). Sweden's biggest chocolate producer, Marabou, makes huge bars of solid milk chocolate, as well as some with dried fruits or nuts. *Daim* are milk chocolate-covered hard toffees, sold in a variety of sizes, from large bars to bite-size pieces, all in bright red wrappers. The Freia company, Norway's chocolate goddess (named for the Norse goddess Freya), makes a wonderful assortment of delights, from *Et lite stykke Norge* ("A little piece of Norway"—bars of creamy milk chocolate wrapped in pale yellow paper) and *Smil* (chocolate-covered soft caramels sold in rolls) to *Firkløver* (bars of milk chocolate with hazelnuts) and the venerable Kvikk Lunsj, similar to a Kit Kat bar. For those who can't decide on one type, the company sells bags of assorted chocolates called *Twist* and red gift boxes of pricey chocolates called *Kong Haakon*, named after Norway's first king.

While chocolate rules, licorice and gummy candies are also popular. Black licorice *(lakrits/lakris/lakrids)* is at its best here—although *saltlakrits* (salty licorice) is not for the timid. Black licorice flavors everything from ice cream to chewing gum to liqueur. Throughout Scandinavia, you'll find stores selling all varieties of candy in bulk. Fill your bag with a variety of candies and pay by the gram. Look around at the customers in these stores...they aren't all children.

Staying Connected

One of the most common questions I hear from travelers is, "How can I stay connected in Europe?" The short answer is: more easily and affordably than you might think.

The simplest solution is to bring your own device—phone, tablet, or laptop—and use it just as you would at home (following the money-saving tips below, such as getting an international plan or connecting to free Wi-Fi whenever possible). Another option is to buy a European SIM card for your US mobile phone. Or you can use European landlines and computers to connect. More details are at RickSteves.com/phoning. For a very practical one-hour talk covering tech issues for travelers, see RickSteves.com/mobile-travel-skills.

USING YOUR PHONE IN EUROPE
Here are some budget tips and options.

Sign up for an international plan. To stay connected at a

Tips on Internet Security

Make sure that your device is running the latest versions of its operating system, security software, and apps. Next, ensure that your device and key programs (like email) are password-protected. On the road, use only secure, password-protected Wi-Fi. Ask the hotel or café staff for the specific name of their network, and make sure you log on to that exact one.

If you must access your financial info online, use a banking app rather than accessing your account via a browser, and use a cellular connection, not Wi-Fi. Never log on to personal finance sites on a public computer. If you're very concerned, consider subscribing to a VPN (virtual private network).

lower cost, sign up for an international service plan through your carrier. Most providers offer a simple bundle that includes calling, messaging, and data. Your normal plan may already include international coverage (T-Mobile's does).

Before your trip, research your provider's international rates. Activate the plan a day or two before you leave, then remember to cancel it when your trip's over.

Use free Wi-Fi whenever possible. Unless you have an unlimited-data plan, save most of your online tasks for Wi-Fi. Most accommodations in Europe offer free Wi-Fi. Many cafés (including Starbucks and McDonald's) offer hotspots for customers; ask for the password when you buy something. You may also find Wi-Fi at TIs, city squares, major museums, public-transit hubs, airports, and aboard trains and buses.

Minimize the use of your cellular network. The best way to make sure you're not accidentally burning through data is to put your device in "airplane" mode (which also disables phone calls and texts) and connect to Wi-Fi networks as needed. When you need to get online but can't find Wi-Fi, simply turn on your cellular network (or turn off airplane mode) just long enough for the task at hand.

Even with an international data plan, wait until you're on Wi-Fi to Skype, download apps, stream videos, or do other megabyte-greedy tasks. Using a navigation app such as Google Maps over a cellular network can require lots of data, so download maps when you're on Wi-Fi, then use the app offline.

Limit automatic updates. By default, your device constantly checks for a data connection and updates app content. Check your device's menu for ways to turn this off, and change your email settings from "auto-retrieve" to "manual" (or from "push" to "fetch").

Use Wi-Fi calling and messaging apps. Skype, WhatsApp, FaceTime, and Google Hangouts are great for making free or low-

Hurdling the Language Barrier

Though each of the Scandinavian countries has its own language, Danish, Norwegian, and Swedish are so closely related that locals can laugh at each other's TV comedies. Danes and Norwegians can read each other's newspapers and can converse somewhat (but with difficulty because of thick accents). Swedes, whose written language is different, have a hard time with printed Danish and Norwegian, but can carry on simple conversations in those languages. Finns (whose language is not related at all) learn Swedish in school, thanks to Sweden's long historical presence in Finland. Estonian is similar to Finnish. If there's ever a language barrier, though, most Scandinavians can easily revert to their common second language—English.

For travelers to Scandinavia, English is all you need; it seems every well-educated Scandinavian speaks it. Still, knowing a few key words in the language of the country you are visiting is good style and helpful.

These languages add a few extra letters (Æ, Ø, Ö, Å, Ä) that affect pronunciation—and also alphabetizing. If you can't find, say, Årjäng in a map index, look after Z. Finnish and Estonian are related and vastly different from the other Scandinavian languages; in fact, Finnish has more in common with Hungarian than with Swedish.

Here are a few Swedish, Norwegian, and/or Danish words you'll see and hear a lot: *hej/hei* (hi), *tack/takk/tak* (thanks), *gammal/gammel* (old), *litten/litt/lille* (small), *stor* (big), *slott/slot* (palace), *centrum/sentrum* (center), *gata/gate/gade* (street), and *öl/øl* (beer).

You'll find a longer list of survival phrases in the introductory chapters for each country in this book. Give it your best shot. The locals will appreciate your efforts.

cost calls or sending texts over Wi-Fi. Just log on to a Wi-Fi network, then connect with friends or family members who use the same service. If you buy credit in advance, with some services you can call or text anywhere for just pennies.

Buy a European SIM card. If you anticipate making a lot of local calls, need a local phone number, or your provider's international data rates are expensive, consider buying a SIM card in Europe to replace the one in your (unlocked) US phone or tablet. SIM cards are sold at department-store electronics counters, some newsstands, and vending machines (you may need to show your

How to Dial

Here's how to dial from anywhere in the US or Europe, using the phone numbers of recommended hotels in Copenhagen, Denmark (33 21 12 17); Stockholm, Sweden (08 5173 6500); and Tallinn, Estonia (680 6630) as examples. Note: If a number starts with 0, drop it when dialing from country to country.

From a US Mobile Phone

Phone numbers in this book are presented exactly as you would dial them from a US mobile phone, from any location. For international access, press and hold the 0 key until you get a + sign, then dial the country code (see the chart) and phone number.

▸ To call the Copenhagen hotel, dial +45 33 21 12 17.
▸ To call the Stockholm hotel, dial +46 8 5173 6500.
▸ To call the Tallinn hotel, dial +372 680 6630.

From a US Landline

Replace + with 011 (US/Canada international access code), then dial the country code and phone number.

▸ To call the Copenhagen hotel from your home landline, dial 011 45 33 21 12 17.
▸ To call the Stockholm hotel, dial 011 46 8 5173 6500.
▸ To call the Tallinn hotel, dial 011 372 680 6630.

Country Codes	
Denmark	45
Norway	47
Sweden	46
Finland	358
Estonia	372
US/Canada	1

passport). If you need help setting it up, buy one at a mobile-phone shop. There are generally no roaming charges when using a European SIM card in other EU countries, but confirm when you buy.

WITHOUT A MOBILE PHONE

It's less convenient but possible to travel in Europe without a mobile device. You can make calls from your hotel and check email or get online using public computers.

Most **hotels** charge a fee for placing calls—ask for rates before you dial. You can use a prepaid international phone card (usually available at newsstands, tobacco shops, and train stations) to call out from your hotel. Dial the toll-free access number, enter the card's PIN code, then dial the number.

Some hotels have **public computers** in their lobbies for guests to use; otherwise ask your hotelier or the TI for suggestions. On a European keyboard, use the "Alt Gr" key to the right of the space bar to insert the extra symbol that appears on some keys. If you

From a European Landline

To call from country to country, replace + with 00 (Europe international access code), then dial the country code and phone number.

▶ To call the Copenhagen hotel from a Norwegian landline, dial 00 45 33 21 12 17.

▶ To call the Stockholm hotel from a Danish landline, dial 00 46 8 5173 6500.

▶ To call the Estonian hotel from a Finnish landline, dial 00 372 680 6630.

▶ To call my US office from a Swedish landline, dial 00 1 425 771 8303.

To call within a country, drop the country code and dial the phone number. Swedish and Finnish numbers require an initial 0 when dialing domestically. Danish, Norwegian, and Estonian numbers do not.

▶ To call the Copenhagen hotel from a Danish landline, dial 33 21 12 17.

▶ To call the Stockholm hotel from a Swedish phone, dial 08 5173 6500.

▶ To call the Tallinn hotel from an Estonian phone, dial 680 6630.

More Dialing Tips

Local Numbers: European phone numbers and area codes can vary in length and spacing, even within the same country. Mobile phones use separate prefixes.

Toll and Toll-Free Calls: It's generally not possible to dial European toll or toll-free numbers from a US mobile or landline (although you can sometimes get through using Skype). Look for a direct-dial number instead.

Calling the US from a US Mobile Phone, While Abroad: Dial +1, area code, and number.

More Phoning Help: See HowToCallAbroad.com.

can't locate a special character (such as @), simply copy and paste it from a web page.

MAIL

You can mail one package per day to yourself worth up to $200 duty-free from Europe to the US (mark it "personal purchases"). If you're sending a gift to someone, mark it "unsolicited gift." For details, visit www.cbp.gov, select "Travel," and search for "Know Before You Go." The postal service works fine throughout Scandinavia, but for quick transatlantic delivery (in either direction), consider services such as DHL (www.dhl.com).

Transportation

Figuring out how to get around in Europe is one of your biggest trip decisions. **Cars** work well for two or more traveling together (especially families with small kids), those packing heavy, and those delving into the countryside. **Trains, buses,** and **boats** are best for solo travelers, blitz tourists, city-to-city travelers, and those who want to leave the driving to others. Short-hop **flights** within Europe can creatively connect the dots. Just be aware of the potential downside of each option: A car is an expensive headache in any major city; with trains and buses you're at the mercy of a timetable; flying entails a trek to and from a usually distant airport, and leaves a larger carbon footprint.

If your itinerary mixes cities and countryside, my advice is to connect cities by train (or bus) and to explore rural areas by rental car. Arrange to pick up your car in the last big city you'll visit, then use it to lace together small towns and explore the countryside. For more detailed information on transportation throughout Europe, see RickSteves.com/transportation.

TRAINS

With a few exceptions, trains cover my recommended Scandinavian destinations wonderfully.

To study schedules and prices in advance, check Bahn.com (Germany's excellent Europe-wide timetable). You'll also find fares, timetable information, and online booking at DSB.dk or Rejseplanen.dk (Denmark), Vy.no (Norway), SJ.se (Sweden), VR.fi (Finland), and Elron.ee (Estonia).

Point-to-Point Tickets

The easiest way to buy most train tickets is online or at stations from self-service kiosks. If you need help, tickets are sold at counters at bigger stations, but this can come with long lines and a surcharge. The cheapest tickets are advance purchase, nonchangeable, and nonrefundable.

Ticket Discounts: Advance booking for specific departures is the best way to save money on point-to-point tickets, especially for longer distances and faster trains in Norway, Sweden, and Finland (but discounts come with refund and exchange limitations). In these countries, discounted tickets go on sale three to four months ahead of travel dates (see websites above). In Denmark, distances are shorter and standard tickets are more affordable, but discounts are available for those willing to lock in a departure time outside of rush hours (sold up to two months ahead).

In Norway, kids (ages 6-17) and seniors (age 67 and older) pay half the full fare on most trains (but not sleepers). In Sweden, kids (2-15) traveling with an adult pay only about 15 percent of the regular rate; youths (under 26) and seniors (65 or over) qualify for last-minute rates sold within 24 hours of departure. In Finland, kids (4-16) save 40 percent on most tickets and seniors (65 or over) save 20 percent. In Denmark, up to two kids ages 4–11 travel free

Rail Pass or Point-to-Point Tickets?

Will you be better off buying a rail pass or point-to-point tickets? It pays to know your options and choose what's best for your itinerary.

Rail Passes

A regional Eurail Scandinavia Pass lets you travel in Denmark, Norway, Sweden, and Finland for three to eight days (consecutively or not) within a one-month period. In addition, single-country rail passes can be a solid value in all four countries. These countries are also covered (along with most of Europe) by the classic Eurail Global Pass.

Discounted rates are offered for seniors (age 60 and up) and youths (ages 12-27). Up to two kids (ages 4-11) can travel free with each adult-rate pass (but not with senior rates). All passes offer a choice of first or second class for all ages.

Rail passes are best purchased outside Europe (through travel agents or Rick Steves' Europe). For more on rail passes, including current prices, visit RickSteves.com/rail.

Point-to-Point Tickets

If you're taking just a couple of train rides, buying individual point-to-point tickets may save you money over a pass. Use this map to add up approximate pay-as-you-go fares for your itinerary, and compare that to the price of a rail pass. Keep in mind that significant discounts on point-to-point tickets may be available with advance purchase.

Map shows approximate costs, in US dollars, for one-way, second-class tickets on faster trains.

with ticket-buying adults on most trains and those under 16 generally ride for half the adult fare.

Rail Passes

One of the great Nordic bargains, the Eurail Scandinavia pass is your best rail-pass deal for a trip through Denmark, Norway, Sweden, and Finland. All Eurail passes allow up to two kids (ages

PRACTICALITIES

4-11) to travel free with an adult. Youth and senior discounts are available.

Those four countries are included in the Eurail Global pass, which covers most of Europe. Single-country Eurail passes are also available for Denmark, Norway, Sweden, and Finland (and for Estonia and Latvia, but those countries are better traveled by bus).

For detailed advice on figuring out the smartest rail-pass options for your train trip, visit RickSteves.com/rail.

Seat Reservations and Sleepers: Passes cover almost all trains in the region, though you'll need paid seat reservations ($5–20) for many longer rides, express trains, and special routes such as the scenic Myrdal-Flåm portion of the Norway in a Nutshell route. If you'll be taking a popular train on a busy day and want to be assured of having a seat, a reservation can be a good investment even if it's not required.

Within tiny Denmark, reservations are rarely necessary. Some reservations aren't available outside Europe, but generally trains don't sell out terribly far in advance. You can usually arrange several reservations at your first train station.

Sleepers on night trains also cost extra. For instance, in Norway, the fee for a two-bed sleeper compartment is about $100 with a second-class rail pass; cheaper shared compartments are available in Sweden and Finland but not Norway.

The national railway websites may not process passholder reservations or accept US credit cards. As a workaround, try ordering by phone: Norway +47 61 05 19 10 (press 9 for English) or email tog@vy.no; Sweden +46 771 757 575 (press 7 for English); Denmark +45 70 13 14 18; Finland +358 923 192 90. US agents such as Rail Europe (see RickSteves.com/rail) may have access to some but not all reservations in this region.

Boat Discounts with a Rail Pass: The Scandinavia and Global rail passes give you discounts on some boat tickets (such as Stockholm to Helsinki, Tallinn, and Riga) without requiring the use of a counted rail-pass travel day.

BUSES

Don't overlook long-distance buses, which are usually slower but considerably cheaper than trains. Big bus carriers include Norway's Nor-Way (www.nor-way.no) and Vy Buss (www.vybuss.com), Sweden's branch of Flixbus (www.flixbus.se), and Finland's Matkahuolto (www.matkahuolto.fi). Denmark is served by Eurolines (www.eurolines.de) and Flixbus www.flixbus.com)—but the train is nearly always the better option in Denmark. Estonia's several carriers (Lux Express is the largest, www.luxexpress.eu) cover more destinations than the national railway; to check schedules and buy tickets for all Estonian bus service, see Tpilet.ee.

BOATS

Boats are romantic, scenic, and sometimes the most efficient—or only—way to link destinations in coastal Scandinavia. Boats can be more expensive than other options, although some international routes may be covered or discounted with a rail pass. Prices vary, but are generally higher in summer and on weekends.

The main overnight links are Oslo to Copenhagen (www.dfds. com; see the Copenhagen chapter), Stockholm to Helsinki (www. vikingline.fi and www.tallinksilja.com; see the Helsinki chapter), and Stockholm to Tallinn (www.tallinksilja.com; see the Tallinn chapter). Advance reservations are recommended for overnight boats, especially in summer and on weekends.

Several companies speed between Helsinki and Tallinn in two to three hours (see the Tallinn chapter). It's possible to connect Bergen or Kristiansand, Norway, with Hirtshals, Denmark, by ferry (www.fjordline.com and www.colorline.com;). Ferries are essential for hopping between the mainland and Scandinavia's (see the Bergen and South Norway chapters) many islands, such as Stockholm's archipelago or Ærø in central Denmark (drivers should reserve in advance for weekends and summer, www.aeroe-ferry.dk; see Central Denmark chapter). Boats are both a necessary and spectacular way to travel through Norway's fjords or along its coast (www.fjordtours.no, www.fjord1.no). Bergen, in Norway, is a departure point for boats to the Arctic (www.hurtigruten.com; see the Bergen chapter).

TAXIS AND RIDE-BOOKING SERVICES

Most European taxis are reliable and cheap. In many cities, two people can travel short distances by cab for little more than the cost of bus or subway tickets. If you like ride-booking services such as Uber, their apps usually work in Europe just like they do in the US: Request a car on your mobile phone (connected to Wi-Fi or a data plan), and the fare is automatically charged to your credit card.

RENTING A CAR

It's cheaper to arrange most car rentals from the US, so research and compare rates before you go. Most of the major US rental agencies (including Avis, Budget, Enterprise, Hertz, and Thrifty) have offices throughout Europe. Also consider the two major Europe-based agencies, Europcar and Sixt. Consolidators such as Auto Europe (www. autoeurope.com—or the sometimes cheaper www.autoeurope.eu) compare rates at several companies to get you the best deal.

For a Scandinavian trip, renting a car for a short time in each country can work well. Use the car to explore the most interesting regions (such as Sweden's Glass Country) and take the train to cover longer distances (connecting Copenhagen and Stockholm).

Wherever you book, always read the fine print. Check for add-on charges—such as one-way drop-off fees, airport surcharges, or mandatory insurance policies—that aren't included in the "total price."

Rental Costs and Considerations

Figure on paying roughly $300 for a one-week rental for a basic compact car. Allow extra for supplemental insurance, fuel, tolls, and parking. To save money on fuel, request a diesel car.

Manual vs. Automatic: Almost all rentals are manual by default—and cars with a stick shift are generally cheaper. If you need an automatic, reserve one specifically. When selecting a car, don't be tempted by a larger model, as it won't be as maneuverable on narrow, winding roads or when squeezing into tight parking lots.

Age Restrictions: Some rental companies impose minimum and maximum age limits. Young drivers (25 and under) and seniors (69 and up) should check the rental policies and rules section of car rental websites.

Choosing Pick-up/Drop-off Locations: Always check the hours of the locations you choose: Many rental offices close from midday Saturday until Monday morning and, in smaller towns, at lunchtime. When selecting an office, confirm the location on a map. A downtown site might seem more convenient than the airport but could actually be in the suburbs or buried deep in big-city streets. Pedestrianized and one-way streets can make navigation tricky when returning a car at a big-city office or urban train station. Wherever you select, get precise details on the location and allow ample time to find it.

Drop-Off Fees and Crossing Borders: Be aware that international trips—say, picking up in Copenhagen and dropping off in Oslo—can be expensive if the rental company assesses a drop-off fee for crossing a border. Even one-way rentals within a country can come with a drop-off fee; always check.

Tell your car-rental company exactly which countries you'll be entering. Some companies levy extra insurance fees for trips taken in certain countries with certain cars (such as BMWs, Mercedes, and convertibles). Double-check with your rental agent that you have all the documentation you need before you drive off (especially if you're crossing borders into non-Schengen countries, where you might need to present proof of insurance).

Picking Up Your Car: Before driving off in your rental car, check it thoroughly and make sure any damage is noted on your rental agreement. Rental agencies in Europe tend to charge for even minor damage, so be sure to mark everything. Find out how your car's gearshift, lights, turn signals, wipers, radio, and fuel cap function, and know what kind of fuel the car takes (diesel is common in Europe). When you return the car, make sure the agent verifies its condition with you.

Car Insurance Options

When you rent a car in Europe the price typically includes liability insurance, which covers harm to other cars or motorists—but not the rental car itself. To limit your financial risk in case of damage to the rental, choose one of these options: Buy a Collision Damage Waiver (CDW) coverage with a low or zero deductible from the car-rental company (roughly 30-40 percent extra), get coverage through your credit card (free, but more complicated), or get collision insurance as part of a larger travel-insurance policy.

Basic **CDW** costs $15-30 a day and typically comes with $1,000-2,000 deductible, reducing but not eliminating your financial responsibility. When you reserve or pick up the car, you'll be offered the chance to "buy down" the deductible to zero (for an additional $10-30/day; this is sometimes called "super CDW" or "zero-deductible coverage").

If you opt for **credit-card coverage,** you must decline all coverage offered by the car-rental company—which means they can place a hold on your card to cover the deductible. In case of damage, it can be time-consuming to resolve the charges. Before relying on this option, quiz your card company about how it works.

If you're already purchasing a **travel-insurance policy** for your trip, adding collision coverage can be an economical option. For

Useful Topographical Words

Knowing some basic terms can be a big help in decoding signs and maps you'll encounter throughout the Scandinavian countries.

English	Danish	Norwegian	Swedish
airport	lufthavn	flyplass	flygplats
bay, inlet	vig	vik	Vik
beach	strand	strand	strand
boulevard	boulevard	allé	boulevard
bridge	bro	bro	Bro
castle	slot, borg	slott	slott
church	Kirke	kirke	kyrka
city	By	by	stad, storstad
city hall	Rådhus	rådhus	stadshus, rådhus
forest	Skov	skog	skog
freeway	Motorvej	motorvei	motorväg
harbor	Havn	havn	hamn
hill	Bakke	bakke	kulle, backe
hospital	sygehuset	sykehus	sjukhus
island	Ø	øy	Ö
island (small)	Holm	holme	holme
lake	Sø	innsjø, vatn	Sjö
market	Marked	marked	marknad

example, Travel Guard (www.travelguard.com) sells affordable renter's collision insurance as an add-on to its other policies; it's valid everywhere in Europe except the Republic of Ireland, and some Italian car-rental companies refuse to honor it, as it doesn't cover you in case of theft.

For more on car-rental insurance, see RickSteves.com/cdw.

Navigation Options

If you'll be navigating using your phone or a GPS unit from home, remember to bring a car charger and device mount.

Your Mobile Phone: The mapping app on your mobile phone works fine for navigating Europe's roads. To save on data, most apps allow you to download maps for offline use (do this before you need them, when you have a strong Wi-Fi signal). Some apps—including Google Maps—also have offline route directions, but you'll need mobile data access for current traffic. For more on using

English	Danish	Norwegian	Swedish
mountain	Bjerg	fjell	berg
palace	palads, slot	slott	palats, slott
park	Have	park	park
pedestrian street	Gågade	gågate	gågata
river	Flod	elv	älv, flod
road	Vej	vei	väg
sea	hav, sø	hav, sjø	hav
sound	Sund	sund	sund
square	torv, plads	torg	torg
street	stræde, gade, vej	gate/gata, vei	gata, väg
subway	S-tog, Metro	T-bane	T-bana
town	By	by	stad, småstad
trail, path	Sti	sti	stig
train station	Banegård	togstasjon	tågstation
tram	Sporvogn	trikk	spårväg
valley	Dal	dal	Dal
north	Nord	nord	norr
south	Syd	sør	söder
east	Øst	øst	öst
west	Vest	vest	väst
center	Centrum	sentrum	centrum

a mapping app without burning through data, see "Using Your Phone in Europe," earlier.

GPS Devices: If you want a dedicated GPS unit, consider renting one with your car ($10-30/day, or sometimes included—ask). These units offer real-time turn-by-turn directions and traffic without the data requirements of an app. The unit may come loaded only with maps for its home country; if you need additional maps, ask. Make sure you know how to use the device—and that the language is set to English—before you drive off.

Paper Maps and Atlases: Even when navigating primarily with a mobile app or GPS, I always make it a point to have a paper map, ideally a big, detailed regional road map. It's invaluable for getting the big picture, understanding alternate routes, and filling in if my phone runs out of juice. The free maps you get from your car-rental company usually don't have enough detail. It's smart to buy a better map before you go, or pick one up at a local gas station, bookshop, newsstand, or tourist shop.

PRACTICALITIES

Driving

Except for the dangers posed by scenic distractions and moose crossings, Scandinavia is a great place to drive. But never drink and drive—even one drink can get a driver into serious trouble.

Road Rules: Seat belts are mandatory, and small children (generally, under 4.5 feet) need a child-safety seat. Be aware of typical European road rules; for example, many countries require headlights to be turned on at all times, and nearly all forbid handheld mobile-phone use. In Europe, you're not allowed to turn right on a red light unless a sign or signal specifically authorizes it, and on expressways it's illegal to pass drivers on the right. Ask your car-rental company about these rules, or check the US State Department website (www.travel.state.gov; search for your country in the "Learn about your destination" box, then click on "Travel and Transportation").

STOP **AND LEARN THESE ROAD SIGNS**

Speed Limit (km/hr) · Yield · No Passing · End of No Passing Zone

One Way · Intersection · Main Road · Expressway

Danger · No Entry · Cars Prohibited · All Vehicles Prohibited

No Through Road · Restrictions No Longer Apply · Yield to Oncoming Traffic · No Stopping

Parking · No Parking · Customs or Toll Road · Peace

Fuel: Gas is expensive—often more than $6 per gallon. Newer US chip credit and debit cards are generally accepted at staffed stations and should work at pay-at-the-pump stations. Carry more than one card and cash just in case. Diesel rental cars are common; make sure you know what type of fuel your car takes before you fill up. Some pumps are color-coded: Unleaded pumps are green and labeled "E," while diesel pumps (often yellow or black) are labeled "B".

On the Road: Roads are good (though nerve-rackingly skinny in western Norway). Signs and road maps are excellent. Local road etiquette is similar to that in the US. There are plenty of good facilities, gas stations, and scenic rest stops. Snow is a serious problem off-season in the mountains.

Tolls: You'll encounter tolls on major bridges in Scandinavia. The most expensive (about $65) is the Øresund Bridge between Sweden and Denmark; other toll bridges include the Svinesund Bridge between Sweden and Norway (about $2) and the Storebælt Bridge between the Danish islands of Zealand and Funen (about $22). Cities such as Oslo, Bergen, and Stockholm charge tolls for entering the city center. Rental cars are typically equipped with devices to automatically collect tolls, which are then charged back to you via your rental company.

Parking: Parking on the street is a headache in major cities, where expensive garages are safe and plentiful. It's usually a good strategy to park on the outskirts and take public transportation into city centers.

Many Scandinavian cities, such as Tallinn and Helsinki, have pay-and-display parking; check signs locally. Denmark uses a parking windshield-clock disk (provided with a rental car but also available free at TIs, banks, and newsstands; set it when you arrive and be back before your posted time limit is up). Even in the Nordic countries, thieves break into cars. Park carefully, use the trunk, and show no valuables.

Signage: As you navigate, you'll find town signs followed by the letters *N, S, Ø (Ö* in Sweden), *V,* or *C.* These stand for north *(nord/norr),* south *(syd/sør/söder),* east *(øst/öst),* west *(vest/väst),* and center *(centrum/sentrum),* respectively; understanding them will save you lots of wrong turns.

FLIGHTS

Copenhagen is usually the most direct and least expensive Scandinavian capital to fly into from the US. Copenhagen is also Europe's gateway to Scandinavia from points south.

This book covers far-flung destinations separated by vast stretches of mountains and water. While boats and trains are more romantic, cheap flights can provide an affordable and efficient way to connect the dots on a Scandinavian itinerary.

To compare flight costs and times, begin with an online travel search engine: Kayak is the top site for flights to and within Europe, easy-to-use Google Flights has price alerts, and Skyscanner includes many inexpensive flights within Europe. To avoid unpleasant surprises, before you book be sure to read the small print about refunds, changes, and the costs for "extras" such as reserving a seat, checking a bag, or printing a boarding pass.

Flights to Europe: Start looking for international flights about four to six months before your trip, especially for peak-season travel. Depending on your itinerary, it can be efficient and no more expensive to fly into one city and out of another. If your flight requires a connection in Europe, see our hints on navigating Europe's top hub airports at RickSteves.com/hub-airports.

Flights within Europe: Flying between European cities is surprisingly affordable. Before buying a long-distance train or bus ticket, first check the cost of a flight on one of Europe's airlines, whether a major carrier or a no-frills outfit like EasyJet or Ryanair. Options include Norwegian Airlines (hubs in Oslo and Bergen, www.norwegian.com), Widerøe (www.wideroe.no; connections throughout Norway and a few international destinations), and Tallinn-based Estonian Air (www.estonian-air.com). Be aware that flying with a discount airline can have drawbacks, such as minimal customer service and time-consuming treks to secondary airports.

Flying to the US and Canada: Because security is extra tight for flights to the US, be sure to give yourself plenty of time at the airport (see www.tsa.gov for the latest rules).

Resources from Rick Steves

BEGIN YOUR TRIP AT RICKSTEVES.COM

My mobile-friendly **website** is *the* place to explore Europe in preparation for your trip. You'll find thousands of fun articles, videos, and radio interviews; a wealth of money-saving tips for planning your dream trip; travel news dispatches; a video library of travel talks; my travel blog; our latest guidebook updates (RickSteves.com/update); and the free Rick Steves Audio Europe app. You can also follow me on Facebook, Instagram, and Twitter.

Our **Travel Forum** is a well-groomed collection of message boards where our travel-savvy community answers questions and shares their personal travel experiences—and our well-traveled staff chimes in when they can be helpful (RickSteves.com/forums).

Our online **Travel Store** offers travel bags and accessories that I've designed to help you travel smarter and lighter. These include my popular carry-on bags (which I live out of four months a year), money belts, totes, toiletries kits, adapters, guidebooks, and planning maps (RickSteves.com/shop).

Our website can also help you find the perfect **rail pass** for your itinerary and your budget, with easy, one-stop shopping for rail passes, seat reservations, and point-to-point tickets (RickSteves.com/rail).

Rick Steves' Tours, Guidebooks, TV Shows, and More

Small Group Tours: Want to travel with greater efficiency and less stress? We offer more than 40 itineraries reaching the best destinations in this book...and beyond. Each year about 30,000 travelers join us on about 1,000 Rick Steves bus tours. You'll enjoy great guides and a fun bunch of travel partners (with small groups of 24 to 28 travelers). You'll find European adventures to fit every vacation length. For all the details, and to get our tour catalog, visit RickSteves.com or call us at +1 425 608 4217.

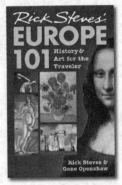

Books: This book is just one of many in my series on European travel, which includes country and city guidebooks, Snapshots (excerpted chapters from bigger guides), Pocket Guides (full-color little books on big cities), "Best Of" guidebooks (condensed, full-color country guides), and my budget-travel skills handbook, *Rick Steves Europe Through the Back Door*. A complete list of my titles—including phrase books, cruising guides, and travelogues on European art, history, and culture—appears near the end of this book.

TV Shows and Travel Talks: My public television series, *Rick Steves' Europe*, covers Europe from top to bottom with over 100 half-hour episodes—and we're working on new shows every year (watch full episodes at my website for free). My free online video library, Rick Steves Classroom Europe, with a searchable database of short video clips on European history, culture, and geography (Classroom.RickSteves.com). And to raise your travel I.Q., check out the video versions of our popular classes (covering most European countries as well as travel skills, packing smart, cruising, tech for travelers, European art, and travel as a political act—RickSteves.com/travel-talks).

Audio Tours on My Free App: I've produced dozens of free, self-guided audio tours of the top sights in Europe. For those tours and other audio content, get my free **Rick Steves Audio Europe app,** an extensive online library organized by destination. For more on my app, see page 30.

Radio: My weekly public radio show, *Travel with Rick Steves*, features interviews with travel experts from around the world. It airs on 400 public radio stations across the US. An archive of programs is available at RickSteves.com/radio.

Podcasts: You can enjoy my travel content via several free podcasts. The podcast version of my radio show brings you a weekly, hour-long travel conversation. My other podcasts include a weekly selection of video clips from my public television show, my audio tours of Europe's top sights, and live recordings of my travel classes (RickSteves. com/watch-read-listen/audio/podcasts).

APPENDIX

Holidays and Festivals

This list includes selected festivals, plus national holidays observed throughout Scandinavia. Many sights and banks close down on national holidays—keep this in mind when planning your itinerary. Before planning a trip around a festival, verify the dates with the festival website, city and national tourist offices, or my "Upcoming Holidays and Festivals" pages at RickSteves.com/europe.

Jan 1	New Year's Day
Jan 6	Epiphany, Sweden and Finland
Feb 24	Independence Day, Estonia
April	Easter Sunday-Monday: April 16-17, 2022; April 9-10, 2023
April 30	Walpurgis Night (bonfires), Sweden and Finland
April/May	Common Prayer Day (fourth Friday after Easter), Denmark
May 1	Labor Day (parades)
May 15	St. Hallvard's Day, Oslo
May 17	Constitution Day (parades), Norway

Late May-early June	Bergen International Festival (performing arts; www.fib.no)
May/June	Ascension Day: May 26, 2022; May 18, 2023
May/June	Pentecost and Whitmonday: June 5-6, 2022; May 28-29, 2023
May-June	Medieval Festival (www.oslomiddelalderfestival.org), Oslo
June 5	Constitution Day, Denmark
June 6	National Day (parades), Sweden
Early June	Old Town Days (music, parades; http://vanalinnapaevad.ee), Tallinn
Early June	Archipelago Boat Day (steamboat parade, (www.skargardstrafikanten.se), Stockholm
Early June	Taste of Stockholm (www.smakapastockholm.se)
Mid-June	Bergenfest (music festival; www.bergenfest.no), Bergen, Norway
Mid-June-mid-Aug	Grieg in Bergen Festival (concert series; www.grieginbergen.com), Bergen, Norway
June 23	Victory Day, Estonia
June 23	St. John's Eve (midsummer festival, Norway and Denmark)
Late June	Midsummer Eve and Day (celebrations, bonfires)
Late June-early July	Roskilde Festival (music, art, www.roskilde-festival.dk), Denmark
Mid-July	Stockholm Jazz Festival (http://stockholmjazz.se)
July	Copenhagen Jazz Festival (www.jazz.dk)
Late July	Food Festival (www.gladmat.no), Stavanger, Norway
Late July-mid-Aug	Hans Christian Andersen Festival (www.hcafestivals.com), Odense, Denmark
Mid-Aug	Chamber Music Festival (www.oslokammermusikkfestival.no), Oslo
Mid-Aug	Jazz Festival (www.oslojazz.no), Oslo
Mid-late Aug	Helsinki Festival (music, dance, film, theater; www.helsinkifestival.fi)
August 20	Day of Restoration of Independence, Estonia
Late Aug-Sept	Aarhus Festival (music, dance, theater; www.aarhusfestuge.dk), Denmark

Mid-Sept	Ultima Contemporary Music Festival (www. ultima.no), Oslo
Mid-Nov–early Jan	Christmas Fair (Tivoli Garden), Copenhagen
Dec 6	Independence Day, Finland
Dec 10	Nobel Prize Award Ceremony, Oslo and Stockholm
Dec 13	St. Lucia Day (festival of lights), Sweden, Norway, and parts of Finland
Dec 24-25	Christmas Eve and Day
Dec 26	Boxing Day
Dec 31	New Year's Eve

Books and Films

To learn about Scandinavia past and present, check out a few of these books and films.

General Scandinavia

A History of Scandinavia: Norway, Sweden, Denmark, Finland, and Iceland (T. K. Derry, 2000). This comprehensive tome weaves together the history and common heritage of these five countries.

Children of Ash and Elm: A History of the Vikings (Neil Price, 2020). Drawing on extensive archaeological and textual evidence, this is an engaging guide to the Viking world.

Scandinavia Since 1500 (Byron J. Nordstrom, 2000). Nordstrom presents a readable account of the region's history.

Scandinavian Folk and Fairy Tales (Claire Booss, 1988). This collection of Scandinavian folklore includes illustrations by local artists.

Denmark
Books

Conquered, Not Defeated (Peter Tveskov, 2003). Tveskov combines historical fact with childhood memories of Denmark under German occupation in World War II.

The Fairy Tale of My Life (Hans Christian Andersen, 1975). Andersen's autobiography chronicles everything from his impoverished childhood to encounters with other literary greats.

The Fairy Tales of Hans Christian Andersen (H.C. Andersen, 2013). The writer's most famous tales—from *The Little Mermaid* to *The Princess and the Pea*—are collected in this anthology.

Hans Christian Andersen: A New Life (Jens Andersen, 2003). The

APPENDIX

author reveals new dimensions to the man behind many famous childhood stories.

Music and Silence (Rose Tremain, 1999). Tremain captures Denmark in the 17th century through the eyes of a lute player at court.

Smilla's Sense of Snow (Peter Høeg, 1992). In this thriller set in snowy Copenhagen, Smilla looks into the murder of her six-year-old neighbor (later adapted as a 1997 movie starring Julia Ormond).

We, the Drowned (Carsten Jensen, 2010). This novel covers the wars and adventures of the seafaring men of Marstal, a port town on the island of Ærø—and the angst of the families they leave behind.

Winter's Tale (Isak Dinesen, 1942). Best known for her memoir *Out of Africa*, Isak Dinesen (a.k.a. Karen Blixen) set most of these short stories in her homeland of Denmark.

Film and Television

Babette's Feast (1987). This Oscar winner for Best Foreign Language Film, about a Frenchwoman taking refuge in rural 19th-century Denmark, is the original foodie movie (based on the novel by Isak Dinesen).

Borgen (2010-2013). In this dramatic political TV series, principal character Birgitte Nyborg juggles her ambitions as the first female prime minister of Denmark with her responsibilities as a wife and mother.

The Bridge (Danish: *Broen;* Swedish: *Bron;* 2011-2018). This crime drama, a coproduction of Swedish and Danish TV, follows the cases and personal lives of a brilliant but obsessive-compulsive Swedish detective and her empathetic Danish collaborator.

Italian for Beginners (2000). Thirtysomethings learn Italian in hopes of finding romance in a small Danish town.

Pelle the Conqueror (1988). A Swedish father and son emigrate to Denmark in the 19th century and work to build a new life in this film based on the 1976 book by Martin Andersen Nexø (1989 Best Foreign Language Film).

Estonia
Books

The Czar's Madman (Jaan Kross, 1992). Accused of insanity, a nobleman from the Livonian region of Estonia is subsequently monitored and scrutinized by his family.

Purge (Sofi Oksanen, 2010). Oskanen explores the Soviet occupation of Estonia and postwar suffering in this powerful novel about two women who reconcile their violent pasts.

Treading Air (Jaan Kross, 1998). This novel follows the life of pro-

tagonist Ullo Paerand, from the 1920s through the Soviet occupation of Estonia.

Truth and Justice (Anton Hansen Tammsaare, 1926). In one of the
cornerstones of Estonian literature, Tammsaare draws from
his own life to describe Estonia's evolution into an independent state.

Film

Autumn Ball (2007). Based on the novel by Mati Unt, this film
explores the isolation of six disparate people living in a Soviet-
era apartment complex.

The Singing Revolution (2006). This documentary follows the evolution of Estonian music as a form of peaceful protest and symbol of patriotism.

Spring (1969). Set in a small town boarding school, this coming-of-
age story is an Estonian classic.

Finland
Books

Burnt-Out Town of Miracles (Roy Jacobsen, 2005). In this fictional-
ized account of the 1939 Winter War, a besieged Finnish town
repels invading Russians with cunning and grit.

Kalevala (Elias Lönnrot, 1835). Regarded as Finland's national
epic, *Kalevala* is a compilation of Karelian and Finnish oral
folklore and poetry.

My Childhood (Toivo Pekkanen, 1966). Toivo Pekkanen chronicles
his family's working-class life in early-20th-century Finland.

Seven Brothers (Aleksis Kivi, 1870). In this Finnish classic, young
brothers must learn to work hard and become productive
members of society.

The Unknown Soldier (Väinö Linna, 1957). This iconic Finnish book
candidly captures native soldiers' responses to World War II.

Film

The Man Without a Past (2002). In this Academy Award-nominat-
ed film, a man is beaten up shortly after arriving in Helsinki,
loses his memory, and must start his life anew.

Mother of Mine (2005). A young Finnish boy is evacuated to Sweden during World War II.

Road North (2012). An estranged father and son reunite for a road
trip to northern Finland.

Uuno Turhapuro (1973-2006). Many Finnish politicians and celebrities make appearances throughout these 19 classic Finnish
comedies about good-for-nothing Uuno, who disrupts and un-
dermines his father-in-law in outlandish situations.

Norway
Books

Beatles (Lars Saabye Christensen, 1984). Four Beatles fans grow up in Oslo in the '60s and '70s.

A Doll's House (Henrik Ibsen, 1879). Ibsen's classic play questions marriage norms and the role of women in a 19th-century man's world.

Growth of the Soil (Knut Hamsun, 1917). This epic tale of a man living in backcountry Norway helped Hamsun win the Nobel Prize in Literature in 1920.

The Ice Palace (Tarjei Vesaas, 1993). Two young girls become unlikely friends—until a tragic disappearance shatters one of their lives.

Into the Ice: The History of Norway and the Polar Regions (Einar-Arne Drivenes and Harald Day Jolle, 2006). This comprehensive overview details expeditions, research, and the history of the polar region from the 19th century to the present.

Kon-Tiki (Thor Heyerdahl, 1948). Heyerdahl chronicles his historic 1947 journey from Peru to Polynesia on a balsa-wood raft. Norwegian filmmakers have catalogued his exploits in two films called *Kon-Tiki:* an Academy-Award-winning documentary (1950) and a blockbuster historical drama that was nominated for an Oscar for Best Foreign Language Film (2012).

Kristin Lavransdatter (Sigrid Undset, 1920-1923). This trilogy (also a 1995 movie) focuses on the life of a Norwegian woman in the 14th century.

My Struggle (Karl Ove Knausgaard, 2012). This six-part autobiography of a father and writer from Oslo is hugely popular in Norway and is quickly gaining worldwide recognition.

Out Stealing Horses (Per Petterson, 2005). A widower in remote Norway meets a neighbor who stirs up memories of a pivotal day in 1948.

The Winter Fortress (Neal Bascomb, 2016). Bascomb uses letters, diaries, and once-secret documents to flesh out the story of the WWII Norwegian commandos who destroyed the heavy water plant at Vemork, striking a blow to the Nazi atomic bomb program.

Film and Television

The Heavy Water War (2015). This six-part miniseries recounts the sabotage of the heavy water plant at Vemork, part of Hitler's atomic bomb program, and touches on morality and collaboration in wartime.

Insomnia (1997). The midnight sun plays a role in this Norwegian thriller about a police detective investigating a small-town murder.

The Kautokeino Rebellion (2008). Based on the true events of 1852, the Sami people of Norway revolt against their exploitation by Norwegian authorities.

The King's Choice (2016). During the German invasion of April 1940, King Haakon and the royal family escape from Oslo and refuse to surrender to the pursuing Nazis.

Lilyhammer (2012-2014). This dark and humorous Netflix series follows a *Sopranos*-style New York mobster who, under the witness protection program, relocates to Lillehammer and adjusts to Norwegian society the only way he knows how.

Max Manus (2008). Based on real events in the life of WWII resistance fighter Max Manus, this film recounts the exploits of Manus and his comrades in Oslo during the Nazi occupation of Norway.

Nobel (2016). In this eight-part thriller, a Norwegian soldier returns home from Afghanistan only to be entwined in a web of political intrigue and murder surrounding the Nobel Peace Prize.

Occupied (2015-2019). A twisty-turny political thriller in which Norway, after discovering a clean source of energy and shutting down oil production in the North Sea, is occupied by Russia with backing from the EU (Netflix).

Trollhunter (2010). Trolls wreak havoc in modern-day Norway in this fun fantasy/thriller that explains the real purpose of those power lines in the Norwegian mountains.

Vikings (2013-2020). This History Channel series centers on the adventures of mythological Vikings Ragnar and Lagertha Lothbrok and their sons.

Sweden
Books

Faceless Killers (Henning Mankell, 1990). This is the first of a string of popular mysteries featuring inspector Kurt Wallander.

The Girl with the Dragon Tattoo (Stieg Larsson, 2005). The first book in Larsson's *Millennium* trilogy, about a punky computer hacker and a disgraced journalist, put Swedish crime fiction on the map. The Swedish and Hollywood film versions of these books are as compelling as the novels.

Hanna's Daughters (Marianne Fredriksson, 1994). This moving novel follows the lives of three remarkable Swedish women from the 1870s through World War II.

A History of the Swedish People (Vilhelm Moberg, 2005). Written by a novelist, this popular history of Sweden is both revealing and entertaining.

In the Heat of the Moment (Viveca Sten, 2018). This who-done-it and the others in the popular 10-book Sandhamn Murders series unfold on the tiny Swedish archipelago island of Sandhamn.

A Man Called Ove (Fredrik Backman, 2014). This dark comedy centers on a cranky widower whose life is devoid of joy—until some lively neighbors move into his housing complex (also an Oscar-nominated motion picture).

Pippi Longstocking (Astrid Lindgren, 1945). Kids of all ages love reading about the adventures of the strong-willed and unconventional nine-year-old living in Sweden.

The Red Room (August Strindberg, 1879). This biting satire on Stockholm society made Strindberg a literary giant.

The Wonderful Adventures of Nils (Selma Lagerlöf, 1906). In this fantastical children's novel (winner of the Nobel Prize for Literature), Nils loves nothing more than eating, sleeping, and tormenting animals—at least until he is shrunken down to their size.

Film and Television

As It Is in Heaven (2004). A famous conductor returns to his village in Sweden, where he finds love and the key to happiness.

Dalecarlians (2005). After living in Stockholm, Mia returns home to her small village and must adjust to the life she left behind.

The Emigrants (1971). A Swedish family faces a rough transition as they move from Sweden to Minnesota in this film starring Max von Sydow and Liv Ullmann (based on the novels by Vilhelm Moberg). The sequel *The New Land* (1972) continues the family's journey.

My Life as a Dog (1985). This bittersweet tale from director Lasse Hallström focuses on a young boy in 1950s Sweden.

The Seventh Seal (1957). In this Ingmar Bergman film (set in Sweden during the Black Death), a knight questions the meaning of life. Other masterpieces from the Oscar-winning Swedish director include *Smiles of a Summer Night* (1955), a turn-of-the-century frolic, and *Fanny & Alexander* (1983), about two children overcoming their father's death.

Together (2000). This satirical view of socialist values is set in a 1970s Stockholm commune.

Wallander (2005-2013). Based on the characters in Henning Mankell's Kurt Wallander detective novels, this Swedish crime series is a study in the Scandinavian temperament and culture.

Welcome to Sweden (2014-2015). In this NBC comedy series starring Greg Poehler (who co-produces the show with his sister

Amy), an American accountant follows his girlfriend back to her home in Stockholm, where he embarks on crazy adventures with her quirky family.

Conversions and Climate

Numbers and Stumblers

- Europeans write a few of their numbers differently than we do. 1 = 1, 4 = 4, 7 = 7.
- In Europe, dates appear as day/month/year, so Christmas 2023 is 25/12/2023.
- Commas are decimal points and decimals commas. A dollar and a half is $1,50, one thousand is 1.000, and there are 5.280 feet in a mile.
- When counting with fingers, start with your thumb. If you hold up your first finger to request one item, you'll probably get two.
- Scandinavians number their weeks. Instead of saying, "Spring break is the third week in March," they'd say, "Spring break is week 12."
- On escalators and moving sidewalks, Europeans keep the left "lane" open for passing. Keep to the right.

Metric Conversions

A **kilogram** equals 1,000 grams (about 2.2 pounds). One hundred **grams** (a common unit at markets) is about a quarter-pound. One **liter** is about a quart, or almost four to a gallon.

A **kilometer** is six-tenths of a mile. To convert kilometers to miles, cut the kilometers in half and add back 10 percent of the original (120 km: 60 + 12 = 72 miles). One **meter** is 39 inches—just over a yard.

1 foot = 0.3 meter	1 square yard = 0.8 square meter
1 yard = 0.9 meter	1 square mile = 2.6 square kilometers
1 mile = 1.6 kilometers	1 ounce = 28 grams
1 centimeter = 0.4 inch	1 quart = 0.95 liter
1 meter = 39.4 inches	1 kilogram = 2.2 pounds
1 kilometer = 0.62 mile	32°F = 0°C

Clothing Sizes

When shopping for clothing, use these US-to-European comparisons as general guidelines (but note that no conversion is perfect).

Women: For pants and dresses, add 30 in Scandinavia (US 10 = Scandinavian 40). For blouses and sweaters, add 8 for most of Europe (US 32 = European 40). For shoes, add 30-31 (US 7 = European 37/38).

APPENDIX

Men: For shirts, multiply by 2 and add about 8 (US 15 = European 38). For jackets and suits, add 10. For shoes, add 32-34.

Children: Clothing is sized by height—in centimeters (2.5cm = 1 inch), so a US size 8 roughly equates to 132-140. For shoes up to size 13, add 16-18, and for sizes 1 and up, add 30-32.

Scandinavia's Climate

First line, average daily high; second line, average daily low; third line, average days without rain. For more detailed weather statistics for destinations in this book (as well as the rest of the world), check Wunderground.com.

	J	F	M	A	M	J	J	A	S	O	N	D
DENMARK • Copenhagen												
	37°	37°	42°	51°	60°	66°	70°	69°	64°	55°	46°	41°
	29°	28°	31°	37°	45°	51°	56°	56°	51°	44°	38°	33°
	14	15	19	18	20	18	17	16	14	14	11	12
ESTONIA • Tallinn												
	25°	25°	32°	45°	57°	66°	68°	66°	59°	50°	37°	30°
	14°	12°	19°	32°	41°	50°	54°	52°	48°	39°	30°	19°
	12	12	18	19	19	20	18	16	14	14	12	12
FINLAND • Helsinki												
	26°	25°	32°	44°	56°	66°	71°	68°	59°	47°	37°	31°
	17°	15°	20°	30°	40°	49°	55°	53°	46°	37°	30°	23°
	11	10	17	17	19	17	17	16	16	13	11	11
NORWAY • Oslo												
	28°	30°	39°	50°	61°	68°	72°	70°	60°	48°	38°	32°
	19°	19°	25°	34°	43°	50°	55°	53°	46°	38°	31°	25°
	16	16	22	19	21	17	16	17	16	17	14	14
SWEDEN • Stockholm												
	30°	30°	37°	47°	58°	67°	71°	68°	60°	49°	40°	35°
	26°	25°	29°	37°	45°	53°	57°	56°	50°	43°	37°	32°
	15	14	21	19	20	17	18	17	16	16	14	14

Fahrenheit and Celsius Conversion

Europe takes its temperature using the Celsius scale, while we opt for Fahrenheit. For a rough conversion from Celsius to Fahrenheit, double the number and add 30. For weather, remember that 28°C is 82°F—perfect. For health, 37°C is just right. At a launderette, 30°C is cold, 40°C is warm (usually the default setting), 60°C is hot, and 95°C is boiling. Your air-conditioner should be set at about 20°C.

Packing Checklist

Whether you're traveling for five days or five weeks, you won't need more than this. Pack light to enjoy the sweet freedom of true mobility.

Clothing

- ☐ 5 shirts: long- & short-sleeve
- ☐ 2 pairs pants (or skirts/capris)
- ☐ 1 pair shorts
- ☐ 5 pairs underwear & socks
- ☐ 1 pair walking shoes
- ☐ Sweater or warm layer
- ☐ Rainproof jacket with hood
- ☐ Tie, scarf, belt, and/or hat
- ☐ Swimsuit
- ☐ Sleepwear/loungewear

Money

- ☐ Debit card(s)
- ☐ Credit card(s)
- ☐ Hard cash (US $100-200)
- ☐ Money belt

Documents

- ☐ Passport
- ☐ Tickets & confirmations: flights, hotels, trains, rail pass, car rental, sight entries
- ☐ Driver's license
- ☐ Student ID, hostel card, etc.
- ☐ Photocopies of important documents
- ☐ Insurance details
- ☐ Guidebooks & maps

Toiletries Kit

- ☐ Basics: soap, shampoo, toothbrush, toothpaste, floss, deodorant, sunscreen, brush/comb, etc.
- ☐ Medicines & vitamins
- ☐ First-aid kit
- ☐ Glasses/contacts/sunglasses
- ☐ Sewing kit
- ☐ Packet of tissues (for WC)
- ☐ Earplugs

Electronics

- ☐ Mobile phone
- ☐ Camera & related gear
- ☐ Tablet/ebook reader/laptop
- ☐ Headphones/earbuds
- ☐ Chargers & batteries
- ☐ Phone car charger & mount (or GPS device)
- ☐ Plug adapters

Miscellaneous

- ☐ Daypack
- ☐ Sealable plastic baggies
- ☐ Laundry supplies: soap, laundry bag, clothesline, spot remover
- ☐ Small umbrella
- ☐ Travel alarm/watch
- ☐ Notepad & pen
- ☐ Journal

Optional Extras

- ☐ Second pair of shoes (flip-flops, sandals, tennis shoes, boots)
- ☐ Travel hairdryer
- ☐ Picnic supplies
- ☐ Water bottle
- ☐ Fold-up tote bag
- ☐ Small flashlight
- ☐ Mini binoculars
- ☐ Small towel or washcloth
- ☐ Inflatable pillow/neck rest
- ☐ Tiny lock
- ☐ Address list (to mail postcards)
- ☐ Extra passport photos

INDEX

INDEX

INDEX

MAP INDEX

Explore Europe

At ricksteves.com you can browse through thousands of articles, videos, photos and radio interviews, plus find a wealth of money-saving travel tips for planning your dream trip. And with our mobile-friendly website, you can easily access all this great travel information anywhere you go.

TV Shows

Preview the places you'll visit by watching entire half-hour episodes of *Rick Steves' Europe* (choose from all 100 shows) on-demand, for free.

your travel dreams into affordable reality

Radio Interviews

Enjoy ready access to Rick's vast library of radio interviews covering travel tips and cultural insights that relate specifically to your Europe travel plans.

Travel Forums

Learn, ask, share! Our online community of savvy travelers is a great resource for first-time travelers to Europe, as well as seasoned pros.

Travel News

Subscribe to our free Travel News e-newsletter, and get monthly updates from Rick on what's happening in Europe.

Classroom Europe®

Check out our free resource for educators with 500+ short video clips from the *Rick Steves' Europe* TV show.

Rick's Free Travel App

Get your FREE **Rick Steves Audio Europe**™ app to enjoy…

- Dozens of self-guided tours of Europe's top museums, sights and historic walks
- Hundreds of tracks filled with cultural insights and sightseeing tips from Rick's radio interviews
- All organized into handy geographic playlists
- For Apple and Android

With Rick whispering in your ear, Europe gets even better.

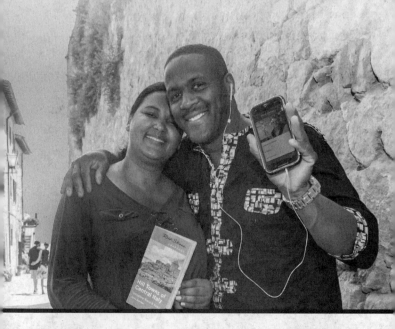

Find out more at ricksteves.com

Gear up for your next adventure at ricksteves.com

Light Luggage

Pack light and right with Rick Steves' affordable, custom-designed rolling carry-on bags, backpacks, day packs and shoulder bags.

Accessories

From packing cubes to moneybelts and beyond, Rick has personally selected the travel goodies that will help your trip go smoother.

Shop at ricksteves.com

Save time and energy

This guidebook is your independent-travel toolkit. But for all it delivers, it's still up to you to devote the time and energy it takes to manage the preparation and logistics that are essential for a happy trip. If that's a hassle, there's a solution.

Rick Steves Tours

A Rick Steves tour takes you to Europe's most interesting places with great

with minimum stress

guides and small groups. We follow Rick's favorite itineraries, ride in comfy buses, stay in family-run hotels, and bring you intimately close to the Europe you've traveled so far to see. Most importantly, we take away the logistical headaches so you can focus on the fun.

Join the fun

This year we'll take thousands of free-spirited travelers—nearly half of them repeat customers— along with us on 50 different itineraries, from Athens to Istanbul. Is a Rick Steves tour the right fit for your travel dreams?

Find out at ricksteves.com, where you can also check seat availability and sign up. Europe is best experienced with happy travel partners. We hope you can join us.

See our itineraries at ricksteves.com

BEST OF GUIDES

Full-color guides in an easy-to-scan format. Focused on top sights and experiences in the most popular European destinations

Best of England
Best of Europe
Best of France
Best of Germany
Best of Ireland
Best of Italy
Best of Scotland
Best of Spain

COMPREHENSIVE GUIDES

City, country, and regional guides printed on Bible-thin paper. Packed with detailed coverage for a multi-week trip exploring iconic sights and venturing off the beaten path

Amsterdam & the Netherlands
Barcelona
Belgium: Bruges, Brussels,
  Antwerp & Ghent
Berlin
Budapest
Croatia & Slovenia
Eastern Europe
England
Florence & Tuscany
France
Germany
Great Britain
Greece: Athens & the Peloponnese
Iceland
Ireland
Istanbul
Italy
London
Paris
Portugal
Prague & the Czech Republic
Provence & the French Riviera
Rome
Scandinavia
Scotland
Sicily
Spain
Switzerland
Venice
Vienna, Salzburg & Tirol

Rick Steves books are available from your favorite bookseller.
Many guides are available as ebooks.

POCKET GUIDES

Compact color guides for shorter trips

Amsterdam
Athens
Barcelona
Florence
Italy's Cinque Terre
London
Munich & Salzburg
Paris
Prague
Rome
Venice
Vienna

SNAPSHOT GUIDES

Focused single-destination coverage

Basque Country: Spain & France
Copenhagen & the Best of Denmark
Dublin
Dubrovnik
Edinburgh
Hill Towns of Central Italy
Krakow, Warsaw & Gdansk
Lisbon
Loire Valley
Madrid & Toledo
Milan & the Italian Lakes District
Naples & the Amalfi Coast
Nice & the French Riviera
Normandy
Northern Ireland
Norway
Reykjavík
Rothenburg & the Rhine
Sevilla, Granada & Southern Spain
St. Petersburg, Helsinki & Tallinn
Stockholm

CRUISE PORTS GUIDES

Reference for cruise ports of call

Mediterranean Cruise Ports
Scandinavian & Northern European
  Cruise Ports

Complete your library with...

TRAVEL SKILLS & CULTURE

Study up on travel skills and gain insight on history and culture

Europe 101
Europe Through the Back Door
Europe's Top 100 Masterpieces
European Christmas
European Easter
European Festivals
For the Love of Europe
Travel as a Political Act

PHRASE BOOKS & DICTIONARIES

French
French, Italian & German
German
Italian
Portuguese
Spanish

PLANNING MAPS

Britain, Ireland & London
Europe
France & Paris
Germany, Austria & Switzerland
Iceland
Ireland
Italy
Spain & Portugal

Credits

RESEARCHERS
To help with this edition, Rick relied on...

Glenn Eriksen

A solo backpacking trip across Europe and Scandinavia back in the '70s turned out to be Glenn's first step on the road to Rick Steves' Europe. Today, as a guidebook editor and researcher, he indulges his love for the Old Country while helping Rick's readers "keep on travelin'." When not on the road, Glenn lives in Seattle with his wife, Kathy, and enjoys hiking, photography, and keeping in touch with his Norwegian roots.

Cameron Hewitt

Born in Denver and raised in central Ohio, Cameron settled in Seattle in 2000. Ever since, he has spent three months each year in Europe, contributing to guidebooks, tours, radio and television shows, and other media for Rick Steves' Europe, where he serves as content manager. Cameron married his high school sweetheart (and favorite travel partner), Shawna, and enjoys taking pictures, trying new restaurants, and planning his next trip.

Pål Bjarne Johansen

A tour guide and guidebook researcher for Rick Steves' Europe (covering Scandinavia and Spain), Pål grew up in the Norwegian countryside near the Swedish border and has family ties in Denmark. He discovered his passion for travel and adventure at a young age and has backpacked much of the world. When he's not working for Rick Steves, you'll find Pål skiing the Norwegian woods in winter and sailing the seven seas in summer.

Suzanne Kotz

Suzanne, an editor with Rick Steves' Europe, began her travel career riding in a station wagon with her six siblings from Michigan to Florida for spring break. Since then, she's broadened her destinations to include much of Europe and parts of Asia. A librarian by training and a longtime editor of art publications, she's happiest with a garden trowel or a good book in her hands, or when planning a meal for family and friends in Seattle.

CONTRIBUTOR
Gene Openshaw

Gene has co-authored more than a dozen Rick Steves books, specializing in writing walks and tours of Europe's cities, museums, and cultural sights. He also writes for Rick's public television series, produces audio tours on Europe, and is a regular guest on Rick's public radio show. Outside of the travel world, Gene has co-authored The Se-attle Joke Book. As a composer, he has written an opera called Mat-ter, a violin sonata, and dozens of songs. He lives near Seattle, where he enjoys giving presentations on art and history, and roots for the Mariners in good times and bad.

ACKNOWLEDGMENTS

Thanks to Thor, Hanne, Geir, Hege, and Kari-Anne, our Norwegian family. Special thanks to Jane Klausen for her expertise in all things Danish. Thank you to Risa Laib for creating the color introduction for this book (and for her 25-plus years of dedication to the Rick Steves guidebook series). Thanks to these translators for their help with the survival phrases: Marita Bergman, Unni-Marie Kvikne, Mati Rummes-sen, and Christina Snellman. And, in loving memory of Berit Kristian-sen, whose house was my house for 20 years of Norwegian travel.

PHOTO CREDITS

Front Cover: Geiranger Fjord, Norway © Dr. Wilfried Bahnmüller, im-ageBROKER, Alamy Stock Photo

Back Cover: Dreamstime.com (left to right): Stortorget, Gamla Stan, Stockholm © Dimbar76; smørrebrød sandwich, Denmark © Artmim; Oslo Opera House © Dmitry Chulov

Dreamstime.com: 7 (middle) © Epixx; 7 (bottom) © Njoyhurghada; 16 (middle right) © Rpbmedia; 26 (bottom) © Perboge; 665 (top) © Dimmex

National Museum, Oslo: 239 Jacques Lation; 240 (top), 685 Børre Høstland

Additional Credits: 190 (bottom) Jacob Due, Foto/medie afdelingen Moesgaard; 238 MIR/Statsbygg/Kleihues + Schuwerk

Additional Photography: Kyle Bonnell, Dominic Arizona Bonuc-celli, Orin Dubrow, Rich Earl, Glenn Eriksen, Tom Griffin, Cameron Hewitt, David C. Hoerlein, Jack Juliussen, Suzanne Kotz, Cathy Lu, Gene Openshaw, Jennifer Schutte, Carrie Shepherd, Rick Steves, Ian Watson. Photos are used by permission and are the property of the original copyright owners.

Avalon Travel
Hachette Book Group
1700 Fourth Street
Berkeley, CA 94710

Text © 2021 by Rick Steves' Europe, Inc. All rights reserved.
Maps © 2021 by Rick Steves' Europe, Inc. All rights reserved.

Printed in Canada by Friesens.
16th Edition. First printing July 2021.

ISBN 978-1-64171-418-1

For the latest on Rick's talks, guidebooks, tours, public television series, and public radio
show, contact Rick Steves' Europe, 130 Fourth Avenue North, Edmonds, WA 98020,
425/771-8303, www.ricksteves.com, rick@ricksteves.com.

Hachette Book Group supports the right to free expression and the value of copyright. The
purpose of copyright is to encourage writers and artists to produce the creative works that
enrich our culture. The scanning, uploading, and distribution of this book without permission is a theft of the author's intellectual property. If you would like permission to use material from the book (other than for review purposes), please contact permissions@hbgusa.
com. Thank you for your support of the author's rights. The publisher is not responsible for
websites (or their content) that are not owned by the publisher.

Rick Steves' Europe

Managing Editor: Jennifer Madison Davis
Assistant Managing Editor: Cathy Lu
Editors: Glenn Eriksen, Suzanne Kotz, Rosie Leutzinger, Jessica Shaw, Carrie Shepherd
Editorial & Production Assistant: Megan Simms
Researchers: Glenn Eriksen, Cameron Hewitt, Pål Bjarne Johansen, Suzanne Kotz
Research Assistance: Rich Earl, Lisa Friend, Robyn Stencil, Laura Terrenzio
Contributor: Gene Openshaw
Graphic Content Director: Sandra Hundacker
Maps & Graphics: David C. Hoerlein, Lauren Mills, Mary Rostad
Digital Asset Coordinator: Orin Dubrow

Avalon Travel

Senior Editor & Series Manager: Madhu Prasher
Associate Managing Editors: Jamie Andrade, Sierra Machado
Indexer: Stephen Callahan
Production: Lisi Baldwin, Rue Flaherty, Jane Musser
Cover Design: Kimberly Glyder Design
Maps & Graphics: Kat Bennett, Mike Morgenfeld

*Although every effort was made to ensure that the information was correct at the time of going to
press, the author and publisher do not assume and hereby disclaim any liability to any party for any
loss or damage caused by errors, omissions, bad herring, or any potential travel disruption due to
labor or financial difficulty, whether such errors or omissions result from negligence, accident, or any
other cause.*

COLOR MAPS

Scandinavia • Copenhagen • Oslo • Norway's Sognefjord •
Bergen • Stockholm • Helsinki • Tallinn

SIGHTS

1 Amagertorv
2 Amalienborg Palace & Square
3 Amalienborg Museum
4 Børsen (Old Stock Exchange)
5 Cathedral of Our Lady
6 Christiania
7 Christiansborg Palace
8 City Hall
9 Copenhagen University
10 Danish Jewish Museum
11 Gammeltorv & Nytorv
12 Gefion Fountain
13 Gråbrødretorv
14 House of Amber
15 Illum Dep't Store
16 Kongens Nytorv
17 Little Mermaid Statue
18 Magasin du Nord Dep't Store
19 Meatpacking District (Restaurants)
20 Museum of Copenhagen
21 Museum of Danish Resistance
22 National Gallery of Denmark
23 National Museum
24 Ny Carlsberg Glyptotek
25 Nyhavn
26 Our Savior's Church
27 Rådhuspladsen (City Hall Square)
28 Rosenborg Castle & Treasury
29 Rosenborg Gardens
30 Round Tower
31 Royal Library ("Black Diamond")
32 Strøget (Pedestrian Street)
33 Thorvaldsen's Museum
34 Tivoli Gardens
35 Train Station (Hovedbanegården)

400 Meters
400 Yards

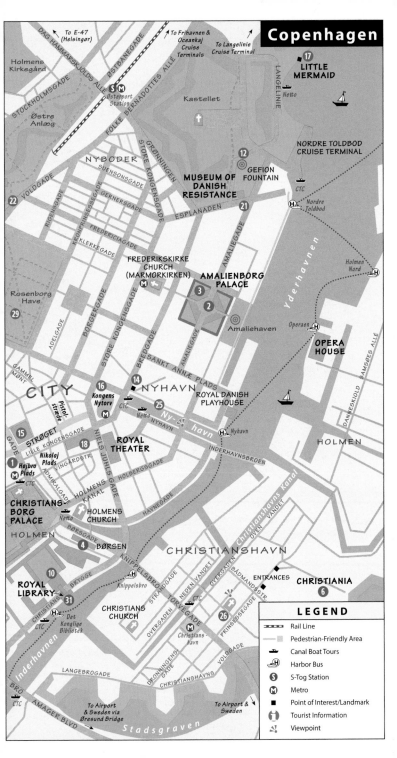

Copenhagen

17 LITTLE MERMAID

Netto

To E-47 (Helsingør)

To Frihavnen & Oceankaj Cruise Terminals

To Langelinie Cruise Terminal

DAG HAMMARSKJÖLDS ALLÉ

ØSTBANEGADE

Holmens Kirkegård

STOCKHOLMSGADE

S Østerport Station

Østre Anlæg

ØSTRE ANLÆG

Kastellet

LANGELINIE

NYBODER

VOLDGADE

22

SUENSONSGADE

RIGENSGADE

KRONPRINSESSEGADE

GERNERSGADE

FREDERICIAGADE

KLERKEGADE

STORE KONGENSGADE

GRØNNINGEN

FOLKE BERNADOTTES ALLÉ

12 GEFION FOUNTAIN

MUSEUM OF DANISH RESISTANCE

ESPLANADEN

21

NORDRE TOLDBOD CRUISE TERMINAL

CTC

H Nordre Toldbod

Rosenborg Have

29

ADELGADE

BORGERGADE

FREDERIKSKIRKE CHURCH (MARMORKIRKEN)

M

AMALIEGADE

3

2 AMALIENBORG PALACE

Amaliehaven

Yderhavnen

Holmen Nord **H**

Operaen **H**

OPERA HOUSE

BAMSØES ALLÉ

DANNESKIOLD

GAMMEL MONT

CITY

Pistol- stræde

16 Kongens Nytorv **M**

14 NYHAVN

STORE KONGENSGADE

BREDGADE

SANKT ANNÆ PLADS

AMALIEGADE

ROYAL DANISH PLAYHOUSE

CTC

25 *Netto* Nyhavn

HOLMEN

15 STRØGET

LILLE KONGENSGADE

NIELS JUHLS GADE

18

Nikolaj Plads

1 Højbro Plads **M**

CTC

ROYAL THEATER

INGARDSTR.

ADMIRALGADE

HOLMENS KANAL

HOLBERGSGADE

H Nyhavn

INDERHAVNSBROEN

INDERHAVNEN

CHRISTIANS BORG PALACE

HOLMEN

Netto

HOLMENS CHURCH

HAVNEGADE

BØRSGADE

4 BØRSEN

KNIPPELSBRO GADE

CHRISTIANSHAVN

Christianshavns Kanal

OVEN VANDET

10

ROYAL LIBRARY

BRYGGE

H Knippelsbro

31

CTC Det Kongelige Bibliotek

CHRISTIANS CHURCH

STRANDGADE

OVERGADEN NEDEN VANDET

TORVEGADE

CTC

OVERGADEN OVEN VANDET

BÅDMANDSSTR.

ENTRANCES

6 CHRISTIANIA

26

M Christians- havn

PRINSESSEGADE

DRONNINGENS GADE

LANGEBROGADE

BRO

AMAGER BLVD

CHRISTIANSHAVNS VOLDGADE

To Airport & Sweden via Øresund Bridge

To Airport & Sweden

Stadsgraven

LEGEND

- ▬▬▬ Rail Line
- Pedestrian-Friendly Area
- ⛴ Canal Boat Tours
- **H** Harbor Bus
- **S** S-Tog Station
- **M** Metro
- ■ Point of Interest/Landmark
- **⑂** Tourist Information
- ⤴ Viewpoint

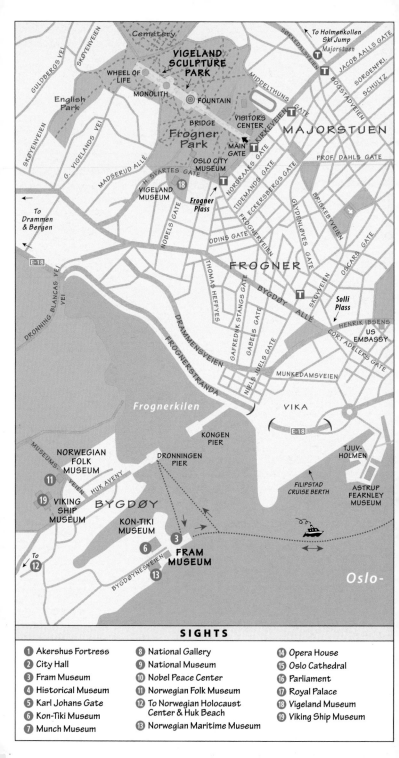

SIGHTS

1. Akershus Fortress
2. City Hall
3. Fram Museum
4. Historical Museum
5. Karl Johans Gate
6. Kon-Tiki Museum
7. Munch Museum
8. National Gallery
9. National Museum
10. Nobel Peace Center
11. Norwegian Folk Museum
12. To Norwegian Holocaust Center & Huk Beach
13. Norwegian Maritime Museum
14. Opera House
15. Oslo Cathedral
16. Parliament
17. Royal Palace
18. Vigeland Museum
19. Viking Ship Museum

Oslo

BEYER BRIDGE

RINGNES BREWERY

SANNERGATE

SCHLEPPEGRELLS GATE

VALLEGATA

COLLETTS GATE

UELANDS GATE

MARIDALSVEIEN

THERESES GATE

SOFIES GATE

ULLEVÅLSVEIEN

GEITMYRSVEIEN

WALDEMAR THRANES GATE

BJERREGAARDS GATE

ST. HANS-HAUGEN

GAMLE AKER CHURCH

ÅMOT BRIDGE

THOR. MEYERS GATE

MARKVEIEN

FOSSVEIEN

Olaf Ryes Plass

HELGESENS GATE

SOFIENBERGGATA

GRÜNER-LØKKA

To E-6 & Airport

TRONDHEIMSVEIEN

SARS GATE

Botanic Garden

HEIMDALSGATA

LAKKEGATA

NORBYGATA

TØYENGATA

VIBES GATE

ROSENBORGGATA

JOSEFINES GATE

PILESTREDET

INKOGNITOGATA

PARKVEIEN

STEENBERGGATA

ULLEVÅLSVEIEN

AKERSVEIEN

AKERSBAKKEN

MARIDALSVEIEN

Akers River

NORDRE GATE

HAUSMANNS GATE

Vår Frelsers Cemetery

ST. OLAF'S CHURCH

TREFOLDIGHETS CHURCH

Youngstorget

MØLLERGATA

GRUBBEGATA

AKERSGATA

TORGGATA

HAMMERS BORGGATA

C. KROGHS GATE

STORGATA

NYLANDSVEIEN

Oslo Spektrum

Grønland

GRØNLAND

Slotts-parken

ROYAL PALACE 17

National-theatret

KRISTIAN IV's GATE

4

UNIV.-GATA

8

GATE

NATIONAL THEATER

KARL JOHANS GATE

16 Stor-tinget

CENTER

5

15

Stortorvet

Jernbane-torget

BRUGATA

BISKOP GUNNERUS GATE

SCHWEIGAARDS GATE

RUSELØKKVEIEN

MUNKEDAMSVEIEN

9

10

2

CITY HALL

Råd-hus-plassen

TOLLBUGATA

PRINSENS

KIRKEGATA

DRONN.

SKIPPERGATE

STRANDGATA

TRAIN STATION

BARCODE PROJECT

162

AKER BRYGGE MALL

STRANDEN

NORWEGIAN RESISTANCE MUSEUM

1

RÅDHUSGATA

MYNTGATA

AKERSHUSSTRANDA

AKERSHUS FORTRESS

14 OPERA HOUSE

REVIERKAIA CRUISE BERTH

Bjørvika

DRONNING EUFEMIAS GATE

OPERAGATA

7 MUNCH MUSEUM

Bispe-vika

KONG HÅKON 5s GATE

RUINS OF MEDIEVAL OSLO

162

Pipervika

SØNDRE AKERSHUSKAIA CRUISE BERTH

VIPPETANGEN (AKERSHUS) CRUISE BERTH

DFDS TICKET OFFICE

fjord

To Copenhagen, Denmark

GRESHOLMEN

N

KONGSVEIEN

To Ekeberg Sculpture Park

HOVEDØYA

LEGEND

Pedestrian-Friendly Area

 T-bane (subway)

T Tram #12

Tourist Information

Viewpoint

1,000 Meters

1,000 Yards

Bergen

To Norwegian Fisheries Museum

SKOLTEN CRUISE TERMINAL

(B)

SKUTEVIKSTORGET

E85

BERGENHUS FORTRESS

SKOLTEGRUNNS-KAIEN

INTERNATIONAL FERRIES

HÅKON'S HALL

NORDNES

Harbor

FESTNINGS-KAIEN

9

14

TOTEM POLE

AQUARIUM

1

STRANDGATEN

C. SUNDTS GATE

HARBOR FERRIES

ROSEN-KRANTZ TOWER

POOL

HAUGEVEIEN

SWIMMING BEACH

Nordnesparken

STRANDSIDEN

NYKIRKEN

NORDNESVEIEN

C. SUNDTS GATE

STRANDGATEN

HOLBERGSALLM.

HAUGEVEIEN

Puddefjorden

KLOSTERGATEN

SKOTTEGATEN

NØSTEGATEN

ENGEN

HURTIGRUTEN TERMINAL (COASTAL CRUISES)

NØSTEGATTEN

555

JEKTEVIKEN/DOKKEN CRUISE PORT

TORBORG NEDREAXASGATE

SIGHTS

1. Aquarium
2. Bergenhus Fortress
3. Bryggens Museum
4. Cathedral
5. Fish Market
6. Fløibanen Funicular
7. Fortress Museum
8. To Gamle Bergen
9. Håkon's Hall
10. Hanseatic Museum
11. KODE Art Museums
12. Leprosy Museum
13. Ole Bulls Plass
14. Rosenkrantz Tower
15. St. Mary's Church
16. Theta Museum
17. Torgallmenningen (Main Square)
18. Bus to Ulriken643 Cable Car
19. Bybanen Tram to Troldhaugen, Fantoft Stave Church & Airport

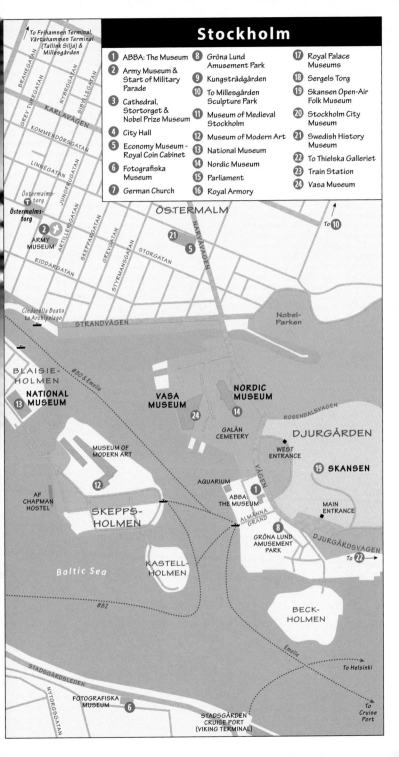

Stockholm

1. ABBA: The Museum
2. Army Museum & Start of Military Parade
3. Cathedral, Stortorget & Nobel Prize Museum
4. City Hall
5. Economy Museum - Royal Coin Cabinet
6. Fotografiska Museum
7. German Church
8. Gröna Lund Amusement Park
9. Kungsträdgården
10. To Millesgården Sculpture Park
11. Museum of Medieval Stockholm
12. Museum of Modern Art
13. National Museum
14. Nordic Museum
15. Parliament
16. Royal Armory
17. Royal Palace Museums
18. Sergels Torg
19. Skansen Open-Air Folk Museum
20. Stockholm City Museum
21. Swedish History Museum
22. To Thielska Galleriet
23. Train Station
24. Vasa Museum

To Frihamnen Terminal, Värtahammen Terminal (Tallink Silja) & Millesgården

BRAHEGATAN
GREY TUREGATAN
NYBROGATAN
SIBYLLEGATAN

KARLAVÄGEN

KOMMENDÖRSGATAN

LINNEGATAN

Östermalms-torg
Östermalmstorg

JUNGFRUGATAN

ÖSTERMALM

To 10

ARTILLERIGATAN
SKEPPARGATAN
GREVGATAN
STYRMANSGATAN
STORGATAN
NARVAVÄGEN

2 ARMY MUSEUM

21

5

RIDDARGATAN

Cinderella Boats to Archipelago

STRANDVÄGEN

Nobel-Parken

BLAISIE-HOLMEN

#80 & Emelie

NATIONAL MUSEUM 13

VASA MUSEUM

24

NORDIC MUSEUM

14

ROSENDALSVÄGEN

DJURGÅRDEN

GALÄN CEMETERY

MUSEUM OF MODERN ART

12

WEST ENTRANCE

VÄGEN

19 SKANSEN

AQUARIUM

AF CHAPMAN HOSTEL

SKEPPS-HOLMEN

ABBA: THE MUSEUM 1

MAIN ENTRANCE

ALLMÄNNA GRAND

8

GRÖNA LUND AMUSEMENT PARK

DJURGÅRDSVÄGEN

To 22

KASTELL-HOLMEN

Baltic Sea

#82

BECK-HOLMEN

Emelie

To Helsinki

STADSGÅRDSLEDEN

NYTORGSGATAN

FOTOGRAFISKA MUSEUM

6

STADSGÅRDEN CRUISE PORT (VIKING TERMINAL)

To Cruise Port

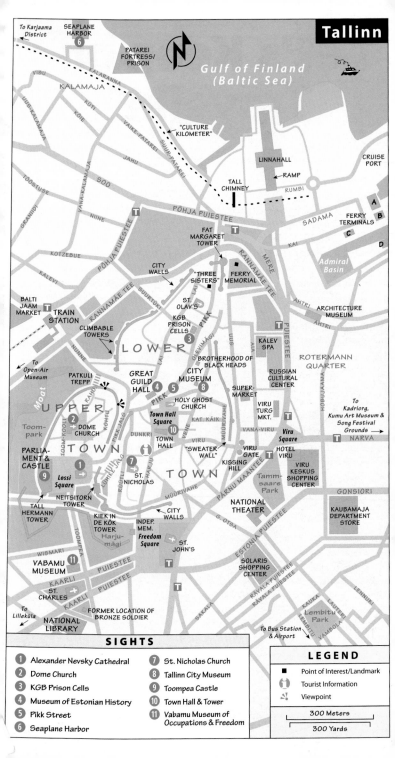

Tallinn

To Karjaama District

SEAPLANE HARBOR ⑥

PATAREI FORTRESS/ PRISON

KALARANNA

KALAMAJA

VIBU

UUS-KALAMAJA

KOIE

KUTI

JAHU

NIINE

SOO

TOOSTUSE

GRANIIDI

KOTZEBUE

KALEVI

VAIKE-PATAREI

SUUR-PATAREI

VANA-KALAMAJA

"CULTURE KILOMETER"

N

Gulf of Finland (Baltic Sea)

LINNAHALL

TALL CHIMNEY

RAMP

RUMBI

CRUISE PORT

PÕHJA PUIESTEE

SADAMA

FERRY TERMINALS

A

B

C

D

Admiral Basin

BALTI JAAM MARKET

TRAIN STATION

To Open-Air Museum

PÕHJA PUIESTEE

RANNAMÄE TEE

NUNNE

CITY WALLS

CLIMBABLE TOWERS

SUURTUKI

LAI

FAT MARGARET TOWER

"THREE SISTERS"

ST. OLAV'S

KGB PRISON CELLS ③

PIKK

OLEVIMÄGI

FERRY MEMORIAL

RANNAMÄE TEE

MERE

KAI

AHTRI

AHTRI

ARCHITECTURE MUSEUM

ROTERMANN QUARTER

LOWER

BROTHERHOOD OF BLACK HEADS

KALEV SPA

PUIESTEE

AIA

UUS

To Kadriorg, Kumu Art Museum & Song Festival Grounds

NARVA

Moat

Toompark

UPPER TOWN

PATKULI TREPP

TOOM-KOOLI

DOME CHURCH ②

RAHU

KOHTU

PIKK JALG

PIKK

RÜÜTLI

DUNKRI

GREAT GUILD HALL ④

⑤

CITY MUSEUM ⑧

HOLY GHOST CHURCH

KAT. KÄIK

VENE

MÜÜRIVAHE

SUPER-MARKET

RUSSIAN CULTURAL CENTER

VIRU TURG MKT.

VANA-VIRU

Viru Square

T

Town Hall Square

TOWN HALL ⑩

⑩

ST. NICHOLAS ⑦

KULLASSEPA

KUNINGA

LÜHIKE JALG

LOSSI Square ①

Toompea

PARLIAMENT & CASTLE ⑨

TALL HERMANN TOWER

NEITSITORN TOWER

TOOMPEA

WISMARI

KIEK IN DE KÖK TOWER

Harju-mägi

INDEP. MEM.

Freedom Square

CITY WALLS

MÜÜRIVAHE

"SWEATER WALL"

VIRU GATE

KISSING HILL

Tammsaare Park

PÄRNU MAANTEE

HOTEL VIRU

VIRU KESKUS SHOPPING CENTER

KAUBAMAJA DEPARTMENT STORE

GONSIORI

NATIONAL THEATER

G. OTSA

ESTONIA PUIESTEE

SOLARIS SHOPPING CENTER

KAVALA PUIESTEE

RÄVALA PUIESTEE

SAKALA

LENNUKI

Lembitu Park

LAUTERI

KAUKA

VAMBOLA

ST. JOHN'S

VABAMU MUSEUM ⑪

KAARLI PUIESTEE

ST. CHARLES

To Lilleküla

KAARLI PUIESTEE

NATIONAL LIBRARY

FORMER LOCATION OF BRONZE SOLDIER

To Bus Station & Airport

SIGHTS

① Alexander Nevsky Cathedral
② Dome Church
③ KGB Prison Cells
④ Museum of Estonian History
⑤ Pikk Street
⑥ Seaplane Harbor
⑦ St. Nicholas Church
⑧ Tallinn City Museum
⑨ Toompea Castle
⑩ Town Hall & Tower
⑪ Vabamu Museum of Occupations & Freedom

LEGEND

■ Point of Interest/Landmark

ℹ Tourist Information

📐 Viewpoint

300 Meters

300 Yards

Let's Keep on Travelin'

SCOTCH PLAINS PUBLIC LIBRARY

3 9523 00240 043 6

Your trip doesn't need to end.

Follow Rick on social media!